The Letters of Charlotte Brontë

The Letters of Charlotte Brontë

with a selection of letters by
family and friends

EDITED BY
MARGARET SMITH

VOLUME ONE
1829–1847

CLARENDON PRESS · OXFORD

Oxford University Press, Great Clarendon Street, Oxford OX2 6DP
Oxford New York
Athens Auckland Bangkok Bogota Bombay
Buenos Aires Calcutta Cape Town Dar es Salaam
Delhi Florence Hong Kong Istanbul Karachi
Kuala Lumpur Madras Madrid Melbourne
Mexico City Nairobi Paris Singapore
Taipei Tokyo Toronto
and associated companies in
Berlin Ibadan

Oxford is a trade mark of Oxford University Press

Published in the United States
by Oxford University Press Inc., New York

First published 1995

British Library Cataloguing in Publication Data
Data available

Library of Congress Cataloging in Publication Data
Data available

ISBN 0-19-818597-9

3 5 7 9 10 8 6 4

Printed in Great Britain
on acid-free paper by
Bookcraft Ltd,
Midsomer Norton, Somerset

IN HONOUR OF

PROFESSOR MILDRED CHRISTIAN, PH.D., 1901–1989,

WHOSE SCHOLARLY WORK ON

CHARLOTTE BRONTË

LAID THE FOUNDATION OF THIS EDITION

ACKNOWLEDGEMENTS

This edition owes much to the scholarly work over many years of the late Mildred G. Christian, former Professor of English at Newcomb College of Tulane University, who located many of the manuscripts of the Brontës' letters, and made a valuable collection of Bronteana, including photographs of some material which is no longer accessible. Her generous bequest of her working-papers, photographs, and books to the Brontë Society has helped to further the study and understanding of the Brontë family and their writings; and I gratefully acknowledge her pioneering work.

To Professor Ian Jack and Professor Kathleen Tillotson I offer sincere thanks for their support, guidance and co-operation in the field of Brontë studies. The approval and encouragement of the Brontë Society Council has been greatly appreciated, and the patience and practical assistance of the staff of the Brontë Parsonage Museum have been unfailing. I am grateful for the help of the present Director of the Museum, Ms Jane Sellars, and of the former Curator, Dr Juliet R. V. Barker. Dr Barker has continued to give unstinted help and information, and has generously allowed me to benefit from her own scholarly research. Ms Kathryn White has patiently answered my questions and cheerfully endured my many demands upon her time during my visits to the Museum library. I owe a special debt of gratitude to Mrs Barbara Whitehead, who has kindly shared with me her detailed knowledge of the Nussey family.

I acknowledge with thanks a substantial grant from the Leverhulme Trust which enabled me to examine personally manuscripts and other material in this country and abroad.

To the authorities of the following institutions I offer my thanks for permission to publish or to quote from letters or other documents in their collections: the Bodleian Library, Oxford; Brown University Library, Providence, Rhode Island; Brigham Young University; the British Library; the Brotherton Collection, Leeds University Library; the Brontë Society, Haworth; Cliffe Castle Museum, Keighley; George Dunlop Papers, Rare Book and Manuscript Library, Columbia University Library, New York; the Fales Library, New York University; the Fitzwilliam Museum, Cambridge; Guildhall Library, London; the Houghton Library, Harvard University; the Huntington Library, San Marino, California; Special Collections and Archives, Knox College Library, Galesburg, Illinois; the King's School, Canterbury; Leeds City Museum; Manchester Central Library; the Trustees of the National Library of Scotland; the Gilbert and Amy Angell Collier Montague Collection, Rare Books and Manuscripts Division, the New York Public Library, Astor, Lenox and Tilden Foundations; the Century Company Records, Rare Books and Manuscripts Division, The New York Public Library, Astor, Lenox and Tilden Foundations; the Henry W. and Albert A. Berg Collection; the Pforzheimer Library; the Pierpont Morgan Library, New York, MA 2696 and MA 4500; the Manuscripts Division, Department of Rare Books and Special Collections, Princeton University Libraries; the Rosenbach Museum and Library, Philadelphia; the John Rylands Library of the University of Manchester; Rutgers University Library, New Jersey; Sheffield University Library; the Friends Historical Library of Swarthmore College,

Pennsylvania; St. Andrew's University Library; the Master and Fellows of Trinity College, Cambridge; the Board of Trinity College, Dublin; the Special Collections Division, University of British Columbia Library; Whitby Literary and Philosophical Society; West Yorkshire Archive Services at Calderdale (Halifax), Kirklees (Huddersfield), and at Bradford, Leeds and Wakefield; and the Beinecke Library, Yale University. I thank the Harry Ransom Humanities Research Center, University of Texas at Austin, for allowing me to consult documents in their collection.

I thank the following for permission to publish or quote from manuscripts in their possession: Mr Alan Gill; Ms L. Glading; John Murray (Publishers) Ltd.; Mr A. M. I. Parmeter; Mr William Self; Professor Mark Seaward; Charles Scribner's Sons; Mr G. A. Yablon; and Dr T. J. Winnifrith. For permission to publish copyright material published by them, I thank Basil Blackwell Publishers Ltd., and for permission to quote from *Victorian Ouseburn: George Whitehead's Journal* I thank Mr Helier Hibbs. Professors John Chapple and Arthur Pollard kindly allowed me to quote from their edition of *The Letters of Mrs Gaskell* (Manchester University Press, 1966); and I thank Mrs Trevor Dabbs for allowing me to quote from some of the manuscript letters of Mrs Gaskell and from the Rylands Library manuscript of Mrs Gaskell's *Life* of Charlotte Brontë. Branwell Brontë's letter to Wordsworth of 10 January 1837 is published by permission of the Wordsworth Trustees, Dove Cottage, Grasmere. Quotations from Abraham Shackleton's Weather Diaries are made by permission of the City of Bradford Metropolitan Council, Arts, Museums and Libraries Division. The Richmond portrait of Charlotte Brontë is reproduced by permission of the National Portrait Gallery, London; other illustrations by permission of the Brontë Society, Haworth.

I am grateful to the family of the late C. K. Shorter for permission to publish MSS by Charlotte Brontë, and to Mrs D. Lewens for her kind permission to quote from the letters of her father, C. K. Shorter. I gratefully acknowledge the permission of the late Mr John Nussey to publish MSS by Ellen Nussey. Mr Nussey also most patiently and kindly answered my many queries about Ellen Nussey's family and acquaintances.

I have appreciated the help, advice, information, encouragement or hospitality offered to me by the people named above, and by Dr Christine Alexander, Dr Donald Anderle, Dr Peter Aynscough, Professor Robert Barnard, Dr B. Benedicz, Dr A Betteridge, Professor James Boulton, Dr Lisa Brower, Dr M. N. Brown, Ms Lesley Byrne, Dr Diana Chardin, Mrs Paule Chicken, Dr Edward Chitham, Mr John Christian, Ms Kathleen Collins, Mr John Cumberland, Mrs Ann Dinsdale, Professor Angus Easson, Mrs Victoria Fattorini, Ms Sarah Fermi, Monsieur François Fierens, Mr Wayne Furman, Professor S. R. Gannon, Mrs Cathy Geldard, Dr Stephen Gill, Dr Vincent Giroud, Mr D. S. Goodes, Mr Douglas C. Grant, Mrs Audrey Hall, Dr Mihai Handrea, Mr Arthur Hartley, Mrs Margaret M. Hartley, Dr Cathy Henderson, Ms Judith Hodge, Ms Sarah S. Hodson, Dr Philip Kelley, Mr Charles Lemon, Mrs Christine Lingard, Dr Peter McNiven, Dr Jean Macqueen, Miss Laurie Marriott, Dr Bernard Meehan, Mrs Virginia Murray, Ms Christine Nelson, Miss Christine Penney, Dr Robert E. Parkes, Ms Jean E. Preston, Mr J. G. Sharps, Dr Christopher Sheppard, the late Mrs Eunice Skirrow, Mr Matthew Smith, Dr John D. Stinson, the late Miss Chris Sumner, Dr Margaret M. Sherry, Ms Judy Smith, Mrs Joyce E. Tripp, Dr Emily C. Walhout, Dr Alexander Wainewright, Ms Helen Walasek, Dr Robert Woof, Mr J. G. N. Wooler, and Ms Georgianna Ziegler. To the many other people who have allowed me to consult or to publish documents in their collections I give grateful acknowledgement. The staff of the following libraries have been especially helpful: Birmingham University Library; Birmingham Reference Library; Bradford City Library; the Mitchell Library, Glasgow; Humberside County Libraries; the National Postal Museum; the Penzance Library; Warwickshire County Archives; and the Wellcome Institute for Medical Research. The help of other people and libraries will be acknowledged in future volumes.

Finally I am grateful for the support, expertise, and patience of Kim Scott Walwyn, Frances Whistler, and Vicki Reeve of the Oxford University Press.

CONTENTS

LIST OF ILLUSTRATIONS

(between pp. 318–319)

ABBREVIATIONS AND SYMBOLS

For books the place of publication is London unless otherwise indicated. Reference to letters in *Shorter* and W & S (see below) is by number, not page.

AB	Anne Brontë
AB *Diary*	Anne Brontë, MS Diary Paper
ABN	Arthur Bell Nicholls
AG	*Agnes Grey*
Alexander *Bibliography*	Christine Alexander, *A Bibliography of the Manuscripts of Charlotte Brontë* (Keighley, 1982)
Alexander *EEW*	*An Edition of the Early Writings of Charlotte Brontë*, edited by Christine Alexander (Oxford, vol. i, 1987; vol. ii, parts 1 and 2, 1991)
Alexander *EW*	Christine Alexander, *The Early Writings of Charlotte Brontë* (Oxford, 1983)
Allott	Miriam Allott, *The Brontës: The Critical Heritage* (1974)
AR	Amelia Ringrose
Aylott	Aylott and Jones
Barker	Juliet R. V. Barker, *The Brontës* (1994)
BB	Branwell Brontë
BCP	*Book of Common Prayer*
Berg	Henry W. and Albert A. Berg Collection, The New York Public Library, Astor, Lenox, and Tilden Foundations
Biographical Notice	*Wuthering Heights and Agnes Grey* . . . A New Edition Revised, with a Biographical Notice of the Authors . . . By Currer Bell (Smith, Elder and Co., 1850)
BL	British Library
Bon	Bonnell Collection, Brontë Parsonage Museum, Haworth
BPM	Brontë Parsonage Museum, Haworth
Brewer	E. C. Brewer, *A Dictionary of Phrase and Fable* (revised and corrected by Ifor H. Evans, 1978)
Bronteana	*Bronteana: The Rev. Patrick Brontë, A. B., His collected Works and Life*, edited by J. Horsfall Turner. (Bingley, 1898)
Brotherton	Brotherton Collection, Brotherton Library, University of Leeds
B.S.	Brontë Society
BST	*Brontë Society Transactions*. References are to volume, part, and page[s]; e.g. 17. 90. 339–40
Cadman	Cadman Collection, Brontë Parsonage Museum
CB	Charlotte Brontë
CBCircle	Clement K. Shorter, *Charlotte Brontë and her Circle* (1896)
CH	Constantin Heger
Chadwick	Mrs E. H. Chadwick, *In the Footsteps of the Brontës* (1914)
Chitham *ABP*	Edward Chitham, *The Poems of Anne Brontë* (1979)
CKS	Clement King Shorter

CP	*The Letters of Mrs. Gaskell*, edited by J. A. V. Chapple and Arthur Pollard (Manchester, 1966)
DNB	*Dictionary of National Biography*
Dugdale	Thomas Dugdale, *Curiosities of Great Britain: England and Wales Delineated* (published in parts, *c*.1837–41)
ECG	Elizabeth Cleghorn Gaskell
EJB	Emily Jane Brontë
EJB *Diary*	Emily Jane Brontë, MS Diary Paper
EJK	Elizabeth Jane Kingston
EN	Ellen Nussey
EN *Diary* 1844	Ellen Nussey, MS Diary, Texas
EN *Diary* 1849	Ellen Nussey, MS Diary, BPM
FHG	Francis Henry Grundy
Fitzwilliam	Fitzwilliam Museum, Cambridge
Fraser *CB*	Rebecca Fraser, *Charlotte Brontë* (1988)
Gérin *AB*	Winifred Gérin, *Anne Brontë* (1959)
Gérin *BB*	Winifred Gérin, *Branwell Brontë* (1961)
Gérin *CB*	Winifred Gérin, *Charlotte Brontë: The Evolution of Genius* (Oxford, 1967)
Gérin *EJB*	Winifred Gérin, *Emily Brontë* (Oxford, 1971)
GHL	George Henry Lewes
Gr.	Grolier Collection, BPM
Grundy	Francis Henry Grundy, *Pictures of the Past* (1879)
GS	George Smith
Hatfield	Typescript copy of *Nussey*, Hatfield papers, BPM
Hatfield *EBP*	*The Complete Poems of Emily Jane Brontë*, edited by C. W. Hatfield (1941)
HC	Hartley Coleridge
HM	MS in Huntington Library, San Marino, California
HN	Henry Nussey
HN *Diary*	Henry Nussey, MS Diary, BL MS Egerton 3268A
Hours at Home	Letters of CB published in Scribners' *Hours at Home*, vol. xi (New York, 1870)
Huxley	Leonard Huxley, *The House of Smith Elder* (1923)
Infernal World	Daphne du Maurier, *The Infernal World of Branwell Brontë* (1960)
i.w.	illegible word or words
JBL	Joseph Bentley Leyland
JE	*Jane Eyre*
Law-Dixon	MS formerly in the collection of Sir Alfred J. Law, at Honresfeld, Littleborough, Lancashire
Leyland	Francis A. Leyland, *The Brontë Family, with Special Reference to Patrick Branwell Brontë* (2 vols.; 1886)
LD	John Lock and W. T. Dixon, *A Man of Sorrow: The Life, Letters and Times of the Rev. Patrick Brontë* (1965)
Life	E. C. Gaskell, *The Life of Charlotte Brontë* (2 vols.; 1857). (First edition unless otherwise stated)

Life 1900	E. C. Gaskell, *The Life of Charlotte Brontë*, with an introduction and notes by Clement K. Shorter (Haworth Edition, 1900)
Lowell, Harvard	Amy Lowell Collection, Harvard University Library
Mayhall	John Mayhall, *The Annals of Yorkshire from the Earliest Period to the Present Time* (2 vols.; Leeds, 1862)
MGC	Mildred G. Christian
MGC *Census*	Mildred G. Christian, *A Census of Brontë Manuscripts in the United States*, in 5 parts, *The Trollopian* (1947–8)
Miscellaneous Writings	*The Miscellaneous and Unpublished Writings of Charlotte and Patrick Branwell Brontë* (2 vols.; 1936, 1938). (Part of the Shakespeare Head Brontë edition)
Montague	Montague Collection, New York Public Library
MS	Holograph manuscript
MT	Mary Taylor
Murray	Archives held by John Murray (Publishers)
MW	Margaret Wooler
Needham	Ellen Nussey's copies of letters from CB, bought by Mrs Needham of Blackburn in 1898; now in BPM
Neufeldt *BBP*	*The Poems of Patrick Branwell Brontë*, edited by Victor A. Neufeldt (London, 1990)
Neufeldt *CBP*	*The Poems of Charlotte Brontë*, edited by Victor A. Neufeldt (London, 1985)
Nussey	*The Story of the Brontës: Their Home, Haunts, Friends and Works. Part Second—Charlotte's Letters* (Printed for J. Horsfall Turner; Bingley, 1885–9). (The suppressed edition)
NYPL	New York Public Library
OCEL	*Oxford Companion to English Literature*, edited by Margaret Drabble (Oxford, 1985)
ODEP	*Oxford Dictionary of English Proverbs* (Oxford, 1970)
OED	*Oxford English Dictionary*
Oxon	J. Foster, *Alumni Oxonienses 1715–1886* (4 vols.; London and Oxford 1887, 1888)
PB	The Revd Patrick Brontë
Pforzheimer	Pforzheimer Collection, New York Public Library
Pierpont Morgan	Pierpont Morgan Library, New York
Pigot's *Directory* + date	[James] Pigot & Co's *National Commercial Directory* (1830) Pigot & Co's Royal National and Commercial Directory (Manchester, 1841)
PM	Postmark[s]
Poems 1846	*Poems by Currer, Ellis, and Acton Bell* [Charlotte, Emily, and Anne Brontë], (1846)
Princeton, Parrish Collection	Morris L. Parrish Collection, Drawer A–B, Princeton University Library
Princeton, Taylor Collection	Robert H. Taylor Collection, Princeton University Library
Problems	Edward Chitham and Tom Winnifrith, *Brontë Facts and Brontë Problems* (1983)

Regional History	*A Regional History of the Railways of Great Britain* (15 vols.; 1960–91)
Reid	T. Wemyss Reid, *Charlotte Brontë: A Monograph* (1877)
Robinson *EB*	A. M. F. Robinson [later Darmesteter, later Duclaux], *Emily Brontë* (1883)
Rosenbach	Rosenbach Museum and Library, Philadelphia
Rutgers-Symington	Papers of J. Alexander Symington at Rutgers University
Rylands	John Rylands Library of the University of Manchester
Rylands MS *Life*	E. C. Gaskell, holograph MS of *The Life of Charlotte Brontë* in Rylands
SE	Smith, Elder and Co.
SG	Seton-Gordon Collection, BPM
Shackleton	Abraham Shackleton, MS Weather Records, Cliffe Castle Museum, Keighley, Yorkshire
Shorter	Clement K. Shorter, *The Brontës: Life and Letters* (2 vols.; 1908) Letters in *Shorter* are identified by their numbers. Reference to material other than letters is by volume and page.
Sixty Treasures	Juliet R. V. Barker, *Sixty Treasures* (Haworth, 1988)
Stevens	*Mary Taylor, Friend of Charlotte Brontë: Letters from New Zealand and Elsewhere*, edited by Joan Stevens (Oxford, 1972)
Stockett-Wise	Correspondence of C. W. Hatfield and Davidson Cook in the Stockett/Thomas J. Wise Collection, University of British Columbia Library
Tenant	Anne Brontë, *The Tenant of Wildfell Hall*
TLS	*The Times Literary Supplement*
Texas	The Harry Ransom Humanities Research Center, University of Texas at Austin
UBC	University of British Columbia, Vancouver, Canada
Venn	J. A. Venn, *Alumni Cantabrigienses 1752–1900*, part 2, (6 vols.; Cambridge, 1922–54)
W & S	*The Brontës: Their Lives, Friendships and Correspondence*, edited by T. J. Wise and J. A. Symington (4 vols.; Shakespeare Head Brontë (Oxford, 1932) Letters in W & S are identified by their numbers; other material is referred to by vol. & page.
WH	*Wuthering Heights*
Whitehead	Barbara Whitehead, *Charlotte Brontë and her 'Dearest Nell'* (Otley; 1993)
White's *Directory* + date	William White, *History, Gazetteer and Directory of the West Riding of Yorkshire* . . . (2 vols.; Sheffield, vol. i, 1837; vol. ii, 1838) William White, *Directory of . . . Leeds* (Sheffield, 1843) William White, *Directory and Topography of Leeds, Bradford, . . . and the whole of the Clothing Districts of the West Riding of Yorkshire* (Sheffield, 1847)
Winnifrith *Background*	Tom Winnifrith, *The Brontës and their Background: Romance and Reality* (1973)
Winnifrith *BBP*	*The Poems of Patrick Branwell Brontë*, edited by Tom Winnifrith (Oxford, 1983)

Winnifrith *CBP*	*The Poems of Charlotte Brontë*, edited by Tom Winnifrith (Oxford, 1984)
Wright	*The English Dialect Dictionary*, edited by Joseph Wright (6 vols.; 1898–1905)
Wroot	*Sources of Charlotte Brontë's Novels: Persons and Places*, by Herbert E. Wroot (Shipley, 1935; Publications of the Brontë Society, Supplementary Part to No. 4 of vol. 8)
WSW	William Smith Williams
WYAS + location	West Yorkshire Archive Service: repositories at Bradford, Calderdale (Halifax), Kirklees (Huddersfield), Leeds, and Wakefield

Symbols

< >	Deleted in MS by author
\ /	Added in MS by author
*	Word deleted in MS by Ellen Nussey
**	Placed before and after conjectural readings of phrases or longer passages deleted by Ellen Nussey
[ ]	Added by editor
—	Digits or letters missing or obscured in postmark

Unless otherwise indicated page references to novels by the Brontës are to the Clarendon editions published by Oxford University Press under the general editorship of Ian Jack:

Anne Brontë, *Agnes Grey*, edited by Hilda Marsden and Robert Inglesfield, 1988
Anne Brontë, *The Tenant of Wildfell Hall*, edited by Herbert Rosengarten, 1992
Charlotte Brontë, *Jane Eyre*, edited by Jane Jack and Margaret Smith, 1969; revd. 1975
Charlotte Brontë, *The Professor*, edited by Margaret Smith and Herbert Rosengarten, 1987
Charlotte Brontë, *Shirley*, edited by Herbert Rosengarten and Margaret Smith, 1979
Charlotte Brontë, *Villette*, edited by Herbert Rosengarten and Margaret Smith, 1984
Emily Brontë, *Wuthering Heights*, edited by Hilda Marsden and Ian Jack, 1976.

INTRODUCTION

I thank you again for your last letter which I found as full or fuller of interest than either of the preceding ones—it is just written as I wish you to write to me—not a detail too much—a correspondence of that sort is the next best thing to actual conversation—though it must be allowed that between the two there is a wide gulph still—

I imagine your face—voice—presence very plainly when I read your letters.

When Charlotte Brontë wrote these words to Ellen Nussey on 19 January 1847 their friendship had lasted for sixteen years, and they had written to each other some hundreds of letters. At their best Charlotte's letters to her have some of the immediacy of good conversation—a quality which was to shock her husband Arthur Nicholls soon after their marriage in 1854. 'Men don't seem to understand making letters a vehicle of communication—they always seem to think us incautious. I'm sure I don't think I have said anything rash—however you must burn it when read. Arthur says such letters as mine never ought to be kept—they are dangerous as lucifer matches—so be sure to follow a recommendation he has just given "fire them"—or "there will be no more." . . . I can't help laughing—this seems to me so funny; Arthur however says he is quite serious and looks it, I assure you'.[1]

Fortunately Ellen disobeyed orders and retained most of the letters she received. The result is that we have some 380 intimate and revealing letters written with a fine disregard for their possible incendiary qualities, in the confidence of a tried and trusted friendship. Letters to Ellen greatly outnumber those to other recipients in the present volume; and though the publication of *Jane Eyre* in 1847 greatly increased the volume and range of her correspondence, she continued to reveal to Ellen the daily life and many of the feelings she could not fully share with those who first knew her as the famous Currer Bell.

Charlotte met Ellen in 1831 as a fellow-pupil at Miss Margaret Wooler's school at Roe Head, Mirfield in Yorkshire. The school was about 18 miles away from her home in Haworth parsonage, where Charlotte had lived since her father, the Revd Patrick Brontë, had moved there with his family in April 1820. She had been born at Thornton near Bradford on 21 April 1816, and was the third child in a family of six. Her eldest sister Maria was born in 1813, and was to become the serious, quiet, patient child whom Charlotte portrayed as Helen Burns in *Jane Eyre*. Both Maria and Elizabeth Brontë, born in 1815, were to die of tuberculosis in 1825. Patrick Branwell Brontë, the only boy in the family, was the next in age to Charlotte, being born on 26 June 1817; their younger sisters

[1] EN ?27.10.1854.

were Emily Jane, born 30 July 1818, and Anne, born 17 January 1820. Their mother, Maria Branwell Brontë, a Cornishwoman whom Patrick had met when she visited relatives at Woodhouse Grove School near Leeds, seems to have been an attractive, loving, woman, capable of a gentle liveliness, conventionally educated, and somewhat naïvely pious, as her essay on 'The Advantages of Poverty in Religious Concerns' shows. It was perhaps intended to be published as a tract, but was not printed until C. K. Shorter included it as appendix I in his *The Brontës: Life and Letters* in 1908. Mrs Brontë died of cancer on 15 September 1821. Many years later on 16 February 1850, Mr Brontë put into Charlotte's hands a 'little packet' of her mother's letters, yellow with time, and she wrote: 'it was strange to peruse now for the first time the records of a mind whence my own sprang—and most strange—and at once sad and sweet to find that mind of a truly fine, pure and elevated order. They were written to papa before they were married—there is a rectitude, a refinement, a constancy, a modesty, a sense—a gentleness about them indescribable. I wished She had lived and that I had known her.'[2]

After Mrs Brontë's death the children were cared for by her sister, Elizabeth Branwell, who earned the girls' respect and Branwell Brontë's love, and by their servant Tabitha Aykroyd, whose protective devotion they repaid with an equal loyalty. In 1824 Mr Brontë took his four elder daughters to the newly established 'Clergy Daughters' School' at Cowan Bridge in Lancashire, which was to be unforgettably portrayed as Lowood school in *Jane Eyre*. Maria, already desperately ill, was brought home on 14 February 1825, and died on 6 May. After Elizabeth was sent home on 31 May Mr Brontë lost no time in fetching his younger daughters back to Haworth; and Charlotte was therefore at home when Elizabeth died on 15 June.

Charlotte's closeness to the remaining members of the family gave her security and stability so long as she remained at home, but her suppressed anxiety came to the surface when she was separated from it, as a pupil at Miss Wooler's school from January 1831 until 20 June 1832, and again as a teacher there from 29 July 1835 until 22 December 1838. Emily accompanied her as a pupil in 1835, but was too homesick to remain; after her return home, Anne took her place at the school. The letters of 1835–8 reflect Charlotte's panic about Anne's illness in 1837, her fears about her own spiritual well-being, her worries about the health of her friends Mary Taylor and Ellen Nussey, and her clinging dependence on their affection. Charlotte's loss of her mother is echoed in the motherless state of the heroines of her novels, but is less obvious in her letters. An underlying tension is however betrayed in her letter to her cousin Eliza Kingston on 8 May 1846: 'all of us enjoy better health when the air is serene and mild—I fancy most of us possess

[2] MS BPM Gr. E 17, W & S 527. Maria's letters were first printed in full in *CBCircle* in 1896, 34–51.

the Constitution of Mamma's family—Myself and my sister Anne especially—'.[3] Charlotte's appreciation of motherly qualities in older women who gave her some of the warm affection she needed is evident in many of her letters: she came to have a lasting love and respect for Margaret Wooler, her elder by 24 years, finding in her the 'rectitude', refinement, and good sense she associated with her mother; and she responded with courteous affection and gratitude to Ellen's mother, the elderly Mrs Nussey.

Our knowledge of Charlotte and her family before 1829 derives mainly from later recollections, but from that date onwards there is an abundance of evidence in their writings in prose and verse and in the letters of Charlotte, Branwell, and Mr Brontë. Because so few letters to Charlotte have survived I have included complete letters from her friends and family to other people wherever they illuminate her life more clearly than piecemeal quotations or summaries could do.

Early Letters, 1829–35

Charlotte's first letter was written in September 1829 to her father. Throughout her life her strongest loyalty was to him, and she already shows both a dutiful affection and an awareness of what will most please and interest him—his young family's pleasant progress in 'reading, working, and learning' their lessons, and in making drawings which their uncle thinks good enough to keep. The correspondence with Ellen Nussey began in May 1831 with 'C's first letter written at School'—in laborious copperplate and with the self-conscious courtesy of an exercise designed to please both teacher and friend. Seventeen other letters to Ellen during this period show a development from this hesitant beginning through sententious advice to more natural schoolgirl gossip and teasing, and eventually to an ardent adolescent fondness.

The letters tell us little, at this stage, of Charlotte's secret world of imagination, shared only with her family. She and Branwell were writing prolifically, creating miniature magazines filled with precocious reviews, poems, and stories in imitation of the journals seen or taken at the parsonage. The children shared their father's lively interest in politics, his enlightened Toryism, and his enthusiasm for the Duke of Wellington; in their early stories these preoccupations were curiously mingled with exotic and romantic scenes deriving from the Arabian Nights or 'Sir Charles Morell's' (James Ridley's) *The Tales of the Genii*. Together Branwell and Charlotte invented an imaginary kingdom of Angria, and filled it with the adventures of heroes and villains, lovers and ladies modelled on the characters of Scott's novels and Byron's poems, or soldiers modelled on the military heroes of the Peninsular War. Their style was

[3] MS Berg; ?previously unpublished.

joyfully experimental and varied, precocious in its forays into rough satire, elaborately picturesque description, or dramatic dialogue, and full of echoes of their reading—not only of Scott and Byron, but also of Shakespeare, Milton, Southey, Coleridge, Burns, and the writers in *Blackwood's Edinburgh Magazine*. Thus there is a curious undercurrent beneath the surface of Charlotte's correspondence, and I have drawn attention to it where oblique references or ironic contrasts might otherwise be missed. For example on 4 July 1834 Charlotte solemnly advised Ellen not to read Shakespeare's comedies or Byron's *Don Juan*—even though Ellen would find that bad poems were 'invariably revolting' and she would never wish to read them over twice. Yet in the same month Charlotte wrote *The Spell: An Extravaganza*—a lurid, amoral and entertaining tale in which Charlotte's casual and unabashed quotations from *Don Juan* show her own complete familiarity with the poem.[4]

While there are no completely new letters in this early period, the texts of several letters are fuller and more accurate than those in previous editions: those of 11 May 1831, 13 January 1832, 21 July 1832, 5 September 1832, and 8 May 1835 are now manuscript based. The personality of Charlotte's friend Mary Taylor of Gomersal, the 'Rose Yorke' of *Shirley*, is brought into clearer focus: her enthusiasm for art, and her radical politics, both encouraged by her father, are revealed in the letter to Ellen Nussey of 13 January 1832. In contrast Charlotte's contemptuous dislike of Whig politicians is emphasized in her letter of 8 May 1835, written in the year of an important election in which both Mr Brontë and Branwell took an active interest.

1836–8

After three years at home, from June 1832 until July 1835, Charlotte had returned as a teacher to Roe Head school. She continued to teach there in 1836 and 1837, and moved with the school to Heald's House, Dewsbury Moor, early in 1838. She finally left her employment there on 22 December 1838, as her father told Mrs Gaskell on 30 July 1855.[5] From October 1835 until ?December 1838 Charlotte had the quiet company of her sister Anne—who however was a pupil, and at her age could not, perhaps, be her sister's confidante. The contrast between Charlotte's inner and outer worlds is very marked at this period. Her mundane life of lessons with recalcitrant or stupid pupils, of mechanical 'repetitions' or oral examinations, and of reluctant attention to the dress or discipline of the younger girls within the small, enclosed, almost conventual world of the school, was sharply at odds with her inner life. Her imaginary heroes were plumed, dashing, and amorous, her heroines bejewelled, silken, haughty, or dying for love's sake. After one wearisome schoolday she 'crept up to the

[4] See Alexander *EEW*, ii. pt. 2, 148–238. [5] MS Rylands.

bed-room to be alone for the first time' and resigned herself 'to the Luxury of twilight & solitude . . . the toil of the Day succeeded by this moment of divine leisure—had acted on me like opium & was coiling about me a disturbed but fascinating spell such as I never felt before. What I imagined grew morbidly vivid. I remember I quite seemed to see with my bodily eyes, a lady standing in the hall of a Gentleman's house as if waiting for some one . . . She was very handsome—it is not often we can form from pure idea faces so individually fine'.[6]

At the same time Charlotte's fondness for Ellen Nussey was becoming extreme; Charlotte was desolate when Ellen was away from her home in nearby Birstall, hated to be separated from her, and longed for her return. Because Ellen had a docile, unquestioning, conventional piety she seemed doubly unattainable and admirable. Charlotte in contrast was afflicted with feverish doubts and fears; 'longing for holiness which I shall never, never obtain . . . darkened in short by the very shadows of Spiritual Death!'[7] Her self-torments culminated in a nervous crisis in May 1838. Charlotte later recalled this 'dreadful doom' of Hypochondria and realized that she could have been no better company for Miss Wooler than 'a stalking ghost'.[8] Fortunately a period of recuperation at home and the lively company of Mary and Martha Taylor, during their visit to Haworth, restored her to a healthier frame of mind and enabled her to return to her work.

The letters of this period record vividly but disturbingly the erratic fluctuations of Charlotte's moods. Refreshed by a holiday at home in summer 1836, she could write with cheerful mockery of the Miss Uptons 'setting out accoutred in grand style . . . in gay green dresses—fit for a ball-room rather than for walking four miles on a dusty road' and could sign off to her 'kind, sincere Ellen Scribble' as her 'affectionate Coz Charlotte Scrawl'.[9] She could also impale the butterfly character of Amelia Walker as sharply and with as little mercy as Jane Austen might have done: 'Miss Amelia changed her character every half hour. Now she assumed the sweet sentimentalist, now the reckless rattler. Sometimes the question was "Shall I look prettiest lofty?" and again "Would not tender familiarity suit me better?" ' Amelia's unfortunate brother William is also demolished: 'William Walker though now grown a tall—well built man is an incorrigible "Booby" from him I could not extract a word of sense.'[10]

But for the most part Charlotte is strained, self-absorbed, and often self-abasing; she hates herself for her 'miserable and wretched touchiness of

[6] Roe Head Journal fragment MS BPM Bon 98(8).
[7] EN 5 and 6.12.1836; MS BPM Bon 162.
[8] MW ?Nov./Dec. 1846; MS Fitzwilliam.
[9] EN Aug./Sept. 1836; MS BPM Gr. E 26.
[10] EN *c*.7.7.1836; MS HM 24412.

character' and her 'idiocy'; she abhors and despises herself as a 'coarse commonplace wretch' in contrast to her extravagantly praised darling Ellen. Though she could not control her morbid sensibility she could express and even analyse it, and her observation of her own experience was to contribute ultimately to her novels. The emotional crises of Caroline Helstone and Lucy Snowe are presented with a similar intensity. Ridicule makes Charlotte 'wince as if [she] had been touched with a hot iron: things that nobody else cares for enter into my mind and rankle there like venom';[11] Lucy Snowe's mental pain wrung her heart, brimmed her eyes, and scalded her cheek 'with tears hot as molten metal'.[12] In contrast Ellen's notes are 'meat and drink' to Charlotte, as Paul Emanuel's letters were for Lucy 'real food that nourished, living water that refreshed'.[13]

By the end of 1838 Charlotte's equilibrium was more or less restored; she had gradually emerged, spiritually, from her slough of despond, and the return of a healthy self-respect and a sense of humour allowed her to greet Ellen's home-coming from her visits to relatives with a normal and moderate pleasure. By January 1839 she had definitely 'come through' and was capable of laughing at and resisting Ellen's repeated invitations to stay at Brookroyd.

Charlotte's correspondence with the poet Robert Southey in 1836–7 marks an important stage in her development as a writer. On 29 December 1836 she had written to ask the ageing poet if he would give his opinion on her poems. The original MS of her letter is missing, but an early copy MS of his reply makes it clear that she had written in the intense and 'exaltée' vein characteristic of this period about her ambition to be 'for ever known' as a poetess, and that she had imagined the laureate 'stooping from a throne of light & glory'.[14] With this in mind one can more readily appreciate the kindly caution of Southey's advice that Charlotte's habitual daydreams will induce 'a distempered state of mind'; and one can perhaps see his notorious dictum that 'Literature cannot be the business of a woman's life' as more pardonable in its full context. Southey had warned Charlotte that she should not cultivate her talent 'with a view to distinction', but he had also generously acknowledged that she possessed '& in no inconsiderable degree . . . "the faculty of Verse" '. A rational, steady confidence in her ability was precisely what she needed; and she later told Mrs Gaskell that 'Mr. Southey's letter was kind and admirable; a little stringent, but it did me good'.[15]

The letters of 1836–8 present a number of textual problems. Many are

[11] EN 26.9.1836; MS BPM Bon 161.
[12] *Villette* 220.
[13] EN 5 and 6.12.1836; MS BPM Bon 162; *Villette* 713.
[14] Southey to CB 12.3.1837; MS BL Add. 44355.
[15] *Life* i. 172.

undated, and Ellen Nussey's later annotations on her letters from Charlotte show that she was unsure of the dates. She may also have destroyed or lost several letters, for none survives which can be definitely placed in the second half of 1837, and comparatively few in 1838; and the MSS of four of the twenty letters to Ellen have not been located. Evidence derived from the original MSS, from postmarks, and from Henry Nussey's diary has led to the dating of three letters in 1838 (February / March, 24 August, 2 October) compared with dates in 1836 and 1837 in previous editions. Other letters have been more tentatively placed, using the evidence of paper, content, or dated contemporary material such as the Roe Head Journal or the book presented to Anne Brontë on 14 December 1836. The resulting sequence is reasonably coherent, but the lack of complete MS documentation means that it cannot be definitive. Two letters not printed by Wise and Symington in the Shakespeare Head edition of 1932 make a pleasant addition to the record: one is the brief friendly note to Ann Greenwood of Spring Head written on 22 July [1836], and the other is the lively and interesting letter about the Miss Uptons—one of the splendid collection of forty-four autograph letters acquired by the Brontë Society from the Grolier Club sale at Christie's in New York on 25 March 1980. My text differs slightly from that in *BST* 17. 90. 353–4, and I have supplied an approximate date of August / September 1836.

1839–41

For the first five months of 1839 Charlotte was at home. In March she received and refused a proposal of marriage from Ellen's brother, the Revd Henry Nussey. In May she took a temporary post as a governess in the family of John Benson Sidgwick at Stonegappe near Skipton. Some time after her return in July she was astonished to receive another proposal of marriage, this time from the Revd David Pryce, whom she had met only once, and again sent a refusal. In September she saw the sea for the first time, when she went with Ellen to Easton and Bridlington on the Yorkshire coast. The parsonage was enlivened in 1840 by the frequent company of the handsome young William Weightman, who had become Mr Brontë's curate in August 1839. In November 1840 Charlotte sent the opening chapters of a novel to the poet Hartley Coleridge, son of S. T. Coleridge, and was not (so she said) unduly cast down by his opinion that her novel would not 'make an impression upon the heart of any Editor in Christendom'. From the end of February until December 1841 she was a governess to the children of Mr and Mrs John White of Rawdon, near Leeds; she endured the last few weeks the more willingly because she had decided to go abroad. She and her sister Emily planned to acquire the extra skills in French, German, and music which would enable them to set up a school of their own.

There is a welcome new self-assurance and vigour about many of the letters of 1839–41. Released in December 1838 from 'governess drudgery' at Heald's House, Dewsbury Moor, Charlotte knew that she must eventually resume the yoke; but she was in a healthier state of mind, more resilient than she had been, less self-condemning, less clinging in her affection for Ellen Nussey, and less violently assailed by religious fears. She found satisfaction in writing some of her most accomplished Angrian tales. Novelettes such as 'Henry Hastings'—'A young man of captivating exterior, elegant dress'—and 'Caroline Vernon' have a more coherent structure, more mature characterization and a wider social range than her previous prose works. They bear a recognizable relation to Charlotte's real experience: Elizabeth Hastings comes from a rough wild countryside of moors and mountains, and has been a governess; the exotic Zamorna for a time resembles a country gentleman like Mr Sidgwick, wearing a 'broad-brimmed hat of straw', watching the hay-makers 'busily engaged' in his fields, and chatting with his dialect-speaking companion about tillage and manure, bog-soil and wheat-planting. Nevertheless Zamorna soon resumes his usual character as a glamorous seducer, and as Christine Alexander says, 'More than any other of her manuscripts, *Caroline Vernon* reverberates with Byronic echoes.'[16] It was probably in 1839 that Charlotte made a conscious effort to bid 'farewell to Angria': 'I long to quit for awhile that burning clime . . . the mind would cease from excitement and turn now to a cooler region where the dawn breaks grey and sober, and the coming day for a time at least is subdued by clouds.'[17] Between 1839 and 1841 Charlotte wrote the various MS fragments now gathered together as *Ashworth*: chapters of a novel in which Angrian characters have been transformed into Alexander Ashworth, a 'Cow-Jobber—& Horse-Jockey' adored by 'the smutty—intelligent mechanics of Manchester & [of] the West-Riding of Yorkshire', and his brother William, 'quieter in manner but not more cordial in feeling'. These characters were to reappear as the Crimsworths in *The Professor*, the early chapters of which were probably written at this period. In concentrating the interest of that novel on the younger brother and in giving him an acute intelligence, a longing for liberty and self-fulfilment, and in making him seek these ideals abroad, Charlotte expressed her own frustrations and that strong 'wish for wings' which was to take her to Mme Heger's school in Brussels in 1842.

The letters of this period anticipate Charlotte's major novels in content, tone, and style more often, and more obviously, than in previous years. When she refuses Henry Nussey's proposal she tells him that it is her habit to study character: she has observed him, and helpfully if rather tactlessly describes the kind of calm and reasonable wife he should marry—not, she says firmly, a

[16] *EW* 196. [17] MS BPM Bon 125, quoted in *Miscellaneous Writings*, ii. 404.

romantic and eccentric enthusiast like herself: 'Her character should not be too marked, ardent and original—her temper should be mild, her piety undoubted, her [spirits] even and cheerful, and her "personal attractions" sufficient to please your eye and gratify your just pride.'[18] Charlotte's prescription sounds slightly absurd but was probably offered in good faith. Transformed into an insistence on spiritual affinity in marriage, the conviction expressed here was to be at the heart of *Jane Eyre*.

Almost equally important was Charlotte's experience of being an 'inferior' and an outsider when she worked as a private governess. In her letters to Ellen and her sister Emily she described her detestation of her humiliating position in Mrs Sidgwick's household, and the strain of controlling her real feelings and disguising her essential self in her uncongenial surroundings. 'I used to think I should like to be in the stir of grand folks' society but I have had enough of it—it is dreary work to look on and listen. I see now more clearly than I have ever done before that a private governess has no existence, is not considered as a living and rational being except as connected with the wearisome duties she has to fulfil.'[19] Charlotte's heroines were to be animated by a similar rebellious spirit.

Many of the letters of this period are vigorous in praise or blame, emphatic, lively, or enthusiastic. 'Have you forgot the Sea by this time Ellen?', she writes in October 1839. 'Is it grown dim in your mind? or you can still see it dark blue and green and foam-white and hear it—roaring roughly when the wind is high or rushing softly when it is calm?'[20] Even in writing to the sedate Henry Nussey she refers to the 'glorious changes' of the sea. Her longing for change is expressed in her impatience, her wish for wings; 'a fire was kindled in my very heart which I could not quench—I so longed to increase my attainments to become something better than I am . . . Mary Taylor cast oil on the flames.'[21]

This enthusiasm coexists, as it does in Charlotte's novels, with an increasingly astringent satirical tone. She reacts strongly to the pettiness and bigotry of the curates, as she does in *Shirley*, and is contemptuously amused by the affectation of her 'august relations' the Branwell Williams.[22] Her outspokenness can be enjoyably unladylike or positively slangy: she will 'take a running leap and clear' the entire 'circle of dilemmas' Ellen has raised around her.[23] The invitation to go to the seaside drives her 'clean daft', Ellen is to be scolded with 40-horse power for her presents, and the curates need 'kicking or horse-whipping'. She signs herself 'Caliban' or 'Charivari' or 'Ça ira', and is full of

[18] HN 5.3.1839; MS William Self.
[19] EJB 8.6.1839.
[20] EN 24.10.1839; MS HM 24419.
[21] EN 7.8.1841; MS HM 24428; EN 2.11.41; MS HM 24429.
[22] EN 7.4.1840, 14.8.1840.
[23] EN 20.1.1839; MS BPM B.S. 40.5.

rebellious energy. 'I cannot be formal in a letter,' she tells Henry Nussey; 'if I write at all I must write as I think.'[24]

The most attractive letters of this period reflect the spirit of youthful exuberance introduced into the Brontës' lives by William Weightman. 'Have you lit your pipe with Mr Weightman's valentine?' she asks Ellen, in a cheerful letter anticipating the pleasure of a visit to Brookroyd. 'Huzza for Saturday afternoon after next! I'll snap my fingers at Mrs W[hite] & her imps Good night my lass!'[25] The atmosphere of heightened sexual consciousness aroused by the flirtatious Mr Weightman's visits to the parsonage is evident in several passages printed here for the first time. Sentences edited out of a letter to Ellen in the manuscript of Mrs Gaskell's *Life* read: 'Our letters are assuming an odd tone. We write of little else but love and marriage, and, ?verily, I have a sort of presentiment that you will be married before you are many years older. I do not wish you to reciprocate the compliment'.[26] Another passage which Ellen was determined to obliterate beyond retrieval has in fact been retrieved; it appears to confirm that Mary Taylor's behaviour in the presence of Branwell Brontë had been 'wrought to a pitch' of such intensity that 'Mr Weightman thought her mad'.[27]

A brief note to Maria Taylor of Stanbury, the daughter of a Haworth church trustee, kindly provided by one of her descendants, has not been published before. It probably dates from September 1839, and shows that Charlotte continued to be on friendly terms with this family.

A more substantial addition to the letters printed by Wise and Symington in 1932 is Charlotte's letter to Hartley Coleridge of 10 December 1840, which can now be readily compared with her draft version. Wise and Symington printed only the extracts from the draft given by Mrs Gaskell in the *Life*, and assumed, as she did, that it was 'apparently a reply to one from Wordsworth'.[28] In both the draft and the fair copy Charlotte uses the sardonic and flamboyant style she had developed for her satirical persona Charles Townshend in the Angrian stories—one of which she had sent to Coleridge for his opinion. No doubt piqued by his criticism, and protected by her anonymity, she clearly enjoyed writing this showy letter and elaborating it with extra flourishes in her final version. She mocks her own literary ambitions along with the absurdity, real or pretended, of the 'great' novelists. Her lively iconoclasm mingles with a wry affection for the tales she read in childhood, so 'infinitely superior to any trash of Modern literature'. Her references to Richardson's work are particularly interesting, for his novels are recalled in both *The Professor* and *Jane Eyre*.

[24] HN 9.5.1841; MS William Self.
[25] EN ?1.4.1841; MS HM 24427.
[26] EN 15.5.1840.
[27] EN 20.11.1840; MS HM 24426.
[28] See W & S 100, and the History of the Letters, below, p. 62.

1842–4

The year 1842 began with a slight coolness on the part of Ellen Nussey, who thought Charlotte had neglected her. She did not pay a farewell visit to Haworth before Charlotte set off with her father, Emily, and Joe and Mary Taylor for Brussels, where Mary joined her sister Martha at a school just outside the city, and Charlotte and Emily became pupils at Mme Heger's pensionnat. After five months of tuition, mainly in French, they were invited to stay on after the summer vacation, Charlotte to teach English and Emily music in return for their board and tuition. The end of the year was overshadowed by the deaths of Martha Taylor in Brussels and of William Weightman and Miss Branwell in Haworth. Charlotte and Emily hurried back to England, but were too late for their aunt's funeral. Charlotte was somewhat comforted by a happy reunion with Ellen Nussey. On 29 January 1843 she returned alone to the pensionnat, where she continued to teach English, to learn German, and to improve her knowledge of French. For a time during the first half-year she gave lessons in English to Mme Heger's husband Constantin Heger and his brother-in-law, and became increasingly devoted to M. Heger. By midsummer Charlotte's friends, the Dixons and Wheelwrights, had left Brussels, and Mme Heger's former kindness had changed to a cool reserve. Charlotte felt miserably isolated and homesick, and returned to Haworth in January 1844. Her father's deteriorating eyesight made it impossible for her to leave him again; she and her sisters therefore decided to start a school at the parsonage, but no pupils were to be had. Though Charlotte was not unduly depressed by this failure, her separation from M. Heger caused her great distress, and in October Mary Taylor's decision to emigrate to New Zealand made her feel 'as if a great planet fell out of the sky'.

Charlotte's two years in Brussels were of crucial importance in her life and writing. M. Heger's inspired teaching of French literature, his generous gifts of French books, his lessons in composition and literary analysis all widened Charlotte's insular horizons, developed her conscious appreciation of different styles of writing, and encouraged her to control and shape the material suggested for composition. She delighted in being the pupil of a cultured, intelligent master, and his autocratic, choleric, volatile temperament combined with his real kindness only added to the piquancy of the situation.

Letters written in Charlotte's first year in Brussels show a new sense of satisfaction: 'we are completely isolated in the midst of numbers—yet I think I am never unhappy—my present life is so delightful so congenial to my own nature.'[29] The full text of this letter reveals her amused observation of

[29] EN May 1842; MS Law-Dixon.

M. Heger's capricious behaviour: 'he is very angry with me just at present because I have written a translation which he chose to stigmatise as peu correct—not because it was particularly so in reality but because he happened to be in a bad humour when he read it.' In July she admitted to 'brief attacks of home-sickness' and found most of the pupils 'singularly cold, selfish, animal and inferior—they are besides very mutinous and difficult for the teachers to manage'.[30] These girls were to figure in *The Professor* as the monstrous Aurelia, Adèle, and Juanna Trista—violently overdrawn so as to contrast with the suave and subtle principal of the school, Mlle Reuter. In spite of her jaundiced view of the Belgian girls, Charlotte wrote that she had been happy in Brussels because she had 'always been fully occupied with the employments' that she liked. Charlotte and Emily continued to impress the Hegers with their intelligence and eagerness to learn, and M. Heger wrote warmly of their 'progrès très remarquable dans toutes les branches de l'enseignement'.[31] There was no doubt that the Hegers would welcome a return of their English pupils. But Brussels would have sad associations for them: Charlotte told Ellen that she had 'seen Martha's grave—the place where her ashes lie in a foreign country Aunt—Martha—Taylor—Mr Weightman are now all gone—how dreary & void everything seems'.[32] Charlotte's journey to the 'Protestant Cemetery, outside the gate of Louvain' was to be movingly recalled in *The Professor* and *Shirley*.

Charlotte's equilibrium was gradually restored. For a time her whole family, including Anne, was at home; and after Anne's return to her work as a governess, Charlotte broke through 'ceremony, or pride, or whatever it is' and was happily reunited with Ellen at Brookroyd. Other friends welcomed the travellers back. Two recently discovered notes to Mrs Taylor of Stanbury mention her 'kind invitation' to visit, though in the end only Branwell could go. Charlotte and Emily decided that they had to stay at home to prepare for the arrival of Ellen at Haworth.[33]

The year 1843 began well with teasing and lively letters to Ellen, full of affectionate 'nonsense'. The manuscript of the first, written on 6 January, shows Charlotte playfully extending the 'nothing' she has to tell her friend by spinning it out into single lines. On 6 March, writing from Brussels, she again teases Ellen about her admirer Mr Vincent, and finishes her letter with an absurd little sketch of a very plain and dumpy Charlotte waving good-bye to an apparently newly married Ellen. She felt lonely, but M. and Mme Heger had received her cordially and had offered her the use of their private sitting-room.

[30] EN July 1842; MS HM 24431.
[31] Letter to the Revd P. Brontë, 5.11.1842.
[32] EN 10.11.1842; MS Harvard.
[33] MSS of ?Dec. 1842, WYAS Calderdale (Halifax) and BPM B.S. 103.2.

Not wishing to intrude on them, she did not accept the offer and so, as she told Ellen 'I am a good deal by myself'. But she had twice enjoyed the friendly hospitality of Mary Taylor's relatives, the Dixon family. Two letters to Mary Dixon, the second one previously unpublished, show clearly the change that took place in the course of this year. In the first letter, written in the spring while Mary was still in Brussels, Charlotte cheerfully agrees to sit to Mary for her portrait, and jokes about her 'unfortunate head': 'the features thereof may yield good practice as they never yet submitted to any line of regularity—but have manifested each a spirit of independance, edifying to behold.'[34] The second letter, written on 16 October 1843, is markedly different in tone: 'I, isolated as I am, am not likely soon to forget you—I think of you often, by way of refreshment and contrast when I am weary of the Belgians—'. Longing for society, Charlotte has disinterred Mary's portrait from the bottom of a trunk and has been 'comforted by discovering a certain likeness'.[35]

The redating of a letter from 15 November 1843 (the date given for W & S 166) to June or July confirms other evidence that Charlotte's depression had begun before the long summer vacation. She told Emily on 29 May that she was convinced Mme Heger did not like her—'why, I can't tell'—and that M. Heger had 'withdrawn the light of his countenance'. By June or July the silence and loneliness of the pensionnat during the occasional days of holiday weighed down her spirits 'like lead', yet Mme Heger never came near her on such days: 'I fancy I begin to perceive the reason of this mighty distance & reserve it sometimes makes me laugh & at other times nearly cry.'[36]

During the long vacation the school was empty save for the uncongenial company of one of the teachers. Charlotte's attempt to escape from her nightmarish state by endlessly wandering through the streets of Brussels ended in her 'real confession' in the Catholic cathedral. It was an experience confided to Emily alone, with the request that 'Papa' should not be told. Most fully and hauntingly recreated in *Villette*, Charlotte's intense emotions were also echoed in *Shirley*. In both novels images of an enclosed, oppressive, tomb-like existence are associated with the deprivation of companionship and the loss of love. Charlotte was to admit in her last letter to Emily of 1843 that her mind was shaken 'for want of comfort'.[37]

This bleak ending to a year which had been so hopefully begun is softened a little by 'Mademoiselle Sophie's' affectionate note to Charlotte of 17 December.[38] Charlotte had found this teacher more likeable than her other colleagues,

[34] M. Dixon, early 1843; MS Berg.

[35] MS Princeton, Taylor Collection.

[36] EN June/July 1843; MS Pierpont Morgan MA 2696.

[37] EJB 19.12.1843.

[38] Not in W & S but printed in Gérin *CB* 589.

and would perhaps be slightly comforted by Sophie's assurance that more than one person would be thinking of her.

In a letter of 23 January 1844 Charlotte told Ellen that she would not 'forget what the parting with Monsr Heger' had cost her: 'It grieved me so much to grieve him who has been so true and kind and disinterested a friend.' The full text of the letter shows why she had refused his request to take one of his little daughters back to Haworth as a pupil: 'this however I refused to do as I knew it would not have been agreeable to Madame.'[39] The shape of Charlotte's major novels is already foreshadowed: in all, a privileged rival comes between the heroine and her 'master'.

Though there is an undertone of sadness in most of the letters of 1844—a consciousness of lost illusions, a longing to see M. Heger again, a pity for George Nussey's mental illness—there are pleasant and sometimes surprising touches of warmth and humour from time to time. There is a charming letter, not to be found in W & S, to a former pupil, the little Victoire Dubois.[40] There is a revival of an enjoyably forthright and slangy style in several of the letters to Ellen, and some comedy in the misdeeds of Ellen's 'infamous little bitch', Flossy junior. Charlotte is animated by a desire for action and for the achievement of her ambition to set up a school. Her two surviving letters to M. Heger in this year, written on 24 July and 24 October, show a conscious effort to atone for a previous letter to him which was 'peu raisonnable, parceque le chagrin me serrait le cœur' 'hardly rational, because sadness was wringing my heart'; in July she stresses that she will try to succeed in her plan for a school, that she is regularly learning passages of French by heart, and that she is convinced she will see him again. Her letter of October is over-excited, effusive, less controlled—but again positive in its joyful anticipation of a reply.

Access to original manuscripts of letters and to a manuscript diary kept by Ellen in 1844 has enabled me to redate six letters to her written during this year, so that the letters to M. Heger are now correctly placed within the sequence of those to Ellen and to other friends. A letter from Charlotte's pupil Mathilde, full of gratitude for Charlotte's kindness to her, shows that she too could inspire devotion. Ellen's long letter to Mary Gorham of 21 May 1844 also gives an attractive picture of Charlotte and Mary Taylor 'walking & talking with all their might in the garden' at Hunsworth, and greeting Ellen and her brother with a ' "bless you" burst[ing] forth in all the power of friendship & affection'.[41]

[39] MS Law-Dixon.
[40] 18.5.1844; MS BPM B.S. 51.
[41] MS BPM; quoted in part in *Whitehead* 108.

1845

Although Mary Taylor reported on 4 January that Charlotte was 'very well', her first letter is a cry of despair to M. Heger, whose failure to reply had become almost unbearable. Depressed by his silence and by the thought of Mary Taylor's imminent departure for New Zealand, Charlotte spent an unhappy week in February with the Taylors at Hunsworth. Recovering a little in the spring, perhaps because M. Heger had at last written to her, she was pleased when her sister Anne returned home in June, having decided to give up her post as governess in the Robinsons' family at Thorp Green. Charlotte felt free to leave her father in her sisters' care while she stayed with Ellen at Hathersage in Derbyshire. There she enjoyed a visit to the Peak cavern at Castleton, met some of the Eyre family, and saw their ancestral home, North Lees Hall, where, it was said, a mad woman had once been kept in an upper room. She was greatly shocked when she returned to Haworth on 26 July to find that Branwell had been dismissed from his tutorship at Thorp Green for conduct 'bad beyond expression'. Branwell had reacted to his dismissal by 'stunning or drowning his distress of mind' so that 'no one in the house could have rest'; and he was sent away for a week to recuperate. He let it be known that his employer's wife, Lydia Robinson, had showed him 'a degree of kindness which . . . ripened into declarations of more than ordinary feeling', and that he had daily enjoyed 'troubled pleasure, soon chastised by fear'.

For the rest of the year Branwell's behaviour, despite his sporadic efforts to find work and to write poetry, was a dragging burden on the family, who had to suffer his drinking, his bouts of lethargy, and fits of irritability. In spite of this, his sisters were trying to conquer their own depression by writing. By 31 July Anne had begun the third volume of *Passages in the Life of an Individual*—possibly a draft of *Agnes Grey*. Charlotte wrote poems, and looked out the beginning of a story about two brothers she had written before she went to Brussels. On to this she grafted more chapters of what was to become *The Professor*. In the autumn she made her famous discovery of a manuscript 'volume of verse in . . . Emily's handwriting', found in it 'a peculiar music—wild, melancholy, and elevating' and with difficulty persuaded her that 'such poems merited publication'. The sisters' dream of becoming authors now 'took the character of a resolve' and they agreed to arrange a selection of their verse. They carefully selected sixty-one poems—twenty-one each by Emily and Anne, nineteen by Charlotte—revised them to remove Angrian and Gondal names and to make other changes to fit them for publication, made fair copies of their own poems, and decided how they should be arranged. They must have worked steadily, for the collection was ready to be sent to publishers in January the following year. Nevertheless this absorbing work could not distract Charlotte completely from the pain of her separation from M. Heger; humiliated by her inability to control either her regrets or her impatience, she feared above all that he might become estranged from her. No other letter to M. Heger survives after her *cri de cœur* of 18 November.

Though it comes to the surface only in the two pitiable letters to Heger, this undercurrent of suppressed pain lies beneath all the letters written in 1845 to friends who could not be allowed to suspect its existence or its cause. Charlotte found some relief in revealing to Ellen her surface miseries, which were accountable enough: 'I can hardly tell you how time gets on here at Haworth . . . life wears away—I shall soon be 30—and I have done nothing yet—sometimes I get melancholy—at the prospect before and behind me—yet it is wrong and foolish to repine—undoubtedly my Duty directs me to stay at home for the present . . . I feel as if we were all buried here—I long to travel—to work to live a life of action.'[42] Charlotte was to endow Jane Eyre with the same urgent desire to escape confinement, and to speak for all women 'in silent revolt against their lot'.[43]

Charlotte's depression was transformed into angry rebellion in a letter to Ellen of 2 April 1845, which ends, 'Write again soon—for I feel rather fierce and want stroking down'. Her ferocity has been aroused by reflecting on the way women are expected to behave if they wish to 'escape the stigma of husband-seeking they must act & look like marble or clay—cold—expressionless, bloodless—for every appearance of feeling of joy—sorrow—friendliness, antipathy, admiration—disgust are alike construed by the world into an attempt to hook in a husband'. Defiantly, she advises Ellen *not* 'to live only by halves because if you shewed too much animation some pragmatical thing in breeches (excuse the expression) might take it into its pate to imagine that you designed to dedicate your precious life to its inanity'.[44] Charlotte's furious eloquence may well be a healthy reaction to a letter of good advice from Brussels, perhaps dictated by Mme Heger. Charlotte's defence of women's right to show themselves as they are and to defy misconstruction—'well-meaning women have their own Consciences to comfort them after all'—shows a welcome resilience. The heroines of her fiction would be condemned by some reviewers for a similar 'unregenerate and undisciplined spirit'.

Charlotte's concealed torments may also have helped her to understand and pity the suffering of others. Her self-pitying letter to M. Heger of 8 January was followed only a few days later by one expressing her deep concern for Ellen and her brother George, and her strong wish to give them comfort and hope. Affectionate messages and wishes for George's recovery continue throughout the year; and the pattern of personal grief and altruistic compassion is repeated

[42] EN 24.3.1845; MS Law-Dixon. [43] *JE* 132 [44] MS HM 24437.

in November. In her letter to M. Heger of 18 November Charlotte admits that she is enslaved to her obsession with him; when he does not write 'j'ai la fièvre—je perds l'appétit et le sommeil—je dépéris'. Yet two days later she sets aside her own feelings to reassure Ellen that her news about George is 'quite cheering . . . for I have ever remarked, that after much distress comes a proportionate degree of happiness'.[45] Earlier in the year she wrote a friendly and sympathetic letter to the schoolmaster's wife, Mrs Rand, with a kiss for her 'dear little baby'.[46] In June she described her father's increasing blindness with a full understanding of what it meant for him: 'can it be wondered at—that as he sees the most precious of his faculties leaving him, his spirits sometimes sink? It is so hard to feel that his few and scanty pleasures must all soon go—he now has the greatest difficulty in either reading or writing . . . I try to cheer him, sometimes I succeed temporarily.'[47]

Charlotte's reaction to Branwell's dismissal was one of shock rather than compassion. It was complicated by her repression of her feelings for M. Heger, by her apparent refusal to admit that her attraction to him might be interpreted as sexual and therefore comparable to Branwell's involvement with Mrs Robinson, and by her contempt for the moral weakness of a brother who had formerly been her closest companion. Charlotte's attitude to him was a complex one. Since discussion of it requires careful scrutiny of her letters, accurate texts and dates are especially important in this crucial year. Wise and Symington give incorrect dates for several letters of 1845 and for Charlotte's visit to Hathersage: Ellen Nussey's letters to Mary Gorham and Emily's Diary Paper of 30 July 1845 show that her visit lasted from about 3rd July until 26 July, not from 26 June until 19 July. Charlotte's letter to Ellen referring to Branwell's week at Haworth was written later than 24 June—probably on or about the 27th; and Emily's letter to Ellen, asking her to assure Charlotte that 'all are well at home' must have been sent on or about 16, not 11 July. The manuscript of Charlotte's discreet letter to Mrs Nussey refusing her invitation to go to Brookroyd shows that she wrote on 28 not 23 July. Any speculation about Branwell's movements must therefore take these dates into account.

More evidence for Charlotte's attitude to moral duty and family responsibility is revealed in the full text of her letter to Ellen of 31 July 1845, in a paragraph deploring John Nussey's failure to help his mother to care for his brother Joseph, an alcoholic whose presence was a 'burthen' on the Nussey family; John should have regarded this 'call' upon him as 'one of the most sacred' he could have. Ellen understandably deleted this paragraph in the

45 EN 20.11.1845.
46 26.5.1845; MS Pierpont Morgan.
47 EN 13.6.1845; MS HM 24439.

holograph, a Grolier manuscript not available to Wise and Symington. The full text of the letter to Ellen of 8 September 1845 also reveals a strong concern for family loyalty, along with great sympathy for the distress caused by George Nussey's mental illness. Charlotte satirically attributes to Henry Nussey's wife 'warm-hearted—sisterly kindness . . . justice and gratitude' and condemns her meanness and her coldness towards Ellen. Charlotte's ideas of sisterly duty are emphatically implied by contrast.

A letter to Ellen of ?10 September 1845, published here for the first time, has been recreated from two fragments, one in the Beinecke Library at Yale and one in the Brontë Parsonage Museum. This also shows Charlotte's ability to share Ellen's anxieties and a concern for just and compassionate dealings within the family: 'Surely—surely—Richard will do justice to his sick brother, his aged Mother—his utterly unprotected sisters.' But Charlotte also realizes the difficulty of making right decisions; she can give Ellen 'no dogmatical advice' on whether to take a situation.

Some of Branwell's letters of 1845 have also been newly arranged and dated to give a better record of his activities. The text of his application for the secretaryship of a railway company of ?23 October is included. Its presence, and Branwell's confidence that he can produce 'full testimonials', help to balance the impression of him given by Charlotte in her letter of 4 November, when she cannot say 'one word . . . in his favour'. It is unfortunate that Branwell no longer felt able to confide in his sisters, for they seem to have remained in ignorance of his writings and publications in 1845. He had written several poems on exile, a long, unfinished but quite impressive poem about the death of a loved sister, and the first volume of a proposed three-volume novel, 'And the Weary are at Rest'. Two of his poems, 'Real Rest' and 'Penmaenmawr' had been published in the *Halifax Guardian* for 8 November and 20 December 1845.

1846

Branwell's 'Letter from a Father' was printed in the *Halifax Guardian* on 18 April, and he also had the 'materials for a respectably sized volume', but despaired of getting them published. His sisters had already offered their poems to a publisher on 28 January. Following the advice of Chambers & Co. of Edinburgh, Charlotte wrote to the firm of Aylott and Jones, who published mainly theological works by clergymen. Charlotte later explained the decision to adopt pseudonyms: 'Averse to personal publicity, we veiled our own names under those of Currer, Ellis, and Acton Bell; the ambiguous choice being dictated by a sort of conscientious scruple at assuming Christian names positively masculine, while we did not like to declare ourselves women, because—without at that time suspecting that our mode of writing and thinking was not what is called "feminine"—we had a vague impression that authoresses are liable to be looked on with prejudice; we had noticed how critics sometimes use for their chastisement the weapon of personality, and for their reward, a flattery, which is not true praise.'[48] The sisters had to pay for the printing, publication, and advertising of their work, which appeared in late May. Almost all Charlotte's letters to Aylott and Jones survive. They are clear, workmanlike and efficient, respectful but confident and decisive in tone, providing a new note in the correspondence.

In spite of the dismal sales of the *Poems*—the volume 'stole into life' and only two copies were sold—there were discerning reviews in *The Critic* and *The Athenaeum* on 4 July and in the *Dublin University Magazine* for October. For Charlotte the activity of polishing and revising creative work, and of organizing the publication was reviving and pleasurable; it provided an emotional satisfaction to counterbalance her unfulfilled longing for a response from M. Heger and her angry grief over Branwell's behaviour. In addition Charlotte had already turned her Brussels experiences to account in *The Professor*, transforming them by imagining for her teacher-pupil heroine a happy marriage with her 'master'. M. Heger's silence and Branwell's 'intolerable' behaviour no longer dominated her life, even though the death of Lydia Robinson's husband on 26 May 'served Branwell for a pretext to throw all about him into hubbub and confusion with his emotions' and he was 'continually screwing money out of' his father, 'sometimes threatening that he will kill himself if it is withheld from him'.[49]

Charlotte's earlier comment that 'pleasures and pains' were 'strangely mingled in this life' was prophetic of much of her experience in this and later years. On 6 April she had asked Aylott and Jones whether they would publish 'a work of fiction—consisting of three distinct and unconnected tales' which the 'Bells' were preparing for the press. They were advised to try other firms; and so, in Charlotte's words, *The Professor*, *Wuthering Heights*, and *Agnes Grey* 'were perseveringly obtruded upon various publishers for the space of a year and a half; usually, their fate was an ignominious and abrupt dismissal'.[50] Charlotte's application to Henry Colburn, the publisher of innumerable three-decker novels, has survived, along with Colburn's scribbled instructions on the back of the letter. The document shows that Charlotte hoped, rather naïvely, to impress him with the vague statement that the three authors had 'already appeared before the public'.[51] The shrewd and experienced Colburn required to know what the Bells had written before 'allowing the M.S—' to be sent to him. He was unlikely to be impressed by their answer—though he might have

[48] *Biographical Notice* p. ix.
[49] EN 17.6.1846; MS BPM Gr. E 11.
[50] *Biographical Notice* p. x.
[51] H. Colburn 4.7.1846; MS Princeton Parrish Collection.

seen the two favourable reviews which had appeared on the day Charlotte wrote to him.

None of the three novels was accepted in 1846. Charlotte was to tell Mrs Gaskell that 'her tale came back upon her hands, curtly rejected by some publisher, on the very day when her father was to submit to his operation' for cataract—25 August. Charlotte had taken her father to Manchester for his operation, and her much-travelled novel must have been forwarded to her there. Mrs Gaskell continues in the heroic style: 'But she had the heart of Robert Bruce within her, and failure upon failure daunted her no more than him. Not only did "The Professor" return again to try his chance among the London publishers, but she began, in this time of care and depressing inquietude,—in those grey, weary, uniform streets . . . there and then, did the brave genius begin "Jane Eyre".'[52]

Charlotte told Ellen nothing about the poems or the novels, and at this stage Ellen could have guessed nothing. Charlotte's affection for her remained undiminished—'never a day passes, and seldom an hour, that I do not think of you and the scene of trial in which you live—move and have your being.'[53] But she delayed her New Year visit until February—that is until the *Poems* had been prepared and accepted for publication. Charlotte's letters to Ellen continue to be personal and confidential on family matters. Ellen is told of Branwell's 'stupifying' himself with drink but also of Mr Brontë's patience during his months of blindness and of his fortitude during his operation—a fortitude inherited by Anne Brontë, who is admired for her 'extraordinary heroism of endurance'.[54] Charlotte values Ellen's friendship because she recognizes her own failings: she is 'too sore—too demonstrative and vehement' in contrast to her usually mild-tempered and equable friend. Their characters complement each other: 'It is not in my nature to forget your nature—though I daresay I should spit fire and explode sometimes if we lived together continually, and you too would be angry now & then and then we should get reconciled and jog on as before.'[55] Charlotte's advance in self-knowledge and maturity is also evident in her correspondence with Miss Wooler. In a long letter of 30 January Charlotte explains why she lets Emily manage their railway investments in spite of her occasionally 'unreasonable and headstrong notions'. 'You my dear Miss Wooler know full as well as I do the value of sisters' affection to each other; there is nothing like it in this world, I believe, when they are nearly equal in age and similar in education, tastes and sentiments.'[56] In November or December she writes movingly to Miss Wooler of her joy in the change from

[52] *Life* ii. 7.
[53] EN 23.1.1846; MS HM 24442.
[54] EN 13.12.1846; MS HM 24450.
[55] EN 28.12.1846; MS HM 24451.
[56] MW 30.1.1846; MS Fitzwilliam.

her father's helpless blindness when he 'sat all day-long in darkness and inertion—Now—to see him walk about independently—read, write &c. is indeed a joyful change'.[57] In the same letter she writes, 'I pity Mr Thomas [Margaret Wooler's brother] from my heart'. She understands his suffering under the 'tyranny of Hypochondria' for she recalls the 'preternatural horror' of her own similar experience. Her rather unusual epithet occurs also in *Jane Eyre*, in the Red Room episode in chapter 2 which Charlotte must have written not long before this letter. Both letter and novel powerfully evoke the 'concentrated anguish of certain insufferable moments' when life seemed a 'waking Nightmare': Jane's terrifying experience echoes that of her creator.

Charlotte's letters to Ellen in 1846 show a similar sensitivity towards abnormal states of mind. The complete texts of her letters of 17 June, 10 July, 31 August, 13 and 29 September, and 17 November reveal the continuing tragedy of George Nussey's mental deterioration, Charlotte's sympathy for him and his mother and sisters, and her indignant criticism of other Nussey relatives. The letter of 13 September is typical in its warm compassion: 'Poor George! time passes—winter, spring and summer, and his ?natural self delays to return—How can his brothers decline to give assistance in his case?'[58] From the letter of 29 September we learn that Joe Taylor had visited George—an act of kindness which would please both Ellen and Charlotte. In the same letter Charlotte's rather sour comment on Richard Nussey's getting 'spliced at last . . . look out for squalls occasionally' shows that Ellen's brother married in 1846 and not 1848 as the garbled text of W & S 387 implies.

Four letters have been added to those printed by Wise and Symington. The first is a previously unpublished letter of 22 January written to the former Haworth schoolmaster Mr Rand on Mr Brontë's behalf, showing a courteous and kindly interest in his family, and especially in the progress of his little son. A brief note to Ellen of about 5 February asks her to ensure that Mary Taylor's letter from New Zealand is being circulated amongst her friends. Charlotte's letter of 21 February to Aylott and Jones, selecting long primer type for the *Poems* and commenting on the paper and layout, was apparently untraceable in 1932, but is now at Princeton. The fourth letter was written on Mr Brontë's behalf on ?3 March to Charlotte's cousin Eliza Kingston; it is interesting because it adds to our scanty knowledge about the Brontës' relationship with the Branwell family.

1847

This year was to be the *annus mirabilis* for the sisters, with the publication of the best-selling *Jane Eyre* on 19 October and of *Wuthering Heights* and *Agnes*

[57] MS Fitzwilliam.
[58] MS BPM Bon 189.

Grey in December. But at the beginning of the year Emily and Anne's novels and Charlotte's *The Professor* were still going the rounds of the publishers, and no more copies of the *Poems* had been sold. In March Charlotte felt that her youth had 'gone like a dream—and very little use have I ever made of it—What have I done these last thirty years—? Precious little'.[59] Branwell had continued to write, but left most of his poems unfinished. The *Halifax Guardian* accepted another of his melancholy poems, 'The End of All',[60] in which the speaker recognized that even achievement in battle would not console him for the death of his wife: 'I could not bear the thoughts which rose, | Of what *had* been, and what *must* be.'[61] In the following week the sisters recognized that their poems were 'a drug' on the market, and, *faute de mieux*, sent complimentary copies of what they could not sell to half a dozen famous writers 'in acknowledgment of the pleasure and profit we have often and long derived from your works'.[62] The gesture was perhaps an admission that their future as writers must lie in fiction, not verse.

By this time *Jane Eyre* was almost complete. Charlotte had still to write the concluding chapters, but she had begun to make a fair copy on 16 March. She had aimed to give her novel 'a more vivid interest than belongs to "The Professor" '. The turning point came in July, when *Wuthering Heights* and *Agnes Grey* were accepted for publication by Thomas Cautley Newby, and *The Professor* was sent to Smith, Elder and Company's discerning reader William Smith Williams.

> Ere long, in a much shorter space than that on which experience had taught him to calculate—there came a letter, which [Currer Bell] opened in the dreary expectation of finding two hard hopeless lines, intimating that Messrs. Smith and Elder 'were not disposed to publish the MS.,' and, instead, he took out of the envelope a letter of two pages. He read it trembling. It declined, indeed, to publish that tale, for business reasons, but it discussed its merits and demerits so courteously, so considerately, in a spirit so rational, with a discrimination so enlightened, that this very refusal cheered the author better than a vulgarly-expressed acceptance would have done. It was added, that a work in three volumes would meet with careful attention.
>
> I was just then completing *Jane Eyre*, at which I had been working while the one volume tale was plodding its weary round in London: in three weeks I sent it off; friendly and skilful hands took it in.[63]

Charlotte's brief note of 24 August accompanying the manuscript of *Jane Eyre* has been in recent years the most prized of all her letters, and has changed hands in the sale-rooms for ever-increasing sums.

59 EN 24.3.1847; MS BPM Bon 191.
60 5 June 1847.
61 Neufeldt *BBP* 296–8.
62 De Quincey 16.6.1847; MS Berg.
63 *Biographical Notice* pp. x–xi.

Though Charlotte was overjoyed by Smith, Elder's acceptance of her novel, and grateful for their courtesy and advice, she was by no means subservient in her dealings with them. Until quite recently her complete correspondence with the firm was not available, but in 1974 Mrs Elizabeth Seton-Gordon, a granddaughter of the publisher George Smith, most generously presented to the Brontë Society her unique collection of documents relating to Charlotte Brontë. They included more than ninety letters to George Smith or his publishing house, and several to his mother, in whose home Charlotte was to stay during some of her visits to London. Fifteen of the letters were transcribed by Professor Arthur Pollard and published in *BST* 18. 92. 101–14. These and many others, hitherto published only in part, are included in the present edition. They add much to our understanding of the relationship between Charlotte and her publisher.

A letter of 7 August to Smith, Elder was quoted by Mrs Gaskell in the *Life*,[64] but unaccountably omitted by Wise and Symington, who normally reprinted from the *Life* when MSS were not available. It shows Charlotte's tenacity in pressing for the publication of *The Professor*, which she rather naïvely thought might 'serve as an introduction' to a more exciting work and make the 'success of the second . . . more probable'.[65] W. S. Williams, who had sound literary judgement, and George Smith, who was an extremely astute business man, would have none of *The Professor* at this date (or indeed until after Charlotte's death), but they had great difficulty in dissuading Charlotte from later attempts to revise and publish it. When in 1851 her 'martyrised MS' was 'withdrawn for the ninth time' she said ironically, 'Of course my feelings towards it can only be paralleled by those of a doting parent towards an idiot child'.[66]

In 1847 Charlotte reluctantly accepted the decision that *Jane Eyre* must come first—but in the form in which she had written it, not with 'improvements'. A letter of 12 September shows her remarkable firmness on the matter and her confidence in her own work:

> my engagements will not permit me to revise 'Jane Eyre' a third time, and perhaps there is little to regret in the circumstance; you probably know from personal experience that an author never writes well till he has got into the full spirit of his work, and were I to retrench, to alter and to add now when I am uninterested and cold, I know I should only further injure what may be already defective. Perhaps too the first part of 'Jane Eyre' may suit the public taste better than you anticipate—for it is true and Truth has a severe charm of its own.[67]

64 ii. 25.
65 MS BPM SG 3.
66 Vol. ii, GS 5.2.1851; MS BPM SG 45.
67 SE 12.9.1847; MS BPM SG 3/1B.

Charlotte's confidence was of course justified. The novel was an outstanding success, and most reviewers had indeed been impressed by the 'truth' of her 'Do-the-Girls' school in the first part and by the 'force, vigour and freshness' of the whole work. By 18 December a second edition was called for, and Charlotte drafted a preface for it. The revised second edition, dedicated to Thackeray, was to appear in January 1848, and the third, with a few additional corrections, in April of the same year. To this she added a note explaining that her 'claim to the title of novelist' rested on *Jane Eyre* alone. Her sisters' works had appeared by 14 December, and Charlotte was indignant on their behalf about Newby's careless presentation and tardy publishing of their novels, and about his clever advertising which implied that both were by the author of *Jane Eyre*. She was grateful for the care Smith, Elder had taken with her novel, and naturally pleased with the many enthusiastic reviews. A few, like G. H. Lewes, took exception to the melodramatic plot, and *The Spectator* condemned the novel for its improbability and 'a low tone of behaviour (rather than of morality)'.[68] Charlotte was somewhat perturbed by this, but was amused by the contrasting views of other papers. The *Sunday Times* thought Rochester was 'morose and savage' 'with the repulsive manners of a boor', and considered that some of the scenes were 'too disgusting to be quoted'. The *Newcastle Guardian* in contrast found the tone quite healthy and moral and concluded, surprisingly, that the novel was 'a simple and well-told narrative of events common in every-day life'. The reviewer, as Charlotte said, seemed 'to think it a mild potion which may be "safely administered to the most delicate invalid." / I suppose the public must decide when critics disagree'.[69]

The publication of *Jane Eyre* brought in its wake a great enrichment of Charlotte's correspondence. Her formal letters to Smith, Elder soon gave place to a personal correspondence with W. S. Williams. He was to become a trusted friend and adviser, the recipient of some of her most revealing letters on her reading and on the composition of her works, and on the sorrows of her private life—especially in 1848–9, when Branwell, Emily, and Anne died. Another new correspondent was George Henry Lewes, whose criticism she valued (with reservations) and who was to elicit her famous remarks on the supremacy of imagination and passion in the novel, and her question, 'Can there be a great Artist without poetry?'[70]

Charlotte continued to write to Ellen Nussey throughout the year, but revealed neither the frustrations nor the triumphs of her literary life. In September she received some of the proofs of *Jane Eyre* during a visit to Ellen: she 'occasionally sat at the same table with her friend, correcting them; but they

[68] WSW 10.11.1847, n. 3.
[69] WSW 11.12.1847; MS Harvard.
[70] Vol. ii, GHL 18.1.1848; MS BL Add. 39763.

did not exchange a word on the subject.'[71] Ellen continued to be a comfort. To her Charlotte confessed her frequent moods of 'self-weariness' or her feeling that she was a 'consummate ass'.[72] She derided herself for having the honour of being a nuisance to her friends, and admitted on occasion to feeling particularly 'old and ugly' or 'grey sunk and withered'.[73] There were minor squabbles, as when Ellen postponed a visit in May, and Charlotte growled angrily about the snobbish Ann Nussey who cared nothing whether 'little people like us of Haworth are disappointed or not, provided great nobs like the Briar Hall gentry are accommodated'.[74] This letter was sent defiantly, with 'a large amount of wormwood and gall', but Charlotte quickly climbed down and asked for forgiveness. Her friendship withstood such strains, and was neither exclusive nor petty: she did not think of being jealous of Ellen's other friends, such as Amelia Ringrose, in whose welfare she took a kindly interest. Her brief note to Amelia, written on 24 December, was the first of many courteous letters to this friend who had been George Nussey's fiancée and who was to be the wife of Charlotte's old acquaintance Joe Taylor. Charlotte was later to see and criticize the weaknesses of her character, but she maintained an amicable relationship with her to the end of her life, and became very fond of her little daughter 'Tim'.

The Seton-Gordon collection provides most of the additional material in 1847—most notably, the three letters of 7 August, 12 and 18 September. Apart from this, envelopes postmarked 14 and 18 July and 28 August help to date visits to and by Ellen, and show how Charlotte arranged them to suit the progress of her writing. A letter to Ellen of ?15 October has been pieced together from two fragments, one in the Beinecke Library at Yale and the other in the Kirklees archives in Yorkshire—a fragment printed as if it were a complete letter in W & S 310. The full text gives Charlotte's shrewd assessment of Amelia Ringrose's '<u>religious</u> hypochondria' and her sensible advice that a visit in Ellen's company 'to some cheerful watering-place' would be the best remedy. Other letters can now be read in their unexpurgated versions, as in the letter to Ellen of 19 January 1847 where Charlotte is rudely outspoken about Mrs Joshua Nussey—'Is she a frog or a fish—? She is certainly a specimen of some kind of cold-blooded animal.'[75] Four letters have been redated[76] and the draft version of the last of these shows that Charlotte selected her words with care in her early letters to her publishers, as indeed may be assumed from their formal style. In the final version of her letter Charlotte is assured enough to omit her request

[71] *Life* ii. 28.
[72] EN 19.1.1847; MS BPM B.S. 57.5.
[73] EN 24.3.1847, MS BPM Bon 191; EN 14.2.1847, MS HM 24452.
[74] EN 20.5.1847; MS BPM Bon 192.
[75] MS BPM B.S. 57.5.
[76] EN ?23.8.1847 and ?29.10.1847, SE 8.10.1847, WSW 18.12.1847.

for 'alterations or additions' to her preface, but she still feels, perhaps too strongly, the 'severe humiliation' of the *Observer's* analysis of the plot in *Jane Eyre*. On the reverse of the draft her poem, 'He saw my heart's woe discovered my soul's anguish', is a reminder that she had indeed gone through a 'valley of humiliation' during and after her years in Brussels. In spite of the valley, or perhaps because of it, Charlotte had reached an astonishingly high peak of achievement. As Mrs Gaskell wrote, 'The whole reading-world of England was in a ferment to discover the unknown author' of *Jane Eyre*.[77] Thus the end of the present volume also marks the beginning of a new life in which, because of her fame, 'the lights and shadows must always fall with a certain difference'.

[77] *Life* ii. 37.

THE HISTORY OF THE LETTERS

I. 1855–62: Mrs Gaskell and the 'Life of Charlotte Brontë'

A letter from Charlotte Brontë's friend Ellen Nussey initiated the writing of Mrs Gaskell's *Life*, in which many of Charlotte's letters were first used. On 6 June 1855 Ellen wrote to Charlotte's widower, the Revd A. B. Nicholls, to say how much she had been 'hurt and pained' by an article in *Sharpe's London Magazine* for June 1855, entitled 'A few words about "Jane Eyre" '.[1] The article, published barely two months after Charlotte's death, must have shocked Ellen by recalling that Mr Rochester had used 'real wicked oaths, like a bold, bad, live man', causing the public to clamour at this 'improper' innovation as if 'the writer had chosen to go to the opera *sans culottes*'. It referred to the *Quarterly's* decision that *Jane Eyre* was written by a 'strange man' with thoroughly masculine notions of 'female attire'; and it was grossly inaccurate about the Brontës' lives. The writer asserted that Mr Brontë had married at Penzance, had caused his wife's relatives to cut off intercourse with her, and had left it to the servants to educate his children. Ironically enough whole sections of this cheap and nasty article derived from an earlier letter of Mrs Gaskell to Catherine Winkworth of 25 August 1850, based in part on gossip,[2] and written before Mrs Gaskell had gained a rather more intimate knowledge of Charlotte and her family.

Ellen Nussey felt strongly that readers of the *Sharpe's* article would 'imbibe a tissue of malign falsehoods'; those who had known Charlotte best spoke of her with 'reverence & affection', and justice should be done to her and to her aged father. If the famous novelist Mrs Gaskell, fitted for the task by her friendship with Charlotte and by her ability as a writer, would undertake 'this just and honourable defence', Ellen would gladly supply her with facts sufficient 'to set aside much that is asserted'.[3]

Mr Nicholls responded that a reply would give the *Sharpe's* article 'an importance which it would not otherwise have obtained', and that Mr Brontë

[1] *Sharpe's London Magazine* N.S. v. 339–342. The article may have been the one previously offered to Dickens by Frank Smedley (1818–64, a novelist and possibly an acquaintance of C. Winkworth), who had edited *Sharpe's* from 1847–9 and had continued to contribute to it. In an admirable letter of rejection Dickens refused to publish 'so soon after Miss Brontë's death' details that might be 'saddening or painful to her husband'; he had 'no sympathy whatever with the staring curiosity' that such details would gratify. I am grateful to Professor Kathleen Tillotson for her discussion of this article. See G. Storey, K. Tillotson, and A. Easson (eds.), *The Letters of Charles Dickens* (Oxford, 1993), vii. 610, Dickens to Frank Smedley 5.5.1855.

[2] CP letter 75.

[3] EN to ABN 6.6.1855, MS J.G. Sharps; W & S 954.

was only amused by the remarks on his behaviour—'I have not seen him laugh as much for some months.'[4]

By 16 June 1855, however, Mr Brontë had changed his mind. He had seen too many false statements by 'a great many scribblers', and he asked Mrs Gaskell to write a 'long or short' account of Charlotte's life and to make some remarks on her works. He and Mr Nicholls would give her such information as she might require.[5] Mrs Gaskell had already told George Smith, Charlotte's publisher, that she would like simply to write down her 'own personal recollections' of Charlotte so that 'people would honour her as a woman . . . when her wild sad life, and the beautiful character that grew out of it' were made public.[6] Having accepted Mr Brontë's invitation to write an account, Mrs Gaskell visited the Haworth parsonage in July 1855; and Mr Nicholls somewhat reluctantly passed on to Ellen Nussey her request to see Charlotte's letters:

> The greatest difficulty seems to be in obtaining materials to shew the development of Charlotte's Character—For this reason Mrs G. is anxious to see any of her letters—Especially those of any early date . . . we should feel obliged by your letting us have any that you may think proper—not for publication, but merely to give the writer an insight into her mode of thought—of course they will be returned after a little time. I confess that the course most consonant with my own feelings would be to take no steps in the matter but I do not think it right to offer any opposition to Mr Bronté's wishes—.[7]

A letter from Mrs Gaskell to Ellen assured her that she had the eager support of Mr Brontë, and that Mr Nicholls though reluctant realized the need for a 'full and authorized <account> 'history' of Charlotte's life if one were to be written at all. He had therefore brought down all the materials he could furnish her with 'in the shape of about a dozen letters addressed principally to her sister Emily; one or two to her father & her brother; and one to her aunt. The dates extend from 1839 to 1843.' Mrs Gaskell added that she would like to make Ellen's personal acquaintance, since she was 'the person of all others to apply to'.[8] Ellen accordingly reread and arranged her collection of 'more than five hundred letters', selected a number for Mrs Gaskell's perusal, and took the precaution of erasing many of the proper names in them. She also made the condition that she must see any extracts from the 330 that Mrs Gaskell chose to

[4] ABN to EN 11.6.1855; W & S 955.

[5] PB to ECG 16.6.1855, MS Rylands; W & S 956 as 16 July.

[6] ECG to G. Smith 4.6. [1855], MS Murray; CP letter 242.

[7] ABN to EN 24.7.1855, MS Brotherton; W & S 957. George Smith's insistence that Mr Nicholls should transfer copyright in the 'materials of the biography' to Mrs Gaskell caused him intense pain. ABN to GS 1.12.1856, MS Murray.

[8] ECG to EN 24.7.1855, MS Manchester Central Library; CP letter 257.

use.[9] Ellen handed over most of the letters when Mrs Gaskell visited her at Brookroyd in August 1855.

Though Ellen claimed that she still had 'près de 500 lettres' when she wrote to M. Heger in 1863,[10] she told Katharine Cortazzo and her mother in 1882 'that she had formerly had at least 500 but that only 300 were left. "I must have burnt or lost 200 or more, at least I cannot find them." '[11] In a letter of 18 November 1892 to T. J. Wise she wrote: 'I regret I ever destroyed any letters—over 500 I had at C's death—The appeal from Mr. Bronte and Mr. N. for Mrs. Gaskell to have the use of the letters caused me to destroy a large number at once.'[12] Ellen's memory was unreliable well before the 1880s, and her vagueness makes her statements unsatisfactory. Horsfall Turner printed about 370 letters for her between 1885 and 1889, most of them from original MSS, as Ellen's anxiety about the latter was to show.

But it is true that there are longish gaps in the correspondence—notably from mid-June 1837 to the end of that year, when further insight into Charlotte's emotional attachment to Ellen, religious self-searchings, and eventual nervous 'hypochondria' in the period 1836–8 would have been especially welcome. The date of Ellen's return from London in 1837 is unknown, but her absence alone would not account for the complete dearth of letters in the second half of the year.[13] A later gap extends from late June to early October 1853, when Charlotte was secretly corresponding with Mr Nicholls, and again from that date until 1 March 1854, just over a month before her engagement to him. The survival of a single letter in eight months certainly hints that others may have been destroyed. A letter to Ellen from Mary Hewitt of 21 February 1854 shows that there had been an estrangement, only recently healed, between the friends. Ellen's dislike and jealousy of Mr Nicholls may well account for the rift. She had written a strange letter to Mary Taylor on 12 August 1853 and was roundly told off for her pains. Mary wrote from New Zealand on 24 February 1854: 'You talk wonderful nonsense abt. C. Bronte in yr letter. What do you mean about "bearing her position so long, & enduring to the end? & still better—"bearing our lot whatever it is." If its C's lot to be married shdn't she bear that too? or does your strange morality mean that

[9] See CP letters 264a, 264b, and 267. Ellen mentioned these figures to William Scruton in 1885 or 1887: see *BST* 1. 8. 35. She told him that her reading was 'done, but in a fashion. The sheets were sent to me hurriedly with such urgent requests to forward them at once to London that I had barely time to glance through them'. Mrs Gaskell referred to a series of 350 letters (CP letter 271).

[10] See M. Heger's reply, 7.11.1863; W & S 1009, as 7.9.1863.

[11] Helen H. Arnold, 'The Reminiscences of Emma Huidekoper Cortazzo', *BST* 13. 68. 220–1.

[12] MS Brotherton. See pp. 52–56 and p. 55, n. 15. In a letter of 14.11.1892, written before he had acquired Ellen's collection, T.J. Wise referred to 400 letters. (MS BPM). Margaret Wooler also destroyed confidential material, assuring A.B. Nicholls on 30.4.1855 that she would retain no letter which might give pain. (Letter in private hands.)

[13] The dates of several letters in 1836–8 are unknown and have been conjecturally supplied, but no letter can be confidently placed in this half-year. W & S 64 and 65 belong to 1838, not 1837.

she shd refuse to ameliorate her lot when it lies in her power. How wd. she be inconsistent with herself in marrying? Because she considers her own pleasure? If this is so new for her to do, it is high time she began to make it more common.'[14]

Other gaps are indicated by references in extant letters, and by the survival of envelopes without their contents.[15] Horsfall Turner printed a number of letters, including seven for the period 1831–8, of which the MSS remain unlocated. But they may not have been destroyed. 'Missing' holographs continue to come up for sale, and Turner had used copies provided by Ellen for some letters. If Ellen did destroy MSS, it was likely to be (as she said) before lending her collection to Mrs Gaskell, who read the letters Ellen provided, selected extracts, and returned them. Ellen did not accuse Mrs Gaskell of losing or keeping any of her letters, though she made other complaints about her after the publication of the *Life*.

While Mrs Gaskell had the excellent intention of allowing Charlotte Brontë to tell her own life-story in her own words wherever that was possible, she chose her quotations so that readers would 'honour the woman as much as they have admired the writer'[16] and be convinced of her essential 'purity of mind'.[17] Other constraints were imposed by her wish not to hurt the feelings of Charlotte's surviving friends. She wrote to George Smith on 26 December 1856:

> I am indeed vexed I let you see the MS at all in so unfinished a state . . . for I had often to trust long pieces of copying letters to one of my daughters, & I told her just to write straight on, and I should take out what it was undesirable to have published when I read it over with Mr Gaskell . . . I should have thought you might have felt quite sure that I was going to take 'out' all that ought to be considered as private or personal . . . before it was published . . . I should certainly have scored out, so that no one could have read it through my marks all that related to any one's appearance, style of living &c, in whose character as indicated by these things the public were not directly interested.[18]

The Rylands Library MS of the *Life* is indeed marked by near-impenetrable deletions. Mrs Gaskell's quotations do not necessarily reflect the tenor of a complete letter, for her own selectiveness was compounded by Ellen's censorship of dubious passages.[19] Unlike Lockhart in his biography of Scott, Mrs Gaskell rarely sought to 'improve' the style of the letters she

[14] MS BL Ashley 5768; *Stevens* 120.

[15] e.g. for missing letters to EN of 14.7.1847 and 18.7.1847.

[16] ECG to G. Smith, 31 May [1855]; CP letter 241.

[17] The page-headings in early editions of the *Life* were carefully phrased to suit this intention: see e.g. ii. 275, 'Self-Abnegation' and ii. 281, 'Her repugnance to Impropriety'. The headings were devised by either George Smith or W. S. Williams, but were presumably approved by Mrs Gaskell. See CP letters 334 and 335.

[18] CP letter 326.

[19] See e.g. EN 20.11.1840 and notes.

quoted,[20] and she did retain surprisingly strong stuff. There is no toning down of Charlotte's comment that a high wind has 'produced the same effects on the contents of my knowledge-box that a quaigh of usquebaugh does upon those of most other bipeds. I . . . am strongly inclined to dance a jig, if I knew how. I think I must partake of the nature of a pig or an ass—both which animals are strongly affected by a high wind.'[21]

But Mrs Gaskell certainly expurgated other letters, and she or her assistant copyists not infrequently changed or misread single words, paraphrased a sentence, or misrepresented by omissions, which were not invariably indicated.[22] Her version of EN 7.4.1840 presents the flirtatious curate William Weightman ('Mr. W.') only as the preacher of a 'noble, eloquent' discourse and the giver of a lecture at the Keighley Mechanics' Institute, and not as the attractive young man whom Charlotte had nicknamed 'our friend Miss Celia Amelia', whose eyes sparkled with delight. In the same letter 'a most stormy meeting' becomes 'a stirring meeting', 'snivel' becomes 'sniggle', and the good Yorkshire use of 'nay' is oddly transformed into the French '*mais*'.[23] On the other hand Mrs Gaskell could quote accurately and fully letters she particularly admired, such as Charlotte's long letter to Margaret Wooler of 30 January 1846. Here she was 'Acting on the conviction . . . that where Charlotte Brontë's own words could be used, no others ought to take their place'.[24]

Thus, while it is unwise to rely on the text of the letters in the *Life* when the manuscript is lacking, Mrs Gaskell's direct access to MSS and the fact that she had charmed so many correspondents into yielding up their treasured letters mean that the *Life* cannot be ignored as a source.[25] I have retrieved from the Rylands MS of the *Life* and from the early editions a number of phrases and a few longer passages which occur in no other texts—in, for example EN 19.6.1834, 20.2.1837, 3.3.1841, and 15.5.1840, where Charlotte admits that she and Ellen 'write of little else but love and marriage'. This last is a passage lightly scored through in the MS and not printed in the first edition. Charlotte's reference to a local bankruptcy, 'The oldest family in Haworth failed lately' in her letter to Miss Wooler of 28 August 1848 survives in the printed editions

[20] Davidson Cook, who saw some of Scott's original MSS in the Law Collection, noted Lockhart's alterations. See C. W. Hatfield to D. Cook, 7.6.1927, Stockett-Wise. For John Forster's rewriting of some of Dickens's letters, see Madeline House and Graham Storey (eds.), *The Letters of Charles Dickens* (Oxford, 1965), i. pp. xii–xiii.

[21] EN 29.9.1840; *Life* i. 219.

[22] Mrs Gaskell's principal amanuenses were her daughters Marianne and Meta, and her friend 'Snow' (Julia) Wedgwood.

[23] *Life* i. 214–15. Mrs Gaskell used the word 'sniggled' for 'snickered, laughed at' in *Cousin Phillis* pt. 4.

[24] *Life* i. 339.

[25] Mrs Gaskell saw letters to most of Charlotte's friends and acquaintances, including her publishers and the writer and critic G. H. Lewes. Most surprisingly M. Heger allowed her to see (or to hear) Charlotte's letters to him of 1844 and 1845, and copied out for her use passages from the first two. See CH 24.7.1844, 24.10.1844 and notes.

of the *Life* but not in other texts of the letter. Only the first half of the relevant manuscript is now extant, but the authenticity of the passage is suggested by Charlotte's immediately preceding letter to Ellen of 18 August.[26]

The *Life* also remains the primary source for a few letters of which the later versions are clearly derivative. These include the letters to Emily of July 1839 (to 'Mine Bonnie love') and 1 October 1843, and the incomplete letter to Mr Brontë of 2 June 1843.

The dispersal of Brontë manuscripts started, in a small way, even before the publication of the *Life*, and increased as a result of it, for it caused an immense resurgence of interest in the lives and works of the Brontë sisters. Autographs and mementoes were eagerly sought, and already valuable. Mrs Gaskell promised the brother of the poet William Johnson Cory (1823–92) 'a set of her books and gave him half a letter with the signature of C Brontë' some time before 1863.[27] On 7 July 1864, during the American Civil War, Mrs Gaskell sent a collection of autograph letters to Abigail B. Adams 'to be sold for the benefit of the Sanitary Commission. I give them with all my heart.' They included a 'Letter from *Miss Brontë*' sent with the comment 'this is, & ought to be very valuable,—it is a very rare autograph'.[28]

By the end of 1858 Mr Brontë was reduced to cutting up one at least of the few letters he had received from Charlotte into small sections—all he could spare, he told the recipients apologetically. A letter on mourning paper, written a few days after the death of Anne Brontë at Scarborough, can be imperfectly pieced together from the five fragments that survive in five scattered locations—Haworth, Dublin, Texas, New York, and Pennsylvania. By the time it was written, on 9 June 1849, Charlotte and Ellen Nussey had moved away from Scarborough to the 'quieter and more lonely' resort of Filey, with its 'black desolate reef of rocks', as Charlotte described it to her father. An empty envelope postmarked a few days later from Bridlington shows that she wrote home once again after leaving Filey.[29]

In 1861 and 1862 Mr Nicholls also sent out tiny fragments of a letter or letters from Charlotte. The fragments which survive are too small and too few to form a coherent whole. One regrets this loss the more because Mr Nicholls had either destroyed or refused to produce Charlotte's other letters to him when

[26] See *Life* ii. 76. EN 18.8.1848 is based on 2 separate MSS, BPM Gr. E 13 and B.S. 65. *Shorter* 303 and W & S 387 did not use the Grolier MS, and part of their postscript belongs to a different letter. For the family referred to see Sarah Fermi, 'A "Religious" Family Disgraced', *BST* 20. 5. 289–95.

[27] W. Cory to Lord Rosebery 8.11.1863, quoted in *Extracts from the Letters and Journals of William Cory, Author of 'Ionica'* selected and arranged by Francis Warre Cornish (Oxford, 1897), 99.

[28] CP letter 552. This was CB's letter to Mrs Gaskell of 18.6.1851, now at Harvard. It had been sold to George Peabody at the 'Great Sanitary Bazaar', and was given to Harvard by Mrs M. L. Peabody.

[29] See *LD* 520 and Margaret Smith, 'A Reconstructed Letter', *BST* 20. 1. 42–7. The fifth fragment came to light through the kindness of its owner after the publication of this article.

Mrs Gaskell was seeking material for the *Life*, and we cannot know what she wrote to the man who was to become her loved and loving husband.[30]

In January 1857 Ellen had complimented Mrs Gaskell on what she had read of the *Life* in manuscript, considering it an accurate record of life at the parsonage. Ellen was therefore alarmed by the public controversy that followed its publication, fearing that she would be regarded as the source of the untrue and objectionable stories about Mr Brontë's violence, or the descriptions of Branwell's degradation. She asked Mrs Gaskell to insert some corrections, and a disclaimer on her behalf, in the third edition.[31] Mrs Gaskell complied,[32] but Ellen remained unhappy and on the defensive, saying repeatedly that she had lent her letters only at Mr Nicholls's urgent request. She told George Smith on 1 June 1860 that this exonerated her from a promise she had made to Mr Nicholls after Charlotte's funeral that she would not show the letters to others and would eventually destroy them. Ellen's wish to protect Charlotte's reputation was now complicated by an anxious concern to protect her own, and by an increasing resentment against Mr Nicholls. He had apparently blamed her for allowing certain passages where he 'appeared too prominently' to be printed in the *Life*, but Ellen maintained that her request for their removal had been ignored by Mrs Gaskell.[33] Ellen's grudge against Mr Nicholls caused her, illogically enough, to refuse to face the fact of his ownership of copyright in his wife's letters, so that while her censorship of their content was taken to inordinate lengths, she made repeated efforts to have them published in this censored form without admitting that his permission should be sought.

II. 1863–84: Ellen Nussey and the Letters. Projected Editions and Early Selections

In 1863, two years after Mr Brontë's death, with Mr Nicholls detached from the immediate scene by his removal to Ireland, Ellen amazingly and ineptly

[30] Mr Nicholls 'brought me down all the materials he could furnish me with'. ECG to EN [24] July [1855]; CP letter 257. The fragments may have dated from 1853 or 1854, during Mr Nicholls's exile from the parsonage. It seems unlikely that Mr Nicholls would cut up Charlotte's letters to other people; but he did give away envelopes addressed to Mr Brontë, one postmarked 8 June 1851.

[31] For the controversy see e.g. *LD* 504–14 and W & S appendix I. Ellen's comments are recorded in ECG to ?WSW ?19.1.1857, CP letter 335, and EN to GS 30.7.1857, MS Murray. The 1st edn. of the *Life* in Mar. 1857 had been quickly followed by a 2nd edn. in May, just before Mrs Gaskell's retractation of her allegations about Branwell Brontë's 'seducer' appeared in *The Times* on 30 May. Sales were discontinued, and unsold copies withdrawn. The 3rd edn., 'Revised and Corrected', appeared in Nov. 1857.

[32] See *Life* 3rd edn. ch. 7. Mrs Gaskell added 2 sentences explaining that Ellen had responded to requests by Mr Brontë and Mr Nicholls, had 'most carefully and completely effaced the names of the persons and places' in the letters, and that her information had referred 'solely to Miss Brontë and her sisters, and not to any other individuals'. cf. *Life* 1st edn. i. 127.

[33] EN to GS 1.6.1860; MS Murray.

decided to ask M. Heger to help her produce an edition of the letters. He replied courteously that Charlotte's letters would still be of interest even after the publication of the *Life*, for in them 'rien ne déguise le mouvement intime de sa pensée et en quelque sorte les battements de ce pauvre cœur malade' ('nothing disguises the innermost movement of her thoughts and, as it were, the beatings of this poor sick heart',)[1]—a phrase that must surely have alarmed Ellen. But he suggested that one should not publish confidential letters where more is revealed to 'la curiosité maligne des lecteurs' than the writer would have wished. As for translating the letters into French, he considered that the spontaneity of intimate letters gave them 'une grâce, un charme *intraduisibles*'. He thus gently and gracefully excused himself from complying with what must have been an embarrassing request—adding that in any case, 'faute de loisir', he could not assist Ellen in her pious plan to 'ajouter à la gloire, à la considération de [son] amie', ('to add to the glory and reputation of her friend'). Mrs Gaskell's careful editing of the *Life* had concealed Charlotte's early impression of M. Heger as a 'little, black, ugly being' sometimes looking like 'an insane Tom-cat—sometimes . . . a delirious Hyena', (EN May 1842) and she had suppressed any hint of Charlotte's later emotional dependence on him, but he must have been far from desiring further revelations of her 'cœur malade'.[2]

Ellen gave up the idea of publication for the time being, but on 19 December 1868 she had occasion to write to George Smith: could a local photographer make *carte-de-visite* photographs of Charlotte Brontë (presumably taken from the Richmond portrait) for sale at a church bazaar without infringing upon the copyright of her publisher?[3] Perhaps encouraged by his 'kind permission', she told him in her letter of 14 January 1869 that friends 'especially the Miss Woolers' had often urged her to have Charlotte's letters published.[4] Since the *Life* appeared Ellen had realized 'they would be of considerable value some day', though she had not intended to make use of them herself. But now she saw a very good use for any money raised by them. Could she send him 'for perusal some of the early letters' which she had copied out 'expunging a little here & there, of course there would be more of this to do if they came to

[1] C. Heger to EN ?7.11.1863; W & S 1009, as '7 Septembre, 1863'. The Rutgers-Symington transcript of the MS, which was formerly in the Law Collection, dates '7 9bre 1863', i.e. 'November'. The Swarthmore College copy of M. Heger's draft (erroneously dated 16 Octobre '1865') shows more clearly M. Heger's own perception of Charlotte's 'heart-sickness': 'ces lettres où l'on peut voir le mouvement intime et sans doute sentir les battements de ce pauvre cœur malade.' Mrs Chadwick, whose transcript differs slightly from W & S 1009, noted that 'malade' had been altered twice in the first draft, into 'blessé' [wounded], but finally left 'as it now stands'. (*Chadwick* 278.)

[2] See the notes to CH 24.7.1844 and 24.10.1844 for Mrs Gaskell's discreet omissions from M. Heger's extracts from the letters.

[3] MS Murray. Smith had originally commissioned the portrait, and had permitted its reproduction in the *Life*, which was of course published by his own firm.

[4] MS Murray.

printing) & one or two specimens from letters of a more recent date'? She had 'frequent proofs from America that the interest in the Brontë family is still very lively & real'.[5]

George Smith replied that Mr Nicholls owned the copyright in his wife's letters, and it might not be easy to obtain his permission to print them; but if they proved suitable for publication it would be worthwhile to seek his consent. Smith would therefore be glad to see Ellen's copies.[6] Ellen, who had previously complained to him that Mr Nicholls, for no good cause, had been 'in a savage humour'[7] with her ever since the *Life* came out, was 'a little vexed' to find that Mr Nicholls had 'any power whatever over the letters especially after the use he got me to give of them to Mrs. Gaskell'.[8] Nevertheless she sent copies of 'about 4 years of the correspondence—they are almost verbatim copies I mean the omissions are not very extensive'. She had omitted little about herself because in writing of her friend, Charlotte had shown 'freedom & expression of herself'.

Clearly Ellen had retained enough of this freedom in the letters to make George Smith apprehensive—he had after all published the rather too revealing *Villette* as well as the *Life*. The letters, he acknowledged, expressed 'without reserve' Charlotte's inmost feelings. 'How these revelations of her emotions would strike the public mind if they were published separately, and whether they would heighten the impression of her character made by Mrs Gaskell's biography appears to me an important consideration.'[9] He tactfully suggested that Ellen might instead incorporate 'some of the most characteristic letters, or passages from them . . . in a brief and simple narrative of [her] friendship': 'Mr Nicholls could not make any objection to such a publication, especially if it took place in the "Cornhill Magazine." ' Ellen replied warily but no doubt sincerely that she was too preoccupied with work for a Church 'Sale of Work' to accept immediately, but asked what he would pay her if she wrote 'anything producible which I feel very diffident about'. Could he find out whether Mr Nicholls possessed any of her own letters to Charlotte?[10] He would do well to give them up since she had letters from Charlotte that he would surely give almost a fortune to possess. Smith, realizing from the tone of Ellen's allusions to Mr Nicholls that he would be unlikely to give her permission to publish the letters, replied that articles such as he had suggested might be printed without applying to Mr Nicholls, and that Ellen might expect to receive '£50 or

[5] In *Scribner's Monthly* for May 1871, p. 18, Ellen identifies Henry J. Raymond as the American who had advised 'a further publication of C. B.'s letters', saying they would be a 'considerable success'.

[6] GS to EN 18.1.1869, MS BPM Cadman; W & S 1012.

[7] EN to GS 20.2.1868, MS Murray.

[8] EN to GS 19.1.1869, MS Murray.

[9] GS to EN 12.2.1869, MS BPM Cadman; W & S 1014.

[10] EN to GS 16.2.1869, MS Murray.

thereabouts' for two or three articles.[11] This was a comparatively modest offer: the firm had paid £62 13*s*. 8*d*. for the fourteen-page 'The Last Sketch' (Charlotte's 'Emma' with a preface by Thackeray) in the *Cornhill* for April 1860—a publication for which Mr Nicholls had given a willing and courteous permission.[12]

In reply Ellen requested the return of her copied letters and elaborated on her 'insuperable aversion' to writing to Mr Nicholls, even for the sake of retrieving her own letters.[13] It was an aversion which would have serious consequences for the later publication of the correspondence. Her somewhat cool note of thanks to Smith for the return of her copies and his equally cool acknowledgement on 5 March 1869, accompanied by his recognition of the impasse in her relations with Mr Nicholls, marked the end of her second attempt to publish her letters.[14]

Some two years later, on 10 May 1871, Ellen sent to George Smith a copy of the American magazine, *Scribner's Monthly*, for that month, 'containing a few Reminiscences of CB's early life, such as a schoolfellow can give'. She had, she said, inadequately performed the task which she was 'urged into—but as I was assured that it would be only an American issue I ventured on the attempt.'[15] George Smith can hardly have been pleased with her admission that she had often wished for his judgement on the matter. *Scribner's*, and not the *Cornhill*, had acquired Ellen's invaluable recollections of Charlotte's early days at Roe Head school and her memories of the Brontë family as they appeared to her on her early visits to the parsonage, along with illustrations of Haworth, of Roe Head, of Ellen's home, the Rydings, and of other places associated with the Brontës. Ellen did not tell George Smith—nor had she told Mr Nicholls—that the 'Reminiscences' followed the publication of a selection of Charlotte's letters in Scribner's earlier magazine, *Hours at Home*, from June to September 1870.[16] They had been prepared for Scribner's by the Hon. John Bigelow, a diplomat and literary editor who had been the American consul in Paris from 1861 to 1864 and had later visited England. He had selected letters from 'some three hundred' placed in his hands by Ellen Nussey 'with a view to their

[11] GS to EN 24.2.1869, MS BPM Cadman; W & S 1017.

[12] MS Notebook, Smith, Elder papers, National Library of Scotland MS 23185. See Margaret Smith, 'New Light on Mr Nicholls', *BST* 19. 3. 97–106.

[13] EN to GS 27.2.1869; MS Murray; W & S 1018 (part). In a letter to C. K. Shorter of 26.4.1895 Mr Nicholls said that he had not seen any of Ellen's letters, which had probably been destroyed. (MS Brotherton.)

[14] EN to GS 4.3.1869, MS Murray, and GS to EN 5.3.1869, W & S 1019. Smith also drily confirmed his refusal to comply with Ellen's repeated requests for gifts of books for her church bazaar.

[15] EN to GS 10.5.1871; MS Murray. For the 'Reminiscences' see Appendix.

[16] *Hours at Home* (New York), xi; excerpts from 114 letters to EN from CB and 1 from EJB of 22.5.1843. A printed announcement on the back cover of the Sept. number advised that *Scribner's Monthly* would be issued 'early in October for November' in place of the old magazine, in response to popular demand, and that it would be edited by Dr. J. G. Holland.

publication'[17] in the spring of 1870. Scribner's had offered Ellen £100 for the series, doubling George Smith's offer.[18] Richard Watson Gilder, the editor of *Hours at Home*, proclaimed that these new letters revealed Charlotte's womanhood, and were 'touchingly characteristic' in their 'quaint, old-womanly, sad tone'. Brief sympathetic comments and quotations from the *Life* were added to give a semblance of coherence. The publication of course evaded A. B. Nicholls's control, since American law offered no copyright protection to foreign writers until 1891.

T. J. Winnifrith suggests, rightly, I think, that Ellen provided for *Hours at Home* the copies she had made for George Smith (no doubt with later additions), and that these might well be the heavily bowdlerized and inaccurate copies bought by a Mrs Needham of Blackburn at the sale of Ellen's possessions in 1898.[19] Noting that the copies correspond closely in order and text to the versions in *Hours at Home*, he demonstrates their inadequacy by collating them with later texts. He remarks that the Needham copies include two letters not printed by Wise and Symington, one 'a mere scrap' dated 3 July 1833, the second 'in the spring of 1853' referring to the Upjohns.[20] The manuscripts of both these letters have survived and are now in the BPM as B.S. 40.2 and the mutilated B.S. 86.5, which I date tentatively as 16 March 1853. The Needham texts of the early letters are fuller than those in *Hours at Home*. In spite of their palpable errors, they preserve a few readings which may be authentic, notably in Charlotte's letter to Ellen of 18 October 1832.

The *Hours at Home* text is unsatisfactory on almost all counts. It was intended to be supplementary to the *Life*, passages already published there being enclosed within square brackets. Heavily edited, and sometimes absurd in its rewording or misreading, it provided a few nearly complete 'new' letters and many disconnected snippets, lacking a meaningful context and in some cases out of chronological order. Omissions were rarely indicated, and most personal names were reduced to arbitrary and inconsistent initials. Comparison of the *Hours at Home* version of EN 13.3.1835 with the fuller text in *Nussey* 32–3[21] reveals minor variants in wording, and the omission of proper names and several complete sentences (including the postscript and Charlotte's admission,

[17] J. B. 'To the Editor of Hours at Home', *Hours at Home* xi. [101]. For Bigelow, see his *Retrospections of an Active life* (New York, 1913).

[18] Ellen planned to use the money for a memorial window to the Brontës in Haworth church. See *Whitehead* 215.

[19] The copies are now in the BPM. See T. J. Winnifrith, 'Charlotte Brontë's Letters to Ellen Nussey', *Durham University Journal*, Dec. 1970, 16–18 and his study of texts and transmission in *Background* ch. 2 and notes, and appendix B.

[20] *Durham University Journal*, Dec. 1970, 16. The MSS of W & S 855, 880, 884, and 885 have now been located.

[21] The suppressed edn. of the letters printed for J. Horsfall Turner between 1885 and 1889. See pp. 43–52.

'I fancy he thought me very stupid'). There is also an unfortunate misprint, when Charlotte's impression of Ellen is said to be 'unhappily incapable of erasure'.[22] The editing is capricious: Charlotte's teasing advice that Ellen should wear 'white pantaloons and smart boots' at the Birstall rout is retained, but Ellen's gift of a bustle is merely 'the other gift' and a 'roll of muslin' becomes 'the transparency' in EN ?14.1.1843.

The *Hours at Home* letters had been chosen to correct what Ellen saw as Mrs Gaskell's inadequate emphasis on Charlotte's religious faith, and to show that she was above all dutiful, self-sacrificing, and patiently resigned. For Ellen the publication was part of a crusade, to be continued in her 'Reminiscences', which were to be her defence of Charlotte from 'the oft-made charge of irreligion'.[23] Ellen wished to show through the letters that her friend had a 'trustful, obedient faith' and that her whole life was a 'practical illustration of [Christ's] teachings . . . daily she was a Christian heroine, who bore her cross with the firmness of a martyr saint!'[24]

As a quarry for full, accurate, and unbiased texts *Hours at Home* is therefore negligible, but it cannot be entirely ignored. Where no holograph manuscript survives, it may occasionally retain an authentic reading not found in later copies, and I have recorded the more likely of these in the notes. For example the *Hours at Home* text of EN 18.9.1845 ends 'and I promise to write you a regular long letter next time' instead of 'all continue the same here. Good bye' as in *Nussey* 134. Perhaps both versions derive from a fuller original MS. In EN 20.11.1845 Charlotte refers to the unpleasant Mrs Joshua Taylor as an 'old woman' instead of an 'old lady', as in *Nussey* 136, and ends her letter 'Write again soon. Good-by.'[25] Such variants are of little consequence, but when all sources are secondary, they are worth consideration. One *Hours at Home* reading (deriving from the Needham copy) has been used in the text of the present volume: Ellen is unlikely to have added a phrase to Charlotte's rash venture into inaccurate schoolgirl French of 18 October 1832, where she might well have addressed Ellen as 'mon amie chère et chérit'.[26]

Early in 1876 Ellen met Thomas Wemyss Reid,[27] the editor of the *Leeds*

[22] *Hours at Home*, xi 107.

[23] 'Reminiscences of Charlotte Brontë', *Scribner's Monthly*, May 1871, 18.

[24] Ellen had in mind such attacks as that by Elizabeth Rigby (Lady Eastlake) in the *Quarterly Review* for Dec. 1848, where *JE* is said to be 'pre-eminently an anti-Christian composition . . . a murmuring against God's appointment . . . a proud and perpetual assertion of the rights of man'. See also WSW 15.12.1847 notes 3 and 7.

[25] *Hours at Home* xi. 295, 296.

[26] Ibid. 104. *Needham* reads 'et cherit'.

[27] T. W. Reid (1842–1905) was knighted in 1894. An experienced journalist, he became the head of the reporting staff of the *Leeds Mercury* in 1866 and its editor from 1870 to 1887, after which he was the manager of Cassell's publishing firm until his death. He wrote biographies of CB, 1876–7, W. E. Forster, 1888, Lord Houghton (Richard Monckton Milnes) 1890, and others. In his *Charlotte Brontë* (1876, 1877) he used information provided by Lord Houghton, who had met CB in London and had exerted himself to help Mr Nicholls. Reid's correspondence with EN began in 1873.

Mercury, who had given a lecture on the Brontës which interested her. They planned that he should weave some of Charlotte's letters into a sketch of her life and character. Ellen wrote to him very cordially on 10 May to suggest that the sketch might be enlarged: it would be 'the most desirable thing possible' if he could 'write another Memoir' of Charlotte 'without that fearful history of her brother', for it was unjust that 'one so pure & excellent . . . should have anything connected with her printed Life that is unsuited for the reading of the young & innocent'. She would put as much material as she possibly could into his hands.[28] Reid replied that it would be a 'very great pleasure & privilege' to write a Life free from some of the defects in Mrs Gaskell's story: he thought the letters she had sent him were charming.[29]

By 26 May 1876 Reid had arranged with Macmillan to publish his preliminary sketch in the August–October numbers of *Macmillan's Magazine*, to be followed by an enlarged version of the 'monograph' in volume form. Ellen would see the proofs, and he would alter or omit at her request any of the material she had provided.[30] This included some of Charlotte's letters to Margaret Wooler, who was to share with Ellen one third of the £100 Reid received for the two publications. Ellen duly saw the proofs, answered his questions about the Brontës, and as he said in his preface, helped him 'with much valuable counsel and advice in the decision of many difficult points'.

Ellen had for example told Reid about her family's homes, about their excursion with the Brontës to Bolton Priory, and about Mr Nicholls's friend, the Revd Sutcliffe Sowden. But Ellen was ageing, her memory was treacherous, and her accounts often biased. She could not remember whether the Nusseys had moved to Brookroyd in 1836 or 1837, she called Mr Nicholls's friend 'Snowdon',[31] and she alleged that the Brontës, in their 'rickety dogcart' redolent of some rural farmyard,[32] were awed by the carriage in which Ellen's relatives had travelled to the Priory. In her letters to Reid she referred venomously to Mr Nicholls as pigheaded, obtuse, selfish, and sadistic, and to Mr Brontë as an 'old villian' who had tried to turn Charlotte's faithful heart from her. She insisted that Charlotte, in contrast to these monsters, should be shown in all her nobility.[33]

Ironically enough, while Reid complied with Ellen's wishes by playing down the effect of Branwell's disastrous life on the 'pure' Charlotte, he showed instead that her deepest emotional experiences had been in Brussels. Her time

[28] EN to Reid 10.5.1876; MS Berg.

[29] Reid to EN 11.5.1876 and 26.5.1876, MSS BPM Cadman; W & S 1024 and 1025.

[30] Reid to EN 26.5.1876, 13.11.1877, MSS BPM Cadman; W & S 1025, 1028.

[31] EN to Reid 4.7.1876, 7.7.1876, MSS Berg. See also Barbara Whitehead's comments on Ellen's wishful thinking in *Whitehead* 219–20.

[32] *Reid* 30.

[33] EN to Reid 3.11.1876, 7.7.1876, MSS Berg.

there had been the turning-point in her life, and it had been the arena for a sharp contest with temptations.[34] This was perceptive on Reid's part, and it drew back a little the veil with which Mrs Gaskell had so carefully concealed Charlotte's feelings for M. Heger. It cannot have been to Ellen's liking, and its effect on her was to make her yet more fanatically defensive of Charlotte's saint-like virtue.[35]

The magazine articles were drawn to the attention of Mr Nicholls, who broke his long silence to write in some agitation to Wemyss Reid. In the last chapter Charlotte's sole failure of duty, when 'she allowed inclination to blind her' to the right path, was said to have 'coloured the whole of her subsequent life. But her own condemnation of herself was more sharp and bitter than any which could have been passed upon her by the world.'[36] Mr Nicholls objected that the passage 'from its obscurity, is, I think, liable to misconstruction'.[37] Wemyss Reid retained this paragraph in his 1877 volume, but added a footnote reference to Charlotte's own confession of her failure in duty.[38] He also retained letters referring to James Taylor ('Mr. X') and Charlotte's reactions to the possibility of marriage with him.[39] Though 'Mr. X's' departure for India had been disguised as a journey to Australia, Mr Nicholls expressed an understandable distaste for the publication of his wife's frank analysis of her feelings for a previous suitor, and he wrote: 'Had I known that these letters were in existence I should have asked [Ellen Nussey] to destroy them'; but he felt himself to blame for not having cautioned her that his wife's letters were not 'hers for publication—I could not however imagine that she would have been so unmindful of what was due to the memory of the dead and the feelings of the living'.[40] Yet Reid had in fact portrayed with no lack of sympathy Charlotte's complex emotions as well as her integrity and refusal to compromise: 'if X—be the only husband fate offers to me, single I must always remain.'[41] Wise and Symington were later to confuse matters by including parts of a letter to Mrs Gaskell within Charlotte's letter to James Taylor of 1 January 1851.[42] In the present edition the complete texts of Charlotte's surviving letters to Taylor should give a little more insight into this difficult relationship.

Reid's monograph was an altogether more coherent production than the

[34] *Reid* ch. 6.

[35] See e.g. the notes to EN 23.1.1844. On the whole EN praised Reid's volume, which 'entranced' her. (EN to Reid 10.5.1877, MS Berg.)

[36] *Macmillan's Magazine* xxxv. 16 (Nov. 1876). In EN 14.10.1846 CB admitted that she returned to Brussels 'against [her] conscience'.

[37] ABN to Reid 6.11.1876, MS Berg.

[38] *Reid*, 232.

[39] *Macmillan's Magazine* xxxiv. 497–8 (Oct. 1876); extracts from CB's letters to EN 30. 1–23.4.1851.

[40] ABN to Reid 6.11.1876, MS Berg.

[41] CB to EN 23.4.1851, MS BPM Gr. E 22; *Reid* 123. [Reid's text.].

[42] MS Texas; W & S 631. CB unhelpfully misdated her letter '1850'. Her letter to Mrs Gaskell was written on 22.1.1851 (MS Rylands; W & S 640).

Hours at Home series. It related Charlotte's life to her writing, and as Reid intended, it complemented Mrs Gaskell's *Life*. He had put some of her more solemn quotations into context, illustrating occasions when Charlotte showed the 'happy levity of youth'.[43] He had chosen extracts from a hundred letters to Ellen and twelve to Miss Wooler, and had quoted from them at some length. These and the excellent facsimile of Charlotte's letter to Ellen of 25 August 1852,[44] were new to readers at the time. His work is still of value, and it has been used occasionally, and with caution, in the commentary of the present edition—as in the notes to EN 11.9.1833. Nevertheless Reid cannot be relied on. He repeated the myths about Patrick Brontë's neglect of his wife, his vanity, violence, and injustice—eliciting a protest from Mr Nicholls, who thought the character 'very much overdrawn' and insisted that Mr Brontë had 'never uttered an unkind or angry word to' him personally.[45] Reid's intentions were good, for he wished Charlotte to 'speak for herself, and tell her own story to the world'.[46] Unfortunately too many of his extracts from her letters, edited and proof-read by Ellen, were silently abridged, inaccurate, misdated, or placed in a misleading context. Where no manuscript survives, his texts are of value in little more than their partial agreement with other late copies. The addition of the name 'Ellen' in EN 14.12.1836 and of 'us' in a letter of early June 1837 (p. 171) are his only contributions to the text of the letters in the present volume.

In 1877 Reid suggested the eventual deposit of the letters in the British Museum, an idea which pleased Ellen, who asked him to find further information on the matter 'from the authorities'.[47] On 13 November he reported that he was 'not letting the British Museum matter rest; but [he was] forced to act very cautiously because of the possibility of Mr. Nicholls appearing on the scene'.[48] No action had been taken by 2 February the following year, when Ellen was still wishing for 'the Letters to be in safe-keeping (ie) in the British Museum if they would buy them'.[49] When she consulted George Smith on 3 May 1878, he declined to give an opinion on their marketable value and doubted whether she could legally sell them to 'the Trustees of the British Museum without [Mr Nicholls's] sanction'.[50] It is a great pity that Ellen's relationship with Mr Nicholls made any request from her or sanction by him equally unlikely, for the way was left open to a much less scrupulous adviser than George Smith or Wemyss Reid. T. J. Wise was to exploit Ellen's wish to

[43] *Reid* 35.
[44] *Reid* opp. 134. The MS is now in the Huntington library, HM 24498. Even here Reid's quotation on pp. 135–6 is inaccurate.
[45] ABN to Reid 6.11.1876, MS Berg.
[46] Reid to EN 11.5.1876, MS BPM Cadman; W & S 1024.
[47] EN to Reid 10.5.1877, MS Berg.
[48] Reid to EN 13.11.1877, MS BPM Cadman; W & S 1028.
[49] EN to Reid 2.2.1878, MS Berg.
[50] GS to EN 10.5.1878, MS BPM Cadman; W & S 1029.

sell the letters into the safe-keeping of a museum in order to gain possession of the greater part of her collection, under false pretences, in 1892.[51]

In 1884 Ellen again asked Wemyss Reid about the eventual deposit of her letters in the Museum. He had spoken to Lord Houghton, one of the Trustees, who

> did not encourage the idea that the Museum would buy the letters from you . . . I feel it is very difficult to advise you on the subject. If they went to the British Museum, they would be open to everybody and perhaps an unscrupulous use might be made of them. I have always felt that something more could be made out of them when Mr. Nicholls died, but not before; but even then it would need to be done very tenderly and discreetly.

Reid was 'greatly touched' by Ellen's thought of leaving the letters to him—perhaps this was on condition that he in turn should leave them to the Museum. He pointed out that she might well survive him, and wished her to 'take no step of this kind without the fullest consideration of it from all sides'.[52]

Between 1878 and 1882 Ellen lent a number of her letters to the Revd Alpheus Wilkes,[53] who planned to write a book on the Brontës. By 10 February 1879 he had written '14 books full' of his 'first rough MS', but in June 1882 this was still unfinished, for Ellen had discouraged him by finding his manuscript verbose and badly organized. He gave up the idea, and Ellen accused him of failing to return the letters she had lent him.[54] Pained and indignant, he replied that he had 'scrupulously and religiously returned . . . every letter written by the Brontës', and he reminded her that she had once told him 'some of the letters had been taken away . . . by some person who had been living under [her] roof' and by another named person.

Meanwhile she had sent other letters to a Brontë enthusiast, the effusive Sidney Biddell,[55] with the request that he would select two or three for sale[56] in aid of the fund for a Brontë memorial in Haworth church, but they were apparently not sold. Biddell returned what was probably a separate loan of eleven letters on 24 November 1882, and yet another on 15 February 1885.

Ellen's control of the letters was becoming precarious, and she seems to have alternated between generous trustfulness and anxious concern about their security. William Scruton, who visited Ellen in 1885 and 1887, was told by her that she had 'nothing left' of Emily Brontë's handwriting 'but a few

[51] See p. 54.

[52] Reid to EN 24.3.1884, MS BPM Cadman. Reid (1842–1905) was much younger than Ellen (1817–97). He was obviously reluctant to take the responsibility of ownership or disposal of the letters during the lifetime of Mr Nicholls, who in fact outlived him by a year.

[53] Alpheus Wilkes, BA London 1865, ordained priest 1869, curate of Stowmarket in Suffolk 1868–70, Titchwell near Lyme Regis 1870–3; at this date Vicar of West Barsham, Norfolk.

[54] Wilkes to EN 2.11.1878, 2.6.1882, MSS BPM Cadman; W & S 1030, 1038. See also *Whitehead* 222.

[55] Sidney Biddell or Biddle, (b. 1830), entered Trinity College Cambridge 1848; BA 1853, MA 1856; entered Lincoln's Inn 1853, called to the Bar 1856.

[56] Biddell to EN 18.4.1882, MS BPM Cadman; W & S 1036

envelopes addressed by her, which had once contained letters lent to a gentleman who had not had the graciousness to return them. The last letter of Emily's that she possessed she had given to the late Lord Houghton, who had been very anxious to possess one'.[57] She disposed of other individual letters or autographs from time to time before her sale of the remainder in 1892—as in September 1887 when a single letter (EN ?28.5.1836) and an autograph signature were offered to Miss Ingilby of Ripley in return for a donation for 'deserving objects' in memory of Charlotte Brontë.[58]

In 1882 Ellen had confided to Biddell her fear that unscrupulous people might publish her letters without her knowledge or supervision; she suspected that Alpheus Wilkes intended 'giving out' such a garbled edition 'at some future date'.[59] Biddell, either forgetting or ignoring the question of copyright, suggested that she might prevent this by preparing 'a little volume containing nothing but' Charlotte's letters to her, with a short preface and notes; he was sure the work would have a great sale, and he would be the 'go-between and arrange all business matters'.[60] His suggestion was made on the spur of the moment, and Ellen did not take it up at the time; but it was the germ of her next undertaking, the production of just such a volume in collaboration with Joseph Horsfall Turner of Idel, near Leeds, who had been introduced to her by William Scruton.

III. 1885–91: Horsfall Turner and the Suppressed Edition

Turner was a respected local antiquarian who edited *Yorkshire Notes and Queries* and had published *Haworth Past and Present: A History of Haworth, Stanbury, and Oxenhope* in 1879. In the 1880s he was gathering together 'autobiographical matter to form a book of appeal in order to test the statements of the many authors who . . . were spreading and re-spreading erroneous notions respecting' the Brontë family.[1] He was also interested in the Nussey family, and, naturally, in Ellen Nussey as a source of information about the Brontës. In 1885 she lent him her Brontë letters, with permission to make a facsimile of one of them to 'enrich' the pages of *Yorkshire Notes and Queries*.[2] The letters were then returned to Ellen.

What happened next was described by Horsfall Turner in *Bronteana: Rev. Patrick Brontë's Collected Works* (Bingley, 1898), the only part of the 'book of

[57] See *BST* 1. 8. 36.

[58] EN to Francis Spencer, 1.8.1887, 1 of 2 letters accompanying the CB MSS sold as Lot 53 at Phillips' sale rooms on 14.11.1991.

[59] This is evident in Biddell's reply of 24.11.[1882]; W & S 1041.

[60] Biddell to EN 24.11.[1882]; W & S 1041.

[1] J. Horsfall Turner, *Bronteana* (Bingley, 1898), p. [ix].

[2] Turner to EN 23.12.1885, MS BPM Cadman.

appeal' to be published.[3] He explained that his friend F. A. Leyland's contribution to 'the honour of the [Brontë] family', his two-volume defence of Branwell Brontë published in 1886,[4] had only resulted in mystification:

His work so displeased Miss Nussey . . . that she desired to counteract some of his assertions, but she also wished to thwart a clergyman of East Anglia, who had got access to her Brontë correspondence with the object of bringing out a Brontë biographical work. She had sought my acquaintance, and I had agreed to print the letters at her death, and add other matters which I still have in MS. respecting the Brontë and Nussey families. During her visits to my home and my repeated visits to Fieldhead, where she then resided, we came to the conclusion that the most satisfactory insight into the personal life of Charlotte Brontë could alone be obtained from her letters arranged in chronological order, but as it might be advantageous for Miss Nussey to see them in type and make notes, we agreed to print but not publish them during her life time.

On March 18th, 1887, she again sent me her collection, with a note, the first sentence of which read,—'I am sending off by train from Drighlington this evening a very precious parcel to you, just all that I had put together to come to you after my decease.'

Sometime before this date she had made her will in which the letters were designed to come to me, and, with the sum to be realized by their sale, it was agreed to place a memorial in Birstall Church by approval of our mutual friend the Rev. Canon Kemp.

On receiving the parcel a second time I immediately commenced printing the letters in chronological order but added no notes or comments (though I had many), because my scheme involved several volumes. The printing continued for two years, and just as the last of the Nussey letters were worked off—leaving the Taylor, Wheelwright and a few odd letters to be added—Miss Nussey changed her mind, desired to dispose of some of the original MS. letters in a way contrary to her own first suggestion.[5]

The correspondence of Ellen Nussey and Horsfall Turner in 1886–7 supports much of this account. On 7 September 1886 he suggested a meeting at Ellen's home: 'It is with a view to have your editorial supervision that I suggest the present private printing, and no one else can do it to perfection.'[6] This is not inconsistent with a plan to publish after Ellen's death, though since the agreement was not put into writing,[7] one cannot determine when the final printing was to be carried out, nor how many copies were to be printed. But Ellen clearly knew that the letters were being set up in type, and that she was to correct and annotate proofs. On 16 November Turner assured her that he was hurrying the printer, John Harrison of the firm of Thomas Harrison of Bingley,

[3] The full title was to have been *The Story of the Brontës: Their Homes, Haunts, Friends, and Works.* Charlotte's letters were to form 'Part Second'.

[4] Francis A. Leyland, *The Brontë Family with special reference to Patrick Branwell Brontë* (2 vols., 1886).

[5] *Bronteana* pp. [ix]–x.

[6] Turner to EN 7.9.1886, MS BPM Cadman.

[7] Ellen's 'statement of facts' prepared on 16.9.1889 and sent to G. Smith on 9.11.1889 declared that 'there was no written agreement'. MS Murray.

with other work 'so as to begin with the letters'.[8] By March 1887 Ellen was seeing proofs and adding comments. Turner wrote on 8 March:

'Do not . . . hurry, if you prefer to add further notes. The paper chosen is equal to that on which the "Works" and "Life" are printed.'[9]

On 20 August he reassured her that the work was confidential:

Mr John Harrison is the only person that sees a line of MS. or a line of print. I have him under pledge besides knowing him intimately. Your letter refers to getting quite through the correspondence. You will see we have only reached 1845. Yours of this morning, however, states that friends desire an autograph. By all means, at your discretion, I will send such as you indicate, and compare with the printed copy. I ask your pardon for any seeming neglect or real omission, assuring you that any such was quite unintentional.[10]

Turner's letters to Ellen in the BPM Cadman Collection, which continue until 21 April 1888, maintain this respectful tone; he was co-operating with her wishes and giving her every opportunity to 'make as full notes as ever' she could at her own 'time and leisure'.[11] Printing continued until spring 1889,[12] when an increasingly acrimonious dispute arose. Mr Turner was no doubt aggrieved by Ellen's decision not to bequeath the letters to him,[13] but she too believed she had cause for complaint. The matter was eventually settled with the help of Ellen's solicitor, H. F. Killick, who later wrote that she had not been satisfied with the printing, and had thought more material should have been omitted.[14]

Ellen's decision to halt the printing in 1889 was not the result of intervention by Mr Nicholls.[15] None of her somewhat inconsistent accounts of the Turner affair refers to a veto by him at this stage, and in a letter to her friend and adviser George Armytage of 16 November 1889, when she was still planning to have the book published, she cheerfully acknowledged that Mr Nicholls was Charlotte's representative 'if he chose to act—But I do not myself see the question in a serious light—For how could he in conscience come down on any such publication after the use my letters have had by his request for the

[8] MS BPM Cadman.

[9] Ibid. 8.3.1887.

[10] Turner to EN 20.8.1887, MS BPM Cadman.

[11] Turner to EN 14.1.1888, MS BPM Cadman.

[12] The imprint of the suppressed edn. reads: 'Printed for J. Horsfall Turner, Idel, Bradford; | By Thomas Harrison & Sons, Bingley. | 1885–9'. (p. 384.)

[13] See *Bronteana* p. x.

[14] See the undated note signed by H. F. Killick on a leaf inserted in his copy of the suppressed edn., presented to him by EN on 20.8.1895, and now in the BPM. A note by Mr Killick on the other side of the leaf is dated '21 Jany 1918'. He was mistaken in thinking that the letters were entrusted to Turner in 1889.

[15] The misconception that Mr Nicholls intervened in 1889 arose from the sentence beginning 'At the same time' in *CBCircle* 24 and *Shorter* i. 18–19. C. K. Shorter refers only to the 'possibility' of a veto.

memoir'.[16] In a statement prepared on 16 September 1889 and sent to George Smith on 9 November Ellen said she had entrusted the letters to Mr Turner 'on the express understanding that they were not to see daylight till after' her decease. 'The Letters were passed to me in proof for correction—I then, (& after) made a request for the return of the original letters—This request was disregarded . . . My Will was not made as he states—it was in prospect.' She added that the eventual publication would be 'for the benefit of the Poor of Birstall' if 'the sale realised sufficient after the sum of 300 had been secured by Mr. T. as compensation for his efforts & fulfilment of conditions. No entry has been made at the Stationers Hall as said to be necessary by him).'[17] This is a rather more credible account than Ellen's two later memoranda of 18 July 1894, alleging that the letters were entrusted to Mr Turner with her strict instruction that the parcel must not be opened until after her death, and that she was horrified to hear later that 1,000 copies were being put 'in type'.[18] This version can only be attributed to the fragile memory of Ellen at the age of 77, convinced she had been cheated and betrayed, and defending her good name 'for the information of those I leave behind'.

In 1889 Ellen had also told George Smith about the recovery of her letters. Mr Turner had 'threatened when I wrote for the return of the original letters to publish forthwith the letters he had in type unless I paid him a certain sum for the *half* of them (ie) originals'.[19] On legal advice she agreed to pay him £100 providing he returned 'all my letters & 1,000 sheets of the printed letters'.[20] The manuscripts were retrieved by 25 October 1889, the printed sheets, '12 large weighty packages', by 9 November. By 16 November Ellen was again in possession of her manuscripts, but had left the sheets in Mr Killick's office for the time being.[21] She later alleged that the MSS were handed over to her so hurriedly that she could not examine them properly, and that she subsequently realized fifty to sixty autographs and some pen and ink drawings were missing.[22]

[16] MS WYAS Calderdale (Halifax).

[17] EN to GS 9.11.1889, MS Murray.

[18] MS Texas.

[19] EN to GS 9.11.1889, MS Murray.

[20] Ibid.

[21] EN to George Armytage 25.10.1889 and to Mrs George Armytage 16.11.1889, MSS WYAS Calderdale (Halifax).

[22] See EN's 2 memoranda of 18.7.1894, MSS Texas. One of these refers to missing 'letters & autographs', terms which were sometimes used interchangeably; it is not clear whether EN refers to separate items in this case. CB drew 1 sketch on the MS of EN 6.3.1843. See pl. 3. A printed note to this letter in *Nussey* reads 'Humorous pen-and-ink sketch, illustrating this "Good bye across the Channel" '. EN wrote in one of the copies of *Nussey* on this page, the word 'Stolen'. (*Hatfield* 168.) But Ellen may have mislaid the drawing, which at some stage was detached from the rest of the letter, for in Oct. 1889 she proposed to use drawings for an American publication. See p. 49. The MS is BPM B.S. 50.4, part of Horsfall Turner's collection purchased by the Brontë Society in 1974, and probably originally bought by Mr Turner from T. J. Wise before 1896. See EN 12.11.1840 n. 2 for another MS with sketches, now missing.

While it is true that Charlotte's signature has been cut from a number of her letters, and that others now at Yale and in the BPM are more extensively mutilated, it is impossible to know who was responsible.[23] The words written in some MSS to replace missing signatures and text are most often in Ellen's handwriting, but this does not necessarily mean that it was she who took the 'autographs'; she could have replaced the text by reference to her own copies or to the printed sheets.

Regrettable as the outcome of the Turner affair undoubtedly was, it had resulted in the recording of some letters for which the manuscript has since disappeared. Though the comparison of *Nussey* texts with surviving manuscripts shows that they vary greatly in their degree of fidelity to the original, and though some were based on copies by Ellen which would also have been censored, they cannot be ignored as source material. Collation shows that C. K. Shorter took some of his texts in *Charlotte Brontë and her Circle* in 1896 directly from the copy of *Nussey* which Ellen had 'placed in [his] hands' some 'three or four years' before, with the request that he 'would write something around what might remain of the unpublished letters'.[24] Shorter's copying of the *Nussey* texts was not impeccable. His alterations of punctuation mean that *Nussey* is more likely to record some at least of the accidentals of the original manuscript, even though neither Ellen nor Horsfall Turner's printer attempted faithful reproduction of Charlotte's expressive but informal pointing. When no manuscript survives, and when the Wise and Symington texts simply reprint Shorter's versions, *Nussey* is the preferred copy-text unless there are good reasons for using the *Life* or a composite text.[25] The advantage of printing from *Nussey* in such cases can become amusingly obvious when manuscripts come to light. MS BPM Grolier E 19 shows that *Nussey* was correct in reading 'what are the results of the operation?' in EN 24.4.1850; but Ellen added in the margin of BPM *Nussey* Copy 1 the words 'tooth drawing'[26] and in Copy 2, 'tooth-extraction'. C. K. Shorter, understandably taking her note as an emendation rather than a gloss, printed 'what are the results of the tooth extraction'. It was this version (*Shorter* 431) which was reproduced in W & S 548.

Useful information about the content if not the text of the letters can be derived from some of Ellen's notes on the proofs and on some of the other printed sheets which were later bound in volume form. She commented on Charlotte's letter to her of 14 August 1839, 'The visit to the seaside was at length realised. Charlotte sobbed with emotion & was for some time fixed to the point of observation'; and on the letter of 17 March 1840, '<u>buoyancy</u> of spirit

[23] See e.g. EN ?Jan. 1844, p. 340, EN?5.2.1846, EN?10.9.1845, and notes.

[24] *CBCircle* 24. Ellen gave Shorter an interleaved copy with a list providing 'much information respecting living personages & their names'. EN to T. J. Wise, Nov. [?1892], BL MS Ashley B169.

[25] See e.g. EN ?20.2.1837, ?10.1.1842, ?4.3.1844 and notes.

[26] BPM *Nussey* Copy 1, 227.

was the gift of the present time'.[27] But her notes have to be used with caution; some are obviously prejudiced or inaccurate, or written in defence of Charlotte's 'purity of mind'. In some her hostility to Mr Nicholls is evident, along with her continuing uneasy defensiveness about her use of the letters. This resulted in at least one distinct *suppressio veri*. In a letter of November 1854 Ellen pledged herself to destroy Charlotte's letters if Mr Nicholls pledged himself 'to no censorship in the matter communicated'.[28] She later added a pencil note on the MS of this letter, 'Mr N continued his censorship so the pledge was void'. Charlotte's reply reads, in part, 'Arthur thanks you for the promise . . . on my asking him whether he would give the pledge required in return—he says "yes we may now write any dangerous stuff we please to each other".'[29] Ellen deleted the whole of this passage in *Nussey* and added a pencilled footnote, 'he never did give the pledge'.[30] C. K. Shorter, using a copy of *Nussey* provided by Ellen, omitted the sentence 'Arthur thanks you for the promise' and replaced it with 'Arthur wishes you would burn my letters'.[31] This is of course not in the manuscript—Ellen had already promised to burn them. Shorter was also misled by a false identification of someone mentioned in the same letter. His text refers to a Mrs Hewitt's loss of a child, but the manuscript shows that Charlotte was sympathizing with the elderly Mrs Cockill's loss of her grown-up daughter, the 'poor Elizabeth' already mentioned in the letter. Probably Ellen, her memory failing, had informed Shorter that the blank left in *Nussey* should be filled with the name of her close friend Mrs Thomas S. Hewitt, the former Mary Gorham.[32] W & S 923 reproduces this corrupt text.

In the present edition I have quoted, selectively, from Ellen's notes in the various *Nussey* copies, but it should be realized that they may often reveal more about Ellen than Charlotte Brontë. I have also used *Nussey* as a source for two letters to Ellen Nussey not printed in full elsewhere—a curt message from A. B. Nicholls dated 18 June 1861 describing in a single sentence Mr Brontë's last illness and death, and a long, affectionate, and informative letter from Mary Taylor of 28 January 1858 giving her reasons for staying in New Zealand, and referring to the frail health of her niece 'Tim', Charlotte Brontë's much-loved 'grandchild', the daughter of the widowed Amelia Taylor.[33]

[27] BPM Killick copy and copy 2, 65; Killick copy, 70.

[28] EN to 'the Revd The Magister' [A. B. Nicholls], [Nov. 1854]; MS Texas. W & S 922 reads '*no* authorship'.

[29] EN 7.11.1854; MS Pierpont Morgan.

[30] BPM Killick copy, 333.

[31] *Shorter* 686.

[32] Some of EN's identifications can be verified by external evidence—e.g. the surnames of 2 of CB's pupils, Lister and Marriott, in EN ?14.12.1836.

[33] BPM Killick copy, 382–4. Other copies of *Nussey* used in the present edn. are BPM copies 2 and 3; a copy formerly belonging to Robertson Nicoll, transcribed by C. W. Hatfield (BPM typescript); and Ashley 169, the British Library copy which formerly belonged to T. J. Wise, and was probably the one given to him by EN. I have not seen Horsfall Turner's 'proof-copy', now in private hands. There are also copies in the Bodleian Library, and the Houghton Library, Harvard.

Once Ellen had recovered her letters she planned to publish them, in some form, without delay. 'Mr. Killick, as others, who know of the affair with Mr. Turner, urges an immediate Publication, so I must begin to prepare, for my kind Friends who have offered to negociate for me with American Publishers.'[34] She hoped to add interest by inducing M. Heger 'to give up something . . such as the Devoirs CB wrote when his pupil', and by using photographs and possibly drawings by Charlotte—'The Americans are so fond of illustrations'.[35] She had sought advice from Augustine Birrell, the barrister and man of letters whose amiable *Life of Charlotte Brontë*, with its interesting new information about Mr Brontë's early love, Mary Burder, had appeared in 1885. He had advised her to publish what she meant to do 'at once & in America'; he was sorry he could not undertake to edit, but he would use his influence with Scribner's to negotiate good terms for her.[36] By 7 November 1889 he had seen Charles Scribner's representative in London and found that the firm was 'nervous' about the legal aspect of publication. Ellen should therefore write to George Smith, who might have got the copyright from Mr Nicholls, and ask if he would be willing to publish either on his own account or with Scribner's.[37] When Ellen contacted George Smith, tempting him with the prospect of the 'immense sale' forecast by her friends 'the A[merican] Consul & his wife', he warned her that Charlotte's legal representative, whoever he was, 'might come forward, and the publisher . . . might be put to heavy legal and other expenses'. He would not dare to print the letters without the copyright owner's sanction.[38]

Birrell advised Ellen that Mr Nicholls would have been Charlotte's appointed executor, and that Ellen did not own the copyright in the letters written to her; but she still hoped for an American publication as the consul wished to 'employ a Legal Friend' on her behalf. The matter was temporarily in abeyance, and she was glad of a little repose—'fearing only the mice feasting on the 1,000 Sheets'.[39] The sheets were to have a more spectacular and less demeaning fate—but not yet; Ellen evidently wished them to be preserved intact for the time being. On 2 December 1889 Birrell assured her that 'The Letters could be published in America at once—without asking anybody's

[34] EN to G. Armytage 25.10.1889; MS WYAS Calderdale (Halifax). The friends were Augustine Birrell and Sir George and Lady Morrison. For the Morrisons see *Whitehead* 233–7.

[35] Ibid.

[36] A. Birrell to EN 9.10.1889, MS BPM Cadman.

[37] A. Birrell to EN 7.11.1889, MS BPM Cadman. When Birrell read the *Nussey* volume he considered there was little unused that might be of interest except what could not 'with propriety' be published, but he admitted that Americans might think differently. (Birrell to EN 15.1.1890, MS BPM Cadman.)

[38] GS to EN 12.11.1889, copy MS Murray.

[39] EN to Mrs G. Armytage 16.11.1889, MS WYAS Calderdale (Halifax). The American consul in Bradford was Claude Meeker, a Brontë enthusiast and early supporter of the Brontë Society founded in 1893.

leave—but copies could not, (legally) be introduced into this country—if Mr Nicholls objected'.[40] She pooh-poohed the idea of an intervention by Mr Nicholls.

Spurred on by a new adviser and would-be editor, Sir George Morrison, Ellen resumed her campaign in August 1890. In November 1890 she wrote to Charles Scribner's suggesting the publication of a volume of letters with additions by herself.[41] Scribner's responded with 'very lively interest', and asked for copies of the letters so that they could judge the 'scope and nature of the unpublished material'. They proposed that the work might include a portrait of Charlotte Brontë and a facsimile letter.[42] Ellen accordingly sent a packet of the printed sheets, with sensitive matter—especially a 'great deal' about Mr Nicholls—heavily deleted. She explained that Mr Turner had been legally bound not to use her material, and that she hoped to have the printed copies destroyed when the new volume appeared.[43] Scribner's observed that much of the material had been printed in the *Life* or the Reid monograph—not mentioning the parent firm's former magazine, *Hours at Home*—but they offered an advance of £50 on a competently edited, complete, and consecutive edition, and a royalty of 15 per cent of the retail price. They asked Ellen to approve a preface by Charles Scribner making clear that the completeness and not the novelty of the collection was its chief attraction. Ellen was willing to comply but diffident about editing, and on the advice of William Wright, delayed her reply. Scribner's could not proceed without her co-operation, and she in turn could not understand their delay in writing to her. When she did write her suggestions were hardly practical: the work should not be advertised, she thought, because she shunned publicity.[44]

The correspondence trailed on, with long gaps, until 20 June 1892, when at Ellen's request the sheets and illustrations were returned to her: Scribner's had refused to raise their offer when she promised to send a second, revised copy with an additional account of Anne Brontë's death. The affair ended with cool courtesy on Scribner's part and confused regrets on Ellen's. She had been distressed by their delays and distracted by Dr Wright's proposals to take the original letters into his care.[45]

[40] MS BPM Cadman.

[41] EN to Charles Scribner's Sons, New York; 24.11.1890, MS Princeton.

[42] Scribner's to EN 13.12.1890, MS BPM Cadman.

[43] EN to Charles Scribner's Sons, New York; 15.1.1891, MS Princeton. The copies had been destroyed by 7.11.1892, when EN referred in a letter to G. Armytage to the 'destruction of the printed mass'. (MS WYAS Calderdale (Halifax).)

[44] On 20.11.1889 A. Birrell had warned EN that publicity might cause Mr Nicholls to intervene. (MS BPM Cadman.)

[45] Most of EN's letters to Scribner's are at Princeton, and an incomplete series of her letters to and from Scribner's can be found in the BPM general and Cadman collections. William Wright, DD, was the Secretary of the British and Foreign Bible Society in London. His book, *The Brontës in Ireland*, (1893), was devastatingly attacked by Angus Mason Mackay in 'A Crop of Brontë Myths', *Westminster Review* (Oct. 1895), and *The Brontës: Fact and Fiction* (1897). Horsfall Turner revealed more of Wright's historical inaccuracies and inconsistencies in *Bronteana* 267–304, concluding charitably that 'we are persuaded he has been very much misled'. (301.) See E. Chitham, *The Brontes' Irish Background* (1986), for a comparatively favourable modern view of Wright.

Wright, who had been given Ellen's address by Horsfall Turner,[46] had toyed with the ideas of a joint editorship of the letters with Ellen, or of adding an essay on the Brontës' Irish connections to the Scribner publication. He had offered to buy the MSS from her for £50, arrange them and return any 'compromising' ones to her for destruction, though 'If the collection shd. ever be handed over to the British Museum, it ought to be as complete as possible.'[47] Meanwhile Ellen would have peace of mind since he had a 'good Safe at Home & a Strong Room in the Bible House where the letters wd be safe'; Ellen could reclaim them at any time on returning what they cost him.[48] No other person could claim them 'after our death', and they would 'find a resting place in some national Repository'. After a period of warm admiration for and high hopes in her new adviser, Ellen decided that his suggestions were 'presuming interference' and declined his offer. On 16 April 1892 he accepted her decision, relieved that it freed him from 'responsibility and embarrassment',[49] and perhaps recalling his own words in a letter to Ellen of 19 November 1891, 'The Brontë subject is the most prickly I have ever had to do with.'[50]

By 2 November 1892 Ellen no longer dismissed the notion of intervention by Mr Nicholls,[51] and at her request, all but about twelve copies of the printed sheets had been destroyed, with the help of her friend the Revd John Ridley, the minister of Brownhill church in Birstall. He later described the sheets, some of them folded ready for binding:

> I never appreciated before that closely packed paper took so much burning. The martyrdom was exceedingly prolonged; there were probably more than 30,000 sheets to get rid of. It took weeks of my spare time. My garden was at the top of a hill and the Yorkshire winds were fierce . . . Whilst some were burning, many were steeped almost to pulp in the largest tub I could find, and then buried . . . I was glad for my own sake when my task was done, but more so for Miss Nussey's peace of mind. I really believe that the whole transaction, the printing and subsequent difficulties connected with it, worried her into weakened health. Poor old lady![52]

The whole sad farce of the years 1890–2, the abortive negotiations with publishers, and the culminating funeral pyre, had at least led Ellen to think about the value of her manuscripts, and to annotate two copies of the printed sheets—a mixed blessing for future editors, as I have indicated.[53]

46 *Bronteana* 270.

47 Wright to EN 6.7.1891, MS BPM Cadman.

48 Ibid.

49 Wright to EN 16.4.1892, MS BPM Cadman.

50 MS BPM Cadman.

51 'Mr N[icholls] would certainly issue an Injunction the Publishers have discovered if Letters appeared in book form.' EN to G. Armytage, 2.11.1892; MS WYAS Calderdale (Halifax). See p. 53: C. K. Shorter had warned EN of the certainty of an injunction in his letter of 18 Sept. He and Wise may have advised or insisted on the destruction of the copies.

52 J. Ridley to C. K. Shorter; W & S iv. 289.

53 See pp. 47–8.

Much of her editing consisted of deletions of material she considered too private or too revealing of Charlotte's fallible human nature, and she added in the margins appeals for decision on further omissions. She deleted quite innocuous comments, such as the doctors' opinion that Mary Taylor's complaints arose 'from a disordered stomach'.[54] Opposite a passage about Mrs Smith and her family, in which Charlotte said she liked George Smith 'better even as a son and brother than as a man of business' Ellen wrote, 'Should this pass? Please consider.'[55] Endless reconsideration of this kind was clearly impracticable in a transatlantic correspondence such as she had engaged in with Scribner's. Ellen needed a sympathetic but decisive editor closer to home; and, increasingly troubled by the possession of valuable manuscripts and by suspicions that some had been stolen from her, she needed someone to ensure their safe-keeping. She also hoped for a fair financial return for her letters and for any publication based on them.

IV 1892–1912: C. K. Shorter and T. J. Wise

Nothing, then, could have seemed more propitious than the intervention of Clement Shorter's[1] acquaintance T. J. Wise.[2] Ellen had already met Shorter in August 1889, when he was 'very eager to write on the Brontes',[3] and visited her before the publication of his introduction to *Jane Eyre* in the Camelot series: at her request, he discreetly omitted any reference to her as a source of biographical information. Ambitious, enthusiastic, and enterprising, he wished to make a name for himself, and as early as January 1890 was toying with the idea of writing a new life of Charlotte Brontë. In September that year he offered to assist Sir George Morrison to edit Charlotte's letters, but Ellen politely told him that his assistance was not needed 'at the present time'; no doubt he would distinguish himself in due course.[4] Delighted with his promotion to the editorship of the *Illustrated London News* at the end of 1890, and confirmed in his confidence in himself as a man of letters, Clement Shorter several times reminded Ellen of her 'half-promise' to lend him a copy of the Turner volume;

[54] See BL Ashley 169 p. 43, where EN 2.10.[1838] is dated 1836.

[55] EN ?4.12.1849, BL Ashley 169 p. 210.

[1] For the journalist Clement King Shorter, 1857–1926, see J. M. Bulloch (ed.), *C. K. S., An Autobiography: A Fragment* (privately printed, 1927), and John Gross, *The Rise and Fall of the Man of Letters* (1969), 203–5. He was best known as CKS of the *Sphere*, founded in 1900.

[2] Thomas James Wise, 1859–1937, known at this date as a keen bibliophile and private publisher with a special interest in Keats, Shelley, and Browning. His activities as a producer of fake early editions were not fully revealed, though they were suspected, before the publication of John Carter and Graham Pollard's *An Enquiry into the Nature of Certain Nineteenth Century Pamphlets* in 1934. See also F. E. Ratchford, *Letters of Thomas J. Wise to John Henry Wrenn* (New York, 1944), and John Collins, *The Two Forgers* (Aldershot, 1992).

[3] EN to G. Armytage, 7.11.1892; MS WYAS Calderdale (Halifax). The Camelot *JE* was published in 1889.

[4] EN to CKS 6.9.1890, copy MS by EN, BPM.

in June 1891 she told Scribner's that she was still being 'teased & worried by men of the Press grasping at the Letters'.[5] A year later, when her negotiations with Scribner's had broken down, she at last turned to Shorter and asked him if he would edit the letters.[6] Naturally he expressed an interest, and she sent him a 'parcel of interesting matter'; he warned her, however, that he had obtained legal advice that Mr Nicholls owned perpetual copyright in the 'written words' of the letters and would certainly 'move for an injunction' if they were published separately as a book. To avoid this difficulty, Shorter had thought of writing a new biography, and had approached Macmillan, who declined to publish. George Smith had likewise refused, but offered to buy the original letters from Ellen to prevent their ever being published. Shorter was sorry he was so helpless; 'What more can I do'.[7] By October 1892 he was assuring Ellen that a happy solution was in sight: whereas George Smith would deprecate the writing of a new *Life*, and would not purchase the manuscripts unless she could 'prove that no copy of any kind was preserved anywhere', Shorter had a friend who only bought literary letters for their own sakes; he would give Ellen £100 for the MSS, and would not prevent Shorter from writing a biography of which Ellen would have two thirds of all the profits.[8] The unnamed friend was T. J. Wise (at this date eminent and highly respected), who had begun his quest for Brontë manuscripts, and foresaw a profitable deal. By the end of October the offer had been raised to £125, and Ellen was assured that 'Mr Wise may be thoroughly relied on.' All the originals were needed so that Shorter could deal with the life satisfactorily.[9]

On 2 November 1892 Ellen wrote urgently to George Armytage: great pressure was being put upon her to sell the letters; what ought she to demand? Not more than £125 was offered, and she was reluctant to part with them; but 'it would be a relief for the responsibility to rest on those who could fight their own battles, & not trouble me any further—For the Subject never rests. I should I suppose have a guarantee from the Purchaser as to the use he would make of the letters . . . Do you know any thing of a Mr Wise as a Collector of original Letters? He is I am informed negociating with Smith & Elder for CB Letters.'[10] Mr Armytage replied that he thought the price was too low, and he recommended her to sell the MSS at auction; but Ellen believed Mr Nicholls

[5] EN to Scribner's 16.6.1891, MS Princeton.

[6] See CKS to EN 23.6.1892: 'It would indeed please me much to edit a volume of Miss Brontes letters but first I should have to see What are the legal conditions.' MS BPM.

[7] CKS to EN 18.9.1892, MS BPM. Shorter had hoped to write a new life in the 'English Men of Letters' series for Macmillan, who had recently published extracts from CB's letters to W. S. Williams in their *Magazine* (May–Oct. 1891).

[8] CKS to EN; n.d.; annotated by EN '[Post Sept 18/92]'.

[9] CKS to EN, n.d.; annotated by EN 'Received Oct 29th 1892'. Unfortunately Shorter's handwriting becomes a scribble when he reassures Ellen about Wise. His words may be: 'He will never use them [the letters] ?unworthily or ?indiscreetly.'

[10] EN to G. Armytage 2.11.1892, MS WYAS Calderdale (Halifax).

could prevent her doing this, and she admitted that she had already lent Shorter an annotated copy 'not yet complete.'[11] Mr Armytage reluctantly conceded that she had better make 'as good a bargain as possible', but should retrieve her printed copies from Dr Wright and Shorter as their existence would devalue the manuscripts.[12] Ellen replied in haste, 'It appears from the knowledge pressed upon me . . . that I can only do now, as I did, for Mrs. Gaskell & Mr. Reid. A proper & true portrait of C. B. is very desirable in these days of evil inventions from people who certainly ought to know better . . . I intend to keep the original letters—at any rate some time longer. It is not for money, except to use in Charlotte's memory & to do good to others as she might herself have done.'[13]

Less than nine days later Ellen had capitulated to pressure and promises. Wise, seeing his prey wriggling on the hook, and alarmed lest she should escape, wrote to her directly and at great length. By turns bullying and cajoling, self-righteous and oily, he assured her that £125 was *not* a 'ridiculous' sum, but a fair price for her 400 letters; indeed he was even then arranging to buy *unpublished* letters from Charlotte to Mr Williams for only 4*s* 6*d*. each. But if she would send the letters, he would consider raising the offer—or she might even name her own figure, for he and Shorter did not 'want the letters for any commercial purpose, but . . . to enhance the honor & reputation of their gloriously gifted writer'. One of his chief reasons for wanting them was his desire to keep Ellen's collection intact, to 'set them safe for the use of future generations' as part of his library, one of the finest in the world—as she would learn from the description he enclosed. He had already arranged to bequeath his library to the nation, for he intended that at his death it should go to the South Kensington Museum. He loved Charlotte Brontë through her books, and would give his money and care so that Charlotte's letters should never be 'scattered abroad & distributed' or even destroyed.[14] Ellen, assured by both parties that nothing would be done with the letters to give her pain, yielded. On 18 November 1892 she thanked Wise for his 'enclosure' and 'especially for the promises you give'; she anticipated 'with considerable emotion Mr. Shorter's coming work' and would be glad to give every further aid in her power. She named, no doubt at Wise's request, other correspondents of Charlotte Brontë, and added, pathetically, 'It is no doubt wise to part with the Letters as

[11] EN. to G. Armytage, 7.11.1892, MS WYAS Calderdale (Halifax). See p. 47, n. 24.

[12] G. Armytage to EN 8.11.1892, copy MS WYAS Calderdale (Halifax).

[13] EN to G. Armytage 9.11.1892; MS WYAS Calderdale (Halifax). EN believed that Shorter would achieve 'brilliant success' in his delicate task. (EN to T. J. Wise ?Nov. 1892, MS B.L. Ashley B169.)

[14] T. J. Wise to EN 14.11.1892, on Shelley Society notepaper, MS BPM. The 'South Kensington Museum' was renamed the Victoria and Albert Museum in 1899 when Queen Victoria laid the foundation stone of the new building.

I have now done—but can you not imagine what it has cost? A second parting as it were!'[15]

Wise later claimed that Ellen had sold him about 140 letters in two separate lots for a total of £185, and that he had never owned as many as 300;[16] but it is clear from the correspondence of 1892 that he expected to receive 400. He later tried to obtain additional letters from Charlotte to Henry Nussey, and repeatedly requested as much material as possible so that Shorter could present a true picture in his book, *Charlotte Brontë and her Circle*, which appeared in 1896. Ellen therefore furnished Shorter with 'a great deal of interesting information', as he acknowledged in his preface. She also entrusted 'Mr Shorter only' with private papers 'to help him in his essay work, not to use for print in the least' and alleged that in spite of her appeals, these were not returned.[17] Both men, she believed, had deceived her: 'They have Kept what was only lent for perusal and defy my demands for the return of what was most precious to me.'[18] On 22 June 1896 she begged Shorter to return what she had lent him, 'more especially, the sacred treasured letters from CB's death bed, & Canon Heald's letter on "Shirley".'[19] Shorter responded that he would return Canon Heald's letter (and later honourably did so), but he had evidently found Wise impervious to pleading: 'As for the other letters Mr. Wise considers he bought the whole of them & will not part with them . . . He seems to have satisfied your lawyers last time that he had actually bought all your letters.' As Shorter said, he could not interfere.[20]

Wise had not only appropriated additional letters but had begun to dispose of Brontë manuscripts before 1895. Keeping the best for his Ashley Library, he sold, exchanged, or (rarely) gave away his acquisitions, with the result that today they are to be found in widely scattered locations throughout the USA and the British Isles, and probably further afield still. Ironically enough, the 1932 edition nominally coedited by Wise was seriously hampered by his own former activities, for many of the holograph letters were no longer available to his fellow-editors.

Ellen had discovered the fact of the dispersal, but not the name of its originator, in May 1895, by which time Mr John Waugh had lent some of her letters to the recently founded Brontë Society. Her *idée fixe* about Horsfall Turner meant that she suspected him of retaining some of her letters and then

15 MS Brotherton. The recipient's name is not given, but in the context of this correspondence it must be Wise.

16 Undated note in Waugh correspondence, MS BPM Cadman. In *Bronteana*, published in 1898, Horsfall Turner wrote, 'Mr. Wise, Mr. Law, Mr. Waugh, and I have the largest collections of letters that I am at present aware of.' (p. xiii.) See also p. 29, n. 12.

17 Statement by EN, 26.7.1895, MS BPM.

18 Quoted in *Whitehead* 252.

19 EN to CKS 22.6.1896, copy MS in EN's hand, BPM.

20 CKS to EN 24.6.1896, MS BPM.

selling them to Mr Waugh. But Waugh had bought them from the London booksellers Pearson & Co., who assured him that they had acquired the letters from a gentleman who had bought them from Ellen herself. Ellen, still with Mr Turner in mind, but not naming him, told Mr Waugh that she had never sold the 'gentleman' any letters, and denied receiving a cheque from him.[21] Her denial was reported to Wise, who wrote angrily to Ellen's solicitors on 24 July, claiming that he could produce a receipt for the sale of the letters, and the counterfoil of his own cheque dated 17 November 1892.[22] (Had he bought two separate lots of letters, as he claimed, one would have expected two receipts.) He threatened legal action unless Ellen withdrew her false statements and offered him a full apology. Wise repeated his assertions in a private letter to Waugh of 25 July, adding that he could prove that Ellen had sold 'hundreds' of letters.[23] To Ellen he wrote coolly that he had her receipt for £125, and that he had exchanged some of her Brontë letters 'which, as they had already been fully published, I could manage to spare, much as I disliked to part with them'. With 'duplicate letters' by Shelley and Dickens, Ellen's letters had been exchanged for 'some of the Coleridge things' he wanted. He insisted that she must write to himself, to Waugh, and to Pearson's admitting that she had made a mistake.[24] Shorter, writing to Ellen on 25 July, was 'really very vexed to find that the letters owned by Mr Waugh came from Mr Wise'; he did not know that Wise had parted with any, but he had a 'perfect right to do so' and Ellen must extricate herself as best she could—'I am sorry that you have been unnecessarily worried'.[25] On 26 July Ellen wrote agitated notes, with a flurry of underlinings, to explain that she had not thought of Mr Wise in connection with Mr Waugh's letters, for she had understood that the letters Wise had bought would ultimately go to 'Kensington Museum'.[26] He replied to her solicitors on 29 July acknowledging her apology and dismissing the question of the Museum as irrelevant; such a bequest had certainly not been one of the 'conditions of sale'. He asserted that he had informed Ellen as long ago as January 1893 that he was 'collating' his Brontë letters and weeding out those already printed or 'devoid of interest'.[27] Ellen had perforce to let the matter rest; but she was not mollified by Wise's pretence of regret that he had parted with her letters and remained convinced that the truth would one day be revealed; she considered Wise had betrayed Shorter as well as herself.[28]

Shorter, preoccupied with his work as a journalist, made little progress with

[21] EN to J. Waugh, 12.7.1895; MS BPM Cadman.
[22] MS BPM Cadman.
[23] MS BPM Cadman.
[24] T. J. Wise to EN 23.7.1895, MS BPM.
[25] MS BPM.
[26] MS Texas.
[27] T. J. Wise to H. F. Killick, 29.7.1895, MS BPM.
[28] EN to H. F. Killick, 20.8.1895, inserted in BPM Killick copy of *Nussey*.

his book until March 1895, when his great *coup* was something that Ellen had never been likely to achieve, an *entente cordiale* with Mr Nicholls. He had discovered Mr Nicholls' address in December 1889, probably through an advertisement in the *Star*,[29] but had taken no action. Now, realizing that he needed new material, since so many of Ellen's letters had already been used, he decided to make contact with Mr Nicholls—who was known to have retained Brontë manuscripts. A letter to Mr Nicholls elicited 'a cordial invitation to visit him in his Irish home', and on 31 March 1895 Shorter received 'the cordial handclasp of the man into whose keeping Charlotte Brontë had given her life. It was one of many visits, and the beginning of an interesting correspondence. Mr Nicholls placed all the papers in his possession in my hands.'[30] Shorter rejoices in the discovery of these long-hidden treasures—the 'MSS of childhood', Charlotte's letters to her brother and sister from Brussels which 'even to handle will give a thrill to the Brontë enthusiast', the love-letters of Maria Branwell to Patrick Brontë, the four small scraps of Emily and Anne's diary papers. He presents his readers with an engaging picture of his own excitement and Mr Nicholls's gracious response. He had indeed won the confidence of Mr Nicholls, whose cordiality towards him continued during the production of the *Circle*, with a slight cooling in early 1896; and he was to write appreciatively on 30 October 1896 praising Shorter's 'kind and loving spirit' in treating 'a delicate subject'.[31] Shorter in turn referred to him with respectful warmth in all the books he published after their meeting. He wrote of Mr Nicholls's 'kindly assistance', the 'entirely creditable' story of his life, his magnanimity towards and respect for Mr Brontë, his love for Charlotte, and the 'unmixed blessedness' of his second marriage.[32] He had Mr Nicholls's authority for saying that he had never discouraged Charlotte from continuing to write after her marriage. 'The qualities of gentleness, sincerity, unaffected piety, and delicacy of mind are his; and he is beautifully jealous, not only for the fair fame of Currer Bell, but—what she would equally have loved—for her father, who also has had much undue detraction in the years that are past.'[33]

Shorter's warmth of good will towards Mr Nicholls is attractive, and contrasts strongly with the attitude of William Wright, who had alleged that the 'beast' Nicholls had 'wronged' the Irish Brontës. Wright had also assured Ellen Nussey that he might let Nicholls 'have a few pounds £5 or £10. for his consent [to publish] & I wd. take care that his consent shd. be irrevocable.'[34] When, on

[29] In the *Star* (*c.* 27/28.11.1889) Shorter accused Mr Nicholls of sanctioning the 'shameless destruction' of the 'Brontë church' by the Revd John Wade.

[30] *CBCircle* 24.

[31] ABN to CKS 30.10.1896, MS Brotherton.

[32] In his introduction to the Camelot *JE* (1889) Shorter had referred to CB's allegedly disastrous marriage and had said that Mr Nicholls disapproved of her writing.

[33] *CBCircle* 501–2.

[34] William Wright to Ellen Nussey 24.2.1891; MS BPM Cadman.

23 November 1895, Shorter acquired the copyright in Charlotte Brontë's MSS from Mr Nicholls, he paid the considerable sum of £150. For this he obtained copyright in all her MSS which were then, or might be in the future, in his hands, over which Mr Nicholls had any rights, or which Shorter had received or might receive from Ellen Nussey.[35]

He was therefore able to print not only the Nussey and Nicholls MSS, but all the other material he gathered together in 1895 and 1896. The W.S. Williams letters were on loan to him, as was the 'bundle' of Charlotte's letters to James Taylor lent by Mrs Lawry of Muswell Hill and later sold by her to Wise for £25.[36] Shorter had also persuaded the Wheelwright sisters to lend him their ten letters, which he duly copied and returned. 'Tish' (Laetitia) Wheelwright and her sisters liked the young man who told them he had seen their name in the Court Directory. He did not have access to the Heger letters, and had been mistakenly assured by 'Dr. Heger of Brussels that Miss Brontë's correspondence with his father no longer existed'.[37] He did not use the original MSS of letters to Mrs Gaskell, and had not been allowed access to George Smith's collection.

Despite these limitations, *Charlotte Brontë and her Circle* was the most important and substantial work on the Brontës to appear since the *Life* of 1857. The early Brontë manuscripts were listed, and though later scholarship has corrected much in this early catalogue, their scope could be realized for the first time. Excellent facsimiles of pages from Emily Brontë's Diary Papers were included, along with a well-reproduced drawing of Anne Brontë by Charlotte. Shorter's selection of letters to W. S. Williams gave new insights into Charlotte's literary life, and the transcriptions of these letters and of those to Laetitia Wheelwright were fuller and much more accurate than the correspondence with Ellen Nussey, where Shorter was too often hampered by Ellen's previous editing. Shorter also had to rely for some letters on copies made by or for Wise before he sold the originals. Many years later C. W. Hatfield was to comment on the accuracy of Shorter's transcript of one of Charlotte's stories, 'The Search after Hap[p]iness'; in comparison, Wise's transcript of the same story contained 'so many differences that it seems impossible for it to have been made from the same manuscript'.[38] In *Charlotte Brontë and her Circle* Shorter also took pains to correct Mrs Gaskell's quotations of the letters which Mr Nicholls had lent him, and I have used several of his texts, including Charlotte's letter to Miss Branwell of 29 September 1841. Shorter underlined the importance of

[35] A copy of the MS agreement is in the BPM.

[36] Wise bought the MSS in June 1906. They are now in Texas.

[37] *CBCircle* 26. On the authority of Laetitia Wheelwright, who knew CB in Brussels, Shorter emphatically denied that Charlotte's letters to M. Heger had betrayed an undue 'exaltation'. (*CBCircle* 108–10.)

[38] C. W. Hatfield to Davidson Cook, 10.12.1925; Stockett-Wise.

this text: it had been *'Corrected and completed from original letter in the possession of Mr A. B. Nicholls'*.[39] But it is true that caution is necessary. Like Mrs Gaskell, Shorter often failed to indicate omissions, and both here and in his later editions he could be careless: in the Haworth edition of the *Life*, published in 1900, his version of a letter to George Smith of 21 March 1852 has startling references to 'Penn on the Marshes' instead of 'Penn & the Quakers' and to W. E. Forster's letter on 'Communion' instead of 'Communism'. Mrs Gaskell had made sixteen errors in copying a letter to Smith of 14 February 1852, but Shorter apparently did not notice them, and added another of his own in his note. Wise and Symington were to use this text in 1932.[40]

Wise for his part bought from Mr Nicholls, through Shorter, a great collection of valuable manuscripts. Some he retained for his own Ashley Library, others such as the complete MS of *The Professor* were lent to the Brontë Museum for an exhibition in April 1897. *The Professor* was sold, probably in 1899, to J. Pierpont Morgan of New York. Other MSS, ineptly arranged but handsomely bound, were sold from 1898 onwards by the bookseller H. Gorfin on commission, along with Wise's forged 'first issue' pamphlets. Manuscripts by Branwell Brontë were split up and sold as Charlotte's, fragments were detached from other MSS and sold separately, collections of letters from other sources than Mr Nicholls were sold together for no better reason than the variety of their signatures.[41] A sale at Sotheby's in July 1910 included ninety letters from Charlotte Brontë to Ellen Nussey, written between 1833 and 1855.

Wise has been justly execrated for the diaspora of Brontë material and for the confusion of MSS only now being sorted out by such scholars as V. A. Neufeldt and Christine Alexander. In his favour it may be said that the honour of becoming a Vice-President of the Brontë Society in 1899 was not entirely undeserved. He gave fourteen 'representative' letters and a drawing by C. Brontë[42] to the Society in 1899 and later spent £44 5s. *od*. on its behalf for the 'sweepings' of Brontë MSS at the Nicholls sale in July 1907—where he was outbid by Reginald Smith for Emily Brontë's Gondal Poems MS.

These were among the items which Mr Nicholls had either kept back or failed to find in 1895–6. After careful enquiry he had agreed to let Wise have his collection of Mary Taylor's letters to Charlotte,[43] but he was more cautious

[39] *CBCircle* 97.

[40] See W & S 759 and 749.

[41] Collectors appreciated such variety; the Montague Collection of letters in NYPL includes the signatures C Brontë, C B Nicholls, CB (with the name 'Currer Bell' underlined in the text), and a note in the third person from 'Miss Brontë'.

[42] Entered in the BPM Stock Book 1900. There were 7 letters to EN, 5 to W. S. Williams, 1 to Henry Nussey, and 1 to Mercy Nussey. CB's drawing of a seascape was made at Roe Head and is dated 12.1.1833 (MS HAOBP: Br. P. C20.)

[43] See ABN to CKS 22.5.1895; MS Brotherton. Shorter acknowledged permission to publish given by Mary Taylor's nephew Joshua Taylor. (*CBCircle* 25.)

about Charlotte's own letters. On 7 May 1895 he asked Shorter to return 'the letters I told you of' when he had read them,[44] and on 4 June, after some hesitation sent eleven letters from Charlotte to her father, with permission to use them, though he considered Charlotte's reference to Cardinal Wiseman might be hurtful.[45] Wise probably acquired this group of letters. But an emphatic warning accompanied eight letters belatedly discovered and sent to Shorter on 21 January 1896: he was to *return* them and not allow Wise to appropriate them.[46] The packet contained six letters to Emily, one to Mr Brontë and one to Miss Branwell. This tallies with a group of eight unlocated manuscript letters dated between June 1839 and October 1843, and the likelihood is that Mr Nicholls eventually destroyed them to prevent their getting into the wrong hands.[47] Shorter had indeed prevented Wise from obtaining these manuscripts, for the letter to Miss Branwell was 'in the possession of Mr A. B. Nicholls' in 1896,[48] and Mr Nicholls still had the letter to Emily of 1 April 1843 in 1900.[49] But early in 1896 Wise's unscrupulous use of private letters had been forcibly brought home to Mr Nicholls, when Sotheby's printed extracts from Charlotte's letter to Ellen Nussey of 16 May 1853 in their catalogue of items for auction on 28 February 1896. The letter, describing Mr Nicholls soon after Charlotte had refused his proposal—'white, shaking, voiceless' at the Whitsunday service, as he lost command of himself in full view of the communicants—was 'most painful' to him, and he asked Shorter to secure it on his behalf. He must have determined there and then to prevent similar publicity of sensitive matter in the unsold family letters. On 17 April 1896 he emphatically required Shorter to return some letters after use, and added that he would ensure that they should 'never be distributed'.[50] Certainly we now have to rely on the edited texts in the *Life*, *CBCircle*, or Shorter's 1908 compilation, for the group of eight letters referred to above, and indeed for all Charlotte's letters to Emily Brontë.[51] But Mr Nicholls either did not obtain or did not destroy the letter which had hurt him so much, for it is now among the MS letters at Princeton.

[44] MS Brotherton.

[45] MS Brotherton. Shorter went ahead in spite of this warning, and printed CB's account of Wiseman 'simpering and bowing like a fat old lady'. (CB to PB 7.6.1851, MS Pierpont Morgan; *CBCircle* 461–2.) See K. Tillotson's account of Shorter's transactions in *BST* 19. 1. 10–13.

[46] MS Brotherton.

[47] The letters are EJB 8.6.1839, 2.4.1841, 7.11.1841, 29.5.1843, 2.9.1843, 19.12.1843; the incomplete PB 2.6.1843; and the letter to Miss Branwell of 29.9.1841. Shorter did not print EJB July 1839 or EJB 1.10.1843, the only other known letters from CB to Emily, in *CBCircle*, and may not have seen the MSS.

[48] *CBCircle* 97.

[49] See Shorter's footnote to Mrs Gaskell's extract from the letter in *Life* 1900, ch. 12.

[50] MS Brotherton.

[51] CB must have written many more letters to Emily than the 8 whose texts are known. No letters from Charlotte to her sister Anne survive.

It is ironic that had Wise, rogue as he was, purchased the letters to Emily, the full text of these confidential letters might still have been available in manuscript. That he did pay for the material he was allowed to have there is no doubt, for Mr Nicholls acknowledged the receipt of several cheques from him, satisfied that he had been given 'full value'.[52] Mr Nicholls was unsure of his rights and duties as a 'Literary Executor', and he had to ask Shorter what the term meant; but even without that knowledge he was willing to give Shorter exclusive rights to publish his MSS on the terms Shorter had specified in a letter—i.e. that the publishers would pay him for their use.[53] Evidently this was the only condition put into writing. But Mr Nicholls's letter of 28 December 1895 shows that he, like Ellen Nussey, had relied on a promise, Wise's 'assurance' that his letters and MSS would be 'given to the Nation'.[54] As a previous letter makes clear, he had understood from Shorter that they were to find a 'safe resting place' in the South Kensington Museum.[55] Wise made notes on both these letters, denying that he had made any such suggestion. On the December letter he added that Shorter had constantly pressed him to give such an assurance, but Wise had told him clearly that he had no intention whatever of doing so. It is a neat and nasty denial, perverting Shorter's good will into a weapon against him and thereby putting the onus of the deception on him; and it must have been made after Shorter's death when there was no fear of contradiction.[56]

Mr Nicholls, at any rate, still trusted Shorter in 1900, when his 'kind and generous assistance' was acknowledged in the production of Shorter's liberally annotated Haworth edition of the *Life*, published by Smith, Elder in 1900.[57] Shorter had aimed to add 'no single note or line that Mrs Gaskell . . . would not . . . have cordially approved'.[58] For this publication by his own firm George Smith had allowed Shorter to use 'a number of hitherto unpublished letters by Miss Brontë addressed either to him or to his

[52] See e.g. ABN to CKS 26.4.1895, 2.5.1895, 11.9.1895, and 14.11.1895 in the Brotherton MSS. In 1917 Shorter said he thought Wise paid £400 for 'the whole of the little manuscripts' acquired from Nicholls. Possibly this sum did not include payment for the letters: Wise first told Wrenn in 1907 that he 'bought the Brontë Manuscripts for £1500.0.0.' but later in the year quoted £1,100. See Ratchford, *Letters of Thomas J. Wise to John Henry Wrenn* 471 and n. 2.

[53] ABN to CKS 18.6.1895, MS Brotherton. Symington and Wise acquired these letters from Mr Nicholls to Shorter for the Brotherton Collection, and it is probably significant that this letter of 18 June is incomplete, and that 6 lines have been heavily deleted in the letter of 11.11.1895.

[54] MS Brotherton.

[55] ABN to CKS 24.6.1895; MS Brotherton.

[56] C. W. Hatfield reported to Davidson Cook on 13.3.1928 that 'Mr Symington . . . has recently been on a short visit with Mr Wise to Mrs Shorter at Great Missenden and has purchased all Clement Shorter's note books and letters relating to Brontë matters; and a large part of the contents of the library'. (Stockett-Wise.) Shorter died in 1926.

[57] *Life* 1900, p. xxxiv.

[58] Ibid. p. xix. Mrs Gaskell would not have approved of the inclusion of CB's comments on the Hegers in EJB 29.5.1843, or of CB's confession in a Catholic cathedral in EJB 2.9.1843.

firm'.[59] Shorter rightly believed they would add 'special interest', and he used them along with information on people and places, and letters to and from Mr Brontë and Mrs Gaskell, to enhance and elucidate the *Life*. The illustrations included an excellent facsimile of Charlotte's letter to George Smith's mother of 9 January 1850, with its lively half-serious attack on Thackeray's cynical attitude to women, and its self-mocking postscript on the slow progress of the 'little socks' Charlotte had been knitting while in London—'they continue much the same'.[60] Shorter's accurate transcription of the letter shows what he could do when he tried; and his additions to the *Life* opened out and made more attractively human Mrs Gaskell's ideal portrait of her noble heroine.

Not all his quotations were so meticulously transcribed. In GS 31.10.1850 Charlotte, according to Shorter, thanked George Smith for enclosing a 'scribe' in his letter; he had actually enclosed a 'squib', an anti-Puseyite satire. In the same letter Charlotte is made to say the opposite of what she wrote; in Shorter's version she must 'now . . . dissuade' Smith from calling on T. C. Newby. Shorter had misread 'not' as 'now', and altered the next sentence to suit. Wise and Symington reprinted this faulty text in 1932 (no. 616) and added a new error, a 'godly' instead of a 'goodly' rosary.

In his preface to the 1908 *Life and Letters* Shorter attributed the merits of his 1896 volume to 'the happy accident which placed in his hands' so much new material. Since its publication 'correspondents from all parts of the world' had sent him new documents and letters. His 1908 volumes therefore added 'extremely valuable new material', in chronological order, to that of 1896. The expiry of the copyright in Mrs Gaskell's *Life* had enabled him to include whatever she had quoted in her biography—notably, extracts from Charlotte Brontë's letters to her and to George Smith; unfortunately, he had been allowed neither access to the original MSS of these letters, nor permission to reprint his own notes to Smith, Elder's Haworth *Life*. He did however direct readers to that edition, where they could find 'sixty-five letters to . . . Mr George Smith, and to his mother, that are not obtainable elsewhere'.[61] The result of Smith's prohibition was that the 1908 volumes contained only a miscellaneous collection of snippets from the Smith and Gaskell letters, many of them to be reprinted in the same form in 1932, supplemented by a limited selection of letters on loan from George Smith's daughters.

Shorter's access to manuscripts still owned by Wise or Buxton Forman was an advantage, but many others had already crossed the Atlantic, and Shorter too often had to use the suppressed edition of 1885–9, with the sometimes dubious asset of information Ellen had previously supplied. Ironically (like

[59] *Life* 1900, pp. xxi–xxii.

[60] Ibid., opp. 442. Thanks to Smith's granddaughter, Mrs Seton-Gordon, the completed 'little socks', Mrs Smith's 'memento of Currer Bell', are now in the BPM.

[61] *Shorter* i. 2, n. 1.

Wise and Symington in 1932) he no longer had access to many of the holograph manuscripts now in the New York Public Library and the Harvard, Princeton, and Yale collections, since they had been sold to private collectors. Thus he had to use Ellen's abridged and expurgated versions of the letters of, for example, 9/10.12.1841, ?6.1.1843, and 4.4.1847.[62] He also garbled some texts by combining together unrelated letters, or by separating single letters into fragments. Misled by a sequence of quotations in the *Life*, he combined into one several extracts from Charlotte's letters to W. S. Williams of 19 March and 3 April 1850,[63] and his composite version was reprinted as W & S 537 in 1932.

Nevertheless the two substantial volumes of 1908 were a considerable achievement. Shorter had incorporated corrections and additions to the material he published in 1896,[64] and he had managed to amass or to reproduce quantities of information from people who had known or who were related to the family and friends of the Brontës. His appendix II reprinted 'The Brontës at Thornton' from the *Bookman* for October 1904. This was an article by Professor Moore Smith, grandson of the Brontës' friend and benefactor Elizabeth Firth—the Mrs Franks to whom Charlotte wrote in May 1831 and on 2 June 1836.[65] Appendix VI reprinted the 'Personal Reminiscences of Charlotte Brontë' by John Stores Smith, another of Charlotte's correspondents, from the *Free Lance* of 7 March 1868.[66] Imperfect as they were, Shorter's 1908 volumes provided a groundwork for the more substantial Shakespeare Head edition of 1932.

V. 1913: The Heger Letters

A crucial step forward in the understanding of Charlotte Brontë was taken in 1913, when for the first time her feelings for Heger were clearly revealed by the publication of her letters to him. M. Heger had shown the letters to Mrs Gaskell in May 1856, but she had concealed their full significance. Wemyss Reid had recognized that Charlotte's Brussels experience was the turning-point in her life, and other writers had speculated about her relationship with M. Heger. In 1894 Frederika Macdonald, shown the letters by M. Heger's daughter Louise, had advised secrecy precisely because she realized the complexity of the emotions they betrayed: they revolutionized her own view of Charlotte, she told Robertson Nicoll, but made her more interesting and 'strangely romantic and reckless'. The public might not understand that hers was not an 'ordinary improper affection' but 'a consuming sentiment burning

62 *Shorter* 96, 116 (as '*January 10th, 1843*') and 218.

63 *Shorter* 424.

64 e.g. he added 2 corrective notes from the *Yorkshire Daily Observer* of 5 and 13 August 1907 to his account of Maria Branwell. (*Shorter* i. 32, 33.)

65 *Shorter* ii. 410–23.

66 *Shorter* ii. 435–44.

down self-respect and self-restraint'. Mme Heger had kept the letters, but had not revealed how she had finally dealt with Charlotte (who for a time had written twice a week); 'At last M. Heger let Madame write for him stiffly but not unkindly saying C. might write every six months'.[1]

It was almost twenty years later, on 6 June 1913, that Constantin Heger's son Dr Paul Heger and his sisters offered to the British Museum Charlotte's four surviving letters to their father, in order to show how groundless were the suspicions resulting from 'the natural speculations of critics and biographers'.[2] The letters were published, with translations and an explanation by Marion H. Spielmann, in *The Times* for 29 July 1913.

When Paul Heger assured Shorter in 1896 that the letters no longer existed, he did so in good faith, for his sister Louise had not told him of their survival until she had 'passed her seventieth year'—that is some time after 1909.[3] On 6 October 1913 Spielmann visited Louise Heger in Brussels and heard from her the 'whole curious story of the documents'.[4] Her father had torn up and thrown away all but one of the letters, but the prudent Mme Heger had 'saved them, all but the first, and pieced them together with cotton or with gum'.[5] Louise explained that her mother had retrieved the letters because she considered the 'affection expressed by the pupil for the teacher *un peu exagérée*, and, moreover, because one or more of these letters had been addressed to M. Heger, not to the school-house in the Rue d'Isabelle, but to the Athénée Royal'.[6] Mme Heger thought Charlotte 'might take some unexpected step in relation to the family to whom she had never cared to make herself agreeable . . . These letters, then, might be evidence, if there were need, that would dispel any misapprehension that might arise. She became convinced of the justice of her view when Charlotte Brontë was leaving Brussels and let loose the burning valedictory words (as I am assured)—"Je me vengerai" . . . It was a simple measure of self-defence to be held in reserve. So Madame Heger kept the letters and said nothing.'[7]

[1] F. Macdonald to Robertson Nicoll 26.2.1894, MS Brotherton originally catalogued as from EN. Frederika Macdonald, a former pupil at the Pensionnat Heger, published an article entitled 'The Brontës in Brussels' in the *Woman at Home* for July 1894, referring to CB's letters to M. Heger and her 'strong and enthusiastic attachment to her master in literature'.

[2] Paul Heger to the Principal Librarian of the British Museum, 6.6.1913, translated by M. H. Spielmann, *The Times*, 29.7.1913.

[3] M. H. Spielmann, *The Inner History of the Brontë–Heger Letters* (1919), reprinted from the *Fortnightly Review* for Apr. 1919.

[4] Ibid. 2. The first surviving letter, that of 24.7.1844, which was not the first CB had written, was repaired with 'thin paper strips', those of 24.10.1844 and 8.1.1845 were sewn with cotton thread, and the fourth, 18.11.1845, was intact. (Spielmann, *The Times*, 29.7.1913.)

[5] Ibid. 2.

[6] The boys' school in which M. Heger was a teacher, in the rue des Douze Apôtres near the rue d'Isabelle.

[7] Ibid. 3. Possibly the unlikely valediction was 'remembered' by the Heger family after their reading of *Villette*. Clearly it could not have 'justified' a view of letters which had not been written 'when Charlotte Brontë was leaving Brussels'.

Twenty-one years later Louise Heger, distressed after hearing a lecturer denouncing the Hegers for cruelty towards Charlotte Brontë, was shown the letters by her mother, who explained why she had kept them safely in her jewel-box: 'J'ai gardé ces lettres—elles pourront avoir une grande importance.' After her mother's death in January 1890, Louise handed the letters 'in fear and trembling' to her father, who 'recognised them with astonishment, and, with a frown, flung them into the basket along with the other papers discarded and destroyed'.[8]

Rescued and preserved a second time by Louise, the letters were eventually shown by her to her brother Paul some time after 1909. Two years later the family at length decided to seek the opinion of the art-critic Marion Spielmann, a trusted friend, who believed they might safely be given to the British Museum; for English people, unlike the French, would understand that the letters were Charlotte's 'confession of honest admiration of a man, and of her gratitude'.[9] Dr Paul Heger gave Spielmann permission to publish the letters in *The Times*, but was 'no whit responsible' for their publication, and wished for no payment. He agreed that any fee should be handed directly to the Royal Literary Fund.[10]

The opportunist and far from altruistic T. J. Wise forthwith pirated Spielmann's text in an exclusive edition, boldly entitled *The Love Letters of Charlotte Brontë to Constantin Heger*, 'Printed for private circulation only. 1914'. For this title, in a printing of only thirty copies, Wise doubtless demanded a high price from his wealthy clients, though he graciously gave a copy to the Brontë Society—openly defying or ignoring Shorter's claim that *The Times* publication had breached his copyright. Shorter for his part included the Heger letters in *The Brontës and their Circle* (1914), an enlarged version of his 1896 volume.

Most readers would agree that the letters show a good deal more than gratitude and admiration. A discreet deletion in the letter to Heger of 24 October 1844 shows that Charlotte first wrote of her never-ending 'affection' for him, before emending the tell-tale word to 'respect'. But there is no discretion at all in her next letter of 8 January 1845: her burning impatience for some response from Heger is evident in her rapid handwriting, rushing sentences, and disregarded slips of the pen as well as in her excited, demanding words—sent as they were written without rereading, except for the last hasty deletion. Spielmann's transcriptions are reasonably accurate, though he omitted the apt reference to Louise Heger's look of 'vérité'.[11] I have made my own transcriptions and have added conjectural readings of the deleted matter, and of M. Heger's barely legible jottings of tradesmen's names and addresses on the last letter.[12]

[8] Ibid. 4. [9] Ibid. 7. [10] Ibid. 6 and *The Times* 29.7.1913. [11] CH 24.7.1844.
[12] CH 18.11.1845, annotation and n. 15.

VI. 1914–32: Towards the Shakespeare Head Edition

Shorter continued to use the privilege of his copyright by publishing limited editions, but the editorial work for these was done by C. W. Hatfield,[1] who produced for him books such as *Thackeray and Charlotte Brontë: Hitherto Unpublished Letters to her Publisher* 'for private circulation only' in 1919. For this Hatfield had extracted material from the typescript copies of letters to George Smith, sent to him 'many years ago' by Shorter.[2] He later offered to add 'unpublished bits' from the same collection to the proofs of the Shakespeare Head edition.[3]

Shorter also conceived the idea of a 'Library edition of the novels, poems and letters of all the family' of the Brontës,[4] to be published by Hodder and Stoughton, but he did not live to carry out this grand design. Hatfield, who refers in his correspondence to Shorter's 'carelessness', also acknowledges his 'characteristic generosity'.[5] By 1926, the year of Shorter's death, Hatfield had gathered together 'a large number of unpublished poems by Charlotte, a large number of letters which [had] not yet been printed, and hundreds of corrections and additions to the letters which [had] been published,' all of which he hoped to get included in a Library edition of the kind Shorter had planned.[6] Much of Hatfield's collection had been handed over to him by Shorter himself. Hatfield was a modest and retiring person who cared for the accuracy of the Brontë productions, and was singularly indifferent to his personal gain or prestige. 'Do not think that the probable lack of remuneration has any weight with me at all', he wrote to Alexander Symington[7] on 1 July 1932, when he had been supplying transcripts and corrections for the Shakespeare Head edition

[1] C. W. Hatfield died on 15 July 1941 at the age of 65. A Customs and Excise officer whose Brontë hobby made him a magpie collector of all the documents he could accumulate—by entirely fair means, it should be said—he was a Vice-President of the Brontë Society for 14 years, contributed many articles and transcriptions to the Society *Transactions*, supplied corrections for Symington's 1927 catalogue of the Brontë museum items, and prepared a catalogue of the Bonnell collection at Haworth in 1932. His edn. of Emily Brontë's poems in 1941, with its carefully established texts and MS collations, was the most scholarly work on the Brontës produced by that date.

[2] Hatfield to Davidson Cook 13.4.1928; Stockett-Wise.

[3] Hatfield to Symington 27.4.1932; BPM Symington papers.

[4] Hatfield to Davidson Cook 12.1.1926; Stockett-Wise.

[5] 'I have never been able to understand why Mr Shorter did not let me see that second volume of the E[mily] B[rontë] works for it would have saved us from the only adverse criticism which the 1923 volume received. It must have been due to his usual carelessness, and with his characteristic generosity as soon as he realized it he made me a present of his own copy with his bookplate in it, and he does not now possess one himself.' (Hatfield to Davidson Cook, 4.6.1926, Stockett-Wise.)

[6] Hatfield to Davidson Cook 12.1.1926; Stockett-Wise.

[7] J. Alexander Symington, librarian to Sir Edward, later Lord Brotherton of Roundhay Park Leeds, and after Lord Brotherton's death in 1930 Curator of the Brotherton Collection at Leeds University. He was a life-member of the Brontë Society from 1924, a member of the Brontë Society

for over a year.[8] While it is not clear why he did not pursue the idea of his own 'Library' edition, it is certain that his name did not appear in the half-title of the Shakespeare Head *Correspondence* volumes,[9] though his help was acknowledged with 'particular gratitude and thanks' (along with that of Butler Wood, Davidson Cook, and Symington's secretary Miss Marian Wood). At least his name stood first in the list.[10] Symington, who had pressed for a more prominent acknowledgement, ensured that Hatfield shared with him the honours of *The Miscellaneous and Unpublished Writings* in 1936 and 1938—though still in the prefatory note and not in the half-title. On 24 March 1936 Symington told Hatfield that Wise himself had 'never even yet put pen to paper in connection with the whole of the volumes already published in this edition'.[11]

The first eleven volumes of the Shakespeare Head edition, containing the Brontës' novels, appeared in their handsome tawny orange livery in 1931, with statements of editorial policy but no editorial acknowledgement. Alexander Symington, rather than Hatfield, must have seemed a fairly obvious choice as editor of the ensuing four volumes of correspondence. He had been librarian to Sir Edward (later Lord) Brotherton, who was a life-member of the Brontë Society and one of its Vice-Presidents from 1924 until his death in 1930. Symington had acquired for the Brotherton Library at Roundhay Hall, Leeds, a fine collection of Bronteana, including some of Branwell Brontë's manuscripts, his letters to J. B. Leyland, Charlotte's letters to Amelia Ringrose, and (together with T. J. Wise) all C. K. Shorter's remaining papers and correspondence. In 1924 he had produced a privately printed limited edition of one of the Branwell documents, *And the Weary are at Rest*. His key-position as Curator of the Brontë Museum at Haworth from 1926 gave him access to the Society's collections, he had contributed a full transcript of the Leyland letters to the *Brontë Society Transactions* for 1925, and he had supervised the unpacking and installing of the valuable Bonnell Collection of MSS, letters, and other Bronteana in the Museum in 1930. He was in contact with the still-honoured and powerful T. J. Wise, a Vice-President of the Society (though, curiously, only an annual member). He knew Hatfield and had acknowledged his annotation of the Leyland letters, and his assistance in the preparation of the *Catalogue of the Museum and Library* at Haworth in 1927.

Council from 1925 to 1930, and Curator, Librarian, Bibliographical Secretary, and Editor of *Brontë Society Transactions* from 1926 to 1930.

[8] BPM Symington papers.

[9] The half-title page is headed 'The Shakespeare Head Brontë | EDITED BY THOMAS JAMES WISE, HON. M.A. OXON | HONORARY FELLOW OF WORCESTER COLLEGE | AND JOHN ALEXANDER SYMINGTON | BROTHERTON LIBRARIAN'.

[10] W & S i. p. ix.

[11] BPM Symington papers.

At a comparatively late stage, when Symington had been preparing the new edition for about a year, Wise was brought in as a coeditor—indeed he seems to have told Mrs Edgerley of the Brontë Society that he and not Symington would edit.[12] He had been brought in for three reasons: he was a 'name', and as Symington assured Basil Blackwell on 23 December 1931, they were likely to have 'an exceptionally wonderful reception for our edition. There is no doubt Mr. Wise will have a tremendous selling power.'[13] In the second place, the co-operation of the Brontë Society had not been forthcoming, especially in response to Blackwell's request for the loan of the Museum's Branwell Brontë manuscripts for the preparation of the new edition. Symington told Mr Butler Wood, a Brontë Council member and Vice-President, that Wise had 'temporarily taken over the reins for us to get this difficult gee-gee the Brontë Council out of our path'.[14] Symington did not elaborate on the third reason for calling in Wise, and for Wise having to write a 'final strong letter to the "d—d old woman" as he calls her', Mrs Mabel Edgerley, the Secretary of the Brontë Society.[15] Her hostility to any edition undertaken by Symington was nevertheless understandable. Symington had resigned suddenly from his curatorship of the Brontë Museum in 1930, after his installation of the Bonnell Collection. It had become 'evident that certain items were missing and that other Museum material also could not be found . . . some of the missing items were never recovered'.[16] Wise had to be 'very firm' with Mrs Edgerley, who capitulated on the understanding that he was to edit. To Hatfield Symington merely said that Wise had 'kindly consented to associate himself' with the editing.[17]

To do him justice, Symington worked quite hard, according to his lights, on the new edition of the letters. He took as his basis Shorter's 1908 edition and intended to add to it new notes and newly discovered correspondence. He was aware of the need for accurate texts, and he was most fortunate in retaining Hatfield's co-operation, for Hatfield had been 'adding to and amending Shorter's two large volumes ever since they were published'.[18] Symington took the trouble to secure photostats of all the Brontë letters in the splendid Huntington Collection in California, the Pierpont Morgan Library, the New York Public Library, the collection of the Historical Society of Pennsylvania, and the Buffalo Public Library. Hatfield had been in touch with the Bonnells in New York, and still had copies which Henry Bonnell had made of the manuscripts from his collection which were to remain in the USA. Symington asked for but

[12] *BST* 8.42.37.
[13] BPM Symington papers.
[14] Symington to Basil Blackwell, ?Nov. or Dec. 1931, BPM Symington papers.
[15] Symington to Basil Blackwell, 30.11.1931, BPM Symington papers.
[16] Charles Lemon, *A Centenary History of the Brontë Society*, (Haworth, 1993), 34.
[17] Symington to Hatfield 26.10.1931, BPM Symington papers.
[18] Hatfield to Symington 17.6.1931, BPM Symington papers.

was not sent transcripts of Charlotte Brontë's letters to James Taylor in the Wrenn collection in Texas.

In England he had access to the Brotherton Collection, and Hatfield had made transcripts of other manuscripts, including many of those at Haworth. Symington also had the expert help of Hatfield's friend Davidson Cook, whose enthusiasm—primarily for Scott and Burns—had gained him the entrée to Honresfeld, and the privilege of studying and copying some of the Brontë manuscripts in Sir Alfred Law's collection there. It was Davidson Cook who had sent to Hatfield photographs of the volume of Emily Brontë's poems at Honresfeld. On 13 May 1931 Symington wrote to Hatfield, 'Friend Davidson Cook has very kindly lent me his transcripts of the manuscripts in the Law Collection, and is arranging for me to be able to borrow any which it will be necessary to see.[19] Symington asked 'Mr. Cockerell of the Fitzwilliam Museum Cambridge' for complete transcripts of the Wooler letters, and tried but failed to locate the MSS of the Mary Burder letters to and about Mr Brontë. He was allowed to use the George Smith letters in the Haworth edition, and was lent some original MSS by Smith's daughters Mrs Henry Yates Thompson and Mrs Reginald Smith.[20] Finally he had the advantage of access to Wise,[21] who could, he hoped, 'clear up our queries in connection with his manuscripts' and he proposed to work on the manuscripts themselves when they were returned from exhibition at the Central Public Library in Hampstead.[22]

Symington's efforts to seek out the major collections, his special attention to texts derived from photostats or manuscripts to which he had direct access, and his acceptance of many corrections provided by Hatfield combined to make the Shakespeare Head edition an immense improvement on Shorter's 1908 volumes. He questioned Hatfield's views when they did not tally with the evidence of the photostats, holding out against Hatfield's advice that the 'Eleonora' paragraph in *Shorter* 78 should be retained despite the MS evidence because it was 'certainly written by' Charlotte to Ellen Nussey.[23] Between them Symington and Hatfield successfully redated, combined, separated, corrected, or printed in full many of the faulty texts of 1908.

They could not be blamed for failing to trace manuscripts dispersed long ago in private sales or gifts by Wise and others, or for lacking access to some of the

[19] Symington to Hatfield, BPM Symington papers. The Law Collection has been inaccessible to scholars since about 1972.

[20] See W & S i. pp. viii and ix.

[21] Symington to Hatfield 24.9.1931, BPM Symington papers.

[22] The loan of the Brontë section of the 'wonderful Ashley Library of T. J. Wise, Esq., M.A.' and the 'unrivalled beauty' of the exhibits were acknowledged with profuse expressions of gratitude in the Hampstead Library catalogue of the exhibition in 1931. Symington may not have been allowed access to the manuscripts after the exhibition closed.

[23] EN 20.11.40. See Symington to Hatfield 2.3.1932 and Hatfield to Symington 3.3.1932, BPM Symington papers.

Smith, Gaskell, and Kay-Shuttleworth letters. But they too often relied on second or third-hand copies: Symington's assistant had not been allowed to handle the incomplete and difficult crossed letter which was then in the Batley Museum, EN ?15.10.1847. There is no record of Symington checking her copy.[24] He took on trust Wise's transcripts of some MSS in his Ashley Library—'I have not seen the originals of these, but I cannot doubt the word of my Editor-in-Chief!'[25]—even though Hatfield had warned him how unreliable copies supplied by Wise could be. But Hatfield also transmitted to him some distinctly unreliable copies, based on those of Henry Bonnell. These are probably the source of the poor texts of some MSS now in the Pierpont Morgan Library. There are for example ten errors in EN 10.11.1834 (W & S 33) and Charlotte's emphatic capital initials for the 'Sin of Dancing' and 'Frivolity' are not reproduced. Symington and Hatfield also failed to check some MSS available at the British Museum. Since they relied on excerpts in the Haworth *Life* for Charlotte's letters to G. H. Lewes, her appreciation of Jane Austen's 'clear common sense and subtle shrewdness' in contrast to the 'windy wordiness' of Eliza Linton did not appear in the edition.[26]

Symington had hoped to 'put at the foot of each letter the name of the collection or Library where the original' was to be found.[27] His failure to do this, and to indicate where a printed text had been used as copy, has earned the edition blame which might have been more fairly assigned to Mrs Gaskell, Ellen Nussey, or Shorter.[28] The variety of printed sources, alongside more faithfully reproduced MS-based texts, helped to cause inconsistencies in the style of punctuation, as Symington acknowledged in his preface; but both Hatfield and Symington thought Charlotte's punctuation and spelling sometimes needed to be modified or 'corrected'.[29] Symington also seems to have wearied of well-doing towards the end of his editorial work: on 10 February 1932 Hatfield regretted Symington's failure to rewrite Shorter's 1908 introduction properly, though he admitted it would be a tedious business to correct the numerous errors.[30]

Since 1932 more holograph letters to and from the Brontë family have become available. Mildred Christian located Brontë MSS in the principal North

[24] The letter is in 2 separate parts, 1 formerly in Batley, now in the WYAS Kirklees archives, and 1 at Yale.

[25] Symington to Hatfield 8.3.1932, BPM Symington papers.

[26] Some of the shortcomings of the Wise and Symington edn. are described in T. J. Winnifrith, *The Brontës and their Background* ch. 2, and in Margaret Smith, 'The Letters of Charlotte Bronte: Some New Insights into her Life and Writing', *Brontë Society and Gaskell Society Joint Conference Papers* (Keighley, 1990), 57–72.

[27] Symington to Hatfield 5.10.1931, BPM Symington papers.

[28] A fairly short, conventionally punctuated letter to Ellen Nussey, with proper names omitted or supplied in square brackets, is likely to derive from *Nussey* via *Shorter*.

[29] See Hatfield to Symington 12.2.1932, Symington to Hatfield 18.2.1932, BPM Symington papers.

[30] Hatfield to Symington, BPM Symington papers.

American libraries in her *Census* of 1947–8,[31] since when more have been added to the substantial holdings in the Pierpont Morgan Library, New York Public Library, Princeton, Yale, and Harvard libraries. The Harry Ransom Humanities Research Center at Austin in Texas, the New York Public Library, Princeton and Rutgers University libraries, and the University of British Columbia have also acquired valuable collections of nineteenth- and twentieth-century correspondence relating to the Brontës.

In Britain the Brontë Society's unsurpassed collection continues to be enriched by purchase or donation. Outstanding additions have been the Seton-Gordon Collection, most generously given to the Society by George Smith's granddaughter in 1974, and the Grolier Collection bought in 1980. Mildred Christian's much-appreciated bequest of her working-papers, photocopies, books, and photographs has given access to some valuable documents, including photostats of twenty-one important letters from Charlotte in the Law Collection. The Brontë Society also possesses a unique collection of Brontë-related MSS, artefacts, and documents, and has published in its *Transactions* facsimiles of autograph letters in its own and other archives.

The John Rylands Library of the University of Manchester has letters from Charlotte Brontë and her father to Mrs Gaskell, and the manuscript of Mrs Gaskell's *Life*. These MSS, which were not used by Wise and Symington, help to establish an accurate record of Charlotte's friendship with her future biographer. The many smaller collections in public and private libraries in Britain and the USA have been listed in the Acknowledgements.

In the present edition letters are transcribed from the original manuscript wherever possible, and the source of each text is given. The aim throughout, in the presentation and notes, has been to enhance our understanding of the woman who wrote some of the most memorable and compelling novels of the nineteenth century.

[31] Mildred G. Christian, *A Census of Brontë manuscripts in the United States*, 5 parts, *The Trollopian*, later *Nineteenth-Century Fiction* (1947–8).

THE MANUSCRIPTS

Most of the surviving holograph MSS of Charlotte Brontë's letters have been well preserved. A few have been damaged in the past by clumsy mounting or unsuitable storage, but most of these have been conserved by modern methods and are accessible and legible. Charlotte normally wrote in ink which has faded to a light or medium brown, and used a clear cursive hand. The few exceptions are described in the notes. She rarely gave a full address at the beginning of a letter, but most often signed her name formally as C Brontë, Currer Bell, C Bell or (after her marriage) C B Nicholls. In letters to Ellen Nussey she sometimes used Charlotte, CB or a nickname. Her deletions consist of straight strokes, scribbles, or very occasionally more thorough deletion with the addition of extra ascenders and descenders. Most of the heavy deletions in darker ink were made by Ellen Nussey, who also scraped out parts of some names of people or places. Some letters have been mutilated for the sake of the signatures.

Charlotte Brontë naturally wrote more neatly or formally to some correspondents than others, but the development of her handwriting may be roughly divided into four periods.

1829–37: a carefully formed, fairly well-spaced copperplate style, sloping to the right, with elongated ascenders and descenders, usually written with a fine-pointed pen. A final 'd' is not usually looped back, 'y' may be finished with either a narrow downward loop or a long shallow backward curve. A long 's' is habitually used in the address for the first 's' in 'Miss' and 'Nussey', and occasionally elsewhere. Letters in this and, less often, in later periods, may be wholly or partly cross-written. The size of the writing is appropriate to the paper used: normally large double sheets of watermarked wove or laid, with an average leaf-size of about 186 mm. × 228 mm. Smaller double sheets of watermarked paper *c.*113 mm. × 185 mm. were used between June and October 1836.

1838–40: the gradual development of a more loosely formed, bolder, irregular hand, retaining long ascenders and descenders, and often with wider spacing between lines and words. Thicker pens and darker ink may be used. A final 'y' may be finished with a straight descender, a smooth backward curve, or an angled hook. The ascender of a final 'd' may be straight or looped backward. Letters of late 1839 and early 1840 are often noticeably untidy. The long 's' is retained in 'Miss' and 'Nussey'. A smaller, neater version of this hand develops towards the end of 1840. Large double sheets of unwatermarked paper range from a leaf-size of *c.* 183 mm. × 224 mm. to *c.* 204 mm. × 258 mm.

1841–3: a transition from a small but slightly irregular and disjointed hand with occasional blotted loops to a neat, regularly sloped, very small, clear style.

The tail of a final 'y' may be sharply angled, or have a narrow loop. Medial and final 'd' are often neatly curved backward, an initial 'd' may also have a full round loop formed anti-clockwise and recrossing the stem to link with the next letter. The long 's' is retained in 'Miss' in a formal address, as it would be in almost all remaining letters to the end of Charlotte's life; but by the end of 1842 'Nussey' usually lacks the long 's'. The paper size varies according to whether Charlotte was away from home or not, but typically consists of double sheets of unwatermarked wove with an average leaf-size of *c.*114 × 188 mm. A few large or watermarked papers were used.

1844–55: the handwriting has settled into more or less its final form by 1844–5. It is usually small, fluent, even, slightly and regularly sloped to the right, written with a fine nib, and with most ascenders and descenders pleasantly proportioned and harmoniously related to the flow of the script. Hasty notes to Ellen Nussey may be less regular. Sharply angled 'y' tails give place on the whole to a wider angle or smoother curve, but the curving stroke may be prolonged backward to the beginning of a word or beyond. The looped-back 'd' continues and may be a loosely formed open letter; final 'd' may be a straight ascender, or it may loop or curve back towards the beginning of a word.

Small double sheets of unwatermarked cream paper are the norm in this period with leaf-sizes ranging from *c.* 91 × 138 mm. to 117 × 186 mm., but there are occasional sequences of watermarked laid paper, or of double sheets with distinctive embossed devices on the first leaf. For several months after the deaths of Branwell, Emily, and Anne Brontë greyish black-bordered mourning stationery is normally but not invariably used.

It should be emphasized that there are exceptional handwriting styles and types of paper in all periods.

See the examples of handwriting illustrated between pages 318 and 319.

TEXTUAL POLICY

The aim has been to include all known letters to or from Charlotte Brontë, together with a selection of contemporary letters and other material referring to her or illuminating her own references. Wherever possible, texts are based on original holograph manuscripts. Most transcriptions have been made from (or checked against) the manuscripts, and the rest from photocopies. Letters for which the manuscripts have not been traced are based on secondary sources: copy manuscripts, quotations from or transcriptions in printed sources, summaries or references in sale catalogues or elsewhere. As with all such material, complete fidelity to the original manuscript cannot be assumed. The relative value of the major secondary sources has been indicated in the introductory history of the letters. Composite texts have been produced where individual secondary texts appear to be incomplete, and where variants may derive from the original manuscript. A note on the text gives the source of such variants. No attempt has been made to list all variants between secondary sources. Where two secondary texts are substantially the same, the earlier is normally preferred. Fragmentary letters and references to missing letters are placed in the main chronological sequence if an approximate date can be provided. Undatable fragments and references will be printed together at the end of Volume III, as will a list of forgeries.

Most letters written before and some written after 1840 were sent folded and sealed, with the address of the recipient on the outer fold. Addresses so written are described as 'integral' in the notes. Letters written during and after 1840 could be enclosed in envelopes. A few manuscript letters are accompanied by their original envelopes. The BPM has separate collections of envelopes, many of them annotated by Ellen Nussey. These have been matched with the appropriate letters wherever possible, using evidence derived from paper, size, stamps, seals, wafers, postmarks, address, or annotation.

Format and Conventions

The heading of each letter is given in a standardized form. Letters from Charlotte Brontë are headed 'To [recipient]', with the date. The heading of a letter from any other person begins with the name of the sender, as for example 'Emily J. Brontë to Ellen Nussey'. A reference in the notes to 'EN 15.4.1839' signifies a letter from CB to Ellen Nussey.

Date: dates provided by the author are included in the heading of the letter in a standardized form, and are not repeated in the text unless they occur between the body of the letter and a postscript. Dates derived from postmarks or other reasonably reliable evidence are given in square brackets. A query is used to indicate dates derived from handwriting, paper, watermarks, separate envelopes, from the content of the letter, or from external sources, such as Ellen Nussey's diaries and letters to other friends, or the diary papers written by Emily and Anne Brontë. Evidence for the suggested date is given in a note where necessary.

The sender's address is recorded before the letter in the form in which it occurs in the MS. If no address is given in the MS, the probable place of origin is given in square brackets.

Source: If the holograph manuscript has been located, it is the source of the text, and is identified after each letter. For ease of reference the *number* of the letter in the Wise and Symington edition of 1932 is given, if a version or part of the letter appears there. A page reference to the first publication, if any, is given for letters not in W & S. The source of a letter for which the manuscript has not been located is given in a note on the text. See below.

The recipient's address is given after the letter if there is manuscript evidence for it, along with postmarks if any.

Contemporary annotations by recipients or owners of manuscripts such as Ellen Nussey or A. B. Nicholls are recorded. Other annotations such as postage costs, library reference numbers and descriptions are normally omitted.

Notes on the text are given for obscure or mutilated manuscripts, and for letters not based on holograph manuscripts, to explain the choice of copy-text[s] and the inclusion of variants if any. Here and throughout the notes letters in *Shorter* and W & S are identified by their numbers, other material by volume and page.

Spelling: archaic or irregular spellings are recorded as written, without *'sic'*, provided their meaning is recognizable. Forms such as 'M^{r}' 'Esqr' have been standardized to 'Mr.', 'Esqr.'. Abbreviated words are so recorded if they are readily comprehensible ('Yrs', 'affectly') but are expanded if not ('ev[enin]g', 'morn[in]g'). Initials used for proper names are expanded on their first use in a letter, but retained thereafter. Capital initials are retained where they are clearly intentional.

Punctuation: authorial punctuation is followed as faithfully as possible. Alterations or additions, indicated by square brackets, are occasionally made in order to prevent misunderstanding or confusion. Where CB fails to supply a full-stop, a longer-than-usual space between words indicates the appropriate sentence division.

Lacunae: words or single letters inadvertently omitted by the writer are supplied in square brackets. Lacunae caused by the mutilation, repair, or imperfect mounting of a manuscript are indicated by '[. . .]'. Conjectural readings may be supplied in square brackets. Notes give the reason for the lacunae and if necessary the source of the material supplied. Omissions in a text based on a secondary source are indicated by '. . .'.

Additions and Deletions: authorial additions or insertions in MSS are enclosed within ` '. Other additions are given in square brackets. Matter deleted by the author is enclosed within angle brackets < >. Proper names in letters to Ellen Nussey which have been wholly or partly deleted by her are preceded by a single asterisk, with the addition of a query if her deletion makes the reference uncertain. Phrases or longer passages deleted by Ellen Nussey are enclosed within pairs of asterisks (** **) and the readings given must be assumed to be conjectural. A note is given when the obliteration is exceptionally thorough or confusing. The suggested readings of such passages derive from the visible shapes of letters, word divisions indicated by varying density of deletion, differing ink colours, and context. Deciphering has occasionally been assisted by the use of a light-table or ultra-violet light.

References: the place of publication of books referred to in the notes is London unless otherwise indicated.

Volume Division. The present volume is designed to be the first of three. Each volume will include biographical notes and a chronology appropriate to the period covered, and an index. A comprehensive index will be provided at the end of the third volume.

A CHRONOLOGY OF CHARLOTTE BRONTË

1816	21	April	Charlotte Brontë born at Thornton, Bradford, Yorkshire, third child of Patrick and Maria Brontë
1817	26	June	Patrick Branwell Brontë born
1818	30	July	Emily Jane Brontë born
1820	17	January	Anne Brontë born
	20	April	The Brontës move to Haworth, near Keighley, Yorkshire
1821	15	September	Mrs Brontë dies of cancer
1824	21	July	CB's elder sisters Maria (born 1813) and Elizabeth (born 1815) taken to the Clergy Daughters' School at Cowan Bridge
	10	August	Charlotte taken to Cowan Bridge
	25	November	CB joined by Emily
1825	14	February	PB brings Maria Brontë home
	6	May	Maria dies of pulmonary tuberculosis
	31	May	Elizabeth Brontë is brought home
	1	June	PB brings Charlotte and Emily home
	15	June	Elizabeth Brontë dies of pulmonary tuberculosis
1825–30			Brontë children at home under the supervision of their aunt Elizabeth Branwell
1829	15	January	PB writes to *Leeds Intelligencer* supporting civil rights for Catholics
		March	CB writes *The History of the Year*
1829–41			CB writes about 180 poems, 120 stories, and a number of other prose pieces in minute script, many of them set in Angria, an imaginary kingdom invented by BB and CB. She also sketches and copies engravings
1831	17	January	Charlotte arrives at Miss Wooler's school, Roe Head, Mirfield, Yorkshire. Meets Ellen Nussey and Mary Taylor, both born in 1817, who become her close friends and principal correspondents
1831	14	December	CB wins French prize
1832	*c.*20	June	Leaves Roe Head school
		Summer	Appointed first superintendent of newly opened National Sunday school at Haworth
		September	CB's first visit to EN at Rydings, Birstall
1833	19	July	EN's first visit to Haworth
1834		Summer	CB's pencil copies of two engravings, 'Bolton Abbey' and 'Kirkstall Abbey', exhibited in Leeds
1835			BB has drawing lessons from William Robinson of Leeds
	29	July	CB returns to Roe Head as a teacher, accompanied by EJB as a pupil

	mid-October	AB replaces EJB at Roe Head
	7 December	BB asks the editor of *Blackwood's Magazine* to take him on in place of James Hogg, but receives no reply to this or later letters
1836		CB's 'Roe Head Journal' reveals her conflict between her imaginary world and her duty to teach 'dolts' in the schoolroom She confides her religious doubts and fears to EN, whom she loves and admires intensely
	17–24 June	CB and AB stay with Mrs Franks in Huddersfield
	29 December	CB sends specimens of her poetry to Robert Southey and tells him of her ambition to be 'for ever known' as a poet
1837	10 January	BB sends a poem to Wordsworth and acknowledges his ambition to be a poet. Wordsworth does not reply
1837	12 March	Southey writes to CB acknowledging her 'faculty of verse' but advising her to 'write poetry for its own sake . . . not with a view to celebrity'. CB values his advice. She continues to teach at Roe Head
	December	AB ill at Roe Head; CB quarrels with Miss Wooler for failing to realize Anne's danger, and returns with Anne to Haworth
1838	January	CB agrees to return to Roe Head
	Feb./Mar.	CB's nervous depression made worse by EN's absence in London and later in Bath
	?Feb./Mar.	Miss Wooler's school moves from Roe Head to Heald's House, Dewsbury Moor
	23 March	CB's 'hypochondria' increases and she goes home on doctor's advice
	?late April	CB returns to Dewsbury Moor
	late May	CB back at Haworth
	*c.*3–9 June	Mary and Martha Taylor stay at Haworth
	?August–22 December	CB's last term as a teacher at Dewsbury Moor
	Sept/Oct–?March 1839	EJB endures 'governess slavery' at Law Hill school near Halifax; returns to Haworth at the end of six months
1839	5 March	CB rejects a proposal of marriage from EN's brother the Revd Henry Nussey
	8 April	AB goes as a governess to the Inghams of Blake Hall, Mirfield
	May–July	CB becomes a governess to the Sidgwicks at Stonegappe near Skipton and at Swarcliffe near Harrogate
	late July	CB refuses a proposal of marriage from the Revd David Pryce
	July–Dec.	Writes a substantial novelette, 'Caroline Vernon'
1839	August	The Revd William Weightman becomes curate to Mr Brontë
	Sept./Oct.	CB and EN stay with the Hudsons at Easton near Bridlington and in Ann Booth's lodgings at Bridlington Quay
	December	AB leaves Blake Hall
1840	January	BB becomes tutor to the sons of Robert Postlethwaite at Broughton-in-Furness, Lancashire

	20	April	BB writes to Hartley Coleridge, asking him for his opinion on his poem, 'At dead of midnight' and his translations of two of Horace's Odes
	1	May	BB meets Hartley Coleridge and is encouraged by him
	?8	May	AB goes as governess to the family of the Revd Edmund Robinson of Thorp Green, near York
	27	June	BB sends translation of Book I of Horace's Odes to Hartley Coleridge
		June	BB is dismissed from his post at Broughton
	31	August	BB becomes assistant clerk at Sowerby Bridge railway station
	?	November	CB sends the opening chapters of a MS novel (?*Ashworth*) to Hartley Coleridge
	10	December	CB writes to Hartley Coleridge acknowledging his candid opinion that her novel is unlikely to be accepted by a publisher
1841		Jan./Feb.	The Taylors of Gomersal disperse after the death of Joshua Taylor on 28.12.1840; Mary and Martha eventually go abroad
		?end Feb.	CB becomes governess to the family of John White of Upperwood House, Rawdon, near Leeds
	1	April	BB becomes clerk in charge at Luddenden Foot station
1841	30	June	CB returns home
		July	C, EJ, and AB plan to start a school of their own, possibly at Bridlington
		late July	CB returns to Upperwood House
		September	Miss Wooler invites CB to take over the school at Dewsbury Moor, but CB decides to go abroad
	29	September	CB asks her Aunt Elizabeth Branwell for a loan so that she and Emily can study abroad for six months
	24	December	CB returns home from Upperwood House
1842	8	February	PB, CB, and EJB leave with Mary and Joe Taylor for Brussels; CB and EJB become pupils at Mme Heger's pensionnat
	3	March	BB dismissed from Luddenden Foot for negligence
		July–Aug.	CB and EJB meet the Wheelwrights at the pensionnat and visit their apartment in Brussels
		September	CB and EJB stay on at the pensionnat, CB teaching English and EJB music in return for board and tuition
	6	September	W. Weightman dies of cholera at Haworth
	12	October	Martha Taylor dies of cholera in Brussels
	29	October	Elizabeth Branwell dies of internal obstruction in Haworth. She leaves money to her nieces
	8	November	CB and EJB return to Haworth
	29	November	AB returns to Thorp Green
1843	?21	January	BB goes to Thorp Green, where he is to be tutor to Mr Robinson's son Edmund
	29	January	CB returns alone to the pensionnat Heger as a teacher. She gives English lessons to M. Heger and his brother-in-law

		March	She enjoys the company of Mary Dixon, a cousin of the Taylors
	1	May	CB's feeling of depression and isolation at the pensionnat increases
1843		Aug./Sept.	CB lonely and homesick in Brussels during long vacation; goes to confession at Ste Gudule
		October	CB distrusts Mme Heger and gives in her notice, but M. Heger countermands it
by	17	Dec	CB decides to come home
1844	1	January	CB leaves Brussels
	3	January	CB arrives at Haworth to find her father's eyesight is rapidly deteriorating
		end Jan.	CB wishes to start a school but cannot leave her father
		May	Reunion of CB and EN with Mary Taylor, returned from teaching in Germany
		July	CB tries to get pupils for a school at the parsonage
	24	July	CB writes to M. Heger: if her sight permitted, she would write a book and dedicate it to him; she longs for an answer from him
	24	October	Joe Taylor takes another letter from CB to M. Heger: she is grieved by his six months' silence, and counts on having news of him on J. Taylor's return
	26	October	CB has heard that Mary Taylor is to emigrate to New Zealand
	14	November	CB recognizes failure of attempt to start a school
		late Dec	Mary Taylor stays at the parsonage until ?3 January
1845	8	January	CB writes to M. Heger in despair; she is tortured by his failure to reply, and she cannot bear to lose his friendship
		February	She spends a miserable week with the Taylors
	12	March	Mary Taylor sails from Gravesend, arriving in Wellington, N.Z., on 24 July
		May	The Revd Arthur Bell Nicholls becomes curate to Mr Brontë
	11	June	AB receives her final payment from Mr Robinson
1845	30	June–2 July	AB and EJB go for an excursion to York
	?3	July	CB begins a three-week visit to EN who is at her brother Henry's vicarage in Hathersage, Derbyshire
	17	July	BB receives dismissal from Mr Robinson for 'proceedings . . . bad beyond expression' (?an affair with Mrs Robinson). BB drinks to drown his distress.
	26	July	CB returns to Haworth
	29	July	John Brown takes BB to Liverpool and North Wales to recuperate
	31	July	AB has begun third volume of *Passages in the Life of an Individual*, possibly a draft of *Agnes Grey*
	?	Sept./Oct.	CB discovers and reads poems by EJB; Anne offers hers. They plan to publish a selection, and begin to prepare it
	18	November	Last surviving letter from CB to M. Heger: she admits she cannot master her thoughts of him. Begs for a letter

	20 December	BB's poem 'Penmaenmawr', published in *Halifax Guardian*, contains covert references to Mrs Robinson as his 'Angel'
1846	28 January	CB asks publishers Aylott and Jones if they would publish a collection of poems
	6 February	Sends MS of poems as work of 'Currer Ellis and Acton Bell'
	3 March	CB pays Aylott & Jones £31 10s. for printing the poems
	6 April	CB asks whether Aylott and Jones would publish three tales—i.e. *The Professor*, *Wuthering Heights*, and *Agnes Grey*
	mid-April	Aylott and Jones refuse but offer advice
	c.22 May	*Poems* published at 4s.
1846	26 May	The Revd E. Robinson dies. BB believes that Mrs Robinson is prevented from seeing him; he is distraught
	4 July	*Poems* well reviewed in *Athenaeum* and *Critic* but only two copies are sold
	4 July	CB sends the '3 tales' to the publisher H. Colburn, who rejects them. During the next year they are sent to and rejected by four more publishers Mr Brontë is now blind
	19 August	CB takes her father to Manchester for an eye operation
	25 August	PB operated on for cataract in the left eye. *The Professor* is returned, rejected, on the same day, and CB begins writing *Jane Eyre*
	December	CB continues to write *Jane Eyre* but tells EN that 'nothing happens at Haworth' except trouble with BB
1847	24 March	CB feels her 'youth is gone like a dream'
	16 June	*Poems* remain unsold. CB and her sisters send complimentary copies to ?Wordsworth, Tennyson, De Quincey, Hartley Coleridge, John Lockhart, and Ebenezer Elliott
	July	T. C. Newby agrees to publish *Wuthering Heights* and *Agnes Grey*
	15 July	CB sends *The Professor* to Smith, Elder and Co.
	7 August	CB acknowledges Smith, Elder's reasons for rejecting *The Professor*, but mentions that a work of 'more vivid interest' is nearly completed
	24 August	CB sends MS of *Jane Eyre* to Smith, Elder by rail
	12 September	CB accepts Smith, Elder's terms for publication of *Jane Eyre*, but refuses to revise it 'a third time'
	9–23 Sept	CB stays with EN at Brookroyd, correcting proofs of *JE* while there but not admitting authorship
1847	19 October	Publication of *Jane Eyre: An Autobiography*, edited by Currer Bell, in three volumes
	26 October	CB has received the first of many favourable reviews
	29 October	CB continues to correspond with EN about Amelia Ringrose, not mentioning *Jane Eyre*
	6 November	CB writes first letter to G. H. Lewes, in reply to one from him

	17 November	EJB and AB have received last proof-sheets of *Wuthering Heights* and *Agnes Grey*
	14 December	CB has written three beginnings to her next novel but has discarded them; she wishes to recast *The Professor*
		EJB and AB have received their six copies of *Wuthering Heights A Novel*, by Ellis Bell and *Agnes Grey. A Novel*, by Acton Bell, published together in three volumes
	21 December	CB sends a revised preface for second edition of *JE*, which will appear on 22.1.1848 with a dedication to Thackeray
	31 December	CB disclaims authorship of *WH* and *AG*

Main Events 1848–55

1848	c.27 June	*The Tenant of Wildfell Hall* by Acton Bell published in three volumes by T. C. Newby
	7–11 July	CB and AB go to London to prove the separate identity of the 'Bells'; they meet George Smith and William Smith Williams
	24 September	BB dies of chronic bronchitis and marasmus (wasting of the body)
	19 December	EJB dies of pulmonary tuberculosis
1849	28 May	AB dies of pulmonary tuberculosis
	26 October	*Shirley. A Tale* by Currer Bell published in three volumes by Smith, Elder and Co.
1849	Nov.–Dec.	CB visits London; meets Thackeray
1850	May–June	CB visits London; sits for her portrait to George Richmond
	3–6 July	CB visits Edinburgh in the company of George Smith
	August	CB meets Mrs Gaskell during a visit to the Kay-Shuttleworths at Briery Close, near Windermere
1851	5 April	CB dubious about possible marriage to James Taylor
	May–June	She visits London for the Great Exhibition
		Begins writing *Villette*
1852	20 November	*Villette* completed
1853	January	Last visit to London
	28 January	*Villette* by Currer Bell published in three volumes by Smith, Elder and Co.
	April	Visits Mrs Gaskell in Manchester
	November	Writes 'Emma', the opening chapters of a new novel
1854	29 June	CB marries the Revd A. B. Nicholls
1855	31 March	CB dies at Haworth, of phthisis according to the death certificate, but possibly of hyperemesis gravidarum, excessive sickness during pregnancy
	16 June	Mr Brontë asks Mrs Gaskell to write an account of CB's life, with 'some remarks on her works'. She agrees, and begins to gather material for the *Life*, which will be published by Smith, Elder, in 1857, followed by *The Professor, A Tale* by Currer Bell, in two volumes.

BIOGRAPHICAL NOTES

Elizabeth Branwell, 2 December 1776–29 October 1842

Elizabeth Branwell, one of the eleven children of Thomas Branwell and his wife Anne, née Carne, was born in Penzance in Cornwall. Her father died in 1808, leaving £50 per annum to each of his daughters. In 1815 Elizabeth stayed with her sister Mrs Maria Brontë's family at Thornton, where she became an affectionate friend of Elizabeth Firth, and with her acted as godmother at the baptism of the Brontës' second daughter Elizabeth. Mr Brontë later appreciated her help during his wife's mortal illness at Haworth in 1821, when she 'afforded great comfort to my mind, which has been the case ever since, by sharing my labours and sorrows, and behaving as an affectionate mother to my children'.[1] After her sister's death Elizabeth moved permanently to Haworth. Ellen Nussey recalled her as 'a very small antiquated little lady'.[2]

'Aunt Branwell' helped to educate Charlotte, Emily, and Anne at home, allowed them to read the romantic tales in her ancient copies of the *Lady's Magazine*, and gave them a copy of Scott's *Tales of a Grandfather* in 1828. But, as Mr Brontë told Mrs Gaskell, she was 'unaware of the fermentation of unoccupied talent going on around her. She was not her nieces' confidante' and her discipline was sometimes felt to be oppressive. Nevertheless 'she and her nieces went on smoothly enough; and though they might now and then be annoyed by petty tyranny, she still inspired them with sincere respect, and not a little affection. They were, moreover, [as Charlotte acknowledged,] grateful to her for many habits she had enforced upon them, and which in time had become second nature: order, method, neatness in everything; a perfect knowledge of all kinds of household work; an exact punctuality, and obedience to the laws of time and place'.[3]

Since Miss Branwell had been brought up as a Wesleyan Methodist, it is unlikely that she held the Calvinistic beliefs attributed to her by Winifred Gérin in *AB* 34–5, or that she exercised a 'tyranny of the spirit' over Anne Brontë.

In practical terms she contributed much to the Brontë family. She paid for her board at the parsonage, and encouraged the girls in their plans to set up their own school, offering them a loan of £100 for this purpose. When Charlotte suggested that some of the money might be used to finance a period of study abroad, Miss Branwell agreed, and offered a further sum to enable her

1 PB to the Revd John Buckworth, 27.11.1821; W & S 11.

2 See Appendix, p. 597.

3 *Life* i. 208–9.

nieces to have a separate room.[4] By her will she left the residue of her estate to be divided equally amongst her four nieces—Charlotte, Emily, Anne, and their cousin Elizabeth Jane Kingston. Their investment of this money enabled them to pay for the publication of the *Poems* in 1846 and *Agnes Grey* and *Wuthering Heights* in 1847.

Eanne Oram's article, 'Brief for Miss Branwell' in *BST* 14. 74. 28–38 is well-informed, and is accompanied by a reproduction of an attractive miniature of Elizabeth Branwell at the age of 23.

Anne Brontë, 17 January 1820–28 May 1849

Anne was three months old when the family moved from Thornton, her birthplace, to Haworth on 20 April 1820, and her mother died on 15 September the following year. Anne was therefore brought up and educated mainly by her Aunt Elizabeth Branwell at the Haworth parsonage until she was 15. Her father also gave her some tuition. She was the playmate of Emily, and with her created the exotic imaginary land of Gondal.

In October 1835 she took the place of the homesick Emily as a pupil at Roe Head school, Mirfield. Quiet and industrious, with some talent for languages, she won a prize for good conduct in December 1836. Towards the end of 1837 she suffered a crisis of faith and became 'wretchedly ill'. She gained spiritual comfort from a Moravian minister, the Revd James La Trobe, but continued to be in pain and to have difficulty in breathing. Charlotte, in great anxiety, told her father of Anne's illness, and accompanied her back to Haworth in December. After another year at school Anne decided to become a governess. By her own wish she travelled alone on 8 April 1839 to Blake Hall near Mirfield, where she found Joshua Ingham's children 'desperate little dunces', excessively indulged and ill-behaved; yet she was 'not empowered to inflict any punishment'.[5] Her tribulations there until she left in December 1839 are echoed in those of her heroine Agnes Grey at Wellwood. At home she met the young curate William Weightman and was admired by him. Her poem, 'I will not mourn', written in December 1842, probably shows her attempts to control her grief for his death.

In May 1840 she became governess to the daughters of the Revd Edmund Robinson at Thorp Green, Little Ouseburn, near York. She may also have taught his son Edmund. Though she loved the woods and meadows near the house, and persevered with her studies in Latin and German, her 'drooping spirit' longed for home. Charlotte compassionately described her as a persecuted stranger amongst insolent people.[6] Though Anne wished to leave, she 'rendered herself so valuable in her difficult situation' that the Robinsons 'entreated her to return to them'.[7] She remained at Thorp

[4] EN 20.1.1842. [5] EN 15.4.1839. [6] EN 7.8.1841. [7] EN 10.1.1842.

Green until June 1845. She continued to write her Gondal stories and poems, and more profound poems of spiritual self-scrutiny akin to those of her favourite poet William Cowper. Her gentle firmness eventually gained her the respect and affection of her pupils; but her humiliations and her anxiety about their moral welfare are painfully recalled in the Horton Lodge episodes of *Agnes Grey*. Her perturbation increased after Branwell became Edmund Robinson's tutor in January 1843. It is probable that she became aware of an attraction between Mrs Robinson and Branwell, for she did not contradict his later assertion that Mr Robinson's discovery of their affair was the cause of his dismissal.

Anne's contributions to the 'Bells' ' *Poems* in 1846, and her novel *Agnes Grey*, published with and overshadowed by *Wuthering Heights* in December 1847, gained mild approval from some reviewers, but made comparatively little impact. In contrast, the publication of her second novel, *The Tenant of Wildfell Hall*, in June 1848 convinced a writer in the *North American Review* for October that the 'Bells' had a sense of the depravity of human nature 'peculiarly their own'. 'Acton Bell' was accused of writing also *Wuthering Heights* and 'certain offensive' portions of *Jane Eyre*, and of taking a morose satisfaction in analysing human brutality. Anne, who had witnessed her brother's continuing degradation with pain and revulsion, had already written a preface to the second edition of *The Tenant* to explain that she intended to impress her moral warning on readers by telling the unadorned truth.

After Emily's death in December 1848, tubercular symptoms became evident in Anne's declining health. As courageous as her sister but more amenable, she accepted medical help and wished strongly for recovery. Her journey to Scarborough in May 1849 was undertaken in the hope of improvement; but she died, within sight of the sea, on 28 May, three days after her arrival.

Emily Jane Brontë, 30 July 1818–19 December 1848

Emily, the fifth child of Patrick and Maria Brontë, was born at Thornton, but the family moved to Haworth in April 1820. At the age of 6 she was the 'pet nursling' at Cowan Bridge school, to which she was taken on 25 November 1824. Mr Brontë brought Emily and Charlotte home on 1 June 1825 after an outbreak of 'low fever' at the school. Emily's diary note of 24 November 1834, written with Anne, mentions her domestic duties and music-lessons, reflects her lifelong love of animals and birds—'I fed Rainbow, Diamond Snowflake Jasper phaesant'—and shows that she and Anne had already begun writing their stories of the imaginary land of Gondal.[8] The impression given is of a

[8] Gérin *EJB* 39.

cheerful, untidy, normal girl, young for her age and happier to go out to play than to do her lessons. Charlotte wrote: 'My sister Emily loved the moors . . . She found in the bleak solitude many and dear delights; and not the least and best loved was—liberty.'[9]

When Charlotte returned as a teacher to Roe Head school on 29 July 1835, Emily accompanied her as a pupil, but soon fell ill. Charlotte, convinced that Emily would die if she remained away from home and from the freedom of the moors, obtained her recall to Haworth in October of the same year. At home Emily 'took the principal part of the cooking upon herself, and did all the household ironing; and after Tabby [the servant] grew old and infirm, it was Emily who made all the bread for the family; and any one passing by the kitchen-door, might have seen her studying German out of an open book, propped up before her, as she kneaded the dough.'[10]

In October 1838 Emily again left home to be a teacher at Elizabeth Patchett's school at Law Hill near Halifax; there she endured for six months the appalling drudgery of 'Hard labour from six in the morning until near eleven at night, with only one half hour of exercise between.'[11] The surrounding area, a vast sweep of upland with isolated farms and buildings such as High Sunderland Hall, with its grotesquely carved entrance, may be recalled in *Wuthering Heights*.

The years 1836–40 were, Law Hill notwithstanding, Emily's richest creative period as a poet, for she was inspired both by freedom and by the longing for it. Her poems also tell us almost all we know of Gondal, still being chronicled with enthusiasm in 1845.[12]

On 12 February 1842 Emily went with Charlotte to Mme Heger's pensionnat in Brussels. With less knowledge of French than Charlotte, she was more isolated, but she worked 'like a horse' at her lessons, mastered more German as well as French, and was proficient enough in music to give piano lessons to the younger Wheelwright sisters. Emily and Charlotte returned to Haworth in early November 1842 on hearing of their Aunt Branwell's death, and Emily stayed on there to keep house for her father. Although she supported Charlotte's plan to establish a school at the parsonage in 1844, Emily did not regret their failure to attract any pupils. She was contented, in good health, and had probably begun to write *Wuthering Heights*.

In autumn 1845 Charlotte 'accidentally lighted on a MS. volume of verse' in Emily's handwriting. Convinced of the 'genuine' quality of her sister's poems and of their 'peculiar music—wild, melancholy, and elevating', Charlotte at length persuaded her to consent to publication. The discriminating reviewer in

[9] Prefatory Note to 'Selections from poems by Ellis Bell' in *Wuthering Heights* (1850).
[10] *Life* i. 150.
[11] EN 2.10.1838.
[12] EJB Diary Paper 31.7.1845, p. 408 and Gérin *EJB* chs. 3–8.

the *Athenaeum* for 4 July 1846 praised the poems of 'Ellis Bell' for 'an evident power of wing that may reach heights not here attempted'.[13]

By summer 1847 the publisher Thomas Cautley Newby had accepted *Wuthering Heights* and Anne's *Agnes Grey*, but he delayed publication until December, when he exploited the success of Currer Bell's *Jane Eyre* by advertising the novels as if they were by the same author. Reviewers were startled, shocked, or baffled by the 'savagery' they discerned in *Wuthering Heights*, but some were aware of its uniqueness and power. Sales were encouraging, and Newby wrote to Emily on 15 February 1848 offering to accept her next work 'upon the understanding that its completion be at your own time'.[14]

Emily lived to see Anne's *The Tenant of Wildfell Hall* published in June 1848, but after the death of Branwell on 24 September her health rapidly declined. Her spirit remaining 'inexorable to the flesh', she refused all medical help until it was too late, and died, wasted with consumption, after a 'hard, short conflict' on 19 December 1848.

Patrick Branwell Brontë, 26 June 1817–24 September 1848

Branwell Brontë was born at Thornton near Bradford, but was under three years old when the family moved to Haworth, and only four when his mother died. He came to regard his Aunt Branwell, who was fond of him, as a mother. Mr Brontë educated him at home, and encouraged his interest in politics. Like Charlotte, Branwell was an avid reader of *Blackwood's Edinburgh Magazine*, and from the age of 11 he wrote prolifically, imitating the style of magazine reviews, composing poems and dramas, and collaborating with Charlotte in endless sagas of Glasstown and Angria. Throughout his life he thought of himself as a poet, and from 1835 onwards begged influential writers—Wordsworth, Macaulay, James Martineau, Leigh Hunt, Hartley Coleridge—and (repeatedly) the editor of *Blackwood's* to acknowledge his talent. He published poems in reputable local newspapers five years before his sisters produced their *Poems* in 1846: twelve appeared in the *Halifax Guardian* between 5 June 1841 and 5 June 1847, and others in the *Bradford Herald* and *Leeds Intelligencer* in 1842.

Branwell's other ambition was to be an artist. In 1835 his father paid for him to study painting with William Robinson of Leeds, who had been taught by Sir Thomas Lawrence. Mr Brontë was prepared to support his application to train in the Royal Academy Schools; but Branwell seems to have done no more than draft an enquiry to the Secretary of the Academy. He did, however, rent a room in Bradford in 1837 or 1838, and attempted to earn his living as a portrait

13 *Allott* 61. 14 W & S 347.

painter. His surviving efforts show his lack of skill, though he achieved a memorable painting of his sister Emily.

During 1839, following his failure as an artist, he read with his father in preparation for a post as tutor to the sons of Robert Postlethwaite at Broughton-in-Furness in Lancashire. He sent from Broughton to his boon companion John Brown of Haworth an obscene account of a drinking party at Kendal in January 1840.[15] But two poems written at Broughton, one of them a competent sonnet on Black Comb, show his continuing poetic ambition and ability. He was dismissed, probably in disgrace, from his post at Broughton and returned home in June 1840.

His next post was that of a railway clerk, first at Sowerby Bridge Station from 31 August 1840, and then from April 1841 at Luddenden Foot near Halifax. While there he became friendly with the sculptor Joseph Bentley Leyland and with the young railway engineer Francis Grundy, who was to record his vivid but inaccurate recollections of Branwell in *Pictures of the Past* (1879). Dismissed from his clerkship owing to the dishonesty of a porter for whom he was responsible, Branwell returned home depressed and ill in March 1842. He grieved deeply over the deaths of his father's curate, William Weightman, in September 1842 and of Aunt Branwell on 29 October.

In January 1843 Branwell became the tutor of Edmund Robinson, the son of Anne Brontë's employer at Thorp Green. A year later Charlotte heard that he and Anne were 'wondrously valued' in their situations,[16] but during his holidays at Haworth that summer he was 'toujours malade'—possibly Charlotte's euphemism for his drinking. On 17 July 1845 he received a letter from Mr Robinson dismissing him for conduct 'bad beyond expression'.[17] In the following October he told Grundy that Mrs Robinson had declared 'more than ordinary feeling for him' while he was at Thorp Green. Branwell's behaviour and his family's reaction to it are described in more detail in the Introduction.

In an effort to distract his mind and to earn some money he turned again to his writing; he planned an epic and began or continued a novel, but he completed neither. His reading of part of an unfinished manuscript to Leyland and a local schoolmaster, William Dearden, may have led to Dearden's claim that Branwell had written part of *Wuthering Heights*. In late October 1845 he failed to secure the secretaryship to a newly formed railway company.

After the death of Mr Robinson on 26 May 1846, Branwell claimed that Mrs Robinson was distraught, and that she would have married him but for a clause in Mr Robinson's will forbidding her to see him again on pain of losing all the property he bequeathed to her. The clause did not exist, though Branwell may

[15] Copy MS BPM B. S. 137.5. [16] EN 23.1.1844. [17] EN 31.7.1845.

have been led to believe that it did. Mrs Robinson's feelings and motives at this point remain unknown; but it is certain that she married a rich elderly relative, Sir Edward Dolman Scott, on 8 November 1848 soon after Branwell's death. When in March 1857 Mrs Gaskell alleged in the *Life* of Charlotte Brontë that Branwell had been seduced and ruined by a 'profligate woman', she was threatened with a libel action by solicitors acting for Lady Scott, and was compelled to withdraw the first two editions of the *Life*. Whatever the truth may have been, Branwell seems to have lost direction in his life after May 1846. He spent whatever money he was given on drink or drugs; if he had no money he incurred debts which had to be paid by his family. He grew physically weak, and on 22 September 1848 was found exhausted in the village and had to be helped back to the parsonage. He died two days later of 'chronic bronchitis and marasmus'—a wasting of the flesh without apparent disease. Charlotte recalled, in a letter written on 2 October, her 'aspirations and ambitions for him once—long ago' and felt 'a bitterness of pity for his life and death'.

The Revd Patrick Brontë, 17 March 1777–7 June 1861

Charlotte Brontë's father was born in Emdale, County Down, Ireland, the eldest of a family of ten children. In about 1798, after five or six years as a schoolmaster, he became a tutor in the family of the Revd Thomas Tighe, a Church of Ireland rector of evangelical sympathies. With Tighe's help Patrick Brontë began to study theology, and was entered as a sizar at St John's College Cambridge on 1 October 1802. He won prizes each year, was awarded small exhibitions in 1803 and 1805, and gained his BA degree in 1806. In the same year he was appointed curate at Wethersfield in Essex and ordained a deacon of the Church of England. Ordination to the priesthood followed in 1807.

In Wethersfield he fell in love with a farmer's daughter, Mary Mildred Burder, and wrote several letters to her after he moved to Glenfield in Leicestershire for a short time in 1808, and to Wellington in Shropshire in January 1809. The Burder family disapproved of their engagement, which was broken off, probably by Patrick, in or before 1810. In Wellington he met the Methodist schoolmaster John Fennell, and a fellow-curate, William Morgan, both of whom were to become relatives by marriage. A curacy at the Yorkshire woollen town of Dewsbury followed from December 1809 until early 1811, when Patrick moved to the parish of Hartshead cum Clifton, a rural area about four miles west of Dewsbury. Both parishes were involved in the Luddite risings at this period, and some of Patrick's memories of them were to be recalled in Charlotte Brontë's *Shirley* in 1849.

From 1810 onwards Patrick Brontë wrote and published conventional didactic and occasional verse and moral tales, sermons in pamphlet form, and articles on matters of faith and doctrine. His first publication was *Winter*

Evening Thoughts, a 'Miscellaneous Poem', printed for Longmans of London and John Hurst of Wakefield in 1810. His *Collected Works* were published by J. Horsfall Turner in *Bronteana* (Bingley, 1898), and they are described and quoted at length in J. Lock and W. T. Dixon, *A Man of Sorrow* (1965). His articles 'On Conversion' in William Morgan's periodical *The Pastoral Visitor* for July, September, and October 1815 are reprinted in *BST* 19. 6. 271–5. His many letters to newspapers show a lively concern for the social, religious, and political questions of his day, well represented in *Barker*.

In July 1812 Patrick was invited by John Fennell to examine the pupils in classics at the new Methodist school at Woodhouse Grove, Rawdon, near Leeds. His courtship of Fennell's niece Maria Branwell began in the same year, and they were married at Guiseley church on 29 December 1812. Their first daughter Maria was baptized at Hartshead on 23 April 1814, and a second daughter, Elizabeth, was born there on 8 February 1815. In May 1815 Patrick and his family moved to Thornton, a village near Bradford, where his three younger daughters and his son were born. The family was warmly befriended at Thornton by Dr John Scholefield Firth and his daughter Elizabeth (1797–1837), later Mrs Franks.

When Patrick Brontë was nominated to the perpetual curacy of Haworth in 1819 by the Vicar of Bradford, the Revd Henry Heap, he was at first rejected by the Haworth Church Trustees, as an assertion of their right to choose their own minister, but he was finally accepted by them in February 1820, and the family moved to Haworth in April.

After Mrs Brontë's death from cancer on 15 September 1821, her sister Elizabeth Branwell became the housekeeper at the parsonage. Mr Brontë may have proposed, unsuccessfully, to Elizabeth Firth in 1821, and to Isabella Dury, the sister of his friend Theodore Dury, Rector of Keighley, in 1822 or 1823. His proposal of marriage to Mary Burder in 1823 met with a sharp refusal.

In 1824 Mr Brontë took his four older daughters to the Clergy Daughters' School at Cowan Bridge in Lancashire. All the children were brought home in 1825. Maria and Elizabeth, already suffering from tuberculosis, died soon after their return, Maria on 6 May and Elizabeth on 15 June, and their father decided that the other children should be educated at home for the time being. The work of looking after his extensive parish, especially during a smallpox epidemic in the early months of 1830, led to exhaustion and acute illness in June and July of that year. In January 1831 he arranged for Charlotte to go as a pupil to Roe Head school Mirfield, not far from the home of Mrs Franks.

In summer 1831 he obtained a grant from the National School Society towards the building of a Sunday School in Haworth, opened in 1832. The Parliamentary Reform Act passed in that year was supported by Mr Brontë, a Tory who believed in moderate reform. Before the Parliamentary elections of

1835 his support for Peel antagonized the powerful Whigs in Haworth. His opposition to the Whig candidate, Lord Morpeth, was intensified by the Whig espousal of church disestablishment, a policy Mr Brontë opposed in his pamphlet, *Signs of the Times* (Keighley, 1835). Strong objections by Dissenters to the payment of Church rates meant that Patrick and his curate William Hodgson were involved in much local dissension in the late 1830s.

In 1839 he helped to prepare his son Branwell for a post at Broughton-in-Furness by reading with him works by Virgil, Homer, and Horace, and the four gospels in Greek. After Branwell's return from Broughton his father supported his application for a railway clerkship in August/September 1840. In February 1842 Mr Brontë accompanied Charlotte and Emily on their journey to Brussels, and took the opportunity to visit the field of Waterloo. He was deeply grieved by the death of his young curate William Weightman on 6 September 1842, and in his funeral sermon said that they had been 'always like father and son'.[18] The death of Miss Branwell on 29 October 1842 meant that the housekeeping at the parsonage was taken care of by Emily and the servants.

In 1844 rumours that Mr Brontë had been drinking to excess may have been caused, as he said, by the smell of a lotion for his eyes, which were very weak. Cataracts developed, and he had to depend increasingly on the assistance of the Revd A.B. Nicholls, his curate from May 1845. His troubles were increased by the dismissal of Branwell in disgrace from his tutorial post to Edmund Robinson in July 1845. By mid-1846 Mr Bronte was almost completely blind; in August Charlotte took him to Manchester, where a successful operation for cataract was performed by Dr William James Wilson. At home he suffered the constant burden of Branwell's drinking bouts, unstable temper, and deteriorating health. When Branwell died on 24 September 1848 his father 'cried out for his loss like David for that of Absalom—my son my son!—and refused at first to be comforted'.[19] The death of Emily on 19 December 1848 and of Anne on 28 May 1849 meant that Mr Bronte became increasingly protective of and dependent on his only remaining daughter: he was proud of Charlotte's success as a novelist, and took pleasure in her friendship with her publishers and with Mrs Gaskell.

He continued to work for local causes, and in 1849–50 took the lead in organizing a petition to the Board of Health to procure a much-needed supply of clean water for Haworth. Though a government inspection revealed the appallingly insanitary conditions in the village, vested interests delayed progress until 1856.

In 1851 Mr Brontë welcomed a visit to the parsonage by James Taylor, a member of the Smith, Elder publishing firm, and would have permitted

[18] *Bronteana* 258. [19] WSW 2.10.1848.

Charlotte to marry him providing the marriage was deferred for five years. She was not attracted to him and did not become engaged; but when she told her father of Mr Nicholls's proposal on 13 December 1852, he was violently opposed to the match. He was gradually brought round to a more favourable view during Mr Nicholls's absence from Haworth from May 1853 until April 1854, when he consented to their engagement. Charlotte had stipulated that she should not leave the parsonage, and that her father's 'seclusion and convenience' should remain uninvaded.[20] After her marriage on 29 June 1854 Mr Brontë remained on amicable terms with Mr Nicholls, who continued to respect and care for him after Charlotte's death on 31 March 1855.

Between 1855 and 1857 Mr Brontë co-operated with Mrs Gaskell in her writing of Charlotte's *Life*. The finished work gave him both 'pleasure and pain', but he thought it well done, and asked only for the correction of 'a few trifling mistakes', despite her misrepresentation of him as a violent man and harsh husband. In August–September 1856 Mr Nicholls read to him Charlotte's unpublished novel *The Professor*, and together they decided what deletions should be made before its publication by Smith, Elder in June 1857.

Mr Brontë was bedridden for a few months before his death on 7 June 1861. He left the residue of his estate to his 'beloved and esteemed son-in-law' Mr Nicholls. Though Mr Brontë became somewhat prejudiced, self-absorbed, and reclusive with age, he was a man of integrity, with a strongly held Christian faith, a lively social conscience, and a deep attachment to his family; his influence on Charlotte Brontë can hardly be over-estimated.

Constantin Georges Romain Heger, 10 July 1809–6 May 1896

Constantin Heger was born in Brussels, where his father was a prosperous jeweller. In 1815 the family was bankrupted when a loan to a friend was not repaid. In 1825 Constantin was sent to Paris, where he became a secretary to a solicitor; he was attracted to a career in law but could not afford to pursue it. On his return to Brussels in 1829 he became a teacher of French at the Athénée Royal, and married Marie-Josephine Noyer in the following year. When the Belgian Revolution began in September 1830, Heger fought as a nationalist in the cause of Belgian liberty. His wife's brother was killed during the fighting, and he had the further grief of losing his wife and child on 26 September 1833 during a cholera epidemic.

Not long afterwards M. Heger met Mlle Claire Zoë Parent (13.7.1804–9.1.1890), the directress of a girls' school in the rue d'Isabelle, and began giving literature lessons in her school. They married on 3 September 1836. Their

[20] EN 11.4.1854.

daughters Marie, Louise, and Claire were born before Charlotte and Emily Brontë arrived at the pensionnat in February 1842, and their son Prospère was born on 28 March 1842, followed by Victorine on 14 January 1843 and Paul on 4 December 1846. The marriage was a happy one. M. Heger became Principal of the Athénée in 1853, but resigned after two years because he could not accept the utilitarian educational methods advocated by the General Inspector of Schools. At his own request he resumed the teaching of the youngest class in the school.

Both the Hegers were well known and respected in Brussels for their educational achievements, high principles, and generosity in charitable work. M. Heger had the distinction of being invited more than once to speak at the Athénée prize-givings, where his fluent oratory was applauded. He gave Charlotte Brontë a printed copy of his *Discours* of August 1843.[21] She benefited from his inspired teaching of French Romantic literature, and from his gifts of books such as the works of Bernardin de St Pierre. He recognized and encouraged her talents, and inspired in her a deep attachment.

Two letters written by the poet Thomas Westwood from Brussels on 21 November 1869 and 21 February 1870 describe M. Heger and allege that he showed the 'broken-hearted' letters Charlotte wrote to him from Haworth to another former pupil; Westwood thought him 'a finished specimen of a Jesuit, but with all that a worthy & warm-hearted man'.[22]

Mme Heger's elder daughters assisted her at the pensionnat in the 1860s until her retirement some time before 1869, and continued to run the school (transferred to the avenue Louise) after their mother's death until its closure in 1894. M. Heger retired from teaching in about 1882. His obituary in *L'Indépendence Belge* on 9 May 1896 praised his passionate belief in the importance of education, and the dynamism and authority of his teaching. He had a profound effect on Charlotte Brontë's life and writing. She endowed M. Paul Emanuel in *Villette* with M. Heger's swarthy features, whirlwind energy, fiery temper, high intelligence, and dramatic eloquence.[23]

Ellen Nussey, 20 April 1817–26 November 1897

Ellen Nussey, Charlotte Brontë's closest friend for twenty-four years, was the twelfth child of John Nussey (1760–1826), a cloth merchant of Birstall Smithies in Yorkshire, and his wife, née Ellen Wade (*c.*1771–1857). Four of John Nussey's older children were born in his uncle Richard Walker's pleasant park-surrounded house called Rydings—remembered by Charlotte when she imagined Thornfield in *Jane*

[21] See CH 24.10.1844 n. 8.

[22] Copy MS, Brown University MS 640.

[23] Different facets of M. Heger's life and character are dealt with in *Life* chs. 11 and 12, Gérin *CB* chs. 13–15, Enid L. Duthie, *The Foreign Vision of Charlotte Brontë* (1975), chs. 2 and 3, and Fraser *CB* chs. 9–11. See also pp. 11–17, 33–4 in the present volume.

Eyre. Ellen was born in a house in Smithies Moor Lane, but after John Nussey's death his wife and family moved back into Rydings. Ellen's eldest brother John (1794–1862) was already living in London, where he had been appointed Royal Apothecary to George IV. He later shared his general practice with his brother William (1807–38). Their brother Joshua (1798–1871) was also in London as Curate of St Margaret's and St John's, Westminster; he later moved to Batheaston near Bath, and then to Oundle. Ellen paid long visits to these relatives in the 1830s.

In summer 1836 Ellen's mother, with her younger daughters and sons, moved to Brookroyd in Birstall, a smaller house than Rydings. As a child Ellen first attended a small local school, then the Gomersal Moravian Ladies' Academy, and finally from 25 January 1831 Margaret Wooler's school at Roe Head, where she first met Charlotte Brontë. The development of their friendship until 1847 is described in the Introduction.

Charlotte did not reveal the secret of the 'Bells' ' authorship (though Ellen may have guessed it) until Ellen stayed at the parsonage in December 1848, after the death of Emily Brontë on 19 December. On 9 January 1849 Ellen was given copies of the sisters' four novels to take home with her. She accompanied Charlotte and Anne on Anne's last journey to Scarborough in May 1849; she tended the dying Anne, and helped to make her funeral arrangements. Her presence comforted Charlotte in the following weeks, when she continued to write *Shirley*, transforming reality into the happy ending of the 'Valley of the Shadow of Death'. Ellen took a special interest in this novel, and came to see Caroline as a portrait of herself.

In the 1850s Charlotte's life took on new dimensions when she was courted as a celebrity and introduced to the 'lions' of London society; but Ellen remained her confidante and solace. Charlotte wrote to W. S. Williams on 3 January 1850:

> Just now I am enjoying the treat of my friend Ellen's society and she makes me indolent and negligent—I am too busy talking to her all day to do anything else . . . When I first saw Ellen I did not care for her—we were schoolfellows—in the course of time we learnt each others faults and good points—we were contrasts—still we suited—affection was first a germ, then a sapling—then a strong tree: now, no new friend, however lofty or profound in intellect—not even Miss Martineau herself could be to me what Ellen is, yet she is no more than a conscientious, observant, calm, well-bred Yorkshire girl. She is without romance—if she attempts to read poetry—or poetic prose aloud—I am irritated and deprive her of her book—if she talks of it I stop my ears—but she is good—she is true—she is faithful and I love her.

Charlotte's preoccupation with Arthur Nicholls during the months before her engagement in April 1854 led to an estrangement from Ellen, who was probably jealous of this new and absorbing attachment. The breach was healed by March 1854, but there was a slight constraint in their relationship after Charlotte's marriage, in spite of Charlotte's renewed affection.

After her friend's death in March 1855 Ellen's loyalty to the memory of an idealized Charlotte became her leading principle for the rest of her life. Its consequences are described in the History of the Letters.

Her diaries for 1844 and 1849, and her 'Reminiscences' give an attractive picture of her personality during the years of her friendship with Charlotte. She was sociable, affectionate, pious, devoted to her family and friends. Her outward life of domestic cares, social visits, church-going, and charity continued largely unchanged after Charlotte's death, though she was increasingly sought out by Brontë enthusiasts and must have spent hours talking or writing to them. After her mother's death in 1857 Ellen and her sisters, Mercy Nussey and the widowed Ann Clapham, moved from Brookroyd to a dwelling in part of the old Gomersal Cloth Hall, and then in 1860 to Laneside in Church Lane, Gomersal. Following the death of Mrs Clapham in 1878, Mercy was taken to a nursing-home in York, while Ellen, after a brief spell at Ingwell House in Birstall, moved to rather chilly quarters in the hamlet of Fieldhead. In 1892 she returned to Ingwell House, and her last home was Moor Lane House in Gomersal, where she died.

Ellen's close ties with her family meant that she took to heart a number of family tragedies; her later life was marred by her anxiety and a degree of paranoia about her treasured letters from Charlotte; and she was worried by dilatory landlords, allegedly unreliable servants, and other domestic problems. But the Ellen of old who had been Charlotte's loved companion was still discernible in her capacity for affection and in a certain charm of manner to her favoured guests. William Scruton, who visited her in 1885, wrote of her 'sweet expression which, when brought into full play by an animated conversation or a humorous story, made her all the more pleasing and attractive . . . Miss Nussey was a good conversationalist, and pleasant indeed was her chat about new books and their authors'.[24] He discovered that she was a good but not a bigoted Churchwoman, and a sound Tory who could nevertheless recognize the ability of some Liberal politicians.

Mary Taylor, 26 February 1817–1 March 1893
Martha Taylor, 1819–12 October 1842

Mary and Martha Taylor were the daughters of a cloth manufacturer, Joshua Taylor (1766–1840) of the Red House, Gomersal. His contacts with foreign buyers and journeys abroad had made him more cosmopolitan than his neighbours, and he was the original of the 'French-speaking Yorkshire gentleman' Mr Yorke in *Shirley*. The two girls met Charlotte Brontë in 1831 as fellow-pupils

[24] William Scruton, 'Reminiscences of the late Miss Ellen Nussey', *BST* l. 8. 23–42. For a more detailed study, see Barbara Whitehead, *Charlotte Brontë and her 'Dearest Nell'* (Otley, 1993).

at Roe Head school, and thought her plain, shy, nervous, and oddly dressed. Mary by contrast was pretty and energetic, clever and intolerant, hard-working but 'quietly rebellious' if she chose not to obey instructions, whereas Martha was piquant rather than pretty, and as Ellen Nussey recalled, 'full of change and variety, rudely outspoken, lively, and original', befitting her nickname of 'Miss Boisterous'. Both girls had adopted the furious radical and republican principles of their father. Mary was the 'fine, generous' and intellectual Rose Yorke of *Shirley*, Martha the less profound but more attractive Jessy. Charlotte delighted in both sisters, and Branwell Brontë was attracted to Mary 'till he began to suspect that she cared more for him and then instantly conceived a sort of contempt for her'.[25] Because she bitterly regretted this too frank revelation of her feelings and deeply resented the response to it Mary became more defiantly insistent on women's right to an independent and self-supporting life.

After their father died on 28 December 1840 Mary travelled on the Continent for a time with her brother John, Martha was sent to an expensive school at the Château de Koekelberg just outside Brussels, and their youngest brother Waring emigrated to New Zealand on 7 November 1841. None of the Taylor children liked their disagreeable mother, the dour and dogmatic 'Mrs Yorke' of *Shirley*, and only the eldest, Joshua, stayed with her for some years. When Mary returned to visit Yorkshire, she stayed with her brothers Joseph and John at their cottage next to Hunsworth Mill.

Mary actively encouraged Charlotte to go abroad in search of education and the means of attaining an independent career. Her lively mind and iconoclastic temperament are shown in the letters she wrote to Ellen Nussey in 1842 from Koekelberg, where she had joined her sister. Charlotte and Emily Bronte's visits there relieved their feelings of isolation in Brussels, and they were greatly shocked and distressed by Martha's death from cholera on 12 October in that year.

By 1843 Mary's 'resolute and intrepid proceedings' had taken her to Hagen in Germany to teach 'nice dull' German boys and to have piano lessons from Friedrich Halle, the father of Sir Charles Hallé. Her amusing account of a fiery and argumentative session with Halle is printed by Joan Stevens as letter 12 in her invaluable collection of material about the Taylors, *Mary Taylor, Friend of Charlotte Brontë; Letters from New Zealand and Elsewhere* (Oxford, 1972).

After a brief visit to England and a happy reunion with Charlotte and Ellen in May 1844 Mary returned to Germany. But her previous contentment gave way to loneliness and disillusion, and she resolved to follow her brother Waring to New Zealand. She left England in March 1845 and arrived in Wellington on 24 July. There she helped her brother to run his general store in Herbert Street, offered 'Instructions on the Piano Forte', and built a five-roomed house with a shop which she at first let and later lived in with her

[25] EN 20.11.40.

cousin Ellen Taylor. She threw herself energetically into the work of making her business prosper, bought a cow, began writing a novel, longed to 'hallack' about the country, and grumbled about the ignorance of middle-class women: 'you are thrown entirely on the men for conversation.'[26]

After Ellen Taylor's death in December 1851 Mary carried on alone. She kept in touch with Ellen Nussey and Charlotte, found *Shirley* more interesting than *Jane Eyre*, and commented 'What a little lump of perfection you've made me!' She was angered by what she called Charlotte's 'sacrifices' to Mr Brontë's wishes, and after Charlotte's death wrote two long letters of recollection of her which were incorporated into the *Life*.[27] In 1859 Mary invested £400 in land in Wellington before leaving it on 20 May, probably for the 'hallacking' around the country that she had promised herself.

On her return to Yorkshire in 1860 she lived in Gomersal and wrote articles on 'The First Duty of Women', published as a series in the *Victoria Magazine* between 1865 and 1870, and as a book in 1870. She argued that women should feel neither indignity nor hardship in working for their living; they should not let themselves be 'driven into matrimony'. In 1875 she contributed to *Swiss Notes by Five Ladies*, an account of an expedition in Switzerland by herself and four young women with Mary as 'the originator, *chaperone*, and moving spirit'. Her novel, *Miss Miles: A Tale of Yorkshire Life Sixty Years Ago* was first published in London in 1890. It portrays the contrasting lives of four women, each in their way struggling against the limitations imposed upon them by convention. Though the novel hardly holds together as a narrative sequence, it is redeemed by its sympathetic insight and its portrayal of the independent, talented, and lively Sarah Miles.

Mary destroyed all but one of Charlotte's letters to her, but later she wished she had kept them. The surviving letter, MT 4.9.1848, Charlotte's graphic account of her whirlwind visit to London with Anne in July 1848, makes one regret all the more the loss of other letters to this unconventional, intelligent friend.

William Smith Williams, 1800–75

At 17 W. S. Williams became an apprentice to the publishers Taylor and Hessey, through whom he met and was kindly regarded by Leigh Hunt, William Hazlitt, and Keats. He felt the 'last kind pressure' of the poet's hand as Keats began his last journey in September 1820.[28] He married in 1825 and at about the same time opened a bookshop. After this closed in 1827 through lack of capital, Williams became a somewhat inefficient book-keeper to the

[26] Letter to CB June–July 1848, *Stevens* letter 16.
[27] See *Stevens* appendix B.
[28] Edmund Blunden, *Keats's Publisher* (1936), 79, 244–5.

lithographic printers, Hullmandel and Walter. He wrote reviews and essays on literary and theatrical topics for the *Spectator*, the *Athenaeum*, and other journals.

In 1845, at George Smith's invitation, he took up the more congenial post of reader to Smith, Elder. Smith found him 'loyal, diligent, of shrewd literary judgment, and pleasant manners'. His sympathetic criticism and kindly courtesy earned him the regard of many distinguished writers, including Charlotte Brontë, who was heartened by his discriminating response to *The Professor* in July 1847. Though her short novel was refused, the firm expressed interest in a three-volume work, and it was Williams who warmly recommended *Jane Eyre* for publication (see the Introduction). Charlotte and Anne Brontë first met Mr Williams in London in July 1848—a 'pale, mild, stooping man' who kindly came early on the Sunday morning to take them to church: 'he was so quiet but so sincere in his attentions—one could not but have a most friendly leaning towards him—he has a nervous hesitation in speech and a difficulty in finding appropriate language in which to express himself—which throws him into the background in conversation—but I had been his correspondent—and therefore knew with what intelligence he could write—so that I was not in danger of underrating him.'[29]

Williams became one of Charlotte's most valued correspondents. She shared with him her opinions on the books she read, many of them sent to her as gifts or loans by the firm. Some of her most poignant letters on the deaths of Branwell, Emily, and Anne were written to Mr Williams, and there is a long, sincere, delicately sympathetic letter from him after the death of Emily. Charlotte in turn sympathized with his anxiety when his wife was ill, took a friendly interest in his efforts to establish his large family in self-supporting careers,[30] exerted herself to provide an introduction to Mrs Gaskell for one of his sons in November 1851, and was delighted when Mrs Gaskell was agreeably impressed by 'Young Mr. Williams'.[31]

Their informal, confidential correspondence seems to have ended in 1853, with a brief, restrained note from Charlotte thanking him for the books she is returning, but refusing further loans.[32] It is likely that he wrote to her after this when she became engaged to Mr Nicholls in April 1854, for his name is in the list of friends to whom wedding cards were to be sent in June. Their relationship was undoubtedly affected by the coolness between Charlotte and George Smith in 1853–4.[33]

Mr Williams remained on friendly terms with other authors whose work was published by Smith, Elder, especially with Thackeray, Ruskin, and G. H. Lewes. Sir Sidney Lee wrote of him:

[29] CB to M. Taylor 4.9.1848; MS Rylands.
[30] See e.g. WSW 3.7.1849, W & S 452.
[31] Vol. iii, ECG 6.2.1852; MS Rylands.
[32] Vol. iii, WSW 6.12.1853; W & S 874.
[33] See Biographical Note on Smith in Vol. ii.

During his association with Smith he did no independent literary work beyond helping to prepare for the firm, in 1861, a 'Selection from the Writings of John Ruskin.' He was from youth a warm admirer of Ruskin, sharing especially his enthusiasm for Turner. Williams retired from Smith, Elder & Co.'s business in February, 1875, and died six months later, aged 75, at his residence at Twickenham (August 21). His eldest daughter was the wife of Mr. Lowes Dickinson, the well-known portrait painter; and his youngest daughter Miss Anna Williams [1845–1924], achieved distinction as a singer.[34]

Margaret Wooler, 10 June 1792–3 June 1885

Margaret Wooler was the eldest of eleven children in the family of Robert Wooler (1770–1838) and his wife Sarah Maud, née Upton. Her father was a maltster, corn miller, and farmer at Rouse Mill, between Batley and Dewsbury in Yorkshire. He owned other property and was evidently prosperous, for his children were well educated. His six daughters all taught either in Margaret Wooler's school or in private families, and two of his sons, William and Thomas, became general practitioners.

Margaret Wooler's nephew, Sir Thomas Clifford Allbutt, described her as 'a woman of unusual brains and accomplishments, especially a fine Italian scholar . . . a keen-witted, ironical, and very independent Yorkshire woman'.[35] She was kind and tactful in her handling of the sensitive, clever, but not conventionally accomplished Charlotte Brontë, her pupil from 17 January 1831 until May 1832. She had established her school at Roe Head, Mirfield, in 1830, and rarely took more than eight or nine pupils at the same time. Her principal assistant was her sister Eliza, and her sisters Katherine, Susannah, and Marianne gave occasional help. Her 'remarkable knack' of making her pupils 'feel interested in whatever they had to learn' inspired them with a healthy desire for knowledge, and helped them to 'think, to analyse, to reject, to appreciate . . . On Saturday half-holidays they went long scrambling walks'. Charlotte remembered, and used in *Shirley*, the tales Miss Wooler 'related during these long walks . . . [of] times when watchers or wakeners in the night heard the distant word of command, and the measured tramp of thousands of sad desperate men receiving a surreptitious military training'.[36]

On 6 July 1835 Charlotte told Ellen Nussey that she had accepted Miss Wooler's invitation to become a teacher at her old school. Although Charlotte was often irritated by the chore of teaching stupid 'dolts', she loved and respected Miss Wooler, did not complain of her regime, and was trusted by her. On the one occasion when Charlotte quarrelled with her for

[34] L. Huxley, *The House of Smith, Elder* (1923), 56.

[35] Sir Humphry Davy Rolleston, *The Right Honourable Sir Thomas Clifford Allbutt: A Memoir* (1929), 3.

[36] *Life* i. 113–14.

her failure to realize the seriousness of Anne Brontë's illness at the school in December 1837, Miss Wooler's eventual response showed dignity and good feeling.[37] Charlotte returned to teach at Roe Head, and then at Heald's House, Dewsbury Moor, to which Miss Wooler moved her school early in 1838. At Christmas 1838, when Charlotte left, Margaret Wooler handed over its management to her sister Eliza, though she remained in the house.

In 1840 Charlotte tried but failed to get more pupils for the school, which was 'in a consumptive state of health'.[38] Towards the end of 1841 she provisionally accepted Miss Wooler's proposal for her to take over the school and 'try and work it up to its former state of prosperity'.[39] But, longing to increase her attainments and 'become something better than' she was, she decided instead to go with Emily to Mme Heger's school in Brussels.

Miss Wooler and her sister closed their school at the end of 1841, but Charlotte retained her friendship, wrote 'respectfully and affectionately' to her, and welcomed her visits to the Haworth parsonage. Miss Wooler moved away from the Dewsbury area for a time. In the spring of 1849 she offered the hospitality of her house in the North Bay at Scarborough to the desperately ill Anne Brontë, but for Anne's sake Charlotte chose warmer lodgings in the South Bay. Miss Wooler probably attended Anne's funeral in Scarborough on 30 May 1849.

By 1853 Miss Wooler had moved to Hornsea further down the coast, where Charlotte spent a 'happy and a pleasant week' with her in October of that year.[40] In June 1854 she was one of the few friends invited to Charlotte's wedding; it was hastily arranged that she should give Charlotte away, when Mr Brontë at the last minute decided not to go to the church. In December 1854 Charlotte assured her that all at the parsonage would be glad to see her if she cared to visit, but before any visit could take place Charlotte became increasingly ill in the few months before her death in March 1855.

Margaret Wooler had moved back to the West Riding by 1867, when she was living in a separate wing at West House, Dewsbury, the home of her brother Dr William Moore Wooler. After his death in 1873 she lived with her sisters Katherine and Eliza in Gomersal. Unlike the rather narrow-minded Katherine, Margaret Wooler could understand and appreciate unconventional women like Mary Taylor, and she admired Charlotte's novels, with some reservations on 'certain phrases, exclamations &c'. Charlotte valued her frankness, and did not fear that she might think *Jane Eyre* coarse.[41]

[37] EN 4.1.1838.
[38] EN 12.11.1840.
[39] *Life* i. 236.
[40] Vol. iii, MW 18.10.1853.
[41] Vol. ii, MW 14.2.1850.

After Charlotte's death Margaret Wooler chose the letters she lent to Mrs Gaskell carefully, burnt one confidential letter which might have hurt the feelings of Mr Nicholls, and cut off parts of other letters. Happily, most of the manuscripts survive in the fine collection of thirty-three holograph MSS given by Sir Clifford Allbutt to the Fitzwilliam Museum in Cambridge.

The Letters,
1829–1847

To the Revd Patrick Brontë, 23 September 1829

Parsonage House, Crosstone.[1]

My Dear Papa,

At Aunts, request[2] I write these lines to inform you that "if all be well" we shall be at home on Friday by dinner time, when we hope ˋtoˊ find you in good health—On account of the bad weather we have not been out much, but notwithstanding we have spent our time very pleasantly, between reading, working,[3] and learning our lessons, which Uncle Fenell[4] has been so kind as to teach us every day, Branwell has taken two sketches from nature, & Emily Anne[5] & myself have likewise each of us drawn a piece from some views of the lakes which Mr Fenell brought with him from Westmoreland,[6] the whole of these he intends keeping—Mr Fenell is sorry he cannot accompany us to Howarth on Friday for want of room, but hopes to have the pleasure of seeing you soon, all unite in sending their kind love with your

Affectionate Daughter, Charlotte Bronte

MS BPM Bon 159. W & S 16.
Address (integral): The Revd. P Bronte, | Howarth, | nr Bradford.
PM: (i) [HA]LIFAX | 23 SE | 1829. (ii) KEIGHLEY
Annotation by PB: 'Charlotte's first letter—'. Either Miss Branwell, or perhaps PB at a later date, altered Charlotte's punctuation after 'Aunts', 'every day' and 'soon', but ignored her spelling errors.

1. Cross Stone, near Todmorden, on the border between Lancs. and Yorks. The Brontë children and their Aunt Elizabeth Branwell were staying with the Revd John Fennell, the children's great uncle. Mr Fennell's wife Jane had died on 26 May 1829.
2. Elizabeth Branwell (1776–1842) had been housekeeping for the Brontë family since the death of her sister Maria (1783–1821), Mr Brontë's wife. See the Biographical Notes on Miss Branwell and Mr Brontë.
3. Needlework.
4. The Revd John Fennell (1762–1841), born at Madeley in Shropshire, and godson of the Revd John Fletcher, the friend of John Wesley. He moved to Penzance as a young man, was a Methodist class-leader there, and married Jane Branwell (aunt of Elizabeth and Maria) in Dec. 1790 at Madron in Cornwall. In 1809 he became the headmaster of a boarding-school at Wellington in Shropshire, where Patrick Brontë had just become a curate to the Revd John Eyton. On 25 Sept. 1811 Mr Fennell was appointed the first governor and 'Commercial and Mathematical Master' of a new school for the sons of Methodist ministers, Woodhouse Grove school at Rawdon, near Leeds, where Patrick was to meet his future wife, Maria. When Mr Fennell became an Anglican he left Woodhouse Grove (in Sept. 1813), and became a curate to the Vicar of Bradford, the Revd John Crosse, and was nominated as the new incumbent of Cross Stone in Apr. 1819. See F. C. Pritchard, *The Story of Woodhouse Grove School* (Bradford, 1978) esp. chs. 1 and 2.
5. See the Biographical Notes.
6. Perhaps Mr Fennell had spent some time in the Lake District after his bereavement earlier in the year. A finely detailed pencil-drawing of Cockermouth by CB (BPM HAOBP: C33) copied from an engraving was probably based on the kind of 'views' referred to here. See Jane Sellars, 'Art and the Artist as Heroine in the Novels of Charlotte, Emily and Anne Brontë', *BST* 20. 2. 57–76, and Christine Alexander, 'Art and Artists in Charlotte Brontë's Juvenilia', *BST* 20. 4. 177–204.

Revd Patrick Brontë to Mrs Franks,[1] *28 April 1831*

Haworth,
Near Bradford,
Yorkshire—

Dear Madam,

Having heard of your kind attention to Charlotte;[2] I have taken the liberty of writing to thank both Mr. Franks[3] and you, for this—and to assure you, that we have not forgotten, in our little Family, your other various acts of kindness. Charlotte, would be highly gratified. She still remembered, having seen you at Kipping, and has often heard us speak of you, whilst we took a retrospective view of Good Old Times. I have just received a letter, from our Mutual Friend, Miss Outhwaite[4]—which has given me some uneasiness. It appears, that Some, whose opinions, I highly value, greatly misunderstand my motives, in being an advocate for temperate reform, both in Church and State, I am, in all respects, <u>now</u>, what I <u>was</u>, when, I lived, in Thornton,—in regard to all political considerations. A warmer, or truer friend—to Church, and state, does not breathe the vital air.[5] But after many years, mature deliberation, I am fully convinced, that, unless, the <u>real</u> friends of our excellent Institutions, come forward, and advocate the cause of Temperate reform[6]—The inveterate enemies—will avail themselves of the opportunity, which this circumstance would give them, and will work on the popular feeling,—already but too much excited—so as to cause, in all probability, general insurrectionary movements, and bring about a revolution—We see, what has been lately done in France[7]—We, know, that the Duke of Wellington's declaration, against reform,[8] was the principal cause, of the removal, of him, & the other Ministers, from power—And there is now, another instance before our eyes, of the impolicy of this perverseness. The Antireformers, have imprudently thrown the Ministers into a minority, and consequently Parliament is dissolved by the King in person, and in all probability, another parliament will soon be returned, which may be less particular than the other, and perhaps go too far in the way of reformation—Both, then, because, I think moderate, or temperate reform, is wanted—and that this would satisfy all wise & reasonable people, and weaken the hands of our real enemies, & preserve the church and state from ruin—I am an advocate for the Bill, which has been just thrown out of Parli[a]ment—It is with me, merely an affair of conscience and Judgment, and sooner than violate the dictates of either of these, I would run the hazard of poverty, imprisonment, and death. My friends—or some of them, at least, may differ from me, as to the <u>line of conduct</u> which ought to be followed—but our <u>motives</u>, and our <u>good wishes,</u> towards, Church, and state, are the same—

But to come nearer home—I have for nearly a year past, been in but a very delicate state of health. I had an inflammation in my lungs, last summer—and was in immediate, and great danger, for several weeks—for the six months, last past, I have been weak in body, and my spirits have often been low—I was for about a month, unable to take the Church Duty.[9] I now perform it—though, with considerable difficulty. I am, certainly, a little better, yet, I fear, I shall never fully recover—I sometimes, think, that I shall fall into a decline. But, I am in the Lord's hands, and hope that he will at the last, give me a happy issue, out of all my troubles, and take me forever, into his heavenly kingdom. We have been much concerned, to hear from time, to time, that you have not been quite so strong as usual—It is our earnest wish and prayer, that the Lord, may support and comfort you, and spare you, long, and in mercy, to your Husband, and your children. I have only been once, at Kipping, since I \`last' saw you, and Mrs Firth,[10] there—The Family were kind—to me, but I missed my old Friends and could not feel comfortable, and I s[oo]n departed, intending, never to call again—Miss Branwell,[11] still continues with me, and kindly superintends my little family, and they all join with me, in the kindest, and most respectful regards. When, you, write to, or see Mrs. Firth, be so kind as to remember us all to her in the most respectful, and affectionate manner. Be so good, also, as to thank Mr. Franks, in our name, for his kind attention to Charlotte, and believe me to be, <very respectfully>, Dear Madam,

Very respectfully, And truly, Your's,

P. Brontë.

MS BPM BS 182. W & S 17.
Address (integral): Mrs. Franks, Vicarage, Huddersfield.
PM: (i) BRADFORD YORKS | AP 29 | 1831 (ii) Bradford Yor[ks] | Py Post[12]

1. Elizabeth Franks, née Firth (1797–1837), the daughter of Dr John Scholefield Firth (1757–1820) of Kipping House, Thornton, by his first wife Elizabeth Holt (1758–1814). Elizabeth Firth and her father had been on friendly terms with the Brontës during Mr Brontë's curacy at Thornton from 1815 to 1820, and were the godparents of his second daughter Elizabeth (1815–25). Elizabeth was also Anne Brontë's godmother, and perhaps stood proxy for Charlotte Branwell at CB's baptism. Elizabeth's daughter Mrs Moore Smith wrote: 'My mother Elizth. Firth stood sponsor for C. B. being then 19 years of age.' (MS notes, Sheffield University Library.) Elizabeth's father and stepmother were Branwell Brontë's godparents.
2. Mrs Franks had sent the parcel described in the following letter of thanks from CB.
3. The Revd James Clarke Franks, MA, BD (1793–1867), Vicar of Huddersfield from 1823 to 1840, who had married Elizabeth Firth on 21 Sept. 1824. As a scholar at Trinity College Cambridge he had won the Hulsean Prize in 1813, and the Norrisian Prize for 4 years running from 1814. He had been chaplain of Trinity in 1819 and Select Preacher from 1819 to 1820. He was the author of a prize essay and several other published theological works. A respected and active vicar of Huddersfield, he had recently organized the rebuilding of St Peter's Church in an ornate Gothic style, the work being completed by 1830.
4. Frances Outhwaite (1796–1849), daughter of Dr Thomas Outhwaite of Bradford and sister of Dr John Outhwaite (1792–1868). She was a former schoolfellow and close friend of Mrs Franks, had been well known to the Brontës at Thornton, and was one of Anne Brontë's godmothers.
5. Patrick Brontë was a Tory and a 'moderate' churchman on the evangelical wing of the Church

of England. The wealthy Dr John Outhwaite was a Tory who scorned deviations from the 'good old faith'. (Obituary, *Bradford Observer* 20.2.1868.)

6. After the Whig Lord John Russell's bill for the reform of the Parliamentary franchise had been defeated by a narrow majority of 299 to 291 on its third reading on 19 Apr. 1831, Parliament was dissolved and a general election called for 6 May.
7. The French Revolution of 1830 had been precipitated by a series of ordinances issued on 25 July by the Bourbon King Charles X which practically destroyed the last vestiges of constitutional government. After violent insurrection in Paris, Charles abdicated and the crown was offered to the more cautious and liberal Louis Philippe.
8. In Nov. 1830.
9. The Revd Thomas P. Plummer officiated at funerals, baptisms, and the sole marriage at Haworth between 20 June and 10 July 1830.
10. Anne Firth, née Greame (?1761–1846), Dr Firth's second wife, whom he married on 6 Sept. 1815.
11. Elizabeth Branwell. See the previous letter, n. 2.
12. This 'penny post' was a cheap local post operated by many large towns before the implementation of the country-wide pre-paid penny post in 1840. By the mid-1830s there were 356 such local posts in England and Wales. See M. J. Daunton, *Royal Mail: The Post Office Since 1840* (1985), 5. For other postage rates see EN 21.7.1832 n. 13.

To Mrs Franks,[1] *[Early May 1831]*

Roe-Head.[2]

Dear Madam

I beg to acknowledge the receipt of the parcel, which arrived the other day from Huddersfield and to thank yourself for the frock and muslin and Miss Outhwaite[3] for the shawl which she has so kindly sent me. My chilblains are quite well I am sorry I was out when Mr Atkinson[4] called the other day. Pray give my love to Mrs Firth[5] and present my thanks to her for her welcome note. The Miss Woolers[6] desire their kind respects to you; they 'are' much obliged to Mr Franks for the loan of "Keith on the prophecies"[7] with which they were greatly pleased. Accept dear Madam my sincere thanks for all the kindness you have shown me, and permit me to subscribe myself

Yours gratefully & affectionately
C Brontë

MS BPM B.S. 38. W & S 18.
Address (integral): Mrs Franks | Vicarage | Huddersfield
PM: not in MS.
Annotation in unknown hand: Has Mr Te— sent the Parcel to [i.w.]

1. See previous letter and n. 1.
2. Roe Head, Mirfield, was an 18th-cent. house to the west of the old turnpike road from Bradford to Huddersfield. It had been rebuilt in 1740 for a local family of coal-owners, the Marriotts, and since 1830 had housed a girls' boarding-school run by Miss Margaret Wooler and three of her sisters. CB had arrived there on 17 Jan. 1831. A small establishment with no more than 10 pupils, it had probably been recommended to Mr Brontë by CB's godparents, the Atkinsons, who lived at Green House, Mirfield. They were said by W. W. Yates to have borne the expenses of

CB's first stay at Roe Head as a pupil (*The Father of the Brontës* (1897), 100) but there is no firm evidence for this. For the house and the district, see H. N. Pobjoy, *A History of Mirfield* (Driffield, 1969). The building survives in an altered and extended form.

3. See previous letter, n. 4. Miss Outhwaite's kindness to the Brontë family had also been shown in visits to Haworth during the illness of Mrs Brontë. The gifts may have been for CB's 15th birthday on 21 Apr.
4. The Revd Thomas Atkinson, MA (1780–1870), a graduate of Magdalene College Cambridge who in 1815 had exchanged livings with PB in order to be nearer Frances Walker of Lascelles Hall near Huddersfield, whom he married on 23 Dec. 1817. He had been perpetual curate at Thornton until May 1815, when he transferred to Mr Brontë's former parish of Hartshead-cum-Clifton. The Atkinsons moved to the Green House, Mirfield, on their marriage, but Mr Atkinson continued as perpetual curate of Hartshead until 1866.
5. See previous letter, n. 10.
6. For Margaret Wooler (1792–1885) who later became a respected friend of CB, see the Biographical Notes. Her sister Katherine Harriet Wooler (3.8.1796–20.11.1884) is said to have been highly intelligent but less amiable than Margaret Wooler. She was 'partner in the school' according to EN's letter to Shorter of 22 Apr. 1896 (Brotherton MS), and EN's correspondent the Revd A. Wilkes had heard that she 'taught French and Mrs Carter drawing'. (Letter of 2 Nov. 1878, W & S 1030.) Susan or Susanna Wooler (1800–72) had married the Revd Edward Nicholl Carter, the curate of Mirfield Parish Church, on 30.12.1830. She helped her sisters at Roe Head (mainly in the teaching of drawing) until the birth of her first child, a son, in Dec. 1832. Mary Anne Wooler (28.10.1801–28.5.1843), usually known as Marianne, was also a teacher at Roe Head for a time. She became the first wife of the Revd Thomas Allbutt on 9 July 1835, in which year he became the Vicar of Dewsbury. She was the mother of Marianne Maria (1840–1906) and of the distinguished physician Sir Thomas Clifford Allbutt (1836–1925). Eliza Wooler (14.6.1808–15.9.1884) seemed to her great-nephew the Revd M. W. Blakeley rather 'austere and proper', but he later realized her kindness. (Max Blakeley, 'Memories of Margaret Wooler and her Sisters', *BST* 12. 62. 113–14.) She gave up teaching for a time, probably in 1837, to look after her ailing father who died on 20 Apr. 1838. At Christmas 1838 Eliza took over the school, which was then at Heald's House Dewsbury, but it declined and was relinquished in 1841. The parents of the Wooler sisters, who were members of a very large family, were Robert Wooler (1770–1838) maltster, corn miller, and farmer of Rouse Mill, Batley, and Sarah Maud, née Upton (1767–1841).
7. Either *Sketch of the Evidence from Prophecy* (Edinburgh, 1823) or *Evidence of the Truth of the Christian Religion derived from the Literal Fulfilment of Prophecy* (Edinburgh, 1828), both by the Revd Alexander Keith (1791–1880), pastor of St Cyrus, Kincardineshire, 1816–40.

To Ellen Nussey,[1] *11 May 1831*

Roe-Head.

Dear Ellen

I take advantage of the earliest opportunity to thank you for the letter you favoured me with last week and to apologize for having so long neglected to write to you, indeed I believe this will be the first letter or note I have ever addressed to you. I am extremely obliged to your Sister[2] for her kind invitation and I assure you that I should very much have liked to hear Mr Murray's[3] lectures on Galvanism[4] as they \would/ doubtless have been both amusing,[5] and instructive. But we are often compelled "to bend our inclinations to our duty" (as Miss Wooler[6] observed the other day) and since there [are] so many holidays this half-year it would have appeared almost unreasonable to ask for an extra holiday; besides we should perhaps have got behind-hand with our lessons so that, everything considered it is perhaps as well that circumstances have deprived us of this pleasure

Believe me to remain
Your affect. friend
C Brontë

MS BPM B.S. 39. W & S 20 as 'May 31st, 1831', from Haworth.
Address (integral): Miss E Nussey | Roe-Head
PM: none.
Annotation by EN: C's first letter written at School | May 11th 31

1. For Ellen Nussey, CB's intimate friend and principal correspondent, see the Biographical Notes. In the *Hatfield* copy of *Nussey* Ellen added a note: 'Charlotte Brontë's first letter to her friend E. written as a school exercise.'
2. Either Ann Nussey (10.9.1795–24.4.1878) EN's eldest sister, or Mercy Mary Nussey (14.4.1801–24.9.1886). Both sisters were quite well-educated, and Ann was to prove herself a capable housekeeper for the family. Mercy had been for a time a Moravian sister at Fairfield near Manchester, and had some experience of teaching. Both were involved with the Gomersal Moravian community. Poems 'Translated from the German' by ?MN, possibly Mercy Nussey, can be found in a collection of Nussey papers among the Hellewell and Sutton Deeds, Bundle 117, WYAS Leeds. A third sister, Sarah Walker Nussey (1809–43) was an invalid, possibly disabled in some way. See *Whitehead* 31–3.
3. Probably John Murray (?1786–1851), FLS, FSA, FGS, FHS, a scientific writer who became well known for his lectures and demonstrations at mechanics' institutes. A 'John Murray F.S.A.' was a member of the Keighley Mechanics' Institute: see *BST* 11. 40. 345. H. A. Cadman mentions lectures on electricity, and the use of an 'electro-magnetic machine' in *Gomersal Past and Present* (Leeds, 1930), 32–5.
4. Electricity developed by chemical action; also the use of this therapeutically, esp. in the alleviation of pain: from Luigi Galvani, 1737–98. In galvanic therapy electrodes were applied to the body, through which the electric current passed. Cf. Anne Orford to Mrs Hering, from Shillingstone, 4 May 1818: 'Mrs. Andree . . . has lately been Galvanised, and Electrified, every thing is tried to restore her to health, but I fear she will never be so well as she has been.' (Letter in private hands.)
5. Possibly in the sense of 'interesting' rather than positively entertaining. Anne Brontë uses the word in the archaic sense of 'beguiling' or 'deceiving' in *Tenant* (1848), ch. 22.
6. Margaret Wooler. Her younger sisters would be referred to as 'Miss Eliza', etc.

To Ellen Nussey, 13 January 1832

Haworth

Dear Ellen

The receipt of your letter gave me an agreeable surprise, for notwithstanding your faithful promises you must excuse me if I say that I had little confidence in their fulfilment, knowing that when School girls once get home[1] they willingly abandon every recollection which tends to remind them of school & indeed they find such an infinite variety of circumstances to engage their attention and employ their leisure hours that they are easily persuaded that they have "no time" to fulfil promises made at school it gave me great pleasure however to find that you and Miss *Taylor[2] are exceptions to the general rule. I was sorry to hear that your Mother[3] & Brother[4] had been ill and likewise that the Miss *Taylors[5] had suffered from bad colds The Cholera[6] still seems slowly advancing but let us yet hope knowing that all things are under the Guidance of a merciful providence. England has hitherto been highly favoured for the disease has neither raged with the astounding violence nor extended itself with the frightful rapidity which marked its' progress in many of the continental countries, I was glad to hear that Mr *Taylor[7] was pleased with Miss Mary's drawings. Tell her I hope she will derive benefit from the perusal of Cobbett's lucubrations[8] but I beg she will on no account burden her Memory with passages to be repeated for my edification lest I should not justly appreciate either her kindness or their merit since that worthy personage & his principles whether private or political are no great favourites of mine Remember 'me' to your Sisters & Mother give my best love to Dear Polly and little Miss Boisterous[9] and accept the same Dearest Ellen

From your affectionate friend
Charlotte Brontë

MS Harvard r.f. MS Eng. 35F. W & S 21.
Address (integral): Miss E. Nussey | Rydings | Birstal | near Leeds
PM: (i) BR[AD]FORD YORKS | JA ?13 | 1832 (ii) *Bradford Yorks* | *Penny Post*
Annotation by ?EN: 2 age of 16—Jan 13—32

1. Both girls were at home for the Christmas holidays. The school term had ended on 14 Dec. 1831, when CB was awarded a prize for French, *Le Nouveau Testament* (Edimbourg, G. Cowie & Co, 1829), originally inscribed 'French prize adjudged to Miss Bronté & presented with the Miss Woolers' kind love. Roe Head Decr 14th 1831.' (BPM. The inscription is almost illegible.)
2. Mary Taylor (1817–93) fourth child of Joshua Taylor of Gomersal. See n. 5. Enterprising and radical, Mary was the 'original' of Rose Yorke in *Shirley*. See the Biographical Notes.
3. The widowed Mrs John Nussey (?1771–1857), née Ellen Wade. EN's father, who like Mr Taylor had been a woollen manufacturer, had died in 1826 aged 66.
4. Three of EN's seven brothers lived locally, carrying on the family business as scribbling millers, woollen manufacturers, and merchants. Joseph (1797–1846) and Richard (1803–72) were not so close to EN as the next in age to her, George (1814–85), whom she frequently mentions and who probably lived at home at this period. Richard, and Henry Nussey (1812–67), then a student at Cambridge, were in good health, for Henry recorded in his diary on 14.1.1832: 'I had the pleasure of seeing my brother Richard here in his route to Town.' (HN *Diary* fol. 18^r.) Possibly Joseph was ill; Henry Nussey referred to his continuing ill-health on 31 July this year. (fol. 28^r.) See *Whitehead* 32 for a list of members of the Nussey family.
5. Mary and her sister Martha (1819–42). See the Biographical Notes. Both were at Roe Head school. Martha was the 'original' for Jessy Yorke in *Shirley*.
6. Asiatic cholera reached Hamburg by 21 June 1831. 'On the 7th November, a vessel arrived from that place to Sunderland, and in a very short time more than thirty fatal cases occurred there.' (*Mayhall* i. 382.) The disease spread rapidly, reaching London on 13.2.1832, and was at its worst in 1832, after which it lingered until 1838. By the end of the epidemic 31,376 out of 82,528

reported cases had proved fatal. The first case in Leeds was on 26.5.1832, in Dewsbury on 19 June, and in Bradford in late Aug. For a detailed account, based on the advance of the disease in Exeter, see G. M. Young (ed.), *Early Victorian England* (1934), i. 156–66.

7. 'Mr Taylor' is the probable reading of the MS; 'Mrs Taylor' is possible but less likely. Mr Taylor, the father of Mary, Martha, and their four brothers, was Joshua Taylor (1766–1840) of the Red House, Gomersal, a cloth manufacturer with premises at Hunsworth Mill on the river Spen. He was also a merchant and a banker, issuing his own notes, but his banking business had failed in 1826, owing, it is said, to the failure of a cousin belonging to the Dixon family in Birmingham. Like Hiram Yorke in *Shirley* he was something of a connoisseur of art, and made sure that his daughters had some training in drawing: in March 1842 Mary Taylor wrote to EN from her Brussels school, 'Before breakfast I draw, after breakfast I practise, say German lessons, & *draw*, after dinner walk out, learn German & *draw*'. (MS Pierpont Morgan, *Stevens* letter 2. (W & S 21 reads, incorrectly, 'I am glad to hear Mr— was pleased with Mercy's drawings.'))
8. *Rural Rides* (1830), a collection of essays selected by the radical William Cobbett (1762–1835) from his *Weekly Political Register*, is probably the work referred to here. In Jan. 1830 'everybody' in and near Leeds had flocked to hear his lectures on means of alleviating the current distress, and 'everybody' talked 'of his person, his performances, and his doctrines'—which would have been congenial to the Taylors but not to the Brontës. See *Mayhall* i. 358, 377.
9. Mary and Martha Taylor respectively.

To Branwell Brontë,[1] *17 May [18]32*

Roe-Head.

Dear Branwell

As usual I address my weekly letter to you—because to you I find the most to say. I feel exceedingly anxious to know how, and in what state you arrived at home after your long, and (I should think very fatiguing journey. I could perceive when you arrived at Roe-Head[2] that you were very much tired though you refused to acknowledge it. After you were gone many questions and subjects of conversation recurred to me which I had intended to mention to you but quite forgot them in the agitation which I felt at the totally unexpected pleasure of seeing you. Lately I had begun to think that I had lost all the interest which I used formerly to take in politics but the extreme pleasure I felt at the news of the Reform-bill's being thrown out <of> 'by' the House of Lords[3] and of the expulsion or resignation of Earl Grey,[4] &c. &c. convinced me that I have not as yet lost all my penchant for politics.[5] I am extremely glad that Aunt has consented to take in Frazer's Magazine[6] for though I know from your description of its general contents it will be rather uninteresting when compared with "Blackwood"[7] still it will be better than remaining the whole year without being able to obtain a sight of any periodical publication whatever, and such would assuredly be our case as in the little wild, moorland village where we reside there would be no possibility of borrowing, or obtaining a work of that description from a circulating library.[8]

I hope with you that the present delightful weather may contribute to the perfect restoration of our dear Papa's health and that it may give Aunt pleasant reminiscences of the salubrious climate of her native place.[9] With love to all believe [me][10] dear Branwell to remain

Your affectionate sister

Charlotte.

MS BPM Gr. A. W & S 19 as 1831. *BST* 17. 90. 351–3 (with poem).
Address: none.
PM: none.

1. CB's brother Patrick Branwell Brontë (26.6.1817–24.9.1848) was at home in Haworth. See the Biographical Notes. This letter, written in very neat handwriting, formal in its style, and lacking address and postmark, looks as if it was a school-exercise. CB either retrieved or retained it, and used the blank fourth page to write the draft of a poem, 'O that thy own loved Son thy noblest born', in the small, upright, print-like script she used for her private writings. For the poem, which consists of eight 9-line stanzas, see Neufeldt *CBP* 149–51; Winnifrith *CBP* 309–11. It appears to be part of the 'Angrian' saga of romantic adventures created by CB and BB, dealing mainly with the young Byronic hero-king Zamorna and his rival the villain Northangerland. See Alexander *EW* and *EEW* i. and ii.
2. See CB to Mrs Franks, May 1831 n. 2. Roe Head is about 18 miles from Haworth, by roads over steep hills and moors.
3. The Whig Reform Bill, eventually passed in June 1832, extended the parliamentary franchise to holders of lands (or houses in boroughs) worth £10 a year, abolished rotten and pocket boroughs, and redistributed parliamentary seats to represent the new industrial towns more fairly. The bill had been defeated in the House of Lords on 7 May. On 8 May the Whig Lords Grey and Brougham advised King William IV that new peers should be created to enable the bill to be carried, and resigned their office on 9 May after his rejection of their advice. Keenly partisan meetings both pro- and anti-reform had taken place in Leeds on 14 May.
4. Charles Grey, the 2nd Earl Grey (1764–1845), took up the cause of parliamentary reform in 1830. As prime minister of the Whig administration of 1831 he introduced a reform bill in Mar. that year, which was defeated once in committee and twice in the House of Lords. After Grey's resignation on 9 May 1832, the Duke of Wellington proved unable to form a Tory government, and Grey returned to office, now with the King's permission to create (Whig) peers. Faced with the threat of a permanent Whig majority, Wellington advised his Tory followers not to vote at all, and so to allow the passing of the bill.
5. In *Life* ch. 3 Mrs Gaskell described the 'vivid interest' in politics shown by the Brontë family from childhood onwards, and in ch. 6 quoted Mary Taylor's letter of 18 Jan. 1856, 'We used to be furious politicians, as one could hardly help being in 1832 . . . [Charlotte] worshipped the Duke of Wellington, but said that Sir Robert Peel was not to be trusted.' (*Life* i. 60, 109–10.)
6. *Fraser's Magazine for Town and Country* (1830–82), founded by William Maginn (1793–1842) and Hugh Fraser, was a reputable and substantial Tory journal to which James Hogg, S. T. Coleridge, Southey, Peacock, Carlyle, and Thackeray among others contributed in the 1830s and 1840s. It was independent of any large publishing house, and guaranteed that 'its opinions [would] neither be sold for lucre, nor biassed by self-interest'.
7. *Blackwood's Edinburgh Magazine* (1817–1905; continued as *Blackwood's Magazine* until 1980). It was begun by the Scottish publisher William Blackwood (1776–1834) as a Tory rival to the *Edinburgh Review*. John Lockhart, John Wilson (writing as 'Christopher North'), and James Hogg, the Ettrick Shepherd, were the principal contributors to the early numbers. It was read by the young Brontës from an early age, and its format was imitated by CB and BB in their own miniature magazines. See Mrs Oliphant, *Annals of a Publishing House, William Blackwood and his Sons, their Magazine and Friends* (1897, 1898), ii. 177–85, and Gérin *BB*, esp. 112–13. In CB's 'The History of the Year', dated 12 Mar. 1829, she writes 'We see the John Bull it is a High Tory

very violent Mr Driver lends us it as likewise Blackwoods Magazine the most able periodical there is'. (BPM MS Bon 80 (11).) If 'Mr Driver' was the 'Rev. Jonas Driver, A.M.' of Haworth who died in Dec. 1831 aged 35, and was buried by Mr Brontë on 22 Dec., the lack of a *Blackwood's* in 1832 is explained. See Haworth Parish Registers, Burials 1831 No. 1859; but see also EN 13.3.1835 n. 6.

8. At this date Haworth had no circulating library, though by 1847 it had a bookseller, John Greenwood. See White's *Directory* for that year. PB did not become a member of the Keighley Mechanics' Institute, founded in 1825, until some time in the year ending 8 Apr. 1833. It had a lending library which in 1841 included 11 volumes of *Blackwood's Edinburgh Magazine* and 'parts', implying that a subscription had been taken out. See Clifford Whone, 'Where the Brontës Borrowed Books', *BST* 11. 60. 344–58, and Ian Dewhirst, 'The Rev. Patrick Brontë and the Keighley Mechanics' Institute', *BST* 14. 75. 35–7. The Haworth Subscription Library which closed on Easter Monday 1844 was probably short-lived. (*Bradford Observer* 8.4.1844) A writer in the *Bradford Observer* for 17.2.1894 described recollections of CB and her sisters trudging the four miles to Keighley where Charlotte procured books 'at a lending library kept by Mr Hudson, a bookseller and druggist in the High Street'. This was Thomas Duckett Hudson of 32 High Street, Keighley, Bookseller, Stationer, Binder, and Chemist. (Pigot's *Directory* for Keighley, 1841.) The recollection is undated, but presumably refers to a later period than 1832. In her letter to G. H. Lewes of 18.1.1848 (in Vol. ii) CB said she had 'no access to a circulating library'. (W & S 341.)
9. Elizabeth Branwell came from Penzance in Cornwall.
10. MS reads 'believe dear'.

To Ellen Nussey, 21 July 1832

Haworth

My dearest Ellen

Your kind and interesting letter gave me the sincerest pleasure I have been expecting to hear from you almost every day since my arrival at home[1] and I \`at' length began to despair of receiving the wished-for letter. You ask me to give you a description of the manner in which I have passed every day since I left School: this is soon done as an account of one day is an account of all. In the morning from nine o'clock till half past twelve I instruct my Sisters & draw,[2] then we walk till dinner after dinner I sew till tea-time, and after tea I either read, write,[3] do a little fancy-work or draw, as I pl[eas]e[†] Thus in one delightful, though somewhat monotonous course my life is passed. I have only been out to tea twice since I came home, we are expecting company this afternoon & on Tuesday next we shall have all the Female teachers of the Sunday-School[4] to tea. A short time since I was rather surprised by the receipt of a letter from Miss L. S. *Brooke[5] it contained no news of consequence but she complained heavily "of the things which she understood had been said of her after she left school." I suppose the little prattling amiable *Maria[6] had given her a full relation of all those disgraceful stories we heard respecting Miss *Leah. I am extremely sorry to hear of the deaths of Mrs ?*Wm *Wooler[7] and Mr *Carr[8] and I doubt not both those individuals will be a serious loss to their respective famillies. Your friend *Harriette *Carr's[9] account of Miss *Isabella *?Slayden[10] 'does not surprise me' You know I had formed no very high opinion of her from the traits Miss *Hall[11] related of her character. I do hope my dearest that you will return to school again for your own sake though for mine I had rather you would remain at home as we shall then have more frequent opportunities of correspondence with each other. Should your Friends decide against your returning to school I know you have too much good sense and right-feeling not to strive earnestly for your own improvement. Your natural abilities are excellent and under the direction of a judicious and able friend (and I know you have many such) you might acquire a decided taste for elegant literature and even Poetry which indeed is included under that general ter[m].† I was very much dissapointed by your [not]† sending the hair.[12] You may be sure my [dear]est† Ellen that I would 'not' grudge double postage[13] to obtain it but I must offer the same excuse for not sending you any. My Aunt and Sisters desire their love to you. Remember me kindly to your Mother & Sisters and accept all the fondest expressions of genuine attachment, from

Your real friend
Charlotte Brontë

P.S Remember the mutual promise we made of a regular correspondence with each other Excuse all faults in this wretched scrawl Give my love to the Miss Taylors[14] when [you]† see them. Farewell my dear dear dear Ellen

MS HM 24403. W & S 23.
Address (integral): Miss E Nussey | Rydings | Birstall | nr Leeds.
PM: (i) BRADFORD YORKS | JY 24 | 1832 (ii) *Bradford Yorks* | *Penny Post*
Text: † indicates loss of Text caused by tear or repair of paper.

1. The school term had probably ended on 20 June. On that date EN had received a volume including Mrs Chapone's *Letters on the Improvement of the Mind* (1824 ed.) inscribed 'Prize | For Good & Lady like conduct, adjudged to Miss Nussey, and presented with the Miss Woolers kind love. | Roe Head. | June 20th 32.' (BPM MS ab 109.) EN recorded in her 'Reminiscences' that as well as taking home 3 prizes at the end of her first half-year at Roe Head in 1831, CB won the right to the silver medal 'for the fulfilment of duties' in each of the three half-years she spent there 'and it was presented to her on leaving school'. See Appendix. See also EN 18. 10.1832 n. 7.
2. Mrs Gaskell wrote, 'At one time, Charlotte had the notion of making her living as an artist, and wearied her eyes in drawing with pre-Raphaelite minuteness, but not with pre-Raphaelite accuracy, for she drew from fancy rather than from nature.' (*Life* i. 144.) For accounts of CB's copying of engravings, and her use of art in her fiction, see Jane Sellars, 'Art and the Artist as Heroine in the Novels of Charlotte, Emily and Anne Brontë', *BST* 20. 2. 57–76, and Christine Alexander, 'Art and Artists in Charlotte Brontë's Juvenilia', *BST* 20. 4. 177–204.
3. All the Brontë children were prolific writers of stories and poems. For CB and BB, see BB 17.5. 1832 n. 1. Emily and Anne Brontë created an imaginary kingdom called Gondal. As late as 31 July 1845, EJB could still record in her 'Diary Paper', 'Anne and I went our first long journey by ourselves together [to York] . . . and during our excursion we were Ronald Macelgin, Henry Angora, Juliet Augusteena . . . The Gondals still flourish bright as ever.' See p. 408.
4. The building in which this had recently been opened still stands, almost opposite Haworth parsonage in Church Lane. It had been erected earlier in 1832 at Mr Brontë's instigation.

5. Leah Sophia Brooke, born 5 Nov. 1815, a fellow-pupil at Roe Head. She was baptized by PB's friend the Revd John Buckworth on 7 Feb. 1816 at Dewsbury Parish Church, and was the first child of Sarah and John Brooke. Her father was a partner in the firm of Halliley, Brooke, and Hallileys, important woollen manufacturers specializing in blankets and carpets, with substantial banking interests in Dewsbury and elsewhere.
6. Anna Maria Brooke, Leah's younger sister, born 31 July 1818. She was a friend of Martha Taylor, who wrote to EN on 19 May 1832, 'I asked Mother if Miss Maria Brooke might come to our house in the holidays & she said she would be very glad to see her any time.' (MS Texas; W & S 22 as 17 May.)
7. The wife of Dr William Moore Wooler (1795–1873) who was a brother of Margaret Wooler of Roe Head; a general practitioner and Licentiate of the Society of Apothecaries (1817). In Pigot's *Directory* for Derbyshire for 1835 he is recorded as a surgeon practising at 9 Friar Gate, Derby, but in 1832 he may have been in York, where his first wife, Sidney Maria, née Allbutt (1806–32) died of cholera. His second wife was Anne Medley (1812–84). He retired before 1844 to West House, Dewsbury, and was the author of *The Physiology of Education* (1859) and *The Philosophy of Temperance, and the Physical Causes of Moral Sadness* (1840), in which he writes of various dangers to health, including 'Excess of Eating producing opacity of intellect', 'The Misery inflicted on the Poor by' the abuse of tea, and smoking, 'this filthy invader of social intercourse'.
8. Charles Carr of Gomersal (1777/8–13.7.1832), a solicitor. (W & S 23 mistakenly reads 'Caris'.)
9. Probably Harriet Carr (18.8.1816–1898), youngest daughter of Charles Carr, and sister-in-law of EN's second cousin Eleanor (Walker) Carr. (W & S 23 reads 'Caris'.)
10. Not traced. The surname has been heavily deleted and may be 'Sugden', a common local name, as in W & S 23.
11. A Roe Head pupil, mentioned also by Martha Taylor in her letter to EN of 19 May: 'When Miss Hall is returned from Lincolnshire She is going to stay with my Sister and they are going to come to see me at school.' (MS Texas; W & S 22 as 17 May.) Not identified, but the Lydia Hall born on 3 Jan. 1817, daughter of a tanner, James Hall and his wife Lydia, of Littletown, would be the right age; she was baptized by the Revd W. M. Heald, the Vicar of Birstall, on 16 Feb. 1817.
12. A lock of EN's hair as a keepsake.
13. Before Jan. 1840 the cost of postage was usually paid by the recipient. 'The lowest rate for a letter of a single sheet [by the general post] was fourpence up to 15 miles, rising to one shilling for a distance up to 300 miles . . . A double letter of two sheets paid twice these rates . . . "heavy" letters were charged by the quarter ounce.' (M. J. Daunton, *The Royal Mail* (1985), 6.)
14. Martha Taylor would be returning to Roe Head, and her sister Mary might return 'to take drawing lessons'. Martha wrote to EN, 'I wonder how we shall go on next half year without you and Miss Bronté I think the schoolroom will look without [*sic*] Miss Bronté . . . I think I shall feel Miss Bronté's loss very much as she has always been very kind to me.' (19 May 1832, MS Texas.)

To Ellen Nussey, 5 September 1832

Haworth

Dearest Ellen

I am really very much indebted to you for your well-filled and very interesting letter; it forms a striking contrast to my brief, meagre epistles but I know you will excuse the utter dearth of news visible in them when you consider the situation in which I am placed; quite out of the reach of 'all' intelligence except what I obtain through the medium of the Newspapers,[1] and I believe you would not find much to interest you in a political discussion or a summary of the accidents of the week. **The Story of the white hen seen at Mrs W ?*Woolers funeral savours very much of the supernatural.[2] You seem to hint that there are suspicions that she was buried alive, if so how agonizing must be the feelings of her relations! I do not wonder at poor Mr ?*Woolers ?derangement.**[3] Papa was very sorry to hear that his old friend Mr *Roberson[4] had suffered from an attack of paralysis, I should think, his age, precludes all hope of his ultimate recovery. It gave me pleasure to learn that you take lessons at Roe-Head once a week as I have no doubt that your improvement will now be rapid, in those two important branches of Female education, French & Music. Your account of Miss *Martha *Taylor's fit of good behaviour amused me exceedingly, I only hope it may be permanent. En passant is Polly[5] yet in the land of the living if she is I wish you would tell her the first time you have an opportunity that I should be very glad to receive a letter from her. I am sorry, <u>very</u> sorry that Miss ?*Kirby[6] has turned out to be so different from what you thought her, but my dearest Ellen you must never expect perfection in this world and I know your naturally confiding, and affectionate disposition had led you to imagine that Miss K— was almost faultless. I now come to the latter part of your letter, I feel greatly obliged to your Mother & yourself for the very kind invitation[7] there contained, When I consulted Papa and Aunt about it they both said that they could not possibly have any objection to my accepting it. It is therefore with great pleasure that I am enabled to return an affirmative answer to your kind and pressing request. I leave it to you to fix the day which may be most convenient to your Mother and Sisters. I think dearest Ellen our friendship is destined to form an exception to the general rule regarding school friendships At least I know that absence has not in the least abated the sisterly affection which I feel towards You. Remember me to your Mother & Sisters and accept every profession of genuine regard which the English Tongue affords from

Your friend
Charlotte Brontë

PS. Do not criticise the execrable Penmanship visible in this letter.

Adieu pour le présent

MS BPM B. S. 39.5. W & S 24 (part).
Address: (integral): Miss E Nussey | Rydings | Birstal | Nr Leeds
PM: (i) BRADFORD YORKSHIRE | SE 6 | 1832 (ii) *Bradford Yorks* | *Penny Post*

1. In her 'History of the Year' dated 12 Mar. 1829 CB records 'papa and Branwell are gone for the newspaper the Leeds Intelligencer—a most excellent Tory newspaper edited by Mr [i.w.] Wood the proprietor Mr Hennaman [i.e. John Hernaman] we ?take 2 and see three Newspapers as such we take the Leeds Intelligencer [. . .] Tory and the Leeds Mercury Whig Edited by Mr Bains and His Brother Soninlaw and his 2 sons Edward and Talbot—We see the John Bull it is a High Tory very violent.' (MS BPM Bon 80 (11).)

2. For Mrs W. Wooler see EN 21.7.1832 n. 7. White birds are sometimes thought to presage disaster. cf. also the idea that the conscience or the soul is like a white bird: see *Brewer*, under 'White'.
3. MGC's reading in her transcript at BPM. A former owner of the MS, Professor Woodward of the Mary Washington College of the University of Virginia, writes, 'The entire passage ['The story of the white hen . . .? derangement'] is crossed out, and this word/phrase has been lined out by two hands and is resistant to interpretation even under ultra-violet light.' Professor Woodward deciphered only 'S—g—t'. See *BST* 14. 74. 46–8. 'derangement' is an acceptable reading: cf. CB's use of the word in EN ?15.10.1847.
4. The Revd Hammond Roberson (1757–1841), MA and Fellow of Magdalene College Cambridge; ' "licensed as Curate to Dewsbury Yorks., [?1779] on the recommendation of Henry Venn, the evangelical vicar of Huddersfield." Opened a school for boys at Squirrel Hall, Liversedge, 1783, which he transferred to Heald's Hall, Liversedge, 1795. V[icar] of Hartshead, 1795–1803. Built a church [Christ Church] at Liversedge, of which he was incumbent until 1841.' (*Venn*) EN gives a lengthy note in *Hatfield* 5–6, part of which reads, 'He was a remarkable man, of an iron will, had great power of control and dignity of deportment. He gave up his residence during the Luddite Riots (1812) as Barracks for the soldiers. Mr. Bronte then incumbent of Hartshead (a contiguous Parish) was united with Mr. Roberson in these exciting times in efforts to quell local disturbances. . . . C.B. never saw him but once when ten years of age, but heard much of him from her Father, and thus combined his character with that of her Father—tabulating them as Mr. Helstone in "Shirley".'
5. Mary Taylor.
6. Professor Woodward reads 'Haigh'. The name is partly deleted, but 'Kirby' seems the more probable reading. For Haigh, see EN 20.6.1833 and notes 4 and 6. I have not identified a likely 'Kirby'.
7. To stay with the Nusseys at Rydings, Birstall. This was a battlemented house (one of CB's models for Thornfield in *JE*) where the younger Nussey children had lived with their mother from about 1827. It was a substantial property with stables, hot-houses, gardens, a park, wood, and plantations. For a history of the house, with illustrations, see J. T. M. Nussey, 'Rydings—Home of Ellen Nussey', *BST* 15. 78. 244–9, and *Whitehead* 26–7, 35. EN commented on 'Charlotte's first visit to her friend EN at Rydings. Branwell was sent as an escort with his sister; he was wild with excitement and delight. He told his sister he was leaving her in Paradise!' (*Hatfield* 27 where it erroneously refers to the visit mentioned in EN 12.1.1835.) The visit probably began in early Oct. See next letter, and Appendix, p. 596.

To Ellen Nussey, 18 October 1832

A Haworth le 18 Octobre, 32.

(a) Ma très chère Amie

Nous sommes encore partu[1] et il y a entre nous dix sept milles de chemin: le bref quinzaine pendant lequel je fus chez vous c'est envolé et desormais il faut compter ma visite agréable parmi le nombre de choses passées.

(b) J'arrivait à Haworth en parfaite sauveté sans le moindre accident ou malheur. Mes petites sœurs[2] couraient hors de la maison pour me rencontrer aussitôt que la voiture se fit voir, et elles m'embrassaient avec autant d'empressement, et de plaisir comme si j'avais été absente pour plus d'[un] an. Mon Papa, ma Tante, et le monsieur dont mon frére avoit parlé,[3] furent tous assemblés dans le Salon, et en peu de temps je m'y rendis aussi. C'est souvent l'ordre du Ciel que quand on a perdu un plaisir il y en a un autre prêt à prendre sa place. Ainsi je venois† de partir de trés chérs amis, mais tout à l'heure je revins à des parens aussi chers et bons. [Dans le moment même][4] que vous me perdiez (ose-je croire que mon depart vous était un chagrin?) vous attendites l'arrivée de votre frére, et de votre soeur. J'ai donné a mes sœurs les pommes que vous leur envoyiez avec tant de bonté; elles disent qu'elles sont sûr† que Mademoiselle <Ellen>ˋE—ˊ. e[s]t trés aimable et bonne; l'une et l'autre sont extremement impatientes de vous voir; j'espère qu'en peu de mois elles auront ce plaisir.[5] . . .

(a) Je n'ai plus de temps et pour le présent il faut conclure. Donnez mes plus sincéres amitiés a [Mademoiselle Mercy] et maintenant ma bien aimee, ma précieuse E[llen] mon amie chere et chérit,[6] Croyez-moi de rester a vous pour la vie,

Charlotte.

P.S.—You cannot imagine in what haste I have written this. If you do not like me to write French letters tell me so, and I will desist, but I beg and implore your reply may be in the universal language,[7] never mind a few mistakes at first, the attempt will contribute greatly to your improvement. Farewell sweet one†.[8] Write soon, very soon; I shall be all impatience till I hear from you.

MS untraced. W & S 25.

To Ellen Nussey, 18 October 1832: Translation

[CB's command of French was obviously imperfect. The translation provides what she probably intended to say.]

My very dear friend,

Once more we are parted[1] and there are seventeen miles of road between us; the brief fortnight during which I was with you has gone by, and from now on my pleasant visit must be reckoned among the number of things past. I arrived in Haworth in perfect safety without the least accident or mishap. My little sisters[2] ran out of the house to meet me as soon as the carriage came in sight, and they hugged me with as much eagerness and pleasure as if I had been away for over a year. My father, my aunt, and the gentleman my brother had mentioned[3] were all assembled in the parlour, and in a very short time I went there too. Heaven often ordains that when one has lost one pleasure, another is ready to take its place. Thus I had just left very dear friends, but I returned straightaway to equally dear and good relatives. At the very moment[4] when you lost me (dare I believe that you regretted my departure?) you were awaiting the arrival of your brother and sister. I have given my sisters the apples you so kindly sent for them; they say they are sure that Miss Ellen is very amiable and good; both of them are extremely impatient to see you; I hope that in a few months' time they will have that pleasure.[5] I have no more time and must finish for the present. Give my most sincere friendly greetings to Miss Mercy; and now my well-beloved, precious Ellen, my dear and cherished[6] friend, believe that I am your friend for life,

Charlotte.

[The letter continues in English as printed.]
Address: not in sources.
PM: not in sources.
Text: (b) Rylands MS *Life*, an incomplete text supplemented by (a) *Nussey* 21–2 and *Hours at Home* xi. 104, and by readings from *Needham* (marked with a dagger). The name 'Mademoiselle Mercy' is supplied from *Shorter* 7. W & S 25 reproduces *Shorter* 7, with one correction of a faulty accent. Some corrections were introduced in the printed editions of the *Life*. Errors in the present text may derive from CB or from the various early copyists: I have not attempted to correct them.

1. All texts read 'partu', which may be a misreading of 'partis'. Seventeen miles was the approximate distance from EN's home in Birstall to Haworth.
2. Emily was 14, Anne 12. See the *Chronology*.
3. Branwell had accompanied Charlotte to Birstall. The visitor he mentioned has not been identified.
4. All sources have 'bons dans le moment. Même', a reading that hardly makes sense.
5. After 'plaisir' *Needham* has an ellipsis, and *Nussey* prints 2 square brackets.
6. *Hours at Home*, which was intended to supply material not in the *Life*, prints the conclusion only (from 'Donnez mes' to the end), including the words 'et chérit'. *Needham* has 'et cherit'; other texts omit these two words.
7. French, the common language of international diplomacy and European culture, especially since the 'Enlightenment'. CB's enthusiasm for the language is shown by her translation of the first book of Voltaire's epic, *La Henriade*, in Aug. 1830. (MS in the Houghton Library, Harvard.) At the end of her first year at Roe Head CB was given a small French Testament as a prize. (BPM. See *BST* 4. 21. 202 and EN 13. 1. 1832 n.1).
8. Ellen deleted the words 'sweet one' in *Needham*. They are omitted in all other texts.

To Ellen Nussey, 1 January 1833

Haworth

Dear Ellen

I believe we agreed to correspond once a month, that space of time has elapsed since I received your last interesting letter and I now therefore hasten [to] reply. Accept my congratulations on the arrival of the "New Year" every succeeding day of which will I trust find you <u>wiser</u> and <u>better</u> in the <u>true</u> sense of those much-used words. The first day of January always presents to my mind a train of very solemn and important reflections and a question<s> more easily asked than answered frequently occurs viz: How have I improved the past year and with [what] good intentions do I view the dawn of its successor? these my dearest Ellen are weighty considerations which (young as we are) neither you nor I can too deeply or too seriously ponder. I am sorry your too great diffidence arising I think from the want of sufficient confidence in your own capabilities prevented you from writing to me in French as I think the attempt would have materially contributed to your improvement in that language. You very kindly caution me against being tempted by the fondness of my Sisters to consider myself of too much importance and then in a parenthesis you beg me not to be offended. O Ellen do you think I could be offended by any good advice you may give me? No, I thank you heartily and love you if possible better for it. I received a letter about a Fortnight ago from Miss *Taylor[1] in which she mentions the birth of Mrs *Carters little boy[2] and likewise tells me that you had not been at *Roe-Head for upwards of a month but does not assign any reason for your absence. I hope it does not arise from ill health. I am glad you like Kenilworth[3] [it] is certainly a splendid production more resembling a Romance than a Novel and in my opinion one of the most interesting works that ever emanated from the great Sir Walter's pen. I was exceedingly amused at the characteristic and naïve manner in which you expressed your detestation of Varney's character,[4] so much so indeed that I could not forbear laughing aloud when I perused that part of your letter: he is certainly the personification of consummate villainy and in the delineation of his dark and[5] profoundly artful mind Scott exhibits a wonderful knowledge of human nature as well as surprising skill in embodying his perceptions so as to enable others to become participators in that knowledge. Excuse the want of <u>news</u> in this very barren epistle for I really have none to communicate. Emily and Anne beg to be kindly remembered to you. Give my best love to your Mother and Sisters and as it is very late permit me to conclude with the assurance of my Unchanged, Unchanging, and Unchangeable affection for you.

Adieu my Sweetest Ellen
I am Ever yours
Charlotte

MS BPM B.S. 40. W & S 26.
Address (integral): Miss 'E' Nussey | Birstal | nr | Leeds
PM: (i) BRADFORD YORKS | JA 2 | 18–3 (ii) *Bradford Yorks* | *Penny Post*

1. Mary Taylor. See EN 13.1.1832 n. 2.
2. Born Dec. 1832, ?d. in infancy; first child of Susan Carter, née Wooler, and the Revd Edward Nicholl Carter (22.12.1800–29.2.1872), the curate of Mirfield Parish Church, who was to become the first curate-in-charge of the new Christ Church, Lothersdale on 30 Nov. 1838, and Vicar of Heckmondwike in 1842. The Revd E. N. Carter is said to have prepared CB for confirmation while she was a pupil at Roe Head; at Heckmondwike, 'he was dearly loved, and . . . the church of St. Saviour's was built in his memory'. For Mrs Carter, see CB to Mrs Franks May 1831 n. 6, and for her husband see Subscription Lists of the Diocese of Ripon for 1838 (WYAS Leeds) *BST* 12. 62. 113–14, and *BST* 18. 94. 270.
3. CB wrote 'Kenilworth its is'. Sir Walter Scott's *Kenilworth* was published in 3 vols. in 1821. As Christine Alexander points out, CB's own writings in 1833–5 show that she 'devoured the works of Scott and Byron with something bordering on obsession', appropriating into her own saga 'the abducted heroines of *Ivanhoe* and *Kenilworth*'. (Alexander *EEW* ii. pt. 1, p. xxi.)

4. In Scott's novel Richard Varney inveigles Amy Robsart into a secret marriage with Queen Elizabeth's favourite, the Earl of Leicester, and ultimately causes Amy's death.
5. CB wrote 'dark and and profoundly'.

To Ellen Nussey, 20 June 1833

Haworth.

Dear Ellen

I know you will be very angry because I have not written sooner; my reason, or rather my motive for this apparent neglect was, that I had determined 'not to write' until I could ask you to pay us your long-promised visit. Aunt thought it would be better to defer it until about the middle of Summer, as the Winter, and even the Spring seasons are remarkably cold and bleak among our mountains.[1] Papa now desires me to present his respects to Mrs *Nussey & say that he should feel greatly obliged if she would allow us the pleasure of your company for a few weeks at Haworth. I will leave it to you to fix whatever day may be most convenient but dear Ellen let it be an early one. I received a letter from Poll *Taylor[2] yesterday, she was in high dudgeon at my inattention in not promptly answering her last epistle I however sat down immediately and wrote a very humble reply candidly confessing my fault and soliciting forgiveness; I hope it has proved successful. Have you suffered much from that troublesome, though not, (I am happy to hear) generally fatal disease the influenza?[3] We have so far steered clear of it but I know not how long we may continue to escape. Miss *Taylor tells me that *Hannah *Haigh[4] has been elevated to the office of house-keeper at *Colne *Bridge[5] doubtless she will fulfil its duties with great self-complacency. Do you not think Mrs *Bradbury[6] has made an excellent choice of a partner for life? Your last letter Ellen revealed a ?st[ate] of mind which seemed to promise much [?As][7] I read it I could not help wishing, that [my own] feelings more nearly resembled yours: but [un]happily all the good thoughts that enter [my mind] evaporate almost before I have had time [to as]certain their existence, every right resolution <that> 'which' I form is so transient, so fragile, and so easily broken that I sometimes fear I shall never be what I ought. Earnestly hoping that this may not be your case, that you may continue steadfast till the end

I remain Dearest Ellen
Your ever faithful friend
Charlotte Brontë

P. S. Write soon, and let the answer be favourable.

MS HM 24404. W & S 27.

Address: (integral): Miss E Nussey | Rydings | nr Birstall
PM: (i) [BRADF]ORD [remainder torn away] (ii) *Bradford Yorks* | *Py Post*

1. The word was used until the late 18th cent., and evidently in the early 19th cent., for 'elevations of moderate altitude'. (*OED*.) cf. EN's published 'Reminiscences', where the Brontës are said to have lived amid 'the free expanse of hill and mountain', (*BST* 2. 9. 83; W & S i. 116) and *Life* ch. 2, where Mrs Gaskell refers to the beck running down the mountainside and to 'mountain streams'. The South Pennines west of Ponden Kirk reach about 1,400 ft.
2. Mary Taylor.
3. CB was optimistic. Mayhall records that in May 1833 'The influenza was very prevalent at Hunslet [on the outskirts of Leeds and about 5 miles from Birstall], and many cases terminated fatally'. (*Mayhall* i. 401.)
4. A fellow-pupil at Roe Head. Not certainly identified, since the name was one of the commonest in the area. She may have been the daughter of Samuel and Hannah Haigh, christened on 23 June 1816 at St Peter's, Huddersfield, and related to the family of Thomas Haigh, cotton-spinner, of King Street, Huddersfield and Colne Bridge, and to the later Samuel Wood Haigh, also a cotton-spinner at Colne Bridge. (See Pigot's *Directory* for Huddersfield, 1822, and for Kirkheaton, 1841, and documents relating to Samuel Wood Haigh and Thomas Haigh and Sons, WYAS Bradford, C296 Boxes 109–13.) The Hannah Haigh who married Thomas Lumb at Kirkheaton on 5 June 1833 made her mark instead of signing her name, and is unlikely to have been the person CB refers to.
5. A hamlet about 2 miles north of Kirkheaton, near Huddersfield.
6. Probably Ann Haigh of Huddersfield, who married the apothecary Uriah Bradbury of Mirfield on 8 May 1833 at St Peter's Huddersfield, in the presence of 6 witnesses including Thomas Haigh and Joseph Bradbury. Perhaps she was the former housekeeper at Colne Bridge. (Marriage Register of St Peter's, WYAS Calderdale, microfilm copy.) Her son Thomas Haigh Bradbury was christened at Mirfield parish church on 28 July 1834.
7. Square brackets indicate loss of text caused by tears in the paper, or by the mounting strip; the missing words have been supplied from *Needham*.

To Ellen Nussey, 3 July 1833

Haworth

Dearest Ellen

I am extremely sorry to be obliged to tell you that owing to circumstances, I must request you to defer your long-desired visit till the 19th. of the present month.[1] On that day we shall all be most happy to see you, and till then believe me to be

Your most affectionate friend
C Brontë

PS. excuse the brevity of this hasty scrawl as the post is just going off

MS BPM B. S. 40. 2. No publication traced.
Address: not in MS.
PM: not in MS.
Annotation by EN in ink: July 3. 33
Date: CB corrected the date from 'July 4' to 'July 3d —33'.

1. For EN's first visit to Haworth, see Appendix, pp. 596–9.

To Ellen Nussey, 11 September 1833

Haworth.

Dear Ellen

I have hitherto delayed answering your last letter because from what you said I immagined you might be from home. I was at first rather at a loss to understand what you meant by saying that "*George[1] had made a mistake in his arrangements with *Branwell respecting the Gig."[2] but at length I conjectured that the expression must have been in allusion to the agreement of paying the price of a conveyance in equal shares. If <so> this conjecture is correct, allow me to assure you dear Ellen that there is no mistake, for if you recollect your Brother *Richard[3] most kindly disbursed all the expenses incurred at the Inn—which amounted to more than your share of the stipulated sum; consequently we are in reality the debtors, and you the creditors. Since you were here, Emily has been very ill, her ailment was Erysipelas in the arm, accompanied by severe bilious attacks, and great general debility: her arm was obliged to be cut in order to remove the noxious matter which had accumulated in the inflamed parts, it is now I am happy to say nearly healed, her health is in fact almost perfectly re-established though the sickness still continues to recur at intervals. Were I to tell you of the impression you have made on every one[4] here you would accuse me of flattery. Papa and Aunt are continually adducing you as an example for me to shape my actions and behaviour by, Emily & Anne say "they never saw any one they liked so well as Miss *Nussey" and Tabby[5] whom you have absolutely fascinat[ed] talks a great deal more nonsense about your ladyship than I chuse to repeat. You must read this letter dear Ellen without thinking of the writing for I have indited it almost all in the twilight. It is now so dark that notwithstanding the singular property of "seeing in the night-time" which the young ladies at Roe Head used to attribute to me, I can scribble no longer. All the family unite<s> with me in wishes for your welfare. Remember me respectfully to your Mother and Sisters, and supply all those expressions of warm and genuine regard which the increasing darkness will not permit me to insert

Charlotte Brontë

MS HM 24405. W & S 28.
Address (integral): Miss E. Nussey | Rydings | Nr Birstall
PM: (i) BRADFORD YORKS | SE 12 | 1833 (ii) *Bradford Yorks* | *Penny Post*

1. EN's brother George. See EN 13.1.1832 n. 4. She was fond of this kind-hearted brother, and was to be greatly distressed by his later mental illness. See EN 13.10.1843 and 30.12.1844 notes.
2. The gig used by the Brontës for an excursion probably in late Aug., to the picturesque ruins of Bolton Priory in Wharfedale, where they met EN's 'friends and relatives who were to take [Ellen] home'. EN's account of the visit is given in EN's MS 'Reminiscences' (King's School

Canterbury), and in Wemyss Reid, *Charlotte Brontë* (2nd edn., 1877), ch. 4, q.v. See Appendix, p. 602. EN was condescending about the Brontës' hired gig: 'Their conveyance is no handsome carriage, but a rickety dogcart, unmistakably betraying its neighbourship to the carts and ploughs of some rural farmyard. The horse, freshly taken from the fields, is driven by a youth [i.e. Branwell Brontë] who, in spite of his countrified dress, is no mere bumpkin.' (*Reid* 30.) For CB's careful copy of an engraving of Bolton Priory, exhibited in Leeds in 1834, see *BST* 20. 2. 58, reproducing BPM MS C73, and Christine Alexander, *Charlotte Brontë's Paintings* (Canberra, 1993).

3. See EN 13.1.1832 n. 4. Richard Nussey's fiancée Elizabeth Charnock was probably one of the party.
4. EN's visit to Haworth, made probably during late July and part of Aug., was 'on the whole . . . a happy visit to all parties,' as ECG records in *Life* ch. 7 (i. 133.) See Appendix, p. 596 for EN's account.
5. Tabitha Aykroyd, née Wood, 'who died Feby. 17th. 1855 in the 85th. year of her Age. Faithful Servant of the Brontë Family for over thirty years', as her tombstone in Haworth churchyard records. She was a widow of 53 when Mr Brontë engaged her as a general servant in 1824, and his children became much attached to her, regarding her as one of the family. EN describes her as 'very quaint in appearance' in her 'Reminiscences'; 'We were all "childer" and "bairns", in her estimation.' Hannah, the servant at Moor House in *JE*, probably has many of Tabby's traits.

To Ellen Nussey, 11 February 1834

Haworth

Dear Ellen

My letters are scarcely worth the postage and therefore I have till now, delayed answering your last communication; but upwards of two months having elapsed since I received it, I have at length determined to take up the pen in reply lest your anger should be roused by my apparent negligence. It grieved me extremely to hear of your precarious state of health; I trust sincerely that your medical advisor is mistaken in supposing you have any tendency to pulmonary affection,[1] dear Ellen that would indeed be a calamity; I have seen enough of Consumption to dread it as one of the most insidious, and fatal diseases incident to humanity, but I repeat it I hope nay pray that your alarm is groundless; If you remember I used frequently to tell you at school that you were, constitutionally nervous   guard against the gloomy impressions which such a state of mind naturally produces, cheer up, take constant and regular exercise and all I doubt not will yet be well. What a remarkable Winter we have had! Rain and wind continually but an almost total absence of frost or snow.[2] Has general ill-health been the consequence of the wet weather at Birstall or not? with us an unusual number of deaths have lately taken place. According to custom I have no news to communicate   indeed I do not write either to retail gossip or to impart solid information, my motives for maintaining our mutual correspondence are in the first place to get intelligence from you, and in the second that we may remind each other of our separate existences: without some such medium of reciprocal converse; according to the nature of things you, who are surrounded by society and friends, would soon forget that such an 'insignificant' being as myself, ever lived; I however in the solitude of our wild little hill village, think of my only un-related friend, my dear ci-devant school companion daily, nay almost hourly. Now Ellen, don't you think I have very cleverly contrived to make a letter out of nothing? Good-bye dearest, that God may bless you[3] **and <*i.w*>you** is the earnest prayer of

Your ever faithful friend
Charlotte Brontë

Write to me very soon.

MS HM 24406, W & S 29.
Address (integral): Miss E Nussey | Birstall | nr Leeds
PM: (i) BRADFORD YORKS | FE 12 | 1834 (ii) *Bradford Yorks* | *Penny*—

1. Pulmonary tuberculosis. Both CB's elder sisters had died of this disease, Maria (1813–6 May 1825) being terminally ill when her father took her home from Cowan Bridge school on 14 Feb. 1825. The Cowan Bridge Register records of Elizabeth Brontë 'Left in ill-health, May 31, 1825. Died June 15, 1825, in decline.' The *Leeds Mercury* reported on 18 June 1825 that Elizabeth died of an 'affection' of the lungs, the term used by CB here.
2. Mayhall recorded that on 31 Dec. 1833 'Yorkshire and the adjacent counties were visited by one of the most tremendous hurricanes ever remembered.' (*Mayhall* i. 413.) Dec. 1833 was described as 'very windy and wet'. Only three days without rain were recorded in Jan. 1834, 8 Jan. being also 'darksome' and 21 to 24 'wet, and windy'. The weather improved from 7 Feb. (*Shackleton*.)
3. After 'bless you' about 15 words have been heavily deleted; they may include 'and . . . your . . . and . . . health. . . friend.' EN may have confirmed an earlier deletion by CB.

To Ellen Nussey, 20 February 1834

Haworth

Dearest Ellen,

Your letter gave me real, and heartfelt pleasure, mingled with no small degree of astonishment. Mary *Taylor had previously informed me of your departure for London[1] and I had not ventured to calculate on receiving any communication from you while surrounded by the splendours, and novelties of that great city, which has been called the mercantile metropolis of Europe. Judging from human Nature, I thought that a little country girl, placed for the first time in a situation 'so well' calculated to excite curiosity, and to distract attention, would lose all remembrance for a time at least of distant and familiar objects, and give herself up entirely to the fascination of those scenes which were then presented to her view. Your kind, interesting and most welcome epistle, showed me however that I had been both mistaken, and uncharitable in my suppositions, I was greatly amused at the tone of nonchalance which you assumed while treating of London, and its wonders, which seem to have excited anything rather than surprise in your mind: did you not feel awed while gazing at St. Paul's and Westminster Abbey? had you no feeling of intense, and ardent interest, when in St Jame's you saw the Palace, where so many of England's Kings, had held their courts, and beheld the representations of their persons on the walls You should not be too much afraid of appearing country-bred, the magnificence of London has drawn exclamations of astonishment, from travelled Men, experienced in the World, its wonders, and beauties. Have you yet seen any of the Great Personages whom the sitting of Parliament now detains in London? The Duke of Wellington,[2] Sir Robert Peel,[3] Earl Grey,[4] Mr Stanley,[5] Mr O'Connel[6] &c? If I were you Ellen, I would not be too anxious to spend my time in reading whilst in Town, make ˋuseˊ of your own eyes for the purposes of observation now and for a time at least lay aside the spectacles with which authors would furnish us in their works. It gives me more pleasure than I can express to h[ear] of your renewed health, About a week before I received yours, I had written to you supposing you to be still at *Birstall, fearing that that letter may be sent in mistake for the present one I have hastened to return an answer with as little delay as possible. According to your wish I direct this to Miss M *Nussey *Rydings.[7] I shall be quite impatient dear Ellen till I receive another letter from you pray continue to remember me give my love to your Sisters and accept the kindest wishes, from

Your affectionate friend
C Brontë

PS. will you be kind enough to inform me of the number of performers in the kings Military Band—[8]

MS HM 24407. W & S 30.
Address (integral): Miss M. Nussey | Rydings | Birstall
PM: (i) BRADFORD YORKS | FE 21 | 1834 (ii) *Bradford*—| *Penny*—

1. CB addresses the letter to EN's sister Mercy at Birstall for forwarding to London, where EN was staying with her eldest brother John (1794–1862), a general practitioner, of 4 Cleveland Row, St James's. He had qualified as a licentiate of the Society of Apothecaries in 1818, and was an apothecary to George IV and his successors. He had married Mary Walker (1799–1868), his second cousin, in 1825. CB's questions and comments probably took into account the royal connection and West End address. See John T. M. Nussey, 'Walker and Nussey—Royal Apothecaries 1784–1860', *Medical History* (London), 14. No. 1, Jan. 1970.
2. Arthur Wellesley, 1st Duke of Wellington (1769–1852), commander of the British forces in the Peninsular campaigns during the Napoleonic Wars and at the battle of Waterloo which ended them in 1815. He was greatly admired by the Brontës. The early stories of CB and BB were woven round their heroic versions of the Duke and his sons. See e.g. *Life* ch. 5, Alexander *EW* 24–5, and CB's list of contents of her *Tales of the Islanders* in Alexander *EEW* i. 212–14.
3. Sir Robert Peel (1788–1850), Tory statesman. He had been Home Secretary under Lord Liverpool from 1822 to 1827, then under Wellington from 1828 to 1830, and was to become Prime Minister in November 1834.
4. See BB 17.5.1832 n. 4.
5. Edward George Stanley (1799–1869), statesman; Irish Secretary under Grey from 1830 to 1833. As Colonial Secretary he had carried the act for the abolition of slavery in 1833. He could be a

brilliant and persuasive speaker in Parliament, but his 3 premierships were short-lived. He succeeded his father as Earl of Derby in 1851.

6. Daniel O'Connell (1775–1847), Irish politician, known as 'The Liberator'. An able barrister, he worked for Catholic Emancipation and for the repeal of the 1800 Act of Union between Great Britain and Ireland. He had been elected MP for County Clare in 1828, and for Dublin in 1832.
7. See EN 5.9.1832 n. 7.
8. After 'Military Band' *Shorter* 12 and W & S 30 read 'Branwell wishes for this information', but there is no sign of this sentence in the MS or in the earliest printed version of it in *Life* ch. 7 (i. 137). Shorter might have seen a manuscript fragment, or he might have incorporated a gloss by EN, who would know of Branwell's talent and enthusiasm for music. His fascination with brass and 'reed' bands, and his extravagant delight in the 'stupendous' new organ installed in Haworth church in Mar. 1834 are amusingly satirized by CB in 'My Angria and the Angrians', completed on 14.10.1834. (Alexander *EEW* ii. pt. 2, 247–53.)

To Ellen Nussey, 19 June 1834

[Haworth]

My own dear [Ellen],

I may rightfully and truly call you so now.[1] You have returned or are returning from London, from the great City, which is to me [almost] as apocryphal[2] as Babylon, or Nineveh,[3] or ancient Rome. You are withdrawing from the world (as it is called,) and bringing with you,—if your letters enable me to form a correct judgement—a heart as unsophisticated, as natural, as true, as that you carried there. I am slow very slow to believe the protestations of another; I know my own sentiments, because† I can read my own mind, but the minds of the rest of man and woman-kind[4] are to me as† sealed volumes, hieroglyphical scrolls,[5] which I can not easily either unseal or decipher. Yet time, careful study, long acquaintance overcome most difficulties; and in your case, I think they have succeeded well in bringing to light, and construing that hidden language, whose turnings, windings inconsistencies and obscurities so frequently baffle the researches of the honest observer of human nature. [How many after having, as they thought, discovered the word friend in the mental volume, have afterwards found they should have read false friend! I have long seen "friend" in your mind, in your words in your actions, but now distinctly visible, and clearly written in characters that cannot be distrusted, I discern true friend.] I am truly <thankful>'grateful'[6] for your mindfulness of so obscure a person as myself, and I hope the pleasure is not altogether selfish; I trust, it is partly derived from the consciousness that my friend's character is of a higher, a more steadfast order than I was once perfectly aware of. Few girls would have done, as you have done—would have beheld the glare, and glitter, and dazzling display of London with dispositions so unchanged, heart so uncontaminated. I see no affectation in your letters,[7] no trifling no frivolous contempt of plain, and weak admiration of showy persons and things. [I do not say this in flattery—but in genuine sincerity. Put such an one as A[melia] W[alker][8] in the same situation and mark what a mighty difference there would be in the result! I say no more: remember me kindly to your excellent sisters, accept the good wishes of my Papa, Aunt, Sisters and Brother, and continue to spare a corner of your warm affectionate heart for

Your true and grateful friend
Charlotte Brontë.]

MS untraced. W&S 31.
Address: not in sources.
PM: not in sources.
Text: based on Rylands MS *Life* fos. 127–8; omissions supplied in square brackets from *Nussey* 28–9.† indicates a word supplied from *Needham*. W & S 31 derives from *Shorter* 13, which imperfectly reproduces either *Nussey* or a manuscript, possibly a copy MS by EN. *Hours at Home* 106 prints only the sections in square brackets, with minor variants in accidentals.

1. *Nussey*, *Shorter*, W & S read '*now* you'.
2. *Shorter* and W & S read 'almost apocryphal'.
3. Both Babylon and Nineveh, two of the 'lost cities of the ancient world', were memorably painted by John Martin (1789–1854). Nineveh was the city to which God commanded Jonah to go in Jonah 1: 2: 'Arise, go to Nineveh, that great city, and cry against it; for their wickedness is come up before me.' Excavations of the ruined city had begun in the 1820s. Martin's 'Fall of Nineveh', analysed in *Blackwood's Edinburgh Magazine* for July 1828, influenced CB's poem, 'The trumpet hath sounded', written on 11 Dec. 1831. (Neufeldt *CBP* 91–3, Winnifrith *CBP* 133–5.) For Martin's influence on CB's writing and for her fascination with ruined cities see Gérin *CB* 43–50 and Christine Alexander, 'Art and Artists in Charlotte Brontë's Juvenilia', *BST* 20. 4. 177–204, both with illustrations.
4. *Nussey*, *Shorter*, W & S read 'men and women-kind'.
5. *Nussey*, *Shorter*, W & S read 'as sealed'. *Shorter* and W & S omit the word 'scrolls'.
6. *Nussey*, *Shorter*, W & S read 'really grateful'.
7. *Nussey*, *Shorter*, W & S read 'your letter'.
8. Amelia Walker (?*c*.1818–25.5.1892), a fellow-pupil of CB at Roe Head, was the younger daughter of the wealthy Joseph Walker (1779–1862) and his wife Jane of Lascelles Hall, Lepton, near Huddersfield. She was the niece of CB's godmother, Mrs Thomas Atkinson, née Frances Walker, and was to outlive the rest of her family, becoming a rich heiress. For CB's critical view of Amelia, see EN July 1836. CB's pencil drawing of her, dated June 1831, is now in BPM (HAOBP. P. Br. C62), and is reproduced in *BST* 12. 63. opp. p. 33. For Lascelles Hall see EN 7.7.1836 n. 4 and *BST* 19. 6. 287–8.

To Ellen Nussey, 4 July 1834

Haworth

Dear Ellen,

You will be tired of paying the postage of my letters[1] but necessity must plead my excuse for their frequent recurrence, I must thank you for your very handsome present, The bonnet is pretty, neat and simple, as like the Giver as possible It brought *Ellen *Nussey with her fair, quiet face, brown eyes, and dark hair full to my remembrance. I wish I could find some other way to thank you for your kindness than words, the load of obligation under which you lay me is positively overwhelming, and I make no return. In your last you request me to tell you of your faults and to cease flattering you. Now really Ellen how can you be so foolish? I won't tell you of your faults, because I don't know them, what a creature would that be who after receiving an affectionate and kind letter from a beloved friend, should sit down and write a catalogue of defects by way of answer? Imagine me doing so and then consider what epithets you would bestow on me, Conceited, Dogmatical, Hypocritical little Humbug, I should think would be mildest; Why child I've neither time nor inclination to reflect on your faults when you are so far from me, and when besides kind letters and presents and so forth are continually bringing forward your goodness in the most prominent light. Then too there are judicious relatives always round you who can much better discharge that unpleasant office, I have no doubt their advice is completely at your service, Why then should I intrude mine? If you will not hear them, it will be vain—though one should rise from the ?dead to instruct you.[2] [Let] us have no more nonsense about fl[attery] Ellen, if you love me.[3] Mr R[ichard] *Nussey,[4] is going to 'be' married is he? Well his wife-elect appeared to me to be a clever, and aimiable lady as far as I could judge from the little I saw of her and from your account. Now to this flattering sentence must I tack a long list of her faults Ellen? You say it is in contemplation for you to leave Rydings,[5] I am sorry for it, Rydings is a pleasant spot, one of the old family Halls of England, surrounded by Lawn, and wood-land speaking of past times and suggesting (to me at least) happy feelings. Martha *Taylor thought you grown less did she? that's like Martha, I am not grown a bit but as short, and dumpy as ever. I wrote to Mary lately but have as yet received no answer. You ask me to recommend some books for your perusal; I will do so in as few words as I can. If you like poetry let it be first rate, Milton,[6] Shakespeare, Thomson,[7] Goldsmith Pope (if you will though I don't admire him) Scott,[8] Byron,[9] Camp[b]ell,[10] Wordsworth and Southey Now Ellen don't be startled at the names of Shakespeare, and Byron. Both these were great Men and their works are like themselves, You will know how to chuse the good and avoid the evil, the finest passages are always the purest, the bad are invariably revolting you will never wish to read them over twice, Omit the Comedies of Shakspeare and the Don Juan, perhaps the Cain of Byron though the latter is a magnificent Poem and read the rest fearlessly, that must indeed be a depraved mind which can gather evil from Henry the 8th from Richard 3d from Macbeth and Hamlet and Julius Cesar, Scott's sweet, wild, romantic Poetry can do you no harm nor can Wordsworth's nor Campbell's nor Southey's, the greatest part at least of his some is certainly exceptionable, For History read Hume,[11] Rollin,[12] and the Universal History[13] if you can I never did. For Fiction—read Scott alone all novels after his are worthless. For Biography, read Johnson's lives of the Poets,[14] Boswell's life of Johnson,[15]

Southey's life of Nelson[16] Lockhart's life of Burns,[17] Moore's life of Sheridan, Moore's life of Byron,[18] Wolfe's remains.[19] For Natural History read Bewick,[20] and Audubon,[21] and Goldsmith[22] and White of Selborne[23] For Divinity, but your brother Henry[24] will advise you there I only say adhere to standard authors and don't run after novelty. If you can read this scrawl[25] it will be to the credit of your patience. With love to your Sisters, believe me to be

for ever Your's
Charlotte Brontë

MS HM 24408. W & S 32.
Address (integral): Miss E Nussey | Birstall | nr Leeds
PM: (i) BRADFORD YORKS | JY 5 | 1834 (ii) *Bradford Yorks* | *Py Post*

1. See EN 21.7.1832 n. 13.
2. cf. Luke 16: 31 'If they hear not Moses and the prophets, neither will they be persuaded, though one rose from the dead.'
3. Loss of text caused by tears in the paper. Words supplied from *Needham*.
4. For Richard Nussey see EN 13.1.1832 n. 4. He did not marry until Sept. 1846, when his bride was Elizabeth Charnock (b. 1803), daughter of John Charnock, 'Gentleman', of 103 Woodhouse Lane, Leeds. (Leeds Directories from 1830 to 1847 give what is probably the same address in slightly different forms.) See EN 29.9.1846. Mr Charnock also owned a mill, and tenements at Trafalgar Mill, in Meadow Lane, Leeds.
5. See EN 5.9.1832 n. 7. Rydings did not belong to Mrs Nussey, EN's mother, but to her brother-in-law the bachelor Richard Nussey (1763–30.11.1835) who also lived there. On his death it was bought by EN's brother John, the London apothecary, who wished to provide a home for his mother-in-law, Mrs Mary Walker, and her daughters Elizabeth and Catharine. In the event Mrs Nussey, Mercy, and EN did not move to Brookroyd, Birstall, until summer 1836.
6. CB's copy of *Paradise Lost* (1797 edn., Edinburgh) is in the BPM, MS bb39.
7. James Thomson (1700–48), author of *The Seasons* (1726–30). Mrs Brontë's copy, an 1803 edn. inscribed 'Maria Branwell 1804 Penzance' is BPM MS bb213.
8. Sir Walter Scott (1771–1832). CB frequently quotes from his poems and novels in her own fiction. See *The Professor* appendix VII, 333–4. For the influence of his work on her juvenilia, see EN 1.1.1833 n. 3.
9. The works, including *Don Juan*, and the personal myth of George Gordon, Lord Byron (1788–1824) greatly attracted the young Brontës, and influenced their later fiction, esp. in the characterization of Rochester in *JE*. See e.g. Gérin *CB* ch. 4, *JE* Explanatory Notes, and Alexander *EEW* introductions and notes, esp. those to *The Spell*, written on 21 July 1834. (*EEW* ii. pt 2, 148–238.)
10. Thomas Campbell (1777–1844), author of *The Pleasures of Hope* (1799) and many other poems, very popular in their day. He was also the editor of the *New Monthly Magazine* from 1820 to 1830.
11. David Hume (1711–76), Scottish philosopher and historian. The 6 vols. of his *History of England* appeared between 1754 and 1761.
12. Charles Rollin (1661–1741), author of *Histoire ancienne* (1730–8) and *Histoire romaine*, of which 8 vols. were completed by 1741. The Brontës' copy of *Histoire ancienne* was in the Haworth Parsonage Sale on 2.10.1861. See BPM MS BS X H.
13. The novelist Tobias George Smollett (1721–71) contributed to and helped to compile some of the 44 vols. of the 'Modern Part' of the *Universal History* which appeared between 1759 and 1766. One of the proprietors of the *History* was the novelist and printer Samuel Richardson. Another *Universal History* in 25 vols. was produced by the Revd William Fordyce Mavor (1758–1837) in 1802–4. See Neufeldt *BBP* 371.
14. Dr Samuel Johnson (1709–84) published *Lives of the Poets* vols. i–iv in 1779 and vols. v–x in 1781.

15. *The Life of Samuel Johnson* by James Boswell (1740–95), published 1791.
16. CB admired Robert Southey (1774–1843) as a poet (with some reservations) as well as a biographer. See her correspondence with him, *infra*, March 1837. His *Life of Nelson* (1813), expanded from an article in the *Quarterly Review* of February 1810, was described by Macaulay as 'the most perfect and the most delightful of his works'.
17. *Life of Robert Burns* (1828) by John Gibson Lockhart (1794–1854), one of the writers to whom CB sent a copy of *Poems by Currer, Ellis, and Acton Bell* on 16 June 1847 'in acknowledgment of the pleasure and profit we have often and long derived from your works'. See p. 530.
18. *The Life of Sheridan* (1825) and *The Letters and Journals of Lord Byron*, with a *Life* by Thomas Moore (1830). The Brontës derived much of their knowledge of Byron from Moore's *Life*, and copied engravings from it. See Christine Alexander, 'Art and Artists in Charlotte Brontë's Juvenilia', *BST* 20. 4. 181–2.
19. Charles Wolfe (1791–1823), poet, author of 'The Burial of Sir John Moore at Corunna'. His *Remains* were published in 1829.
20. Thomas Bewick (1753–1823) wood-engraver; perhaps most famous for the finely observed illustrations in *The History of British Birds* (1797, 1804) of which Mr Brontë owned a copy. CB and her sisters copied Bewick's engravings, and in *JE* the child Jane finds the opening pages of the book, and its illustrations, mysterious and 'strangely impressive'. (Ch. 1.) See Joan Stevens, 'A Sermon in Every Vignette', *Turnbull Library Record* (Mar. 1968), 12–28.
21. John James Audubon (1785–1851), American ornithologist. In *BST* 18. 94. 271–8 Ronald Berman ('Charlotte Brontë's Natural History') points out that Audubon's splendidly illustrated *Birds of America* (1827–38) would have been too costly for the parsonage family to own, but CB might have seen the early volumes of Audubon's *Ornithological Biography* (1831–9) of which Mr Brontë eventually owned a full set.
22. Oliver Goldsmith (1728–74), the poet, playwright, and essayist, was also the author of an unreliable work on natural history, *A History of Earth and Animated Nature* (1774).
23. *The Natural History and Antiquities of Selborne* (1789) by Gilbert White (1720–93).
24. Henry Nussey (28.2.1812–1867). In 1834 Henry was a student at Magdalene College Cambridge, strongly in sympathy with the evangelical and related missionary movements, and planning to take holy orders after gaining his BA in 1835. His diary reveals an earnest and conscientious young man, capable of strong affection and gratitude towards his friends, especially the younger Revd W. M. Heald (1803–75) of Birstall. He was Curate to the Revd T. Allbutt in Dewsbury from Sept. 1835 until July 1837 and to Mr Heald from Aug. 1837 until Feb. 1838, when he became ill and 'harassed in mind'. He later recalled with shame an unspecified sin committed on 7 Mar 1838., and his distress was increased by the illness and death of his brother William in June 1838. Nervous stress, and a head injury caused by a fall from a horse, combined to hamper his ability to speak in public, and though he was conscientious in his pastoral duties at his next curacy at Burton Agnes near Bridlington, his Vicar, the Revd C. H. Lutwidge asked him to 'relinquish' it 'on acct. of the inadequacy of [his] powers to fulfil its duties'. (*HN Diary* fol. 36.) From Dec. 1838 until Apr. 1844 he was a curate at Donnington and Earnley with Almodington near Chichester in Sussex, small rural communities where he lived a fairly peaceful life. He admired his Rector the Revd Henry Browne as a 'truly excellent & clever man', and was able to preach more effectively and to undertake some tutorial work as his health improved. He felt confident enough to propose to Margaret Anne Lutwidge (1809–69), the sister of Charles Henry, whom he had met at Burton Agnes, and immediately after her refusal, to propose to CB. He accepted both their refusals with pious resignation as the 'Will of the Lord'. (See HN 5.3.1839 n. 1.) In Apr. 1844 he was licensed to the curacy of Hathersage and Derwent in Derbyshire, and became the Vicar of Hathersage in Aug. the same year. His marriage to the wealthy Emily Prescott took place at Everton in Lancs. on 22 May 1845. His 3 years at Hathersage were marred by dissension over the setting up of a school, by other disputes with his parishioners, and by his own ill health. He and his wife travelled on the Continent from July 1847 for the sake of his health, but he was never afterwards well enough to resume clerical duties. The later years of his marriage were not happy. He settled eventually in Nice, where it is presumed that he died in 1867. Parts of his diaries and several letters and sermons are preserved in BL MS Egerton 3268A.
25. The letter is crossed and is difficult to decipher.

To Ellen Nussey, 10 November 1834

Haworth.

Dear Ellen

I have been a long while, a very long while without writing to you; a letter I received from Mary *Taylor this morning reminded me of my neglect and made me instantly sit down to atone for it if possible. She tells me your Aunt *Nussey of Brookroyd[1] is dead and that poor *?Sarah[2] is very ill; for the last I am truly sorry but I trust her case is not yet without hope. You should however remember that death, should it happen, will undoubtedly be great gain to her, for existence must have possessed but little enjoyment. Can you give me any particulars respecting the failure of Messrs Haliley Brooke and Co.[3] or rather, their suspension of payment, for I hope it may not yet prove a decided failure. Do you know whether the fortunes of Mrs. Brooke,[4] Mrs. Buckworth,[5] Mrs. Carter,[6] and Mrs Jackson[7] were in their brother's ?hands What was the immediate cause of the stoppage and what dividend is expected to remain for the creditors when affairs are settled? I am thus particular in my enquiries, because Papa is anxious to hear the details of a matter so seriously affecting his old friend at Dewsbury[8]—and because I cannot myself help feeling interested in a misfortune which must fall heavily on some of my late school-fellows. Poor Leah and Maria Brooke![9] In your last dear Ellen you asked my opinion respecting the amusement of Dancing, and whether I thought it objectionable when indulged for an hour or two in parties of Boys and Girls. I should hesitate to express a difference of opinion from Mr *Allbut[10] or from your excellent Sister, but really the matter seems to me to stand thus. It is allowed on all hands that the Sin of Dancing[11] consists not in the mere action of "shaking the shanks" (as the Scotch say) but in <its> the consequences that usually attend it nam[ely][12] Frivolity and waste of time. When it is us[ed] only, as in the case you state, for the [ex]ercise and amusement of an hour among young people (who surely may, without any breach of God's ordinances be allowed a little light-heartedness) these consequences cannot follow. Ergo[13] (according to my manner of arguing) the amusement at such times is perfectly innocent. Having nothing more to say, I will conclude with the expression of my sincere and earnest attachment for, Ellen, your own dear self.

Charlotte Brontë

Pray write soon. forgive mistakes, erasures bad-writing &c. Farewell

MS Pierpont Morgan MA 2696. W & S 33.
Address (integral): Miss E Nussey, | Rydings, | Birstall.
PM: (i) BRADFORD | YORKS | NO 11 | 1834 (ii) *Bradford Yorks* | *Py Post*
Annotation by EN on address panel: 34 | Nov 10 an opinion on dancing

1. Ann Nussey (1764–4.10.1834), daughter of Joshua Nussey (1715/16–1792) of Birstall Smithies and his wife Mercy (1733–96), EN's grandparents. Brookroyd, a comfortable but less spacious and impressive house a short distance from Rydings, was to be the home of EN, her mother, and her sister Mercy from summer 1836. See *Whitehead* 66, 71, and 134.
2. Sarah Walker Nussey (1809–43), EN's invalid and possibly disabled sister.
3. Halliley, Brooke, and Hallileys, woollen manufacturers and merchants of Aldams Mills, Westgate, Dewsbury. The failure, one of several in the woollen trade at this period, was caused by the 'stoppage' of the London house of Halliley and Carter. See the *Leeds Mercury* 25.10.1834, 5: 'At a meeting of the creditors of Messrs Halliley, Brooke, and Hallileys, of Dewsbury, merchant manufacturers, held this week, it was judged expedient to wind up the Concern through the medium of the Gazette.' On 22.11.1834 the *Leeds Mercury* reprinted the notice of bankruptcy from the *London Gazette* of 18 Nov. The Hallileys purchased the mill back from the receivers by taking out a mortgage, and continued to operate it and presumably to make profits which would then be used to pay off the mortgage.
4. Mrs John Brooke, née Sarah Halliley, daughter of the former head of the firm John Halliley who had died on 18 Aug. 1828. John Brooke, one of the senior partners, had married Sarah at Dewsbury Parish Church on 30 May 1808, the Revd John Buckworth being the officiating minister. Like the other three ladies, she was a sister of the present head of the firm, John Halliley junior.
5. Mrs John Buckworth, née Rachel Halliley (b. 1781), sister of Mrs Brooke. She was married on 28 Jan. 1806. With Mrs Jackson, she was one of the beneficiaries under the will of John Halliley senior.
6. Not traced. Perhaps this sister had married a member of the London firm of Halliley and Carter.
7. The wife of the Revd Thomas Jackson, née Sophia Halliley (b. 1798).
8. The Revd John Buckworth (1779–2.4.1835), a graduate of St Edmund Hall, Oxford, BA 1805, MA 1810; the husband of Rachel Halliley. He was a talented evangelical preacher and hymn-writer who had been the Vicar of Dewsbury from Dec. 1806. Mr Brontë had had rooms in the vicarage at the beginning of his curacy at Dewsbury in Dec. 1809, and remained on very friendly terms with the Buckworths when he moved to Hartshead in Mar. 1811. The Hallileys and Brookes were members of the congregation at St Stephen's, Dewsbury, and were well known to PB.
9. See EN 21.7.1832 notes 5 and 6.
10. The Revd Thomas Allbutt (1800–67), who had been admitted as a sizar to PB's old college, St John's Cambridge, on 3 July 1828, but migrated to St Catharine's on 30 Jan. 1829; BA 1833, MA 1838. He was a friend of Henry Nussey in Cambridge, and became the curate to Mr Buckworth at Dewsbury in 1832 and vicar there after Mr Buckworth's death in 1835. In 1862 he moved to become rector of Debach-cum-Boulge in Suffolk. For his first wife, née Marianne Wooler, see CB to Mrs Franks May 1831 n. 6. He married his second wife Sarah Isabella Chadwick, née Skelton, on 18.9.1849. His sister Sidney Maria was the first wife of Dr William Moore Wooler, brother of Margaret Wooler.
11. The dangers of indulging in worldly amusements were often emphasized in evangelical writings. CB's views are more liberal than those of her father in his moral tale, *The Maid of Killarney* (1818), where Captain Loughlean objects to dancing 'because it has a natural tendency towards' abuse: it is 'the destroyer of constitutions, the underminer of morals, the consumer of time. Consider . . . the trifling and giddy manners of a ball-room.' (*Bronteana* 152.)
12. Loss of text caused by a fold in the paper.
13. Therefore (Latin).

To Ellen Nussey, 12 January 1835

Haworth

Dearest Ellen

I thought it better not to answer your very kind letter too soon—lest I should (in the present fully occupied state of your time) appear, intrusive. I am happy to inform you that Papa has given me permission to accept the invitation it conveyed, & erelong I hope once more to have the extreme pleasure of seeing almost the only, and certainly the dearest friend I possess (out of our own family). I leave it to you to fix the time—only requesting you not to appoint too early a day, let it be at least a fortnight or three weeks from the date of the present letter. I am greatly obliged to you for your kind offer of meeting me at Bradford,[1] but Papa thinks that such a plan would involve much uncertainty, and would besides be productive of too much trouble to you. He recommends therefore that I should 'go' direct in a Gig from Haworth to Rydings,[2] at the time you shall determine, or if that day should prove unfavourable, on the first subsequently fine one. Such an arrangement would leave us both free and if it meets with your approbation, would perhaps be the best we could finally resolve on. It gave me great pleasure to hear that poor *Sarah[3] is nearly recovered but *Mercy's illness counterbalances that, I hope however both are alike—convalescent by this time. Excuse the brevity of this epistle dear Ellen for I am in a great hurry, and we shall I trust soon see each other face to face,[4] which will be better than a hundred letters. Give my respectful love to your Mother and Sisters, Accept the kind remembrances of all our family and believe me in particular to be

Your firm and faithful friend
Charlotte Brontë

P.S. You ask me to stay a month when I come, but as I do not wish to tire you with my company, and as besides Papa, and Aunt both think a fortnight amply sufficient, I certainly shall not exceed that period.

Farewell, dearest, dearest Ellen

MS HM 24409. W & S 34.
Address (integral): Miss E Nussey | Rydings | nr Birstall
PM: (i) BRADFORD YORKS | JA 12 | 1835 (ii) *Bradford Yorks* | *Py Post*

1. Bradford is about 12 miles from Haworth and 6 from Rydings, Birstall.
2. The gig, a 'light two-wheeled one-horse carriage' (*OED*), would be hired in Haworth. cf. the 'rickety dogcart' scorned by EN in EN 11.9.1833 n. 2.
3. See EN 10.11.1834 n. 2
4. A phrase often used in the Bible. See e.g. 3 John 1: 14.

To Ellen Nussey, 13 March 1835

Haworth

Dear Ellen,

I suppose by this time you will be expecting to hear from me. You did not fix any precise period when I should write, so I hope you will not be very angry on the score of delay, &c. Well, here I am, as completely separated from you as if a hundred instead of seventeen miles intervened between us. I can neither hear you, nor see you, nor feel you, you are become a mere thought, an unsubstantial impression on the memory which however is happily incapable of erasure. My journey home was rather melancholy, and would have been very much so but for the presence and conversation of my worthy companion. I found K[elly][1] a very intelligent man and really not unlike Cato,[2] (you will understand the allusion.) He told me the adventures of his sailor's life, his shipwreck, and the hurricane he had witnessed in the West Indies, with a much better flow of language than many of far greater pretentions are masters of. I thought he appeared a little dismayed by the wildness of the country round Haworth, and I imagine he has carried back a pretty report of it. He was very inquisitive, and asked several questions respecting the names of places, directions of roads, &c., which I could not answer. I fancy he thought me very stupid.

What do you think of the course Politics are taking? I make this inquiry because I now think you have a[3] wholesome interest in the matter, formerly you did not care greatly about it. B[aines][4] you see is triumphant. Wretch! I am a hearty hater, and if there is any one I thoroughly abhor, it is that man. But the opposition is divided, red-hots and luke-warms; and the Duke[5] (par-excellence the Duke) and Sir Robert Peel[6] show no signs of insecurity, though they have already been twice beat; so "courage, mon amie." Heaven defend the right:[7] as the old chevaliers used to say, before they joined battle. Now Ellen, laugh heartily at all this rodomontade, but you have brought it on yourself, don't you remember telling me to write such letters to you as I write to Mary Taylor?[8] Here's a specimen; hereafter should follow a long disquisition on books, but I'll spare you that. Give my best and sincerest love[9] to your mother and sisters. Every soul in this house unites with me in best wishes to yourself.

I am, dear Ellen,
Thy friend,
Charlotte.

P.S.[10] Did Kelly request you to send the umbrella I left to the Bulls Head Inn,[11] Bradford? Our carrier called for it on Thursday but it was not there. I suppose the people of the Inn have lost it. Happily it was of no great value, so it does not much signify.

MS untraced. W & S 35.
Address: not in source.
PM: not in source.
Text: *Nussey* 32–4 with one emendation from Rylands MS *Life* in l. 21. The extract in *Life*, from 'What do you think' to 'joined battle', is probably MS-based. W & S 35 derives from *Shorter* 17, which may be a careless version of *Nussey*, or of a separate EN or T. J. Wise copy. The unreliable edited text in *Hours at Home* reads 'unhappily incapable' in l. 8. (xi. 107.)

1. The driver: not traced. CB had returned in a carriage to Haworth, presumably after the fortnight's visit to EN which had been planned for Feb. Kelly is said to have been a manservant of the Nussey family.
2. The name used for a man of simple habits, severe morals, and blunt speech, like the Roman censor Cato, 234–149 BC; or the 'young and noble Cato', the austere conspirator in *Julius Caesar* and protagonist of Addison's play, *Cato*. The precise point of the allusion remains obscure. For the first usage, cf. *The Professor* 183 and n.
3. *Life* reads 'you take a'.
4. Rylands MS *Life* reads 'Baines'; although the name is not deleted the printed *Life*, like *Nussey*, reads 'B.' (i. 142.) Edward Baines (1774–1848), the proprietor of the *Leeds Mercury*, had been elected on 9 Jan. as the Whig MP for Leeds with 1,803 votes in the General Election which followed the dissolution of the first reformed parliament in Dec. 1834. He was a Dissenter and had supported Catholic Emancipation, parliamentary reform, and the abolition of church rates. Shorter, followed by W & S, reads 'Brougham', which may be right; but it seems more likely that Shorter expanded 'B' in his source to 'Brougham' at EN's suggestion, or on the grounds that the Whig Henry Peter Brougham (Lord Brougham, 1778–1868) would be anathema to CB, and ignored the fact that Brougham was not 'triumphant' at this period.
5. The Duke of Wellington. See EN 20.2.1834 n. 2 and 8.5.1835 n. 4. He was first 'beat' when he resigned the premiership rather than accept parliamentary reform in 1830.
6. See EN 20.2.1834 n. 3 and 8.5.1835 n. 4. As Home Secretary in Wellington's administration from January 1828, Peel had resigned with Wellington in 1830. In her Diary Paper of 24 Nov. 1834 EJB had written 'This morning Branwell went down to Mr Driver's and brought news that Sir Robert Peel was going to be invited to stand for Leeds', but the Tory candidate proved to be Sir John Beckett, elected along with Baines in Jan. 1835. The rumour about Peel had probably circulated from James Driver's grocer's and draper's shop in Haworth. (See White's *Directory* (1838), ii. 442.)
7. cf. *Richard II*, I iii. 101, 'Receive thy lance, and God defend the right.' 'Heaven . . . right!' omitted in *Life* i. 143.
8. The Taylors of the Red House, Gomersal, like the Yorkes in *Shirley*, were convinced and argumentative radicals. cf. BB 17.5.1832 and n. 5.
9. *Shorter* and W & S read 'Give my sincerest love'.
10. *Shorter* and W & S omit the third sentence of the postscript.
11. A substantial coaching-inn in Westgate, Bradford. See Gérin *BB* 143–4, and William Scruton, *Pen and Pencil Pictures of Old Bradford* (Bradford, 1889), 168–9, with illustration.

To Ellen Nussey, 8[May] 1835

Haworth.

Dearest Ellen

Judging by the date of your letter, (April 1st.) precisely one month and four days intervened between the period in which it was written and that which brought it to my hands. I received it last Monday and till that time it continued to lie snugly enclosed in the umbrella at the Bull's Head Inn Bradford,[1] our Carrier having neglected to inquire for it. Poor Mr. Buckworth,[2] who was only ill when you wrote, is now, dead and buried! He had a troubled sojourn in Dewsbury; but undoubtedly he has now found rest in heaven Mr T Allbut[3] according to the papers has succeeded him. Will Miss Marianne Wooler change her name soon? I should suppose all cause of delay is now removed. The Election! The Election![4] that cry has rung even amongst our lonely hills like the blast of a trumpet. how has it roused the populous neighbourhood of Birstall? Ellen, under what banner have your brothers ranged themselves? the Blue or the Yellow? Use your influence with them entreat them if it be necessary on your knees to stand by their country and Religion in this day of danger. Oh! I wish the whole West-Riding of our noble [Yorkshire would feel the][5] necessity of exertion [. . .] were animated by [. . .] That traitor to his [. . .] had the meannes[s. . .] with a plebeian [. . .] that he became [. . .] the "accident of [. . .] would 'then' soon be [. . .] to Castle Howard[6] [. . .] of the old and [. . .] which he has [. . . Oh how I wish] Stuart Wortley[7] the Son of the mos[t] patriotic ?<Representative> 'Patrician' Yorkshire owns would be elected the Representative of his native Province, Lord Morpeth[8] was at Haworth last week and I saw him, My opinion of his Lordship is recorded in a letter I wrote yesterday to Mary Taylor. it is not worth writing over again. so I will not trouble you with it here. Give my regards "tender and true" to your Sister Mercy. Surely Mr Harrison[9] is not going to leave for ever—No—No—let us think of nothing so distressing, he will I trust attend better to his own interests which I immagine lie very much in the neighbourhood of Birstall if the Man were only clear-sighted enough to discern them. Tell Miss Mercy that if she will excuse me for asking a favour to which I have so little title, a letter from her would afford me the greatest possible pleasure—Remember me to your Mother and believe my own dear Ellen that I remain

Yours with true affection
Charlotte Brontë

PS. Aunt & my sisters beg their kindest love to you.

MS BPM Bon 160. W & S 36.
Address (integral): Miss E Nussey | Birstal | nr Leeds
PM: BRADFORD YORKS | MY 9 | 1835
Annotations include 'pub in H at H'—i.e. 'published in *Hours at Home*'. See Introduction, pp. 36–8
Date: CB dates 'Haworth. March 8th.—35.' The first sentence and the postmark show that this is a slip for 'May'.

1. See EN 13.3.1835 n. 11.
2. Mr Brontë's friend and former vicar, the Revd John Buckworth of Dewsbury (1779–1835) who had died on 2 Apr. He had 'enjoyed but indifferent health and frequently travelled in the south of England because of its warmer climate'. (*LD* 45.) In PB's *Cottage Poems* (1811), written while he was a curate at Dewsbury, he gives pride of place to his 'Epistle | to the Rev, J— B—, (Vicar of Dewsbury) | whilst journeying for the recovery of his | health.' See EN 10.11.1834 n. 8.
3. The Revd Thomas Allbutt had been Mr Buckworth's curate. He took over from Mr Buckworth the editorship of the *Cottage Magazine* as well as becoming Vicar of Dewsbury; according to EN

in a letter to Shorter of 22 Apr. 1896, Mr Allbutt had once been the 'editor of a newspaper at the Staffordshire potteries'. (MS Texas.) The Allbutt family came from Shelton, Hanley, in Staffs. See Mrs Franks May 1831 n. 6 and EN 10.11.1834 n. 10. for his marriage to Marianne Wooler—delayed no doubt owing to Mr Allbutt's previous small income as a curate.

4. The withdrawal of Lord Althorp in Nov. 1834 weakened Melbourne's Whig administration; William IV dismissed the Whigs ('yellows') and asked the Duke of Wellington to form a government. The general election of Jan. 1835 brought in a weak minority Tory ('blue') government under Peel, who had to resign after being beaten on the question of Irish church revenues. Lord Melbourne reluctantly returned to office in Apr. at the head of a disunited Whig government. Mayhall records that on 16 May 'A West-Riding election took place *vice* Lord Morpeth [see below], who was appointed a member of the Whig ministry. The hon. John Stuart-Wortley, the eldest son of Lord Wharncliffe, was brought out by the tories, in opposition to Lord Morpeth. The result of the poll was . . . Lord Morpeth, 9,066. Hon. J.S. Wortley, 6,259.' (*Mayhall* i. 426.)
5. Loss of text caused by the tearing away of about a quarter of the leaf. W & S (like *Needham*) read 'our noble [Yorkshire would feel the] necessity of exertion . . .' They omit the 7 cryptic phrases which follow, then read, '[Oh, how I wish] Stuart Wortley.' 'the accident of' was probably 'of birth'. The general drift is clear enough: CB appears to believe that Lord Morpeth has betrayed his noble lineage by standing in the Whig interest, and she hopes that the Tory John Stuart-Wortley will be elected.
6. The great baroque mansion near York, designed by Sir John Vanbrugh for the 3rd Earl of Carlisle at the end of the 17th cent. and built during the 18th. In 1835 it was the family home of George Howard, the 6th Earl of Carlisle, whose eldest son, Lord Morpeth, was contesting the election.
7. John Stuart-Wortley (1801–55), son of the 1st Baron Wharncliffe, a leading Tory statesman who had shown great personal courage during the reform riots in Yorkshire in 1832. John Stuart-Wortley had been Tory MP for Bossiney from 1823 to 1832, and was eventually to represent the West Riding from 1841 to 1845, when he became the 2nd Baron Wharncliffe on the death of his father. The *DNB* describes him as 'an enlightened agriculturist and a cultivated man.'
8. George William Frederick Howard (1802–64), Viscount Morpeth, who was to become the 7th Earl of Carlisle on the death of his father, the 6th Earl, in Oct. 1848. As the Whig MP for Morpeth from June 1826 he had supported various liberal reforms, and as one of 4 MPs for Yorks. from Aug. 1830 he had spoken in favour of the Reform Bill—and had offended PB by referring to the rural churches as so many 'dark lanterns'. From Dec. 1832 he was MP for the West Riding of Yorks, and had been re-elected in Jan. 1835. In May 1851 he introduced himself to the by then famous Currer Bell in London and talked in a 'courteous kind fashion'. (See her letter to PB of 31.5.1851, in Vol. iii). He was 'able and kind-hearted' with cultivated tastes and 'great fluency of speech'. (*DNB*.)
9. Not identified. Apparently he was thought to be 'interested' in Mercy Nussey.

To Ellen Nussey, 2 July 1835

[Haworth]

Dear Ellen

I had hoped to have had the extreme pleasure of seeing you at Haworth this summer, but human affairs are mutable, and human resolutions must bend to the course of events—We are all about to divide, break up, separate, Emily is going to school Branwell is going to London,[1] and I am going to be a Governess[2] This last determination I formed myself, knowing that I should have to take the step sometime, and "better sune as syne"[3] to use the Scotch proverb and knowing also that Papa would have enough to do with his limited income should Branwell be placed at the Royal Academy, and Emily at Roe-Head. Where am I going to reside? you will ask—within four miles of Yourself dearest at a place neither of us are wholly unacquainted with, being no other than the identical Roe-Head mentioned above. Yes I am going to teach, in the very school where I was myself taught—Miss *Wooler made me the offer and I preferred it to one or two proposals of Private Governesship which I had before received—I am sad, very sad at the thoughts of leaving home but Duty—Necessity—these are stern Misstresses who will not be disobeyed. Did I not once say Ellen you ought to be thankful for your independence? I felt what I said at the time, and I repeat it now with double earnestness: if any thing would cheer me, it is the idea of being so near you—surely you and Polly[4] will come, and see me—it would be wrong in me to doubt it—you were never unkind yet. Emily, and I leave home on the 29th. of this month, the idea of being together consoles us both somewhat—and in truth since I must enter a situation "my lines have fallen in pleasant places"[5]—I both love, and respect Miss *Wooler—What did you mean Ellen by saying that you knew the reason why I wished to have a letter from your sister *Mercy? the sentence hurt me though I did not quite understand it. My only reason was a desire to correspond with a person I have a regard for; give my love both to her and to *Sarah and Miss *Nussey,[6] remember me respectfully to Mrs. *Nussey, and believe me my dearest friend

Affectionately, warmly Yours
C Brontë

July 2nd. —35
My paper has I see got somehow disgracefully blotted, but as I really have not time to write another letter, I must beg you to excuse its slovenly appearance—pray let no one else see it—for the writing into the bargain is shameful.

MS HM 24410. W & S 38.
Address (integral): Miss E Nussey | Rydings | nr. Birstall
PM: (i) BRADFORD YORKS | JY 6 | 1835 (ii) *Bradford Yorks* | *Penny Post*

1. An undated draft letter from Branwell Brontë to the Secretary of the Royal Academy survives. It reads, 'Sir Having an earnest desire to enter as probationary Student in the Royal Academy, but not being possessed of information as to the means of obtaining my desire I presume to request from you as Secretary to the Institution an answer to the questions—Where am I to present my drawing? At what time? and especially can I do it in August or September.' (BPM MS Bon 147.) On the reverse of the MS draft are verse fragments in minuscule handwriting. See Neufeldt *BBP* nos. 55, 56, and notes. The brownish-white wove paper watermarked 'J GREE[N] & SON | 1834' is the same as that used by CB for several letters in 1836. There is no firm evidence that Branwell ever went to London. Ch. 9 in Gérin *BB*, where it is assumed that he did so, is based on unauthenticated reports and on one of Branwell's stories, his 'History of Angria'. He had, however, been receiving lessons in painting from the Leeds artist, William Robinson (1799–1839), a portrait-painter, who had studied under Sir Thomas Lawrence at the

Academy. Mr Brontë wrote to Robinson on 7.9.1835 to say that Branwell hoped to be with him 'on Friday next, in order to finish his course of lessons'. (W & S 40.)

2. The term was used for a teacher in a school as well as in a private house. CB was to teach at Roe Head, filling the vacancy left when Marianne Wooler married on 9 July, and Emily would be a pupil there.
3. Better soon than later. (Scottish proverb.) *ODEP* gives 'As good soon as syne', but quotes also from Scott, *Rob Roy* ch. 18, giving the form used here. cf. *Villette* 382: the dormouse 'must one day go the way of all flesh, "As well soon as syne." '
4. Mary Taylor.
5. cf. Psalm 16: 6, 'The lines are fallen unto me in pleasant places; yea, I have a goodly heritage.'
6. Sarah Walker Nussey and Ann Nussey.

Revd Patrick Brontë to Mrs J. C. Franks,[1] *6 July 1835*

Haworth, near Bradford,
Yorkshire

My dear Madam,

As two of my dear children, are soon to be placed near you,[2] I take the liberty of writing to you a few lines, in order to request both you and Mr. Franks, to be so kind, as to interpose with your advice and counsel, to them, in any case of necessity—and if expedient to write to Miss Branwell, or me, if our interference should be requisite. I will charge them, strictly, to attend to what you may advise, though, it is not my intention, to speak to them, of this letter. They, both, have good abilities, & as far as I can judge their principles, are good also, but they are very young, and unacquainted with the ways of this delusive, and insnaring world, and though, they will be placed under the superintendance, of Miss Wooler, who will I doubt not, do what she can for their good, yet, I am well aware, that neither they, nor any other, can ever, in this land of probation, lie beyond the reach of temptation. It is my design, to send my son, for whom, as you may remember, my <?warm>, kind, and true friends, Mr. Firth,—and Mrs. Firth,[3] were sponsors,—to the Royal Academy, for Artists, in London[4]—and my dear little Anne, I intend, to keep at home, for another year,[5] under her Aunt's tuition, and my own.—For these dispositions, I feel indebted, under God, to you, and Miss Outhwaite,[6] and Mrs. Firth, and other kind Friends,—and for every act of kindness, I feel truly grateful. It has given us all unfeigned pleasure, to learn, that your health, is nearly restored, and that Mr. Franks and your 'dear' little children,[7] are all well. Several years ago, I saw in Bradford, a fine little child of yours, whom I took into my arms, and would have nursed, but it took the alarm, and would not stay with me; and so I was obliged to return it to Miss Outhwaite, in whom it placed greater confidence. My own health, is generally but very delicate, yet through a gracious providence, and with great care, I am for the most part, able to perform my various ministerial duties. Indeed, I have never been very well, since I left Thornton.[8] My happiest days were spent there.[9] In this place, I have received civilities, and have I trust, been civil to all, but I have not tried to make any friends, nor have I met with any whose mind, was congenial, with my own. I have not been, at Thornton, or Kipping, for many years. The last time I was there, I travel'd over some of my ancient paths, and thought of my Dear Wife and children, whom death had removed,[10] and when I was in the church, and reflected, that my beloved Friend,[11] with whom I was wont to take sweet counsel, was beneath my feet, sadness came over my heart, and afterwards, as I walked round your garden, I call'd to mind all my dear friends who were removed from thence—by the vicissitudes of life—and I soon found the whole aspect of affairs to be entirely changed—and so I return'd home, fully intending, to visit Thornton and Kipping no more, unless I should be in a great measure forced, by reason of circumstances. I have heard however, that some alterations, and perhaps, a few improvements have been made there—But of these you must know more than I do—as probably you often revisit the place of your nativity, and the scenes of your early youth. Amidst all the chances, changes, and trials of this mortal life,[12] we have still the glorious conviction, on our minds, that we may have our hope immoveably anchor'd in heaven,[13] by the Throne of God, in whom there is no variableness, neither shadow of turning.[14] And I trust this blessed consideration, will be a never failing source of comfort to you, during the remainder of your journey through life—and especially at that last hour when you will step out of time, into eternity. We are now, as members of the Church of England placed under peculiar trials, outwardly, from the numerous, and inveterate enemies of both the church and state, and we may have enemies within—Yet still, if we look to the Lord, in humility, patience, and faith, and use the appropriate scriptural means, we shall at last come off, more than conquerors,[15] over death and hell, and obtain houses, not made with hands, eternal in the heavens.[16]

Be so good, as to give my very kind and respectful regards, to Mr. Franks—and to my old and kind Friends, Mrs. Firth, and Miss Outhwaite, when you see them—And also excuse, the trouble, which I have here given you—And believe me, My Dear Madam,

ever Yours, very sincerely
And truly,
P. Brontê.

MS BPM B.S. 184. W & S 39.
Address (integral): Mrs. Franks, | Vicarage, | Huddersfield.
PM: (i) BRADFORD YORKS | JY 7 | 1835 (ii) *Bradford Yorks* | *Penny Post*

1. See PB to Mrs Franks 28.4.1831 notes 1 and 3.
2. Roe Head school is about $4\frac{1}{2}$ miles from Huddersfield. 'On the 29th of July, 1835, Charlotte went. . .as teacher to Miss Wooler's. Emily accompanied her as a pupil.' (*Life* i. 149.)

3. Anne, née Greame (?1761–1846), Mrs Franks's stepmother, the second wife of Dr John Scholefield Firth to whom she was married on 6 Sept. 1815.
4. See the previous letter, and n. 1. Branwell's preliminary visit to the Academy may have been planned for Sept.
5. In the event Anne was to replace Emily, who was unhappy at Roe Head, from late Oct. See Edward Chitham, *A Life of Anne Brontë* (Oxford, 1991), 44. Anne's pencil drawing of an oak tree, dated 27.10.1835 (MS BPM Bon 15) was done at Roe Head.
6. See PB to Mrs Franks 28.4.1831 n. 4.
7. The Franks had 5 children: John Firth (1826–1917), James Coulthurst (1828–?1928), Henry James (1830–54), Elizabeth (1831–97), and William Walker (1833–64).
8. In 1820. The Brontës' first 2 daughters, Maria and Elizabeth, had been born at Hartshead. The other children were born in Thornton, which at that time was a straggling village 4 miles west of Bradford.
9. Elizabeth Firth's (Mrs Franks's) diary from 1815 onwards records much friendly visiting between her family and the Brontës. She is said to have refused a proposal of marriage by Mr Brontë after his wife died. For an incomplete transcript of the Firth Diaries see W & S i. 36–45. The MS is in Sheffield University Library.
10. The Brontë family had been complete at Thornton. Mrs Brontë died at Haworth in 1821, and Maria and Elizabeth in 1825.
11. Mrs Franks's father. Mr Brontë had returned several times to visit Dr Firth at Thornton and had comforted him in his last illness. He took his funeral service on 2 Jan. 1821. (Diary of Elizabeth Firth, Dec. 1820 and 2 Jan. 1821.)
12. 'Assist us mercifully, O Lord . . . that, among all the changes and chances of this mortal life, [thy servants] may ever be defended.' (*BCP*, Holy Communion, Collect after the Offertory.)
13. cf. Hebrews 6: 19.
14. James 1: 17.
15. Romans 8: 37.
16. 2 Corinthians 5: 1.

To Ellen Nussey, 10 May 1836

Roe-Head

My dearest Ellen

Just now I am not at all comfortable; for if you are thinking of me at all at this moment I know you are thinking of me as an ungrateful, and indifferent being. You imagine I do not appreciate the kind, constant heart whose feelings were revealed in your last letter; but I do—"Why then did I not answer it?" you will say. Because I was waiting to receive a letter from Miss *Wooler that I might know whether or not I should have time enough to give you an invitation to Haworth before the school re-opened.[1] Miss *Wooler's letter when it came summoned me instantly away and I had no time to write. Do you forgive me? I know you do, you could not preserve ˋinˊ anger[2] against me long if you would I defy you. You seemed kindly apprehensive about my health. I am perfectly well now and I never was very ill. I was struck with the note you sent me with the umbrella. it shewed a degree of interest about my concerns which I have no right to expect from any earthly creature.[3] I won't play the hypocrite I won't answer your kind, gentle friendly questions in the way you wish me to. Don't deceive yourself by imagining that I have a bit of real goodness about me. My Darling if I were like you I should have my face Zion-ward[4] though prejudice and error might occasionally fling a mist over the glorious vision before me. for with all your single-hearted sincerity you have your faults. but I am not like you. If you knew my thoughts; the dreams that absorb me; and the fiery imagination[5] that at times eats me up and makes me feel Society as it is, wretchedly insipid you would pity and I dare say despise me. But Ellen I know the treasures of the Bible I love and adore them. I can see the Well of Life[6] in all its clearness and brightness; but when I stoop down to drink of the pure waters they fly from my lips as if I were Tantalus.[7] I have written like a fool. Remember me to your Mother and Sisters. Good-bye.

Charlotte

Roe-Head May 10th. 36
come and see me soon. don't think me mad this is a silly letter[8]

MS HM 24411. W & S 44.
Address (integral): Miss E Nussey | Rydings
PM: none.

1. CB and AB had been at Roe Head from 20.1.36 until late Mar., after which they had returned home for the Easter holiday. Easter Sunday was on 3 Apr. in 1836. For the term dates see the end of CB's poem, 'But once again' in which the farewell to Haworth is dated 'Jany 19 1836'. Neufeldt *CBP* 191.
2. Possibly an error for 'persevere in anger'; the original reading, 'preserve anger' would have been acceptable.
3. Mary Taylor described CB's mood at this period: 'Three years after [the Roe Head schooldays] I heard that she had gone as teacher to Miss Wooler's. I went to see her, and asked how she could give so much for so little money, when she could live without it. She owned that, after clothing herself and Anne, there was nothing left, though she had hoped to be able to save something. She confessed it was not brilliant, but what could she do?' (Quoted by Mrs Gaskell from a letter by Mary Taylor, *Life* ch. 8, i. 152–3.) In the evenings, however, CB 'used to sit alone, and "make out" '—i.e. to imagine events in a fantasy world. (*Ibid.* i. 153.)
4. cf. John Bunyan, *The Pilgrim's Progress*, (*Christian*): 'I come from the City of *Destruction*, but am going to Mount *Zion*.' (Clarendon ed., ed. J. B. Wharey, rev. R. Sharrock; Oxford, 1960; 25.)
5. In Feb. 1836 and again in the Easter holidays CB had continued to write her exotic stories of Byronic passion and violence, imagining e.g. the Angrian queen's 'voluptuous ottoman' defiled by the chieftain Quashia, 'stupified with drunken sleep'. In 'Passing Events', written between about 18 and 29 Apr. and 24–28 June 1836, the cynical narrator satirizes Methodism. See Alexander *EW* 146–50; and for the date of the MS, *BST* 20. 3. 121–5. CB's poems at this period include lines like 'Our western tenderness does so enhance | The ardour of our women's souls & spirits | That nought on earth such fire divine inherits.' (Neufeldt *CBP* 197, ll. 109–11.)
6. cf. John 4: 14: [Jesus said] 'the water that I shall give him shall be in him a well of water springing up into everlasting life'.
7. In Greek mythology Tantalus, a son of Zeus, offended the gods and was punished by an insatiable thirst: the waters of the river in which he was plunged receded whenever he tried to drink them.
8. The postscript is written in minute print-style handwriting at the foot of the page.

To Ellen Nussey, [?28 May 1836]

[Roe Head]

My dear Ellen

You are far too kind and frequent in your invitations. You puzzle me, I hardly know how to refuse.[1] and it is still more embarrassing to accept. At any rate I cannot come this week for we are in the very thickest melée of the Repetitions.[2] I was hearing the terrible fifth section when your note arrived. But Miss Wooler says I must go to Gomersall[3] next Friday as she promised for me on Whitsunday;[4] and on Sunday Morning I will join you at Church if it be convenient and stay at Rydings till Monday Morning There's a free and easy proposal– – – – Miss Wooler has driven me to it, she says her character is implicated! I am very sorry to hear that your Mother has been ill. I do hope she is better now and that all the rest of the family are well.

Will you be so kind as to deliver the accompanying note to Miss *Taylor when you see her at Church on Sunday. Dear Ellen excuse the most horrid scrawl ever penned by mortal hands, remember me to your Mother and Sisters and believe me

E Nussey's friend
Charlotte.

MS: present location unknown. W & S 47.
Address: none.
PM: none.
Date: EN annotates '36'. The paper, a single sheet 113 mm. × 181 mm. of off-white wove with no watermark, is consistent with an 1836 date. The address may have been on an otherwise blank page: the paper has been torn at the left-hand edge. EN assured the Miss Ingilby who acquired the letter from her in Sept. 1887 that the date 'I feel certain [is] about June in the year 36'.
Text: the MS, sold by Phillips of London on 14 Nov. 1991.

1. Mrs Gaskell writes: 'Miss Wooler was always anxious to afford Miss Brontë every opportunity of recreation in her power; but the difficulty often was to persuade her to avail herself of the invitations which came . . . [She] was too apt to consider, that allowing herself a holiday was a dereliction of duty.' (*Life* i. 152.)
2. Oral tests requiring answers learnt by heart. cf. the reports on Elizabeth Firth when she was at Crofton Hall, Wakefield: 'Miss Firth repeated the first set of English questions extremely well without any mistake. April 11th 1811. Richmal Mangnall.' (MS Sheffield University Library.)
3. i.e. to Mary Taylor's home at the Red House.
4. 22 May. 'Next Friday' would be 3 June if the conjectural date of the letter is accepted. A later date for CB's visit would probably have been too close to the likely end of term. See the next letter.

To Mrs Franks,[1] *2 June 1836*

Roe-Head

Dear Madam

I have been obliged to delay answering your kind invitation until I could fix a time for accepting it. Till this Morning Miss Wooler had not decided when her school should break up; she has now fixed upon Friday the 17th. of this month for the commencement of the Vacation. On that day if all be well Anne and I hope to have the very great pleasure of seeing you at Huddersfield. We are both extremely glad to hear that your health is at least partially recovered,[2] and I <u>do</u> hope the fine Weather we have recently had may contribute to confirm it. Changes I have no doubt have taken place in your little family since I last saw it. John must now be grown a very fine boy indeed, and dear little Henry and Elizabeth must also have risen some grades in the ascent of life[3] When I first heard of Miss Outhwaite's accident[4] it shocked me much but I trust her good constitution will soon get the better of its effects. I feel anxious to know how she recovers. We propose coming by the four or five o'clock coach on Friday 'afternoon' and returning by an early Morning coach on Monday.[5] as papa I fear will scarcely be willing to dispense with us longer at home even though we should be staying with so valued a friend as yourself. Excuse what is faulty in this hasty scrawl my dear Madam, and do not think me negligent in having so long delayed to answer your kind note because I really could not help it, accept my own, and my Sister's[6] respectful and sincere love and believe me to be

Affectionately Yours
C. Brontë.

MS Sheffield. W & S 49.
Address: (integral): Mrs. Franks | Vicarage | Huddersfield
PM: none visible: possibly concealed by mounting.

1. See PB to Mrs Franks 28.4.1831 n. 1.
2. Mrs Franks's daughter, Mrs Elizabeth Moore Smith, wrote: 'My mother's health failed in 35—after influenza but she lived until Sep./37.' (MS notes, Sheffield University Library.)
3. See PB to Mrs Franks 6.7.1835 n. 7. Mrs Moore Smith noted 'My brother Henry died March 30/54 just a year before C.B.' (MS Sheffield.) John Firth Franks (1826–1917) was the Vicar of Bekesbourne, Kent, from 1868 to 1879.
4. A broken arm. See the next letter.
5. 17–20 June; but Mr Brontë 'countermanded' this arrangement, so that his daughters probably stayed until 24 June. See next letter, and EN 7.7.1836.
6. Anne had replaced Emily at Roe Head in Oct. 1835. CB later wrote: 'Liberty was the breath of Emily's nostrils; without it, she perished. The change from her own home to a school . . . was what [Emily] failed in enduring . . . Every morning when she woke, the vision of home and the moors rushed on her, and darkened and saddened the day that lay before her . . . her white face, attenuated form, and failing strength threatened rapid decline. I felt in my heart she would die if she did not go home, and with this conviction obtained her recall. She had only

been three months at school.' (Prefatory note to 'Selections from Poems by Ellis Bell' (1850); repr. in the Clarendon *WH* 446.)

Revd Patrick Brontë to Mrs J. C. Franks, 13 June [1836]

Haworth,
Near Bradford, Yorkshire

My Dear Madam,

My 'dear' little Charlotte, has <?written to me to say> 'informed me,' that you, and Mr. Franks,[1] have been so kind as to invite her, and Anne, to pay you a visit for a week, but, that, through impatience, as is very natural, they had curtail'd that invitation to a few days—I have written to them, to countermand, this intention—I esteem it, as a high privilege, that they should be under your roof, for a time—where, I am sure, they will see, and hear nothing, but what, under providence, must necessarily tend, to their best interest, in both the worlds—You, I have long known, Mr Frank's character, I am well acquainted with, through the medium of authentic report—And hence, I came to this conclusion—I have written to Charlotte, and Anne, to this effect—but as my letter, may not reach them—(owing to a bye post[2]) in due time, I will thank you, to communicate to them, this intelligence. I will, send the Horse, and Gig for them, to your house—and if necessary, they may, return from thence, by Roe-Head.—In these sentiments, Miss Branwell[3]—perfectly agrees with me—and at the same time, joins with me, and my Family, in the most respectful, and kind compliments, and regards, to you and Mr. Franks, and to Mr. and Mrs. Atkinson[4]—when you see them—For many, years, I have visited no friends, in Bradford—but, having heard, that our old friend, Miss Outhwaite,[5] had broken her arm, I went over, a few days ago, to that Town, where I saw, those, who awaken'd in me, many lively recollections of "Auld Lang Syne."[6] On some, perhaps, on all, time had made a difference—but, there was only one, whom I did not at first, recognise—They complimented me, in general, on renewing my age[7]—but perhaps, this was owing to their kind partiality—Sincerely, and ardently wishing, and praying for your health, and happiness, both here, and hereafter, I remain, My Dear Madam,

Your old Friend,
and obliged Servant,
P. Brontê.

MS BPM B.S. 186. W & S 50.
Address (integral): Mrs. Franks, | Vicarage, | Huddersfield, | Yorkshire.
PM: (i) BRADFORD YORKS | JU 14 | 1836 (ii) *Bradford Yorks* | —
Date: based on postmark and content. PB mistakenly dates '1835'.

1. See PB to Mrs Franks 28.4.1831 notes 1 and 3.
2. A short road connecting a place to one of the main post roads.
3. PB's sister-in-law Elizabeth Branwell had stayed with the Brontës at Thornton from mid-1815 until 28 July 1816, and Elizabeth Firth's (Mrs Franks's) diary for that period shows a warm friendship with her: 'I took leave of Miss Branwell. She kissed me and was much affected.' (Sheffield University Library, MS Diary for 28 July 1816.)
4. Mrs Atkinson, CB's godmother, was Mrs Franks's cousin. See CB to Mrs Franks May 1831, n. 4.
5. See PB to Mrs Franks 28.4.1831 n. 4.
6. The phrase ('old times long ago'), best-known as part of Robert Burns's song, 'Should auld acquaintance be forgot' (1788) appealed to all the Brontës. BB wrote a variant on the song in Aug. 1837 (Neufeldt *PBB* 193) and CB was to use 'Auld Lang Syne' as a chapter-title in *Villette*.
7. Perhaps an echo of Psalm 103: 5, 'thy youth is renewed like the eagle's'.

To Ellen Nussey, [c.7] July 1836

[Haworth]

My dear Ellen

Every day during the last fortnight I have been expecting to hear from you, but seeing that no intelligence arrives I begin to get a little anxious. When will you come? but three weeks now remain, and you seem resolved to defer your visit nearly till the last. I hope no whim has got into your head which makes you consider your presence indispensable at home. I do think they could do without you for a little while, and above all and seriously Ellen I hope no little touch of anger[1] is still lingering in your mind; write to me very soon and dispel my uncertainty or I shall get impatient almost irritable—

When I was at *Huddersfield whom do you think I saw? Amelia *Walker[2] She and her Sister and Mamma and Papa and Brother[3] were all at the Vicarage when we arrived there on Friday. They were monstrously gracious, Amelia almost enthusiastic in her professions of friendship!! She is taller, thinner, paler and more delicate looking than she used to be—very pretty still, very lady-like and polished, but spoilt utterly spoilt by the most hideous affectation I wish she would copy her Sister who is indeed an example: that affable unaffected manners and a sweet disposition may fascinate powerfully without the aid of beauty We spent the Tuesday at *Lascelles-*Hall[4] and had on the whole a very pleasant day. Miss Amelia changed her character every half hour. now she assumed the sweet sentimentalist, now the reckless rattler. Sometimes the question was "Shall I look prettiest lofty?" and again "Would not tender familiarity suit me better?" At one moment she affected to inquire after her old school-acquaintance the next she was detailing anecdotes of High-Life. At last I got so sick of this that I turned for relief from her to her Brother. but *William *Walker though now 'grown' a tall—well built man is an incorrigible "Booby" from him I could not extract a word of sense. Papa Aunt and all the rest unite in kind regards to you. Remember me affectionately and respectfully to your Mother and Sisters. I hope the former is now quite well. write soon very soon Fix the day, and believe me

Truly yours
Charlotte

MS HM 24412. W & S 51.
Address (integral): Miss E Nussey | Brookroyd | Birstall
PM: (i) BRADFORD YORKS | JY — | 1836 (ii) *Bradford Yorks* | *Py Post*
Annotation by EN on address panel: Ju 36 | Haworth | in vacation time
Date: CB's 'fortnight' would be the period at Haworth since she and Anne returned from their visit to Mr and Mrs Franks at Huddersfield, probably on 24 June. This would give a conjectural date of 7 July for the letter.

1. Possibly EN was displeased by the brevity of the visit to Rydings that CB had suggested in her letter of ?28 May, since it might be her last opportunity to see EN in her old home before the move to Brookroyd. See EN 4.7.1834 n. 5.
2. Amelia Walker's father Joseph Walker (1779–1862) was Mrs Franks's cousin. See EN 19.6.1834 n. 8. Amelia had been a fellow-pupil of CB and EN at Roe Head.
3. Amelia was the younger daughter of Joseph and Jane Walker. Her sister Jane and her brother William are both recorded as aged 25 in the inexact 1841 census, where Amelia's age is given as 20. She was probably born between 1818 and 1821. See EN 19.6.1834 n. 8.
   William died in 1848.
4. One of two halls at Lepton, about 2 $\frac{1}{2}$ miles east of Huddersfield. Amelia's home was the late 16th-cent. 'Old Hall', from which the New Hall (1649) was divided by a narrow lane. Both buildings had Georgian and later additions. In 1809 Joseph Walker had inherited the Old Hall (originally acquired by his grandfather, a Huddersfield Merchant, in about 1751) and had 'gentrified' it by laying out extensive park-like grounds. He had, however, neglected the rest of the estate buildings, some of which were used as commercial premises: by 1845, when the Walkers moved to Torquay, several Huddersfield firms, including Jessops, 'fancy waistcoating manufacturers', were established or held sales there. See K. Brickhill, *The Halls at Lascelles Hall* (1983; typescript, WYAS Kirklees Archives) and Williams's *Directory* for Huddersfield, 1845.

To Miss Ann Greenwood,[1] *22 July [?1836]*

My dear Anne

Should the weather prove favourable we shall be very happy to wait upon yourself and Sister[2] at the time mentioned in your note—which I presume from the date is this afternoon.

I am affectionately Your
C Brontë

MS BPM B.S. 58. No publication traced.
Address (integral): Miss A Greenwood | Spring Head[3]
PM: not in MS.
Date: the cream wove paper with a rectangular embossed design and part of a watermark, 'N & SON | 34' matches paper marked 'J GREEN & SON | 1834' used for 4 letters in 1836. This note could not postdate 1838, the year of Ann Greenwood's death.

1. Ann Greenwood (1820–38). The Greenwood memorial tablet in Haworth church records the deaths of Ann's parents, Joseph and Grace (Cockcroft) Greenwood, and continues: 'ALSO in memory of Ann their daughter, who departed this life, December the 6th 1838 in the 19th year of her age.' Joseph Greenwood (1786–1856) was a mill-owner, and a Haworth Church Trustee, related to but not on good terms with most of the wealthy mill-owning Greenwoods of Keighley and Bridge House, Haworth. On 28 June 1836 he was appointed a magistrate after a campaign on his behalf led by Patrick Brontë. For more information on the Bridge House Greenwoods, see Sarah Fermi, 'A "Religious" Family Disgraced: New Information on a Passage Deleted from Mrs Gaskell's *Life of Charlotte Brontë*', *BST* 20. 5. 289–95. For information on Joseph Greenwood's appointment to the magistracy I am indebted to Dr Juliet R. V. Barker. The BPM has portraits of the Spring Head family: see *BST* 12. 64. 319.
2. Martha Clapham Greenwood (1818–76). Ann's other sister, Sarah, had died on 6 May 1833 'in the 17th year of her age'.
3. A hamlet in the Worth valley, dominated by the Greenwood worsted mill, and about half a mile from Haworth parsonage. The Greenwoods lived in a large house near the mill. CB's note would have been delivered by hand.

To Ellen Nussey, [?August/September 1836]

[Roe Head]

Dear Ellen when your note arrived, Miss Wooler and les demoiselles,[1] were just setting out accoutred in grand style. my ladies in gay green dresses—fit for a ball-room rather than for walking four miles on a dusty road; they looked most terribly blank at the recall—what was to be done they could not lose all their trouble in dressing and preparing, they must go out somewhere so off they trotted to Mr Kitson's,[2] leaving orders that your messenger should wait for about an hour and that if they did not return in that <if they> time I should send him off with the tidings that they would do themselves the pleasure of waiting upon you to-morrow.

Ellen you are far too kind what right have either Anne or I to receive presents from you, but you will give and we must take "it is more blessed to give than to receive".[3] you leave nothing for us to do but to iterate and reiterate "thank you." I had written a foolish note to you before the boy came but it is in Miss E Upton's custody. she will deliver it to you if they should go tomorrow. I shall be sorry if the delay of the messenger should occasion you any inconvenie[nce] but it is not my fault Miss Wooler's dictum must be obeyed, at least by me

Is your Sister[4] returned? remember me affectionately to her if she is, Give my love also to Miss Mercy and to your Mother and believe me my own darling, my kind, sincere Ellen Scribble[5]

Your affectionate Coz[6]
Charlotte Scrawl

Tuesday afternoon
I am now at liberty to announce that to-morrow my Superior and their Serene Highnesses, the Ladies E & H. will shower the light of their glorious green apparel upon you, id est that they will come to Brook-royd.[7]

I am thine
Charles Thunder

I've sent one note within the other, write me just a scrap and send it by the *Uptons to-morrow do—do it will cheer me. any-thing

MS BPM Gr. E 26. *BST* 17. 90. 353–4.
Address (integral): Miss E. Nussey | Brook-royd
PM: none.
Date: the cream wove paper with a rectangular embossed design and a watermark, 'J GREEN & SON | 1834' matches that of the dated letter to EN of 26.9.1836, and the paper used in CB's Roe Head Journal fragment, 'I'm just going to write'. (BPM Bon 98(7), dated on internal evidence *c*.October 1836.) CB's reference to the Uptons in this letter and on 26 Sept. also supports the conjectural date.

1. Miss Wooler's visitors were probably Elizabeth Upton (b. 1804) and Harriet Upton (b. 1811), daughters of a Leeds insurance agent, Thomas Everard Upton, and perhaps relatives of Miss Wooler's mother, née Sarah Maud Upton.
2. Not identified. The name was a fairly common one in the area. A Miss Kitson and 'A. M. Kitson' who signed their names in an album along with several pupils of Roe Head may have been of the same family. (Album in private hands.) A Dr John Kitson lived at Field Head, Mirfield 'at the beginning of the nineteenth century'. (H. N. Pobjoy, *A History of Mirfield* (Driffield, 1969), 102.)
3. cf. Acts 20: 35.
4. Ann Nussey.
5. EN's spidery handwriting was often difficult to decipher, as her letters to Mary Gorham of 1844–52 in the BPM show. She later developed a more legible hand.
6. 'Cousin', as in e.g. Shakespeare's *Much Ado About Nothing*, III. iv. 39 and 97. CB teasingly pretends that her own hasty (but not illegible) writing shows their kinship.
7. The first postscript is written in dark ink in an upright style no doubt intended to fit the masculine pseudonym—a private joke on CB's part, since she used the initials 'C. T.' (for 'Charles Townshend') for some of her Angrian stories, such as 'Passing Events', written in Apr. and June 1836. The Greek word 'Brontë' means 'thunder'.

To Ellen Nussey, 26 September 1836

[Roe Head]

Last Saturday afternoon[1] being in one of my sentimental humours I sat down and wrote to you such a note as I ought to have written to none but M *Taylor who is nearly as mad as myself; to-day when I glanced it over it occurred to me that Ellen's calm eye would look at this with scorn, so I determined to concoct some production more fit for the inspection of common Sense.[2] I will not tell you all I think, and feel about you Ellen. I will preserve unbroken that reserve which alone enables me to maintain a decent character for judgment; but for that I should long ago have been set down by all who know me as a Frenchified—fool. You have been very kind to me of late, and gentle and you have spared me those little sallies of ridicule which owing to my miserable and wretched touchiness of character used formerly to make me wince as if I had been touched with a hot iron: things that nobody else cares for enter into my mind and rankle there like venom. I know these feelings are absurd and therefore I try to hide them but they only sting the deeper for concealment. I'm an idiot!—

I was informed that your brother *George was at Mirfield church last Sunday.[3] Of course I did not see him though I guessed his presence because I heard his cough (my short-sightedness makes my ear very acute) Miss *Uptons[4] told me he was there: they were quite smitten he was the sole subject of their conversation during the whole of the subsequent evening Miss Eliza described to me every part of his dress and likewise that of a gentleman who accompanied him with astonishing minuteness. I laughed most heartily at her graphic details, and so would you if you had been with me.

Ellen I wish I could live with you always, I begin to cling to you more fondly than ever I did. If we had but a cottage and a competency of our own I do think we might live and love on till Death without being dependent on any third person for happiness

Farewell my own dear Ellen
[Unsigned]

MS BPM Bon 161. W & S 52.
Address (integral): Miss E Nussey | Brook-royd
PM: none.
Date: written by CB on the back of the letter.

1. 24 Sept.
2. cf. *Villette* ch. 23: 'I wrote to these letters two answers—one for my own relief, the other for Graham's perusal. To begin with: Feeling and I turned Reason out of doors . . . dipped in the ink an eager pen, and, with deep enjoyment, poured out our sincere heart. When we had done . . . Reason would leap in, vigorous and revengeful, snatch the full sheets, read, sneer, erase, tear up, re-write, fold, seal, direct, and send a terse, curt missive of a page. She did right.' (363–4.)
3. George Nussey was at this period a good-looking young bachelor of 22. See EN 11.9.1833 and 30.12.1844, notes.
4. See the previous letter, n. 1.

To Ellen Nussey, [?October 1836]

[?Roe-Head]

Weary with a day's hard work—during which an unusual degree of Stupidity[1] has been displayed by my promising pupils I am sitting down to write a few hurried lines to my dear Ellen. Excuse me if I say nothing but nonsense, for my mind is exhausted, and dispirited. It is a Stormy evening[2] and the wind is uttering a continual moaning sound that makes me feel very melancholy—At such times, in such moods as these Ellen it is my nature to seek repose in some calm, tranquil idea and I have now summoned up your image to give me rest There you sit, upright and still in your black dress and white scarf—your pale, marble-like face—looking so serene and kind—just like reality—I wish you would speak to me—. If <it> we should be separated if it should be our lot to <life> live at a great distance and never to see each other again. in old age how I should call up the memory of my youthful days and what a melancholy pleasure I should feel in dwelling on the recollection of my Early Friend Ellen Nussey!

If I like people it is my nature to tell them so and I am not afraid of offering incense to your vanity. It is from religion that you derive your chief charm[3] and may its influence always preserve you as pure, as unassuming and as benevolent in thought and deed as you are now. What am I compared to you I feel my own utter worthlessness when I make the comparison. I'm a very coarse common-place wretch!

Ellen (I have some qualities that make me very miserable some feelings that you can have no participation in—that few very few people in the world can at all understand I don't pride myself on these peculiarities, I strive to conceal and suppress them as much as I can. but they burst out sometimes[4] and then those who see the explosion despise me and I hate myself for days afterwards). we are going to have prayers so I can write no more of this trash yet it is too true.

I must send this note for want of a better. I don't know what to say. I've just received your epistle and what accompanied it, I can't tell what should induce your Sisters to waste their kindness on such a one as me. I'm obliged to them and I hope you'll tell them so—I'm obliged 'to' you also, more for your note than for your present the first gave me pleasure the last something very like pain. Give my love to both your Sisters and my thanks the bonnet is too handsome for me I dare write no more. When shall we meet again

C Brontë

MS HM 24383. W & S 46.
Address (integral): Ellen Nussey | Brook-royd
PM: none.
Annotation in ink by EN: 18 36 or 7
Date: the cream wove paper is the same size as that used in EN 26.9.1836, the reference to stupid pupils is comparable to that in CB's Roe Head journal fragment of Oct. 1836, and the stormy weather of the same month is recorded in contemporary newspapers. See the notes below.

1. CB's impatience and frustration with her pupils, 'those fat-headed oafs', is a recurring theme in her private writings of this period. See e.g. the Roe Head Journal BPM Bon. 98(7): 'I'm just going to write because I cannot help it . . . Miss W[oole]r in the back-ground, Stupidity the atmostphere, school-books the employment, asses the society, what in all this is there to

remind me of the divine, silent, unseen land of thought'. (Printed in an edited version in Norton *Jane Eyre* (1987), 416.)

2. The Journal fragment quoted above, written in Oct. 1836, was also written during a high wind: 'pouring in impetuous current through the air, sounding wildly unremittingly . . . with a rapid gathering stormy swell.' *The Times* for 5 Oct. 1836 printed a report from Harwich dated 1 Oct.: 'It has blown tremendously heavy all day from S.S.W., thick, with heavy squalls and rain', and there were later reports of ships blown off course during the gales.
3. EN remained a devout member of the Church of England throughout her long life.
4. CB may be referring to her irresistible urge to write her passionate and romantic stories, or to her hot temper, or both. In the Roe Head fragment already quoted she describes her pupils gaping with astonishment 'all wondering why I write with my eyes shut'; and in a letter to Branwell Brontë written from Mme Heger's school in Brussels on 1.5.1843 CB describes how she gets 'red-in-the face with impatience at [her pupils'] stupidity—but don't think I ever scold or fly into a passion—if I spoke warmly, as warmly as I sometimes used to do at Roe-Head they would think me mad.'

To Ellen Nussey, [?October/November 1836]

[Roe Head]

All my notes to you Ellen are written in a hurry—I am now snatching an opportunity—Mr J *Wooler[1] is here, by his means it will be transmitted to Miss EW[2]—by her means to Henry by his means to you—I do not blame you for not coming to see me I am sure you have been prevented by sufficient reasons but I do long to see you and I hope I shall be gratified momentarily at least e'er long—Next Friday if all be well I shall go to Gomersall[3]—On Sunday I hope I shall at least catch a glimpse of you Week after week I have lived on the expectation of your coming, Week after week I have been disappointed—I have not regretted what I said in my last note to you The confession was wrung from me by sympathy and kindness such as I can never be sufficiently thankful for I feel in a strange state of mind still gloomy[4] but not despairing. I keep trying to do right, checking wrong feelings, repressing wrong thoughts—but still—every instant I find—myself going astray—I have a constant tendency to scorn people who are far better than I am—A horror at the i[dea] of becoming one of a certain set—a dread lest if I made the slightest profession, I should sink at once into Phariseeism, merge wholly into the ranks of the self-righteous. In writing at this moment I feel an irksome disgust at the idea of using a single phrase that sounds like religious cant—I abhor myself—I despise myself—if the Doctrine of Calvin[5] be true I am already an outcast—You cannot imagine how hard rebellious and intractable all my feelings are—When I begin to study on the subject I almost grow blasphemous, atheistical in my sentiments, don't desert me—don't be horrified at me, you know what I am—I wish I could see you My darling, I have lavished the warmest affections of a very hot, tenacious heart 'upon you'—if you grow cold—its over—love, to your Mother and Sisters.

C Brontë

MS HM 24413. W & S 48.
Address (integral): Miss E. Nussey | Brookroyd
PM: not in MS.
Annotation (i) at head, in pencil: 8/20; (ii) [in ink]: 1837; (iii) [on address panel by EN]: Roe Head | 36 or 7.
Date: the cream wove paper watermarked 'J GREEN & SON | 1834' resembles that used in 4 other letters, beginning with that to EN postmarked 'JY— | 1836' (p. 148), and used also in the Roe Head Journal fragment dated 'October 14th. 1836'. (BPM MS Bon 98(8).) The hectic tone and religious scruples, esp. the reference to Calvin, are akin to other letters of this period.

1. One of Margaret Wooler's brothers: either John (1793–1845) or James Upton Wooler (1811–92), who were to take over Rouse Mill after their father's death in 1838. They are named as millers and maltsters in Pigot's *Directory* for Dewsbury, 1841.
2. Margaret Wooler's sister Eliza (1808–84), who was probably looking after her elderly parents at Rouse Mill at this time, and would be able to contact Henry Nussey. Henry was curate to the Revd Thomas Allbutt at All Saints Church, Dewsbury, from Sept. 1835 to July 1837, and Rouse Mill was in his parish. For this curacy see White's *Directory* i. (1837) and Dewsbury Parish Church Marriage Registers. Henry Nussey also officiated at Dewsbury on 13 Nov. and 24 and 26 Dec. 1837.
3. To visit Mary Taylor.
4. Mary Taylor wrote to Mrs Gaskell describing CB's state of mind when she was a teacher at Roe Head: 'She seemed to have no interest or pleasure beyond the feeling of duty, and, when she could get [the opportunity], used to sit alone, and "make out". She told me afterwards, that one evening she had sat in the dressing-room until it was quite dark, and then observing it all at once, had taken sudden fright . . . From that time . . . her imaginations became gloomy or frightful; she could not help it, nor help thinking. She could not forget the gloom, could not sleep at night, nor attend in the day.' (*Life* i. 153.)
5. CB no doubt refers to the extreme form of Calvinism developed by some of the followers of John Calvin (1509–64): the belief that individuals were predestined by God to be either 'Elect' (saved by grace to Eternal Life) or 'Reprobate' (eternally damned or 'outcast'). cf. the reference to 'Ghastly Calvinistic doctrines' in the next letter, and CB's poem 'Look into thought' (Neufeldt *CBP* 209) written about Oct./Nov. 1836, where she longs for 'a breeze bearing life through that vast realm of death' but finds that 'The spirit lay dreadless & hopeless beneath'.

To Ellen Nussey, [5 and 6 December 1836]

[Roe Head]

I am sure Ellen you will conclude that I have taken a final leave of my senses, to forget to send your bag—when I had had 'it' hanging before my eyes in the dressing-room for a whole week.[1] I stood for ten minutes considering before I sent the boy off I felt sure I had something else to entrust to him besides the books, but I could not recollect what it was—These aberrations of Memory, warn me pretty intelligibly that I am getting past my prime.

I hope you will not be much inconvenienced by my neglect, I'll wait till to-morrow to see if *George will call for it on his way to Huddersfield[2] and if he does not I'll try to get a person to go over with it to Brookroyd on purpose. I am most grieved lest you should think me careless—but I assure you it was merely a temporary fit of absence which I could not avoid. I wish exceedingly that I could come to see you before Christmas, but it is impossible—however I trust ere another three weeks elapse I shall again have my Comforter beside me, under the roof of my own dear quiet home—If I could always live with you, and 'daily' read the bible with you, if your lips and mine could at the same time, drink the same draught from the same pure fountain of Mercy[3]—I hope, I trust, I might one day become better, far better, than my evil wandering thoughts, my corrupt heart, cold to the spirit, and warm to the flesh[4] will now permit me to be. I often plan the pleasant life which we might lead together, strengthening each other[5] in that power of self-denial, that hallowed and glowing devotion, which the first Saints of God often attained to—My eyes fill with tears when I contrast the bliss of such a state brightened by hopes of the future with the melancholy state I now live in, uncertain that I have ever felt true contrition, wandering in thought and deed, longing for holiness which I shall never, never obtain—smitten at times to the heart with the conviction that *?your Ghastly Calvinistic doctrines[6] are true—darkened in short by the very shadows of Spiritual Death! If Christian perfection[7] be necessary to Salvation I shall never be saved, my heart is a real hot-bed for sinful thoughts and as to practice when I decide on an action I scarcely remember to look to my Redeemer for direction.

I know not how to pray—I cannot bend my life to the grand end of doing good I go on constantly seeking my own pleasure pursuing the Gratification of my own desires, I forget God and will not God forget me? And meantime I know the Greatness of Jehovah I acknowledge the truth the perfection of his word, I adore the purity of the Christian faith, my theory is right, my Practice—horribly wrong.

Good-bye Ellen
C Brontë

Write to me again if you can your notes are meat and drink to me. Remember me to the Family I hope Mercy is better
Monday Morning
Roe-Head
I wish I could come to Brookroyd for a single night but I don't like to ask Miss Wooler She is at Dewsbury and I'm alone at this moment eleven o'clock on Tuesday night I wish you were here all the house in bed but myself I'm thinking of you my dearest
Return me a scrap by the Bearer if it be only a single line to satisfy me that you have got your bag safely. I met your brother *George on the road <yesterday> 'this afternoon' I did not know it was he until after he was past and then Anne told me—he would think me amazingly stupid in not moving[8]—can't help it

MS BPM Bon 162, W & S 53.
Address (integral): Miss E Nussey | Brookroyd
PM: none.
Date: the cream wove paper watermarked 'J GREEN & SON | 1834' resembles that used in 4 other letters of 1836, beginning with the letter to EN of July 36. In that year a Monday and Tuesday 3 weeks before Christmas would be 5 and 6 Dec.; the date given in W & S 53 is 6 Dec.

1. EN had evidently responded to CB's longing for her to visit Roe Head; see e.g. CB's last 2 letters.
2. George Nussey would pass Roe Head on his way to Huddersfield market, held on Tuesdays.
3. cf. Revelation 7: 17, 'For the Lamb . . . shall lead them unto living fountains of waters.'
4. cf. Romans 8: 9, 'But ye are not in the flesh, but in the Spirit, if so be that the Spirit of God dwell in you.'
5. cf. Philippians 1: 27, 'stand fast in one spirit, with one mind striving together for the faith of the gospel'.
6. See previous letter, n. 5. 'your' is conjectural; EN deleted all but the loop of the first letter, fearing perhaps that the word would be taken to mean her personal doctrines rather than a generalized 'people's' Calvinism.
7. cf. Matthew 5: 48, 'Be ye therefore perfect, even as your Father which is in heaven is perfect.' CB's soul-searching echoes current evangelical writings, such as Legh Richmond's *Domestic Portraiture* (1833), the homilies printed in the Anglican journal, *The Record* (1828–1948) to which Henry Nussey subscribed, and *The Cottage Magazine* (to which PB had contributed), edited at the time by Revd Thomas Allbutt, the Vicar of Dewsbury.
8. Bowing or nodding the head as a sign of recognition.

To Ellen Nussey, [?14 December 1836]

[?Roe Head]

My dear Ellen,

You will excuse a very brief and meagre answer to your kind note, when I tell you that at the moment it reached me, and that just now whilst I am scribbling a reply, the whole house is in the bustle of packing and preparation, for on this day we all go HOME.[1]

Your palliation of my defects is kind and charitable, but I dare not trust its truth, few would regard them with so lenient an eye as you do. Your consolatory admonitions are kind, [Ellen;] and when I can read them over in quietness and alone, I trust I shall derive comfort from them, but just now in the unsettled, excited state of mind which I now feel, I cannot enter into the pure scriptural spirit which they breathe. It would be wrong of me to continue the subject, my thoughts are distracted and absorbed by other ideas. You do not mention your visit to Haworth. Have you spoken of it to the family? Have they agreed to let you come?—but I will write when I get home. Ever since last Friday I have been as busy as I could be in finishing up the half-year's lessons which concluded with a terrible fag in Geographical Problems: (think of explaining that to Misses M[arriott][2] and L[ister])[3] and subsequently in mending Miss E. L's[4] clothes. I am very sorry to hear that poor—[5] is again ill. Give my love to her, &c. Miss Wooler is calling for me—something about my [protégée's] nightcaps—Good bye.

We shall meet again ere many days, I trust.

C. Brontë.

MS untraced. W & S 54.
Address: not in source.
PM: not in source.
Text: *Nussey* 45; '[Ellen;]' added from *Reid* 50; 'protégée's' corrected from *Hours at Home* xi. 110.
Date: the last day of the school term was probably 14 Dec. 1836. See n. 1.

1. Anne Brontë was given a copy of Isaac Watts's *The Improvement of the Mind; with a Discourse on the Education of Youth* (1741) in J. F. Dove's English Classics edn. of 1826. It was inscribed by Miss Wooler, 'Prize for good conduct. Presented to Miss A. Brontë with Miss Wooler's kind love. Roe Head, December 14, 1836.' (Inscription recorded in *Life* 1900 147 n. 1.)
2. Possibly a daughter of George Marriott (d. 1825), former owner of Roe Head, whose widow was still living there with her family in 1841: either Lydia, born in 1817, or Elizabeth, born in 1819. Lydia married Henry John Watkinson in Spring 1841. (Information by courtesy of Miss Laurie Marriott of York.)
3. Probably Harriet or Harriette Lister, b. ?1818, who was to marry William Clement Drake Esdaile in 1846. EN wrote to Shorter on 22 Apr. 1896, 'Mrs. Ingham of Blake Hall was a Miss Cunliffe Lister. A sister was a pupil of Miss W's . . . Mrs I. was an amiable conventional woman—her sister Harriet clever—but refractory, was a pupil in Charlotte's time of teacher.' (Brotherton MS.) The two pupils are unflatteringly referred to in CB's Roe Head Journal, e.g. on 14.10.1836: 'After tea we took a long weary walk. I came back abymé to the last degree for Miss L[ister] & Miss M[arriot]t had been boring me with their vulgar familliar trash all the time we were out if those Girls knew how I loathe their company they would not seek mine so much as they do.' (BPM MS Bon 98(8).) cf. also CB to R. Southey 16.3.1837 n. 5. For 'abymé' (= abimé, overwhelmed) cf. Fanny Burney, *Cecilia* iii. bk. 5, ch. 1; 'I am quite *abimé*, Sir, to incommode you.'
4. Possibly Ellen Lister, unrelated to Harriet Cunliffe Lister. Mr John Nussey suggested that she might be a relative of the Marriotts. The passage quoted above from the Roe Head Journal begins: 'In the afternoon Miss E— L— was trigonometrically oecumenical about her French Lessons she nearly killed me between the violence of the irritation her horrid wilfulness excited and the labour it took to subdue it to a moderate appearance of calmness.' (BPM MS Bon 98(8).)
5. In her previous letter CB had written 'I hope Mercy is better'. EN had probably deleted her sister's name in the MS or copy supplied to Horsfall Turner. See also the reference to Mercy in the next letter.

To Ellen Nussey, [29 December 1836]

[Haworth]

My dear Ellen

I am sure you will 'have' thought me very remiss in not sending my promised letter long before now, but I have a sufficient and a very melancholy excuse in an accident that befell our old faithful Tabby[1] a few days after my return home—She was gone out into the village on some errand, when as she was descending the steep street her foot slipped on the ice, and she fell—it was dark and no one saw her mis-chance, till after a time her groans attracted the attention of a passer-by She was lifted up and carried into a druggist's[2] near and after examination it was discovered, that she had completely shattered, and dislocated one leg Unfortunately the fracture could not be set till six o'clock the next morning as no Surgeon was to be had before that time, and she now lies at our house, in a very doubtful and dangerous state. Of course we are all exceedingly distressed at the circumstance for she was like one of our own family—Since the event we have been almost without assistance a person has dropped in now and then to do the drudgery but we have as yet been able to procure no regular Servant, and consequently the whole work of the house as well as the additional duty of nursing Tabby falls on ourselves. Under these circumstances I dare not press your visit here at least until she is pronounced out of danger—it would be too selfish of me—Aunt wished me to give you this information before but Papa, and all the rest were anxious that I should delay until we saw whether matters took a more settled aspect, and I myself kept putting it off from day to day most bitterly reluctant to give up all hope of the pleasure I had anticipated so long

However Ellen remembering what you told me, namely that you had commended the matter to a higher decision than ours <and that ours>, and that you were resolved to submit with resignation to that decision whatever it might be I hold it my duty to yield also and to be silent: it may be all for the best I fear if you had come during this severe weather your visit would have been of no advantage to you for the moors are blockaded with snow[3] and you would never have been able to get out—After this disappointment I never dare reckon with certainty on the enjoyment of a pleasure again it seems as if some fatality stood between you and me, I am not good enough for you, and you must be kept from the contamination of too intimate society.

I would urge your visit yet, I would entreat and press it but the thought comes across me "Should Tabby die while you are in the house?" I should never forgive myself—No it must not be—and in a thousand ways the Consciousness of that, mortifies and disappoints me most keenly. And I am not the only one who is disappointed, All in the house were looking forward to your visit with eagerness Papa says he highly approves of my friendship with you and he wishes <you> 'me' to continue it through 'life'. I hope your Sister *Mercy is better and that all the rest of the family are well Give my love to your Mother and Sisters and believe me, vexed and grieved

Your friend
C Brontë

If you don't write soon in my crabbed state of mind I shall conclude that you've cut me

MS BPM B.S. 40.4. W & S 55.

Address (integral): Miss E Nussey | Brookroyd | Birstall | Nr. Leeds.
PM: (i) BRADFORD YORKS | DE 29 | 183 [*sic*] (ii) *Bradford Yorks* | *Penny Post*
Annotation in ink by EN: 31 Dec 29—37
Date: Mrs Gaskell accepted EN's date of 1837, but Chitham presents convincing evidence for 1836 in *Problems* 29–30. See notes below.

1. For Tabitha Aykroyd (?1771–1855), the Brontës' much-loved servant, see EN 11.9.1833 n. 5. Chitham notes that Abraham Shackleton recorded a temperature below freezing on 15 Dec. This followed records of 'some sleet' on 9 and 10 Dec., 'a little snow, frosty' on 11, and 'some rain, snow still' on 12, all of which would make for precarious conditions by 15 Dec., and no doubt for 'a few days' afterwards.
2. Kept by Elizabeth Hardaker. See White's *Directory* for 1838, ii. 441. The steep main street of Haworth was paved with 'setts', or as Mrs Gaskell writes, 'flag-stones . . . placed end-ways, in order to give a better hold to the horses' feet; and, even with this help, they seem to be in constant danger of slipping backwards'. (*Life* i. 5.) She describes the druggist as 'a clever, intelligent Yorkshire woman' who also held 'the position of village doctress and nurse'. 'Betty' Hardaker told Mrs Gaskell that the young Brontës ' "struck" eating' until Tabby was allowed to stay and be nursed at the parsonage. (*Life* i. 180, 182.) In his ed. of the *Life* Shorter adds that Betty was 'called in to see Charlotte during her last illness. She died in 1888.' (*Life* 1900, 164.)
3. *Shackleton* records snow in late Dec., beginning with 'much snow' on 24, and Mayhall noted that on 31 Dec. the Leeds mail-coaches and others were delayed 'owing to the snow, which choaked the roads'. (*Mayhall* i. 441.) Elizabeth Barrett Browning wrote to Hugh Boyd from London on 29 Dec. 1836, '[I] shd. have forseen that all the mails as well as the females, myself included, would be blocked up by the snow this week!!' (Philip Kelley and Ronald Hudson (eds.), *The Brownings' Correspondence* (Winfield, Kan., 1985) iii. 213.)

To Robert Southey, 29 December 1836

[This letter from CB, asking the poet's opinion of her literary talents, has not been located. Its substance can be deduced from Southey's comments in his reply of 12 March 1837, q.v.]

Patrick Branwell Brontë to William Wordsworth, 10 January 1837[1]

Haworth—nr Bradford
Yorks

Sir

I most earnestly entreat you to read and pass your judgement upon what I have sent you,[2] because from the day of my birth to this the nineteenth year of my life I have lived among wild and secluded hills where I could neither know what I was or what I could do.—I read for the same reason that I eat or drank,—because it was a real craving of Nature. I wrote on the same principle as I spoke,—out of the impulse and feelings of the mind;—nor could I help it, for what came, came out and there was the end of it, for as to self conceit, that could not receive food from flattery, since to this hour Not half a dozen people in the world know that I have ever penned a line.—[3]

But a change has taken place now, Sir and I am arrived at an age wherein I must do something for myself—the powers I possess must be exercised to a definite end, and as I dont know them myself I must ask of others what they are worth—yet there is not one here to tell me, and still, if they are worthless, time will henceforth be too precious to be wasted on them.

Do pardon me, Sir, that I have ventured to come before one whose works I have most loved in our Literature and who most has been with me a divinity of the mind—laying before him one of my writings, and asking of him a Judgement of its contents,—I must come before some one from whose sentence there is no appeal, and such an one he is who has developed the theory of poetry as well as its practice,[4] and both in such a way as to claim a place in the memory of a thousand years to come.

My aim, Sir, is to push out into the open world and for this I trust not poetry alone that might launch the vessel but could not bear her on—sensible and scientific prose, bold and vigorous efforts in my walk in Life would give a further title to the notice of the world and <u>then</u> again poetry ought to brighten and crown that name with glory—but nothing of all this can be even begun without <u>means</u> and as I dont possess these I must in every shape strive to gain them; Surely, in this day, when there is not a <u>writing</u> poet worth a sixpence[5] the field must be open if a better man can step forward

What I send to you is the prefatory scene of a much longer Subject in which I have striven to develope strong passions and weak principles struggling with a high imagination and acute feelings till as youth hardens towards age evil deeds and short enjoyments end in mental misery and bodily ruin—Now to send you the whole of this would be a mock upon your patience; what you see, does not even <u>pretend</u> to be more than the description of an Imaginative child—But read it Sir and as you would hold a light to one in utter darkness as you value your own kind heartedness <u>return</u> me an <u>Answer</u> if but one word telling me whether I should write on or write no more—

Forgive undue warmth because my feelings in this matter cannot be cool and believe me to be Sir

with deep respect
Your really humble Servant
P B Brontë.

MS Dove Cottage. W & S 57 as 19 Jan.
Address (integral): William Wordsworth Esqre | Rydal Mount | Ambleside | Westmoreland
PM: (i) BRADFORD YORKS | 1 1 JA 1837 (ii) *Bradford Yorks Py Post*
Annotation by Wordsworth's son-in-law Edward Quillinan: 'Given to me by Mrs. Wordsworth this day | Monday the 26th August 1850 at Rydal Mount—E.Q.' Another note reads '?Peter Bradwell—deceased—Bronte | Howarth | nr Bradford'.

Text: enclosed with the letter is a substantial part of a poem, 'The Struggles of flesh with Spirit | Scene 1—Infancy'. The poem begins 'Still, and bright in twilight shining, | Glitters forth the evening star'. See Neufeldt *BBP* 120–6, Winnifrith *BBP* 39–48. The poem is dated 'August 13th 1836'.

1. This letter is included for comparison with CB's correspondence with the poet Robert Southey, Wordsworth's friend and neighbour in the Lake District. Southey's letter to CB of 12 Mar. 1837 shows that she had first written to him, on 29 Dec. 1836, in an exalted strain not unlike Branwell's, referring to Southey on his 'throne of light and glory' and to her own desire to be 'for ever known' as a poet. It seems likely that Charlotte and Branwell had decided together to approach their 'divinities of the mind'.
2. Wordsworth was 'disgusted' with Branwell's letter, and did not reply. See Southey's letter to CB of 22.3.1837, n. 1.
3. In fact Branwell had written repeatedly to the editor of *Blackwood's Edinburgh Magazine* offering his 'services' to the magazine and sending specimens of his writing. On 4 Jan. 1837 he had pressed for a personal interview: 'Will you still so wearisomely refuse me a word . . . Is it pride which actuates you—or custom—or prejudice?—Be a Man—Sir! and think no more of these things! Write to me—Tell me that you will receive a visit—And rejoicingly will I take upon myself the labour, which, if it succeed, will be an advantage both to you and me,—and, if it fail, will still be an advantage, because I shall then be assured of the impossibility of succeeding'. (MS BPM BS 135. W & S 56 prints part of this letter, dating it 9 Jan. 1837.) For Branwell's letter to the Editor of *Blackwood's* of 7.12.1835 see W & S 41. Mrs Oliphant comments that the editor, Robert Blackwood, 'probably thought the writer crazy'. See Margaret Oliphant, *William Blackwood and his Sons* (1897), ii. 177–85.
4. Wordsworth had expounded his poetic theories in a number of essays, most famously in his prefaces to the 2nd edn. of *Lyrical Ballads* (1800) and to his *Poems* of 1815.
5. A singularly tactless remark: Wordsworth himself had published *Yarrow Revisited, and other Poems* in 1835, and Hartley Coleridge, whom Branwell admired and for whom Wordsworth had a protective affection, continued to write verse. Tennyson had published poems in 1827, 1830, and 1832, and Robert Browning was known for his *Paracelsus* (1835).

To Ellen Nussey, [? Early 1837]

Roehead

My dear, dear Ellen,

I am at this moment trembling all over with excitement after reading your note, it is what I never received before—it is the unrestrained pouring out of a warm, gentle, generous heart, it contains sentiments unstained[1] by human motives, prompted by the pure God himself, it expresses a noble sympathy which I do not, cannot deserve. Ellen, Religion has indeed elevated your character. I thank you with energy for this kindness. I will no longer shrink from [answering] your questions.[2] I do wish to be better than I am. I pray fervently sometimes to be made so. I have stings of conscience—visitings of remorse[3]—glimpses of holy [of] inexpressible things which formerly I used to be a stranger to: it may all die away, I may be in utter midnight, but I implore a Merciful Redeemer that if this be the real dawn of the Gospel it may still brighten to perfect day.[4] Do not mistake me, Ellen, do not think I am good, I only wish to be so. I only hate my former flippancy and forwardness. O! I am no better than I ever was. I am in that state of horrid, gloomy uncertainty, that, at this moment I would submit to be old, grey-haired, to have passed all my youthful days of enjoyment and be tottering on the verge of the grave, if I could only thereby ensure the prospect of reconcilement to God and Redemption through His Son's merits.[5] I never was exactly careless of these matters, but I have always taken a clouded and repulsive view of them; and now if possible the clouds are gathering darker, and a more oppressive despondency weighs continually on my spirits. You have cheered me, my darling; for one moment, for an atom of time, I thought I might call you my own sister in the spirit, but the excitement is past, and I am now as wretched and hopeless as ever. This very night I will pray as you wish me. May the Almighty, hear me compassionately! and I humbly trust he will—for you will strengthen my polluted petitions[6] with your own pure requests. All is bustle and confusion round me, the ladies pressing with their sums and their lessons. Miss Wooler is at Rouse Mill,[7] she has said every day this week I wonder Miss Ellen does not come. If you love me <u>do</u> <u>do</u> <u>do</u> come on Friday, I shall watch and wait for you, and if you disappoint me I shall weep. I wish you could know the thrill of delight which I experienced, when as I stood at the dining-room window I saw your brother (George) as he whirled past,[8] toss your little packet over the wall. I dare write no more, I am neglecting my duty. Love to your mother and both your sisters. Thank you again a thousand times for your kindness—farewell my blessed Ellen.

Charlotte.

MS untraced. W & S 45 as 1836.
Address: not in source.
PM: not in source.
Date: ECG may be right in assigning to the 'latter portion of [1836]' (*Life* i. 155) but in its present position it leads naturally to the next letter. EN is CB's 'darling' in both, and the hectic tone continues to convey the unresolved religious crisis of late 1836.
Text: *Nussey* 37 with emendations from Rylands MS *Life* indicated by square brackets. W & S 45 derives from *Shorter* 21, which differs from *Nussey* in punctuation and in some substantives and is probably less reliable. *Life* has many variants and omissions: see i. 155–7.

1. *Shorter* and W & S read 'sentiments unrestrained'.
2. *Nussey*, *Shorter*, and W & S read 'from your questions'.
3. CB must have been guiltily conscious that she had written some of her most impassioned Angrian stories in 1836–7. 'The Return of Zamorna' begins with a satire on religious frenzy at 'Ebenezer Chapel' and ends with the heroine clasped to the 'warm throbbing bosom' of the hero Zamorna. (?Dec. 1836–Jan. 1837; *Miscellaneous Writings* ii. 281–314.)
4. cf. Proverbs 4: 18, 'But the path of the just is as the shining light, that shineth more and more unto the perfect day.'
5. cf. 2 Corinthians 5, esp. verses 18 and 19.
6. *Shorter* and W & S read 'petition'.
7. Rouse Mill was the home of Miss Wooler's parents, Robert and Sarah Maud Wooler. The family property was extensive and valuable. James Upton Wooler, who with his brother John, took over the mill after his father's death, qualified as an elector in 1844 as the 'occupier of Farm, Mill, Buildings and Land, at £300 rent at Rouse Mill' and as the owner of freehold

dwellings, houses, and land in Batley, Carlinghow, Gomersal, and Dewsbury Road. (West Riding Electoral Register 1844, Soothill Township. No. 4189.)

8. Probably on his way to Huddersfield market. cf. EN 5 and 6.12.1836 n. 2.

To Ellen Nussey, [?20 February 1837]

Roe Head

I read your letter with dismay, Ellen, what shall I do without you? [How long are we likely to be separated?][1] why are we so to be denied each other's society. It is an inscrutable fatality. I long to be with you because it seems as if two or three days or weeks spent in your company would beyond measure strengthen me in the enjoyment of those feelings which I have so lately begun to cherish.[2] You first pointed out to me that way in which I am so feebly endeavouring to travel, and now I cannot keep you by my side, I must proceed sorrowfully alone.

Why are we to be divided? Surely, Ellen, it must be because we are in danger of loving each other too well; of losing sight of the <u>Creator</u> in idolatry of the <u>creature</u>.[3] At first I could not say "Thy will be done."[4] I felt rebellious, but I know it was[5] wrong to feel so. Being left a moment alone this morning I prayed fervently to be enabled to resign myself to <u>every</u> decree of God's will—though it should be dealt forth with a far severer hand than the present disappointment. Since then, I have felt calmer and humbler—and consequently happier. Last Sunday I took up my Bible in a gloomy frame of mind; I began to read; a feeling stole over me such as I have not known for many long years, a sweet placid sensation like those that I remember used to visit me when I was a little child, and on Sunday evenings in summer, stood by the open window reading the life of a certain French nobleman[6] who attained a purer and higher degree of sanctity than has been known since the days of the early Martyrs. I thought of my own Ellen, I wished she had been near me that I might have told her how happy I was, how bright and glorious the pages of God's holy word seemed to me. But the "foretaste" passed away,[7] and earth and sin returned. I must see you before you go, Ellen; if you cannot come to Roe Head I will contrive to walk over to Brookroyd, provided you will let me know the time of your departure.[8] Should you not be at home at Easter I dare not promise to accept your mother's and sisters' kind invitation.[9] I should be miserable at Brookroyd without you, yet I would contrive to visit them for a few hours if I could not for a few days. I love them for your sake. I have written this note at a venture. When it will reach you I know not, but I was determined not to let slip an opportunity for want of being prepared to embrace it. Farewell, may God bestow on you all His blessings. My darling—Farewell. Perhaps you may return before midsummer, do you think you possibly can. I wish your brother John[10] knew how unhappy I am; he would almost pity me.

C. Brontë.

MS untraced. W & S 58.
Address: not in source.
PM: not in source.
Date: ECG dates 20 Feb. [1837], adding, mistakenly, that this was 'Soon after Charlotte returned to Dewsbury Moor'. (*Life* i. 166.) In 1837 20 Feb. was a Monday; 'last Sunday' presumably means 12 Feb., the first Sunday in Lent, rather than 19. The future separation alluded to would be EN's visit to the house of her brother John in Cleveland Row, London.
Text: *Nussey* 48 emended from Rylands MS *Life* in ll. 1–2, where the extra sentence sounds authentic. W & S 58 derives from *Shorter* 36, which differs slightly from *Nussey*, mainly in punctuation; and see n. 9 below.

1. 'How long . . . separated?' omitted by *Nussey*, *Shorter*, W & S.
2. If the sequence of letters is correct, these feelings may be the 'glimpses of holy inexpressible things' referred to in the previous letter. CB's soul-searching would be intensified by the Bible-readings and self-examination appropriate to Lent.
3. cf. *JE* 346, where Jane writes of Rochester, 'I could not, in those days, see God for his creature: of whom I had made an idol.' See also Romans 1: 25.
4. Matthew 6: 10.
5. *Life* reads 'I knew it was'. (i. 166.)
6. Perhaps François de la Mothe-Fénelon (1651–1715), the spiritual leader of a devout group at the court of Louis XIV, from which he was exiled in disgrace after the publication of *Les Aventures de Télémaque*, a didactic romance, in 1699. His application of Christian principles to the idea of government and his assertion of the folly and cruelty of war made him *persona non grata* to the king and his sycophants. There was an English translation of a biography of Fénelon by A. M. Ramsay in 1723, and the Keighley Mechanics' Institute Library (founded 1825) had a copy of *The Adventures of Telemachus*. See *BST* 11. 60. 358. CB refers to characters in *Télémaque* in *Shirley* 546.
7. In Hebrews ch. 6, where St Paul adjures his fellow-Christians to 'go on unto perfection', he refers to those 'who have tasted of the heavenly gift, and were made partakers of the Holy Ghost, And have tasted the good word of God, and the powers of the world to come'. (verses 4 and 5.) Evangelical preachers encouraged perseverance by referring to the Christian's 'foretaste of the heavenly banquet' or 'antepast of heaven'.
8. Ellen's visit to London was to last until at least early June. See the letter written to her on 8 June.
9. *Shorter* 36 reads 'sisters' invitation', W & S 58 'sister's invitation'.
10. EN's eldest brother (1794–1862), a general practitioner and one of the apothecaries to the royal family. See EN 20.2.1834 n. 1. John Nussey's son John Thomas Hartley was born on 24 Feb. Barbara Whitehead suggests that Ellen's presence had been 'urgently requested' to help with her brother's older children 'during the arrival of the baby'. (*Whitehead* 72.)

Robert Southey[1] to Charlotte Brontë, 12 March 1837

Keswick

Madam,

You will probably ere this have given up all expectation of receiving an answer to your letter of Decr. 29.[2] I was on the borders of Cornwall when that letter was written. It found me a fortnight afterwards in Hampshire. During my subsequent movements in different parts of the country, & a tarriance of 3 busy weeks in London, I had no leisure for replying to it. And now that I am once more at home & am clearing the arrears of business wh had accumulated during a long absence, it has lain unanswered till the last of a numerous pile—not from disrespect or indifference to its contents, but in truth, because it is not an easy task to answer it, nor a pleasant one to cast a damp over the high spirits & the generous desires of youth.

What you are I can only infer from your letter, wh appears to be written in sincerity, tho' I may suspect that you have used a fictitious signature.[3] Be that as it may, the letter & the verse bear the same stamp,[4] & I can well understand the state of mind wh they indicate. What I am, you might have learnt by such of my publications[5] as have come into your hands: but you live in a visionary world & seem to imagine that this is my case also, when you speak of my "stooping from a throne of light & glory."[6] Had you happened to be acquainted with me, a little personal knowledge wd. have tempered your enthusiasm. You who so ardently desire "to be for ever known" as a poetess,[7] might have had your ardour in some degree abated, by seeing a poet in the decline of life, & witnessing the effect wh age produces upon our hopes & aspirations. Yet I am neither 'a' disappointed man, nor a discontented one, & you wd. never have heard from me any chilling sermonisings upon the text that all is vanity.[8]

It is not my advice that you have asked as to the direction of your talents, but my opinion of them. 'and' Yet the opinion may be worth little, & the advice much. You evidently possess & in no inconsiderable degree what Wordsworth calls "the faculty of Verse."[9] I am not depreciating it when I say that in these times it is not rare. Many volumes of poems are now published every year without attracting public attention, any one of wh, if it had appeared half a century ago, wd. have obtained a high reputation for its author. Whoever therefore is ambitious of distinction in this way, ought to be prepared for disappointment.

But it is not with a view to distinction that you shd. cultivate this talent, if you consult your own happiness. I who have made literature my profession, & devoted my life to it, & have never for a moment repented of the deliberate choice, think myself nevertheless bound in duty to caution every young man who applies as an aspirant 'to me' for encouragement & advice, against taking so perilous a course. You will say that a woman has no need of such a caution, there can be no peril in it for her: & in a certain sense this is true. But there is a danger of wh I wd with all kindness & all earnestness warn you. The daydreams in wh you habitually indulge[10] are likely to induce a distempered state of mind, & in proportion as all the "ordinary uses of the world" seem to you "flat & unprofitable",[11] you will be unfitted for them, without becoming fitted for anything else. Literature cannot be the business of a woman's life:

& it ought not to be. The more she is engaged in her proper duties, the less leisure will she have for it, even as an accomplishment & a recreation. To those duties you have not yet been called, & when you are you will be less eager for celebrity. You will then not seek in imagination for excitement, of wh the vicissitudes of this life & the anxieties, from wh you must not hope to be exempted (be your station what it may) will bring 'with' them but too much.

But do not suppose that I disparage the gift wh you possess, nor that I wd. discourage you from exercising it, I only exhort you so to think of it & so to use it, as to render it conducive to your own permanent good. Write poetry for its own sake, not in a spirit of emulation, & not with a view to celebrity: the less you aim at that, the more likely you will be to deserve, & finally to obtain it. So written, it is wholesome both for the heart & soul. It may be made next to religion the surest means of soothing the mind & elevating it. You may embody in it your best thoughts & your wisest feelings, & in so doing discipline & strengthen them.

Farewell Madam! It is not because I have forgotten that I was once young myself that I write to you in this strain—but because I remember it.[12] You will neither doubt my sincerity, nor my good will. And however ill what has been said may accord with your present views & temper, the longer you live the more reasonable it will appear to you. Tho' I may be but an ungracious adviser, you will allow me therefore to subscribe myself,

With the best wishes for your happiness, here & hereafter,
Your true friend
(Sd) Robert Southey

MS BL Add 44355 (Copy MS, Gladstone papers). Holograph MS now BPM. B.S. IX, S. W & S 59 (part).
Address: To Miss Charlotte Brontë | Haworth | Bradford | *Yorkshire.*
PM: not in source, which is a copy of the original.
Annotation at the end, in unknown hand: Copy | Mr Southey to | Miss Bronte | 12 March 1837
Text: based on the copy, in an unknown hand, in the Gladstone papers in the BL. This is slightly fuller than the version in *The Life and Correspondence of the late Robert Southey* (6 vols. vi. 327–30), edited by his son the Revd Charles Cuthbert Southey in 1850. Mrs Gaskell recalled in *Life* i. 172: 'I was with Miss Brontë [in August 1850] when she received Mr. Cuthbert Southey's note, requesting her permission to insert the . . . letter in his father's life. She said to me, "Mr. Southey's letter was kind and admirable; a little stringent, but it did me good." '

1. Robert Southey (1774–1843), poet, biographer, essayist, and editor, had been Poet Laureate since 1813. His return home to Greta Hall, Keswick, had been a sad one, since he found his wife Sarah 'in the same hopeless state as when I left her,—perhaps with fewer remains of reason, & weaker in body.' (Letter to Mrs Septimus Hodson, 1 Mar. 1837; MS Huntington Library.)
2. This letter has not been located.
3. CB had used her real name: see the address, and her reply of 16 Mar.
4. CB described her first letter to Southey as the 'crude rhapsody' of one who seemed an 'idle dreaming being'. (See next letter.) We do not know which verses she sent to Southey: a long Byronic poem in 'Don Juan' metre of 19 July 1836 and a 'visionary' poem of 3 stanzas written in Oct. 1836 were recent productions. See Neufeldt *CBP* no. 116, 'And when you left me' and no. 117, 'Look into thought'.

5. Southey's long 'oriental' poems such as 'Thalaba the Destroyer: A Rhythmical Romance' (1801) and 'The Curse of Kehama' (1810) would appeal to CB, whose juvenile tales were similarly exotic. His *A Vision of Judgment* (1821), in praise of the late king George III, had however been hilariously parodied by the Brontës' much-admired Byron in his satire, *The Vision of Judgment* (1822). CB had recommended the 'greater part' of his verse, and his *Life of Nelson*, in her letter to EN of 4.7.1834.
6. 'But you live . . . light & glory': omitted from Cuthbert Southey's *Life* (and from W & S 59.) This and the other omissions noted later may have been made at CB's request.
7. 'who so ardently . . . poetess': omitted from Cuthbert Southey's *Life* and from W & S 59. Branwell Brontë had written in similarly high-flown terms to Wordsworth. See his letter of 10.1.1837.
8. cf. Ecclesiastes 1: 2.
9. Not traced. Wordsworth might have used the phrase in conversation, or Southey might recall *Excursion* v. 76–80: 'Oh! many are the Poets that are sown | By Nature; men endowed with highest gifts, | The vision and the faculty divine; | Yet wanting the accomplishment of verse.'
10. CB's imaginary Angrian characters and adventures filled her daydreams. See e.g. the Roe Head Journal fragment, 'All this day I have been in a dream': 'I quite seemed to see with my bodily eyes, a lady standing in the hall of a gentleman's house.' (BPM Bon 98(8), 14 Oct. 1836.) Amidst the 'stupidity' of the Roe Head schoolroom she wrote at about the same period: 'what in all this is to remind me of the divine, silent, unseen land of thought, dim now & indefinite as the dream of a dream, the shadow of a shade'. A 'glorious' blast of wind reminds her of her villain-hero Northangerland: 'O it has wakened a feeling that I cannot satisfy . . . now I should be agonized if I had not the dream to repose on.' (BPM Bon 98(7), *c.* Oct. 1836.)
11. cf. *Hamlet* I. ii. 133–4.
12. Southey had fairly rapidly retreated from the ardent utopian and republican ideals of his young manhood, evident in the impractical vision of a communist 'Pantisocracy' in the backwoods of America, and in his anti-royalist drama, *Wat Tyler*, of 1794. His acceptance of a government pension in 1807 and of the laureateship in 1813 led to Peacock's satirical portrayal of him as the time-serving Mr Feathernest in *Melincourt* (1817).

To Robert Southey, 16 March 1837

[?Roe Head][1]

Sir,

I cannot rest till I have answered your letter, even though by addressing you a second time I should appear a little intrusive; but I must thank you for the kind & wise advice you have condescended to give me. I had not ventured to hope for such a reply; so considerate in its tone, so noble in its spirit. I must suppress what I feel, or you will think me foolishly enthusiastic.

At the first perusal of your letter I felt only shame, and regret that I had ever ventured to trouble you with my crude rhapsody;—I felt a painful heat rise to my face, when I thought of the quires of paper[2] I had covered with what once gave me so much delight, but which now was only a source of confusion; but, after I had thought a little and read it again and again, the prospect seemed to clear. You do not forbid me to write; you do not say that what I write is utterly destitute of merit. You only warn me against the folly of neglecting real duties, for the sake of imaginative pleasures; of writing for the love of fame; for the selfish excitement of emulation. You kindly allow me to write poetry for its own sake, provided I leave undone nothing which I ought to do,[3] in order to pursue that single absorbing exquisite gratification. I am afraid, Sir, you think me very foolish. I know the first letter I wrote to you was all senseless trash from beginning to end; but I am not altogether the idle dreaming being it would seem to denote. My Father is a clergyman of limited, though competent, income, and I am the eldest of his children. He expended quite as much in my education as he could afford in justice to the rest. I thought it therefore my duty, when I left school, to become a governess.[4] In that capacity, I find enough to occupy my thoughts all day long,[5] and my head & hands too, without having a moment's time for one dream of the imagination. In the evenings, I confess, I do think, but I never trouble any one else with my thoughts. I carefully avoid any appearance of pre-occupation, and eccentricity, which might lead those I live amongst to suspect the nature of my pursuits. Following my Father's advice,—who from my childhood has counselled me just in the wise and friendly tone of your letter—I have endeavoured not only attentively to observe all the duties a woman ought to fulfil, but to feel deeply interested in them. I don't always succeed, for sometimes when I'm teaching or sewing I would rather be reading or writing; but I try to deny myself; and my Father's approbation amply rewarded me for the privation. Once more allow me to thank you with sincere gratitude. I trust I shall never more feel ambitious to see my name in print; if the wish should rise, I'll look at Southey's letter, and suppress it. It is honour enough for me that I have written to him, and received an answer. That letter is consecrated; no one shall ever see it, but Papa and my brother and sisters. Again I thank you. This incident I suppose will be renewed no more; if I live to be an old woman I shall remember it thirty years hence as a bright dream. The signature which you suspected of being fictitious is my real name. Again, therefore, I must sign myself,

C. Brontë.

P.S.—Pray, Sir, excuse me for writing to you a second time; I could not help writing, partly to tell you how thankful I am for your kindness, and partly to let you know that your advice shall not be wasted; however sorrowfully and reluctantly it may be at first followed. C. B.

MS untraced at the time of first publication; now BPM B.S. 40.25. W & S 60.
Address: not in source.
PM: not in source.
Text: Rylands MS *Life* fos. 154–6. W & S 60 reproduces *Shorter* 29, which is probably based on a printed edn. of the *Life* with a few insignificant punctuation variants and the reading 'may at first be followed' in the last sentence.

1. Southey replied to CB at Haworth, and she may have used that address or written from there; but by 23 or 24 Mar. she was at Roe Head, since Emily Brontë had to forward Southey's reply of 22 Mar. there, and it is unlikely that CB returned to Haworth for a few days so soon before Easter (26 Mar.).

2. Mrs Gaskell, one of the first people outside CB's family to see her early writing, wrote in the *Life* 'I have had a curious packet confided to me, containing an immense amount of manuscript, in an inconceivably small space; tales, dramas, poems, romances, written principally by Charlotte, in a hand which it is almost impossible to decipher without the aid of a magnifying glass.' (*Life* i. 83–4.) For a fuller account, see Alexander *EW* and the facsimiles of some of CB's MSS reproduced there.
3. cf. *BCP*, 'A general Confession to be said' at Morning Prayer: 'Almighty and most merciful Father . . . We have left undone those things which we ought to have done.'
4. Here, a teacher in a school. CB did not become a private governess until 1839. cf. EN 2.7.1835.
5. In spite of this disclaimer, CB had felt herself 'breathing quick and short' in the schoolroom at Roe Head as she 'beheld the Duke lifting up his sable crest . . . "Miss Brontë, what are you thinking about?" said a voice that dissipated all the charm, and Miss Lister thrust her little, rough black head into my face! "Sic transit" etc.' (Alexander *EEW* ii. pt. 2, 385; MS dated 'Decbr 19th Haworth 1835' at Huntington.)

Robert Southey to Charlotte Brontë, 22 March 1837

Keswick.

Dear Madam,

Your letter has given me great pleasure, & I should not forgive myself if I did not tell you so. You have received admonition as considerately & as kindly as it was given.[1] Let me now request that if you ever should come to these Lakes while I am living here, you will let me see you.[2] You will then think of me afterwards with more good will, for you will then perceive that there is neither severity nor moroseness in the state of mind to which years & observation have brought me.

It is, by God's mercy, in our power to attain a degree of self-government which is essential to our own happiness, & contributes greatly to that of those around us.—Take care of over-excitement, & endeavour to keep a quiet mind; 'even for your health it is the best advice that can be given you.' Your moral & spiritual improvement will then keep pace with the culture of your intellectual powers.

And now Miss Bronte, God bless you! Farewell,
& believe me to be
Your sincere friend
Robert Southey.

MS BPM, on loan. W & S 61.
Address (i) (integral): To | Miss Bronté | Haworth. | near Bradford | Yorkshire. (ii) on covering sheet, in Emily Brontë's hand: Miss Bronté | Roe Head | Mirfeild | Dewsbury
PM: (i) KESWICK (ii) BRADFORD | MA— | 18— (iii) *Bradford Yorks* | *Py Post*
Annotation (i) on outer wrapper by CB: Southey's Advice | To be kept for ever | Roe-Head April 21 | My twenty-first birthday 1837; (ii) above the word 'Southey's' CB has scribbled 'melpomene' [i.e. the Muse of Tragedy].

Text: MS in private hands. W & S 61 follows the text in Cuthbert Southey's *Life* of his father, vi. 330–1.

1. Southey wrote to Caroline Bowles from Keswick on Easter Monday (27 Mar.) 1837: 'I sent a dose of cooling admonition to the poor girl whose flighty letter reached me at Buckland. It was well taken, and she thanked me for it. It seems she is the eldest daughter of a clergyman, has been expensively educated, and is laudably employed as a governess in some private family. About the same time that she wrote to me, her brother wrote to Wordsworth, who was disgusted with the letter, for it contained gross flattery to him, and plenty of abuse of other poets, including me. I think well of the sister from her second letter, and probably she will think kindly of me as long as she lives.' (Edward Dowden (ed.), *The Correspondence of Robert Southey with Caroline Bowles* (1881), 348.) For Branwell Brontë's letter to Wordsworth see p. 160.
2. CB's first visit to the Lake District took place in Aug. 1850. Southey had died in 1843.

To Ellen Nussey, [early June 1837]

[?Roe Head][1]

My dear Ellen,

I have long been waiting an opportunity of sending a letter to you, as you wished, but as no such opportunity offers itself, I have at length determined to write by post, fearing if I delayed any longer you would attribute my tardiness to indifference. I can scarcely realise the distance that lies between [us], or the length of time that may elapse before we meet again.[2] Now, Ellen, I have no news to tell you, no changes to communicate. My life since I saw you last has passed on as monotonously and unvaryingly as ever, nothing but teach, teach, teach, from morning till night. The greatest variety I ever have is afforded by a letter from you, or a call from the Taylors, or by meeting with a pleasant new book. 'The Life of Oberlin'[3] and Legh Richmond's 'Domestic Portraiture'[4] are the last of this description I have perused. The latter work strongly attracted, and strangely fascinated, my attention. Beg, borrow, or steal it without delay; and read the 'Memoir of Wilberforce,'[5] that short record of a brief, uneventful life, I shall never forget; it is beautiful, [not on account of the language in which it is written,] not on account of the incidents it details, but because of the simple narration it gives of the life and death of a young, talented, and sincere Christian. Get the book, Ellen (I wish I had it to give you), read it, and tell me what you think of it. Yesterday I heard you had been ill since you were in London. What has been your complaint? Are you happier than you were? Try to reconcile your mind to circumstances, and exert the quiet fortitude of which I know you are not destitute. Your absence leaves a sort of vacancy in my feeling which nothing has yet offered of sufficient interest to supply. I do not forget ten o'clock, I remember it every night, and if a sincere petition for your welfare will do you any good, you will be benefited.[6] I know the Bible says, 'The prayer of the Righteous availeth much,'[7] and I am not righteous, nevertheless I believe God despises no supplication that is uttered in sincerity. Give my most affectionate love to your sister,[8] and a kiss for me to your little favourite niece Georgiana,[9] whom I never saw, but whom I almost love in idea for her aunt's sake. My own dear Ellen, good-bye; I can write no more, for I am called to a less pleasant avocation. Do return before winter. I don't know how I shall get over next half-year without the hope of <u>seeing</u> you. Write soon, a long, long letter. Excuse my scrawl.

[unsigned]

MS untraced. W & S 62.
Address: as given in *Nussey, Shorter* 26, and W & S 62: Miss Nussey, | Cleveland Row, | London
PM: not in source. This letter, with that of 8 June, was perhaps enclosed with letters from EN's family: see next letter and notes.
Date: the W & S dating to 1837 is correct. Shorter assigned the letter to 1836, but EN was at home during the spring and summer of that year.
Text: W & S 62, which derives from *Shorter* 26, correcting 'Leigh' to 'Legh' and 'Georgina' to 'Georgiana'. *Reid* 46–7 and *Nussey* 41 omit several phrases and names, and have minor variants. *Reid* supplies 'us' in the second sentence. The extract in *Life* i. 159 (from 'My life since' to 'sincere Christian') has variants and omissions, and the additional phrase 'not on account of . . . written', given here in square brackets.

1. W & S date from 'DEWSBURY MOOR, June 1837', but Miss Wooler did not move her school to Heald's House, Dewsbury Moor until early 1838. See EN 4.1.1838 n. 1 and 5.5.38 n. 1.
2. EN had been staying at her brother John's house, 4 Cleveland Row, St James's, London, since late Feb. or early Mar. See EN 20.2.1837 n.10.
3. Thomas Sims, *Brief Memorials of J. F. Oberlin* (London, 1830). Johann Friedrich Oberlin (1740–1826) was a Lutheran pastor and philanthropist who established schools for children of working parents at Walderbach in Alsace, and encouraged progressive agricultural and industrial methods in the Strasbourg area.
4. The Revd Legh Richmond (1772–1827) was best known for his tract *The Dairyman's Daughter* (1809) of which 2 million copies were sold. An evangelical clergyman, originally converted by reading William Wilberforce's *Practical View of the Prevailing Religious System*, he was a prolific writer for the Religious Tract Society. CB may have known that her father had heard him preach at a Church Missionary service on one of his visits to Bradford, on 7 Nov. 1817. (Information by courtesy of Dr Juliet R. V. Barker.) An edn. of his *Domestic Portraiture*, ed. E. Bickersteth from Richmond's draft papers and notes, appeared in 1834.
5. i.e. Wilberforce Richmond. *Domestic Portraiture* exemplifies 'the successful application of religious principle in the education of a family' 'in the memoirs of three of the deceased children of the Rev. Legh Richmond': his eldest son, Samuel Nugent Legh Richmond, born 1798, his second son Wilberforce Richmond, born 1807, and his third daughter, 'H'. The memoirs of the lame and delicate Wilberforce include affectionate letters from his father to him as a child, but also expressions of hope that 'Willy' as a young man is 'beginning to be truly sensible of the evil and danger of sin, and the necessity of seeking God betimes.' Wilberforce replies very much in the vein of CB's soul-searching letters of this period.
6. CB and EN had probably made a pact that they would pray at 10 o'clock each evening.
7. cf. James 5: 16.
8. EN's sister-in-law Mary Walker Nussey (1799–1868), wife of John.
9. Georgiana Mary, (1829–81), eldest daughter of John and Mary Nussey.

To Ellen Nussey, 8 June 1837

[Roe Head]

My dearest Ellen

The enclosed[1] as you will perceive was written before I received your last—I had intended to send it by this but what you said altered my intention

I scarce dare build a hope upon the foundation your letter lays—we have been disappointed so often—and I fear I shall not be able to prevail on them to part with you but I will try my utmost and at any rate there is a chance of our meeting soon with that thought I will comfort myself[2]

You do not know how selfishly glad I am that you still continue to dislike London and the Londoners—it seems to afford a sort of proof that your affections are not changed—Shall we really stand once again together on the Moors of Haworth? I dare not flatter myself with too sanguine an expectation I see many doubts and difficulties—But with Miss Wooler's leave which I have asked and in part obtained I will go to-morrow and try to remove them—

Give my love to my little sweet correspondent Georgiana[3] and believe me my own Ellen

Yours always a[nd] truly
C Brontë

MS HM 24414. W & S 63.
Address: none. The note was folded small, perhaps to be included in a Nussey family packet.
PM: none.

1. The previous letter. 'by this' may read 'by the'—perhaps a slip for 'by the post'.
2. EN was presumably still in London, but was expected to return shortly. Meanwhile CB hoped to persuade Ellen's family to let her visit Haworth on her return, the date of which remains unknown, owing to the lack of letters for the rest of 1837.
3. See the previous letter, n. 9.

To Ellen Nussey, [4 January 1838]

[Haworth]

Your letter Ellen was a welcome surprise even though it contained something like a reprimand—I had not however forgotten our agreement—I had prepared a note to be forthcoming against the arrival of Your Messenger—But things so happened that it was of no avail—You were right in your conjectures respecting the cause of my sudden departure[1]—Anne continued—wretchedly ill—neither the pain nor the difficulty of breathing left her[2]—and how could I feel otherwise than very miserable? I looked upon her case in a different light to what I could 'wish' or expect any uninterested person to view it in—Miss *Wooler thought me a fool—and by way of proving her opinion treated me with marked coldness—we came to a little eclairsissement [*sic*] one evening[3]—I told her one or two rather plain truths—which set her a crying—and the next day unknown to me she wrote to Papa[4]—telling him that I had reproached her—bitterly—taken her severely to task &c. &c.—Papa sent for us the day after he had received her letter—Meantime I had formed a firm resolution—to quit Miss *Wooler and her concerns for ever—but just before I went away she took me into her room—and giving way to her feelings which in general she restrains far too rigidly—gave me to understand that in spite of her cold repulsive manners She had a considerable regard for me and would be very sorry to part with me—If any body likes me I can't help liking them—and remembering that she had in general been very kind to me—I gave in and said I—would come back if she wished me—so—we're settled again for the present—but I am not satisfied I should have respected her far more if she had turned me out of doors instead of crying for two days and two nights together—I was in a regular passion my "warm temper" quite got the better of me—Of which I don't boast for it was a weakness—nor am I ashamed of it for I had reason to be angry—Anne is now much better—though she still requires a great deal of care—however I am relieved from my worst fears respecting her—

I approve highly of the Plan you mention except as it regards committing a verse of the Psalms to Memory—I do not see the direct advantage to be derived from that—We have entered on a new Year—will it be stained as darkly as the last—with all our sins, follies, secret vanities—and uncontrolled passions and propensities?—I trust not—but I feel in nothing better—neither humbler nor purer—It will want three weeks next Monday to the termination of the holidays—Come to see me my dear Ellen as soon as you can—however bitterly I sometimes feel towards other people—the recollection of your mild steady friendship consoles and softens me—I am glad you are not such a passionate fool as myself—Give my best love to your Mother and sisters, excuse the most hideous scrawl that ever was penned—and believe me

Always tenderly
[Signature cut off]

MS BPM Bon 163. W & S 66.
Address (integral): Miss Ellen Nussey | Brook-royd | Birstall | nr Leeds
PM: (i) BRADFORD YORKS | JA 5 | 1838 (ii) *Bradford Yorks* | *Penny Post*
Annotation by EN: After A's 'B's' illness at Roe Head Jan 38

1. From Roe Head. Miss Wooler's school moved to Heald's House, Dewsbury Moor, before May 1838, but not (as previously thought) in 1837. It is not included in White's *Directory* for Dewsbury for 1837, but appears in William Robson's *Commercial Directory of London, Cheshire . . . York and the West Riding* (2 vols.) for 1840–1. See EN 5.5.1838 n. 1.
2. Anne Brontë's illness sounds like bronchitis, but was described by Bishop James La Trobe as gastric in origin. According to William Scruton, the Bishop, minister of the Moravian church

at Mirfield from 1836 to 1841, had been asked by Anne to visit her. He recalled that 'She was suffering from a severe attack of gastric fever which brought her very low, and her voice was only a whisper; her life hung on a slender thread . . . The words of love, from Jesus, opened her ear to my words, and she was very grateful for my visits . . . her heart opened to the sweet views of salvation, pardon, and peace in the blood of Christ'. (*BST* 1. 8. 27, in 'Reminiscences of the late Miss Ellen Nussey.')

3. EN wrote to C. K. Shorter on 22 Apr. 1896: 'I enclose a copy of the chronicled death of good Miss Wooler—You make me laugh by your added question, Did she and C. B. quarrel? They did righteously. They neither understood each other. Poor C. B. was full of agony for her suffering sister, seeing and feeling much further than Miss W., who had never had a day's illness in her life—She knew nothing as dear C. B. knew in a physical point of view—so C. thought her hard and unfeeling so torture exploded at last, and poor Miss Wooler was taken by surprise by C's vehemence and injustice as she thought. They had it out, as people say, and were all the better friends afterwards.' (Brotherton MS.)
4. Mrs Gaskell paraphrased this letter in the first and second edns. of the *Life*: 'Miss Wooler felt these reproaches keenly, and wrote to Mr. Brontë about them. He immediately sent for his children, who left Dewsbury Moor the next day. Meanwhile, Charlotte had resolved that Anne should never return as a pupil, nor she herself as a governess.' (*Life* i. 183.) The second and third sentences were altered in the 3rd edn., probably at the request of Mr Brontë or Miss Wooler, to read: 'He immediately replied most kindly, expressing his fear that Charlotte's apprehensions and anxieties respecting her sister had led her to give utterance to over-excited expressions of alarm. Through Miss W—'s kind consideration, Anne was a year longer at school than her friends intended.' (*Life* 3rd edn., i. 190–1.)

To Ellen Nussey, [?February/March 1838]

[?Roe Head or
Dewsbury Moor]

My dear Ellen

We were at breakfast when your note reached me and I consequently write in great hurry[1]—Your trials seem to thicken—I trust God will either remove them or—give you strength to bear them   If I could but come to you and offer you all the little assistance either my head or my hands could afford—but that is impossible—I scarcely dare offer to comfort you *about *William[2] lest my consolation should seem like mockery—I know that in cases of sickness Strangers cannot measure what relations feel—One thing, however I need not remind you of—You will have repeated it over and over to [yourself] before now—"God does all for the best"[3] and even should the worst happen, and Death seem finally to destroy hope—remember Ellen that this will be but a practical test of the strong faith and calm devotion which have marked you a Christian so long—I would hope however that the time for this test is not yet come that your brother may recover and all be well—It griev[es] me to hear that your own health is so indifferent once more   I wish I were with you to lighten at least by Sympathy the burden that seems so unsparingly laid upon you

Let me thank you Ellen for remembering me in the midst of such hurry and affliction we are all apt to grow selfish in distress—this so far as I have found is not your case—When shall [I] see you again? the Uncertainty in which the answer to that question must be involved gives me a bitter feeling—through all changes, through all chances[4] I trust I shall love you as I do now—We can pray for each other and think of each other—Distance is no bar to recollection—You have promised to write to me soon and I do not doubt that you will keep your word Give my love to *Mercy and your Mother—take with you my blessing and affection and all the warmest wishes of a warm heart for your welfare

C Brontë

Miss W[ooler] sends her love

MS Brotherton. W & S 43 as '[ROE HEAD, March 1836?]'.
Address: (integral): Miss Ellen Nussey | Brookroyd
PM: none.
Annotation by EN in pencil, illegible except for 'W's illness'.
Date: from William Nussey's illness: see n. 2. *Hours at Home* xi. [197] implies and *Reid* 53–4 explicitly dates '1838'.

1. EN's brother John is said to have been staying at Brookroyd when he was summoned back to London by the news of William Nussey's illness. EN was to travel to London with him.
2. After a medical training EN's brother William Nussey (1807–38) became, as Henry Nussey records, 'a joint apothecary w[ith] my eldest brother to the Queen's household' and lived with the John Nusseys at 4 Cleveland Row, St James's, London. Pigot's *Metropolitan Directory* for 1838 describes both brothers as surgeons. In Aug. 1838 Henry recalled that William 'had laboured since Feby. last under some malady of the brain, & fm. what I have heard laboured under deep convictions of sin, & felt persuaded from the first that his sickness wd. be unto death. Poor fellow!' (HN *Diary* 7.8.1838, fol. 34^{v}). William committed suicide on 7 June 1838. See *Whitehead* 77.
3. cf. Romans 8: 28, 'We know that all things work together for good to them that love God.'
4. cf. *BCP*, Collects after the Offertory: 'Assist us mercifully, O Lord . . . that among all the changes and chances of this mortal life, we may ever be defended by Thy most gracious and ready help.'

To Ellen Nussey, 5 May 1838

[Dewsbury Moor][1]

My dearest Ellen

Yesterday I heard that you were ill[2]—Mr and Miss *Heald[3] were at Dewsbury-Moor and it was from them I obtained the information. This Morning I set off to Brookroyd to learn further particulars; from whence I am but just returned. Your Mother is in great distress about you—she can hardly mention your name without tears—and both She and *Mercy wish very much to see you at home again—Poor girl you have been a fortnight confined to your bed and while I was blaming you in my own mind for not writing—you were suffering in sickness without one kind female friend to watch over you. I should have heard all this before and have hastened to express my sympathy with you in this crisis, had I been able to visit Brookroyd in the Easter Holidays but an unexpected summons back to Dewsbury-Moor in consequence of the illness and death of Mr *Wooler prevented it.[4] Since that time I have been a fortnight and two days quite alone—Miss *Wooler being detained in the interim at *Rouse-Mill. You will now see Ellen that it was not neglect or failure of affection which has occasioned my silence—though I fear you will long ago have attributed it to those causes—If you are well enough do write me just two lines—just to assure me of your convalescence. not a word however if it would harm you, not a syllable. They value you at home Ellen. Sickness and absence call forth expressions of attachment which might have remained long enough unspoken if their object had been present and well. *Mercy told me that *George is quite miserable about 'you' and that his anxiety is making him look wretchedly ill I wish your friends (I include myself in that word) may soon cease to have cause for so painful an excitement of their regard. As yet I have but an imperfect idea of the nature of your illness—of its extent—or of the degree in which it 'may have' now subsided—When you can let me hear all, no particular however minute will be uninteresting to me. How have your spirits been? I trust not much overclouded—for that is the most melancholy result of illness. You are not I understand going to Bath[5] at present; they seem to have arranged matters strangely. I feel impatient to hear your own account of your future plans and prospects—When I parted from you near White-lee Bar[6] I had a more sorrowful feeling than ever I experienced before in our temporary separations it is foolish to dwell too much on the idea of presentiments—but I certainly had a feeling that the time of our re-union had never been so indefinite or so distant as then. I doubt not my dear Ellen that amidst your many trials—amidst the sufferings that you have of late felt in yourself and seen in several of your relations[7]—you have still been able to look up and find support in trial, consolation in affliction, and repose in tumult—where human interference can make no change. I think you know in the right spirit how to withdraw yourself from the vexation, the care, the meanness of Life and to derive comfort from purer sources than this world can afford <it>. You know how to do it silently, unknown to others—you can avail yourself of that hallowed communion, the Bible gives us with God. I am charged to transmit your Mother's and Sister's love—Receive mine in the same parcel, I think it will scarcely be the smallest share. Farewell, my dear Ellen

C Brontë

MS BPM Bon 164. W & S 67.
Address (integral): Miss Ellen Nussey | No 4 Cleveland Row | St. James's | London

PM: (i) DEWSBURY (ii) C | 7 MY 7 | 1838
Annotation in pencil by EN: May 5 —38 When I was ill in London

1. One reason for the move from Roe Head to Heald's House, Dewsbury Moor—possibly in Feb. or Mar. 1838 and certainly before Easter (15 April)—would be Miss Wooler's need to be nearer her parents at Rouse Mill while her father was ill. CB later referred to her own depression, or 'hypochondria' at Heald's House: 'I endured it but a year. When I was at Dewsbury-Moor—I could have been no better company for you than a stalking ghost.' (Letter to Margaret Wooler, ?Nov. 1846. See p. 505.)
2. EN was no doubt under stress owing to her brother William's illness.
3. The Revd William Margetson Heald the younger (1803–75), son of the Revd William Margetson Heald, 'surgeon and divine' (1767–1837) whom he succeeded as Vicar of Birstall. A graduate of Trinity College Cambridge, and a good friend of Henry Nussey, he was 'spiritual, scholarly, gentle, liberal-minded and generous'. With his father, he was the prototype for the Revd Cyril Hall in CB's *Shirley*. See his letter to EN of 8.1.1850, printed in *W&S* 513. The character of Miss Heald (his sister Harriet) is reflected in that of Margaret Hall in *Shirley*; she was to call ' "Jane Eyre" a "wicked book", on the authority of the "Quarterly"—an expression which—coming from her—I will here confess—struck somewhat deep'. (CB to WSW 21.9.1849.)
4. Mr Robert Wooler died on 20 Apr. 1838.
5. EN was still in London in early June, as the next letter shows, but CB addressed her letters of 24 Aug. and 2 Oct. to 'Bath-Easton, Bath, Somersetshire', where Ellen was staying with her brother the Revd Joshua Nussey (1798–1871) and his wife Anne Alexander Nussey (1788–1875).
6. The toll-gate at White Lee, south-west of Brookroyd, Birstall.
7. Both Henry and William Nussey had been ill. Henry recorded that during his visit to London in autumn 1837 he had spent 'abt ten days' with William, 'myself being very much out of bodily health, & harassed in mind'. (HN *Diary* 4.8.1838, fol. 35^{r}.) There had also been some personal crisis in Henry's life on 7 Mar. 1838, a day he associated with sin and humiliation, followed by gratitude to God 'in rescuing me from the jaws of death & destruction before I went to B[urton] A[gnes] & since my arrival there'. (HN *Diary* 7.3.1839, fol. 63^{v}, and 9.12.1838, fol. 39^{v}.)

To Ellen Nussey, 9 June 1838

Haworth

My dear Ellen

I received your packet of dispatches on Wednesday—it was brought me by Mary and Martha *Taylor who have been staying at Haworth for a few days they leave us to-day and I am hastily scrawling this letter to be ready for transmission by them to your friends[1] when they return. You will be surprised when you see the date of this letter.[2] I ought to be at Dewsbury-Moor you know—but I stayed as long as I was able and at length I neither could nor dared stay any longer My health and spirits had utterly failed me[3] and the medical man whom I consulted[4] enjoined me if I valued my life to go home So home I went, the change has at once roused and soothed me—and I am now I trust fairly in the way to be myself again—A calm and even mind like yours Ellen cannot conceive the feelings of the shattered wretch who is now writing to you. when after weeks of mental and bodily anguish not to be described

something like tranquillity and ease began to dawn again. I will not enlarge on the subject to me every recollection of the past half year is painful—to you it cannot be pleasant. Mary *Taylor is far from well[5]—I have watched her narrowly during her visit to us—her lively spirits and bright colour might delude you into a belief that all was well—but she breathes short, has a pain in her chest, and frequent flushings of fever. I cannot tell you what agony these symptoms give me. they remind me so strongly of my two sisters[6] whom no power of medicine could save. I trust she may recover; her lungs certainly are not ulcerated yet, she has no cough, no pain in the side, and perhaps this hectic fever may be only the 'temporary' effects of a severe winter and a late Spring[7] on a delicate constitution—Martha is now very well—she has kept in a constant flow of good-humour during her stay here and has consequently been very fascinating. I fear from what you say I cannot rationally entertain hopes of seeing you before Winter for your own sake, I am glad of it—I do not now fear that society will estrange your heart—and I know it will so polish you, externally—that the mind will be generally appreciated through the medium of the manners.[8] They are making such a noise about me I can not write any more. Mary is playing on the piano. Martha is chattering as fast as her little tongue can run and Branwell is standing before her laughing at her vivacity. My dear Ellen good bye Aunt and my Sisters unite in best love to you Good-bye, love.
P.S. Write to me as often as you can find time.

[Unsigned]

MS BPM B.S. 40.45. W & S 68.
Address (integral): Miss Ellen Nussey | No. 4. Cleveland Row | St James's | London
PM: none.

1. EN's relatives. A common usage at this period. cf. EN 15.4.1839 n. 7.
2. i.e. Haworth; the place, not the time of writing. CB had probably gone home on or soon after 23 May. A volume containing Sir Walter Scott's *The Vision of Don Roderick* and *Rokeby* at the BPM is inscribed by Miss Wooler, 'Presented to Miss Brontë with the Love & best wishes of a sincere Friend—Heald's House. May 23. 1838—'
3. CB was to recall the 'tyranny of Hypochondria' over her 'health and spirits' at Dewsbury Moor: see previous letter, n. 1.
4. Mrs Gaskell adds that CB consulted a doctor 'through Miss Wooler's entreaty'. (*Life* i. 184.) Although Mrs Gaskell alleged that 'Dewsbury Moor was low and damp, and . . . the air did not agree with her' (*Life* i. 182), Charlotte's illness was not purely physical. 'About this time, she would turn sick and trembling at any sudden noise, and could hardly repress her screams when startled . . . and the medical man, whom at length, through Miss Wooler's entreaty, she was led to consult, insisted on her return home. She had led too sedentary a life, he said; and the soft summer air, blowing round her home, the sweet company of those she loved, the release, the freedom of life in her own family, were needed, to save either reason or life.' (*Life* i.184.)
5. Mrs Gaskell writes, 'after a season of utter quiet, [Charlotte's] father sought for her the enlivening society of her two friends, Mary and Martha T[aylor].' (*Life* i.184.) In spite of Charlotte's fears, Mary Taylor was not consumptive; she lived to the age of 76. Martha died, apparently of cholera, at 23. See Biographical Notes.
6. Maria Brontë (1813–25) was already seriously ill when her father brought her home from

Cowan Bridge school on 14 Feb. 1825. She was nursed at home and died on 6 May. Her sister Elizabeth (1815–25) also became ill at Cowan Bridge; she was sent home in the charge of a servant, a Mrs Hardacre, on 31 May 1825 and died on 15 June. Both girls suffered from pulmonary TB, and their illness and death were recalled when CB described the 'pale, wasted' Helen Burns in *JE*.

7. Mayhall recorded the 'most dense' fog for many years on 2 Dec. 1837, and a 'most alarming flood' in which 3 people died at Bradford on 20 Dec., after 'almost incessant rain for several days'. In Jan. 1838 'the frost was so intense, that the principal rivers in England were complet[e]ly frozen over'. (*Mayhall* i. 451–6.)
8. The manuscript may read 'of the manner'.

To Ellen Nussey, 24 August [1838]

Dewsbury-Moor

My dear Ellen

I have been waiting a long time for an opportunity of sending you a letter by private hand—but as none such occurs I have determined to write by post lest you should begin to think I have forgotten you and in revenge resolve to forget me.[1]

As you will perceive by the date of this letter I am again at Dewsbury-Moor engaged in the old business teach—teach—teach. Miss *Eliza *Wooler[2] and Mrs. *Wooler are coming here next Christmas Miss *Wooler will then relinquish the school in favour of her Sister Eliza—but I am happy to say the worthy dame will continue to reside in the house. with all her faults I should be sorry indeed to part with her.

When will you come home? Make haste you have been at Bath long enough for all purposes—by this time you have acquired polish enough I am sure—if the varnish is laid on much thicker I am afraid the good wood underneath will be quite concealed and your old Yorkshire friends won't stand that—come—come I am getting really tired of your absence Saturday after Saturday comes round and I can have no hope of hearing your knock at the door and then being told that "Miss *Ellen *Nussey is come." O dear in this monotonous life of mine that was a pleasant event I wish it would recur again. but it will take two or three interviews before the stiffness—the estrangement of this long separation will quite wear away—I have nothing at all to tell you now except that Mary *Taylor is better and that she and Martha are gone—to take a tour in Wales. Patty[3] came on her pony about a fortnight since to inform me that this important event was in contemplation—she actually began to fret about your long absence and to express the most eager wishes for your return. I heard something from your Sister *Mercy about Mr and Mrs. Joshua[4] wishing you to stay over the Winter don't be persuaded by them

Ellen you've been from home long enough Come back—I've just had a visit from Ann *?Cook[5] she has stayed at home some weeks longer than the regular vacation during this time I have seen a great deal of her—and I don't think her at all altered except that her carriage &c. is improved. She is still the same warm-hearted—affectionate—prejudiced—handsome girl as ever Write to me as soon as ever you get this scrawl. I should be ashamed of such writing as this only I am past all shame—

My <u>own dear Ellen</u> good-bye if we are all spared I hope soon to see you again God bless you—

C Brontë

Miss Wooler is from home or she would send her love I am sure—little *Edward *Carter and his baby Sister[6] are staying with [us] so that between nursing and teaching I have my time pretty well occupied. So far my health keeps up very well—May it but continue to do so

MS HM 24415. W & S 64 as 1837.
Address (integral): Miss Ellen Nussey | Bath-Easton | Bath | Somersetshire
PM: DEWSBURY
Date: the letter forms a natural sequel to that of 9.6.1838, which anticipates EN's 'polish' and refers to Mary Taylor's illness. Mrs Wooler's move to Dewsbury Moor from Rouse Mill follows her husband's death on 20 Apr. 1838. The 1838 dating is supported by the evidence of the paper, an unwatermarked cream wove used also for the next letter, q.v.

1. EN had been away from home since Feb. or early Mar. Her brother William's death in London on 7 June may have hastened her move to Bath, away from the sad associations of her brother John's house.
2. Eliza Wooler (1808–84) had been looking after her mother at Rouse Mill, but had formerly been one of the teachers at her sister's school.
3. Martha Taylor.
4. Ellen's brother the Revd Joshua Nussey (1798–1871) was a graduate of St Catharine's College Cambridge. After graduating BA in 1822 he was ordained a deacon in 1823 and a priest in 1824. He had been Curate of St Margaret's and St John's, Westminster, from 1823 to 1831, and at the village of Batheaston, 3 miles from the centre of Bath, from 1834 until Oct. 1838, when he may have moved to Poughill, Devon, to which he had been appointed Vicar in 1837. He was also 'Domestic Chaplain to Lord Blayney' (Cadwallader Davis Blayney, Baron of Monaghan, 1802–74, Conservative MP for County Monaghan, Ireland, from 1830–1834, when Joshua Nussey had for a time been a curate in Westminster). This appointment continued when he moved to Oundle, Northants, where he was Vicar from 1845 until his death. He had married Anne Elizabeth Alexander (1788–1875) on 3 Mar. 1832. See the photograph in *Whitehead* 215.
5. W & S print 'Ann Carter', but the heavily obliterated surname is short and has no obvious 't' stroke. A Roe Head pupil named 'A. C—k' is mentioned in CB's Journal fragment, 'I'm just going to write' (BPM Bon 98(7)) but is not distinguished from the 'Asses' who disgust CB. In EN 12.1.1840, however, 6 days after the funeral of Ann Cook at Dewsbury on 6.1.1840, CB grieves for 'Anne C—'s death, 'a young, beautiful, and happy girl . . . a warm-hearted, affectionate being, and I cared for her'. Ann, born in 1825, was the daughter of Thomas Cook, an important Dewsbury banker and cloth manufacturer. See EN 12.1.1840 n. 1.
6. The children of Margaret Wooler's sister Susanna (1800–72) and her husband the Revd Edward Nicholl Carter (1800–72), the Curate of Mirfield Parish Church since 1831. Their daughter, Ellen was born in Dec. 1834, Edward in 1835, and Susan Margaret on 10 July 1837. In 'Emily at Law

Hill, 1838: Corroborative Evidence' (*BST* 18. 94. 267–70), Jennifer A. Cox suggests that the children's parents may have been preparing to settle in at Lothersdale, near Skipton, where Mr Carter was to be the curate-in-charge of the newly built church. The Subscription Lists of the Diocese of Ripon show that he was officially licensed to the 'Church or Chapel of Christ Church Lothersdale' on 30 Nov. 1838. (WYAS, Sheepscar, Leeds.)

To Ellen Nussey, 2 October [1838]

Dewsbury-Moor—

My dear Ellen

I should have written to you a week ago but my time has of late been so wholly taken up that till now I have really not had an opportunity of answering your last letter. I assure you I feel the kindness of so early a reply to my <late> tardy correspondence   it gave me a sting of self-reproach—let this admission satisfy you and upbraid me no more

A day or two after I received your last letter I took a walk over to *Brookroyd for the purpose of seeing your Sister *Mercy who you will have heard has been very ill. I found her much better and altogether occupied with her poultry-yard—dove-cote, hen-coop, and more especially—a batch of newly hatched chickens—Mercy has a kindness of heart about her which I like—Your Sister *Anne seemed very dejected—your Mother I thought in somewhat better Spirits than usual—all <seemed> were anxious for Ellen's return. The *Taylors have got home after their Welsh tour.[1] They spent three weeks a[t] Aber[y]stwyth on the Coast—I have not seen *Mary since—but Martha rode over a few days ago to give me an account of their proceedings and from what she said of her Sister I fear her health is not materially improved—the medical men however are of opinion that her complaints do not arise from disease in the lungs, but from a disordered stomach   this seems to afford ground for hope.

My Sister Emily is gone into a Situation as teacher in a large school[2] of near forty pupils[3] near Halifax. I have had one letter from her since her departure   it gives an appalling account of her duties—Hard labour from six in the morning until near eleven at night. with only one half hour of exercise between—this is slavery   I fear she will never stand it—[4]

It gives me sincere pleasure my dear Ellen to learn that you have at last found a few associates of congenial minds—I cannot conceive a life more dreary than that passed amidst sights sounds and companions all alien to the nature within us—from the tenour of your letters it seems that your mind remains fixed as it ever was, in no wise dazzled by novelty or warped by evil example—I am thankful for it. I could not help smiling at the paragraphs which related to your *Sister & *Joshua[5]—there was in them a touch of the genuine unworldly simplicity which forms a part of your character—Ellen depend upon it—all people have their dark side—though some possess the power of throwing a fair veil over the defects—close acquaintance slowly removes the screen and one by one the blots appear; till at length we sometimes see the pattern of perfection all slurred over with blots that even partial affection cannot efface. I hope my next communication with you will be face to face and not as through a letter darkly[6]—Commending you to the care of One above us all I remain still my dear Ellen

Your friend
C Brontë

MS BPM B.S. 40.3. W & S 65 as 1837.
Address: integral: Miss Ellen Nussey | Batheaston | Bath | Somersetshire
PM: D—BURY | OC 6 | 1838
Annotation in pencil by EN: ?named | Remarks on character
Date: CB dates 'Octbr. 2nd— 1836' but the postmark is clearly 1838. Jennifer A. Cox notes that the 'combined postmark' showing both place and date was first introduced for Dewsbury 'on September 22nd 1838' and that the date '1836' must therefore be Charlotte's mistake. ('Emily at Law Hill, 1838: Corroborative Evidence', *BST* 18. 94. 270.)

1. Mary and Martha Taylor had begun their tour in Wales before 24 Aug. See the previous letter. In 1838 Aberystwyth was a market town and seaport with steep and uneven streets and houses 'principally formed of dark slate' with 'a very singular appearance'. The beauty of its surroundings had for some years past made it a popular summer retreat and bathing-place and 'the customary amusements of plays and assemblies during the season add [ed] to the attractions for summer visitants'. (*Dugdale* 11.)
2. Law Hill school, about 1 mile east of Halifax, kept by Miss Elizabeth Patchett (b. 1796). Emily was to stay there for 6 months. See E. Chitham's account of the school in *A Life of Emily Brontë* (Oxford, 1987), ch. 9, and his essay, 'Early Brontë Chronology' in *Problems* in which he establishes the correct date of the present letter and its relevance to Emily Brontë's career. Hilda Marsden speculates that the landscape and buildings of the area may be recalled in *WH*. ('The Scenic Background of "Wuthering Heights" ', *BST* 13. 67. 111–30, and 'The Moorlands: The Timeless Contemporary', Part 2, *BST* 20. 4. 205–12.)
3. The 1841 Census shows that there were then 20 pupils aged between 11 and 15 at Law Hill school, but these would be boarders. Miss Patchett may have had day-pupils as well. See E. Chitham, *A Life of Emily Brontë*, 273.
4. 'Liberty was the breath of Emily's nostrils; without it, she perished. The change from her own home to a school . . . was what she failed in enduring.' (Charlotte Brontë, writing of Emily's brief stay at Roe Head in her prefatory note to 'Selections from poems by Ellis Bell' in her 1850 edn. of *WH* and *AG*; repr. in the Clarendon edn. of *WH* 446. CB does not mention Emily's teaching at Law Hill.)
5. The names are heavily deleted, but the reference is most likely to be to EN's brother Joshua and his wife: see the previous letter, n. 4. Neither CB nor Mary Taylor had a high opinion of Joshua Nussey. Mary Taylor wrote to EN in 1842, 'I would take your opinion on almost any subject in preference to your brother Joshua's though he no doubt has read as much as you & I put together, & a little bit of Charlotte included.' (MS Texas; printed in *Stevens*, letter 7, 36.)
6. cf. 1 Corinthians 13: 12, 'For now we see through a glass, darkly; but then face to face.'

To Ellen Nussey, [20 January 1839]

[Haworth]

My dear, kind Ellen

I can hardly help laughing when I reckon up the number of urgent invitations I have received from you during the last three months[1]—had I accepted all, or even half of them—the *Birstallians would certainly have concluded that I had come to make *Brookroyd my permanent residence—When you set your mind upon a thing you have a peculiar way of hedging one in with a circle of dilemmas so that they hardly know how to refuse you—however I shall take a running leap and clear them all—Frankly my dear Ellen I cannot come—Reflect for yourself a moment—do you see nothing absurd in the idea of a person coming again into a neighbourhood within a month after they have taken a solemn and formal leave of all their acquaintance[2]—? However I thank both you & your Mother for the invitation which was most kindly expressed—You give no answer to my proposal that you should come to Haworth with the Taylors—I still think it would be your best plan—I should have been at Lascelles-Hall[3] before now if Amelia W[alker][4] had not made a mistake about the Huddersfield Coach from Bradford—I go to-morrow—O dear! I wish the visit were well over—I wish you and the Taylors were safely here, there is no pleasure to be had without toiling for it

I feel rather uneasy about the continued application of blisters[5] you have had to undergo does it not produce great weakness? Was the Caustic ordered on account of soreness left by the blisters—or for the removal of inflamation—it appears to me a strange kind of remedy in your Case—When you come here we will give up Medical prescriptions and try what exercise and fresh air will do—I have desired Branwell to make inquiries about your donkey—&c.

You must invite me no more my dear Ellen until next Midsummer at the nearest. I know you will call me a stupid little thing for refusing—but no matter I trust to get a reconciling kiss when you come to Haworth

All desire to be remembered to you Aunt particularly—Angry though you are I will venture to sign myself as usual—(no not as usual, but as suits circumstances)

Yours under a cloud
C Brontë

MS BPM B.S. 40.5. W & S 71.
Address (integral): Miss Ellen Nussey | Brook-royd | Birstall | nr Leeds
PM: (i) BRADFORD YORKS | JA 21 | 1839 (ii) *Bradford Yorks* | *Penny Post*

1. EN must have come home from Bath soon after CB's letter to her of 2.10.1838.
2. On 22 Dec. 1838, at the end of her period of teaching at Miss Wooler's school, which was to be

run by Miss Eliza Wooler from Christmas 1838. See EN 24.8.1838 and Patrick Brontë's letter to Mrs Gaskell of 30.7.1855: Charlotte 'officiated as teacher, from 29th. July 1835, till Decr. 22–1838.' (MS Rylands.) Dewsbury Moor is within walking distance of Brookroyd.

3. One of two halls at Lepton, near Huddersfield. See EN *c.*7.7.1836 n. 4.
4. Amelia Walker was the niece of CB's godmother, Mrs Thomas Atkinson; probably CB could not avoid making the visit. See EN 19.6.1834 n.8.
5. Irritants derived from cantharidae (blister-beetles) applied to the skin in order to produce blisters which withdrew blood from, and so relieved, painful local inflammation. The treatment was widely used for various disorders: cf. a letter from Anne Orford to Mrs Hering from Lyme Regis, 30.8.1817, describing 'a Pain in the Chest . . . which I thank God I am now recovering from, the Pain has been removed by bleeding and a perpetual Blister for a fortnight.' (Letter in private hands.)

To Revd Henry Nussey,[1] *5 March 1839*

[Haworth]

My dear Sir

Before answering your letter, I might have spent a long time in consideration of its subject; but as from the first moment of its reception and perusal I determined on which course to pursue, it seemed to me that delay was wholly unnecessary.

You are aware that I have many reasons to feel grateful to your family, that I have peculiar reasons for affection towards one at least of your Sisters, and also that I highly esteem yourself. do not therefore accuse me of wrong motives when I say that my answer to your proposal must be a decided negative. In forming this decision—I trust I have listened to the dictates of conscience more than to those [of] inclination; I have no personal repugnance to the idea of a union with you—but I feel convinced that mine is not the sort of disposition calculated to form the happiness of a man like you. It has always been my habit to study the characters of those amongst whom I chance to be thrown, and I think I know yours and can imagine what description of woman would suit you for a wife. Her character should not be too marked, ardent and original—her temper should be mild, her piety undoubted, her spirits even and cheerful, and her "personal attractions" sufficient to please your eye and gratify your just pride. As for me you do not know me, I am not the serious, grave, cool-headed individual you suppose[2]—you would think me romantic and [eccentric—you would] say I was satirical and [severe—however I scorn] deceit and I will never for the sake of attaining the distinction of matrimony and escaping the stigma of an old maid take a worthy man whom I am conscious I cannot render happy. Before I conclude let me thank you warmly for your other proposal regarding the school near Donnington.[3] It is kind in you to take so much interest about me but the fact is I could not at present enter upon such a project because I have not the capital necessary to ensure success. It is a pleasure to me to hear that you are so comfortably settled and that your health is so much improved. I trust God will continue<s> his kindness towards you—let me say also that I admire the good sense, and absence of flattery and cant which your letter displayed. Farewell—! I shall always be glad to hear from you as a friend—

[believe me Yours truly
C Brontë.]

MS William Self. W & S 72.
Address (integral): Revd. H. Nussey | Earnley–Rectory | nr Chichester | Sussex
PM: (i) BRADFORD YORKS | MA 6 | [18]39 (ii) *Bradford Yorks* | *Py Post*
Text: The words in square brackets in lines 22, 34, 35 are from a fragment sent by EN to a Miss Ingilby in August 1887 and sold at auction by Phillips of London on 14 Nov. 1991. EN copied the words on to the letter after cutting out the fragment.

1. See EN 4.7.1834 n. 24. From Sept. 1835 until late July 1837 Henry Nussey had been Curate to Margaret Wooler's brother-in-law the Revd. Thomas Allbutt in Dewsbury, and for 6 months, from Aug. 1837 to early Feb. 1838, Curate to the Revd W. M. Heald, the Vicar of Birstall. He would certainly have met his sister Ellen's friend CB during this period, when she was teaching at Roe Head and Dewsbury Moor. By the date of this letter he had already proposed to and been refused by Margaret Anne Lutwidge (1809–69), the sister of his former Vicar, the Revd C. H. Lutwidge, at Burton Agnes in East Yorks. On Friday 1 Mar. 1839 Henry wrote in his Diary, 'On Tuesday last received a decisive reply fm. M.A.L's papa. A loss, but I trust a providential one. Believe not her will, but her fathers. All right. God knows best what is good for us, for his Church, & for his own Glory. This I humbly desire. And his Will be done, & not mine in this or in anything else. Evermore give me this Sp[iri]t of my Lord & Master! Wrote to a York[shir]e Friend, C.B., Brothers John & George also.' (HN *Diary* fol. 62^{r}.) On Sunday 3 Mar. Henry preached on the 'God of Hope'; but on Saturday 9 Mar. he noted, 'Received an unfavourable ?reply fm. C.B. The Will of the Lord be done.' On Monday 11 he returned from Chichester and Donnington to Earnley 'quite ill w[ith] a bilious head ache'. His earnest piety, methodical attitude to marriage, and his suggestion that CB should take charge of a school may have provided some traits in the character of St John Rivers in *JE*. See *Whitehead* 82–3 for a possible Moravian influence.
2. Almost any page of the story CB wrote between 24 Feb. and 26 Mar., beginning 'A young man of captivating exterior, elegant dress and most gentlemanlike deportment' would have convinced Henry Nussey of the truth of this assertion. The tale is printed as 'Captain Henry Hastings' in *Five Novelettes*, (1971). ed. Winifred Gérin, transcribed from the MS in the Widener Collection, Harvard.
3. Henry Nussey was the curate-in-charge at Earnley with Almodington, Sussex, from Dec. 1838 to Apr. 1844, when he was appointed Curate of Hathersage, Derbyshire. The Rector of Earnley, the Revd Henry Browne, had been asked by the Bishop of Chichester to transfer to St George's, Donnington, 4 miles from Earnley. Henry Nussey preached at both churches, but lived at Earnley Rectory near the 'rustic and primitive-look[ing] church' in a district he described as 'a very low & flat neighbourhood near the Sea, but studded I trust w[ith] "trees of righteousness, the planting of the Lord"' (HN *Diary* 2.12.1838, fol. 37^{v}.) Earnley and Donnington were small villages with 153 and 228 inhabitants respectively—in contrast to Haworth, a town with 19 mills and a population of 2,434. (*Dugdale* 708, 639, 945; John James, *History and Topography of Bradford* (1846), 291; Census for Haworth, 1841.)

To Ellen Nussey, 12 March 1839

Haworth—

My dearest Ellen

When your letter was put into my hands—I said "She is coming at last I hope" but when I opened it and found what the contents were I was vexed to the heart. You need not ask me to go to Brookroyd any more—Once for all and at the hazard of being called the most stupid little Wretch that ever existed—I won't go till you've been to Haworth.—I don't blame you I believe you would come if you might perhaps I ought not to blame others—but I'm grieved.

Anne goes to *Blake-Hall[1] on the 8th. of April unless some further unseen cause of delay should occur. I've heard nothing more from Mrs. Thos Brook[2] as yet—Papa wishes me to remain at home awhile longer—but I begin to be anxious to set to work again—and yet it will be hard work after the indulgence of so many weeks to return to that dreary Gin-horse round.[3]

You ask me my dear Ellen whether I have received a letter from *Henry—I have about a week since—The Contents I confess did a little surprise me, but I kept them to myself, and unless you had questioned me on the subject I would never have adverted to it—*Henry says he is comfortably settled at <Donnington>'*?in Sussex'[4] that his health is much improved[5] & that it is his intention to take pupils after Easter—he then intimates that in due time he shall want a Wife to take care of his pupils and frankly asks me to be that Wife. Altogether the letter is written without cant or flattery—& in a common-sense style which does credit to his judgment—Now my dear Ellen there were in this proposal some things that might have proved a strong temptation—I thought if I were to marry so, *Ellen could live with me and how happy I should be. but again I asked myself two questions—"Do I love *Henry *Nussey as much as a woman ought to love her husband? Am I the person best qualified to make him happy—?—Alas Ellen my Conscience answered "no" to both these questions. I felt that though I esteemed *Henry—though I had a kindly leaning towards him because he is an aimiable—well-disposed man Yet I had not, and never could have that intense attachment which would make me willing to die for him—and if ever I marry it must be in that light of adoration[6] that I will regard my Husband ten to one I shall never have the chance again but n'importe.[7] Moreover I was aware that Henry knew so little of me he could hardly be conscious to whom he was writing—why it would startle him to see me in my natural home-character he would think I was a wild, romantic enthusiast indeed—I could not sit all day long making a grave face before my husband—I would laugh and satirize and say whatever came into my head first—and if he were a clever man & loved me the whole world weighed in the balance against his smallest wish should be light as air—

Could I—knowing my mind to be such as that could I conscientiously say that I would take a grave <youn> quiet young man like *Henry? No it would have been deceiving him—and deception of that sort is beneath me. So I wrote a long letter back in which I expressed my refusal as gently as I could and also candidly avowed my reasons for that refusal. I described to him too the sort of Character I thought would suit him for a wife—Good-bye my dear Ellen—write to me soon and say whether you are angry with me or not—.

C Brontë

MS BPM Gr. E 2. W & S 73.
Address (integral): Miss Ellen Nussey | Brook-royd | Birstall | nr Leeds
PM: (i) [B]RADFORD | MA ?13 | 18— (ii) *Bradford Yorks* | *Penny Post*
Annotation by EN in pencil: of *Henry

1. Blake Hall, Mirfield, Yorks., was the home of Joshua Ingham (1802–66) and his wife Mary, née Cunliffe Lister (1812–99). They had married on 28.12.1831. Five of their 13 children had been born by the time Anne became a governess at Blake Hall, the eldest being Joshua Cunliffe (1832–77) and the youngest Harriet (1838–9). Mrs Ingham's sister Harriet had been Anne's fellow-pupil at Roe Head, and Joshua Ingham was related to EN's sister-in-law, Mary Walker Nussey. See EN 14.12.1836 n. 3 and *BST* 15. 79. 334. The Bloomfields in *AG* are said to be based on the Ingham family. See the illustrated article by Susan Brooke, 'Anne Brontë at Blake Hall', *BST* 13. 68. 239–50.
2. The wife of Thomas Brooke, a member of a prosperous family of manufacturers in Honley, 3 miles south of Huddersfield. Thomas Brooke's father William Brooke built Northgate House early in the 19th cent.; on his death Thomas and his brother William took over the 'large and still growing industry . . . concentrated at Armitage Bridge Mills'. See D. F. E. Sykes, *The History of Huddersfield and its Vicinity* (Huddersfield, 1898), 375–7. Sykes describes 2 of the sons of Thomas Brooke, William and John Arthur, as 'staunch conservatives and faithful churchmen', upright magistrates and good employers, and mentions another brother whose name indicates a family connection with the Inghams of Blake Hall, 'the Venerable Joshua Ingham Brooke, M.A.'. William Brooke III considered that with his mother CB 'would have found a home congenial to the "finest fibres" of her heart" '. (*BST* 2. 9. 31.)
3. A 'gin-horse' was used in mines and elsewhere to work a drum or windlass for hoisting or pumping. The animal moved in a circular 'gin-race' or 'gin-ring'.
4. See the previous letter, n. 3. CB's replacement for 'at Donnington' has been heavily deleted and the reading is uncertain.
5. Henry's ill-health during 1838 was one reason for his move to a quiet rural area. A 'fall from a spirited horse' had caused head injuries either just before or while he was at Burton Agnes: 'My head was very much affected by this misfortune, and my ministerial work consequently much impeded.' But Earnley suited him: 'I am now in better health & have better nights of rest than I have had for almost years back, & this air seems to agree w[ith] me very well.' (HN *Diary* 9.12.1838, fol. 39^{v}.)
6. Contrast CB's advice to EN in her letter of 15.5.1840: 'I think, if you can respect a person before marriage, moderate love at least will come after; and as to intense passion, I am convinced that is no desirable feeling.'
7. Never mind, no matter.

To Ellen Nussey, 15 April 1839

Haworth

My dear Ellen

I could not well write to you in the week you requested as about that time we were very busy in preparing for Anne's departure—[1] poor child! She left us last Monday no one went with her—it was her own wish that she might be allowed to go alone—as she thought she could manage better and summon more courage if thrown entirely upon her own ressources. We have had one letter from her since she went—she expressed herself very well satisfied—and says that Mrs. *Ingham is extremely kind,[2] the two eldest children[3] alone are under her care, the rest are confined to the nursery—with which and its occupants she has nothing to do. both her pupils are desperate little dunces—neither of them can read and sometimes they even profess a profound ignorance of their alphabet. the worst of it is the little monkies are excessively indulged and she is not empowered to inflict any punishment. she is requested when they misbehave themselves to inform their Mamma—which she says is utterly out of the question as in that case she might be making complaints from morning till night—"So she alternately scolds, coaxes and threatens—sticks always to her first word[4] and gets on as well as she can"—I hope she'll do, you would be astonished to see what a sensible, clever letter she writes—it is only the talking part, that I fear—but I do seriously apprehend that Mrs *Ingham will 'sometimes' conclude that she has a natural impediment of speech for my own part I am as yet "wanting a situation—like a housemaid out of place"[5]—by the bye Ellen I've lately discovered that I've quite a talent for cleaning—sweeping up hearths dusting rooms—making beds &c so if everything else fails—I can turn my hand to that—if anybody will give me good wages, for little labour I won't be a cook—I hate cooking—I won't be a nursery-maid—nor a lady's-maid far less a lady's companion—or a mantua-maker—or a straw-bonnet maker or a taker-in of plain-work[6]—I will be nothing "but a house-maid"

Setting aside nonsense—I was very glad my dear Ellen to learn by your last letter that some improvement had taken place in your health—for occasionally I have felt more uneasy about you than I would willingly confess to yourself—I verily beli[e]ve that a visit to Haworth would now greatly help to restore you—and there can be no objection on account of cold when the weather is so much milder. However angry you are I still stick to my resolution that I will go no more to Brookroyd till you have been to Haworth—I think I am right in this determination and I'll abide by it. it does not arise from resentment but from reason. I have never for a moment supposed that the reluctance of your friends[7] to allow you to leave home arose from any ill-will to me justice compels me to say that I think the wish to keep you near them in your then precarious state of health was quite natural. but now that you are better that argument does not hold good. With regard to my visit to Gomersall[8] I have as yet received no invitation—but if I should be asked though I should feel it a great act of self denial to refuse yet I have almost made up my mind to do so—though the society of the *Taylors is one of the most rousing pleasures I have ever known. I wish you Good-bye my darling Ellen & I tell you once more I want to see you—Strike out that word darling it is humbug where's the use of protestations?—we've known each other and liked each other a good while that's enough

C Brontë

MS HM 24416. W & S 74.
Address (integral): Miss Ellen Nussey | Brookroyd | Birstall | nr Leeds
PM: (i) BRADFORD YORKS | AP 16 | 1839 (ii) *Bradford Yorks* | *Penny Post*
Annotation in pencil by EN: Annes first trial at ?Mr. Inghams

1. See the previous letter, n. 1. Blake Hall (now demolished) was about 18 miles from Haworth.
2. EN told C. K. Shorter that 'Mrs. I[ngham] was an amiable conventional woman . . . The naughty boy in Anne's time was a Captain but died not so very long ago.' (Letter dated 22 Apr. 1896. Brotherton MS.)
3. Joshua Cunliffe Ingham (1832–77) and Mary Ingham (1834–1922).
4. In dealing with her difficult pupils, Anne's heroine Agnes Grey 'determined always strictly to fulfil the threats and promises [she] made.' (*AG* ch. 3, 28.)
5. Untraced. Perhaps from a currently popular song or verse using the formula typical of advertisements for servants.
6. Plain needlework, as distinguished from embroidery.
7. Ellen's relatives. cf. EN 9.6.1838 n. 1.
8. To the Red House, the home of Joshua Taylor and his family.

To Emily J. Brontë, 8 June 1839

Stonegappe

Dearest Lavinia,[1]

I am most exceedingly obliged to you for the trouble you have taken in seeking up my things and sending them all right. The box and its contents were most acceptable. I only wish I had asked you to send me some letter-paper. This is my last sheet but two. When you can send the other articles of raiment now manufacturing, I shall be right down glad of them.

I have striven hard to be pleased with my new situation.[2] The country, the house, and the grounds are, as I have said, divine. But, alack-a-day! there is such a thing as seeing all beautiful around you—pleasant woods, winding white paths, green lawns, and blue sunshiny sky—and not having a free moment or a free thought left to enjoy them in. The children are constantly with me, and more riotous, perverse, unmanageable cubs never grew. As for correcting them, I soon quickly found that was entirely out of the question: they are to do as they like. A complaint to Mrs. Sidgwick brings only black looks upon oneself,[3] and unjust, partial excuses to screen the children. I have tried that plan once. It succeeded so notably that I shall try it no more.[4] I said in my last letter that Mrs. Sidgwick did not know me. I now begin to find that she does not intend to know me, that she cares nothing in the world about me except to contrive how the greatest possible quantity of labour may be squeezed out of me, and to that end she overwhelms me with oceans of needlework, yards of cambric to hem, muslin nightcaps to make, and, above all things, dolls to dress. I do not think she likes me at all, because I can't help being shy in such an entirely novel scene, surrounded as I have hitherto been by strange and constantly changing faces.[5] [I used to think I should like to be in the stir of grand folks' society but I have had enough of it—it is dreary work to look on and listen.[6]] I see now more clearly than I have ever done before that a private governess has no existence, is not considered as a living and rational being except as connected with the wearisome duties she has to fulfil. While she is teaching the children, working for them, amusing them, it is all right. If she steals a moment for herself she is a nuisance. Nevertheless, Mrs. Sidgwick is universally considered an amiable woman. Her manners are fussily affable. She talks a great deal, but as it seems to me not much to the purpose. Perhaps I may like her better after a while. At present I have no call to her. Mr. Sidgwick is in my opinion a hundred times better—less profession, less bustling condescension, but a far kinder heart. It is very seldom that he speaks to me, but when he does I always feel happier and more settled for some minutes after. He never asks me to wipe the children's smutty noses or tie their shoes or fetch their pinafores or set them a chair. One of the pleasantest afternoons I have spent here—indeed, the only one at all pleasant—was when Mr. Sidgwick walked out with his children, and I had orders to follow a little behind. As he strolled on through his fields with his magnificent Newfoundland dog at his side, he looked very like what a frank, wealthy, Conservative gentleman ought to be.[7] He spoke freely and unaffectedly to the people he met, and though he indulged his children and allowed them to tease himself far too much, he would not suffer them grossly to insult others.

I am getting quite to have a regard for the Carter family. At home I should not care for them, but here they are friends. Mr. Carter was at Mirfield yesterday and saw Anne.[8] He says she was looking uncommonly well. Poor girl, she must indeed wish to be at home. As to Mrs. Collins'[9] report that Mrs. Sidgwick intended to keep me permanently, I do not think that such was ever her design. Moreover, I would not stay without some alterations. For instance, this burden of sewing would have to be removed. It is too bad for anything. I never in my whole life had my time so fully taken up. Next week we are going to Swarcliffe, Mr. Greenwood's place near Harrogate,[10] to stay three weeks or a month. After that time I hope Miss Hoby[11] will return. Don't show this letter to papa or aunt, only to Branwell. They will think I am never satisfied wherever I am. I complain to you because it is a relief, and really I have had some unexpected mortifications to put up with. However, things may mend, but Mrs. Sidgwick expects me to do things that I cannot do—to love her children and be entirely devoted to them. I am really very well. I am so sleepy that I can write no more. I must leave off. Love to all.—Good-bye.

Direct your next dispatch—J. Greenwood, Esq., Swarcliffe, near Harrogate.

C. Brontë

MS untraced. W & S 75.
Address: not in source.
PM: not in source.
Text: *CBCircle* 80–2, with one sentence from *Life* i. 192. W & S 75 reprints *Shorter* 51, but adds the sentence copied from the *Life*, inserted by Hatfield in his copy of *Shorter*: 'I used to think . . . and listen.' Some of the variants in the abridged version in *Life* i. 191–2 are given below. The MS may have been destroyed by Mr Nicholls. See Introduction p. 60.

1. This name is not used elsewhere for Emily Brontë, but there is no doubt that the letter is to her. Both sisters would know James Thomson's verse-tale about the 'lovely young Lavinia' 'Recluse amid the close-embowering woods' in *The Seasons*. ('Autumn', ll. 177–310.)
2. CB had taken a temporary post as governess in the family of John Benson Sidgwick (1800–72) and his wife Sarah Hannah (1803–87), at Stonegappe, then a 'lonely secluded house in a wooded dingle of the moors', in Lothersdale, near Skipton, Yorks. Mr Sidgwick was the principal partner in the High Mills, Skipton, and his wife was the daughter of the manufacturer John Greenwood of Knowle House, Keighley. They had been married at Keighley on 10 June 1827 by Mr Brontë's old friend, the Revd Hammond Roberson of Liversedge. See *Wroot* 10 and *BST* 13. 67. 145–8, Gérin *CB* 141–8, and the baptismal and marriage registers of St Andrew's church, Keighley.
3. Arthur Christopher Benson described his relatives the Sidgwicks as 'extraordinarily benevolent', whereas Charlotte Brontë 'had no gifts for the management of children, and was also in a very morbid condition the whole time'. 'Benson Sidgwick, now Vicar of Ashby Parva, certainly on one occasion threw a Bible at Miss Brontë.' (A. C. Benson, *Life of Edward White Benson* (1899), i. 12.)
4. Rylands MS *Life* reads 'A complaint to the mother only brings black looks upon myself . . . I have tried that plan once, and succeeded in it so notably I shall try no more.'
5. Rylands MS and *Life* both indicate an omission of text after 'faces.' (i. 192.)
6. Text from *Life*. cf. Jane Eyre's feeling of isolation in ch. 17 of the novel.
7. CB's Angrian hero Zamorna has a large Newfoundland dog and watches his haymakers at work in 'Caroline Vernon', a story which includes a letter dated 'June 29th 1839'. See *Five Novelettes* (1971), ed. Winifred Gérin, transcribed from the MS in the Widener Collection, Harvard, 282, 285.
8. Anne Brontë's post as a governess was at Blake Hall near Mirfield. For the Revd Edward Nicholl Carter and his family see EN 24.8.1838 n. 6. Mr Sidgwick was the patron of the living to which he was appointed at the newly built Christ Church in Lothersdale. Mr Carter had prepared CB for confirmation while she was at Roe Head when he was the Curate of Mirfield. In 1842 he was to become the Vicar of Heckmondwike, where he was dearly loved, and where he remained until his death in 1872.
9. Not definitely identified. She may have been the wife of the Revd John Collins, assistant from Mar. 1839 and Curate from January 1840 to the Revd Theodore Dury of Keighley whose wife Anne (1795–1881) was Mrs Sidgwick's sister. See EN 7.4.1840 n. 4.
10. Swarcliffe House and the surrounding land on the Southern slopes of the Nidd valley, about 5

miles from Harrogate, had been bought by Mrs Sidgwick's father John Greenwood (1763–1846) in 1805. In 1850 the house was rebuilt and renamed Swarcliffe Hall by Mrs Sidgwick's brother Edwin Greenwood (1798–1852).

11. Not identified.

To Ellen Nussey, [30 June 1839]

[Swarcliffe]

My dearest Ellen

I am writing a letter to you with pencil because I cannot just now procure ink without going into the drawing-room—where I do not wish to go. I only received your letter yesterday for we are not now residing at *Stonegappe—but at *Swarcliffe[1] a summer residence of Mr *Greenwood's Mrs *Sidgwick's father. it is near Harrogate—& Ripon[2]—a beautiful place in a beautiful country—rich and agricultural—

I should have written to you long since—and told you every detail of the utterly new scene into which I have lately been cast—had I not been daily expecting a letter from yourself—and wondering and lamenting that you did not write for you will remember it was your turn. I must not bother you too much with my sorrows Ellen, of which I fear you have heard an exaggerated account—if you were near me perhaps I might be tempted to tell you all—to grow egotistical and pour out the long history of a Private Governesse's trials and crosses in her first Situation—As it is I will only ask you to imagine the miseries of a reserved wretch like me—thrown at once into the midst of a large Family—proud as peacocks & wealthy as Jews—at a time when they were particularly gay—when the house was filled with Company—all Strangers people whose faces I had never seen before—in this state of things having the charge given me of a set of pampered spoilt & turbulent children[3]—whom I was expected constantly to amuse as well as instruct—I soon found that the constant demand on my stock of animal spirits reduced them to the lowest state of exhaustion—at times I felt and I suppose seemed depressed—to my astonishment I was taken to task on the subject by Mrs *Sidgwick with a stern[n]ess of manner & a harshness of language scarcely credible—like a fool I cried most bitterly—I could not help it—my spirits quite failed me at first I thought I had done my best—strained every nerve to please her—and to be treated in that way merely because I was shy—and sometimes melancholy was too bad. at first I was for giving all up and going home—But after a little reflection I determined—to summon what energy I had and to weather the Storm—I said to myself I have never yet quitted a place without gaining a friend—Adversity is a good school[4]—the Poor are born to labour and the

Dependent to endure I resolved to be patient—to command my feelings and to take what came—<when> the ordeal I reflected would not last many weeks—and I trusted it would do me good—I recollected the fable of the Willow and the Oak[5]—I bent quietly and I trust now the Storm is blowing over me—Mrs. *Sidgwick is generally considered an agreeable woman—so she is I daresay in general Society—her health is sound—her animal spirits are good—consequently she is cheerful in company—but O Ellen does this compensate for the absence of every fine feeling of every gentle—and delicate sentiment?—[6]

She behaves somewhat more civilly to me now than she did at first—and the children are a little more manageable—but she does not know my character & she does not wish to know it I have never had five minutes conversation with her since I came—except while she was scolding me—do not communicate the contents of this letter to any one—I have no wish to be pitied—except by yourself—do not even clatter[7] with *Martha *Taylor about it—if I were talking to you I would tell you much more—but I hope my term of bondage will soon be expired—and then I can go home and you can come to see me—and I hope we shall be happy Good-bye dear—dear Ellen Write to me again very—soon and tell me how you are direct J Greenwoods Esqre Swarcliffe nr Harrogate—perhaps though I may be at home before you write again I don't intend to stay long after they leave *Swarcliffe which they expect shortly to do

[Unsigned]

MS Pierpont Morgan MA 2696. W & S 76.
Address (integral): Miss Ellen Nussey | Brookroyd | Birstal | nr Leeds
PM: [H]ARROGATE | JY 1 | 183—

1. See previous letter, notes 2 and 10.
2. Swarcliffe is about 12 miles South-West of Ripon. Four miles beyond Ripon to the north is a Jacobean house, Norton Conyers, which in 1848 was rented by Frederick Greenwood from the owner, Sir Bellingham Graham; John Greenwood himself was probably at Swarcliffe. It is possible that 'the Sidgwicks came over to visit their relatives bringing their children and their governess'. (Sir James Graham, *A Guide to Norton Conyers*, n.d. but *c.*1988.) Whether they did or not, Charlotte could have heard of Norton Conyers' association with the battle of Marston Moor, and of its legend of a mad woman—reputedly a Lady Graham—kept in a remote attic room. The house, along with Ellen Nussey's former home, Rydings, and the home of the Eyre family at North Lees Hall, Hathersage, may have given CB some ideas for Thornfield Hall in *JE* which, as well as its secret mad woman, has the tomb of 'Damer de Rochester, slain at Marston Moor' in its church.
3. Margaret (b. 1827), William (b. 1829), Mathilda (b. 1832), and John Benson Sidgwick (b. 1835).
4. Perhaps a variant on the proverbial 'Adversity makes a man wise, not rich'. (*ODEP* 4.)
5. cf. Croxall's version of Aesop's Fable of the Oak and the Reed, where the reed survives the storm which has felled the Oak: 'I yield and bend to the blast, and let it go over me.' Croxall's 'application' recommends submission 'where it is impossible for us to overcome'. (Samuel Croxall, *Fables of Aesop and Others: Translated into English. With Instructive Applications . . .* (1809 edn.) 89–90.
6. In her old age Mrs Sidgwick made a very different impression on her great-nephew, Arthur Christopher Benson (1862–1925), who visited her in 1874 and described her as 'a little woman with a sweet face, who received us with gentle cordiality, and won our hearts at once'. (Harry Speight, *Chronicles and Stories of Old Bingley* (1898), 315.) An unnamed correspondent of

C. K. Shorter also claimed that the Sidgwicks were generous and considerate whereas CB was 'difficult' and 'often went to bed all day and left [Mrs Sidgwick] to look after the children . . . when she was much occupied with her invalid father, Mr. Greenwood, at Swarcliffe'. (*BST* 1. 8. 18–19, for the year 1898.). The correspondent was probably one of those named by Shorter in 1908: 'Two clever members of this gifted family [the Sidgwicks and Bensons], Mrs. Alfred Sidgwick the novelist, and Miss G. E. Mitton the biographer and essayist, have also written to me as to the lovable qualities of Mrs. John Sidgwick.' (*Shorter* i. 157, n. 2.)

7. Gossip, tattle (Northern dialect). The writing is untidy, and the word could be 'chatter'.

To Emily J. Brontë, [?July 1839][1]

[?Swarcliffe]

Mine bonnie love, I was as glad of your letter as tongue can express: it is a real, genuine pleasure to hear from home; a thing to be saved till bed-time, when one has a moment's quiet and rest to enjoy it thoroughly. Write whenever you can. I could like to be at home. I could like to work in a mill. I could like to feel some mental liberty. I could like this weight of restraint to be taken off. But the holidays will come. Coraggio.[2]

[Unsigned]

MS untraced. W & S 77.
Address: not in source.
PM: not in source.
Text: Rylands MS *Life*. Mrs Gaskell's transcript of this letter is a late insertion in the Rylands MS *Life*, headed '(To Emily about this time.)' and written on the verso of fol. 175. *Hatfield*, *Shorter* 53, and W & S 77 reproduce *Life* i. 195, dating 'July—1839', with the variants: 'I could feel mental liberty' (*Shorter*), 'I could feel some mental liberty' (*Hatfield*), and 'I could like to feel mental liberty' (W & S).

1. *Hatfield* reproduces a note by EN: 'The following letter was written about this time from Charlotte to Emily . . . It is desirable to note here, that dear C. B. was not in the least physically fitted for the position she occupied—hence her depression and inability to gauge justly her present surroundings.'
2. For CB's knowledge of Italian, see E. Branwell 29.9.1841 and n. 4.

To Ellen Nussey, [?26 July 1839]

[Haworth]

Dear Ellen

Your proposal—has almost driven me "clean daft"—if you don't understand that lady-like expression you must ask me what it means when I see you—the fact is an excursion with you anywhere—whether to Cleethorpes[1] or Canada just by ourselves—without any ninnies to annoy us—would be to me most delightful—I should indeed like to go—but I can't get leave of absence for longer than a week and I'm afraid that wouldn't suit you—must I then give it up entirely? I feel as if I could not—I never had such a chance of enjoyment before—I do want to see you & talk to you and be with you—when do you wish to go?—could I meet you at Leeds? to take a gig from Haworth to Birstal would be to me a serious increase of expense—and I happen to be very low in cash—O Ellen rich people seem to have many pleasures—at their command which we are debarred from—however no repining—if I could take the coach from Keighley to Bradford & from Bradford to Leeds[2] and you could meet me at the Inn where the coach stops—on your way to Cleethorpes for I presume you go by the Leeds & Selby Rail-road[3]—it would be the most convenient plan for me

I left *Stonegappe a week since—I never was so glad to get out of a house in my life but I'll trouble you with no complain[ts] at present—Write to me directly explain your plans more fully—say when you go & I shall be able in my answer—to say decidedly whether I can accompany you or not—I must—I will—I'm set upon it I'll be obstinate and bear down opposition

Good-bye
Yours wilfully
C Brontë

[P.S.—If I find it impossible to stay for longer than a week, could you get some one else to bear you company for the remaining fortnight? Since writing the above I find that aunt and papa have determined to go to Liverpool[4] for a fortnight, and take us all with them. It is stipulated, however, that I should give up the Cleathorpes scheme. I yield reluctantly. But Aunt suggests that you may be able to join us at Liverpool. What do you say? We shall not go for a fortnight or three weeks, because till that time papa's expected assistant[5] will not be ready to undertake his duties.]

MS HM 24417. W & S 78.
Address: not in MS.
PM: not in MS.
Annotation by ?EN in ink: 40 July 26 —39
Date: ?EN's date presumably derives from a postmark on the missing leaf. Rylands MS *Life* gives 'July 20th', which may be right.
Text: MS HM 24417 is a single leaf, lacking a second leaf which must have contained the postscript and address. Text of postscript from W & S 78.

1. A small watering-place at the mouth of the Humber in Lincs.
2. Keighley was on the main coach route between Kirkby Lonsdale, Skipton, and Leeds. There were several coaches to Leeds via Bradford each day.
3. The first railway line opened in connection with Leeds, begun in Oct. 1830 and opened for passengers on 22 Sept. 1834. 'The Leeds office of the company was in Kirkgate, and passengers were conveyed from here to the railway station in Marsh Lane by omnibus, at a charge of fourpence a head. On reaching Selby, after an hour and a half or so in the train, the friends would have to complete the next stage of the journey . . . by coach.' (F. R. Pearson, *Charlotte Brontë on the East Yorkshire Coast* (The East Yorkshire Local History Society, 1957), 10.)

4. A surprising choice, since Liverpool had for many years been a 'great and important commercial town', and was 'rather deficient in promenades or public walks'. However, 'During the season, Liverpool [was] a place of frequent resort for sea-bathing.' (*Dugdale* 1085.) Possibly CB's father and aunt recalled journeys via Liverpool from Ireland and Cornwall respectively.
5. The Revd William Weightman, MA (1814–42). See EN 17.3.1840 and n. 4. Writing to the Revd J. C. Franks on 10 Jan. 1839 for advice and assistance, Patrick Brontë explained that he had obtained 'a grant [of £80 per annum] from the Pastoral Aid Society, in case I can procure a man congenial with their sentiments, and who would be active, as well as zealous.' Patrick was, he said, 'no Bigot'—yet he could not 'feel comfortable with a coadjutor, who would deem it his duty to preach the appal[l]ing Doctrines of personal Election and Reprobation, As I should consider these, decidedly derogatory to the Attributes of God'. (MS BPM B.S. 188, W & S 70.) Mr Weightman was due to arrive in Aug. 1839; he officiated for the first time in Haworth at a baptism and a burial on 19 Aug.

To Ellen Nussey, [4 August 1839]

[Haworth]

My dearest Ellen

I have been a long time in answering your last—but the fact was I really could not give you any definite reply till now and I thought it better to wait till I could say something decided.

The Liverpool journey is yet a matter of talk a sort of castle in the air—but between you and I, I fancy it is very doubtful whether it will ever assume a more solid shape—Aunt—like many other elderly people—likes to talk of such things but when it comes to putting them into actual practise she rather falls off. Such being the case I think you and I had better adhere to our first plan—of going somewhere together independently of other people—

I have got leave to accompany you for a week at the utmost stretch a fortnight but no more where do you wish to go?—Burlington[1] I should think from what Mary *Taylor says would be as eligible a place as any—when do you wish to set off?—arrange all these things according to your own convenience—I shall start no objections—the idea of seeing the SEA—of being near it—watching its changes by sunrise Sunset—moonlight—& noonday—in calm—perhaps in storm—fills & satisfies my mind I shall be dis-contented at nothing—& then I am not to be with a set of people with whom I have nothing in common—who would be nuisance & bores—but with you *Ellen *Nussey whom I like and know & who knows me—

I have an odd circumstance to relate to you prepare for a hearty laugh—the other day—Mr *Hodgson[2]—Papa's former Curate—now a Vicar—came over to spend the day—with us—bringing with him his own Curate. The latter Gentleman by name Mr *Price[3] is a young Irish Clergyman—fresh from Dublin University—it was the first time we had any of us seen him, but however after the manner of his Countrymen he soon made himself at home his character quickly appeared in his conversation—witty—lively, ardent—clever too—but deficient in the dignity & discretion of an Englishman at home you know Ellen I talk with ease and am never shy—never weighed down & oppressed by that miserable mauvaise honte[4] which torments & constrains me elsewhere—so I conversed with this Irishman & laughed at his jests—& though I saw faults in his character excused them because of the amusement his originality afforded—I cooled a little indeed & drew in towards the latter part of the evening—because he began to season his conversation with something of Hibernian flattery which I did not quite relish. however they went away and no more was thought about them.

A few days after I got a letter the direction of which puzzled me it being in a hand I was not accustomed to see—evidently it was neither from you nor Mary *Taylor, my only Correspondents—having opened & read it it proved to be a declaration of attachment—& proposal of Matrimony—expressed in the ardent language of the sapient young Irishman!

well thought I—I've heard of love at first sight but this beats all. I leave you to guess what my answer would be—convinced that you will not do me the injustice of guessing wrong

When we meet I'll shew you the letter. I hope you are laughing heartily. this is not like one of my adventures is it? it more nearly resembles *Martha *Taylor's—I'm certainly doomed to be an old maid Ellen—I can't expect another chance—never mind I made up my mind to that fate ever since I was twelve years old. I need not tell you to consider that this little adventure is told in confidence—write soon

C Brontë

I had almost forgotten to settle about how we are to join if I take the coach from Keighley to Bradford and from thence to Leeds[5]—I think I could arrive in the latter Town by 10 or at <mo> the latest 11 o'clock in the morning—will that be soon enough for your plans? & will it suit your convenience to meet me at the Inn where the coach stops?

If this project should be deemed in any way inconvenient I must contrive some other—on some accounts it would be far better to get to Brookroyd the day before—do you know whether there is any daily coach from Bradford runs anywhere within a mile of you?[6] After all I have not yet ascertained whether my limited time for staying at the sea-side will interfere with what is necessary for your health if it would I throw the whole scheme up at once—write very soon.
What luggage will you take? much or little?

MS HM 24418. W & S 79.
Address (integral): Miss Ellen Nussey | Brook-royd | Birstal | Leeds
PM: (i) BRADFORD YORKS | AU 5 | 1839 (ii) *Bradford Yorks* | *Py Post*
Annotation by EN in ink: 41 Aug 4 39

Date: EN's date may be derived from the postmark.

1. An alternative name for Bridlington on the east coast of Yorks. The old town, with a fine priory church and a number of handsome houses, was a mile inland from Bridlington Quay, 'the resort of many noble and respectable families; having strong recommendations as a bathing-place, in the goodness of the shore, the cheapness and excellence of the provisions, and other accommodations; and the general liveliness of its appearance'. (*Dugdale* 272–3.)
2. The Revd William Hodgson (?1809–74), Patrick Brontë's curate from Dec. 1835 to May 1837. He had been popular in Haworth, where a petition for his continuing to officiate there was signed by 236 people on 30 Apr. 1837. He had supported PB's speech against the New Poor Law in Feb. 1837. See *The Times* 27.2.1837, 6. He became the perpetual curate of Christ Church, Colne, Lancs. in 1837 and remained there until his death. A letter from his son-in-law, E. Olridge-de-la-Hey, ascribes various ghost stories to him in spite of his alleged 'clear head and sound judgment'. (*BST* 1. 8. 15–17.)
3. The Revd David Pryce (1811–40). He had been entered as a pensioner at Trinity College Dublin on 18.10.1830, aged 19, and he obtained his BA in summer 1838. His place of birth is given in *Alumni Dublinenses* as Wicklow. For his death from TB see EN 24.1.1840 n. 6. Mr. Hodgson's daughter apparently gave a rather different account of the visit and proposal. Her husband wrote to C. K. Shorter in 1896 or 1897: 'Mr. Bryce [*sic*] had expressed a wish to Mr. Hodgson that he could find a suitable partner for life, and it was in consequence of this that Mr. Hodgson took him over to see the Brontës. My wife distinctly remembers that her father told her that several letters passed between the two after Mr. Bryce's visit, and that the notion of marriage was given up because both families being consumptive the union would not be a prudent one.' (Clement Shorter, 'New Light on the Brontës', *BST* 1. 8. 16.)
4. Painful diffidence or self-consciousness.
5. According to Pigot's *Directory* for 1841 the *Alexander* (from Skipton) 'calls at the Fleece Inn [Keighley], every morning at seven', and then goes through Bingley and Bradford to Leeds, calling at the Bowling Green Inn, Bradford 'every morning (Sunday excepted) at nine'. From Bradford there were coaches to Leeds 'every hour from eight in the morning until eight at night'.
6. Coaches from Bradford to Dewsbury would pass within a mile of Brookroyd.

To Ellen Nussey, [9 August 1839]

[Haworth]

My dearest Ellen

In the greatest haste I scrawl an answer to your letter—I am very sorry to throw you back in your arrangements but I really cannot go tomorrow—I could not get my <boxes &> baggage & myself to Leeds by 10 o'clock tomorrow morning if I were to be hanged for it—you must write again and fix a day which will give me a little more time for preparation Haworth you know is such an out-of the way place one should have a month's warning before they stir from it[1] You were very kind to try to get me fetched—but indeed Ellen it was wrong of you—do you think I could comfortably have accepted so unreasonable a favour? my best plan will certainly be to <go> come to Brookroyd the day before we start—I'll try to manage it—

Good bye my dearest Ellen
The Post is just going

C Br.

Friday-morning

MS BPM BS 41. W & S 80.
Address (integral): Miss Ellen Nussey | Brookroyd | Birstal | Leeds
PM: (i) BRADFORD YORKS | AU 9 | 1839 (ii) *Bradford Yorks* | *Py Post*
Annotation in pencil by EN: [Written before C's first visit to the Sea side. She sobbed with emotion when she first beheld the Ocean & was for sometime fixed to the spot]
Date: from postmark; 9 Aug. was a Friday.

1. Only one gig was available for hire in Haworth: see the next letter, and compare EN's description of the one-horse 'rickety dogcart' used in 1833. (EN 11.9.1833 n. 2.)

To Ellen Nussey, 14 August 1839

Haworth

My dear Ellen

I have in vain packed my box—and prepared everything for our anticipated journey it so happens that I can get no conveyance this week nor the next. The only gig let out to hire in Haworth is at Harrogate & likely to remain there for aught I can hear—Papa decidedly objects to my going by the coach and walking to Birstal[1] though I am sure I could manage 'it' Aunt exclaims against the weather and the roads and the four winds of Heaven. so I'm in a fix—and what is worse so are <u>You</u>.

On reading over for the second or third time your last letter (which by the bye Ellen was written in such hieroglyphics that at the first hasty perusal I could hardly make out two consecutive words) I find you intimate that if I leave the journey till Thursday I shall be too late I grieve that I should have so inconvenienced you but I need not talk either of Thursday—Friday or Saturday now for the fact is I rather imagine there's small chance of my ever going at all The elders of the House have never cordially acquiesced in the measure, & now that impediments seem to start up at every step opposition grows more open—Papa indeed would willingly indulge me but this very kindness of his makes me doubt whether I ought to draw upon it—& though I could battle out Aunt's discontent I yield to Papa's indulgence—He does not say so but I know he would rather I stayed at home—Aunt means well too I daresay but I am provoked that she reserved the expression of her decided disapproval till all was settled between you and myself.

Reckon on me no more—leave me out in your calculations—perhaps I ought in the beginning to have had prudence sufficient to shut my eyes against such a prospect of pleasure & to deny myself the hope of it—Be as angry as you please with me for disappointing you I did not intend it—I have only one thing more to say—if you do not go immediately to the sea will you come and see us at Haworth will you write to me directly & fix your day an early day—I feel convinced the change of air would do you good. This invitation is not mine only it is Papa's & Aunt's—dear—Ellen do come—if you would come here I would go back with you to Birstal, for a few days ˋifˊ you would have me'—and <the> ˋyourˊ return should be no expense to you of course—This would be cheaper than the sea-side scheme if it would only be as effectual—How is Mr *Taylor?—any better?[2]

Good-bye
C Brontë

MS BPM B.S. 42. W & S 81.
Address (integral): [. . .]llen Nussey | Brookroyd | Birstal
PM: *Bradford Yorks* | *Penny Post*
Annotation in pencil by EN: ?on going to Burlington

1. Birstall is about 6 miles from Bradford and 7 from Leeds.
2. Joshua Taylor of Gomersal (1766–1840), father of Mary and Martha Taylor. He had been very ill for several months, and he died on 28 Dec. 1840. See EN 3.1.1841 n. 1.

To Maria Taylor,[1] [?4 or 11 September 1839]

[Haworth]

Dear Miss Taylor

I find I shall have to go from home tomorrow; I cannot therefore accompany you to call on Miss Metcalf[2] as I intended to have done—I shall probably be from home a fortnight, when I return we can if you please fix another [?day] Give my best regards to your Mother and believe me

Yours faithfully
C Brontë

Wednesday Evening

MS Mr A. F. I. Parmeter. No publication traced.
Address (integral): Miss Taylor | Stanbury
PM: not in source
Date: conjectural. The letter cannot be later than 5 Nov. 1839, when Maria Taylor (1808–75), daughter of Stephen and Mary Taylor of Stanbury, married James Ingham, a woolstapler, of Mankinholes, Bradford. (Information by courtesy of the owner of the letter, Mr A. F. I. Parmeter; see Haworth Marriage Register for the date.) CB had originally had permission for a holiday of 'a week at the utmost stretch a fortnight' (EN 4.8.1839.) In early Sept. EN took her, at very short notice, to Bridlington: see the next letter. If Ellen gave no notice at all, as she implies, the present letter must date from an earlier period.

1. Maria Taylor's father Stephen (1772–1831) had been a gentleman farmer whose family lived at the Manor House, Stanbury, a hamlet about 1 ½ miles from Haworth. Like his sons, he was a trustee of Haworth church, and had been a supporter of Patrick Brontë in his contested admission to the perpetual curacy at Haworth in 1820.
2. Not identified. She may have been a connection of Anthony Metcalfe, brother of a Keighley schoolmaster, whom Patrick Brontë had befriended, though he had failed to help him enter into holy orders. See PB's letter to Mr Metcalfe of 30.6.1831, printed in *LD*, 336.

To Ellen Nussey, 24 October 1839

Haworth

My dear Ellen

You will have concluded by this time that I never got home at all[1]—but evaporated by the way—however I did get home and very well too by the aid of the Dewsbury Coachman—though if I had not contrived to make friends with him I don't know how I should have managed. He shewed me the way to the Inn where the Keighley Coach stopped[2]—carried my box—took my place—saw my luggage put in—and helped me to mount on to the top—I assure you I felt exceedingly obliged to him.

I had a long letter from your *brother *Henry the other day—giving an account of his bride-elect[3] if she be what he describes her—He is amply justified in the step he proposes to take—but Love they say blinds the eyes—so I don't know I have not answered it yet but I mean to soon

Have you forgot the Sea by this time Ellen?[4] is it grown dim in your mind? or you can still see it dark blue and green and foam-white and hear it—roaring roughly when the wind is high or rushing softly when it is calm? How is your health have good effects resulted from the change? I am as well as need be, and very fat

I think of Easton[5] very often and of worthy Mr *Hudson[6] and his kind-hearted help-mate and of our pleasant walks to Harlequin-wood—to Boynton[7]—our Merry evenings—our romps with little Fanchon[8]—&c. &c. if we both live this period of our lives will long be a theme of pleasant recollection. Did you chance in your letter to Mrs *Hudson to mention my spectacles? I am sadly inconvenienced by the want of them—I can neither read, write nor draw with comfort in their absence. I hope Madame Booth[9] won't refuse to give them up

I wonder when we shall meet again—have you yet managed to get any definite period fixed for your visit to us?

Excuse the brevity of this letter my dear Ellen for the truth is I have been drawing all day[10] and my eyes are so tired it is quite a labour to write. Give my best love to your Mother & Sister[11] and to *Sarah & believe me

Your old friend
C Brontë.

MS HM 24419. W & S 83.
Address (integral): Miss Ellen Nussey | Brookroyd | Birstal | nr Leeds
PM: (i) BRADFORD YORKS | OC 25 | 1839 (ii) *Bradford Yorks* | *Penny Post*
Annotation by EN in pencil: 24 Oct 39 | after visiting Easton | Burlington

1. CB had returned home after a 5-week holiday with EN on the east coast of Yorks. EN recalled that 'through the aid of a dear relative' (presumably one of her brothers) she had gone to Haworth in a carriage and taken CB by surprise: 'Branwell was grandiloquent, he declared "it was a brave defeat, that the doubters were fairly taken aback." . . . almost before the horse was rested there was a quiet but triumphant starting'; then after a first experience in railway travelling, the journey was completed in an open fly (a light hired carriage) and finally in a post-chaise. 'Friends in the vicinity of the coast . . . informed of their coming' had arranged for them 'to be driven off not to the bourne they were longing for (the seaside) but two or three miles away from it, here they were (though most unwilling) hospitably entertained and *detained* for a month. . . . At last their kind and generous entertainers yielded to their wishes and permitted them to take wing and go into lodgings for one week, but still protecting them by every day visits, and bounteous provision from their dairy.' (For the full account, see the MS text, Appendix, 605–7.)

   Henry Nussey, whose curacy at Burton Agnes in 1838 was only 6 miles from Bridlington, had probably written to the friends, Mr and Mrs John Hudson. Mr Hudson may have been the son of Thomas and Margaret Hudson, christened on 5.9.1802, or of Thomas and Rachel Hudson, christened on 17.2.1807—both of Burton Agnes.
2. CB would have travelled to Keighley from the Scarborough Hotel in Dewsbury market-place.
3. Not identified, but presumably not the wealthy Emily Prescott (1811–1907), whom Henry Nussey married in 1845. The name may be 'Follett'. See EN 30.4.1840 n. 3. Henry's *Diary* does not help, since it stops short on 14 Mar. 1839.
4. On her first sight of the sea, Charlotte 'was quite overpowered, she could not speak till she had shed some tears . . . her eyes were red and swollen, she was still trembling . . . for the remainder of the day she was very quiet, subdued, and exhausted.' (*Shorter* i. 169.)
5. 'A tiny hamlet of only two or three houses, which lies a short distance inland from Bridlington Quay. The situation is charming . . . At this point, the valley of the Gypsey Race . . . merges almost imperceptibly into the sea plain.' (F. R. Pearson, *Charlotte Brontë on the East Yorkshire Coast* (The East Yorkshire Local History Society, 1957), 12.) For a description of Bridlington and Easton at this period, and for a reproduction of CB's drawing of Easton House, see Gérin *CB* 152–9.
6. Mr John Hudson, a gentleman farmer (d. 1878), married in 1831 to Sophia Whipp (d. 1876) 'described by one who knew her well as "a model of primness and old-world sweetness" '. (Pearson, *CB on E. Yorks. Coast*, 12.)
7. Erskine Stuart, quoting Thomas Holderness of Driffield, writes of 'Easton . . . pleasantly situated in the valley; but here we lose the more enchanting sylvan beauty of the supremely picturesque village of Boynton, with its fir-clad slopes.' (J. A. Erskine Stuart, *The Brontë Country* (1888), 206.) Boynton is about a mile from Easton.
8. W & S read 'Hancheon', but the initial letter differs from those in 'Hudson' and 'Harlequin'. 'Fanchon' would be a diminutive for Frances or Fanny Whipp, a niece of Mrs Hudson, and about 7 years old at the time. She became Mrs North of Bridlington, where she died in 1866.
9. The landlady of the lodging-house to which the friends had been allowed to move for the last week of their holiday. Pigot's *Directory* for 1841 names 'Ann Booth, Garrison Street' as a lodging-house keeper in Bridlington Quay. See Appendix p. 606.
10. EN comments: 'Charlotte would spend even 9 hours a day in drawing and painting—She tried miniature portraits, but never succeeded to her satisfaction.' (*Hatfield* 93.)
11. Ann Nussey. Mercy was housekeeping for her brother Henry at Earnley: see the next letter. The phrasing is odd, because Sarah Walker Nussey, the invalid, was also Ellen's sister. Ellen seems not to have been intimate with her cousin Sarah of White Lee (1819–43).

To Henry Nussey, 28 October 1839

Haworth

Dear Sir

I have delayed answering your last communication in the hopes of receiving a letter from Ellen that I might be able to transmit to you the latest news from Brookroyd; however as she does not write I think I ought to put off my reply no longer lest you should begin to think me negligent. As you rightly conjecture I had heard a little hint of what you allude to before and the account gave me pleasure coupled as it was with the assurance that the object of your regard is a worthy, and estimable woman The step no doubt will by many of your friends be considered scarcely as a prudent one, since fortune is not amongst the number of the young lady's advantages[1] for my own part I must confess that I esteem you the more for not hunting after wealth if there be strength of mind, firmness of principle and sweetness of temper to compensate for the absence of that usually all-powerful attraction. The wife who brings riches to her husband sometimes also brings an idea of her own importance and a tenacity about what she conceives to be her rights little calculated to produce happiness in the married state Most probably she will wish to control where Nature and Affection bind her to submit—in this case there cannot I should think be much comfort

On the other hand it must be considered that when two persons marry without money—there ought to be moral Courage and physical exertion to atone for the deficiency—there should be Spirit to scorn dependence, patience to endure privation & energy to labour for a livelihood—If there be these qualities I think with the blessing of God those who join heart and hand—have a right to expect success and a moderate share of happiness—even though they may have departed a step or two from the stern maxims of worldly prudence The bread earned by honourable toil is sweeter than the bread of idleness[2]—and mutual love and domestic calm—are treasures far-preferable to the possessions rust can corrupt and moths consume away.[3]

I enjoyed my late excursion with Ellen with the greater zest because such pleasures have not often chanced to fall in my way—I will not tell you what I thought of the Sea—because I should fall into my besetting sin of enthusiasm.[4] I may however say that its glorious changes—its ebb and flow—the sound of its restless waves—formed a subject for contemplation that never wearied either the eye—the ear or the mind Our visit at Easton was extremely pleasant I shall always feel grateful to Mr & Mrs. Hudson for their kindness[5]—We saw Burton-Agnes[6] during our stay and called on two of your former parishioners—Mrs. Brown and Mrs. Dalton—I was pleased to hear your name mentioned by them in terms of encomium & sincere regard.[7] Ellen will have detailed to you all the minutiæ of our excursion—a recapitulation from me would therefore be tedious. I am happy to say that her health appeared to be greatly improved by the change of air and regular exercise. I am still at home as I have not yet heard of any situation which meets the approbation of my friends.[8] I begin however to grow exceedingly impatient of a prolonged period of inaction—I feel I ought to be doing something for myself—for my health is now so perfectly re-established by this long rest that it affords me no further pretext for indolence. With every wish for your future welfare, and with the hope that whenever your proposed union takes place it may contribute in the highest sense to your good and happiness, believe me

Your sincere friend
C Brontë

P.S. Remember me to your Sister Mercy—who I understand is for the present your Companion and house keeper.

MS BPM B. S. 43. W & S 84.
Address (integral): Revd. H Nussey | Earnley-Rectory | Chichester | Sussex
PM (i) BRAD[FORD] | OC — | 1839 (ii) *Bradford* — | *Penny Post* (iii) N | 30 OC 30 | 1839

1. See the previous letter, and cf. CB's letter of 5 Mar. refusing Henry Nussey's proposal of marriage.
2. Part of the description of a virtuous woman in Proverbs 31: 27, 'She looketh well to the ways of her household, and eateth not the bread of idleness.'
3. cf. Matthew 6: 19.
4. As in the 18th cent., the word still had overtones of excess and fanaticism. The cautious Henry had recorded seeing the sea at Blackpool with notable restraint: '[I] beheld the Sea (emblem of eternity) for the 1st time in my life, 'tis in reality one of the finest sights beheld with mortal eye, yet was not surprised at it, as it appeared much the same as I imagined it would.' (HN *Diary* 17.7.1832, fol. 28^{r}.)
5. See the previous letter, notes 5 and 6.
6. The small town where Henry Nussey had been curate to the Revd Charles Henry Lutwidge, vicar of the rich living of Burton Agnes with Harpham.
7. Not identified, but after describing his farewell services at Burton Agnes and Harpham, Henry recorded that he 'was becoming truly attached to' his parishioners. (HN *Diary* ?28.11.1838, fol. 37^{r}.)
8. Family, relatives, as in EN 9.6.1838 and 15.4.1839.

To Ellen Nussey, 21 December 1839

[Haworth]

Dear Ellen

You seem to be as usual involved in the troubles and calamities of those nearest to you—I fear you have had much to suffer. More even than your letters express though I am well aware that "the wind is always tempered to the shorn lamb"[1] and the same Fate which traced your path in this life through thorns and briars—gave you a tranquil and resigned temperament, to bear the stings they inflict.

I think with you that the worst must now be over—Your brothers must hitherto have had hopeless work,[2] struggling against evils whose approach their utmost efforts could only retard a moment—but which no exertion they had the power to make could finally prevent: if their energies have not been exhausted by the long contest, they ought now to summon them all for another trial and may better success attend them than they have hitherto known.

We are at present and have been during the last month rather busy as for that space of time we have been without a Servant except a little girl to run errands[3] poor Tabby[4]—became so lame from a large ulcer in her leg that she was à[t] length obliged to leave us—She is residing with her Sister in a little house of her own, which she bought with her savings a year or two since. She is very comfortable and wants nothing. As she is near we see her very often—In the meantime Emily and I are sufficiently busy as you may suppose—I manage the ironing and keep the rooms clean—Emily does the baking and attends to the Kitchen—We are such odd animals that we prefer this mode of contrivance to having a new face among us. Besides we do not despair of Tabby's return and she shall not be supplanted by a stranger in her absence.

I excited Aunt's wrath very much by burning the clothes the first time I attempted to Iron but I do better now. Human feelings are queer things—I <would far> am much happier—black-leading the stoves—making the beds and sweeping the floors at home, than I should be living like a fine lady anywhere else.

I must indeed drop my subscription to the Jews[5] because I have no money to keep it up I ought to have announced this intention to you before. but I quite forgot that I was a subscriber. I intend to force myself to take another situation when I can get one. though I hate and abhor the very thoughts of governess-ship—But I must do it and therefore I heartily wish I could hear of a Family where they want such a commodity as a Governess.

My dear Ellen good bye—May you have a happy Christmas and may the next year be pleasanter to you than the last has been

C Brontë

MS HM 24420. W & S 85.
Address (integral): Miss Ellen Nussey | Brookroyd | Birstal | Leeds
PM: (i) BRADFORD YORKS | DE 23 | 1839 (ii) *Bradford Yorks* | *Py Post*
Annotation in pencil by EN: 21 Dec 39 | C & E at home doing servants work

1. A variant of the proverbial 'God tempers the wind to the shorn lamb.' (*ODEP* 312.)
2. Joseph (1797–1846), Richard (1803–1872), and George Nussey (1814–85) were woollen manufacturers, trading as 'Richard Nussey & Co., scribbling millers' (i.e. carrying out the coarse

'carding' or combing of wool) at Brookroyd Mill, Birstall. A trade depression combined with the Chartist risings of 1839 meant that many firms in the cotton and woollen industries were threatened with bankruptcy. Mayhall records that 'in the latter part of the year there were at least 10,000 persons out of employment in the borough of Leeds'. (*Mayhall* i. 464.)

3. Probably Martha Brown (1828–80), second daughter of the sexton and stonemason John Brown of Haworth.
4. The 68-year-old Tabitha Aykroyd. See EN 11.9.1833 n. 5. Her sister was Susannah Wood.
5. The London Society for Promoting Christianity Amongst the Jews, an interdenominational group founded in 1809, had a Ladies' Auxiliary group in Leeds, begun in 1815. CB refers to the 'Jew-basket' in *Shirley* ch. 7—a fund-raising device for the Society. (See *Shirley* 756, n. to 125.) It was a 'cause very near to' Henry Nussey's heart. (HN *Diary* 9. 12. 1838, fol. 40^{v}.)

To Ellen Nussey, [?28 December 1839]

[Haworth]

My dear Ellen

I write a hasty line to assure you we shall be happy to see you on the day you mention, Friday week.[1] I will do my best to give you what assistance[2] I can while you stay with us, and as you are now acquainted with the neighbourhood and its total want of society, and with our plain monotonous mode of life, I do not fear so much as I used to do that you will be disappointed with the dullness and sameness of your visit.[3]

One thing however—will make the daily routine more unvaried than ever Branwell, who used to enliven us—is to leave us in a few days—to enter the situation of a private tutor in the neighbourhood of Ulverston[4]—How he will like, or settle remains yet to be seen, at present he is full of Hope and resolution.

I who know his variable nature, and his strong turn for active life, dare not be too sanguine.[5] We are as busy as possible in preparing for his departure and shirt-making and collar-stitching fully occupy our time. Friday-week I look forward to with impatience don't change your day

Good-bye my dear Ellen

C Brontë

I think it is your turn to scold about bad writing.[6]

P.S. The bag I was working for you remains just in the state it was four months ago. When you come I'll try to finish it.

MS Beinecke, Yale. W & S 86.
Address: not in MS.
PM: not in MS.
Date: from W & S 86. The MS is a single leaf of the same greyish wove paper used for the dated letters to EN of 21.12.1839 and 12.1.1840; these consist of two conjoint leaves bearing a watermark, not found at any other date, of three feathers above the words RUGG & HARTLEY | 1839. A missing leaf with watermark, address and postmark may have provided the date given by W & S for the present letter.

1. 10 Jan. 1840, if this letter is correctly dated; but Ellen postponed her visit until Feb. See EN 17.3.1840 and notes.
2. Possibly in connection with Ellen's plans to become a governess. cf. EN 12.1.1840, postscript, and 24.1.1840.
3. The curate William Weightman, who was certainly not dull, may have been away from Haworth during the first 3 weeks of Jan. 1840. He officiated frequently at baptisms and burials during Nov. and Dec. 1839, but he did not sign the Haworth registers again, after officiating at a baptism on 29 Dec., until 21 Jan. 1840, when he took a burial service.
4. Branwell was to be the tutor to John (1828–86) and William (1829–1908), sons of Robert Postlethwaite, b. 1786, a retired magistrate. See Timothy Cockerill, 'A Brontë at Broughton-in-Furness', *BST* 15. 76. 34–5, Gérin *BB* 163–9, and Branwell's sonnet, 'Black Comb' in Neufeldt *BBP* 209. The Postlethwaites lived at Broughton, a small market town 9 miles from Ulverston, Lancs., and about 5 miles from the mountain described in Branwell's poem.
5. Branwell Brontë's variable nature is evident in the letters he wrote at this period: see his obscene letter of 13 Mar. 1840 to John Brown (BPM Copy MS 137.5, W & S 90 (part)), and in contrast his courteous plea to Hartley Coleridge for an opinion on his poems, 20.4.1840 (W & S 93). See also *Barker*.
6. CB is honest: the letter is scrawled in the large untidy handwriting typical of her letters of 1839–40.

To Ellen Nussey, [12 January 1840]

[Haworth]

a) Your letter, which I received this morning, was one of painful interest. Anne C.[1] it seems, is dead; when I saw her last, she was a young, beautiful, and happy girl; and now 'life's fitful fever' is over with her, and she 'sleeps well.'[2] I shall never see her again. It is a sorrowful thought; for she was a warm-hearted, affectionate being, and I cared for her. Wherever I seek for her now in this world, she cannot be found, no more than a flower or a leaf, which withered twenty years ago. A bereavement of this kind gives one a glimpse of the feeling those must have, who have seen all drop round them—friend after friend—and are left to end their pilgrimage alone. But tears are fruitless, and I try not to repine.

b) I have not repeated my invitation to you because Aunt has taken it into her head to object to having any visitors during the winter—I did not at first like to tell you of this, but Candour is the best plan after all. the matter has weighed on my mind a long while and made me uncomfortable—now that I have fairly written it down I feel far more easy.

I intend to take full advantage of this penny postage[3] and to write to you often whether I continue at home or "go out" that is as often as I have time.—

All send their love to you—Papa has just been telling me that I am to be sure and say I am much obliged to you for your intimations respecting Mrs H[alli-ley].[4] I told him on the contrary that I should scold you well for their vagueness and for the very illegible writing in which they were conveyed—in solid truth

Ellen I believe I was half an hour in making out the letter—pray write immediately as Mrs. *Halliley is daily expecting my reply and I cannot write till I hear from you

I shall be sure not to mention your name or anything you may say—I have written to Miss Wooler also for information.

Good-bye dear Ellen
C. Brontë

You may answer an advertisement without mentioning your name giving only initials. Some people however require the name Mrs H did. Do you think your health will ever be strong enough for a Governess? Don't leave that consideration out of the question.[5]

MSS: (a) untraced; (b) final page only: BPM B.S. 44. W & S 87.
Address (integral): Miss Ellen Nussey | Brookroyd | Birstall | Leeds
PM: (i) [circular printed stamp] PAID ONE PENNY ['N' printed backwards] (ii)' BRADFORD | YORKS | JA 13 | 1840
Text: (a) Rylands MS *Life* fol. 188^v Mrs Gaskell was quoting an excerpt from a leaf (now missing) sent to her by EN on 15.11.[1855]. *Shorter* 61 and W & S 87, which probably derive from the printed *Life*, supply the surname 'Carter' (erroneously) for Mrs Gaskell's 'Anne C.'. See n. 1. below. (b) BPM MS B.S. 44, the final leaf of the letter.

1. Almost certainly Ann Cook (1825–40), who is likely to be the pupil described in much the same terms, 'still the same warm-hearted—affectionate—prejudiced—handsome girl as ever' in EN 24.8.1838, q.v. The registers of St John's Church, Dewsbury Moor (the church to which Miss Wooler's pupils usually went from Heald's House) record the burial of Ann, daughter of Mr Thomas Cook of Dewsbury, on 6.1.1840. Mrs Gaskell writes: 'In January 1840, Charlotte heard of the death of a young girl who had been a pupil of hers, and a schoolfellow of Anne's, at the time when the sisters were together at Roe Head; and had attached herself very strongly to the latter, who, in return, bestowed upon her much quiet affection.' (*Life* i. 210.) In sending this part of the letter to Mrs Gaskell, EN had explained that Anne Brontë had bestowed on her friend 'a great deal of quiet affection and genial notice. I think the young lady's friends would most probably be gratified if dear C.'s comments on her decease were inserted—they are monied and influential people in this neighbourhood, some of them not very friendly to Currer Bell's emanations. Would they not be won by her kindly thought of one of their own?' (Letter of 15.11.[1855], W & S 963.)
2. cf. *Macbeth* III. ii. 23.
3. Bradford, like many other towns, had been operating a local 'penny post', but the Postal Duties Act of 17 Aug. 1839 had instituted reform of the postal system, and a uniform, prepaid penny rate of postage came into operation throughout the kingdom on 10 Jan. 1840. The printed formula 'PAID ONE PENNY' could be hand-stamped by the post office on letters sent before 6 May 1840, when ready-stamped envelopes and adhesive stamps were introduced. For the previous system, see EN 21.7.1832 n. 13. An interim reform had already operated since 5 Dec. 1839, whereby 'the number of pieces of paper of which a letter may consist [would] be of no importance' as all postages were charged by weight. (*Leeds Intelligencer* 7.12.1839, 8.) From Mar. 1840 CB usually wrote 'Prepaid', 'Paid', or occasionally 'Stamped' on the address panel or envelope.
4. Mrs. Edward Halliley, née Susanna Hirst of Gomersal, sister-in-law of John Halliley Junior of the firm of Halliley Brooke, and Hallileys, woollen and carpet manufacturers of Dewsbury. At the time of the Halliley bankruptcy (for which see EN 10.11.1834 n. 3), Edward Halliley was described as resident in Leeds, a cloth merchant, dealer, and chapman with premises at Low-Close Mill, Sheepscar, Leeds. His children included Frederick Tullock, b. 1831, and Susannah, b. 1832. The advertisement to which CB had replied may have been that in the *Leeds Intelligencer* (the Tory newspaper taken at the parsonage) for Saturday 21 Dec. 1839, 1, though

CB would not have been able to teach music: 'WANTED after the Christmas Recess, by a Family in Leeds, a young Lady, as GOVERNESS, of an amiable disposition, and some experience, willing to make herself generally useful, and competent to teach Music, French and Drawing, with the usual Branches of a good Education. None need apply but Members of the Church of England, stating Age, Reference and Salary. Letters, Post-paid, addressed to H. 181, Post-Office, Leeds.' For Mr Brontë's acquaintance with the Halliley family, see EN 10.11.1834 n. 8.

5. Before this postscript W&S 87 has a paragraph found in *Shorter* 61 but not in MS B.S. 44: '*P.S.*—As far as I can judge, the resolution you mention is a right one, and I wish you may be able to carry it into execution. You seem to doubt your own abilities—you need not.'

To Ellen Nussey, [24 January 1840]

[Haworth]

My dear Ellen

I have given Mrs *Edward *Halliley[1] her coup de grace—that is to say I have relinquished the idea of becoming an inmate of her family—I have no doubt she will be very cross with me especially as when I first declined going she pressed me to take a trial of a month—I am now therefore again adrift, without an object—I am sorry for this but something may turn up erelong

I know not whether to encourage you in your plan of going out or not—your health seems to me the great obstacle—if you could obtain a situation like *Mary *Brooke[2] you might do very well—But you could never live in an unruly, violent family of Modern children such for instance as those at *Blake Hall[3]—Anne is not to return—Mrs. *Ingham is a placid mild woman—but as for the children it was one struggle of life-wearing exertion to keep them in anything like decent order.[4]

I am miserable when I allow myself to dwell on the necessity of spending my life as a Governess. The chief requisite for that station seems to me to be the power of taking things easily as they come and of making oneself comfortable and at home wherever we may chance to be—qualities in which all our family are singularly deficient. I know I cannot live with a person like Mrs *Sidgwick[5]—but I hope all women are not like her—and my motto is "Try again"

Mary *Taylor—I am sorry to hear is ill—have you seen her or heard anything of her lately—Sickness seems very general and Death too at least in this neighbourhood. Mr. *Price[6] is dead—he had fallen into a state of delicate health for sometime and the rupture of a blood-vessel carried him off. He was a strong athletic-looking man when I saw him and that is scarcely six months ago. Though I knew so little of him, and of course could not be deeply or permanently interested in <his> what concerned him—I confess when I suddenly heard he was dead, I felt both shocked and saddened. it was no shame to feel so, was it?

I scold you Ellen for writing illegibly and badly, but I think you may repay the compliment with cent per cent interest—I am not in the humour for writing a long letter so good bye. God—bless you

[Signature cut off]

MS Pierpont Morgan MA 2696. W & S 88.
Address (integral): Miss Ellen Nussey | Brookroyd | Birstal | Leeds
PM: (i) BRADFORD YORKS | JA 25 | 1840 (ii) *Bradford* | *Py P*
Annotation in pencil by EN: Jan Mrs Halliley—Situations

1. See previous letter, n. 4.
2. Probably Maria Brooke, who became a governess, perhaps in a school, and later married a Halifax solicitor, Mr Michael Stocks. See EN 21.7.1832 n. 6, and CB to ?L. S. Brooke, early 1841 (p. 254.)
3. See EN 12.3.1839 n. 1.
4. cf. Anne Brontë's account of the governess's trials in the Bloomfield family in *AG* chs. 2 to 5.
5. CB's employer at Stonegappe, Lothersdale in the summer of 1839. See EJB 8.6.1839 notes 2 and 3.
6. The Revd David Pryce (1811–40), the curate who had proposed to CB in Aug. 1839 after visiting Haworth with his Vicar, the Revd W. Hodgson. See EN 4.8.1839 n. 3. He died at Colne, Lancs., on 17 Jan.

To Ellen Nussey, [17 March 1840][1]

[Haworth]

My dear Mrs. Eleanor

I wish to scold you with a forty horse power for having told *Martha *Taylor that I had requested you "not to tell her everything" which piece of information of course has thrown Martha into a tremendous ill-humour besides setting the teeth of her curiosity on edge with the notion, that there is something very important in the wind which you and I are especially desirous to conceal from her

Such being the state of matters I desire to take off any embargo I may have laid on your tongue which I plainly see will not be restrained and to enjoin you to walk up to *Gomersal[2] and tell her forthwith every individual occurrence you can recollect, including Valentines,[3] "Fair Ellen, Fair Ellen"—"Away fond Love" "Soul divine" and all—likewise if you please the painting of Miss Celia Amelia[4] *Weightman's portrait[5] and that young lady's frequent and agreeable visits—By the bye I inquired into the opinion of that intelligent and interesting young person respecting you—it was a favourable one—She thought you a fine-looking girl and a very good girl into the bargain—Have you received the newspaper which has been despatched containing a notice of her lecture at Keighley?[6] Mr *Morgan[7] came, stayed three days and went by Miss *Weightman's aid we got on pretty well—it was amazing to see with what patience and good temper the innocent creature endured that fat Welchman's prosing—though she confessed afterwards that she was almost done up by his long stories.

We feel very dull without you, I wish those three weeks were to come over again Aunt has been at times precious cross since you went, however she is rather better now I had a bad cold on Sunday and stayed at home most of the day—Anne's cold is better—but I don't consider her strong yet What did your Sister Anne say about my omitting to send a drawing for the Jew-basket?[8] I hope she was too much occupied with the thoughts of going to Earnley[9] to think of it—

I am obliged to cut short my letter—every-body in the house unites in sending their love to you—Miss Celia Amelia—*Weightman also desires to be remembered to you—Write soon again, and believe me yours unutterably—

Charivari[10]

To your hands and *Martha *Taylor's do I resign myself in a spirit worthy of a Martyr that is to say with much the same feeling that I should experience if I were sitting down on the plat[11] to have a tooth drawn you have a peculiar fashion of your own of reporting a saying or a doing and *Martha has a still more peculiar fashion of re-reporting it

MS HM 24421. W & S 91.
Address (integral): Miss Ellen Nussey | Brookroyd | Birstal | nr Leeds
PM: (i) BRADFORD YORKS | MA 17 | 1840 (ii) *Bradford Yorks* | *Py Post*
Annotation in pencil by EN: May 17 40 | M Taylor | W W | chiefly fun

1. EN had stayed at Haworth for 3 weeks, from just before 14 Feb.
2. i.e. to the Taylors' home at the Red House.
3. CB's response to the Valentines, an 11-stanza poem beginning 'A Rowland for your Oliver', is printed in Neufeldt *CBP* 271–2. Ellen Nussey recalled that 'Mr Weightman discovered that none of the party had ever received a valentine—a great discovery! Whereupon he indited verses to each one, and walked ten miles to post them, lest Mr Brontë should discover his dedicatory nonsense, and the quiet liveliness going on under the sedate espionage of Miss Branwell and Mr Brontë himself.' (Note by EN in the copy of *Nussey* used by CKS. See *Shorter* i. 176 n. 1.)
4. EN comments: 'The playful naming of Mr Brontë's first curate. [*sic*] A handsome lively young man fresh from Durham University.' (*Hatfield* 100.) The Revd William Weightman (1814–42), Mr Brontë's second curate, was the son of a brewer in Appleby, Westmorland. He had gained a licentiate in theology in 1839 after 2 years at University College Durham, where he would also have been well grounded in classics: from 1835 to 1839 divinity students had been taught by the Professor of Greek, Henry Jenkyns, since the Chair of Divinity at Durham was vacant. The Subscription Books of the diocese of Ripon show that he was ordained deacon on 27 July 1839 and licensed to the curacy of Haworth on the following day. (WYAS Sheepscar Leeds; see also EN 26.7.1839 n. 5.) The Durham licentiate in theology was equivalent to a BA, and an MA could be conferred 9 terms after the first degree without further examination provided that theology had been studied for at least 3 terms; Mr Weightman would therefore be able to proceed to an MA in June 1842. (See C. E. Whiting, *The University of Durham* 1832–1932, (1932), 60.)
5. Dr Juliet R. V. Barker reproduces a drawing by CB in her article 'A Possible Portrait of William Weightman' (*BST* 19. 4. 175–6) and argues very persuasively that Weightman was the sitter, and that the drawing was made in addition to the portrait in oils or water-colour. Ellen Nussey recalled 'the taking of Mr W's portrait by Charlotte. The sittings became alarming for the length of time required—So the guest had to adopt the black academic gown then in vogue and needed for the picture, as the owner was very proud of its possession—amusing the whole party with his remarks and criticisms of the handsome materials of which it was formed. This period was certainly the chief little era in the Brontë sisters lives of any youthful joyousness and happiness.' (*Hatfield* 100–1.)

6. 'An excellent Classical Scholar, He gave a very good lecture on the Classics at Keighley. "The young ladies at the Parsonage must hear his lecture".' Ellen describes the escort Mr Weightman provided, and the return home at 12 p.m. to a 'disturbed' Miss Branwell with insufficient coffee for the whole party. 'Mr. W. who enjoyed teasing the old lady was very thirsty—The great spirits of the walking party had a trying suppression—except for the twinkling eye fun sustained by some of the party.' (*Hatfield* 100.)
7. The Revd William Morgan (1782–1858), a friend of Patrick Brontë whom he had first met during PB's curacy at Wellington, Shropshire, in 1809. Morgan became perpetual curate at Christ Church, Bradford, in 1815, kept a 'Classical and Mathematical School' in Darby Street for a time in addition to his clerical duties, and edited an evangelical magazine, *The Pastoral Visitor*, to which PB contributed. He had been a 'ten-year man', a mature student (over the age of 24) who had been on the books of Emmanuel College Cambridge from 1813–16 and then of Queens' College Cambridge from 1816–23: a period of ten years in all, which enabled him to obtain a BD after paying fees. He was admitted BD at Queens' College Cambridge in 1823. In 1851 he became Rector of Hulcott, Bucks., and died at 10 South Parade, Bath, in 1858. There are frequent references to him in *LD*; and see Edward Baines' *Directory* (West Riding) (1822), i. 149. CB may have used some of his traits for Dr Boultby in *Shirley*. For *The Pastoral Visitor* see *BST* 19. 6. 271–5.
8. See EN 21. 12. 1839 n. 5 and *Shirley* ch. 7.
9. Ann was to replace Mercy Nussey as their brother Henry's housekeeper at Earnley Rectory. See CB's letter to Henry Nussey 5.3.1839 n. 3.
10. Perhaps derived from 'Charlotte' as 'Eleanor' from 'Ellen'. A 'charivari' was the 'rough music' made with kettles, pans, tea-trays, etc., in public derision of an unpopular person. CB uses the word in *JE* ch. 17 for the uproar of unruly pupils against a governess. When the satirical and radical journal *Punch* was founded in 1841 its full title was *Punch, or, The London Charivari*, in imitation of the French journal *Le Charivari* (1832–1915). In the BPM copy of *Nussey* EN writes, 'Buoyancy of spirit was the gift of the present time.'
11. The grass 'plot' in front of the parsonage.

To Ellen Nussey, [?7 April 1840]

[Haworth]

My dear Mrs Menelaus[1]

I think I'm exceedingly good to write to you so soon—indeed I am quite afraid you will begin to consider me intrusive with my frequent letters—I ought by rights to let an interval of a quarter of a year elapse between each communication and I will in time never fear me, I shall improve in procrastination as I get older. (my hand is trembling like that of an old man so I don't expect you'll be able to read my writing never mind put the letter by in a drawer and I'll read it to you next time I see you)—Little Haworth has been all in a bustle about Church-rates[2] since you were here—we had a most stormy meeting in the School-room[3]—Papa took the chair and Mr *Collins[4] and Mr *Weightman acted as his supporters one on each side—There was violent opposition—which set Mr *Collins' Irish blood in a ferment and if Papa had not kept him quiet partly by persuasion, and partly by compulsion he would have given the Dissenters their kail through the reek.[5] (a Scotch proverb which I'll explain another time—He and Mr *Weightman both bottled up their wrath for that time but it was only to explode with redoubled force at a future period—We had two sermons on Dissent and its consequences preached last Sunday one in the afternoon by Mr *Weightman and one in the evening by Mr *Collins— <Miss Celia Amelia de> all the Dissenters were invited to come and hear and they actually shut up their chapels and came in a body; of course the church was crowded. Miss Celia Amelia[6] delivered a noble, eloquent high-Church, Apostolical succession[7] discourse—in which he banged the Dissenters most fearlessly and unflinchingly—I thought they had got enough for one while, but it was nothing to the dose that was thrust down their throats in the evening—a keener, cleverer, bolder and more heart-stirring harangue I never heard than that which Mr *Collins delivered from Haworth Pulpit last Sunday Evening—he did not rant—he did not cant he did not whine, he did not snivel: he just got up and spoke with the boldness of a man who is impressed with the truth of what he is saying who has no fear of his enemies and no dread of consequences—his Sermon lasted an hour yet I was sorry when it was done I do not say that I agree either with him or Mr *Weightman in all or half their opinions—I consider them bigoted, intolerant and wholly unjustifiable on the grounds of common sense—my conscience will not let me be either a Puseyite[8] or a Hookist[9] nay if I were [a] Dissenter I would have taken the first opportunity of kicking or horse-whipping both the Gentlemen for their stern[10] bitter attack on my religion and its teachers—but in spite of all this I admired the noble integrity which could dictate so fearless an opposition against so ?<loud> 'strong' an antagonist. I have been painting a portrait of Agnes Walton[11] for our friend Miss Celia Amelia—you would laugh to see how his eyes sparkle with delight when he looks at it like a pretty child pleased with a new play-thing. Good bye to you let me have no more of your humbug about <u>Cupid</u> &c. you know as well as I do it is all groundless trash

C Brontë

Mr Weightman has given another [lecture] at the Keighley Mechanic's Institute,[12] and Papa has also given a lecture[13] both are spoken of very highly in the Newspaper[14] and it is mentioned as a matter of wonder that such displays of intellect should emanate from the Village of Haworth "situated amongst the bogs and Mountains and until very lately supposed to be in a state of Semi-barbarism." Such are the words of the newspaper.

MS HM 24422. W & S 92.
Address (integral): Miss Ellen Nussey | Brookroyd | Birstal | nr Leeds
PM: (i) BRADFORD YORKS | AP 8 | 1840 (ii) *Bradford Yorks* | *Py Post*
Date: either 7 or 8 Apr. EN annotates '46 Ap 7—40' in ink, but 'Apl 8 40' in pencil (along with other now illegible words).

1. Helen of Troy, wife of Menelaus—a play on the name 'Ellen'.
2. Rates levied for the maintenance of the church fabric. Nonconformists, who received no benefit, had in many places resisted payment, which for Haworth had risen from 10*d.* in the pound in 1831 to 1*s.* 5*d.* in 1841, according to *LD* 323. Patrick Brontë deprecated compulsory payment, and had suggested that 'the churchwardens [should] make an estimate of the rate, and . . . go round both to churchmen and dissenters and receive what they would be disposed voluntarily to give, and if what might be raised in this way should fall short, a collection should be made in the Church.' (Letter to ?the editor of the *Leeds Mercury*, 1. 10. 1836; *LD* 323.) The meeting referred to in the present letter took place on Thursday 26 Mar. 1840.
3. In the Haworth National School which PB had helped to establish in 1832. The *Bradford Observer* for 2 Apr. 1840 reported a debate of more than 3 hours: 'Nearly the whole of the gentlemen, tradesmen, and many of the ratepayers of the chapelry came together, and a very spirited discussion took place. There were three clergymen belonging to the Church of England and one Dissenting minister.' The outcome was a compromise: 'A motion was passed by a very great majority that no church rate be granted for the chapelry. To extricate the churchwardens, who have bills against them to the amount of 21£, it was agreed that collections be made in the church, and that dissenters help to pay off the debt.' The debate took place at a time of 'peculiar distress' in Haworth, 'owing to the great depression of trade and the want of employment for the poor'. (*Bradford Observer* 2.4.1840 in an article immediately preceding the report of the debate.)
4. The Revd John Collins, MA, b. 1801. Probably the John Collins, son of William Collins 'generosus'—i.e. 'gentleman'—of Antrim, who gained his BA in 1828 and MA in 1832 from Trinity College Dublin. He had assisted the Revd T. Dury at Keighley Parish Church since at least Mar. 1839, was ordained priest by Bishop Longley of Ripon on 4.1.1840, and licensed to a curacy at Keighley the following day, while PB's friend Theodore Dury was still the Rector. Mr Collins remained one of the curates of Mr Dury's successor in July 1840, the Revd W. Busfeild, and occasionally officiated at Haworth—e.g. at baptisms on 23 July and 19 Oct. 1840. For his profligate habits, see EN 12.11.1840, and for his subsequent 'career of vice' and abandonment of his wife, see EN 4.4.1847. His name remains in the Clergy Lists for 1847 and 1848, but with no curacy. See *Alumni Dublinenses*, the Subscription Lists for the Diocese of Ripon, WYAS, Sheepscar, Leeds, Haworth Parish Registers, and Baptismal Register for St Andrew's, Keighley, entry for 17 Mar. 1839.
5. He would have let the Dissenters 'have it', in an abusive tirade. (*ODEP*, 416.) 'Kail' means literally 'cabbage', and 'reek' 'thick smoke' in Scottish dialect. The phrase is used by Scott in *Old Mortality* ch. 14.
6. See previous letter n. 4.
7. The doctrine, unacceptable to Dissenters, that the power of ministering in the Christian church can derive only from a validly consecrated bishop, whose own ordination derives from a continuous succession of bishops going back ultimately to the early church.
8. A follower of Edward Bouverie Pusey (1800–82), a leader of the Oxford Movement, and one of the authors of *Tracts for the Times* (1833 onwards), aimed at the purification of the Anglican church from rationalist and latitudinarian tendencies. His 'Letter to the Bishop of Oxford' in 1839 had shown his loyalty to the English as distinct from the Roman church.
9. A follower of Walter Farquhar Hook (1798–1875) Vicar of Leeds from 1837 to 1859, Dean of Chichester 1859–75. He had been chaplain in ordinary to King William IV in 1827, and to Queen Victoria from 1839. In 1838 he had preached at the Chapel Royal a sermon, 'Hear the Church', affirming the apostolical succession of English bishops.
10. CB wrote 'sterm'.
11. CB has decorated the letter 'W' with a tiny flower-spray. Agnes was born at Crackenthorpe, 3 miles from Mr Weightman's birthplace, Appleby in Westmorland, and baptized on 26 Feb. 1820. After Weightman's death she married a farmer, Jonathan Horn. (Info. from Edward Chitham, *ABP* 18.)
12. CB wrote 'letter at'. The Keighley Mechanics' Institute had been founded in 1825, when it had a membership of 71. Patrick Brontë joined it in the year ending 8 Apr. 1833, and would have been able to borrow books from its library, which included technical and scientific works, as

well as history, biography, etc., and magazines. Lectures were given by members and visiting speakers. See *BST* 11. 60. 344–58 and 14. 75. 35–7.

13. For EN's account of Mr Weightman's previous lecture 'on the Classics' see EN 17.3.1840 n. 6. I have not been able to find out the subject of Mr Brontë's lecture. He also might have lectured on the Classics, or on a topic of general interest such as education or the legal system, on both of which he held strong views, as his letters to newspapers make clear. For his eloquence on topics near to his heart, see his speech on the New Poor Law as 'a nose-hewing, finger-lopping quack, a legal deformity', reported in *The Times* 27.2.1837, 6, cols. 4 and 5; quoted in *LD* 331–2.

14. Not traced.

To Ellen Nussey, [30 April 1840]

[Haworth]

My dear Ellen

I am not ungrateful for the gift nor forgetful of the Giver—I wished before I wrote to finish <u>my bag</u> and send it with the letter of thanks for the very pretty Turkish looking thing you sent me but I can get no cord and tassels at Keighley and as I have no opportunity of going elsewhere I must let it continue to lie by a time longer

I read the letters you sent me with real interest *Anne's[1] character is indeed develloped,[2] I fear she has done mischief, if Miss *?Follett[3] has any heart to break if she was really attached the disappointment she will have to endure is enough to break it in good earnest and finish her business properly. I confess I see as yet no solid ground of objection against the match—As to all your Sister says about her <u>boldness</u> &c. I think ample allowance should be made for censures of that nature passed by a previously prejudiced woman on a Stranger.

I see something else too my <u>dear</u> Ellen in the whole spirit of that letter which makes me thankful you are not like some of your friends Fashion, Wealth, Standing in Society seem to be her sole Standards for measuring the worth of a character. Your *Sister thinks she has given up the world but some of the most absurd notions of that world cling to her like a pestilence

I trust Ellen you will ever eschew these doctrines, still keep "all your truth about you"[4]—*Anne has been originally a clever woman but her judgment has been corrupted—she has utterly lost the power of discriminating character her feelings once perhaps warm have been weakened and perverted and heartless Ambition has done it all—the wish to rise in the world—to be distinguished by those to whose Opinion wealth and fashion have <given> in her eyes given great value—

I do not quite understand the passages relating to a certain Mr *Vincent[5]—and you do not vouchsafe a single word by way of explanation—pray let me know more on the subject without delay—if he is a decent fellow I hope something interesting may come of it—Don't blush he must be one of the right sort however or he shall not have you with my consent. I am afraid you are getting worked off your feet at *Brookroyd—as *Henry says take care of yourself and don't be over-anxious Aunt was vastly pleased with the knitting-needle-case.

C Brontë

MS HM 24423. W & S 94.
Address (integral): Miss Ellen Nussey | Brookroyd | Birstal | nr Leeds
PM: (i) BRADFORD YORKS | MY 1 | 1840 (ii) *Bradford Yorks* | *Py Paid*
Annotation in pencil by EN: May 1 40 | Miss ?F— & Mr V.

1. Ellen's sister Ann, keeping house for Henry Nussey and keeping an eye on his 'bride-elect'. See EN 24.10.1839 n. 3.
2. Thus in MS. Disclosed: a meaning current until 1837 according to *OED*, but used by CB in *Shirley* 203 in 1849.
3. Deleted by EN. W & S may be right in reading 'Halkett', but the initial resembles that in 'Fanchon' in EN 24.10.1839. EN's notes on the address-panel are barely decipherable, but may support the reading 'Follett'.
4. Not traced. Perhaps simply a variant on keeping 'all your wits about you'.
5. The Revd Osman Parke Vincent (?1813–85); like his friend Henry Nussey he was a graduate of Magdalene College Cambridge, where he was admitted in July 1832 but did not matriculate until 1834. He graduated BA in 1839 and proceeded to the MA degree in 1842. On 5 Mar. 1839 Henry Nussey asked Bishop Otter of Chichester to offer the 'excellent curacy' of Sidlesham to Mr Vincent, but it was given to 'Mr Williams of Batley', and Vincent was promised a curacy elsewhere. He moved from one parish to another, mainly in the South of England, for many years before becoming Rector of St Mildred's, Bread Street, London, in 1872. See HN *Diary* 5 and 11.3.1839, fols. 63 and 65^r, *Venn*, and Clergy Lists.

To Ellen Nussey, [15 May 1840]

[Haworth]

My dear Ellen,

I read your last letter with a great deal of interest. Perhaps it is not always well to tell people when we approve of their actions, and yet it is very pleasant to do so; and as if you had done wrongly, I hope I should have had honesty enough to tell you so, so now as you have done rightly, I shall gratify myself by telling you what I think . . .[1]

If I made you my Father Confessor I could reveal weaknesses which you do not dream of—I do not mean to intimate that I attach a high value to empty compliments, but a word of panegyric has often made me feel a sense of confused pleasure which it required my strongest effort[2] to conceal—and on the other hand, a hasty expression which I could construe into neglect or disapprobation, has tortured me till I have lost half a night's rest from its rankling pangs.[3] Do not be over-persuaded to marry a man you can never respect—I do not say love because, I think, if you can respect a person before marriage, moderate love at least will come after;[4] and as to intense passion, I am convinced that is[5] no desirable feeling. In the first place, it seldom or never[6] meets with a requital; and, in the second place, if it did, the feeling would be only temporary; it would last the honeymoon, and then, perhaps, give place to disgust or indifference, worse, perhaps, than disgust. Certainly this would be the case on the man's part; and on the woman's—God help her, if she is left to love passionately and alone.

[Our letters are assuming an odd tone. We write of little else but love and marriage, and, ?verily, I have a sort of presentiment that you will be married before you are many years older. I do not wish you to reciprocate the compliment, because] I am tolerably well convinced that I shall never marry at all. Reason tells me so, and I am not so utterly the slave of feeling but that I can occasionally hear her voice. God bless you.[7]

C. Brontë

MS untraced. W & S 95 (part, with an unrelated postscript).
Address: not in sources.
PM: not in sources.
Date: as in *Life* and *Nussey*.
Text: *Nussey* 73 and Rylands MS *Life* fol. 195. W & S 95 reproduces *Shorter* 70.
Neither indicates an omission after 'what I think' in l. 7. Both differ in punctuation from *Nussey*, which looks as if it follows the MS style more closely, and has an extra sentence at the end. The printed *Life* i. 216–71 omits the passage in square brackets, but this is legible, though deleted, in Rylands MS *Life* fol. 195; it does not occur in any other text. *Hours at Home* xi. 199–200 (July 1870) has minor variants: see e.g. notes 2 and 3 below.

1. A reference to Anne's employment as a governess at Thorp Green Hall near York would be expected at this date if she went there on or about 8 May 1840. Mrs Gaskell begins ch. 9 of the *Life* with the sentence 'The year 1840 found all the Brontës living at home, except Anne', but E. Chitham makes a case for the May date in *ABP* 10–11. The omission of text here might help to account for CB's apparent failure to refer to Anne at all until 2 Apr. 1841: see EJB 2.4.1841. Mrs Gaskell is not a reliable witness; she alleges that Branwell was 'living at home' in 1840, whereas he spent the first 6 months at Broughton-in-Furness and the last 3 at Sowerby Bridge.
2. *Hours at Home* reads 'efforts'.
3. *Hours at Home* reads 'fangs'.
4. CB had nevertheless refused Henry Nussey's proposal because she lacked the 'intense attachment' and 'adoration' for him which she considered essential. See EN 12.3.1839.
5. *Life*, *Shorter*, and W & S read 'convinced that that is'.
6. The reading of Rylands MS *Life*, 'seldom or ever', may reflect CB's MS. cf. Maria Edgeworth, *Castle Rackrent*, 'she seldom or ever wore a thing twice the same way' ((World's Classics edn. 1980) 48), and Emily Brontë's Diary Paper for 31 July 1845, 'seldom or ever troubled with nothing to do'.
7. This sentence is omitted in *Life, Shorter*, and W & S.
8. After the signature *Hours at Home, Nussey, Shorter*, and W & S print a postscript which is actually part of EN 29.5.1840, q.v.

To Revd Henry Nussey, 26 May 1840[1]

Haworth

Dear Sir

In looking over my papers this morning I found a letter from you of the date of last Feby. with the mark upon it unanswered your sister Ellen often accuses me of want of punctuality in answering letters and I think her accusation is here justified.

However I give you credit for as much considerateness as will induce you to excuse a greater fault than this especially as I shall hasten directly to repair it.

The fact is when the letter came Ellen was staying with me, and I was so fully occupied in talking to her, that I had no time to think of writing to others—this is no great compliment, but it is no insult either—you know Ellen's worth—you know how seldom I see her—you partly know my regard for her, and from these premises you may easily draw the inference that her company when once obtained is too valuable to be wasted for a moment—

I hear something of a certain Mr Vincent[2] he is I understand a friend of yours—I hope then he is a good and clever man or else I will take the liberty of saying, he is not deserving of the prize destined for him. This is speaking boldly—but you must excuse it one woman can appreciate the value of another better than a man can do. Men very often only see the outside gloss which dazzles in prosperity—women have opportunities for closer observation and they learn to value those qualities which are useful in adversity

There is much too, in that mild even temper and that placid equanimity which keep<s> the domestic hearth always bright and peaceful—this is better than the ardent nature that changes twenty times in a day—I have studied Ellen and I think she would make a good wife, that is if she had a good husband—if she married a fool or a tyrant[3] there is spirit enough in her composition to withstand the dictates of either Insolence or Weakness, though even then I doubt not her sense would teach her to make the best of a bad bargain.

You will see my letters are all didactic, they contain no news—because I know of none which I think it would interest you to hear repeated. I am still at home—in very good health and spirits and uneasy only because I cannot yet hear of a Situation

I shall always be glad to have a letter from you and I promise when you write again to be less dilatory in answering. I trust your prospects of happiness still continue fair, and from what you say of your future partner,[4] I doubt not she will be one who will help you to get cheerfully through the difficulties of this world and to attain a permanent rest in the next—at least I hope such may be the case   you do right to conduct the matter with due deliberation—for on the step you are about to take depends the happiness of your whole life-time

You must not again ask me to write in a regular literary way to you on some particular topic—I cannot do it at all—do you think I am a Blue-stocking? I feel half-inclined to laugh at you for the idea, but perhaps you would be angry what was the topic to be—Chemistry? or Astronomy? or Mechanics? or Chonchology [*sic*] or Entomology or what other ology? I know nothing at all about any of these—I am not scientific, I am not a Linguist—you think me far more learned than I am—If I told you all my Ignorance I am afraid you would be shocked—however as I wish still to retain a little corner in your good opinion I will hold my tongue

Believe me
Yours respectfully
C Brontë

MS William Self. W & S 96 (part).
Address: not in MS.
PM: not in MS.

1 CB gives the date at the end of the letter, which was probably sent in an envelope with either a printed or adhesive penny stamp. These had been available since 6 May.
2 See EN 30.4.1840 n. 5. W & S 96 omits 'I hear . . . excuse it'.
3 William and Frances Crimsworth discuss this theme in *The Professor* ch. 25.
4 At this date, the Miss ?Follett mentioned in EN 30.4.1840.

To Ellen Nussey, 29 May 1840[1]

[Haworth]

My dear Ellen

In a great hurry I write by return of Post to tell you that I most certainly cannot come next week as I have asked Mary & *Martha *Taylor to come to Haworth. I am very much obliged to you for your Invitation and I hope to be able to accept it some time—I warn you to commit no rash act such as sending the gig improm[p]tu   if you do it will certainly come back empty—don't talk any more of sending for me at all   when I come I will send myself   I cannot write any more—All send their love to you

Give my best love to *Mercy   I shall be glad to see her again   I have no prospect of a Situation any more than of going to the Moon   I have answered advertisements in vain

Good bye   write to me again as soon as you can

C Brontë

MS BPM B.S. 44.5. W & S 95 (part; printed as postscript to EN 15.5.1840).
Address (integral): Miss Ellen Nussey | Brookroyd | Birstal | Leeds
PM: (i) BRADFORD YORKS | MY 30 | 1840 (ii) *Bradford Yorks* | *Py Post*

1 This letter does not appear in full in W & S, but a garbled version of part of it is printed as a postscript to W & S 95, dated 'May 15th, 1840': 'P.S.—Don't talk any more of sending for me—when I come I will *send* myself. All send their love to you. I have no prospect of a situation any more than of going to the moon. Write to me again as soon as you can.' The confusion began with *Nussey* 73.

To Ellen Nussey, [?2 June 1840]

[Haworth]

My dear Ellen

Mary *Taylor is not yet come to Haworth—but she is to come on the condition that I first go and stay a few days there—If all be well, I shall go next Wednesday[1]—I may stay at Gomersal until Friday or Saturday and the early part of the following week I shall pass with you if you will have me—which last sentence indeed is nonsense—for as I shall be glad to see you—so I know you will be glad to see me—This arrangement will not allow much time, but it is the only practicable one which considering all the circumstances I can effect—Do not my dear Ellen urge me to stay more than two or three days because I shall be obliged to refuse you I intend to walk to Keighley[2]—there to take the Coach—as far as Bradford—then to get some one to carry my box—and to walk the rest of the way to *Gomersal—If I manage this I think I shall contrive very well—I shall reach Bradford by about five o'clock—and thus I shall have the cool of the evening for the walk I have communicated the whole arrangement to Mary *Taylor—I desire exceedingly to see both her and you

Good bye
C B[3]

I[f] you have any better plan to suggest I am open to conviction provided your plan is practicable

MS HM 24424. W & S 97.
Address: not in MS.
PM: not in MS.
Annotation in ink by EN: ?D June 2–40

1 2 June (EN's date for the letter) presumably derives from a postmark of either 2 or 3 June on a missing envelope: 'next Wednesday' would be 10 June, since CB was writing on a Tuesday (2nd), or Wednesday.

2 CB planned a walk of about $3\frac{1}{2}$ miles from Haworth to Keighley, and $5\frac{1}{2}$ miles from Bradford to Gomersal.

3 The signature, 'C B', is followed by a diminishing tail of 'C B's:
'CB'
'CB'
'CB'
'CB'

To Ellen Nussey, [end of June, 1840]

[Haworth]

My dear Ellen

I promised to write to you and therefore I must keep my promise. though I have neither much to say, nor much time to say it in.

Mary Taylor's visit[1] has been a very pleasant one to us, and I believe to herself also—She and Mr Weightman have had several games at chess which generally terminated in a species of mock hostility—Mr Weightman is better in health,[2] but don't set your heart on him I'm afraid he is very fickle—not to you in particular but to half a dozen other ladies he has just cut his inamorata[3] at Swansea and sent her back all her letters—his present object of Devotion is Caroline Dury[4] to whom he has just despatched a most passionate copy of verses poor lad, his sanguine temperament bothers him grievously

That Swansea affair seems to me somewhat heartless as far as I can understand it though I have not heard a very clear explanation. he sighs as much as ever. I have not mentioned your name to him yet—nor do I mean to do so until I have a fair opportunity of gathering his real mind. Perhaps I may never mention it at all—but on the contrary carefully avoid all allusion to you. It will just depend upon the further opinion I may form of his character. I am not pleased to find that he was carrying on a regular correspondence with this lady at Swansea all the time he was paying such pointed attention to you. and now the abrupt way in which he has cut her off. and the evident wandering instability of his mind is no favourable symptom at all. I shall not have many opportunities of observing him for a month to come—as for the next fortnight he will be sedulously engaged in preparing for his ordination[5] and the fortnight after he will spend at Appleby and Crackenthorp[6] with Mr & Miss Walton.[7] Don't think about him—I am not afraid you will break your heart—but don't think about him.

Give my love to Mercy and your Mother and beleive me

Yours Sincerely
Ça. ira.[8]

MS BPM B. S. 46. W & S 98.
Address (integral): Miss E Nussey | Brookroyd
PM: not in MS.
Annotation in pencil by EN: W W Mr Weightman
Date: various numbers are pencilled on the manuscript (41, 42 altered to 43) but these probably indicate sequence rather than date. The paper used and the references to Mary Taylor's visit and to Caroline Dury make the conjectural date a likely one. Branwell Brontë must have been at home. See the notes below, and EN 20.11.1840 n. 14.

1. Mary Taylor's visit would have followed CB's planned stay at Gomersall and Birstall from 10 to about 16 or 17 June.

2. Mr Weightman took no baptismal services at Haworth in June, perhaps because of the poor health CB refers to here.
3. Not identified.
4. Caroline Dury (b. 1820) was the daughter of the Rev Theodore Dury, (1788–1850) Rector of Keighley, by his first wife (the daughter of Charles Bourchier) who had died at Hastings in 1820. Mr Dury resigned from his Keighley ministry on 2 July, when the family left for West Mill, Herts. Caroline was still in Keighley when this letter was written, but had moved away by the time CB wrote to EN on 14 July.
5. Mr Weightman was already a deacon: see EN 17.3.1840 n. 4. The Subscription Books of the diocese of Ripon show that he was ordained priest on 18 July 1840. (WYAS, Sheepscar, Leeds.) The ordination service would be preceded by an oral examination for which the study of specific books might be required.
6. Appleby is the pleasant market-town on the river Eden in Westmorland, with a 'richly endowed' free grammar school which William Weightman had attended. The hamlet of Crackenthorpe, Agnes Walton's home, is about 3 miles from Appleby.
7. Mr John Walton and his daughter.
8. 'It will be all right.' 'Ça ira' is the refrain of the famous Revolutionary song first sung in Paris just before the Fête de la Fédération, 14 July 1790. The original refrain, which ended 'Ah! ça ira, ça ira, ça ira! | Malgré les mutins, tout réussira' (We shall succeed in spite of opposition) was altered during the Terror to '. . . ça ira! | Les aristocrates à la Lanterne.' (Hang the aristocrats from the lamp posts.) (See *The Oxford Companion to French Literature* (Oxford, 1984), 98.) CB might have seen extracts from Thomas Carlyle's *The French Revolution* part II, book 1, ch. 6 and 8, where he plays on the phrase.

To Ellen Nussey, [14 July 1840]

[Haworth]

My dear Ellen

will you be so kind as to deliver the enclosed to Martha Taylor—do not go up to Gomersal on purpose with it & do not on any account send—but give it her yourself when you see her at Church—you will think it extraordinary that I should send a letter to Martha under a cover addressed to you—I have a reason for so doing of course but it is not my own reason & therefore I do not think I have any right to communicate it Martha will of course please herself. Do not suppose from this apparent mystery that there is anything of importance in the business—it is I assure you the veriest trifle—but trifles are sometimes magnified into matters of consequence—

I am very glad you continue so heart-whole I rather feared our mutual nonsense might have made a deeper impression on you than was safe Mr Weightman—left Haworth this morning, we do not expect him back again for some weeks—I am fully convinced Ellen that he is a thorough male-flirt his sighs are deeper than ever—and his treading on toes more assiduous—I find he has scattered his impressions far and wide—K[e]ighley has yielded him a fruitful field of conquest, Sarah Sugden[1] is quite smitten so is Caroline Dury[2]—she however has left—and his Reverence has not yet ceased to idolize her memory—I find he is perfectly conscious of his irresistibleness & is as vain as a peacock on the subject—I am not at all surprised at all this—it is perfectly natural—a handsome—clever—prepossessing—good-humoured young man—will never want troops of victims amongst 'young' ladies—So long as you are not among the number it is all right—He has not mentioned you to me & I have not mentioned you to him—I believe we fully understand each other on the subject, I have seen little of him lately and talked precious little to him—when he was lonely and rather melancholy I had a great pleasure in cheering and amusing him—now that he has got his spirits up & found plenty of acquaintances—I don't care & he does not care either

I have no doubt he will get nobly through his examination[3] he is a clever lad

[Unsigned]

MS BPM Bon 165. W & S 101.
Address (integral): Miss Ellen Nussey | Brookroyd | Birstal | Leeds
PM: (i)—DFORD YORK— | JY 15 | 1840 (ii) *Bradford Yor—* | *Py Post*
Annotation includes: W. July 14–40

1. Probably Sarah Sugden (*c.*1814–76), daughter of the magistrate and mill-owner William Sugden (1786–1834) of Eastwood House, Keighley. For William Sugden see Sarah Fermi, 'A "Religious" Family Disgraced: New Information on a Passage Deleted from Mrs Gaskell's *Life of Charlotte Brontë*', *BST* 20. 5. 289–95.
2. See the previous letter, n. 4.
3. When Patrick Brontë offered himself for ordination as a deacon in July 1806 he asked 'when and where his Lordship [the Bishop of London] will hold his Ordination; and (if customary) what books I shall be examined in.' (*LD* 22.) At the *viva voce* examination usually held before the ordination the candidate is examined in the translation of Greek or Latin before the Bishop's chaplain. Mr Weightman was ordained priest by Bishop Longley of Ripon on 18 July. See the Subscription Book of the Diocese of Ripon, WYAS Leeds, and the *Leeds Intelligencer* for 25.7.1840, 7.

To Ellen Nussey, [?14 August 1840]

[Haworth]

My dear Ellen

As you only sent me a note I shall only send you one, and that not out of revenge—but because like you I have but little to say—The freshest news[1] in our house is that we had about a fortnight ago—a visit from some of our South of England relations. John *Branwell *Williams[2] and his Wife and daughter—they have been staying above a month with Uncle Fennell at Crosstone[3]—They reckon to be very grand folks indeed—and talk largely—I thought assumingly I cannot say I much admired them—To my eyes there seemed to be an attempt to play the great Mogul down in Yorkshire—Mr *Williams himself was much less assuming than the womenites[4]—he seemed a frank, sagacious kind of man—very tall and vigorous with a keen active look—the moment he saw me he exclaimed that I was the very image of my Aunt Charlotte.[5] Mrs. *Williams sets up for being a woman of great talents, tact and accomplishment—I thought there was much more noise than work.[6] my cousin Eliza[7] is a young lady intended by nature to be a bouncing good-looking girl Art has trained her to be a languishing affected piece of goods. I would have been friendly with her; but I could get no talk except about the Low-Church Evangelical Clergy the Millennium, Baptist Noel[8]—Botany, and her own Conversion. A Mistaken Education has utterly spoiled 'the lass', her face tells that she <was> 'is' naturally goodnatured—though perhaps indolent—in manner she is something of a sanctified Amelia *Walker[9]—affecting at times a saintly child-like innocence so utterly out of keeping with her round rosy face and tall, bouncing figure—that I could hardly refrain from laughing as I watched her—Write a long letter to me next time and I'll write you ditto Good-bye

[Unsigned]

MS BPM Bon 166. W & S 102 as 13 August.
Address (integral): Miss Ellen Nussey | Brookroyd | Birstal | Leeds
PM: BRADFORD YORKS | AU 14 | 1840

1. This phrasing appears to rule out 8 August as a possible date for Anne Brontë's taking up a post as governess at Thorp Green, Little Ouseburn, near York. She was nevertheless there on 28 August, as her poem, 'Lines written at Thorp Green', shows. See Chitham *ABP* 10–11, 75 and EN 15.5.1840 n. 1.
2. A cousin of Mrs Maria Brontë and Elizabeth Branwell. He was the son of their Aunt Alice Branwell, fourth daughter of Richard and Margaret Branwell, who married 'John Williams, gentleman, Redruth, Cornwall'. (See C. W. Hatfield, 'The Relatives of Maria Branwell,' *BST* 9. 49. 245–52.)
3. See PB 23.9.1829 notes 1 and 4.
4. CB uses this contemptuous term for women in *Shirley*, where the schoolboy Martin Yorke-hates 'all womenites' (176), alleges that it is their nature to be spiteful (178), and would like to outwit them (655). The word does not appear in *OED*.
5. Charlotte Branwell (1791–1848) who married her cousin Joseph Branwell (1789–1857). She was the youngest sister of Mrs Brontë and was married on the same day as she was. (29.12.1812.)
6. A variant of the proverbial 'Great cry and little wool', i.e. 'great Pretences and small Performances'. See *ODEP* 333, and cf. the title-page of 'High Life In Verdopolis': 'Much cry and little wool, as St. Nicholas said when he was shearing the Hog' (Alexander *EEW* ii. pt. 2, 3), and *Villette* 691 and note.
7. Eliza Williams.
8. The Honourable Baptist Wriothesley Noel (1798–1873). A graduate of Trinity College Cambridge, he had been since 1827 the minister of St John's Chapel, Bedford Row, London, and was a very popular evangelical preacher. He was to resign from the Anglican ministry in 1849 and to become a Baptist and the minister of John Street Baptist chapel until 1868. He published controversial pamphlets and devotional works. Henry Nussey had heard him preach a missionary sermon at St Giles' church, Cambridge, 'in a sweet style' on 11 Mar. 1832. (HN *Diary* fol. 21^{v}. St Giles' is near Magdalene, Henry Nussey's college, at the foot of Castle Hill.)
9. See EN 19.6.1834 n. 8.)

To Ellen Nussey, [20 August 1840]

[Haworth]

Dear Mrs. Ellen

I was very well pleased with your capital long letter. A better farce than the whole affair of that letter-opening was never imagined (Ducks and Mr *Weightman included)[1] Bye the bye speaking of Mr *Weightman I told you he was gone to pass his examination at Ripon[2] six weeks ago. He is not come back yet and what has become of him we don't know Branwell has received one letter since he went speaking rapturously of Agnes *Walton describing certain balls at which he had figured and announcing that he had been twice over-head and ears desperately in love—It is my devout belief that his Reverence left Haworth with the fixed intention of never returning—If he does return it will be because he has not been able to get a living—Haworth is not the place for him, he requires novelty[3] a change of faces—difficulties to be overcome He pleases so easily that he soon gets weary of pleasing at all. He ought not to have been a parson. Certainly he ought not.

I told Branwell all you said in your last he said little but laughed—the name you gave him was "*Tastril"[4]

I am glad you have not broken your heart because John *Bradbury[5] is married—and yet it is almost a wonder so profoundly attached as you were to him—and such a handsome, attractive, lively creature as he seemed to be—

Our August Relations[6] as you choose to call them are gone back to London, they never stayed with us they only spent one day at our house—they were visitors of Uncle Fennell's—I fancy Uncle Fennell would be very glad to get rid of them I hope George[7] will be better soon—did Mr Heald[8] accompany him to Scotland—did he stay all night at Brookroyd—? Have you seen anything of Miss *Woolers lately, I wish they 'or somebody else' would get me a Situation I have answered advertisements without number—but my applications have met with no success

I have got another bale of French books[9] from Gomersal, containing upwards of 40 volumes—I have read about half—they are like the rest clever wicked sophistical and immoral—the best of it is, they give one a thorough idea of France and Paris—and are the best substitute for French Conversation I have met with.

I positively have nothing more to say to you for I am in a stupid humour you must excuse this letter not being quite as long as your own

Good bye Mrs Ellen I have written to you soon that you might not look after the post-man in vain Preserve this writing as a curiosity in Caligraphy[10]—I think it exquisite—all brilliant black blots and utterly illegible letters.

Caliban[11]

MS HM 24425. W & S 103.
Address (integral): Miss Ellen Nussey | Brookroyd | Birstall | Leeds
PM: BRADFORD YORKS | AU 21 | 1840
Annotation in ink by ?EN: 52 Aug 20–40

1. C. K. Shorter's note to this letter in *Life* 1900 (194) reads 'Referring to a present of birds which the curate had sent to Miss Nussey'.
2. See EN 14.7.1840 n. 3. Haworth, formerly in the diocese of York, had been included in the new diocese of Ripon in 1836. The Haworth Baptismal Registers show that Mr Weightman had last officiated on 12 July, and he was not to take a baptismal service again until 13 Sept.
3. Possibly deleted in MS.
4. This may be a variant on the fanciful word 'testril' used by Sir Andrew Aguecheek in *Twelfth Night* II. iii instead of 'tester', a sixpence. Probably a private joke or part of a word-game that EN had been playing with the Brontës.
5. Probably a relative of Mrs and Miss Bradbury, friends of the Taylors and Nusseys who lived near enough for the frequent visiting mentioned in EN's 1844 and 1849 diaries.
6. See the previous letter.
7. George Nussey (1814–85), EN's brother, whose periods of mental illness were to become more frequent and to necessitate his eventually becoming a patient at Dr Henry S. Belcombe's Clifton House asylum in York. See EN 13.1.1832 n. 4 and 30.12.1844 n. 1.
8. The Vicar of Birstall. See EN 5.5.1838 n. 3. He was a distant relation of the Nusseys through John Nussey's wife Mary Walker, and Henry Nussey refers to him as his 'dear friend'. (HN *Diary* 27.3.1832, fol. 23^{v}.) His gentle manner would be helpful to George Nussey.
9. Joshua Taylor of Gomersal and his children were good linguists. Mr Yorke in *Shirley* (based on Mr Taylor) spoke French 'with nearly as pure a French accent as Gérard Moore'. (52.) The list of Hunsden's books in *The Professor* (33–4) probably reflects the tastes and radical politics of the Taylors.
10. CB's description of her 'caligraphy' is a fair one: many loops have become blots, and the writing is an angular scrawl.
11. CB's 'stupid humour' and her discontent are no doubt reflected in her self-mocking signature. Shakespeare's Caliban is a 'freckled whelp' who 'never Yields . . . kind answer' and bitterly resents being confined to the 'sty' of a hard rock. (*The Tempest* I ii. 283, 308, 342.)

To Ellen Nussey, [?29 September 1840]

[Haworth]

"The wind bloweth where it listeth. Thou hearest the sound thereof, but canst not tell whence it cometh, nor whither it goeth."[1] That, I believe, is Scripture, though in what chapter or book, or whether it be correctly quoted, I can't justly say. However, it behoves me to write a letter to a young woman of the name of E[llen] N[ussey] with whom I was once acquainted, "in life's morning march, when my spirit was young."[2] This young woman asked me to write to her some time since, though having nothing to say—I e'en put it off, day by day, till at last, fearing that she will "curse me by her gods,"[3] I feel constrained to sit down and tack a few lines together, which she may call a letter or not as she pleases. Now if the young woman expects sense in this production, she will find herself miserably disappointed. I shall dress her a dish of salmagundi,[4]—I shall cook a hash—compound a stew—toss up an omelette soufflée à la Francaise, and send it to her with my respects. The wind, which is very high up in our hills of Judea,[5] though, I suppose, down in the Philistine flats of Batley parish it is nothing to speak of, has produced the same effects on the contents of my knowledge-box that a quaigh of usquebaugh[6] does upon those of most other bipeds. I see everything couleur de rose, and am strongly inclined to dance a jig, if I knew how. I think I must partake of the nature of a pig or an ass—both which animals are strongly affected by a high wind. From what quarter the wind blows I cannot tell, for I never could in my life; but I should very much like to know how the great brewing-tub of Bridlington Bay works,[7] and what sort of yeasty froth rises just now on the waves.

A woman of the name of Mrs. B[rooke],[8] it seems, wants a teacher. I wish she would have me; and I have written to [another woman denominated Peg Wooler,][9] to tell her so. Verily, it is a delightful thing to live here at home, at full liberty to do just what one pleases. But I recollect some fable or other about grasshoppers[10] and ants by a scrubby old knave, yclept AEsop; the grasshoppers sung all the summer and starved all the winter.

A distant relation of mine, one Patrick Boanerges,[11] has set off to seek his fortune, in the wild, wandering, adventurous, romantic, knight-errant-like capacity of clerk on the Leeds and Manchester Railroad.[12] Leeds and Manchester, where are they?[13] Cities in the wilderness—like Tadmor, alias Palmyra—are they not?[14] I know Mrs. Ellen is burning with eagerness to hear something about W[illiam] W[eightman], [whom she adores in her heart, and whose image she cannot efface from her memory.] I think I'll plague her by not telling her a word. To speak heaven's truth, I have precious little to say, inasmuch as I seldom see him, except on a Sunday, when he looks as handsome, cheery and good tempered as usual. I have indeed had the advantage of one long conversation since his return from Westmoreland, when he poured out his whole warm fickle soul in fondness and admiration of Agnes W[alton]. Whether he is in love with her or not I can't say; I can only observe that it sounds very like it. He sent us a prodigious quantity of game while he was away. A brace of wild ducks, a brace of black grouse, a brace of partridges, ditto of snipes, ditto of curlews, and a large salmon. There is one little trait respecting him which lately came to my knowledge, which gives a glimpse of the better side of his character. Last Saturday night he had been sitting an hour in the parlour with Papa; and as he went away, I heard Papa say to him—"what is the matter with you? You seem in very low spirits to-night." "Oh, I don't know. I've been to see a poor young girl, who, I'm afraid, is dying." "Indeed, what is her name?" "Susan Bland,[15] the daughter of John Bland, the superintendent." Now Susan Bland is my oldest and best scholar in the Sunday-school; and when I heard that, I thought I would go as soon as I could to see her. I did go, on Monday afternoon, and found her very ill and weak, and seemingly far on her way to that bourne whence no traveller returns.[16] After sitting with her some time, I happened to ask her mother if she thought a little port wine would do her good. She replied that the doctor had recommended it, and that when Mr. W[eightman] was last there, he had sent them[17] a bottle of wine and a jar of preserves. She added, that he was always good-natured[18] to poor folks, and seemed to have a deal of feeling and kind-heartedness about him. This proves that he is not all selfishness and vanity. No doubt, there are defects in his character, but there are also good qualities. God bless him! I wonder who, with his advantages, would be without his faults. I know many of his faulty actions, many of his weak points; yet, where I am, he shall always find rather a defender than an accuser. To be sure, my opinion will go but a very little way to decide his character; what of that? People should do right as far as their ability extends. You are not to suppose from all this, that Mr. W[eightman] and I are on very amiable terms;[19] we are not at all. We are distant, cold and reserved. We seldom speak; and when we do, it is only to exchange the most trivial and commonplace[20] remarks. If you were to ask Mr. W[eightman's] opinion of my character just now, he would say that at first he thought me a cheerful chatty kind of body, but that on farther[21] acquaintance he found me of a capricious changeful temper never to be reckoned on. He does not know that I have regulated my manner by his, that I was cheerful and chatty so long as he was respectful, and that when he grew almost contemptuously familiar I found it necessary to adopt a degree of reserve which was not natural, and therefore was very painful to me. I find this reserve very convenient, and consequently I intend to keep it up.

[Unsigned]

MS untraced. W & S 104.
Address: not in source.
PM: not in source.
Date: as in *Nussey*, *Shorter*, W & S.
Text: *Nussey* 76–9 with words in square brackets from *Shorter* 76.
Hatfield notes that the MS was formerly in the Law Collection: it has not been located. Mrs Gaskell quotes from the beginning to 'are they not?' and from 'There is one' to 'commonplace remarks' in *Life* i. 218–21. W & S 104 follows *Shorter* 76. Some of the more significant variants between these texts and *Nussey* are given below.

1. cf. John 3: 8.
2. Slightly misquoted from Thomas Campbell, 'The Soldier's Dream', stanza 4: 'I flew to the pleasant fields traversed so oft | In life's morning march, when my bosom was young.' CB had used the same quotation in 'High Life in Verdopolis' (20 Mar. 1834.) See Alexander *EEW* ii. pt. 2, 69.
3. cf. 1 Samuel 17: 43.
4. A dish of chopped meat, anchovies, eggs, and onions; a miscellany.
5. CB compares the hilly area of Haworth with EN's low-lying parish: Birstall and Batley are adjoining townships. Her quotation from Samuel has reminded her of David's Judaean hills compared with the Philistine plain of Shephela.
6. Literally, a wooden drinking cup of whisky. (Scottish dialect.)

7. See EN 24.10.1839 and notes. 'Works' literally means 'ferments'.
8. Possibly the Mrs Thomas Brooke of Northgate House, near Huddersfield referred to in EN 12.3.1839; but see also EN 12.11.1840 n. 3.
9. *Life* and *Nussey* read: 'written to Miss W'.
10. Rylands MS *Life* reads 'some scrubby, old fable about grasshoppers'. Aesop's fable contrasts the grasshoppers with the ants who laboured in summer and therefore had stores laid by for winter.
11. i.e. Branwell Brontë. 'Brontë' is the Greek word for thunder, and in Mark 3: 17 Christ names James and John 'Boanerges, which is, The sons of thunder'. CB's satirical title for her brother hints also at his tendency to bombast: cf. her mockery in 'My Angria and the Angrians', Alexander *EEW* ii. p. 2, 245–53. In June Branwell had been dismissed in disgrace from his post as tutor to Robert Postlethwaite's sons at Broughton-in-Furness. For a discussion of allegations that Branwell fathered an illegitimate child or children at this period, see *Barker*.
12. A new stretch of this still incomplete railroad was to be opened between Hebden Bridge and Normanton on 5 Oct. 1840. From Normanton to Leeds the company shared the tracks of the North Midland Railway. Branwell Brontë was to be a clerk at Sowerby Bridge station, about 6 miles east of Hebden Bridge, until 1 Apr. 1841, when he became 'Clerk in Charge' at Luddenden Foot station, some 2 miles north-west of Sowerby Bridge.
13. CB echoes Byron's *Childe Harold* IV. clxxxii, 'Assyria, Greece, Rome, Carthage, what are they?'
14. *Shorter* and W & S read 'in a wilderness'. Tadmor is the ruined city originally founded by King Solomon 'in the wilderness'. (2 Chronicles 8: 4.) The Romans who captured it in AD 272 carried off its queen Zenobia, whose name CB used for the temperamental wife of Northangerland in her Angrian tales. For CB's fascination with ruined cities see Gérin *CB* 46–9, and notes to *Villette* 560 and *The Professor* 193. In 'The spell' (1834) CB describes desolate surroundings as 'Still as Tadmor in the wilderness, voiceless as Tyre on the forsaken sea.' (Alexander *EEW* ii. p. 2, 155.)
15. Probably the daughter of 'John Bland, Warp Dresser', who lived at 83 Main Street, Haworth, in 1850. See Stephen Wood, Map of Haworth in 1850 based on a collation of the 1851 Census and the 1850 tithe awards, in BPM. No burial of a Susan Bland is recorded in the Haworth registers for 1840–3, and she may be the recipient of a letter from CB of 13.6.1848. (W & S 372.)
16. cf. *Hamlet* III. i. 79–80.
17. *Life* reads 'he had brought them'. (i. 220.)
18. *Shorter* and W & S read 'always good to'. In this Mr Weightman resembles Mr Weston, the clergyman-hero of *AG*. See e.g. ch. 11.
19. Rylands MS *Life* reads 'amicable terms'.
20. *Shorter* and W & S read 'exchange the most commonplace'.
21. *Shorter* and W & S read 'and that on further'.

To Ellen Nussey, [12 November 1840]

[Haworth]

My dear Nell,

You will excuse this scrawled sheet of paper inasmuch as I happen to be out of that article, this being the only available sheet I can find in my desk. I have effaced one of the delectable pourtraitures,[1] . . . but have spared the others[2] . . . being moved to that act of clemency by the recollection that they are not the work of my hand, but of the sacred fingers of his reverence W[illiam] W[eightman]. You will discern that the eye is a little too elevated in the horse's head, otherwise I can assure you it is no such bad attempt. It shows taste and something of an artist's eye. The fellow had no copy for it. He sketched it and one or two other little things when he happened to be here one evening, but you should have seen the vanity with which he afterwards regarded his productions. One of them represented the flying figure of fame inscribing his own name on the clouds.

Mrs B[rooke][3] and I have interchanged letters, she expressed[4] herself pleased with the style of my application, with its candour, &c; (I took care to tell her that if she wanted a showy, elegant, fashionable personage, I was not the man for her,) but she wants music and singing. I can't give her music and singing; so of course the negotiation is null and void; being once up however, I don't mean to sit down till I have got[5] what I want, but there is no sense in talking about unfinished projects, so we'll drop the subject. Consider this last sentence a hint from me to be applied practically. It seems Miss E[liza] Wooler's[6] school is in a consumptive state of health. I have been endeavouring to obtain a reinforcement of pupils for her but I cannot succeed, because Mrs Heap[7] is opening a new school in Bradford.

You remember Mr and Mrs C[ollins]?[8] Mrs C—came here the other day, with a most melancholy tale of her wretched husband's drunken, extravagant, profligate habits. She asked Papa's advice; there was nothing, she said, but ruin before them. They owed debts which they could never pay. She expected Mr C—'s immediate dismissal[9] from his curacy; she knew from bitter experience, that his vices were utterly hopeless. He treated her and her child savagely; with much more to the same effect. Papa advised her to leave him for ever, and go home, if she had a home to go to. She said this was what she had long resolved to do; and she would leave him directly, as soon as Mr B.[10] dismissed him. She expressed great disgust and contempt towards him, and did not affect to have the shadow of regard in any way. I do not wonder at this, but I do wonder she should ever marry a man towards whom her feelings must always have been pretty much the same as they are now. I am morally certain no decent woman could experience anything but aversion towards such a man [as Mr C—.] Before I knew, or suspected his character, and when I rather wondered at his versatile talents, I felt it in an uncontrollable degree. I hated to talk to him,—hated to look at him; though, as I was not certain that there was substantial reason for such a dislike, and thought it absurd to trust to mere instinct, I both concealed and repressed the feeling as much as I could; and, on all occasions, treated him with as much civility as I was mistress of. I was struck with Mary's[11] expression of a similar feeling at first sight; she said when we left him, "That is a hideous man, Charlotte!" I thought "He is indeed." In what precise way he has committed himself in Ireland I know not, but Mrs. C. says he dare not follow her there.

This is a very disagreeable letter on account of the subject, and you must necessarily owe me a grudge for writing such a one; but never mind, I'll send you a better one another time, (if all be well).[12]

C. Brontë.

MS untraced. W & S 105.
Address (as given in *Nussey*): Miss E—N— | Brookroyd | Birstall | Leeds
PM: (as described in *Nussey*): 'Penny adhesive stamp, *Bradford* postal mark, Nov 13, 1840. Without envelope of course.'
Text: *Nussey* 79–80 with additions in square brackets from *Shorter* 77 in lines 7, 15, 39. Mrs Gaskell quotes from 'You remember' to ' "He is indeed" ' in *Life* i. 222–3. *Hours at Home* xi. 200 (July 1870) prints 'Mrs B. and . . . subject'. W & S 105 follows *Shorter* 77. Some of the variants between these texts and *Nussey* are given below.

1. *Nussey* adds in parenthesis '(Old English)'.
2. All texts add 'lead pencil sketches of horse's head[,] and man's head'. For these, see F. C. Galloway, *A Descriptive Catalogue of Objects in the Museum of the Brontë Society at Haworth* (Bradford, 1896), 21 and Introduction, p. 46.
3. See EN 12.3.1839 and 29.9.1840 n. 8. Mrs Richard Thornton of Cottingley Hall, Bingley, also refused an application from CB because she could not teach music. (Harry Speight, *Chronicles and Stories of Old Bingley* (Bingley, 1898), 352. I am grateful to Sarah Fermi for this reference.
4. *Hours at Home* reads 'expresses'.
5. *Hours at Home* reads 'till I get'.
6. *Shorter* 77 and W & S read 'Miss Wooler's' but Shorter's text in his footnote to *Life* 1900, 199 reads 'Miss Eliza Wooler's'. Margaret Wooler's sister had taken over the school at Heald's House, Dewsbury Moor, from Christmas 1838. See EN 24.8.1838 n. 2.
7. Mrs Hannah Heap (?1802–77), widow of the Revd Henry Heap (?1789–1839), the late Vicar of Bradford. Mrs Heap and her unmarried daughter H. M. E. Heap took pupils at 1 Manor Street, West End, Bradford, according to the 1851 Census. Mrs Heap died in Thornton Vicarage, where her son the Revd Richard Henry Heap was the incumbent. (*Bradford Observer* 7.9.1877, 4.)
8. For the Revd John Collins, almost certainly referred to here, see EN 7.4.1840 n. 4 and 4.4.1847 n. 6. W & S suggest that Collins was a prototype of Arthur Huntingdon in the *Tenant*. (W & S 285 footnote.)
9. *Life*, *Shorter*, and W & S read 'instant dismissal'.
10. The Revd William Busfeild, MA (1802–78), Rector of Keighley from 2 July 1840 in succession to the Revd Theodore Dury.
11. Mary Taylor's.
12. *Shorter* and W & S read 'all is well'.

To Ellen Nussey, [20 November 1840]

[Haworth]

My dearest Nell

That last letter of thine treated of matters so high and important I cannot delay answering it for a day—Now Nell I am about to write thee a discourse and a piece of advice which thou must take as if it came from thy Grandmother—but in the first place—before I begin with thee, I have a word to whisper in the ear of Mr *Vincent[1] and I wish it could reach him

In the name of St Chrysostom,[2] St Simeon[3] and St Jude,[4] why does not that amiable young gentleman come forward like a man and say all that he has to say to yourself personally—instead of trifling with kinsmen and kinswomen?—Mr *Vincent I say—walk or ride over to *Brookroyd some fine morning—where you will find Miss Ellen sitting in the drawing room making a little white frock for the <missio> Jew's basket[5]—and say "Miss Ellen I want to speak to you." Miss Ellen will of course civilly answer "I'm at your service Mr *Vincent" and then when the room is cleared of all but yourself and herself just take a chair near her, insist upon her laying down that silly Jew-basket work, and listening to you. then begin in a clear distinct, deferential, but determined voice—"Miss Ellen I have a question to put to you, a very important question—will you take me as your husband, for better for worse—? I am not a rich man, but I have sufficient to support us—I am not a great man but I love you honestly and truly—Miss Ellen if you knew the world better, you would see that this is an offer not to be despised—a kind attatched heart, and a moderate competency—" do this Mr *Vincent and you may succeed—go on writing sentimental and love-sick letters to *Henry and I would not give sixpence for your suit.

So much for Mr *Vincent—now Nell your turn comes to swallow the black bolus[6]—called a friend's advice—Here I am under difficulties because I don't know Mr *V— if I did—I would give you my opinion roundly in two words. Is the man a fool? is he a knave a humbug, a hypocrite a ninny a noodle? If he is any or all of these things of course there is no sense in trifling with him—cut him short at once—blast his hopes with lightning rapidity and keenness.

Is he something better than this? has he at least common sense—a good disposition a manageable temper? then Nell consider the matter You feel a disgust towards him now. an utter repugnance—very likely—but be so good as to remember you don't know him—you have only had three or four days' acquaintance with him—longer and closer intimacy might reconcile you to a wonderful extent. and now I'll tell you a word of truth: at which you may be offended or not as you like—From what I know of your character—and I think I know it pretty well—I should say you will never love before marriage—After that ceremony is over, and after you have had some months to settle down, and to get accustomed to the creature you have taken for your worse half—you will probably make a most affectionate and happy wife—even if the individual should not prove all you could wish—you will be indulgent towards his little follies and foibles—and will not feel much annoyance at them. this will especially be the case if he should have sense sufficient to allow you to guide him in important matters.

Such being the case Nell—I hope you will not have the romantic folly to wait for the awakening of what the French call "Une grande passion"[7]—My good girl "une grande passion" is "une grande folie". I have told you so before—and I tell it you again Mediocrity in all things is wisdom[8]—mediocrity in the sensations is superlative wisdom. When you are as old as I am Nell—(I am sixty at least being your Grandmother) you will find that the majority of those worldly precepts—whose seeming coldness—shocks and repels us in youth—are founded in wisdom. Did you not once say to me in all childlike simplicity "I thought Charlotte—no young ladies should fall in love, till the offer was actually made" I forget what answer I made at the time—but I now reply after due consideration—"Right as a glove[9]—the maxim is just—and I hope you will always attend to it—I will even extend and confirm it—no young lady should fall in love till the offer has been made, accepted—<performed> the marriage ceremony performed and the first half year of wedded life has passed away—a woman may then begin to love, but with great precaution—very coolly—very moderately—very rationally—If she ever loves so much that a harsh word or a cold look from her husband cuts her to the heart—she is a fool—if she ever loves so much that her husband's will is her law—and <till> ˋthat′ she has got into a habit of watching his looks in order that she may anticipate his wishes she will soon be a neglected fool.—Did I not once tell you of an instance of a Relative of mine[10] who cared for a young lady[11] till he began to suspect that she cared more for him and then instantly conceived a sort of contempt for her—? You know to what I allude—never as you value your ears mention the circumstance—but I have two studies—you are my study for the success the credit, and the respectability of a quiet, tranquil character—Mary is my study—for the contempt, the remorse—the misconstruction which follow the development[12] of feelings in themselves noble, warm—generous—devoted and profound—but which being too freely revealed—too frankly bestowed—are not estimated at their real value. God bless her—I never hope to see in this world a character more truly noble—she would die willingly for one she loved—her intellect and her attainments are of the very highest standard—**?yet during her last visit here[13]—she so conducted herself on ?one or two occasions that Mr Weightman thought her ?mad—do not for a moment suspect that she acted in a manner really wrong—her conduct was merely wrought to a pitch of ˋgreat′ intensity ˋand ?irregularity′ seldom equalled—but it produced a most unfortunate impression. I did not value her the less for it, because I understood it, **[14] yet I doubt whether Mary will ever marry.[15]

I think I may as well conclude the letter for after all I can give you no advice worth receiving—all I have to say may be comprised in a very brief sentence. On one hand don't accept if you are certain you cannot tolerate the man—on the other hand don't refuse because you cannot adore him. As to little *Walter *Mitchell[16]—I think he will not die for love of anybody—you might safely coquette with him a trifle if you were so disposed—without fear of having a broken heart on your Conscience—**I am not quite in earnest in this ?recommendation—nor am I in some other parts of this letter but [?3 i.w.]

The enclosed note is for Mercy in reply to a few lines from her—I have just received a note from Henry—his account makes the matter rather more uncertain than Anne's he talks of a Father being in the case, and of the possibility of his raising objections to your own want of fortune. I am sure Ellen you will have prudence enough to communicate this business to as few as possible in its present stage. Impress upon Mercy's mind the necessity of her being equally discreet When you have once decided whether to refuse or accept—it will not so much signify.**[17] His reverence *Henry expresses himself very strongly on the subject of young ladies saying "No" when they mean "Yes"—He assures me he means nothing personal.[18] I hope not. Assuredly I quite agree with him, in his disapprobation of such a senseless course—It is folly indeed for the tongue 'to' stammer a negative—when the heart is proclaiming an affirmative. Or rather it is an act of heroic self-denial of which I for one confess myself wholly incapable—I would not tell such a lie to gain a thousand pounds—Write to me again soon and let me know how all goes on—What made you say I admired Hippocrates?[19] It is a confounded "fib" I tried to find something admirable in him and failed

[Unsigned]

MS HM 24426. W & S 106.
Address (integral): Miss Ellen Nussey | Brookroyd | Birstal | near Leeds
PM: (i) BRADFORD YORKS | NO 21 | 1840 (ii) *Bradford Yor[ks]* | *PY Post*
Annotation by ?EN: Nov 20 –40. The misleading underlining and interpretations of the first deleted passage are by a modern hand.

1. See EN 30.4.1840 n. 5. Four undated lines of verse signed 'O. P. V.' survive among the Nussey papers (Hellewell and Sutton archives, WYAS Sheepscar, Leeds): 'Ellen fair I love Thee! | The Lord Almighty speed Thee. | Ellen dear I leave Thee! | ?And God be with Thee.'
2. St John Chrysostom, the golden-mouthed (*c*.345–407), one of the great fathers of the church, whose festival (in the calendar of the Greek church) is on 13 Nov.; perhaps invoked for his eloquence and wisdom. His prayer, ('Almighty God, who hast given us grace at this time . . . Fulfil now, O Lord, the desires and petitions of thy servants, as may be most expedient for them') is used at Morning and Evening Prayer in the Church of England.
3. The prayer of St Simeon is the *Nunc Dimittis*, Luke 2: 29, used at Evening Prayer: 'Lord, now lettest thou thy servant depart in peace: according to thy word.'
4. The 1st-cent. apostle Judas (not Iscariot), perhaps invoked because he is the patron saint of desperate causes. His festival is on 28 Oct.
5. See EN 21.12.1839 n. 5 and 17.3.1840 n. 8. CB was probably one of the 'feebler souls' who 'would rather see the prince of darkness himself at their door any morning, than that phantom-basket'. (*Shirley* 126.)
6. A bitter pill. A bolus is a large, round, soft pill.
7. cf. EN 15.5.1840, n. 4.
8. A variant on the idea of the 'golden mean' or '*optimus modus*'.
9. cf. Scott's Jonathan Oldbuck: ' "I fancy that phrase comes from the custom of pledging a glove as the signal of irrefragable faith." ' (*The Antiquary* (1829 edn.), ii. ch. 30, 114.)
10. Branwell Brontë.
11. Mary Taylor.
12. Disclosure. cf. EN 30.4.1840 n. 2.
13. Mary Taylor had visited the parsonage in late June 1840 when both Branwell and Mr Weightman were in Haworth. At the time CB believed that Mary had enjoyed her visit: see EN end of June 1840.

14. The words from '?yet during her last visit' to 'I understood it' are heavily deleted in dark ink, presumably by EN, and the reading given is conjectural. Some words were deciphered by J. Stevens. See *Stevens* 17.
15. Mary remained unmarried.
16. Possibly a manufacturer in a small way, Walter Mitchell was the tenant of a 'house shop warehouse and yard' in Birstall rented from Ann Nussey. The high rateable value of his property (£7. 6*s*. 8*d*.) was almost twice as much as that of Ann's other tenants. See the Valuation Book for Gomersal and Birstal for 1840. (Copy in WYAS Kirklees (Huddersfield).)
17. The passage from 'I am not quite' to 'so much signify' is heavily deleted in dark ink by ?EN. It was deciphered in part, with some slight inaccuracies, by R. B. Haselden in 'Scientific Aids for the Study of Manuscripts', *Bibliographical Society Transactions*, Supplement No. 10 (1935), 96 and fig. XII.
18. i.e. Henry is not referring to Charlotte's refusal of his proposal. See HN 5.3.1839.
19. Presumably a local doctor (from Hippocrates, the Greek physician born 460 BC).

Draft: to Hartley Coleridge,[1] *[December 1840]*

[Haworth]

Authors are generally very tenacious of their productions but I am not so attatched to this production but that I can give it up without much distress

You say the affair is begun on the scale of a three volume novel I assure you Sir you calculate very moderately—for I had materials in my head I daresay for half a dozen—No doubt if I had gone on I should have made quite a <Sir Charles Grandison>[2] 'Richardsonian'[3] Concern of it Mr West[4] should have been my Sir Charles Grandison—Percy[5] my Mr B—[6] and the ladies <you> should have represented—Pamela, Clarissa[7] Harriet Byron[8] &c. Of course it is with considerable regret I relinquish any scheme so charming as the one I have sketched—it is very edifying and profitable to create a little world out of your own brain—and people it with inhabitants who are <like> so many Melchisedecs[9] & have no father nor mother but your own imagination—by daily conversation with these individuals—by interesting yourself in their family affairs and enquiring into their histories you acquire a tone of mind admirably calculated to ennable you to cut a solid & respectable figure in practical life

The ideal and the actual are no longer distinct notions in your mind but amalgamate in an interesting medley from whence result looks, thoughts and manners bordering on the idiotic

I am sorry I did not exist <si> fifty or sixty years ago when the lady's magazine[10] was flourishing like a green-bay tree[11]—in that case <I should n> I make no doubt my aspirations after literary fame would have met with due encouragement—and I should have had the pleasure of introducing Messrs Percy & West into the very best society—and recording all their sayings and doings in double-columned-close-printed pages side by side with Count

Albert or the haunted castle[12]—Evelina or the Recluse of the lake[13]—Sigismund or the Nunnery[14] & many other equally effective and brilliant productions—You see Sir I have read the lady's Magazine and know something of its contents—though I will not be quite certain of the correctness of the titles I have quoted—I recollect when I was a child getting hold of some antiquated odd volumes and reading them by stealth with the most exquisite pleasure

You give a correct description of the patient Grizzles[15] of those days—my Aunt[16] was one of them and to this day she thinks the tales of the Lady's Magazine infinitely superior to any trash of Modern literature. So do I for I read them in childhood and childhood has a very strong [?faculty][17] of admiration but a very weak one of Criticism

The idea of applying to a 'regular' Novel-publisher and seeing Mr West and Mr Percy at full-length in three vols is very tempting—but I think on the whole 'from what you say' I had better lock up this precious manuscript—wait patiently till I meet with some Maecenas[18] who shall discern and encourage my rising talent—& Meantime bind myself apprentice to a chemist & druggist if I am a young gentleman or to Mantua maker & milliner if I am a young lady

You say something about my politics—intimating that <I> you suppose me to be a high Tory—belonging to the same party which claims for its head <the> his Serene highness[19] the prince of the powers of the air

I would have proved that to perfection if I had gone on with the work—I would have made old Thornton[20] a just representative of all the senseless frigid predjudices of the <high T> Conservatism—I think I would have introduced a Puseyite[21] too and polished off the high Church—with the best of Warren's jet blacking[22]

I am pleased that you cannot quite decide whether I am 'of the soft or the hard sex' an attorney's clerk or a novel-reading dressmaker I will not help you at all in the discovery and as to my handwriting <you> or the ladylike tricks in my style and imagery you must not draw any conclusion from that—Several young gentlemen curl their hair and wear corsets—and several young ladies are excellent whips and by no means despicable jockies—besides I may employ an amanuensis

Seriously Sir I am very much obliged to you for your kind and candid letter and on the whole I wonder <to> you took the trouble to read and notice the demi-semi novelette of an anonymous Scribe who had not even the manners to tell you whether he was a man or a woman or whether his C T[23] meant Charles Tims or Charlotte Tomkins

MS Pierpont Morgan MA 2696. *BST* 10. 50. 16–18. *Life* i. p. ix (part) and W & S 100 (part) as to Wordsworth.

Text: written on the verso of the wrapper in which Hartley Coleridge had returned CB's manuscript, referred to in the draft. The wrapper had been addressed to 'C.T. | Parsonage | Haworth | near Bradford.' It is postmarked 'Ambleside' and has 6 of the first twopenny blue stamps issued in 1840. Mrs Gaskell, followed by Shorter and W & S, assumed that CB, like her brother, had written to Wordsworth (*Life* i. 211), but a letter from Hartley Coleridge would also have been postmarked 'Ambleside', and CB later told M. Heger that she had sent manuscripts to him. (Heger 24.7.1844.) CB's fair copy of this draft letter, dated 10.12.1840, is clearly addressed to 'Hartley Coleridge Esqr.' (See p. 241)

1. Hartley Coleridge (1796–1849), eldest son of S. T. Coleridge; BA Merton College Oxford. Promising as a youth, he had been dismissed from his fellowship at Oriel College for intemperance in 1819, and had attempted literary work and teaching, at first with little success. His poem 'Leonard Mayburne and Susan Hendrie' in *Blackwood's Edinburgh Magazine* Sept. 1827, 362–73 and his collected poems published in 1833 had been admired, and in 1840 he was editing the works of Massinger and Ford. For an account of his character and of Branwell Brontë's meeting with him on 1 May 1840, see Gérin, *BB* 168–76. Coleridge had drafted, and possibly later sent, an encouraging letter to Branwell on his translations of Horace's Odes, praising him as 'the only young Poet, in whom I could find merit enough to commend without flattery'. (MS draft Texas; transcribed in *TLS* 14.5.1970, 544.) Branwell's contact had no doubt encouraged CB to send Coleridge the opening ch. or chs. of a novel for his opinion.
2. The eponymous hero of Samuel Richardson's novel, 1753–4. In *The Professor* ch. 24 CB compares Hunsden's courteous attention to Frances Henri with that of Grandison to Harriet Byron. (242.)
3. All the novels of Samuel Richardson (1689–1761) are long, and the 7-volume *Sir Charles Grandison* has also an immense cast of characters.
4. The handsome young Arthur Ripley West of CB's incomplete novel *Ashworth* and the related fragments in the Pierpont Morgan Library. See the edn. by Melodie Monahan in *Studies in Philology, Texts and Studies* (Chapel Hill, NC, 1983), where it is suggested that the material sent to Coleridge was an early draft of *Ashworth*.
5. Alexander Percy, a dissolute older character in CB's juvenilia, later renamed 'Ashworth' and temporarily reformed through love of his wife.
6. The dissolute would-be seducer of Pamela in Richardson's novel (1740) who, once married to her, also becomes a reformed character.
7. The tragic heroine of Richardson's *Clarissa, or The History of a Young Lady* (1747–9).
8. Harriet Byron is beloved and eventually married by Sir Charles Grandison.
9. Melchisedec was the priest-king to whom Abraham gave tribute, for he was 'without father, without mother, without descent, having neither the beginning of days, nor end of life; but made like unto the Son of God'. See Genesis 14: 18 and Hebrews 7: 3.
10. *The Lady's Magazine: Or Entertaining Companion for the Fair Sex* which began publication in 1770. cf. *Shirley* ch. 22 where some 'venerable Lady's Magazines' are read by Caroline Helstone. (440 and n.)
11. cf. Psalms 37: 35, 'I have seen the wicked . . . spreading himself like a green bay tree.'
12. Not traced; but cf. *The Mysterious Count; or Montville Castle* (2 vols.; 1803). See Robert Watt, *Bibliotheca Britannica* (4 vols.; Edinburgh, 1824), iii. under 'Count'.
13. *Evelina* was Fanny Burney's famous novel, published in 1778, but this title may be a garbled version of Charlotte Smith's *Ethelinde, or the Recluse of the Lake* (1789), which had been excerpted in a number of Miscellanies. cf. CB's reference to 'Ethelinda' in her fair copy letter of 10.12.1840, and for *Ethelinde* see R. D. Mayo, *The English Novel in the Magazines, 1740–1815* (1962), 248–53 and 448–9.
14. Not traced; but for the form of the title compare Mrs. Radcliffe's *The Italian, or the Confessional of the Black Penitents* (1797). All 3 titles recall Radcliffean Gothic, a fashion which persisted in ladies' periodicals long after its heyday in the 1790s. *The Ladies' Museum* for 1831 includes e.g. 'Secrets of the Confessional: A Tale', 'The Fatal Fortnight', and 'A Tale of the Sixteenth Century'.
15. Patient Griseldas. In Boccaccio's *Decameron*, Chaucer's *Clerk's Tale*, Dekker's *Patient Grissil*, and elsewhere the heroine suffers patiently a series of humiliations and cruelties at the hands of her husband. cf. *The Professor* 256 and n.
16. Elizabeth Branwell, who had looked after the Brontë children since the death of their mother

in 1821. To her, or to her sister Mrs Maria Brontë, the *Lady's Magazines* had belonged. See the fair copy letter to Coleridge of 10.12.1840 and n. 16.

17. This word is supplied by C. W. Hatfield in his transcription, *BST* 10. 50. 17; it may be guesswork, since there is now a hole in the paper at this point.

18. A generous patron. C. Cilnius Maecenas (d. 8 BC) was a distinguished and at one time powerful minister of the Emperor Augustus; he was the benefactor of Horace and Virgil, and it may not be a coincidence that Hartley Coleridge discusses Branwell's translation of Horace's lines on Maecenas in his first Ode. See Coleridge's draft letter, *TLS* 14.5.1970, 544.

19. The devil: presumably an allusion to Robert Peel, whom Queen Victoria had once called a 'nasty wretch' leading a party of 'infernal scoundrels'. According to Mary Taylor, CB said that Peel 'was not to be trusted; he did not act from principle like the rest, but from expediency'. (*Life* i. 110.)

20. Sir Abraham Thornton, alias Mr De Capell, a rich retired merchant in CB's *Ashworth* and the Morgan fragments. Probably a private joke, since Thornton is based in part on the radical Joshua Taylor. See *Ashworth* 62–9.

21. A High Church follower of Edward Bouverie Pusey (1800–82). See EN 7.4.1840 and n. 8.

22. Shoe blacking made by the firm of Robert Warren, 30, Strand, London.

23. Either 'Captain Tree' or 'Charles Townshend', pseudonyms used by CB in her juvenilia. Captain Tree is the 'admirable novelist' of her early work, Townshend the cynical narrator of her stories in the late 1830s. See Alexander *EEW* i. 113 and *EW* 173–5.

To Hartley Coleridge,[1] *10 December 1840*

[Haworth]

Sir

I was almost as much pleased to get your letter as if it had been one from Professor Wilson[2] containing a passport of admission to Blackwood—You do not certainly flatter me very much nor suggest very brilliant hopes to my imagination—but on the whole I can perceive that you write like an honest man and a gentleman—and I am very much obliged to you both for the candour and civility of your reply. It seems then Messrs Percy and West[3] are not gentlemen likely to make an impression upon the heart of any Editor in Christendom? well I commit them to oblivion with several tears and much affliction but I hope I can get over it.

Your calculation that the affair might have extended to three Vols is very moderate—I felt myself actuated by the pith and perseverance of a Richardson and could have held the distaff and spun day and night till I had lengthened the thread to thrice that extent—but you, like a most pitiless Atropos,[4] have cut it short in its very commencement—I do not think you would have hesitated to do the same to the immortal Sir Charles Grandison[5] if Samuel Richardson Esqr. had sent you the first letters of Miss Harriet Byron—and Miss Lucy Selby[6] for inspection—very good letters they are Sir, Miss Harriet sings her own praises[7] as sweetly as a dying swan—and her friends all join in the chorus, like a Company of wild asses of the desert.[8] It is very edifying and profitable to create a world out of one's own brain and people it with inhabitants who are like so many Melchisedecs[9]—"Without father, without mother, without descent, having neither beginning of days, nor end of life". By conversing daily with such beings and accustoming your eyes to their glaring attire and fantastic features—you acquire a tone of mind admirably calculated to enable you to cut a respectable figure in practical life—If you have ever been accustomed to such society Sir you will be aware how distinctly and vividly their forms and features fix themselves on the retina of that "inward eye" which is said to be "the bliss of solitude"[10] Some of them are so ugly—you can liken them to nothing but the grotesque things carved by a besotted pagan for his temple—and some of them so preternaturally beautiful that their aspect startles you as much as Pygmalion's Statue[11] must have startled him—when life began to animate its chiselled features and kindle up its blind, marble eyes.

I am sorry Sir I did not exist forty or fifty years ago when the Lady's magazine was flourishing like a green bay tree[12]—In that case I make no doubt my aspirations after literary fame would have met with due encouragement—Messrs Percy and West should have stepped forward like heroes upon a stage worthy of their pretensions and I would have contested the palm with the Authors of Derwent Priory[13]—of the Abbey[14] and of Ethelinda.[15]—You see Sir I have read the Lady's Magazine and know something of its contents—though I am not quite certain of the correctness of the titles I have quoted for it is long, very long since I perused the antiquated print in which those tales were given forth—I read them before I knew how to criticize or object—they were old books belonging to my mother or my Aunt; they had crossed the Sea,[16] had suffered ship-wreck and were discoloured with brine—I read them as a treat on holiday afternoons or by stealth when I should have been minding my lessons—I shall never see anything which will interest me so much again—One black day my father burnt them because they contained foolish love-stories. With all my heart I wish I had been born in time to contribute to the Lady's magazine.

The idea of applying to a regular Novel-publisher—and 'seeing' all my characters at full length in three Vols, is very tempting—but I think on the whole I had better lock up this precious manuscript—wait till I get sense to produce something which shall at least <u>aim</u> at an object of some kind and meantime bind myself apprentice to a chemist and druggist if I am a young gentleman or to a Milliner and Dressmaker if I am a young lady.

You say a few words about my politics intimating that you suppose me to be a high Tory <and> belonging to that party which claims for its head his Serene Highness the Prince of the Powers of the Air. I would have proved that to perfection if I had gone on with the tale—I would have made old Thornton a just representative of all the senseless, frigid prejudices of conservatism—I think I would have introduced a Puseyite too and polished-off the High Church with the best of Warren's jet blacking.[17]

I am pleased that you cannot quite decide whether I belong to the soft or the hard sex—and though at first I had no intention of being enigmatical on the subject—yet as I accidentally omitted to give the clue at first, I will venture purposely to withhold it now—as to my handwriting, or the ladylike tricks you mention in my style and imagery—you must not draw any conclusion from those—Several young gentlemen curl their hair and wear corsets—Richardson and Rousseau[18]—often write exactly like old women—and Bulwer[19] and Cooper[20] and Dickens[21] and Warren[22] like boarding-school misses. Seriously Sir, I am very <very> much obliged to you for your kind and candid letter—and on the whole I wonder you took the trouble to read and notice the demi-semi novelette of an anonymous scribe who had not even the manners to tell you whether he was a man or woman or whether his common-place "C T"[23] meant Charles Tims or Charlotte Tomkins.[24]

You ask how I came to hear of you[25]—or of your place of residence[26] or to think of applying to you for advice—These things are all a mystery Sir—It is very pleasant to have something in one's power—and to be able to give a Lord Burleigh shake of the head[27] and to look wise and important even in a letter

I did not suspect you were your Father

MS Texas. *TLS* 14.5.1870, 544.
Address (integral): Hartley Coleridge Esqr | Knabbe | Rydal | nr Ambleside | Westmoreland
PM: (i) BRADFORD YORKS | DE 10 (ii) *Bradford Yorks* | *Py Post*

1. See HC Draft, n. 1.
2. John Wilson (1785–1854), in his earlier years a friend of Wordsworth and S. T. Coleridge, but later a harsh critic of Coleridge's *Biographia Literaria*. As 'Christopher North' he was the principal writer of and personality in the 'Noctes Ambrosianae' in *Blackwood's Edinburgh Magazine* from 1822 to 1835. By 'a gross piece of political jobbery' he had been elected to the Chair of Moral Philosophy at Edinburgh University in 1820. (See *DNB*.)
3. See HC Draft, notes 4 and 5.
4. The eldest of the 3 Fates, who severs the thread of life spun by Lachesis and drawn from the distaff by Clotho.
5. See HC Draft, notes 2 and 3.
6. Harriet Byron's cousin and principal correspondent.
7. See e.g. *Sir Charles Grandison* i. letters 2 and 4.
8. cf. Job 24: 5, where the wicked go forth to their work 'as wild asses in the desert'.
9. See HC Draft, n. 9.
10. From Wordsworth's poem, 'I wandered lonely as a cloud', lines 21 and 22, published in 1807 in the same collection as his lines 'To H[artley] C[oleridge] Six Years Old'.
11. Pygmalion fell in love with his own creation, a beautiful marble statue. At his request Aphrodite turned the statue into a living woman, whom he married. (Ovid *Metamorphoses* x. fab. 9.)
12. See HC Draft, notes 10 and 11.
13. *Derwent Priory: A Novel. In a Series of Letters*. [By A. Kendall.] Published in the *Lady's Magazine* XXVII (Jan. 1796)–XXVIII (Sept. 1797) in 22 parts. Later reprinted as *Derwent Priory, or Memoirs of an Orphan, in a Series of Letters* (2 vols.; 1798).
14. Possibly *Grasville Abbey, A Romance*, by G[eorge] M[oore]. Published in the *Lady's Magazine* XXIV (Mar. 1793)–XXVIII (Mar., Aug. 1797) in 47 parts. It was reprinted in 3 vols. in 1801. The story is typically 'Gothic' in its names—'Madam Maserini', 'Felicia', 'Sabina', etc.—and in its melancholy dark passages and suggested horrors.
15. See HC Draft n. 13. The 'recluse' of the title is Charles Montgomery, brought up in a lonely cottage near Grasmere. The story also concerns a Mrs Douglas who had fallen in love, like Jane Eyre, with a man married to an imbecile wife, and who (unlike Jane) had borne him two sons.

16. Before her marriage to Patrick Brontë, Maria Branwell had sent for her books from Penzance, but then 'received a letter from my sister giving me an account of the vessel in which she had sent my box being stranded on the coast of Devonshire, in consequence of which the box was dashed to pieces with the violence of the sea, and all my little property, with the exception of a very few articles, being swallowed up in the mighty deep'. See *Life* i. 42 and 131.
17. See HC Draft notes 19–22.
18. The works of Jean-Jacques Rousseau (1712–78) were widely available in English translation.
19. Edward George Earle Lytton Bulwer, later Bulwer-Lytton (1803–73), at this date known chiefly as a prolific novelist. Emily Brontë noted in her 'Diary Paper' of 26 June 1837 that Branwell Brontë was reading Bulwer's *Eugene Aram* to CB as she worked (i.e. sewed) in Aunt Branwell's room.
20. The novels of James Fenimore Cooper (1789–1851) were popular in England, but his *England, with Sketches of Society in the Metropolis* (1837) had been violently attacked.
21. By this date Dickens had published *Sketches by Boz* (1836–7), *The Posthumous Papers of the Pickwick Club* (1836–7), *Oliver Twist* (1837–9), and *Nicholas Nickleby* (1838–9).
22. Samuel Warren (1807–77), author and lawyer. CB had perhaps read his *Passages from the Diary of a Late Physician* in *Blackwood's Edinburgh Magazine* from Aug. 1830, pt. 2, to Aug. 1837. His *Ten Thousand a-Year* had been appearing in serial form in *Blackwood's* from Oct. 1839 and would be published in 3 vols. after its completion in Aug. 1841.
23. See HC Draft n. 23.
24. The two names are carefully written in slightly larger handwriting as if they are alternative signatures. The remainder of the letter, written below the address panel, is in effect a postscript.
25. CB might have heard of Hartley Coleridge through Branwell. Coleridge lived in Leeds during the early 1830s in the family of a publisher, F. E. Bingley, for whom he produced a biographical work on *Lives of Illustrious Worthies of Yorkshire* in 1835. F. Leyland asserts that Coleridge was 'not unknown to the circle at The George', at Bradford, and was acquainted with Branwell Brontë and [J. B.] Leyland. (*Leyland* i. 252.) Like Branwell, Charlotte admired Coleridge's poems, some of which had appeared in *Blackwood's Edinburgh Magazine*.
26. CB would know Coleridge's 'place of residence' through Branwell's contact with him earlier in 1840. He was looked after by a farmer and his wife, Mr and Mrs Richardson, and moved with them into 'Nab Cottage' or 'The Knabbe', Rydal, near Ambleside, early in 1840.
27. In Sheridan's *The Critic* (1779), Lord Burleigh sits without speaking, '*shakes his head, and exit*'; Puff expounds his meaning at length. (III. i.)

To Ellen Nussey, [3 January 1841]

[Haworth]

My dear Ellen

I received the news <of Mr> in your last with no surprise and with the feeling that this removal must be a relief to Mr *Taylor[1] himself and even to his family—The bitterness of death was past a year ago when it was first discovered that his illness must terminate fatally—all between has been lingering suspense—this is at an end now and the 'present' certainly however sad is better than the former doubt. What will be the consequence of his death is another question—for my own part I look forward to a dissolution and dispersion[2] of the family perhaps not immediately but in the course of a year, or two—It is true causes may arise to keep them together awhile longer—but they are restless active spirits and will not be restrained always.—Mary alone has more energy and power in her nature than any ten men you can pick out in the united parishes of *Birstal and *Gomersal It is vain to limit a character like hers within ordinary boundaries—she will overstep them—I am morally certain Mary will establish her own landmarks So will the rest of them

You seem to suspect me of being concerned in some underhand dealings in this matter of Mr *Vincent[3]—who I rather fear is an ass—I assure you I have had nothing to do either with the hash[4] that has been cooked at *Earnley[5] or the porridge which has been stirred a[t] *Devizes[6]—what I have said on the subject has been communicated to yourself alone. I am ashamed to say I have never even answered *Henry's letter[7]

I should correct myself there is one person to whom I have given a hint of this business nor did my conscience accuse me of a breach of confidence in so doing I mean Mary *Taylor I tell her my own secrets—(most of them at least—<there are one or two> all human beings are aware of some circumstances which it is wisest to lock up safely in their own special craniums) And therefore I consider that I m[ay] fairly & faithfully trust her **with some of yours—such of them at least as I am certain it would not hurt your feelings or your interests to have communicate[d]**

*Henry said that Mr *Vincent was eccentric, what does he mean? There can be but two excuses for eccentricity, singular talent or a diminutive, wee crack in the brain <of> 'from' which of these causes does Mr *Vincent's oddness result? Examine him well Nell—If he is a decent fellow in the main don't stand on trifles—but otherwise—be as dogged as you know uncommonly well how to be

This letter has both bad grammar and bad spelling in it but you'll excuse faults.

C Brontë—

Ellen Helen Eleonora Helena
Nell Nelly—Mrs *Vincent[8]

Does it sound well Nell? I think it does—I'll never come to see you after you are married

MS BPM Gr. E 3. W & S 107 (part). *BST* 17. 90. 354–5.
Address (integral): Miss Ellen Nussey | Brookroyd | Birstal | nr Leeds
PM: (i) BRADFORD YORKS | JA 4 | 1841 (ii) *Bradford Y[orks] | Py P[ost]*
Annotation in pencil by EN: [4 i.w.] About Mr V. & [i.w.]; in ink: Jan 3—41

1. Joshua Taylor of the Red House, Gomersal, who had died on 28.12.1840, leaving his property to his wife. She and her sons Joshua and John were to be executors of his will made on 2.12.1836, but the sons appointed George Lawton of York, 'Notary Public' as their proxy. (Copy of will dated 15.1.1841, WYAS Kirklees, (Huddersfield).)
2. CB's opinion was proved true: only Joshua (1812–80) stayed with Mrs Taylor, and in 1845 he moved away owing to his mother's 'unhappy disposition'. See EN 20.11.1845, and cf. the portrayal of the unpleasant Mrs Yorke in *Shirley*. John (1813–1901) and Joseph (?1816–57) moved to a cottage behind the family's Hunsworth Mill ('Hollows Mill' in *Shirley*), Martha went to a finishing-school in Brussels. Mary was either at the Brussels school or travelling on the Continent, with brief visits to her brothers, until 1845. In that year she emigrated to New Zealand, joining her youngest brother William Waring Taylor (?1820–1903) who had reached Wellington in Apr. 1842.

3. See EN 30.4.1840 and 20.11.1840.
4. A 'hash' can mean a 'muddle', but here it seems to imply a plot. In her letter to Henry Nussey of 11.1.1841 CB disclaims any 'underhand' dealings.
5. The hamlet near Chichester where Henry Nussey was curate.
6. A market town in Wilts. The reference remains obscure.
7. See EN 20.11.1840.
8. The names are written in a clear upright style probably intended to look like print. The postscript is omitted, along with much else, in W & S 107, based on *Shorter* 79. It was mistakenly printed as part of *Shorter* 78 (EN 20.11.1840).

To Henry Nussey, 11 January 1841

[Haworth]

Dear Sir

It is time I should reply to your last or I shall fail in fulfilling my promise of not being so dilatory as on a former occasion. I think I told you I had heard something of Mr Vincent's affair[1] before, but I thought from the long interval that had elapsed between his visit to Brookroyd and his late declaration that some impediment had occurred to prevent his proceeding further. I own I am glad to hear that this is not the case for I know few things that would please me better than to hear of Ellen's being well married. This little adverb well is however a condition of importance—it implies a great deal—fitness of character, temper, pursuits, and competency of fortune—Your description of Mr Vincent seems to promise all these things, there is but one word in it that appears exceptionable—you say he is eccentric. If his eccentricity is not of a degrading or ridiculous character—if it does not arise from weakness of mind—I think Ellen would hardly be justified in considering it a serious objection; but there is a species of eccentricity which, shewing itself in silly and trifling forms often exposes its possessor to ridicule—this as it must necessarily weaken a wife's respect for her husband may be a great evil I have advised Ellen as strongly as my limited knowledge of the business gives me a right to do—to accept Mr Vincent in case he should make decided proposals—In consequence of this advice she seems to suspect that I have had some hand in helping "to cook a certain hash[2] which has been concocted at Earnley". I use her own words which I cannot interpret[3] for I do not comprehend them—you can clear me of any such underhand and meddling dealings. What I have had to say on the subject has been said entirely to herself, and it amounted simply to this "If Mr Vincent is a good, honourable, and respectable man, take him, even though you should not at present feel any violent affection for him—The folly of what the French call "Une grande passion"[4] is not consistent with your tranquil character—do not therefore wait for such a feeling. If Mr Vincent be sensible and good-tempered I do not doubt that in a little while you would find yourself very happy and comfortable as his wife"

You will see by these words that I am no advocate for the false modesty[5] which you complain of and which induces some young ladies to say "No" when they mean "Yes"—but if I know Ellen, she is not one of this class—she ought not therefore to be too closely urged—let her friends state their opinion and give their advice, and leave it to her own sense of right and reason to do the rest—It seems to us better that she should be married—but if she thinks otherwise perhaps she is the best judge—We know many evils are escaped by eschewing matrimony and since so large a proportion of the young ladies of these days pursue that rainbow-shade with such unremitting eagerness—let us respect an exception who turns aside and pronounces it only a coloured vapour whose tints will fade on a close approach.

I shall be glad to receive the poetry[6] which you offer to send me—you ask me to return the gift in kind—How do you know that I have it in my power to comply with that request? Once indeed I was very poetical,[7] when I was sixteen, seventeen eighteen and nineteen years old—but I am now twenty-four approaching twenty-five—and the intermediate years are those which begin to rob life of some of its superfluous colouring. At this age it is time that the imagination should be pruned and trimmed—that the judgment should be cultivated—and a few at least, of the countless illusions of early youth[8] should be cleared away. I have not written poetry for a long while

You will excuse the dullness, morality and monotony of this epistle—and believe me, with all good wishes for your welfare here and hereafter

[Signature cut off]

Jany 11th 1841

MS BPM B.S. 47. W & S 108.
Address (integral): [Revd] H Nussey | Earnley Rectory | nr Chichester | Sussex
PM: (i) BRADFORD YORKS | 14 JA 14 | 1841 (ii) *Bradford Yorks* |—*Post*
Annotation in pencil by EN, replacing missing signature: Your sincere friend | C Bronte

1. See EN 30.4.1840, EN 20.11.1840, and 3.1.1841. CB had received 'a note from Henry' by 20.11.1840.
2. See EN 3.1.1841 n. 4.
3. 'interperet' in MS.
4. See EN 20.11.1840 n. 7.
5. See EN 20.11.1840 and n. 18.
6. The kind of poetry Henry Nussey wrote is revealed by his *Diary* entry for 23.2.1839, where he records that he has written a poem of about 500 lines on 'the Heavenly Canaan', which he hopes to publish in order to give any profits to the London Society for Promoting Christianity Amongst the Jews. (HN *Diary* fol. 61^{v}.)
7. CB sets her poetic period further back in the past than it was in reality: the years 1833–7 (from 17 to 21 years old) show a prolific verse output, followed by 13 poems in 1838, tailing off to 4 in 1839—a pattern that may be related to Southey's advice in his letter of 12.3.1837. Her most recent production was probably her response to Mr Weightman's valentines, dated ?Feb. 1840. (Neufeldt, *CBP* 271–2.)

8. Southey's letter of 12.3.37 shows that CB then wished to 'be for ever known' as a poetess. By 1850 her judgement of her own talent was harshly realistic: in a letter to Mrs Gaskell of 26.9.1850 she disparages her early poems in comparison with those of her sisters, admitting that 'Mine are chiefly juvenile productions; the restless effervescence of a mind that would not be still.'

To Ellen Nussey, [?3 March 1841]

[Upperwood House,
Rawdon]

My dear Ellen,

I told you some time since, that I meant to get a situation, and when I said so my resolution was quite fixed. I felt that however often I was disappointed, I had no intention of relinquishing my efforts. After being severely baffled two or three times,—after a world of trouble in the way of correspondence and interviews,—I have at length succeeded, and am fairly established in my new place. It is in the family of Mr. W[hite],[1] of U[pperwood House, Rawdon].[2]

The house is not very large, but exceedingly comfortable, and well regulated; the grounds are fine and extensive. In taking this place[3] I have made a large sacrifice in the way of salary, in the hope of securing comfort, by which word I do not mean to express good eating and drinking, or warm fire, or a soft bed, but the society of cheerful faces, and minds and hearts not dug out of a lead-mine, or cut from a marble quarry. My salary is not really more than £16. per annum, though it is nominally £20., but the expense of washing will be deducted therefrom. My pupils are two in number, a girl of eight[4] and a boy of six.[5] As to my employers, you will not expect me to say much respecting[6] their characters when I tell you that I only arrived here yesterday. I have not the faculty of telling an individual's disposition at first sight. Before I can venture to pronounce on a character, I must see it first under various lights, and from various points of view. All I can say therefore is, both Mr and Mrs W[hite] seem to me good sort of people. I have as yet had no cause to complain of want of considerateness[7] or civility. My pupils are wild and unbroken, but apparently well disposed. I wish I may be able to say as much next time I write to you. My earnest wish and endeavour will be to please them. If I can but feel that I am giving satisfaction, and if at the same time I can keep my health, I shall, I hope, be moderately happy. But no one but myself can tell how hard a governess's work is to me—for no one but myself is aware how utterly averse my whole mind and nature are to the employment. Do not think that I fail to blame myself for this, or that I leave any means unemployed to conquer this feeling. Some of my greatest difficulties[8] lie in things that would appear to you comparatively trivial. I find it so hard to repel the rude familiarity of children. I find it so difficult to ask either servants or mistress for anything I want, however much I want it. It is less pain to me to endure the greatest inconvenience than to go [into the kitchen to] request its removal.[9] I am a fool. Heaven knows I cannot help it!

Now can you tell me whether it is considered improper for governesses to ask their friends to come and see them. I do not mean, of course, to stay, but just for a call of an hour or two? If it is not absolute treason, I do fervently request that you will contrive, in some way or other, to let me have a sight of your face. Yet I feel at the same time, that I am making a very foolish and almost impracticable demand; yet R[awdon][10] is only four miles from B[radford!][11]

I dare say you have received a valentine this year from our bonny-faced friend the curate of Haworth.[12] I got a precious specimen a few days before I left home, but I knew better how to treat it than I did those we received a year ago. I am up to the dodges and artifices of his lordship's character, he knows I know him, and you cannot conceive how quiet and respectful he has long been. Mind I am not writing against him, I never will do that. I like him very much. I honour and admire his generous, open disposition, and sweet temper,—but for all the tricks, wiles, and insincerities of love, the gentleman has not his match for twenty miles round. He would fain persuade every woman under thirty whom he sees that he is desperately in love with her. I have a great deal more to say, but I have not a moment's time to write it in. My dear Ellen, do write to me soon, don't forget. Good bye

[Unsigned]

MS untraced. W & S 109.
Address: not in source.
PM: *Nussey* has a note, '(the Rawdon postal mark is undated, the word Rawdon is in the usual semicircular form, with two concentric halves to complete it)'.
Text: *Nussey* 83–5, emended from Rylands MS *Life*, with some names completed from W & S 109. Mrs Gaskell quotes from 'I told you' to 'four miles from B—' in *Life* i. 226–8. W & S 109 derives from *Shorter* 82, with two minor variants. *Shorter* and *Nussey* vary mainly in punctuation.

1. John White (?1790–30.10.1860), a Bradford merchant. He had inherited Upperwood House from his uncle William Leavens, a wealthy woolstapler who died in 1818. In his memorial in Calverley church he is described by his widow as 'amiable upright & truly Christian'. See *BST* 13. 67. 147–8 and William Cudworth, *Round About Bradford* (1876), 443–4.
2. The house was on the far side of Apperley Lane from Woodhouse Grove school in Rawdon, about 5 miles north-east of Bradford. It was demolished in the late 19th cent. to make way for Ashdown, now Brontë House, the preparatory school for Woodhouse Grove since 1934, but its portico is incorporated in a summer-house in the grounds. See F. C. Pritchard, *The Story of Woodhouse Grove School* (Bradford, 1978), 55, 318, and map opp. 323. CB's great-uncle John Fennell was appointed the first governor of the school in 1811. See PB 23.9.1829 n. 4.
3. *Life*, *Shorter*, and W & S read 'the place'.
4. Sarah Louisa, b. 1832; christened 21.11.1832 at Guiseley, and said by J. Malham-Dembleby in *The Confessions of Charlotte Brontë* (Thornbury, Bradford, 1954), 214 to have married Samuel Walter Atkinson of Huddersfield and to be buried in Chapeltown Church, Leeds. C. K. Shorter notes that CB gave her pupil a book, now lost, inscribed 'Sarah Louisa White, from her friend C. Brontë, July 20, 1841'. (Shorter *CB Circle* 95.)

5. Jasper Leavens White (?1834–65; christened 30.1.1835 at Guiseley). He died unmarried according to J. Malham-Dembleby, who also reports that John White's grandson Dr Percy Stanhope White possessed a book, *The Beavers and Elephant*, inscribed by CB 'Jaspar Leavens White from his friend C Brontë July 20 –41'. (*The Confessions of Charlotte Bronte*, 205.)
6. *Life* and *Shorter* read 'about their'.
7. W & S read 'consideration'.
8. A letter from a Mrs Strickland of Halsteads, Hastings, in the *Westminster Gazette* for May 1901 is quoted in W & S i. 225: 'My mother, Mrs Slade of Hastings, now in her seventy-ninth year, distinctly remembers meeting the afterwards distinguished authoress at the house of Mr White, a Bradford merchant . . . something like sixty years ago. At that time Miss Brontë was acting as governess to Mr White's children, and my mother has a vivid recollection of seeing her sitting apart from the rest of the family in a corner of the room, poring, in her short-sighted way, over a book. The impression she made on my mother was that of a shy nervous girl, ill at ease, who desired to escape notice and to avoid taking part in the general conversation.' W & S note that Mrs William Slade, a native of Leeds, 'was at a boarding school at Westfield House, Rawdon, when she met Charlotte Brontë'.
9. *Nussey* reads 'to go request', *Shorter* and W & S 'to request': both are probably corruptions of the *Life* reading given here.
10. *Life* reads 'yet this'.
11. A partly deleted reading in Rylands MS *Life*. The printed *Life* and *Nussey* read 'four miles from B—!', *Life* 1900 completes this incorrectly with 'four miles from Birstall!' and *Shorter* 82, followed by W & S, inventively alters this to 'nine miles from Brookroyd'. Upperwood House was 4 miles from Bradford as the crow flies.
12. William Weightman. See EN 17.3.1840, n. 3. Ellen added in a note recorded in *Hatfield* 100 that the valentine verses were 'on beautiful tinted paper'.

To Ellen Nussey, [?21 March 1841]

[Upperwood House, Rawdon]

My dearest Ellen

You must excuse a very short answer to your last most welcome letter—for my time is entirely occupied—Mrs *White[1] expects a good deal of sewing from me—I cannot sew 'much' during the day on account of the children—who require the closest attention. I am obliged therefore to devote the evenings to this business—You are depressed and unhappy I see whatever your uneasiness is owing to—you give me no further explanation of *?Mercy's[2] atrocity. Take comfort Nell—write to me often very long letters—it will do both of us good—This place is better than *Stonegappe[3] but God knows I have enough to do to keep a good heart on the matter what you said has cheered me a little—I wish I could always act according to your advice—Home-sickness afflicts me sorely—I like Mr *White extremely—respecting Mrs *White I am for the present silent—I am trying hard to like her. The children are not such little *devils *incarnate as the *Sedg[wi]cks[4]—but <at times> they are over-indulged & at times hard to manage Do, do, do come to see me—if it be a breach of etiquette never mind if you can only stop an hour, come,—Talk no more about my forsaking you—my dear Nell I could not afford to do so—I find it is not in my nature to get on in this weary world without sympathy & attachment in some quarter—& seldom indeed do we find it—it is too great a treasure to be ever wantonly thrown away when once secured.

I do not know how to wear your pretty little handcuffs—when you come you shall explain the mystery—

I send you the precious valentine[5]—make much of it—remember the writer's[6] blue eyes, auburn hair & rosy cheeks—you may consider the concern addressed to yourself—for I have no doubt he intended it to suit anybody—

Fare—thee—well Nell. C Brontë

MS BPM B. S. 47.5. W & S 110.
Address (integral): Miss Ellen Nussey | Brookroyd | Birstal | Leeds
PM: (i) RAWDEN (ii) LEEDS | MR—?3 | 1841 | G
Date: the figure on the postmark is concealed by a repair strip. W & S and *Shorter* may have used the date given in *Life*, 'March 21st'; but this may be a 'correction' of Rylands MS *Life*, 'March 41'.

1. Mrs John White, née Jane Robson (?1800–78); said by J. Malham-Dembleby in *The Confessions of Charlotte Brontë* (Thornbury, Bradford, 1954), 206, to have died at Charlton House, Bellingham, Northumb. on 22 May 1878 at the age of 77. Perhaps there was a connection with the Charlton family of Heslieside, Bellingham.
2. EN's sister. Her 'atrocity' remains unexplained.
3. See EJB 8.6.1839 n. 2.
4. So spelled in Burke's *Landed Gentry* (1868), 600 (Greenwoods of Keighley and Swarcliffe). CB also uses the spelling 'Sidgwick'.
5. See EN 17.3.1840, 3.3.1841, and notes.
6. The Revd William Weightman's: see previous letter.

To Ellen Nussey, [?1 April 1841]

[Upperwood House]

My dear Nelly

It is 12 o'clock at night but I must just write you a word before <you> I go to-bed—If you think I'm going to refuse your invitation—or if you sent it me with that idea—you're mistaken—as soon as I had read your shabby little note—I gathered up my spirits directly—walked on the impulse of the moment into Mrs *White's presence—popped the question—and for two minutes received no answer—will she refuse me when I work so hard for her? thought I Ye -es -es, drawled Madam—in a reluctant cold tone—thank you Ma'am said I with extreme cordiality, and was marching from the room—when she recalled me with—"You'd better go, on Saturday afternoon then—when the children have holiday—& if you return in time for them to have all their lessons on Monday morning—I don't see that much will be lost" you <u>are</u> a genuine Turk thought I but again I assented & so the bargain was struck—

Saturday after next then—is the day appointed—not next Saturday mind—I don't quite know whether the offer about the gig is not entirely out of your own head—or if *George[1] has given his consent to it—whether that consent has not been wrung from him by the most persevering & irresistible teasing on the part of a certain young person of my acquaintance—I make no manner of doubt that if he does send the "conveyance" (as Miss *Wooler used to denominate all wheeled vehicles) it will be to his own extreme detriment & inconvenience, but for once in my life I'll not mind this or bother my head about it—I'll come—God knows with a thankful & joyful heart—glad of a day's reprieve from labour—if you don't send the gig I'll walk[2]

Now mind Nell—I am not coming to Birstal with the idea of dissuading Mary *Taylor[3] from going **to New Holland[4] or New Zealand**[5]—I've said everything I mean to say on that subject—& she has a perfect right to decide for herself—I am coming to taste the pleasure—of liberty—a bit of pleasant congenial talk & a sight of two or three faces I like—

God bless you—I want to see you again Huzza for Saturday afternoon after next! I'll snap my fingers at Mrs W & her imps Good <by> night my lass!

C Brontë

Have you lit your pipe with *Mr *Weightman's valentine?

MS HM 24427. W & S 111 as 1 Apr. 1841.
Address: not in MS; the letter consists of a single sheet of paper.
PM: not in MS.
Date: CB's letter to Henry Nussey, supposedly of 9 May, says she had EN's invitation 'a fortnight since,' i.e. 24 Apr., giving a date for this letter of *c.*25 Apr. and for her visit of 8 May. This is not compatible with the *Shorter* and W & S date of 1 Apr. for the letter, a more likely date which could derive from a missing sheet with an address and postmark; it would give a date of 10 Apr., i.e. Easter Saturday, for the visit. See HN 9.5.1841, note on date.

1. George Nussey, EN's brother.
2. It would be 9 miles from Upperwood House to Birstall.
3. See EN 3.1.1841 n. 2.
4. Australia was so called from 1644, when the Dutch had extended their previous explorations of the continent to its northern coast. It was officially named Australia in 1817.
5. Emigration was being encouraged in the 1830s and 1840s by the Colonial Reformers inspired by Edward Gibbon Wakefield and by the New Zealand Company set up in Aug. 1838, one of whose directors was Sir William Molesworth (1810–55), Radical MP for Leeds. See *Stevens* 19–22 for possible Taylor contacts who had emigrated to New Zealand in Sept. 1839 and Jan. 1841. *The Times* carried attractive advertisements for the vessels to New Zealand.

To Emily J. Brontë, [?2 April 1841]

Upperwood House [Rawdon]

Dear E. J.,

I received your last letter with delight as usual. I must write a line to thank you for it and the inclosure, which however is too bad—you ought not to have sent me those packets. I had a letter from Anne yesterday;[1] she says she is well. I hope she speaks absolute truth.[2] I had written to her and Branwell a few days before. I have not heard from Branwell yet. It is to be hoped that his removal to another station[3] will turn out for the best. As you say, it looks like getting on at any rate.

I have got up my courage so far as to ask Mrs White to grant me a day's holiday to go to Birstall to see Ellen Nussey, who has offered to send a gig for me. My request was granted, but so coldly and slowly. However, I stuck to my point in a very exemplary and remarkable manner. I hope to go next Saturday. Matters are progressing very strangely at Gomersall. Mary Taylor and Waring[4] have come to a singular determination, but I almost think under the peculiar circumstances a defensible one, though it sounds outrageously odd at first. They are going to emigrate—to quit the country altogether. Their destination unless they change is Port Nicholson,[5] in the northern island of New Zealand!!! Mary has made up her mind she can not and will not be a governess, a teacher, a milliner, a bonnet-maker nor housemaid. She sees no means of obtaining employment she would like in England, so she is leaving it. I counselled her to go to France[6] likewise and stay there a year before she decided on this strange unlikely-sounding plan of going to New Zealand, but she is quite resolved. I cannot sufficiently comprehend what her views and those of her brothers may be on the subject, or what is the extent of their information regarding Port Nicholson, to say whether this is rational enterprise or absolute madness. With love to papa, aunt, Tabby, etc.—Good-bye.

C. B.

P.S.—I am very well; I hope you are. Write again soon.

MS untraced. W & S 112.
Address: not in source.
PM: not in source.
Text: *Shorter* 85, the source for W & S 112. Not in *Life* or *Nussey*.
Date: *Shorter* and W & S give 2 Apr., a Friday. This supports their date of 1 Apr. for the previous letter, since 'next Saturday' would give a date for the visit to EN of 10 Apr.

1. CB had told EN on 24.1.1840 that Anne would not return to her post at Blake Hall. Some time before 28 Aug. 1840 Anne became a governess in the family of the Revd Edmund Robinson, MA (1800–46) and his wife Lydia, née Gisborne (1799–1859), daughter of the evangelical writer and friend of William Wilberforce, the Revd Thomas Gisborne of Yoxall Lodge, Staff. The Robinsons lived at Thorp Green Hall, Little Ouseburn, near York, Mr Robinson being,

nominally at least, one of the curates of Great Ouseburn. A portrait of Lydia Robinson is reproduced in *BST* 18.91. opp. 28. For a discussion of the date of Anne's arrival at Thorp Green, see Chitham *ABP* 10; and see EN 15.5.1840 n. 1 and ?14.8.1840 n. 1.

2. Anne was perhaps well, but she was not happy: in her Diary Paper of 30.7.1841 she writes, 'I dislike the situation and wish to change it for another', though she was in fact to remain at Thorp Green until June 1845. See her Diary Paper and that of EJB for the same date, where Emily sends 'from far an exhortation of Courage courage! to exiled and harassed Anne wishing she was here'.
3. On 1 Apr. Branwell moved from his clerkship at Sowerby Bridge station to become clerk in charge at Luddenden Foot station on the same line, the Leeds and Manchester Railroad. See EN ?29.9.1840 notes 11 and 12.
4. See EN 3.1.1841 n. 2 and *Stevens* 18–22. William Waring Taylor emigrated in Nov. 1841, arriving in Wellington, New Zealand in Apr. 1842. Mary was to emigrate in 1845.
5. Colonel William Wakefield, brother of Edward Gibbon Wakefield, had 'negotiated the sale of large areas of land' around Port Nicholson (i.e. Wellington Harbour) in or after Aug. 1839, and there had been widespread campaigning in Yorkshire for settlers. See *Stevens* 20–1 and Jane Stafford, 'Anne Brontë, *Agnes Grey* and New Zealand', *BST* 20. 2. 97–9.
6. Mary Taylor went on a tour of Europe with her brother John in the summer and autumn of 1841. See EN 7.8.1841. Martha Taylor, like Mary, was eventually to attend a school in Brussels instead of France. See the next letter, n. 8.

To Ellen Nussey, [?4 May 1841]

[Upperwood House, Rawdon]

Dear Nell

I have been a long time without writing to you—but I think knowing as you do how I am situated in the matter of time you will not be angry with me—

*George will have told you that he did not go into the house when we arrived at *Upperwood[1]—for which omission of his Mrs W[hite] was very near blowing me up—She went quite red in the face with vexation when she heard that the gentleman had just driven within the gates and then driven back again—for she is very touchy in the matter of opinion—Mr W 'also' seemed to regret the circumstance from more hospitable and kindly motives—I assure you if you were to come and see me you would have quite a fuss made over you.

During the last three weeks that hideous operation called "A Thorough Clean has been going on in the house—it is now nearly completed for which I thank my stars—as during its progress I have fulfilled the twofold character of Nurse and Governess—while the nurse has been transmuted into Cook & housemaid That nurse by the bye is the prettiest lass you ever saw & when dressed has much more the air of a lady than her Misstress Well can I believe that Mrs W has been an exciseman's daughter[2]—and I am convinced also that Mr W's extraction is very low[3]—yet Mrs W— talks in an amusing strain of pomposity about his & her family & connexions & affects to look down with wondrous hauteur on the whole race of "Tradesfolk"[4] as she terms men of business—I was beginning to think Mrs W— a good sort of body in spite of all her bouncing, and boasting—her bad grammar and worse orthography—but I have had experience of one little trait in her character which condemns her a long way with me—After treating a person on the most familiar terms of equality for a long time—?<after seeing & acknowledging th>—If any little thing goes wrong she does not scruple to give way to anger in a very coarse unladylike manner—though in justice no blame could be attached where she ascribed it all—I think passion is the true test of vulgarity or refinement—Mrs W—when put out of her way is highly offensive—She must not give me any more of the same sort—or I shall ask for my wages & go.

This place looks exquisitely beautiful just now—The grounds are certainly lovely—and all is as green as an emerald—I wish you would just come and look at it—Mrs W— would be as proud as Punch to shew it you Mr W— has been writing an urgent invitation to papa entreating him to come and spend a week here.[5] I don't 'at' all wish papa to come—it would be like incurring an obligation—which I have no wish to do because in my secret soul I mean to leave *Upperwood House when I can get a better place. Somehow I have managed to get a good deal more control over the children lately—This makes my life a good deal easier—Also by dint of nursing the fat baby[6] it has got to know me & be fond of me—occasionally I suspect myself of growing rather fond of it—but this suspicion clears away the moment its mamma takes it & makes a fool of it—from a bonny, rosy little morsel—it sinks in my estimation into a small, petted nuisance—Ditto with regard to the other children

Just please yourself about "Going into place"[7] I don't fancy you would stay long—but the experiment might do good—exertion of any kind is always beneficial

Come and see me if you can in any way get. I want to see you It seems *Martha *Taylor is fairly gone[8]—right enough—

Good bye my lassie
yours insufferably
C Brontë[9]

MS BPM B.S. 48. W & S 113 as 4 May—41.
Address: not in MS.
PM: not in MS.
Annotation by EN in ink: 60 May —41
Date: since the top edge of the double sheet of paper is torn, another leaf, now missing (or an envelope), might have given *Shorter* and W & S the date 4 May. This is ticked by Hatfield in his copy of *Shorter*. Alternatively, they might have assumed that the 3 weeks' 'Thorough Clean' followed CB's visit to EN on ?10 Apr.

1. On CB's return from Birstall.

2. Whatever her 'extraction' was, Mrs White might perhaps boast of 'connections' with the landowning Duncombes of Brook Hall and the Charltons of Bellingham. See EN ?21.3.1841 n. 1. and 7.8.1841 n. 1.
3. The Whites were a Manchester trading family. John White, described as a 'gentleman' in his memorial at Calverley church, had inherited his house and estate from his uncle William Leavens, described by William Cudworth as an influential and wealthy manufacturer, a woolstapler who lived at Micklefield, Yorks., and later at Upperwood House. William Leavens's brother Benjamin 'lived at Waterloo House, the ancestral home of the Leavens family, situated at Apperley' (near Rawdon). (William Cudworth, *Round About Bradford* (1876), 443.)
4. MS may read ' "Tradesfolks" '.
5. Patrick Brontë knew the area well. He had met his future wife when he visited Woodhouse Grove school in 1812 as an examiner in Classics, invited there by her uncle John Fennell. His friendly letter to John White of 22.9.1842 shows that Mr. Fennell's widowed second wife, née Elizabeth Lister, was staying at Upperwood House: 'Miss Branwell, and all at home join with me, in the most respectful and kind regards to you, Mrs. White, Mrs. Fennell and all your amiable family . . . My daughter, has always spoken well of you, and Mrs White, and your Family, but she has been very much engaged—Both my Daughters, who are on the Continent, as well as the one, who is near York, as a governess, are exceedingly well received.' (*LD* 333–4.)
6. Arthur Robson White, (b. ?1840) who was to marry a daughter of the Col. Stott referred to in EN 10.8.1844, q.v.
7. Becoming a governess.
8. Martha Taylor went to a finishing-school in the Château de Koekelberg, Brussels. See *Stevens* appendix D, 171–4.
9. The words 'yours insufferably' and the signature are written in a large print-style hand similar to that used for the signature in the next letter, BPM B.S. 45, to Leah Sophia Brooke.

To ? Leah Sophia Brooke,[1] *n.d. [?early* 1841*]*

Does Miss Mary[2] still retain her situation is she well and happy?

I would write a longer letter to you—but it is getting so very late—and I am sleepy

Remember me respectfully to your mother and kindly to your sisters[3] and believe me my dear Miss Leah

Yours half-asleep but very sincerely
C Brontë

MS BPM B.S. 45. W & S 89 as 1840.
Address: not in MS fragment.
PM: not in MS.
Date: uncertain, but probably some time after EN 24.1.1840, where CB refers to Mary Brooke's satisfactory situation as a teacher. The handwriting and slightly unusual signature resemble that in the previous letter (EN ?4.5.1841). CB's tiredness, late hours, and interest in Mary's post may suggest that she is writing from Upperwood House: cf. her reference to lateness in EN ?10.6.1841 and her constant pleas that she is short of time at Upperwood e.g. in EN ?9.12.1841. The paper bears a watermark which includes the letters 'TURKE'—i.e. TURKEY MILL—as does the paper used in EN ?10.6.1841.

1. Leah Sophia Brooke (b. 1815), was the first child of John and Sarah Brooke of Dewsbury and was christened there on 7 Feb. 1816. See EN 21.7.1832 n. 5. Ellen Nussey believed that the MS fragment was part of a letter to 'Miss Leah Brooke . . . [who] for six months or so, was a schoolfellow of Miss Nussey and of [CB] . . . Mr. Brooke, the father of Leah and Mary, was in his youth and early manhood an attorney's clerk, but showing great commercial ability, he was

offered a place in the works of Mr Halliley, at Aldams Mills [Dewsbury]. Subsequently he was taken into partnership.' (W. W. Yates, *The Father of the Brontës* (Leeds, 1897), pp. xv–xvi.)

2. Anna Maria Brooke (b. 1818). See EN 21.7.1832 n. 6. Ellen Nussey wrote, 'After her father's death, Miss Mary Brooke alone or with a sister, took up the teaching profession, and conducted a school of high repute near Fall Lane, Dewsbury. She was a devoted churchwoman, and highly respected in the town and neighbourhood.' (Yates, *The Father of the Brontës*, p. xvi.)
3. Another sister, Elizabeth Brooke, had been christened at Dewsbury Parish Church, on 6 Aug. 1817.

To Revd Henry Nussey, 9 May [1841]

Upperwood-House, Rawdon.

Dear Sir

I am about to employ part of a Sunday evening in answering your last letter—You will perhaps think this hardly right and yet I do not feel that I am doing wrong—Sunday evening is almost my only time of leisure, no one would blame me if I were to spend this spare hour in a pleasant chat with a friend, is it worse to spend it in writing a friendly letter?

I have just seen my little noisy charge[1] deposited snugly in their cribs—and I am sitting alone in the schoolroom with the quiet of a Sunday evening pervading the grounds and gardens outside my window I owe you a letter—can I choose a better time than the present for paying my debt? Now Mr Nussey you need not expect any gossip or news, I have none to tell you—even if I had I am not at present in the mood to communicate them—you will excuse an unconnected letter. If I 'had' thought you critical or captious I would have declined the task of corresponding with you—When I reflect indeed—it seems strange that I should sit down to write without a feeling of formality & restraint to an individual with whom I am personally so little acquainted as I am with yourself—but the fact is I cannot be formal in a letter if I write at all I must write as I think. It seems Ellen has told you that I am become a Governess again—as you say it is indeed a hard thing for flesh and blood to leave home—especially a good home—not a wealthy or splendid one—my home is humble and unattractive to strangers but to me it contains what I shall find nowhere else in the world—[?the] profound, and intense affection which brothers and sisters feel for each other when their minds are cast in the same mould, their ideas drawn from the same source—when they have clung to each other from childhood and when family disputes have never sprung up to divide them.

We are all separated now, and winning our bread amongst strangers as we can—my sister Anne is near York,[2] my brother in a situation near

Halifax.[3]<Em> I am here, Emily is the only one left at home where her usefulness and willingness make<s> her indispensable. Under these circumstances should we repine? I think not—our mutual affection ought to comfort us under all difficulties—if the God on whom we must all depend will but vouchsafe us health and the power to continue in the strict line of duty, so as never under any temptation to swerve from it an inch—we shall have 'ample' reason to be grateful and contented.

I do not pretend to say that I am always contented—a governess must often submit to have the heart-ache—my employers Mr & Mrs White are kind worthy people in their way—but the children are indulged—I have great difficult[i]es to contend with sometimes—perseverance will perhaps conquer them—and it has gratified me much to find that [the] parents are well satisfied with their children's improvement in learning since I came. But I am dwelling too much upon my own concerns and feelings—It is true they are interesting to me but it [is] wholly impossible they should be so to you and therefore I hope you will skip the last page for I repent having written it—

A fortnight since[4] I had a letter from Ellen urging me to go to Brookroyd for a single day—I felt such a longing to have a respite from labour and to get once more amongst "old familiar faces"[5] that I conquered diffidence & asked Mrs White to let me go—she complied and I went accordingly & had a most delightful holiday—I saw your mother—your Sisters Mercy Ellen & poor Sarah[6] and your brothers Richard and George[7]—all were well—Ellen talked of endeavouring to get a situation somewhere—I did not encourage the idea much—I advised her rather to go to Earnley for a while I think she wants a change—and I daresay you would be glad to have her as a companion for a few months.

I inquired if there was any family of the name of Barrett in this neighbourhood—but I cannot hear of any such—though [I] understand there is a Mr. Mrs & Miss Barwick[8]—the names in pronounciation sound very similar.

My time is out—with sincere good wishes for your welfare and kind love to your Sister Miss Nussey[9]

I remain
Yours respectfully
C Brontë

MS William Self. W & S 114 (part).
Address (integral): Revd. H Nussey | Earnley-Rectory | nr Chichester | Sussex
PM: (i) RAWDON— (ii) LEEDS | MY 18 | 1841 | F (iii) ?C | 19 MY 19 (iv) CH[ICHES]TER |——| 1841
Date: The discrepancy between CB's date, Sunday 'May 9th . .', and the posting date was perhaps caused by her retention of the original date when she began this exceptionally neat copy. 'Charge' in l. 8 and the false start 'Em' in l. 29 look like copying slips. She had probably drafted the letter on or about 25 Apr. See n. 4. below.

1. Thus in MS.

2. See EJB ?2.4.1841 n. 1.
3. See EN 29.9.1840 notes 11 and 12. Luddenden Foot is a hillside village about 5 miles west of Halifax. See Gérin *BB* ch. 14, and *Barker*.
4. This does not tally with the dates for CB's visit (10–11 Apr.) derivable from the letters dated by Shorter and W & S 1 and 2 Apr. (pp. 249 and 251.) External evidence is lacking, and the dates remain uncertain. It seems unlikely that CB had made a second visit.
5. cf. Charles Lamb, 'The Old Familiar Faces':

    I have had playmates, I have had companions,
    In my days of childhood, in my joyful school-days,—
    All, all are gone, the old familiar faces.

6. See EN 10.11.1834 n. 2.
7. See EN 13.1.1832. n. 4.
8. Possibly pronounced 'Barrick'.
9. Ann Nussey, housekeeping for Henry at Earnley.

To Ellen Nussey, [?10 June 1841]

[Upperwood House, Rawdon]

Dear Nell

If I don't scrawl you a line of some sort I know you will begin to fancy that I neglect you in spite of all I said last time we met—You can hardly fancy it possible I daresay that I cannot find a quarter of an hour to scribble a note in—but when a note is written it is to be carried a mile to the post—and that consumes nearly an hour which is a large portion of the day—Mr & Mrs *White have been gone a week—I heard from them this morning they are now at Hexham[1]—no time is fixed for their return—but I hope it will not be delayed long or I shall miss the chance of seeing Anne this vacation—She came home I understand last Wednesday and is only to be allowed 3 weeks holidays—because the family she is with are going to Scarborough[2] I should like to see her to judge for myself of the state of her health I cannot trust any other person's report no one seems minute enough in their observations—I should also very much have liked you to see her—

I have got on very well with the servants & children so far—yet it is dreary, solitary work—You can tell as well as me the lonely feeling of being without a companion—I ?<think> offered the Irish Concern[3] to *Mary *Taylor but she is so circumstanced that she cannot accept it—** her brothers—like George**[4]—have a feeling of pride that revolts at the thought of their Sister "going out" I hardly knew that it was such a degradation till lately—

Your visit did me much good. I wish M. T. would come & yet I hardly know how to find time to be with her—

Good bye—God—bless you
C Brontë

I am very well & I contrive to get to bed before 12 o'clock p.m. ?I can't tell[5] people that I am dissatisfied with my situation—I can drive on—there's no use in complaining I have lost my chance of going to Ireland.

MS BPM B.S. 49. Envelope: Needham Collection, BPM. W & S 115.
Address (envelope): Miss Ellen Nussey | Brookroyd | Birstal | nr Leeds
PM: (i) RAWDEN (ii) LEEDS | JU 11 | 1841
Annotation on letter by EN in ink: 61 June 41

1. A Northumbrian market-town 16 miles from Bellingham, where Mrs White died in 1878. Probably she had family connections in the area.
2. The Revd Edmund Robinson and his family regularly took summer apartments in Scarborough, usually in W. Wood's Lodgings, Cliff, on the sea front. The apartments were 'of different sizes, containing from Five to Fifteen Beds' and, according to the proprietor, were patronized by the 'Nobility and Gentry'. See the *Scarborough Record* for 21 June 1845, and Gérin *BB* 230. In 1841 the Robinsons stayed in No. 2 Cliff.
3. A post as a governess; with whom is not known. cf. Jane Eyre's reluctance to exile herself to educate 'the five daughters of Mrs. Dionysius O'Gall of Bitternutt Lodge, Connaught, Ireland'. (315.)
4. The 4 words are heavily deleted. Perhaps Ellen's brother George had helped to persuade her since May not to 'go out', for no more is heard of it until ?June 1843. See EN ?4.5.1841 n. 7.
5. MS may read 'Don't tell'.

To Ellen Nussey, 1 July 1841

[Haworth]

Dear Nell

I was not at home when I got your letter—but I am at home now—and it feels like Paradise.

I came last night—Mr & Mrs *White only returned last Sunday evening—When I asked for a Vacation—<she> 'Mrs W' offered a week or ten days—but I demanded three weeks and stood to my tackle[1] with a tenacity worthy of yourself lassie. I gained the point—but I don't like such victories.

I have gained another point—you are unanimously requested to come here next Tuesday and stay as long as you can Write to me directly—say if that day is convenient and whether we are to meet you at Keighley—Aunt is in high good humour—I hope she will keep so. I need not write a long letter now

Good bye dear Nell
C B. July 1st.

I have lost the chance of seeing Anne[2] She is gone back to "the Land of Egypt and the House of Bondage"[3] also little black Tom[4] is dead—every cup however sweet has its drop of bitter in it—

Probably you will be at a loss to ascertain the identity of that gentleman but don't fret about it I'll tell you when you come. Keeper[5] is as well, big—and grim as ever—I'm too happy to write—Come lassie—

MS Ms Lynda Glading. W & S 116.
Address: not in MS.
PM: not in MS.
Annotation on verso by ?EN: 'Perhaps one may be available another time with full signature'

1. Literally, my weapons; i.e. 'I did not give way.' cf. Fletcher and ?Shakespeare, *Two Noble Kinsmen* II. iii. 55: 'We'll see the sports; then every man to's tackle!' (*ODEP* 770–1, 'To stand to one's tackling'.)
2. See the previous letter.
3. cf. Exodus 13: 14.
4. In her Diary Paper for 30 July 1841, written at Scarborough, Anne records, 'We have got Keeper, got a sweet little cat and lost it, and also got a hawk.' EN recalled that 'black "Tom" the tabby was every-body's pet'. See Appendix.
5. EJB's drawing of her dog, Keeper, has often been reproduced. See Gérin *EJB* opp. 44, and 'Keeper, Flossie and Cat' opp. 45. EN describes him as 'tawny strong limbed . . . Emily's favorite, he was so completely under her control she could quite easily make him spring and roar like a lion'. His portrait is drawn as that 'stubborn canine character' Tartar in *Shirley*. See EJB 1.10.1843 n. 4.

To Ellen Nussey, [?3 July 1841]

[Haworth]

My dear Ellen

I had forgotten—when I asked you to come on Tuesday that there is no coach from Birstal to Bradford except on Thursday—Moreover Aunt is proposing to pay a visit to Uncle Fennell[1] at Cross-stone—who is very ill—She has fixed 'next' Thursday[2] to go—and as she will probably stay a week or two, she will leave her room at liberty which will be much more comfortable for you than being crowded into our little closet[3]—I wish therefore my dear Ellen you could make it convenient to come on that day—it will be a real pleasure both to Emily & myself to have you with us and a great disappointment if you fail to come

Believe me yours sincerely
C B

Write by return of post

MS BPM Gr. E 1. W & S 117.
Address: not in MS.
PM: not in MS.
Annotation in pencil: 45
Date: The present letter is undated in *Shorter* (No. 100), but misplaced among the letters of 1842. W & S 117 reproduces *Shorter*, not the MS, which was presumably not available, but dates '[HAWORTH, July 3rd 1841]'—a likely date in relation to the dated letters of 1 and 19 July.

1. Mr Fennell's first wife Jane was Elizabeth Branwell's aunt. See PB 23.9.1829 notes 1 and 4. Mr Fennell died on 13 Oct. 1841.

2. Thursday 8 July if CB was writing on Saturday 3 July.
3. Probably the small room now known as Emily's room over the hall at the parsonage.

To Ellen Nussey, 19 July 1841

[Haworth]

My dear Ellen

We waited long—and anxiously for you on the Thursday that you promised to come—I quite wearied my eyes with watching from the window—eye-glass in hand and sometimes spectacles on nose—However you are not to blame—I believe you have done right in going to *Earnley[1] and as to the disappointment we endured why all must suffer disappointment at some period or other of their lives—but a hundred things I had to say to you will now be forgotten and never said—there is a project hatching in this house—which both Emily and I anxiously wished to discuss with you—The project is yet in its infancy—hardly peeping from its shell—and whether it will ever come out—a fine, full-fledged chicken—or will turn addle and die before it cheeps, is one 'of' those considerations that are but dimly revealed by the oracles of futurity Now dear Nell don't be nonplussed by all this metaphorical mystery—I talk of a plain and every day occurrence—though in Delphic[2] style—I wrap up the information in figures of speech concerning eggs, chickens, etcetera etceterorum.

To come to the point—Papa and Aunt talk by fits & starts of our—id est—Emily Anne & myself commencing a School[3]—! I have often you know said how much I wished such a thing—but I never could conceive where the capital was to come from for making such a speculation—I was well aware indeed, that Aunt <u>had</u> money[4]—but I always considered that she was the last person who would offer a loan for the purpose in question—A loan however she <u>has</u> offered or rather intimates that she perhaps <u>will</u> offer in case pupils can be secured,—an eligible situation obtained &c. &c.

This sounds very fair—but still there are matters to be considered which throw something of a damp upon the Scheme—I do not expect that Aunt will risk more than 150£ on such a venture—& would it be possible to establish a <u>respectable</u> (not by any means a <u>shewy</u>) school—and to commence housekeeping with a capital of <u>only</u> that amount? Propound the question to your sister *Anne[5]—if you think she can answer it—if not, don't say a word on the subject—As to getting into debt that is a thing we could none of us reconcile our minds to for a moment—We do not care how modest—how humble our commencement be so it be made on sure grounds & have a safe foundation—<and we>

In thinking of all possible and impossible places where we could establish a

School—I have thought of Burlington[6]—or rather of the neighbourhood of Burlington—do you remember whether there was any other school there besides that of Miss *?Jackson[7] This is of course a perfectly crude, random idea—There are a hundred reasons why it should be an impracticable one—We have no connexions—no acquaintance there—it is far from home &c. Still I fancy the ground in the East-Riding is less fully occupied than in the West[8]—Much inquiry & consideration will be necessary of course before any plan is decided on—and I fear much time will elapse before any plan is executed. Can events **be so ?turned as that you shall be included as an associate in our projects?**[9] This is a question I have not at present the means to answer—

I must not conclude this note without even mentioning the name of our revered friend William *Weightman—He is quite as bonny pleasant—light-hearted—good-tempered—generous, careless, crafty, fickle & unclerical as ever he keeps up his correspondence with Agnes *Walton[10]—During the last Spring he went to *Appleby[11] & stayed upwards of a month—in the interim he wrote to Papa several times & from his letters—which I have seen—he appears to have a fixed design of obtaining Miss *Walton's hand & if she can be won by a handsome face—by a cheerful & frank disposition & highly cultivated talents—if she can be satisfied with these things & will not ?exact further the pride of a sensitive mind & the delicacy of a feeling one—<with> in this case he will doubtless prove successful—

Write to me as soon as you can and address to Rawden—I shall not leave my present situation—till my future prospects assume a more fixed & definite aspect—Good bye dear Ellen

C B

MS BPM Gr. E 4. Envelope: BPM B.S. 104/0.5. W & S 118 (part).
Address (envelope): Miss Ellen Nussey | Earnley Rectory | Chichester | Sussex
PM (i) BRADFORD YORKS | JY 22 | 1841 (ii) *Bradford Yorks* | *Py Post* (iii) C | 23 JY 23 | 1841 (iv) CHICHESTER | JY 24 | 1841
Annotation in pencil on envelope by EN: July 19 —41 | School project

1. In her letter of 9.5.1841 to Henry Nussey CB had suggested that EN should join him there for a few months.
2. Oracular; from the oracle of Apollo at Delphi, on Mount Parnassus in Greece.
3. This idea was not finally dropped until 1845, when the sisters had failed to secure a single pupil for their projected school. See EN 4.11.1845.
4. Since 1808 Elizabeth Branwell and her sisters had each had £50 p.a. from their father's will. See *BST* 14.74.28–38.
5. EN's eldest sister, and not her 70-year-old mother, took care of the housekeeping at Brookroyd. CB again asks for housekeeping advice from her or from Ellen in EN 21.8.1846.
6. An alternative name for Bridlington, where CB and EN had stayed in Sept.—Oct. 1839. See EN 24.10.1839 and notes.
7. Probably Miss Clarissa Jacks' Academy at 'Prospect Place', Quay, Bridlington. (Pigot's *Directory* 1841.) CB and EN had been allowed to stay by themselves for a week at Ann Booth's lodging-house, Garrison Street, Bridlington Quay, not far from Miss Jacks' Academy. (See EN

24.10.1839 n. 9.) (The 'Miss C. S. Jack's Academy, King Street Quay' referred to in Gérin *CB* 173 n. 2 was probably the same school. See White's *Directory* 1840.)

8. The East Riding was less densely populated than the West; but Pigot's *Directory* for 1841 lists 15 schools in Bridlington and nearby Flamborough, of which 3 were probably girls' private schools, all at Bridlington Quay.
9. The greater part of this sentence is heavily deleted and the reading is conjectural.
10. See EN 7.4.1840 n. 11.
11. Mr Weightman's home town. See EN end June 1840 n. 6. He had officiated at baptisms in Haworth church on 4 Apr., but not again until 16 May.

Emily J. Brontë, Diary Paper 30 July 1841[1]

A Paper to be opened
when Anne is
25 years old
or my next birthday after—
if
—all be well—

Emily Jane Brontë July the 30th 1841..

It is Friday evening—near 9 o'clock—wild rainy weather I am seated in the dining room 'alone'—having just concluded tidying our desk-boxes[2]—writing this document—Papa is in the parlour. Aunt up stairs in her room—she has <just> been reading Blackwood's Magazine to papa—Victoria and Adelaide[3] are ensconced in the peat-house—Keeper[4] is in the kitchen—Nero[5] in his cage—We are all stout and hearty as I hope is the case with Charlotte, Branwell, and Anne, of whom the first is at John White Esqre upperwood House, Rawden[6] The second is at Luddenden foot[7] and the third is I beleive at—Scarborough[8]—enditing perhaps a paper corresponding to this—<There> A scheme is at present in agitation for setting us up in a school of our own[9] as yet nothing is determined but I hope and trust it may go on and prosper and answer our highest expectations. This day 4—years I wonder whether we shall still be dragging on in our present condition or established to our heart's content Time will show—

I guess that at the time appointed for the opening of this paper—we (i.e.) Charlotte, Anne and I—<will> <?shall> 'shall' be all merrily seated in our own sitting-room in some pleasant <pnd> and flourishing seminary[10] having just ?gathered in for the midsummer holydays our debts will be paid off and we shall have c<h>ash in hand to a considerable amount. papa Aunt and Branwell will either have been—or be coming—to visit us—it will be a fine warm ?summery evening. very different from this bleak look-out Anne and I will perchance slip out into the garden a <i.w.>minutes to peruse our papers. I hope either this [o]r something better will be the case—

The ?Gondalians[11] <were> are at present in a threatening state but there is no open rupture as yet—all the princes and princesses of the ?royal royaltys are at the palace of In-struction[12]—I have a good many books on hands but I am sorry to say that as usual I make small progress with any—however I have just made a new regularity paper! and I ?me[an] ?verb sap[13]—to do great things—and now I close sending from far an ?exhortation of courage <i.w.>courage! to exiled and harassed Anne wishing she was here

MS untraced, W & S i. 238.
Text: from facsimile, *CBCircle* opp. 146.

1. C. K. Shorter described his acquisition of the Diary Papers of 1841 and 1845 in *CBCircle* 146: 'I have before me a little tin box about two inches long, which one day last year Mr. Nicholls turned out from the bottom of a desk . . . Within were four little pieces of paper neatly folded to the size of a sixpence. These papers were covered with handwriting, two of them by Emily, and two by Anne Brontë. They revealed a pleasant if eccentric arrangement on the part of the sisters, which appears to have been settled upon even after they had passed their twentieth year. They had agreed to write a kind of reminiscence every four years, to be opened by Emily on her birthday . . . The *Gondaland Chronicles*, to which reference is made, must remain a mystery for us. They were doubtless destroyed, with abundant other memorials of Emily, by the heart-broken sister who survived her.' In *Shorter* i. 215 part of the accompanying letter from Mr Nicholls is quoted: 'The four small scraps of Emily and Anne's MSS. I found in the small box I send you. They are sad reading, poor girls!' (Letter to C. K. Shorter, 4.1.189[6].) For Shorter's involvement in the acquisition of manuscripts, see pp. 52–63.
2. Two of these are shown on the tables in the 2 tiny drawings at the top of the Diary Paper. Emily's rosewood desk, now in the BPM, was sold as part of the A. B. Nicholls collection at Sotheby's in 1907. Its miscellaneous contents included mementoes of Brussels, 5 reviews of *WH*, and a letter from T. C. Newby offering to make arrangements for 'Ellis Bell's' next novel. See *Sixty Treasures* 43.
3. Probably the 2 tame geese mentioned in Anne Brontë's Diary Paper. See p. 264. They were named after the Queen and her aunt, the widowed Queen Adelaide.
4. Emily's dog. See EN 1.7.1841 n. 5 and EJB 1.10.1843 n. 4.
5. Probably the hawk referred to in Anne's Diary Paper. The name is usually transcribed, incorrectly, as 'Hero'. Emily's water-colour of a female merlin, dated 'Octr. 27th. 1841' (BPM Bon 34) is often identified with this hawk, but it may be a copy of a plate in Thomas Bewick's *A History of British Birds* (1797, *Land Birds*). See Gérin *EJB* 116–17 and B. Wilks, *The Brontës* (1975), 64.
6. See EN ?3.3.1841 notes 1 and 2.
7. A small station near Halifax. See EN ?29.9.1840, EJB 2.4.1841, and EN 20.1.1842 and notes.
8. See EN ?10.6.1841 n. 2. Anne's Diary Paper follows on p. 264.
9. See EN 19.7.1841 and n. 3.
10. Emily's prediction was not fulfilled. See her Diary Paper for 30.7.1845.
11. The imaginary kingdom of Gondal was the scene of Emily and Anne's early stories and of some of their poems. Since the stories do not survive, our knowledge of Gondal derives from the scanty evidence of the poems, the diary papers, and a few scribbled proper names. See F. E. Ratchford, *Gondal's Queen* (Austin, Tex. 1955), a speculative reconstruction of the Gondal saga later criticized by W. D. Paden in *An Investigation of Gondal* (NY, 1958). Gérin *EJB* and Edward Chitham, *A Life of Emily Brontë* (Oxford, 1987) both use Gondal material, since the

authors believe that 'autobiographical and fictional material is closely intertwined' in Emily's poems. (Chitham, *A Life of Emily Brontë*, 6.)

12. cf. Emily's poem, 'Written on returning to the P. of I. on the 10th of January, 1827', 'The busy day has hurried by', 14 June 1839. Hatfield *EBP* 110–12.
13. 'Verbum sapienti sat est': a word is sufficient to the wise man.

Anne Brontë, Diary Paper 30 July 1841[1]

July the 30th, A.D. 1841.

This is Emily's birthday. She has now completed her 23rd year, and is, I believe, at home. Charlotte is a governess in the family of Mr. White.[2] Branwell is a clerk in the railroad station at Luddenden Foot,[3] and I am a governess in the family of Mr. Robinson.[4] I dislike the situation and wish to change it for another. I am now at Scarborough. My pupils are gone to bed and I am hastening to finish this before I follow them.

We are thinking of setting up a school of our own,[5] but nothing definite is settled about it yet, and we do not know whether we shall be able to or not. I hope we shall. And I wonder what will be our condition and how or where we shall all be on this day four years hence; at which time, if all be well, I shall be 25 years and 6 months old, Emily will be 27 years old, Branwell 28 years and 1 month, and Charlotte 29 years and a quarter. We are now all separate and not likely to meet again for many a weary week, but we are none of us ill that I know of and all are doing something for our own livelihood except Emily, who, however, is as busy as any of us, and in reality earns her food and raiment as much as we do.

How little know we what we are
How less what we may be![6]

Four years ago I was at school. Since then I have been a governess at Blake Hall,[7] left it, come to Thorp Green,[8] and seen the sea and York Minster. Emily has been a teacher at Miss Patchet's school,[9] and left it. Charlotte has left Miss Wooler's,[10] been a governess at Mrs. Sidgwick's,[11] left her, and gone to Mrs. White's. Branwell has given up painting, been a tutor in Cumberland, left it, and become a clerk on the railroad.[12] Tabby has left us,[13] Martha Brown has come in her place.[14] We have got Keeper, got a sweet little cat and lost it, and also got a hawk. Got a wild goose which has flown away, and three tame ones, one of which has been killed.[15] All these diversities, with many others, are things we did not expect or foresee in the July of 1837. What will the next four years bring forth? Providence only knows. But we ourselves have sustained very little alteration since that time. I have the same faults that I had then, only I have more wisdom and experience, and a little more self-possession than I then enjoyed. How will it be when we open this paper and the one Emily has written? I wonder whether the *Gondalian[s]*[16] will still be flourishing, and what will be their condition. I am now engaged in writing the fourth volume of *Solala Vernon's Life*.

For some time I have looked upon 25 as a sort of era in my existence. It may prove a true presentiment, or it may be only a superstitious fancy; the latter seems most likely, but time will show.

Anne Brontë

MS untraced. W & S i. 239.

Text: *CBCircle* 148–9.

1. For the provenance of the diary papers of 1841 and 1845 see EJB Diary Paper 30.7.1841 n. 1.
2. See EN ?3.3.1841 notes 1 and 2.
3. See EN ?29.9.1840, EJB 2.4.1841, and EN 20.1.1842, and notes.
4. See EJB ?2.4.1841 n. 1. and EN 10.6.1841 n. 2.
5. See EN 19.7.1841 and n. 3.
6. cf. Byron, *Don Juan* XV. xcix, 'How little do we know that which we are! How less what we may be!' and the echo of Ophelia's words in *Hamlet* IV. v: 'Lord, we know what we are, but know not what we may be', and of 1 John 3: 2.
7. The home of Joshua and Mary Ingham in Mirfield. See EN 12.3.1839.
8. The Robinsons' home near York.
9. The school at Law Hill, near Halifax, kept by Elizabeth Patchett. She was to marry the Revd John Hope, the incumbent of St Anne's in the Grove, Southowram, near the school, on 27.12.1842. See EN 2.10.1838 n. 2 and Gérin *EJB* ch. 7.
10. CB left her teaching post at Margaret Wooler's school at Heald's House, Dewsbury Moor, on 22.12.1838.
11. CB was a governess in the family of Mr and Mrs John Benson Sidgwick from May to July 1839. See EJB 8.6.1839 n. 2.
12. Branwell had tried to make a living as a portrait painter from *c* 1837 to 1838, had been a tutor in the family of Robert Postlethwaite of Broughton-in-Furness, Cumberland, from Jan. to June 1840, and a railway clerk at Sowerby Bridge station from Sept. 1840 to 31 Mar. 1841, when he moved to Luddenden Foot station. See EN 28.12.1839, 29.9.1840, and Gérin *BB* and *Barker*.
13. Tabitha Aykroyd. See EN 11.9.1833 n. 5.
14. See EN 21.12.1839 n. 3.
15. See the notes to EJB *Diary* 30.7.1841. 'Little Black Tom', the cat, had died, probably in June: see EN 1.7.1841.
16. *CBCircle* prints 'Gondaliand'. See EJB *Diary* 30.7.1841 n. 11. Nothing is known of 'Solala Vernon's Life', but Anne's Gondal poem of 1.1.1840, 'Maiden, thou wert thoughtless once' bears the name 'Olivia Vernon'. See Chitham *ABP* 71–3.

To Ellen Nussey, 7 August 1841

*Upperwood-House

My dear Ellen

This is Saturday evening—I have put the children to-bed and now I am going to sit down and answer your letter. I am again by myself—Housekeeper and Governess—for Mr & Mrs *White are staying with a Mrs *?Duncome[1] of

*Brook-Hall[2] near Tadcaster—to speak truth though I am solitary while they are away—it is still by far the happiest part of my time—the children are now under at least decent control—the servants are very observant and attentive to me and the absence of the Master & Mistress relieves me from the heavy duty of endeavouring to seem always easy, cheerful & conversible with those whose ideas and feelings are nearly as incomprehensible to me, as probably mine (if I shewed them unreservedly) would be to them

*Martha *Taylor it appears is in the way of enjoying great advantages[3]—so is Mary—for you will be surprised to hear that she is returning immediately to the Continent with her brother *John[4]—not however to stay there but to take a month's tour and recreation—I am glad it has been so arranged—it seemed hard that Martha should be preferred so far before her elder Sister—I had a long letter from Mary and a packet—containing a present of a very handsome black silk scarf & a pair of beautiful kid gloves bought at Brussels—of course I was in one sense pleased with the gift—pleased that they should think of me—so far off—amidst the excitements of one of the most splendid capitals of Europe—and yet it felt irksome to accept it—I should think Mary & Martha have not more than sufficient pocket-money to supply themselves I wish they had testified their regard by a less expensive token

Mary's letter spoke of some of the pictures & cathedrals she had seen—pictures the most exquisite—& cathedrals the most venerable—I hardly know what swelled to my throat as I read her letter—such a vehement impatience of restraint & steady work. such a strong wish for wings[5]—wings such as wealth can furnish—such an urgent thirst to see—to know—to learn—something internal seemed to expand boldly for a minute—I was tantalized with the consciousness of faculties unexercised—then all collapsed and I despaired

My dear Nell—I would hardly make that confession to any one but yourself—and to you rather in a letter than "viva voce"—these rebellious & absurd emotions were only momentary I quelled them in five minutes—I hope they will not revive—for they were acutely painful—No further steps have been taken about the project[6] I mentioned to you—nor probably will be for the present—But Emily & Anne & I keep it in view—it is our polar-star & we look to it under all circumstances of despondency—I begin to suspect I am writing in a strain which will make you think I am unhappy—this is far from being the case—on the contrary I know my place is a favourable one for a Governess—what dismays & haunts me sometimes is a conviction that I have no natural knack for my vocation—if teaching only—were requisite it would be smooth & easy—but it is the living in other people's houses—the estrangement from one's real character the adoption of a cold frigid—apathetic exterior that is painful[7]

On the whole I am glad you went with *Henry to Sussex[8]—our disappointment was bitter enough—but that is gone by now—and it is as well you have got a change You will not mention our School-scheme to any one at present—a project not actually commenced is always uncertain—Write to me often my dear Nell—you know your letters are valued—Give my regards to your brother & Sister and believe me

Your loving child (as you choose to call me so)
C B

I am well in health—. I have one aching feeling at my heart (I must allude to it though I had resolved not to)—it is about Anne—she has so much to endure—far far more than I have—when my thoughts turn to her—they always see her as a patient, persecuted stranger[9]—amongst people more grossly <ignorant> insolent, proud & tyrannical than your imagination unassisted <will> can readily depict—I know what concealed susceptibility is in her nature—when her feelings are wounded I wish I could be with her to administer a little balm She is more lonely—less gifted with the power of making friends 'even' than I am—drop the subject

MS HM 24428. W & S 119.
Address (integral): Miss Ellen Nussey | Earnley Rectory | nr Chichester | Sussex
PM: (i) RAWDEN (ii) LEEDS | AU 8 | 1841 | F (iii) E | 9 AU 9 | 1841 (iv) CHICHESTER | AU 10 | 1841

1. Heavily deleted. Perhaps the family was related to the Duncombes of Copgrove, Boroughbridge, who had extensive estates in the North & West Ridings.
2. Brook Hall in the village of Wighill is about 2 miles from the market-town of Tadcaster in Yorks.
3. Mary Taylor had taken her younger sister to Mme Goussaert's 'Château de Koekelberg' finishing-school in Brussels. It was expensive, offering French language and literature, 'cosmography', German, music, drawing, dancing, and gymnastics; Mary Taylor gives a lively account of the teachers there in her joint letter with Martha and CB in Mar./Apr. 1842. See also *Stevens* 27–8, 171–4, and CB to Elizabeth Branwell 29.9.1841.
4. A more likely reading than 'Joshua' for this heavily deleted name. John Taylor, who was to emigrate to New Zealand in 1875/6, was at this period living with his brother Joseph at Hunsworth Mill cottage, and travelling to and from the Continent on business. CB gives an equivocal portrayal of him as 'Mark Yorke' in *Shirley*.
5. cf. the opening of *Villette* ch. 6, where Lucy's 'spirit shook its always-fettered wings half loose' as if she was 'at last about to taste life' on her first visit to London.
6. The school project mentioned in EN 19.7.1841.
7. On 6 Nov. 1852 CB explained to W. S. Williams that she had adopted a 'cold' name for her heroine Lucy Snowe in *Villette* 'for she has about her an external coldness'.
8. Ellen's journey with Henry, presumably on his way back to Earnley from a visit to Birstall, helps to explain the suddenness of her departure.
9. cf. Emily Brontë's allusion to 'exiled and harassed Anne' in her Diary Paper of 30.7.1841, and Anne's portrayal of the Murrays in *AG*. But Anne eventually won the affection of her pupils: see Vol. ii, EN 10.12.1848 where the two younger girls visited her at Haworth and 'were clinging round her like two children'.

To Elizabeth Branwell, 29 September 1841

Upperwood House, Rawdon.

Dear Aunt,

I have heard nothing of Miss Wooler yet since I wrote to her intimating that I would accept her offer.[1] I cannot conjecture the reason of this long silence, unless some unforeseen impediment has occurred in concluding the bargain. Meantime, a plan has been suggested and approved by Mr. and Mrs. White, and others, which I wish now to impart[2] to you. My friends recommend me, if I desire to secure permanent success, to delay commencing the school for six months longer, and by all means to contrive, by hook or by crook, to spend the intervening time in some school on the continent. They say schools in England are so numerous, competition so great, that without some such step towards attaining superiority we shall probably have a very hard struggle, and may fail in the end. They say, moreover, that the loan of £100, which you have been so kind as to offer us, will, perhaps, not be all required now, as Miss Wooler will lend us the furniture; and that, if the speculation is intended to be a good and successful one, half the sum, at least, ought to be laid out in the manner I have mentioned, thereby insuring a more speedy repayment both of interest and principal.

I would not go to France or to Paris. I would go to Brussels, in Belgium. The cost of the journey there, at the dearest rate of travelling, would be £5;[3] living is there little more than half as dear as it is in England, and the facilities for education are equal or superior to any other place in Europe. In half a year, I could acquire a thorough familiarity with French. I could improve greatly in Italian,[4] and even get a dash of German,[5] *i.e.*, providing my health continued as good as it is now. Martha Taylor is now staying in Brussels, at a first-rate establishment there. I should not think of going to the Château de Kockleberg,[6] where she is resident, as the terms are much too high; but if I wrote to her, she, with the assistance of Mrs. Jenkins, the wife of the British Consul,[7] would be able to secure me a cheap and decent residence and respectable protection. I should have the opportunity of seeing her frequently, she would make me acquainted with the city; and, with the assistance of her cousins,[8] I should probably in time be introduced to connections far more improving, polished, and cultivated, than any I have yet known.

These are advantages which would turn to vast account,[9] when we actually commenced a school—and, if Emily could share them with me, only for a single half-year, we could take a footing in the world afterwards which we can never do now. I say Emily instead of Anne; for Anne might take her turn at some future period, if our school answered. I feel certain, while I am writing, that you will see the propriety of what I say; you always like to use your money to the best advantage; you are not fond of making shabby purchases; when you do

confer a favour, it is often done in style; and depend upon it £50, or £100, thus laid out, would be well employed. Of course, I know no other friend in the world to whom I could apply on this subject except yourself. I feel an absolute conviction that, if this advantage were allowed us, it would be the making of us for life. Papa will perhaps think it a wild and ambitious scheme; but who ever rose in the world without ambition? When he left Ireland to go to Cambridge University,[10] he was as ambitious as I am now. I want us all to go on.[11] I know we have talents, and I want them to be turned to account. I look to you, aunt, to help us. I think you will not refuse. I know, if you consent, it shall not be my fault if you ever repent your kindness. With love to all, and the hope that you are all well,—Believe me, dear aunt, your affectionate niece, C. Brontë
Miss Branwell.

MS untraced. W & S 121.
Address: not in source.
PM: not in source.
Text: *CBCircle* 96–7 n. 1. W & S 121 and *Shorter* 92 reproduce *CBCircle*, which is MS-based: the *Circle* text is followed by a note, '*Mrs. Gaskell's "Life." Corrected and completed from original letter in the possession of Mr. A. B. Nicholls*'. Rylands MS *Life* and printed edns. of *Life* have omissions and other variants, the more important of which are given below.

1. Margaret Wooler had invited CB to take over Heald's House school, Dewsbury Moor, which Eliza Wooler had relinquished earlier in the year. In EN 12.11.1840 CB had described the school as 'consumptive'. See also EN 17.10.1841 and 2.11.1841
2. Rylands MS *Life* reads 'to <unfold> impart'.
3. In *The Professor* ch. 6 Hunsden tells Crimsworth he 'may get to Brussels . . . for five or six pounds' (53); and in May 1842 Mr Brontë noted that his travelling expenses on the Continent were one-fifth less than in England. (*LD* 303.)
4. CB had perhaps begun to learn Italian at Roe Head. Her copy of Giovanni Veneroni's *The Complete Italian Master* (1831 edn. privately owned), bears her signature and the date 'Aug 31 1832'. Her teacher would be Margaret Wooler, said by her nephew Sir Thomas Clifford Allbutt to be 'a woman of unusual brains and accomplishments, especially a fine Italian scholar'. (Sir Humphry Davy Rolleston, *The Right Honourable Sir Thomas Clifford Allbutt: A Memoir* (1929), 3.) CB quotes scraps of Italian in her early writings, such as the (inaccurate) 'Maria piangendo' in 'The Spell' (1834) (Alexander *EEW* ii. p. 2, 208), but there is no evidence that she studied Italian in Brussels.
5. CB was to have German lessons in Brussels, and to become competent enough to translate German verse into both English and French. See EN 6.3. [1843] n. 1 and Neufeldt *CBP* 357–69.
6. *Life* i. 237 reads 'Mary is now staying at Brussels, . . . there; I should not think of going to the Château de Kokleberg'. Perhaps Mrs Gaskell silently 'emended' to 'Mary' as being more likely than Martha to secure a residence for CB; but a letter from Martha to EN of 9.9.1841 shows that Mary had only visited the school: 'I am going to begin working again very hard, now that John and Mary are going away.' (W & S 120.)
7. The Rylands MS reading, 'British Consul', has been replaced by 'British Chaplain' in the printed edns. of the *Life*. The Revd Evan Jenkins (?1797–1856) was probably a graduate of Trinity College Cambridge (MA 1829), but the entry in *Venn* is confused. He had been the British Chaplain in Brussels since 1826, and was now also 'Chaplain to H.M. the King of the Belgians'. His brother the Revd David Jenkins, perpetual curate of Pudsey near Leeds since 1814, was well known to Patrick Brontë, whom he had replaced as curate at Dewsbury in 1810, and whom he had also helped by taking some of his duties at Hartshead in 1810–11. See EJB 7.11.1841.
8. The Dixon family, sons and daughters of Mary and Martha's aunt Laetitia, née Taylor (1780–1842), and Abraham Dixon (1779–1850), a former 'foreign commission agent' in Leeds, now apparently making a precarious living in Belgium as an 'inventor'. The Dixons' Brussels house

was 11 rue de la Régence, not far from the pensionnat Heger to which CB and EJB went in 1842. CB was befriended especially by Mr Dixon's daughter Mary (?1809–97). See Gérin *CB* 213 and 220, and William Parson and William White, *Directory of the Borough of Leeds* (1830), 39.

9. *Life* i. 238 reads 'to real account'.
10. Patrick Brontë was born at Emdale, County Down, Ireland on 17.3.1777. He was admitted sizar at St John's College Cambridge on 1.10.1802—i.e. at the age of 25, CB's age when she wrote this letter.
11. *Life* i. 238 reads '*all* to get on'.

To Ellen Nussey, 17 October 1841

[Upperwood House, Rawdon]

Dear Nell

It's a cruel thing of you to be always upbraiding me when I am a trifle remiss or so in writing a letter—I see I <u>can't make</u> you comprehend that I have not quite as much time on my hands as Miss *?Walker[1] of Smithies Lane or Mrs Mary *Mills[2] I never neglect you on purpose I could not do it, you little, teazing, faithless wretch

The humour I am in is worse than words can describe—I have had a hideous dinner of some abominable spiced-up indescribable mess & it has exasperated me against the world at large.

So you are coming home are you? then don't expect me to write a long letter or indeed anything but the very shabbiest of notes—

I am not going to *Dewsbury-Moor[3]—at least as far as I can see at present—it was a decent friendly proposal on Miss *Wooler's part and cancels all or most of her little foibles in my estimation but *Dewsbury-Moor is a poisoned place to me[4]—besides I burn to go somewhere else—I think Nell I see a chance of getting to Brussels—Now, can I persuade you to consider that this is a matter still uncertain and therefore not to be talked of or communicated? Mary *Taylor advises me to this step, my own mind and feelings urge me—

I cannot write a word more I must send this instantly

[Unsigned]

MS Harvard H.E.W. 1.5.4. Envelope: BPM B.S. 104/1. W & S 122(part).
Address (envelope): Miss Ellen Nussey | Earnley Rectory | nr Chichester | Sussex
PM: (i) RAWDEN (ii) LEEDS | OC 17 | 1841 | F (iii) F | 18 OC 18 | 1841 (iv) CHICHESTER | OC 19 | 1841

1. MS may read 'Miss Haller'. If 'Walker' is correct, the reference might be to one of EN's Walker relatives, some of whom still lived locally. William Walker of Smithies Lane appears on the Electoral Registers of 1844 and 1847. EN herself was probably born in a house in Smithies Lane, Birstall.
2. In her 1844 diary EN records frequent visits from a Mrs Mills. She had been a valued servant of Ellen's Aunt Ann Nussey of Brookroyd. (EN *Diary* 1844.) The 1849 diary records her death at the age of 71 on 10 Mar. 1849. (EN *Diary* 1849.)

3. See the previous letter, n. 1.
4. In 1838 CB's intense depression had caused her to leave the school for a time, and she later recalled her 'Hypochondria' there. See EN 9.6.1838 and MW ?Nov./Dec. 1846.

To Ellen Nussey, [2 November 1841]

[Upperwood House]

Dear E. N!

Let us dismiss business matters first—and then quarrel like cat & dog on private concerns afterwards—Mrs *White has already five applications from ex-governesses under consideration—I believe she has nearly completed a bargain with one—It would therefore answer no good end to propose the lady you mention—had there been the remotest chance of success I would have done my possible[1] to oblige you—

Now let us begin to quarrel—in the first place I must consider whether I will commence operations on the Defensive or the Offensive—the Defensive I think—You say & I see plainly that your feelings have been hurt by an apparent want of confidence on my part—You heard from others of Miss *Wooler's overtures[2] before I communicated them to you myself this is true—I was deliberating on plans important to my future prospects & I never exchanged a letter with you on the subject—true again—This appears strange conduct to a friend near & dear—long known & never found wanting—most true—I cannot give you my <u>excuses</u> for this behaviour the word <u>excuse</u> implies confession of a fault & I do not feel that I have been in fault. The plain fact is I <u>was</u> not I <u>am</u> not now certain of my destiny—on the contrary I have been most uncertain—perplexed with contradictory schemes & proposals—my time—as I have often told you is fully occupied—yet I had many letters to write which it was absolutely necessary should be written—I knew it would avail nothing to write to you then to say I was in doubt & uncertainty—hoping this fearing that—anxious eagerly desirous to do what seemed impossible to be done. When I thought of you in that busy interval it was to resolve that you should know all when my way was clear & my grand end attained If I could Ellen I would always work in silence & obscurity & let my efforts be known only by their results—Miss *Wooler did most kindly propose that I should come to *Dewsbury *Moor & attempt to revive the school her sister[3] had relinquished—she offered me the use of her furniture for the consideration of her board[4]—at first I received the proposal cordially & prepared to do my utmost to bring about success—but a fire was kindled in my very heart which I could not quench[5]—I so longed to increase my attainments to become something better than I am—a glimpse of what I felt I shewed to you in ˋone ofˊ my former letters—only a glimpse—Mary *Taylor cast oil on the flames[6]—encouraged me & in her own strong energetic language heartened me on—I longed to go to Brussels—but how could I get? I wished for one at least of my Sisters to share the advantage with me I fixed on Emily[7]—she deserved the reward I knew—How could this point be managed?—In extreme excitement I wrote a letter home which carried the point—I made an appeal to Aunt for assistance which was answered by consent—Things are not settled Yet it is sufficient to say we have a chance of going for half a year—

*Dewsbury-*Moor is relinquished perhaps fortunately so it is an obscure & dreary place—not adapted for a school—In my secret soul I believe there is no cause to regret it—My plans for the future are bounded to this intention if I once get to Brussels—& if my health is spared I will do my best to make the utmost of every advantage that shall come within my reach—when the half year is expired I will do what I can—

You say Ellen you know my reasons for not alluding to the subject of Mr Vincent[8]—the only reason for such neglect of which I am conscious is—the extreme haste in which I wrote my last which made me forget much I had fully intended to say—I am glad Mr *Vincent has fairly & openly proposed—I do not know what to say about your refusal if he is a good—& clever man it seems a pity—for I believe it is better to marry to love than to marry for love—yet on the whole I am convinced you know best & can best decide what will suit your own feelings I greatly fear the assumed petulance of my last note was mistaken by you for reality—if so I must beware how I jest in future—When we two shall meet again God knows Believe me my dear Ellen though I was born in April the month [of] cloud & sunshine I am not changeful—my spirits are unequal & sometimes I speak vehemently & sometimes I say nothing at all—but I have a steady regard for you—& if you will let the cloud & shower only pass by without upbraiding—be sure the sun is always behind—obscured but still existing. Write & say all is forgiven I'm fit to cry

C B

MS HM 24429. W & S 123.
Address (integral): Miss Ellen Nussey | Earnley Rectory | nr Chichester | Sussex
PM: (i) RAWDEN (ii) LEEDS | NO 2 | 1841 | F (iii) C | 3 NO | 1841 (iv) CHICHE[STER] | NO— | 18—

1. My utmost. *OED* compares the French 'faire son possible', giving the date 1797 for the English usage.
2. See E. Branwell 29.9.1841 and EN 17.10.1841 and notes.
3. Eliza Wooler.
4. CB would arrange that meals should be provided for Miss Margaret Wooler, who would continue to live at but not be the head of the school.
5. cf. *3 Henry VI*, IV. viii. 7, and Isaiah 42: 3.
6. cf. Horace *Satires* II. iii. 21, 'Oleum adde camino'.
7. Emily, who had lived at home since about Mar. 1839, was to go to Brussels with CB in Feb. 1842.

8. cf. EN 3.1.1841 and HN 11.1.1841. CB had advised Ellen to 'examine' Mr Vincent well and to accept him if he was 'a decent fellow in the main', but to Henry she had stressed that EN was the best judge of the matter.

To Emily J. Brontë, ?7 November 1841

Upperwood House, Rawdon

Dear E. J.,

You are not to suppose that this note is written with a view of communicating any information on the subject we both have considerably at heart: I have written letters but I have received no letters in reply yet. Belgium is a long way off, and people are everywhere hard to spur up to the proper speed. Mary Taylor says we can scarcely expect to get off before January. I have wished and intended to write to both Anne and Branwell, but really I have not had time.

Mr. Jenkins I find was mistakenly termed the British Consul[1] at Brussels; he is in fact the English Episcopal clergyman.

I think perhaps we shall find that the best plan will be for papa to write a letter to him by and bye, but not yet. I will give an intimation when this should be done, and also some idea of what had best be said. Grieve not over Dewsbury Moor. You were cut out there to all intents and purposes, so in fact was Anne, Miss Wooler would hear of neither for the first half year.

Anne seems omitted in the present plan, but if all goes right I trust she will derive her full share of benefit from it in the end. I exhort all to hope. I believe in my heart this is acting for the best, my only fear is lest others should doubt and be dismayed. Before our half year in Brussels is completed, you and I will have to seek employment abroad. It is not my intention to retrace my steps home till twelve months, if all continues well and we and those at home retain good health.

I shall probably take my leave of Upperwood about the 15th or 17th of December. When does Anne talk of returning? How is she? What does W[illiam] W[eightman] say to these matters? How are papa and aunt, do they flag?[2] How will Anne get on with Martha?[3] Has W.W. been seen or heard of lately?[4] Love to all. Write quickly.—Good-bye.

C. Brontë.

I am well.

MS untraced. W & S 124.
Address: not in source.
PM: not in source.
Date: from source.
Text: *CBCircle* 91–2. W & S 124 reproduces *Shorter* 95, which looks like a slightly tidied up version of

CBCircle. This was used as the copy-text because its accidentals and use of initials for W. Weightman approximate more closely to CB's usual style than those in later versions.

1. See E. Branwell 29.9.1841 n. 7.
2. i.e. in their support for the Brussels school scheme.
3. Martha Brown (1828–80), the new housemaid, daughter of John and Mary Brown of Haworth. John Brown (1804–55), the Haworth sexton, was a friend of Branwell Brontë. Martha had probably run errands for the Brontës while Tabitha Aykroyd was being nursed after breaking her leg in Dec. 1836. 'Tabby' became increasingly lame, and as Anne Brontë noted in her Diary Paper on 30.7.1841, 'Tabby has left us, Martha Brown has come in her place.' Tabby had returned by May 1843, but Martha continued her service at the parsonage, taking the heavier share of the housework. See EN ?10.1.1842 n. 3.
4. The order of CB's two questions about Mr Weightman is odd. Possibly Shorter's text is corrupt. Mr Weightman took no baptismal services at Haworth after 26 Sept. until 18 Oct., but he was in Haworth both before and at the alleged date of this letter. He officiated at burials on 28 Oct., 3 and 6 Nov., and at a wedding on 9 Nov.

To Ellen Nussey, [?9 December 1841]

[Upperwood House, Rawdon]

My dear Ellen

I hear from Mary Taylor that you are come home[1] and also that you have been ill—if you are able to write comfortably—let me know the feelings that preceded your illness and also its effects—I fear you have had too much fatigue of body and anxiety of mind—I wish to see you—Mary T reports that your looks are much as usual I trust & believe this is but a temporary attack which will not return—

I understand your Mother has also been ill and that Mercy is not well—a sorrowful house for you to come home to I expect to get back to Haworth in the course of a fortnight or 3 weeks—I hope I shall then see you—I do not mean that I shall find my way to Brookroyd but that you will track out yours to Haworth—Do not urge your invitation my dear Ellen—unless your own capability for leaving home should become more unlikely than it is at present—It is really with an uneasy mind that I seem so often to hesitate to come when you call—'but' if it should appear in any way practicable I would rather you came to Haworth than I went to Brookroyd

My plans advance slowly and I am not yet certain where I shall go or what I shall do when I leave Upperwood—Brussels is still my promised land[2] but there is the wilderness of Time & Space to cross before I reach it—I am not likely I think to go to the Chateau de Kockleberg[3]—I have heard of a less expensive establishment

So far I had written when I received your letter—I was glad to get it—why don't you mention your illness I had intended to have got this note off two or three days past—but I am more straitened for time than ever just now—we have gone to bed at '12' & 1 o'clock during the last three nights & during the whole day I have not had a moment to myself—I must get this scrawl off to-day—or you will think me negligent—I have 20 things to tell you—I have not time—I have just heard that I must stay here a week or two longer[4]—Mr & Mrs White are going from home the new Governess that is to [be] has been[5] to see my plans &c.

My dear Ellen Good-bye—Believe [me in heart & soul your sincere friend][6]

[Signature cut off]

MS Harvard H.E.W. 1.5.4. W & S 125 (part, as 10 Dec.).
Address: not in MS.
PM: not in MS.
Annotation by EN in ink: 67 Dec 9—41.
Date: EN's annotation may be wrong. In EJB ?7.11.1841 CB hoped to be home on 15 or 17 Dec., i.e. only a week, not 'a fortnight or 3 weeks' after 9 Dec. The abridged and inaccurate text of *Shorter* 96 and W & S 125 is dated 10 Dec.

1. From Earnley Rectory.
2. For their sins the Israelites spent 40 years in the wilderness before they reached the 'promised land' of Canaan, 'a land that floweth with milk and honey'. (See Joshua 5: 6.) Related imagery recurs in CB's novels, e.g. in *The Professor* ch. 19, 176 and ch. 25, 248.
3. See EN ?4.5.1841 n. 8 and 7.8.1841 n. 3.
4. CB eventually reached home on Christmas Eve. (EN ?10.1.1842.)
5. MS reads 'to been has been'.
6. The original ending of the letter has been cut away, and these words are written by EN to replace it.

To Ellen Nussey, [?17 December 1841]

[Upperwood House, Rawdon]

My dear Ellen

I am yet uncertain when I shall leave *Upperwood but of one thing I am very certain when I do leave it I must go straight home—It is absolutely necessary that some definite arrangement should be commenced for our future plans before I go visiting anywhere—that I wish to see you I know—that I intend & hope to see you before long I also know—that you will at the first impulse accuse me of neglect I fear—that upon consideration you will acquit me I devoutly trust[1]—Dear Ellen Come to Haworth if you can—if you cannot, I will endeavour to come for a day at least to *Brookroyd—but do not depend on this—come to Haworth—I thank you for Mr J[enkins'] address[2]—you always think of other people's convenience however ill & afflicted you are yourself—how very much I wish to see you—you do not know—but if I were to go to *Brookroyd now—it would deeply disappoint those at home—I have some hopes of seeing Branwell at Xmas[3] & when I should be able to see him afterwards I cannot tell he has never been at home for the last 5 months.

Good night dear Ellen
C B

Miss Ellen Nussey

MS BPM Bon 167. Envelope: BPM B.S. 104/2. W & S 126.
Address (envelope): Miss Ellen Nussey | Brookroyd | Birstal | Leeds
PM: (i) RAWDEN (ii) LEEDS | DE ?19 | 18— | F
Annotation on envelope in pencil by EN: Dec<39> ' 41 | before leaving Rawden | Mrs G

1. CB's rhetoric echoes the dialogue in *Much Ado About Nothing* I. i. 229 f.; cf. also Falstaff's self-defence in *1 Henry IV*, II iv. 514 f. CB knew both plays well, as her quotations in her novels show: see *The Professor* appendix VII, 334.
2. See E. Branwell 29.9.1841 n. 7 and EJB ?7.11.1841. Mr Jenkins lived at 304 chaussée d'Ixelles, outside the walls of Brussels, beyond the Porte de Namur. (Gérin *CB* 200.) Evan Jenkins's nephew, Joseph Walker Jenkins, was a curate at Batley, the parish adjoining Birstall, and would have been able to give EN his uncle's address. cf. Abraham Dixon to Mary Dixon, 3.5.1842 from Brussels: 'It is possible Mr Jenkins will be in Yorkshire next month, on a visit to his brother at Pudsey, & nephew, the curate to Mr Cassel[s] at Batley.' (MS Leeds City Museum.)
3. BB was still the Clerk in Charge at Luddenden Foot station. He later deplored his life at this period as being one of 'grovelling carelessness . . . malignant yet cold debauchery, the determination to find how far mind could carry body without both being chucked into hell'. (BB to Francis H. Grundy, 22.5.1842; W & S 133.) Gérin assumes in *BB* ch. 14 that Branwell was already a 'mental and physical wreck' at this period; but Neufeldt points out that Branwell had poems published in the *Halifax Guardian* on 5 June and 14 Aug. 1841, soon after he moved to Luddenden Foot, and that he began to enter draft poems in a notebook, the longest being entitled 'The triumph of mind over body'. (Neufeldt *BBP* p. xlv.)

To Mercy Nussey, 17 December [1841]

[Upperwood house, Rawdon]

My dear Miss *Mercy

Though I am very much engaged I must find time to thank you for the kind and polite contents of your note I should act in the manner most consonant with my own feelings if I at once & without qualification accepted your invitation[1]—I do not however consider it advisable to indulge myself so far at present—When I leave Upperwood I must go straight home—whether I shall afterwards have time to pay a short visit to Brookroyd I do not yet know—circumstances must determine that—I would fain see Ellen at Haworth instead—our visitations are not shared with any shew of justice—it shocked me very much to hear of her illness—may it be the first & last time she ever experiences such an attack Ellen I fear has thought I neglected her—in not writing sufficiently long or frequent letters—it is a painful idea to me that she has had this feeling—it could not be more groundless—I know her value & I would not lose her affection—for any probable compensation I can imagine—Remember me to your Mother—I trust she will soon regain her health—

Believe me my dear Miss *Mercy
Yours sincerely
C Brontë

MS BPM B.S. 50. W & S 127.
Address (integral): Miss *Mercy *Nussey
PM: not in MS, presumably enclosed in the preceding letter.
1. Mercy Nussey was evidently housekeeping at Brookroyd in the absence of her elder sister Ann.

To Ellen Nussey, [?10 January 1842]

Haworth

My dear Ellen,

Will you write as soon as you get this and fix your own day for coming to Haworth. I got home on Christmas Eve. The parting scene between me and my late employers[1] was such as to efface the memory of much that annoyed me while I was there, but indeed, during the whole of the last six months they only made too much of me; [I did not deserve it.] Anne has rendered herself so valuable in her difficult situation, that they have entreated her to return to them if it be but for a short time.[2] I almost think she will go back, if we can get a good servant[3] who will do all our work. We want one about forty or fifty years old, good tempered, clean and honest. You shall hear all about Brussels, &c., when you come. Mr W[eightman] is still here; just the same as ever. I have a curiosity to see a meeting between you and him.[4] He will be again desperately in love, I am convinced. Come.

C. B.

MS untraced. W & S 128 as 10 Jan.
Address: not in source.
PM: not in source.
Date: as in source; but see note on text below.
Text: *Nussey* 96–7, with 'I did not deserve it' from *Life* i. 241. *Hours at Home* xi. 203 is dated 4 Jan., which may be right: it has minor punctuation variants and several omissions. W & S 128, based on *Shorter* 99, differs slightly in punctuation from *Nussey*.
1. Mr and Mrs John White. See EN 3.3.1841 n. 1 and 21.3.1841 n. 1.
2. Anne consented to return to her post as governess to the daughters of the Revd Edmund Robinson of Thorp Green, in spite of her strongly expressed dislike of the situation in July 1841, when she wished 'to change it for another'. (AB *Diary* 30.7.1841.) For the Robinsons see EN 2.4.1841 notes 1 and 2, and 7.8.41 postscript and n. 9.

3 Martha Brown, who had taken Tabitha Aykroyd's place, was only 13. See EJB ? 7.11.1841 n. 3. EJB noted in her Diary Paper for 30.7.1845: 'Tabby who was gone in our last paper [1841] is come back and has lived with us—two years and a half and is in good health—Martha who also departed is here too.'

4 For Mr Weightman and EN see EN end of June, 1840.

To Ellen Nussey, [20 January 1842]

[Haworth]

Dear Ellen

I cannot quite enter into your friend's[1] reasons for not permitting you to come to Haworth—but as it is at present—& in all human prohability will be for an indefinite time to come impossible for me to get to *Brookroyd—the balance of accounts is not so unequal as it might otherwise be—

We expect to leave England in less than three weeks[2]—but we are not yet certain as to the day as it will depend on the convenience of a French lady now in London Madame Marzials[3] under whose escort we are to sail. Our place of destination is changed Papa received an unfavourable account from Mr or rather Mrs *Jenkins[4] of the French Schools in Bruxelles—representing them as of an inferior caste in many respects—On further inquiry an institution in Lille in the north of France was highly recommended by Baptist Noël[5] & other clergymen—and to that place it is decided that we are to go. the terms are 50£ for each pupil for board & French alone—but a separate room will be allowed for this sum; without this indulgence they are something lower—I considered it kind in Aunt to consent to an extra sum for a separate room—we shall find it a great privelege in many ways—I regret the change from Brussels to Lille on many accounts chiefly that I shall not see Martha *Taylor—Mary has been indefatigably kind in providing me with information—she has grudged no labour & scarcely any expenses to that end—Mary's price is above rubies[6]—I have in fact two friends you & her stanch & true—in whose faith & sincerity I have as strong a belief as I have in the bible—I have bothered you both—you especially—I am bothering you now—but you always get the tongs & heap coals of fire upon my head[7]—

I have had letters to write lately to Brussels to Lille & to London—I have lots of chemises—night-gowns—pocket-handkerchiefs & pockets to make—beside clothes to repair—& I have been every week since I came home expecting to see Branwell[8] & he has never been able to get over yet—we fully expect him however next Saturday Under these circumstances how can I go 'a' visiting?—

Mrs *Tolson[9] has applied again the salary she offers is 40£—I send you Miss *Outhwaite's[10] letter on the subject you will be kind enough to return it—I shall not go of course you bother & tantalize one to death with talking of conversations by the fireside or between the blankets depend upon it we are not to have any such—for many a long month to come—I get an interesting impression of old-age upon my face & when you see me next I shall certainly wear caps & spectacles

Write long letters to me & tell me everything you can think of about Mr *Vincent[11] & everybody—your darling "his young reverence"[12] as you tenderly call him—is looking delicate & pale—poor thing don't you pity him? I do from my heart—when he is well & fat & jovial I never think of him—but when anything ails him I am always sorry—He sits opposite to *Anne at Church sighing softly—& looking out of the corners of his eyes to win her attention—& *Anne is so quiet, her look so downcast[13]—they are a picture—He would be the better of a comfortable wife like you to settle him you would settle him I believe—nobody else would

[Unsigned]

MS HM 24430. Envelope: BPM B.S. 104/2. W & S 129.
Address (envelope): Miss Ellen Nussey | Brookroyd | Birstal | Leeds
PM: (i) BRADFORD YORKS | JA 20 | 1842 (ii) *Bradford Yorks* | *Py Post* (iii) LEEDS | JA 20 | 1842
Annotation in pencil on envelope by EN: Jan 42 before going to Brussels | Mrs G | 5

1. Thus in MS; but CB means 'friends' ' in the plural, i.e. Ellen's relatives. cf. EN 28.10.1839 and n. 8.
2. CB and EJB eventually left England *en route* for Mme Heger's school in Brussels on 12 Feb. See the next letter, notes 1 and 2.
3. Not identified.
4. Wife of the British Chaplain in Brussels. See E. Branwell 29.9.1841 n. 7. Mrs Jenkins was to change her mind after further enquiries.
5. A leading Evangelical preacher. See EN ?14.8.1840 n. 8. CB's 'grand relatives' the Branwell Williams lived, or had lived, in London, where Noel was the minister at St John's Chapel, Bedford Row. In view of Eliza Williams's enthusiasm for him, the recommendation may have come through this family.
6. cf. Job 28: 18, 'for the price of wisdom is above rubies'.
7. Proverbs 25: 21–2.
8. See EN ?17.12.1841 n. 3. Branwell's failure to check the misdeeds of a peculating railway porter was to lead to his dismissal from his post at Luddenden Foot station at the end of Mar. 1842: his accounts were 'found deficient £11.1.7. He had been discharged in consequence and the amount deducted from his quarter's salary'. A 'Memorial' from 'certain Merchants, Millowners &c, residing at Luddenden Foot, interceding for the re-employment of Mr. Brontë' was rejected. (Captain Law's report to the Directors of the Manchester and Leeds Railway, 4 and 11 Apr. 1842; PRO File Vol. H. No. 27 fos. 174–5, 184.) Through his friend F. H. Grundy, he then tried but failed to obtain work abroad, hoping 'from the few who are generally found willing to take them, and from so many Railways being contemplated, in France &c; situations abroad would be more attainable'. (Letter to F. H. Grundy 9.6.1842, BPM MS B.S. 138; part of incomplete W & S 134.)
9. Possibly the wealthy Mrs Tolson who presented the east window of Bradford Parish Church in memory of her husband Richard Tolson in the 1860s.
10. Anne Brontë's godmother. See PB to Mrs Franks 28.4.1831 n. 4.
11. EN had refused Mr Vincent's proposal of marriage. See EN 30.4.1840 n. 5 and 2.11.1841.
12. William Weightman.
13. This behaviour has encouraged the idea of a mutual affection between Anne Brontë and

William Weightman, for which there is perhaps further evidence in Anne's poem, 'I will not mourn' written in Dec. 1842 soon after Mr Weightman's death on 6 Sept. 1842: death has frowned away

That angel smile that late so much
Could my fond heart rejoice;
And he has silenced by his touch
The music of thy voice. (Chitham *ABP* 87.)

Chitham's discussion of the relationship in *ABP* 15–19 may act as a corrective to Gérin's assumption that Agnes Grey's 'boundless love' for Mr Weston was precisely Anne's feeling for Mr Weightman shortly before his death. (Gérin *AB* 182–8.)

Mary and Martha Taylor and Charlotte Brontë to Ellen Nussey, March-April 1842

[Brussels;[1] March]

My dear Ellen

Do not think that I have forgotten you because I have so many things to do that I can no more write to you now & then, than I used to be able to run down to Brookroyd every other day. As for miss Brontë,[2] I have not seen her since I came here so you may judge that I do not spend my time just as 'I' like. Before breakfast I draw, after breakfast I practise, say German lessons, & draw, after dinner walk out, learn German & draw go to bed sometimes at nine o'clock heartily tired & without a word to throw at any one. If it were not Sunday I could not write to you fortunately the weather is too wet for us to go to church so I have time for everything. In the enumeration of my employments I have forgotten the writing of French compositions. This is the plague of Koekleberg schoolroom. "Avez vous fait votre composition"? "Oui mais je ne puis pas—put a beginning to it." Pouvez "vous m'aider"?[3] Silence! What's the french for invite? "It is eight hours! when shall we have the tea? How many years have you? this is a french girl talking english—the Germans make an equal mess of both languages the german teacher worst of all. I must now tell you of our teachers Miss Evans is a well educated English woman[4] who has been eight years in France whom I should like very well if she were not so outrageously civil that I every now & then suspect her of hypocrisy. The french teacher we have not yet got so I can tell you nothing of her except that she is coming in a few days (which she has been doing ever since Christmas). Madame Ferdinand the music mistress is [a] little thin, black, talkative, French woman. Monsieur her husband a tall broadshouldered man with a tremendous mouth who 'is' constantly telling his pupils that the voice has but a very little hole to get out at & that there are both tongue & teeth to interrupt it on its road & that the orifice ought by all means to be opened as wide as possible—

Then comes M Gauné, a little black old Frenchman with his history written on his face & a queer one it is—I speak either of the face or the history—which you please. He has a good appreciation of the literature of his own country & speaks some curious English. I think him a good master—Mons. Huard—the drawing master is a man of some talent, a good judgement, & an intelligible manner of teaching he would be my favourite if he did not smell so of bad tobacco. Last & least is Mons. ?Sacré not that he appears to me to want sense & being a dancing master he ought not to want manner—but he has the faults of a french puppy & they make it advisable never to exchange more words with him than the everlasting "Oui Monsieur—Non Monsieur"—Martha is considerably improved I can't put out my feet—"Allongez!—plus long![5] more! All our awkwardnesses however are thrown into the shade by those of a belgian girl who does not know right foot from left & obstinately dances with her mouth open. There is also a Mon. Hisard, who makes strange noises in the back school room teaching gymnastics to some of the girls & I had nearly forgotten a grinning, dirty, gesticulating, belgian who teaches Cosmosgraphy & says so often "Ainsi donc! c'est bien compris! n'est-ce pas?"[6] that he has earned himself the names of ainsi donc & Mr Globes. Amongst all this noise & bustle we have every possible opportunity of learning—if we choose. I must except French in which we make very little progress owing to the want of a governess.[7] There are more English & Germans than French girls in the school consequently very little french is spoken & that little is bad. I will write no more till I have seen the Brontës.

March—26th. 1842.

Dear Ellen—Mary Taylor says I am to write to you on this side of her letter—You will have heard that we have settled at Brussels instead of Lille—I think we have done well—we have got into a very good school—and are considerably comfortable—just now we are at Kokleberg spending the day with Mary & Martha Taylor—to us such a happy day—for one's blood requires a little warming—it gets cold with living amongst strangers[8]—You are not forgotten as you feared you would be I will write another letter sometime & tell you how we are placed & amongst what sort of people— <I should be> Mary & Martha are not changed I have a Catholic faith in them that they cannot change—Good-bye—remember me to your Mother & Mercy write to me Ellen as soon as you can

C Brontë

April 4th 1842

Dear Ellen

I am going to add my bit to this to this [*sic*] newspaper which you are to have sometime but no one knows when. We have had holiday for the last ten days & I don't feel at all inclined to begin lessons again. I am tired of this everlasting

German & long for the day after tomorrow when our new French Mistress will come & we shall continue our French—I have the cousin of the Mr Jenkins[9] who took tea with my brother Joe at Brookroyd—sat by me, chattering like a magpie, & hoping it may be true that her cousin will come to Brussels before July. Mary is on the other side of me staring into a german dictionary, & looking as fierce as a tiger. There is a very sweet, ladylike, elegant girl here, who has undertaken to civilize our dragon, & she is actually improving a little under her hands? Would you like to be cracking your head with French & german? by the way, you must excuse me if I send you some unintelligible english for in attempting to acquire other languages I have almost forgotten the little I knew of my own;

But I believe we are going to have prayers so I must put this away, but I will write some more some day. Good night

Martha Taylor

Lest you should think yourself forgotten I take the first opportunity of sending you a letter keep up your spirits—look forward to crossing the channel—sometime—Send me particular news of your Mother by my brothers[10] & any thing else you may have to say.

April 5/42 Mary Taylor

& send me news about every one that I know. It is all the fashion for gentlemen to paint themselves,[11] shall I send you some paint for George.[12] When you see my brother Joe have the kindness to pull him his hair right well for me & give John a good pinch.

Remember me to your Mother & Sisters & believe me to be still
Martha Taylor

MS Pierpont Morgan MA 2696. W & S 130.
Address: not in MS.
PM: not in MS.
Dates: CB's addition to Mary Taylor's letter was written on Easter Saturday, 26 Mar.; the Sunday on which Mary wrote the first section may have been that of the preceding weekend, 20 Mar., but external evidence is lacking.

1. The Brontës' change from Lille to Brussels was influenced by Mrs Jenkins's recommendation of Mme Zoë Heger's school in the rue Isabelle. Mrs Gaskell writes: 'I am not aware of all the circumstances which led to the relinquishment of the Lille plan . . . [Mrs Jenkins] at length, after some discouragement in her search, heard of a school which seemed in every respect desirable. There was an English lady, who had long lived in the Orleans family, amidst the various fluctuations of their fortunes, and who, when the Princess Louise [Louise Marie, daughter of King Louis Philippe of France] was married to King Leopold, accompanied her to Brussels, in the capacity of reader. This lady's granddaughter was receiving her education at the pensionnat of Madame Héger; and so satisfied was the grandmother with the kind of instruction given, that she named the establishment, with high encomiums, to Mrs Jenkins; and, in consequence, it was decided that, if the terms suited, Miss Brontë and Emily should proceed thither.' (*Life* i. 244–5).
2. Mary Taylor had travelled with the Brontës and then joined Martha at the Château de

Koekelberg. (See *Stevens* appendix D for the school, and plate 6, opp. 144, for a painting of the Château in 1887.) Mrs Gaskell explains that 'Mr. Brontë determined to accompany his daughters. Mary and her brother [Joseph], who were experienced in foreign travelling, were also of the party.' (*Life* i. 245.) Emily Brontë notes in her Diary Paper of 30.7.1845 that their journey began on 8 Feb. For their crossing to Ostend on 12 Feb. and their subsequent movements see Gérin *CB* 181–7, and cf. CB's fictional version in *The Professor* ch. 7. Lucy Snowe's journey in *Villette* ch. 6 draws partly on CB's second journey to Brussels in 1843.

3. 'Have you done your composition?' 'Yes but I cannot . . . Can you help me?'
4. Not traced. The number of specialist teachers available at Mme Goussaert's Koekleberg school helps to account for her high fees. Mme Heger also employed visiting teachers, but as M. Heger told Mrs Gaskell, 'on receipt of a letter from Charlotte, making very particular inquiries as to the possible amount of what are usually termed "extras," he and his wife were so much struck by the simple earnest tone of the letter, that they said to each other:—"These are the daughters of an English pastor, of moderate means, anxious to learn with an ulterior view of instructing others, and to whom the risk of additional expense is of great consequence. Let us name a specific sum, within which all expenses shall be included." ' (*Life* i. 245.)
5. 'Stretch them out further!—further!'
6. 'So there you are! It's all clear! isn't it?'
7. A teacher.
8. Mr and Mrs Jenkins, who also invited the Brontë sisters to visit them but found them shy and awkward, would count as strangers, though obviously CB refers principally to the Belgians. For the 'coldness', cf. the recurrent cold images in *Villette*.
9. Probably the Revd Joseph Walker Jenkins, curate to the Revd Andrew Cassels at Batley, near Birstall. (See Pigot's *Directory* for 1841, under 'Dewsbury'.) He was the son of the Revd David Jenkins of Pudsey, and nephew of the Revd Evan Jenkins of Brussels. The Subscription Books of the Diocese of Ripon record that J. W. Jenkins, who had attended St Bees College, Cumberland, was ordained priest on 7 Jan. 1843.
10. John and Joseph Taylor travelled frequently to and from the Continent in the course of their trade as woollen merchants. For John Taylor see EN 7.8.1841 n. 4. Joseph Taylor (?1816–57) aroused CB's lively interest, perplexing her by his mixture of kindness and worldliness and exasperating her by his various flirtations. He is said to have been a 'clever practical & theoretical chemist'. (*BST* 15. 79. 309.) CB used some of his traits in her portrayal of Martin Yorke in *Shirley*.
11. To use cosmetics, a practice scorned as typical of a dandy or a 'foreigner'. cf. Michael Sadleir's description of the English dandies of the 1820s and 1830s such as Lord Normanby, pilloried by William Maginn in 1835 as a 'painted, curled, oiled and padded gentleman'. (Michael Sadleir, *Blessington- d'Orsay* (1933), 107.)
12. George Nussey, whom the Taylors knew well as Ellen's brother and as a fellow wool-merchant.

To Ellen Nussey, [May 1842]

[Brussels]

Dear Ellen

It is the fashion now a days for persons to send sheets of blank paper[1] instead of letters to their friends in foreign parts—

I was twenty-six years old a week or two since—and at that ripe time of life I am a schoolgirl—a complete school-girl and on the whole very happy in that capacity It felt very strange at first to <be under > 'submit to' authority instead of exercising it—to obey orders instead of giving them—but I like that state of things—I returned to it with the 'same' avidity that a cow that has long been kept on dry hay returns to fresh grass—don't laugh at my simile—it is natural to me to submit and very unnatural to command

This is a large school[2] in which there are about 40 externes or day-pupils and 12 pensionnaires or boarders—Madame Heger[3] the head is a lady of precisely the same cast of mind degree of cultivation & quality of character as Miss Catherine Wooler[4]—I think the severe points are a little softened because she has not been disappointed & consequently soured—in a word—she is a married instead of a maiden lady—there are 3 teachers in the school Mademoiselle Blanche—mademoiselle Sophie & Mademoiselle Marie[5]—The two first have no particular character—one is an old maid & the other will be one—Mademoiselle Marie is talented & original—but of repulsive & arbitrary manners which have made the whole school except myself and Emily her bitter enemies—no less than seven masters attend to teach the different branches of education—French drawing—music, singing, writing, arithmetic, and German.

All in the house are Catholics except ourselves one other girl[6] and the gouvernante[7] of Madam's children—an Englishwoman in rank something between a lady's maid and a nursery governess[8] the difference in Country & religion makes a broad line of demarcation between us & all the rest we are completely isolated in the midst of numbers—yet I think I am never <quite> unhappy—my present life is so delightful so congenial to my [own] nature compared to that of a Governess—my time constantly occupied passes too rapidly—hitherto both Emily and I have had good health & therefore we have been able to work well. There is one individual of whom I have not yet spoken Monsieur Heger[9] the husband of Madame—he is professor of Rhetoric a man of power as to mind but very choleric & irritable in temperament—a little, black, ugly being with 'a face' that varies in expression, sometimes he borrows the lineaments of an insane Tom-cat—sometimes those of a delirious Hyena—occasionally—but very seldom he discards these perilous attractions and assumes an air not above a hundred degrees removed from what you would call mild & gentleman-like he is very angry with me just at present because I have written a translation which he chose to stigmatize as peu correct—not because it was particularly so in reality but because he happened to be in a bad humour when he read it—he did not tell me so—but wrote the accusation in the margin of my book[10] and asked <me how it> in brief stern phrase how it happened that my compositions were always better than my translations—adding that the thing seemed to him inexplicable the fact is some weeks ago in a high-flown[11] humour he forbade me to use either dictionary or grammar—in translating the most difficult English compositions into French this makes the task rather arduous—& compels me every now and then to introduce[12] an English word which nearly plucks the eyes out of his head when he sees it.

Emily and he don't draw well together at all—when he is very ferocious with me I cry—& that sets all things straight.

Emily works like a horse and she has had great difficulties 'to contend with'—far greater than I have had <the of> indeed those who come to a French school for instruction ought previously to have acquired a considerable knowledge of the French language[13]—<for the> otherwise they will lose a great deal of time for the course of instruction is adapted to natives & not to foreigners and in these large[14] establishments they will not change their ordinary course for one or two strangers—the few private lessons that monsieur Heger has vouchsafed to give us are I suppose to be considered a great favour & I can perceive they have already excited much spite & jealousy in the school—

You will abuse this letter for being short I daresay, and there are a hundred things which I wish to tell you but I have not time.[15] 'Do write to me and cherish Christian charity in your heart!' Brussels is a beautiful city—the Belgians hate the English—their <moral> external morality is more rigid than ours—to lace the stays without any handkerchief on the neck[16] is considered a disgusting piece of indelicacy—Remember me to Mercy & your Mother, and believe me, my dear Ellen[17]—Yours, sundered by the sea,

C Brontë

MS Law-Dixon W & S 131.
Address: not in source.
PM: not in source.
Annotation by EN: Mrs G Brussels —42
Date: conjectured from CB's reference to her 26th birthday (21 Apr.) 'a week or two since'. Hatfield notes '5?' [May] in his copy of *Shorter* (BPM).
Text: based on a transcript by M. G. Christian, who saw the original pencilled MS in the Law-Dixon Collection. Where the present text follows W & S 131 the MGC reading is given in the notes below. W & S 131, slightly fuller than *Life* i. 255–8, has several obvious misreadings and omissions, and a more formal punctuation system than is usual in CB's MSS.

1. W & S 131, like *Shorter* 103, reads 'shoals of blank paper'. There had been some coolness between EN and CB since EN's failure to visit Haworth in Jan.
2. The school was an early 19th-cent. building on the site of the 17th-cent. mansion of the Guild of Arbalétriers, acquired by Mme Heger in 1830. Its high buildings and enclosed garden and playground form the setting for the greater part of *The Professor* and *Villette*. See Gérin *CB* 187–9, Victor Tahon *La Rue Isabelle et le jardin des arbalétriers* (Brussels, 1912) and Fraser *CB*, photographs opp. 181, 340. For Mme Heger's prospectus, see p. 287.
3. Claire Zoë Heger, née Parent (1804–90), daughter of a French emigré who had fled to Brussels in 1789. Her school at 32 rue d'Isabelle was highly regarded. A 'French lady resident in Brussels' told Mrs Gaskell that Mme Heger had 'quelque chose de froid et de compassé dans son maintien' (something cold and formal in her demeanour) but was nevertheless beloved and appreciated by her pupils. (*Life* i. 252.) Her son Paul remembered her as 'douce et d'une grande fermeté: elle n'eut d'autre orientation dans toute sa vie que de créer du bonheur autour d'elle'. (She was gentle and very firm and her one aim throughout her life was to create happiness around her. See *BST* 17. 90. 374.) Physically attractive, with blue eyes and auburn hair, she married M. Constantin Heger in Sept. 1836. For more details, see Gérin *CB* 189–94. Some of her

traits are embodied in Mlle Zoraïde Reuter in *The Professor* and Madame Modeste Maria Beck in *Villette*.

4. Katherine Harriet Wooler (1796–1884). See Mrs Franks early May 1831 n. 6. EN recollected that she imposed a fine for 'late talking' on several pupils, including CB, at Roe Head. (EN 'Reminiscences'; see Appendix, p. 592.) She was also rather narrow-minded: in 1843 Mary Taylor, writing to EN from Germany where she was earning her living by teaching English to German 'lads', commented 'Miss C. Wooler has cut me dead.' (MT to EN 25. 6. 1843; *Stevens* 46.)
5. For CB's later opinion of these teachers see EN 29.5.1843. Mlle Sophie was well disposed towards CB, and her affectionate farewell letter to CB mentions 'l'amitié que vous m'avez toujours témoignée' (the friendship you have always shown me: Mlle Sophie to CB, 17.12.1843). The other two teachers were acridly portrayed in *Villette* as a 'corrupt' Parisienne, Zélie St Pierre, and an avaricious teacher 'not yet twenty-five'. See e.g. ch. 14. In *The Professor* the Parisian teacher Mlle Zéphyrine is 'perfidious, mercenary and dry-hearted'. (Ch. 12.) See Gérin *CB* 252–3, 403–4.
6. Maria Miller, later Mrs W. P. Robertson; said to be 'fashionable, dashing and worldly' and allegedly the prototype of Ginevra Fanshawe in *Villette*. See Gérin *CB* 208 and the obituary of Frances Wheelwright in *BST* 5. 23. 27 f. CB wrote to Laetitia Wheelwright on 16.6.1852: 'I return that most precious document—the letter of Maria Miller. Selfish indeed is the policy which has dictated it—worldly the adroitness with which the suggestion has been carried out.' (W & S 775.)
7. Martha Trotman. See *BST* 11. 59. [249].
8. MGC reads 'or a nursery governess . . . congenial to my <esn> nature'.
9. Constantin Georges Romain Heger (1809–96), a teacher at the Athénée Royal who also gave lessons in literature and rhetoric at his wife's school. CB was to become deeply attached to him, and used many of his traits in creating the talented, vehement, and temperamental M. Paul Emanuel of *Villette*. See the Biographical Notes.
10. 'Devoirs' by EJB and CB survive, with M. Heger's marginal corrections and comments. For examples of these, and for his own account of his teaching methods, see *Life* i. 258–66, ch. 11. Christine Alexander gives a list of the titles and locations of CB's Devoirs in her *Bibliography*, 179–91. See also Sue Lonoff, 'Charlotte Brontë's Belgian Essays: The Discourse of Empowerment', *Victorian Studies* (Indiana, 1989), xxxii, 387–409.
11. MGC reads 'bright-flower'.
12. MGC reads 'to entertain an'.
13. Mrs Gaskell writes, 'M. Héger's account is that they knew nothing of French. I suspect they knew as much (or as little), for all conversational purposes, as any English girls do, who have never been abroad, and have only learnt the idioms and pronunciation from an Englishwoman.' (*Life* i. 252–3.) CB had read French novels as a 'substitute' for conversation: see EN 20.8.1840.
14. MGC reads 'those large'.
15. MGC reads 'I cannot'.
16. A ladylike term for the upper part of the bosom. cf. the description of an evening dress of 1797, worn with a 'Blue enamelled anchor set with diamonds, suspended upon the neck by a purple velvet riband'. (Quoted by R. W. Chapman in his edition of Jane Austen, *Sense and Sensibility*, Oxford, 1933, [387] and frontispiece.) See also Clarendon *JE* 61 and note.
17. MGC omits 'and believe me, my dear Ellen—'.

Madame Heger's Prospectus[1]

MAISON D'ÉDUCATION
Pour les jeunes Demoiselles,
Sous la direction
DE MADAME HEGER-PARENT,
Rue d'Isabelle, 32, à Bruxelles.

Cet établissement est situé dans l'endroit le plus salubre de la ville.

Le cours d'instruction, basé sur la Religion, comprend essentiellement la Langue Française, l'Histoire, l'Arithmétique, la Géographie, l'Écriture, ainsi que tous les ouvrages à l'aiguille que doit connaître une demoiselle bien élevée.

La santé des élèves est l'objet d'une surveillance active: les parents peuvent se reposer avec sécurité sur les mesures qui ont été prises à cet égard dans l'établissement.

Le prix de la pension est de 650 francs, celui de la demi-pension est de 350 francs, payables par quartiers et d'avance. Il n'y a d'autres frais accessoires, que les étrennes des domestiques.

Il n'est fait aucune déduction pour le temps que les élèves passent chez elles dans le courant de l'année. Le nombre des élèves étant limité, les parents qui désireraient reprendre leurs enfants, sont tenus d'en prévenir la directrice trois mois d'avance.

Les leçons de musique, de langues étrangères, etc., etc., sont au compte des parents.

Le costume des pensionnaires est uniforme.

La directrice s'engage à répondre à toutes les demandes qui pourraient lui être adressées par les parents, relativement aux autres détails de son institution.

OBJETS A FOURNIR:

Lit complet, bassin, aiguière et draps de lit.

Serviettes de table.

Une malle fermant à clef.

Un couvert d'argent.

Un gobelet.

Si les élèves ne sont pas de Bruxelles, on leur fournira un lit garni, moyennant 34 francs par an.

Mme Heger's Prospectus:[1] *Translation*

Establishment for the education of young ladies
under the direction of
Madame Heger-Parent, 32 rue d'Isabelle, Brussels.

This establishment is situated in the healthiest part of the town.

The curriculum, founded on religious principles, basically comprises French language, History, arithmetic, geography and writing, as well as all the skills in needlework which a well-brought-up young lady requires.

The pupils' health is diligently supervised; parents can rely with confidence on the steps which have been taken with regard to health in the establishment.

The price of full board is 650 francs, that of half-board 350 francs, payable quarterly in advance. There are no extra charges apart from [New Year] gifts to the servants.

No deduction is made for the time pupils spend at their homes in the course of the year. Since the number of pupils is limited, parents who wish to withdraw their children must notify the directress three months in advance.

Lessons in music and foreign languages etc. are at the parents' expense.

The pupils' dress is uniform.

The directress promises to reply to all enquiries which parents may make of her about the other details of her establishment.

ARTICLES TO BE PROVIDED:

Bed and bedstead, washbowl, ewer, and sheets.

Table napkins.

A lockable trunk.

Silver fork and spoon.

A cup.

If pupils do not live in Brussels, a bed and bedlinen will be provided at a charge of 34 francs per annum.

1. There are copies of the prospectus in BPM, and it is reproduced in Phyllis Bentley, *The Brontës and their World* (1969), 74. The BPM S. 2611 copy has two official stamps and the handwritten date 1842 with the initials 'S. A. W.', for Sarah Ann Wheelwright (b. 7. 10. 1834), one of Emily Brontë's piano pupils.

To Ellen Nussey, [?July 1842]

[Brussels]

Dear Ellen

I began seriously to think you had no particular intention of writing to me again[1]—however let us have no reproaches, thank you for your letter.

I consider it doubtful whether I shall come home in September or not—Madame Heger has made a proposal for both me and Emily to stay another half year—offering to dismiss her English master and take me as English teacher—also to employ Emily some part of each day <as> in teaching music[2] to a certain number of the pupils—for these services we are to be allowed to continue our <education> 'studies' in French and German—and to have board &c without paying for it—no salaries however are offered—the proposal is kind and in a great selfish city like Brussels and a great selfish school containing nearly ninety pupils (boarders & day-pupils included) implies a degree of interest which demands gratitude in return—I am inclined to accept it—what think you?

Your letter set my teeth on edge—I can but half divine the signification of a great part of it but what I guess makes me wish to know all you must speedily write again and explain yourself—

I don't deny that I sometimes wish to be in England or that I have brief attacks of home-sickness—but on the whole I have borne a very valiant heart so far—and I have been happy in Brussels because I have always been fully occupied with the employments that I like—Emily is making rapid progresse in French, German, Music and Drawing—Monsieur & Madame Heger begin to recognise the valuable points of her character under her singularities.

If the national character of the Belgians is to be measured by the character of most of the girls[3] in this school, it is a character singularly cold, selfish, animal and inferior[4]—they are besides very mutinous and difficult for the teachers to manage—and their principles are rotten to the core—we avoid them—which is not difficult to do—as we have the brand of Protestantism and Anglicism[5] upon us

People talk of the danger which protestants expose themselves to in going to reside in Catholic countries[6]—and thereby running the chance of changing their faith—my advice to all protestants who are tempted to do anything so besotted as turn Catholic—is to walk over the sea on to the continent—to attend mass sedulously for a time—to note well the mum[m]eries[7] thereof—also the idiotic, mercenary, aspect of <u>all</u> the priests—& <u>then</u> if they are still disposed to consider Papistry in any other light than a most feeble childish piece of humbug let them turn papists at once that's all—I consider Methodism,

<Dissenterism,> Quakerism & the extremes of high & low Churchism[8] foolish but Roman Catholicism beats them all.

At the same time allow me to tell you that there are some Catholics[9]—who are as good as any christians can be to whom the bible is a sealed book and much better than scores of Protestants <Don't be alarmed because I say my prayers before>

Give my love to your Mother & *Mercy—believe me present occasionally in spirit when absent in flesh[10]

C B

MS HM 24431. W & S 137.
Address (integral): E Nussey [This letter, which is in pencil, was folded small and was no doubt enclosed in a packet of letters to England, to be taken by a friend travelling from Brussels.]
PM: none.
Annotation by EN: Brussels—42
Date: towards the end of the first half-year in Brussels, as para. 2 implies.

1. Martha Taylor had returned for a visit to England on 8 May and was in Leeds on 22 June 1842, when she wrote to EN, 'I will tell you all about Miss Bront[ës] & my Sister when I see you.' (MS Texas; *Stevens* letter 3.) Perhaps Martha's visit to EN, planned for Thursday 30 June, had encouraged Ellen to renew contact with CB. (Martha Taylor to EN 28.6.18[42], MS Berg; *Stevens* letter 4 as 24 June.)
2. See M. Heger's letter to PB of 5.11.1842, where he explains that Emily was about to receive piano lessons from the best teacher in Belgium. Emily already had 'de petites élèves', three sisters, one of whom she taught during play hours so as not to curtail her own school hours. (C. K. Shorter, on the authority of CB's friend Laetitia Wheelwright. See *CBCircle* 111.)
3. cf. CB's harsh portrayal of pensionnat pupils in *The Professor* and *Villette*.
4. Terms deriving from the then popular pseudo-science of phrenology; cf. the Belgian pupils in *The Professor* ch. 7, whose 'intellectual faculties were generally weak, their animal propensities strong'. (67 and 274 n.)
5. Presumably 'Englishness'.
6. cf. CB's strictures on Catholics in *The Professor* chs. 12 and 17, and the more complex treatment of Catholicism in *Villette*.
7. cf. vol. ii, EN 24.6.1851, where CB finds a confirmation by Cardinal Wiseman 'impiously theatrical'.
8. cf. EN 7.4.1840, 'my conscience will not let me be either a Puseyite or a Hookist'.
9. In *Villette* ch. 42 M. Paul Emanuel, who is based on M. Heger, is singled out for similar praise.
10. A recurrent idea in the epistles of St Paul: e.g. 1 Corinthians 5: 3.

Mary Taylor to Ellen Nussey, ?July 1842[1]

[Brussels]

Dear Ellen

It is very fortunate that you did not quarrel with the first half of your letter to such a point as to put it absolutely out of the world as I should thereby have lost very considerably, as I think it the best half of the two.

The lady who resides at some place illegible, had a daughter here named Isabella Simpson[2] a very superior girl, but she has left & I shall probably never see her any more. As to what you say about reading, I think you are quite in the right to read all that falls into your hands; improving yourself does not consist in cramming your head with good sayings out of good books; you can never live exclusively with good people or read exclusively good works you ought therefore to get into the habit of exercising your judgement on every thing, book, word, or action that falls in your way—beginning with a certain letter that you happen to be reading. There are two mistakes in the opinion you express as to the superiority of one sex over the other. 1st superiority does not consist in book learning & for proof I would take your opinion on almost any subject in preference to your brother Joshua's[3] though he no doubt has read as much as you & I put together, & a little bit of Charlotte included.

You will see by Charlotte's letter[4] that you are not likely to have your heart rejoiced by her presence I am sorry for your sake but not for any other reason. I intend to follow her example myself as speedily as possible; & sincerely hope I have bid adieu to your confounded "patrie" (my own though it be) for ever & a day. The stones will turn another side towards me when I <u>do</u> come back again & if any thing looks at me with its old face I'll knock its teeth down its throat.—Always excepting Ellen Nussey who may look at me with any face she likes. I except also the Carrs[5] who have been very kind to Martha & who knew my Father. I except also Mrs. Nussey, Mrs. Cockhill & Hannah[6] & of all the rest of Birstall parish I can buy the affection—when I am rich enough.

Where in the name of the grand dieu de la foudre[7] (a Koekleberg expression) (it means Jupiter) did you find or steal the description of New Zealand?[8] I never <u>knew</u> anything about the country—which however does not prevent my having described it in some overflow of poetic frensy—if this be the case pray refer me to the volume of my works in which it is to be found—or at least mention <ed> the date of the night on which I dreamed it—

What do you think of Germany[9] instead of New Zealand? I have heard they are nice & savage there too—The few specimens we have here are tamed the[y] still however indulge in certain barbarous habits, such as eating enormously with their mouths open putting both elbows on the table to guard their plate wearing seventeen petticoats (more or less) speaking the truth in the silliest manner possible even to their own disadvantage. Very different are the dapper frenchmen & mincing[10] french women whom we English have the discrimination to imitate. They practise civility ie tell lies till it is only the very wise ones among them that know what the truth is, & they take good care not to tell it.—dieu de la foudre, what's my paper done for?

Adieu My dear Ellen you are as near to me or nearer than when I could see you every day

Mary Taylor.

MS Texas. W & S 138.
Address: not in MS.
PM: not in MS.

1. The absence of letters from CB between July and 10 Nov. 1842 means that letters from Mary Taylor and from Branwell Brontë are the main sources of information about CB and her family for this period. One letter was written by CB 3 weeks before 10 Nov., but it has apparently not been preserved. See EN 10.11.1842.
2. Isabella Simpson's name does not recur in the surviving correspondence of MT or EN, or in EN's diaries, in the 1840s. The John Simpson who took EN's dog Flossy home for her from Hathersage in ?1845 was perhaps a servant. (EN to Mary Gorham, letter 3 in BPM Gorham Collection.)
3. The Revd Joshua Nussey MA (1798–1871). See EN 24.8.1838 n. 4 and 2.10.1838 n. 5.
4. The preceding letter may have been enclosed with Mary Taylor's.
5. Mrs Grace Carr (?1775–1863), widow of the Gomersal solicitor Charles Carr I (d. 1832) and her family. The Carrs were related by marriage to the Nusseys.
6. The widowed Mrs Hannah Cockill (1784–1856) and her daughter Hannah G. Cockill (1810–93) who, with her sisters Sarah (1812–96) and Elizabeth (1813–54) kept a school at Oakwell Hall, Birstall from about 1838 to 1852. (*BST* 17. 88. 210–13.) See also EN ?10. 8. 1844 n. 6.
7. Literally the 'great god of thunder'.
8. Mary's brother William Waring Taylor had sailed to New Zealand on the 'Martha Ridgway' on 7. 11. 1841 and had reached Wellington in Apr. 1842, but Mary could not have heard of his experiences there by July 1842. See *BST* 15. 79. 314–22 and EJB 2.4.1841. For the idea that native Australasians were 'savages' cf. Harriet Martineau, 'Homes Abroad' ch. 7 (No. 10 of *Illustrations of Political Economy* (1832–4), repr. in *Popular Tales* (1862)).
9. Mary went to Germany at the end of 1842 and stayed until Apr. 1844. See the next letter.
10. W & S 138 reads 'amusing', *Stevens* letter 7 'assuming'. The handwriting is difficult to decipher.

Mary Taylor to Ellen Nussey, shortly before 24 September 1842

[Brussels]

Dear Ellen

I did not write to you by Joe because I had two other letters to write during the busy time he staid with us. I thank it very likely however that you will get this letter before Joe arrives[1] as there is no knowing where he will run about to, before he set[s] off home.

I thank you for your chain[2]—I will wear it the moment I want one, & will always hold it ready, for that occasion. I even have some idea of cutting a sly hole in the one I now wear in order to get at this one so much the sooner.

I thank you next for writing to me; to find the same hearty old English expressions of kindness that I know as old friends.—There are plenty of goods here, but I have not tried them so often nor found them so sincere.

In <your> the picture you draw to yourself of the pleasures & advantages of Koekleberg life put in a few colours that I will give you.—A falsehood[3] you can never get to the bottom of. (There are exceptions.) An artificial kind of life that prevents you from ever enjoying any simple or natural pleasures. The continually finding yourself suspected of the same falsehood that all around you are guilty of—but what's the use of grumbling when I'm going away? Going! Going! in to the heart of Germany, 'near' to a place called Iserlohn.[4] There is not another English person within a days journey, nor I think a French one. There are plenty of mountains trees & water, & (I hope) of children to whom I can teach English. How this turns out I will tell you when I have been there a little time. I am invited to pass the winter with Mde Schmidt[5] a German lady who has a daughter at Koekleberg; so that I shall not be frozen to death in the cold weather & when it grows warm I must "fend for myself." Charlotte & Emily are well; not only in health but in mind & hope. They are content with their present position & even gay & I think they do quite right not to return to England though one of them at <Leeds> least could earn more at the beautiful town of Bradford than she is now doing.

Excuse me writing any very sensible reasons for this decision first because I am listening to a lecture in french while I am writing to you in English—& 2ly because if you can't see or rather feel why they are right I could not make you understand them. It is a matter of taste & feeling, & I think you feel pent up enough where you are to see why they are right in staying outside the cage—though it is somewhat cold.

Cold or warm—farewell I am going to shut my eyes for a cold plunge—when I come up again I [will] tell you all what its like

Mary Taylor.

MS Texas. W & S 142.
Address (envelope): Miss E Nussey | Brookroyd | Birstal | 'near' Leeds
PM: (i) HULL | SP 24 | 1842 (ii) LEEDS | SP 24 | 1842 | G

1. Joe Taylor evidently took the letter to England and posted it to EN on landing at Hull, the east-coast port then much used for travel to and trade with the Continent. Postage on foreign letters was expensive; hence the use of travelling friends as carriers.
2. An ornamental watchchain, knitted, crocheted, or otherwise made by hand. In *Villette* Lucy used her 'whole stock of beads and silk' to make a long and rich watchguard for M. Paul. (Chs. 28 and 29.)

3. In Madame Beck's pensionnat in *Villette* 'Not a soul . . . but was above being ashamed of a lie . . . they thought nothing of it.' (Ch. 9, 114)
4. Iserlohn lies to the south of the Ruhr and about 14 miles south-east of Dortmund. Mary's description applies quite well to Nachrodt and Hagen, west of Iserlohn, to which she eventually went.
5. Not traced.

P. B. Brontë to Francis H. Grundy,[1] *25 October 1842*

[Haworth]

My dear Sir,—

There is no misunderstanding. I have had a long attendance at the deathbed of the Rev. Mr. Weightman,[2] one of my dearest friends, and now I am attending at the deathbed of my aunt,[3] who has been for twenty years as my mother. I expect her to die in a few hours.

As my sisters are far from home, I have had much on my mind, and these things must serve as an apology for what was never intended as neglect of your friendship to us.

I had meant not only to have written to you, but to the Rev. James Martineau,[4] gratefully and sincerely acknowledging the receipt of his most kindly and truthful criticism,—at least in advice, though too generous far in praise,—but one sad ceremony must, I fear, be gone through first. Give my most sincere respects to Mr Stephenson,[5] and excuse this scrawl; my eyes are too dim with sorrow to see well. Believe me, your not very happy but obliged friend and servant,

P. B. Brontë.

MS untraced. W & S 143.
Address: not in source.
PM: not in source.
Text: *Grundy* 83.

1. Francis Henry Grundy (b. ?1822), son of a Unitarian clergyman, the Revd John Grundy (1782–1843). F. H. Grundy, a railway engineer, was working on the construction of Yorkshire railways in the early 1840s and lodging in Halifax when he met BB, then a railway clerk at Luddenden Foot. (See EJB ?2.4.1841 n. 3 and EN 20.1.1842 n. 8.) Ch. 3 of Grundy's *Pictures of the Past* (1879) includes a lively, sympathetic, but inaccurate account of BB, and several letters or part-letters from him.
2. Mr Weightman had died of cholera, after a fortnight's suffering, on 6 Sept. at the age of 28. His memorial tablet in Haworth Church records that he was buried on 10 Sept.: 'He was three years curate of Haworth, and by the congregation, and parishioners in general, was greatly respected, for his orthodox principles, active zeal, moral habits, learning, mildness, and affability: his useful labours will long be gratefully remembered by the members of the congregation; and Sunday School teachers, and scholars.' In his memorial sermon on 2 Oct. Mr Brontë could not speak of him without great emotion: he had regarded him as a son, and praised 'his preaching, and practising . . . neither distant nor austere, timid nor obtrusive, not bigoted,

exclusive, nor dogmatical'. Patrick Brontë, *A Funeral Sermon for the Late Reverend William Weightman, M.A.* (Halifax, 1842).

3. Elizabeth Branwell lingered for another 4 days, until 29 Oct., when she died a painful death from 'internal obstruction'. (EN 10.11.1842.)
4. The Revd James Martineau (1805–1900) was a distinguished Unitarian divine, the brother of Harriet Martineau; he was a colleague of the Revd John Grundy at Paradise Street Chapel, Liverpool, from 1832, and sole pastor from 1835. From 1840 to 1857 he was Professor of Mental and Moral Philosophy and Political Economy at Manchester New College. Grundy praised him as a 'prince among men . . . He taught me to think'. See *Grundy* 45–6. Branwell Brontë, who would know of James Martineau as a writer and reviewer, had evidently asked for his opinion on some of his work.
5. George Robert Stephenson (1819–1905), civil engineer, nephew of the railway pioneer George Stephenson, and friend of F. H. Grundy. He worked in the drawing office of the Manchester and Leeds Railway from 1837 to 1843.

P. B. Brontë to Francis H. Grundy, 29 October 1842

[Haworth]

My dear Sir,—

As I don't want to lose a real friend, I write in deprecation of the tone of your letter. Death only has made me neglectful of your kindness, and I have lately had so much experience with him, that your sister would not now blame me for indulging in gloomy visions either of this world or another. I am incoherent, I fear, but I have been waking two nights witnessing such agonising suffering as I would not wish my worst enemy to endure; and I have now lost the [guide] and director[1] of all the happy days connected with my childhood.[2] I have suffered such sorrow since I last saw you at Haworth, that I do not now care if I were fighting in India[3] or —, since, when the mind is depressed, danger is the most effectual cure. But you don't like croaking, I know well, only I request you to understand from my two notes that I have not forgotten you, but myself.—

Yours, etc.,
[P. B. Brontë]

MS untraced. W & S 144.
Address: not in source.
PM: not in source.
Text: *Grundy* 83–4. W & S 144 is probably a corrected version of Grundy's text. See n. 1.

1 *Grundy* 84 prints 'pride and director', an obvious error.

2 Miss Branwell must have been a surrogate mother to BB, who was only 4 years old when his mother died. Elizabeth Branwell died at the age of 66 on the day this letter was written, and was buried at Haworth on 3 Nov., the Revd James C. Bradley officiating. (Haworth Parish Register.) For her will, see EN 10.11.1842 n. 2.

3 In a letter to Grundy of 9 June 1842 (W & S 134) Branwell had referred to Grundy's failure to obtain a situation for him, and to his own 'great desire for activity': 'wherever coming years

may lead—Greenland's snows or sands of Afric,' but the present reference is more specific. In 1839 India had been the scene of fierce fighting on the north-west frontier with Afghanistan, and in 1841 the British garrison had been massacred by the Afghans at Kabul. In 1842 a second Afghan expedition was sent from Britain to relieve Jalalabad and to reinstate the Shah Shuja. BB's poem on the Afghan War, printed in the *Leeds Intelligencer* on 7 May 1842, includes the lines

England's children—England's glory,
Moslem sabres smite and quell.

See Neufeldt *BBP* 223–4.

Mary Taylor to Ellen Nussey, 30 October and 1 November 1842

[Brussels]

My dear Ellen

You will have heard by this time the end of poor Martha;[1] & with my head full of this event & still having nothing to say upon it, or rather not feeling inclined to say it, I scarcely know why I write to you. But I don't wish you to think that this misfortune will make me forget you more than the rest did; having the opportunity of sending you a letter postage free I just write to tell you I think of you. You will wish to hear the history of Martha's illness—I will give you it in a few months if you have not heard it then; till then you must excuse me. A thousand times I have reviewed the minutest circumstances of it but I cannot without great difficulty give a regular account of them.—There is nothing to regret, nothing to recall—not even Martha—She is better where she is—But when I recall the sufferings that have purified her my heart aches—I can't help it & every trivial accident sad or pleasant reminds me of her & of what she went through.

I am going to walk with Charlotte & Emily to the protestant cemetery[2] this afternoon (Sunday 30 Oct) It is long since I have seen them[3] & we shall have much to say to each other. I am now staying with the Dixons[4] in Brussels. I find them very different to what I expected. They are the most united affectionate family I ever met with. They have taken me as one of themselves & made me such a comfortable happy home that I should like to live here all my life.

This I could do if I had not a counter liking (so consistent we are) to go into Germany & another to live at Hunsworth.[5] I have finally chosen to go to Germany—activity being in my opinion the most desirable state of existence both for my spirits, health, & advantage. I shall finish my letter after I have seen Charlotte. Well I have seen her & Emily. We have walked about six miles to see the cemetery & the country round it. We then spent a pleasant evening with my cousins & in presence of my Uncle & Emily one not speaking at all; the other once or twice. I like to hear from you & thank you very much for your letter. Remember me to your sister Mercy & your Mother, & to all who inquire about me, if you think they do it more from kindness than curiosity. To Miss Cockhill[6] Mary[7] & all the Misses Wooler, particularly to Miss Wooler, Miss Bradbury[8] & the Healds.[9]

Mary Taylor.

11 Rue de la Regence
1 Novbr 1842

If this letter should not reach you for some time after the date, it will not be because it has been delayed on the road but because an opportunity did not occur of sending it sooner by a private hand.

Mary Dixon wishes me to begin again to express her kind remembrances to you & your sister.

MS Berg. W & S 145.
Address: not in source.
PM: not in source.

1. Martha Taylor died on 12 Oct. of 'what was probably cholera'. (*Stevens* 39.) cf. EN 10.11.1842, 'Mr Weightman's illness was exactly what Martha's was.' For her illness and funeral, see Gérin *CB* 211–13.
2. The cemetery was outside the city beyond the 'porte de Louvain', as CB writes in *The Professor* ch. 19, 167. In *Shirley* CB recalled her visit to 'Jessie Yorke's' (Martha's) grave, and the 'howling, rainy autumn evening too—when certain who had that day performed a pilgrimage to a grave new-made in a heretic cemetery, sat near a wood-fire on the hearth of a foreign dwelling. They were merry and social, but they each knew that . . . they had lost something whose absence could never be quite atoned for so long as they lived'. (*Shirley* ch. 23, 460.)
3. Mary would be able to meet the Brontës more readily during this visit to the rue de la Régence, which runs southwestwards from the Place Royale, a short distance from the rue d'Isabelle.
4. For Mary's uncle Abraham Dixon (1779–1850) see E. Branwell 29.9.1841 n. 8. His wife Laetitia (Taylor) Dixon had died earlier in the year, possibly in Leeds where she had been living with her daughter Mary in the family's English home at 35 Springfield Place, Little Woodhouse, Leeds. Mr Dixon seems to have been an impractical though amiable person. His son Abram, sending a gift of money to his mother from Birmingham on 26.9.1838, had written that his father would send her help 'the very moment he has it in his power. He sends his love &c . . . He seems to be getting on just as usual; stumbling from scheme to scheme & disappointment to disappointment.' (Dixon Papers, Leeds City Museum.) CB was to meet the fourth son, George Dixon (1820–98), at this period working for the Birmingham firm of Rabone, (makers of writing desks, precision tools, etc.) and travelling between England and the Continent on business, later to become a distinguished educational reformer and MP for Birmingham. See *DNB*. Mary Dixon (1809–97) Abraham's only surviving daughter, was rather delicate, and the family letters show concern for her health. She was to become a friend and correspondent of CB.
5. i.e. to the cottage near the Taylor family's Hunsworth Mill, about a mile from Gomersal, where Mary's brothers John and Joe were living. See EN 3.1.1841 n. 2.
6. Hannah Cockill. See MT to EN ?July 1842 n. 6.
7. Probably Mary Carr (b. 1811), sister of the solicitor Charles Carr II (1807–80), who was to marry the younger Revd W. M. Heald on 23. 4. 1844.

8. See EN 20.8.1840 n. 5.
9. William Margetson Heald, the Vicar of Birstall, and his sister Harriet. See EN 5.5.1838 n. 3.

Constantin Heger to Revd P. Brontë, 5 November 1842

[Brussels]
Samedi, 5 9$^{bre.}$

Monsieur!

Un événement[1] bien triste décide Mesdemoiselles vos filles à retourner brusquement[2] en Angleterre: ce départ qui nous afflige beaucoup a cependant ma complète approbation; il est bien naturel qu'elles cherchent à vous consoler de ce que le ciel vient de vous ôter, en se serrant autour de vous, pour mieux vous faire apprécier ce que le ciel vous a donné et ce qu'il vous laisse encore. J'espère que vous me pardonnerez, Monsieur, de profiter de cette circonstance pour vous faire [par]venir l'expression de mon respect; je n'ai pas l'honneur de vous connaître personellement,[3] et cependant j'éprouve pour votre personne un sentiment de sincère vénération, car en jugeant un père de famille par ses enfants on ne risque pas de se tromper, et sous ce rapport l'éducation et les sentiments que nous avons trouvés dans mesdemoiselles vos filles, n'ont pu que nous donner une très haute idée de votre mérite et de votre caractère. Vous apprendrez sans doute avec plaisir que vos enfants ont fait du progrès très remarquable dans toutes les branches de l'enseignement, et que ces progrès sont entièrement [dûs] à leur amour pour le travail et à leur persévérance; nous n'avons eu que bien peu à faire avec de pareilles élèves; leur avancement est votre œuvre bien plus que la nôtre; nous n'avons pas eu à leur apprendre le prix du temps et de l'instruction, elles avaient appris tout cela dans la maison paternelle, et nous n'avons eu pour notre part, que le faible mérite de diriger leurs efforts et de fournir un aliment convenable à la louable activité que vos filles ont puisée dans votre exemple et dans vos leçons.[4] Puissent les éloges [mérités] que nous donnons à vos enfants vous être de quelque consolation dans le malheur qui vous afflige; c'est là notre espoir en vous écrivant, et ce sera, pour Mlles Charlotte et Emily une douce et belle récompense de leurs travaux.

En perdant nos deux chères élèves nous ne devons pas vous cacher que nous éprouvons à la fois et du chagrin et de l'inquiétude; nous sommes affligés parce que cette brusque séparation vient briser l'affection presque paternelle[5] que nous leur avons vouée, et notre peine s'augmente à la vue de tant de travaux interrompus, de tant de choses bien commencées, et qui ne demandent que quelque temps encore pour être menées à bonne fin. Dans un an, chacune de vos demoiselles eût été entièrement prémunie contre les éventualités de l'avenir; chacune d'elles acquérait à la fois et l'instruction et la science d'enseignement; Miss Emily allait apprendre le piano; recevoir les leçons du meilleur professeur[6] que nous ayons en Belgique, et déjà elle avait elle-même de petites élèves;[7] elle perdait donc à la fois un reste d'ignorance, et un reste plus gênant encore de timidité; Miss Charlotte commençait à donner des leçons en français,[8] et d'acquérir cette assurance, cet aplomb si nécessaire dans l'enseignement; encore un an tout au plus, et l'œuvre était achevée et bien achevée. Alors nous aurions pu, si cela vous eût convenu, offrir à Mesdemoiselles vos filles ou du moins à l'une de[s] deux une position qui eût été dans ses goûts, et qui lui eût donné cette douce indépendance si difficile à trouver pour une jeune personne. Ce n'est pas, croyez le bien Monsieur, ce n'est pas ici pour nous une question d'intérêt personnel, c'est une question d'affection; vous me pardonnerez si nous vous parlons de vos enfants, si nous nous occupons de leur avenir, comme si elles faisaient partie de notre famille; leur qualités personnelles leur bon vouloir, leur zèle extrême sont les seules causes qui nous poussent à nous hasarder de la sorte. Nous savons, Monsieur, que vous pèserez plus mûrement et plus sagement que nous la conséquence qu'aurait pour l'avenir une interruption complète dans les études de vos deux filles; vous déciderez ce qu'il faut faire, et vous nous pardonnerez notre franchise, si vous daignez considérer que le motif qui nous fait agir est une affection bien désinté[r]essée et qui s'affligerait beaucoup de devoir déjà se résigner à n'être plus utile à vos chers enfants.

Agréez, je vous prie, Monsieur, l'expression respectueuse de mes sentiments de haute considération.

C. Heger.

MS untraced. W & S 146.

Constantin Heger to Revd P. Brontë, 5 November 1842: Translation

Sir,

A very sad event[1] has caused your daughters' sudden return to England;[2] this departure, which grieves us very much, has nevertheless my full approval; it is very natural that they should seek to console you for what heaven has just taken from you by rejoining your family circle, so that you will more readily appreciate what heaven has given you and what it has still left you. I hope that you will forgive me, sir, for taking advantage of this circumstance to send you this expression of my respect; I have not the honour of knowing you personally,[3] and yet I feel for you yourself a sentiment of sincere veneration, for in judging the father of a family by his children there is no risk of being mistaken; and in this respect the education and opinions we have found in your daughters could only give us a very high idea of your worth and your character. No doubt you will be pleased to hear that your children have made very notable progress in all the branches of instruction, and that this progress is entirely owing to their love of work and their perseverance; in dealing with such pupils we have had but little to do; their progress is your handiwork much more than ours; we have not had to teach them the value of time and instruction, they had learnt all that in their father's house, and we for our part have had the minor merit of guiding their efforts and providing suitable material to foster the admirable activity that your daughters have derived from your example and your lessons.[4] May the well-deserved praise that we give to your children be some consolation to you in the sorrow that afflicts you; that is our hope in writing to you, and for Miss Charlotte and Miss Emily it will be a sweet and genuine reward for their labours.

We must not conceal from you that in losing our two dear pupils we feel both regretful grief and anxiety; we are grieved because this sudden separation breaks up the almost fatherly affection[5] which we have devoted to them, and our distress is increased by the realization that there are so many incomplete tasks, so many things which have been well begun, and which only need a little more time to be satisfactorily completed. In a year's time each of your daughters would have been fully prepared for all future contingencies; each was both improving her knowledge and learning how to teach. Miss Emily was about to learn the piano—to receive lessons from the best teacher[6] we have in Belgium, and she herself already had little pupils;[7] consequently she was losing both the remaining traces of ignorance and a more embarrassing residue of timidity; Miss Charlotte was beginning to give lessons in French,[8] and to gain the assurance and aplomb so essential in teaching; in another year at the most the work would have been completed and well completed. Then we would have been able, if you were agreeable, to offer to your daughters or at least to one of the two a position which would have suited her, and which would have given her that precious independence which is so hard for a young person to find. This is not, please believe me sir, this is not a question of our personal advantage, but a question of affection; you must pardon me if we speak to you of your children and concern ourselves with their future as if they formed part of our family; their personal qualities, their good will, their extreme zeal are the only reasons leading us to venture in this way. We know, sir, that you will assess more maturely and wisely than we the effects which a total interruption of their studies would have on your daughters' future; you will decide what needs to be done, and you will forgive our frankness, if you will kindly consider that we are motivated by a disinterested affection which would be sorely troubled if it had to submit to being no longer of use to your dear children.

I beg you sir to accept the respectful expression of my high regard.

C. Heger.

Address: Au Révérend Monsieur Brontë, Pasteur Évangelique, &c. &c.

Text: Rylands MS *Life* (fos. 251–3) looks like a fairly careful copy from the letter M. Heger wrote for the sisters to take home to their father. ECG introduces it by saying that she was 'tempted to <give> 'copy' it'. Minor slips have been silently corrected. W & S 146, dated '5 Nbre', and *Shorter* 112 ('5 Obre') correct the Rylands MS readings 'prévenir' (l. 10) to 'parvenir', 'du' (l. 18) to 'dûs' and 'méritées' (l. 25) to 'mérités'.

1. The Brontës' aunt Elizabeth Branwell had died on 29 Oct. Her nieces heard the news of her illness too late for them to reach England before she died. See BB to F. H. Grundy 25 and 29.10.1842 and EN 10.11.1842.
2. Gérin comments, 'Too late now to reach home in time for the funeral, they waited for Sunday's [6 Nov.] steam-packet from Antwerp, rather than rush their departure by taking Friday's boat from Ostend.' (Gérin *CB* 213–14.) But CB writes as if they got the news of Miss Branwell's death on the Thursday, i.e. on 3 Nov., too late for the Friday's boat. See the next letter.
3. Though Mr Brontë had accompanied his daughters to Mme Heger's pensionnat on the morning of 15 Feb. 1842, he had not met M. Heger, who, as Gérin says, would have been 'teaching in his own boys' school at that hour'. (Gérin *CB* 187.)
4. Mrs Gaskell wrote in ch. 4 of the *Life*: 'I do not know whether Miss Branwell taught her nieces anything besides sewing, and the household arts . . . Their regular lessons were said to their father.' (i. 62.) But M. Heger may mean moral rather than academic lessons.
5. This expression, and the encouraging words which follow, must have persuaded CB that her return to the pensionnat would be both welcome to the Hegers and advisable for her own career.
6. cf. EN ?July 1842. EJB was about to have lessons from M. Chapelle, brother-in-law of M. Heger's first wife, and teacher of music at the Brussels *conservatoire*. Mme Beck's pensionnat in *Villette*, with its 4 pianos and its singing lessons, probably reflects a similar emphasis on musical accomplishment, and CB's description of M. Paul's brother, 'a noted pianiste, and also the first music teacher in Villette' echoes M. Heger's phrasing here. See *Villette* ch. 11, 142 and ch. 20, 302.
7. Three of the five daughters of Dr Thomas Wheelwright, MD, MRCS 1807 (1786–1861), a London physician who had brought his family to Brussels for their education. All his daughters attended Mme Heger's school from July 1842, continuing to go there daily throughout the vacation for various lessons. The Brontë sisters also remained in the school 'during the whole time', preparing 'their French, drawing, German, and literature for their various masters; and to these occupations Emily added that of music, in which she was somewhat of a proficient; so much so as to be qualified to give instruction in it to the three younger sisters of my informant'. (*Life* i. 270.) Mrs Gaskell's informant was the eldest daughter, Laetitia Elizabeth (1828–1911), who was to become a friend and correspondent of CB. Writing from Hastings in Nov. 1915, Joseph J. Green, a Wheelwright descendant, described Laetitia as a handsome woman who 'ruled the roast' at home: 'she was a good French linguist and musician, and a woman of fine presence, vivacious manners', with 'literary tastes and instincts . . . a devout churchwoman'. The next sister, Emily (1829–88), was the 'flower of the flock in Christian character . . . an excellent French linguist and pianist'. Emily Brontë's reluctant pupils, who resented her teaching them during recreation, were Frances (1831–1913), Sarah Ann (1834–1900), and Julia (b. 30 Oct. 1835) who 'contracted typhus or typhoid fever' at the pensionnat Heger and died on 17 Nov. 1842: Joseph Green had been told that Julia 'was a great favourite in the Heger establishment, and was much caressed by the principals, pupils, and staff'. (Joseph J. Green, in transcript in Symington Papers, Rutgers University Library; in the *Friends' Quarterly Examiner* for Nov. 1915 Julia is said to have died from cholera.) Frances Wheelwright told Green that the sanitation at the Heger pensionnat 'was of a primitive and wholly inadequate character' and this might account for Julia's death. Mme Heger wrote most sympathetically to the Wheelwrights on the death of the 'little angel for whom we weep'. (Letter of 21.11.1842, owned and translated by W. Gérin, *CB* 216.) See *BST* 5. 23. 27–9 and *CBCircle* 100–2.

8. CB was teaching English, but had necessarily to use French to do so. *The Professor* and *Villette* dramatize the difficulties of a foreign teacher faced with a class of 'Bruxelloises'.

To Ellen Nussey, 10 November [1842]

Haworth

My dear Ellen

I was not yet returned to England when your letter arrived—We received the first news of Aunt's illness—Wednesday Novbr 2nd—we decided to come home directly—next morning a second letter informed us of her death. We sailed from Antwerp on Sunday[1]—we travelled day & night and got home on Tuesday morning[2]—of course the funeral and all was over. We shall see her no more—Papa is pretty well   we found Anne at home   she is <in> pretty well also—You say you have had no letter from me for a long time—I wrote to you three weeks ago[3]—When you answer this note I will write to you again more in detail—Martha *Taylor's illness[4] was unknown to me till the day before she died—I hastened to Kokleberg the next morning—unconscious that she was in great danger—and was told that it was finished, she had died in the night—Mary was taken away to Bruxelles[5]—I have seen Mary frequently since—she is in no way crushed by the event—but while Martha was ill she was to her, more than a Mother—more than a Sister watching—nursing—cherishing her—<more>'so' tenderly, so unweariedly—she appears calm and serious now—no bursts[6] of violent emotion—no exaggeration of distress—I have seen Martha's grave—the place where her ashes lie in a foreign country   Aunt—Martha- *Taylor—Mr *Weightman[7] 'are now' all gone—how dreary & void everything seems—Mr *Weightman's illness was exactly what Martha's was—he was ill the same length of time & died in the same manner—Aunts disease was internal obstruction. she also was ill a fortnight

Good bye my dear Ellen

MS Harvard H.E.W. 1.5.4. Envelope: T.J. Winnifrith. W & S 147.
Address (envelope): Miss Ellen Nussey | Brookroyd | Birstal | Leeds
PM: (i)—?NO (ii) BRADFORD YORKS | NO 10 | 1842 (iii) LEEDS | NO 10 | 1842 | F
Annotation on envelope by EN in pencil: Nov 10–42 | Miss Branwel[l] | Mr Weightman | & M Taylor | all dead

1. They sailed on the steam-packet 'Wilberforce'. See *The Times*, Tuesday 8.11.1842, 7: 'Custom House Nov 7. Vessels Entered Inwards: Wilberforce from Antwerp.'
2. 8 Nov. For Elizabeth Branwell's death see BB to F. H. Grundy 25 and 29.10.1842. The funeral had taken place on 3 Nov. For Miss Branwell's will see W & S i. 277–8 and *Barker* 409, 913. She bequeathed to her Brontë nieces and nephew various personal mementoes; her money was to be equally divided among her nieces C, E, and AB, and Eliza Jane Kingston.
3. This letter appears not to have survived.

4. See MT to EN 30.10. and 1.11.1842.
5. i.e. to the Dixons, within the city. The Koekelberg school was a 'maison de campagne . . . avec jardin, plantations et avenue' 1 km. north-west of the city. (*Stevens* 171–4.) In *Villette* the Brettons' 'château', 'La Terrasse', with its 'lawn-terrace', high forest-trees, and avenue in a retired spot 'about half a league without the Porte de Crécy' may owe something to the Château de Koekelberg. (Chs. 16 and 20.)
6. MS may read 'bouts'.
7. Mr Weightman had died on 6 Sept. See BB to F. H. Grundy 25.10.1842.

To Ellen Nussey, [?22 November 1842]

[Haworth]

Dear <Madam> 'Ellen'

I hope your brother *George is sufficiently recovered now to dispense with your constant attendance—Papa desires his compliments to you and says he should be very glad if you could give us your company at Haworth for a little while—Can you come on Friday next[1]—? I mention so early a day because Anne leaves us to return to York[2] on Monday—and she wishes very much to see you before her departure—I think *George is too good-natured to object to your coming—there is little enough pleasure in this world and it would be truly unkind to deny to you and me that of meeting again 'after so long a separation'—do not fear to find us melancholy or depressed—we are now all much as usual—you will see no difference from our former demeanour Send me an immediate answer

C B

Give my love & best wishes to your *Mother & *Mercy
Tuesday Morning

MS Harvard H.E.W. 1. 5. 4. W & S 148 (part, as 20 Nov.)
Address: not in MS.
PM: not in MS.
Annotation (i) in ink by EN: 73 Nov 20; (ii) in pencil by unknown hand: p 105—42? | pub in H at H [i.e. in *Hours at Home*.]
Date: the nearest Tuesday to EN's date, 20 Nov., was 22 Nov.

1. 25th Nov.? But CB went to Brookroyd instead. See the next letter.
2. Anne would have travelled via York to reach Thorp Green. See EJB ?2.4.1841 n.1.

To Ellen Nussey, [25 November 1842]

[Haworth]

My dear Ellen,—

I hope that invitation of yours was given in real earnest, for I intend to accept it. I wish to see you, and as in a few weeks I shall probably again leave England, I will not be too delicate and ceremonious and so let the present opportunity pass.

Something says to me that it will not be too convenient to have a guest at Brookroyd while there is an invalid[1] there. However, I listen to no such suggestions. I find, however, that I cannot come on Monday, because Anne's present arrangements will not suit that day. She leaves Haworth on Tuesday at six o'clock in the morning, and we should reach Bradford at half-past eight—an early hour for you to be there with the gig.

If Tuesday will not suit you write immediately and tell me so. The circumstances of its being Leeds market-day[2] may perhaps render it inconvenient. If so, I will defer my visit to any day you please.

There are many reasons why I should have preferred your coming to Haworth; but as it appears there are always obstacles which prevent that—I'll break through ceremony, or pride, or whatever it is, and like Mahomet go to the mountain which won't or can't come to me.[3]

The coach stops at the Bowling-Green Inn—in Bradford.[4]

Give my love to Mercy and your Mother.

C. Brontë.

MS untraced. Envelope: BPM B.S. 104/3. W & S 149.
Address (envelope): Miss Ellen Nussey | Brookroyd | Birstall | Leeds
PM: (i) BRADFORD YORKS | NO 25 | 1842 | 2 (ii) *Bradford Yorks* | *P Post* (iii) LEEDS | NO 25 | 1842 | F
Annotation by EN in pencil on the envelope: Nov 25 —42 | Coming to Brookroyd
Text: *Shorter* 114. *Hours at Home* xi. 203 and *Nussey* 103 are incomplete, but perhaps closer to the MS in punctuation. Not in *Life*. W & S 149 reproduces *Shorter* 114.

1. Probably George Nussey. See the previous letter.
2. Richard (or less probably Joseph) Nussey might have needed the gig in order to attend one of the Leeds markets, either that in the Mixed Cloth-Hall, 'held on Tuesdays and Saturdays, and only for an hour and a half each day . . . The market-bell rings at six o'clock in the morning in summer, and at seven in winter', or in the White Cloth-Hall 'after the conclusion of those at the Mixed Cloth-hall'. (*Dugdale* 1052–3.) 'Tuesday' would be 29 Nov. W & S note that CB 'spent a week with Ellen Nussey at Brookroyd (Nov. 29th to Dec. 5th) and gave her friend's sister [Mercy] a book, Hemans's *Songs of the Affections*, on the day she left for home . . . The book is now in the Brontë Parsonage Museum'. (i. 284 and n. 1.)
3. 'When Mohammed was asked by the Arabs for miraculous proofs of his teaching he ordered Mount Safa to come to him, and as it did not move, he said, "God is merciful. Had it obeyed my words, it would have fallen on us to our destruction. I will therefore go to the mountain, and thank God that He has had mercy on a stiffnecked generation." ' (See *Brewer* under 'Mohammed'.)

4. The large coaching-inn at 104 Bridge Street, Bradford at which most of the Keighley coaches going on to Leeds stopped; a fine 'old English hostelry', with a large open frontage, balcony, and bay-windows, and 'unlimited accommodation for "man and beast" '. It was of 17th-cent. origin, rebuilt in 1750, and for many years ranked as the best inn of the town. (See William Scruton, *Pen and Pencil Pictures of Old Bradford* (1889), 167 and 177.)

To Mrs Taylor,[1] *Stanbury, [?December 1842]*

[Haworth]

Mr and the Miss Brontës'[2] Compliments to Mrs & Miss Taylor,[3] and they will if the weather be fine, do themselves the pleasure of accepting their kind invitation.—

Monday Morning

MS WYAS Calderdale. RMP 746b. No publication traced.
Address: none
PM: not in MS
Date: The handwriting closely resembles that of EN 10.11.1842. The note was written when Branwell and at least 2 of his sisters were at home, as they were in Dec. 1842. EN's visit to Haworth in late December would cause the sisters to withdraw their acceptance, as the next letter shows.

1. Possibly Mrs Mary Taylor, née Wright, the widow of Stephen Taylor (1772–1831), who had been a leading member of the Haworth Church Trustees. The Taylors lived in the Manor House in Stanbury, a hamlet about a mile from Haworth, and might well offer a 'kind invitation' at about Christmas time on the return of Charlotte and Emily from Brussels.
2. Anne Brontë may not have been at home: she had returned to Thorp Green on 29 Nov., and possibly did not come back again for Christmas. In her Diary Paper for 30.7.1845 Emily Bronte recorded that 'Branwell went to Thorpgreen as a tutor, where Anne still continued—January 1843' (See p. 408.) Anne's poem, 'My soul is awakened', dated 30 Dec. 1842 was, according to her MS note, 'Composed in the long-Plantation on a wild bright windy day'—i.e. at Thorp Green. Branwell probably joined her there on 21 Jan. 1843: Mr Robinson normally paid his salary quarterly on the 21st of the month.
3. Not identified. Perhaps a sister-in-law of Mrs Taylor, or the young Mary Ann Taylor (b. 1833), daughter of the widower George Taylor and granddaughter of Mrs S. Taylor.

To Mrs Taylor,[1] *Stanbury, [?December 1842]*

[Haworth]
Wednesday Morning

The Miss Brontës are very sorry to be obliged, after all, to decline Mrs Taylor's kind invitation.

They have received a letter announcing the arrival of a friend[2] and are compelled to stay a[t] home to prepare for and receive her.

Mr Branwell will—if all be well do himself the pleasure of accepting the invitation

MS BPM B.S. 103.2. Facsimile *BST* 18.94.301.
Address (integral): Mrs Taylor, | Stanbury
PM: not in MS.
Annotation on verso, in the hand of A. B. Nicholls: 'This note is in the handwriting of Charlotte Brontë | A. B. Nicholls.'
Date: probably 2 days after the previous letter. The next occasion when Branwell and his sisters were at home just before a visit from Ellen Nussey would give dates of 24 and 26 June 1844 for these two notes. These are unlikely because on 23 June 1844 CB had written a note inviting Ellen to visit Haworth, an invitation which did not reach Birstall until 26 June. (See EN *Diary* 1844.)

1. Possibly Mrs Stephen Taylor. A note on the letter in *BST* 18.94.302 assumes that the recipient was Mrs George Taylor, but she had died at the age of 33 and was buried by Mr Brontë on 25 July 1842, on the same day as her 9-day-old baby Sarah.
2. EN stayed at Haworth at the end of Dec./early Jan. See EN ?6.1.1843.

To Ellen Nussey, [c.?6 January 1843]

[Haworth]

Dear Nell

It is a singular state of things to be obliged to write and have nothing worth reading to say—[1]

I am glad you got home safe.[2] You are an excellent good girl for writing to me two letters.

Especially as they were such long ones.

Branwell wants to know why you carefully exclude all mention of his name when you particularly send your regards to every other member of the family.

He desires to know whether—& in what he has offended you?

Or whether it is considered improper for a young lady to mention the gentlemen of a house?

We have been one walk on the moors since you left.

We have been to Keighley[3] where we met a person of our acquaintance—who uttered an interjection of astonishment on meeting us—and when he could get his breath informed us that he had heard I was dead and buried.

You say nothing about Mr *George's pocket-book[4] in your last—has he found it?

I don't know what to think about *Joe *Taylor coming so often to *Brookroyd

There exists a tragedy intitled the "rival Brothers"[5]

Do you imagine the two particular letters in *Joe's pocket were from *John?[6]

I've got down into the realms of nonsense so I'll drop it—

I have been as solid as a large dumpling since you left.

*?Fairles's[7] note I return because it must be precious Annes I keep—
Alas for *O P V[incent]![8] Alas! Alas!

[Unsigned]

MS Harvard H.E.W. 1.5.4. W & S 150 as 10 Jan.
Address: not in MS.
PM: not in MS.
Annotation by EN: 75 Jan 43
Date: on ?14 Jan. CB wrote that she had 'found the bustle' last Saturday, i.e. 7 Jan. The present letter must precede that date.

1. CB gives her 'nothing' a semblance of substance by spacing it out in the MS.
2. CB's visit to Brookroyd, probably from 29 Nov. to 5 Dec., had been followed by EN's return visit to Haworth in late Dec. or early Jan.
3. In the *Life* Mrs Gaskell writes of this period: '[they] went often down the long road to Keighley, for such books as had been added to the library there during their absence from England'. (i. 281.) There was a library in the Keighley Mechanics' Institute (see BB 17.5.1832 n. 8 and EN 7.4.1840 n. 12) and one kept by Thomas Duckett Hudson at 32 High Street, Keighley. (See Pigot's *Directory* 1841 and *Bradford Observer* 17.2.1894.) In Jan. 1848, however, CB said that she had 'no access to a circulating library'. (Letter to G. H. Lewes, 18.1.1848.)
4. 'A book-like case for papers, bank-notes, bills, etc, to be carried in the pocket.' (*OED*.)
5. CB may mean, if she is to be taken seriously, *The Brothers* (a comedy not a tragedy) by Richard Cumberland (1732–1811) in which an elder brother dispossesses the younger and courts his sweetheart (*OCEL*); or the anonymous novel, *The Rival Brothers*, published by Symonds in London in 1786.
6. John Taylor, elder brother of Joe Taylor. See EN 7.8.1841 n.4 and Mar./Apr. 1842 n. 10.
7. Perhaps someone EN had met when staying with her brother Henry at Earnley. cf. Henry's *Diary* 21.1.1839: 'Today going to call upon Mr. Fairles's Friend, I was invited by his Squire, Mr. Gibbs to dine at his house.' (fol. 53^v.) The *Clergy Lists* for 1845–50 name the Revd 'Septimus Fairles' as the English Chaplain in Bonn.
8. The curate whose proposal EN had refused. See EN 30.4.1840 and 2.11.1841.

To Ellen Nussey, [?14 January 1843]

[Haworth]

Dear Nell

My striped dress is not cut cross-ways—I am much obliged to you for transferring the roll of muslin—I found the brush under the sofa and last Saturday I found the bustle[1]—for which you deserve smothering.

I will deliver Branwell your message—You have left your bible—how can I send it?

I cannot tell precisely what day I shall leave home, but it will be the last week in this month—are you going with me?

I admire exceedingly the costume you have chosen to appear in at the *Birstal rout[2]—I think you say pink petticoat, black jacket and a wreath of roses—beautiful! For a change I would advise a black coat—velvet stock[3] & waistcoat—white pantaloons & smart boots—

I have adressed you in this note as plain Ellen—for though I know it will soon be Mrs J *Taylor—I can't for the life of me tell whether the initial J stands for *John *or *Joe[4] It is a complete enigma.

When I have time I mean to write Mr *Vincent's elegy—poor man! the manufacturers are beating him hollow—

My adress is, Miss Brontë
Chez Mde Heger-Parent
No 32 Rue d'Isabelle
Bruxelles Belgium

Write to me again—that's a good girl—very soon—in a fortnight you know there will be no more scribbling

Respectful remembrances to your *Mother and *Mercy—[5]

C Br—

MS BPM Gr. E 5. Envelope BPM B.S. 104/4. W & S 151 as 15 Jan.
Address (envelope): Miss Ellen Nussey | Brookroyd | Birstall | Leeds
PM: (i) BRADFORD YORKS | JA —4 | 1843 | ?2 (ii) *Bradford Yorks* | *Py Post*
Annotation by EN in pencil on the envelope includes: Jan —43 amusing | Mrs G
Date: CB was to leave Leeds *en route* for Belgium on 27 Jan., about a fortnight after the present letter, for which 14 Jan. would be a likely date. Only '4' is visible in the postmark.

1. *OED* gives 1788 for the first use of 'bustle' as a pad or lady's'dress improver' to fill out the skirt.
2. 'A fashionable gathering or assembly, a large evening party or reception, much in vogue in the 18th and early 19th centuries.' (*OED*.)
3. 'A kind of stiff close-fitting neckcloth, formerly worn by men generally, now only in the army.' (*OED*.)
4. See previous letter notes 5 and 6.
5. The name 'Mercy' is followed by one or two heavily deleted illegible words.

To Ellen Nussey, 30 January [1843]

Bruxelles

Dear Nell

I left Leeds for London[1] last Friday at 9 o'clock owing to delay we did not reach London till 10 at night 2 hours after time—I took a cab the moment I arrived in Euston Square—and went forthwith to London Bridge wharf—the packet lay off that wharf and I went on board the same night[2]—next morning we sailed, we had a prosperous & speedy voyage—and landed at Ostend at 9—next morning I took the train at 12[3] and reached rue d'Isabelle—at 7 Sunday evening—Mde *Heger received me with great kindness—I am still tired with the continued excitement of 3 days travelling—I had no accident—but of course some anxiety—

Good bye dear Ellen

Miss *Dixon[4] call[e]d this afternoon—Mary *Taylor had told her I should be in Brussels the last week of January—You may tell *Joe *Taylor she looked very elegant & ladylike I am going there[5] on Sunday D.V. address Miss Brontë

Chez Mde Heger-Parent
No 32 rue d'Isabelle
Bruxelles Belgium

MS Trinity College Cambridge MS Cullum K7[4]. W & S 152.
Address (integral): E Nussey
PM: none.

1. CB's journey, begun on 27 Jan., involved a connection at Normanton with the express train from York to London via Derby and Rugby.
2. CB sailed on Saturday 28 Jan. on the 'Earl of Liverpool', 'cleared outwards with cargo' by the Custom House on 27 Jan. (*The Times* 28.1.1843, 3.) CB later described to Mrs Gaskell 'her sense of loneliness, and yet her strange pleasure in the excitement of the situation, as in the dead of that winter's night she went swiftly over the dark river to the black hull's side, and was at first refused leave to ascend to the deck.' (*Life* i. 282.) For Lucy Snowe's journey to 'Boue-Marine' in *Villette* ch. 6, CB combined her own first journey in 1842 in the company of her father, EJB, and the Taylors, including their sightseeing in London, with this second journey, when she was unaccompanied.
3. CB reached Ostend at 9 p.m. on Saturday, and must have stayed there overnight before taking the midday train to Brussels on Sunday 29th. A garbled text in *Shorter* 118 and W & S 152 has misled later commentators on the timing of her journey. cf. CB's description of the 'Boue-Marine' (Ostend) hotel in *Villette* ch. 7.
4. See Mary Taylor's letter to EN 30.10.1842 n. 4.
5. i.e. to the Dixons' home at 11, rue de la Régence, Brussels.

Mary Taylor to Ellen Nussey, 16 February 1843[1]

[Germany]

Dear Ellen

Your descriptions & opinions of the Miss Woolers &c &c are more interesting than you imagine. Why do you not send me more of them? It is something very interesting, to me [to] hear the remarks exclamations &c that people make when they see any one from "foreign parts". I know well how you would spend the month you talk of when Miss Brontë was with you & how you would discuss all imaginable topics & all imaginable people all day & half the night. Tell me something about Emily Brontë: I can't imagine how the newly acquired qualities can fit in, in the same head & heart that is occupied by the old ones. Imagine Emily turning over prints or "taking wine" with any stupid fop & preserving her temper & politeness! Do you know your specimens of "people with good taste who admire "The Sea"[2] shocked me by its vulgarity.

"The Sea" is but a simple air. You should admire elaborate fantasias made on elaborate subjects that want three hands or 12 fingers to play them—where you are left to invent now & then a "brilliant Appogiatura, Cadence, Harfenspiel[3] or what not to modulate through the fifth into the next key or from a minor seventh close, to a" the devil knows what!

—If you can't understand it all, remember I've been learning German, & how is it possible to keep ones brain ?a [. . .] this land of Swedenborg,[4] philosophy, abstract ideas &—cabbage.[5] This last word is a 'literal' translation of a German one, always applied to any thing very confused—my letter for instance.—However I thrive with it all I am decidedly better—better than I have been since I left England [&] Brussels, or perhaps my moral condition there did not agree with me. I felt overpowered with weakness—now I am cheerful & active. Do not think if I don't write to you often that I forget you I write a public letter which I hope you see, & when I have written all the news I have what can I put in your letter? I will wait a day or two & if I ?find a great secret I will put it at the bottom of this page—

Yours ? < i.w.>

I find nothing to say, that I have not said in the public letter & I must close my packet to day for fear an estafette[6] comes to know why I don't write. I have heard from Charlotte since her arrival—she seems content at least but fear her sister's absence [?will] have a bad effect. When people have so little amusement they cannot afford to lose any. However we sh[all] see. Present my remembrances to miss Heald[7] if she sent any to me & I have really forgotten, & your letters are so abominably written that I cannot afford time to read it over again Cannot you take pains & write neatly, as I do? I fully understand your regrets at being forced to remain at home but there is always your Mother for a reason & perhaps if you left her you might regret as much that you had not remained by her. Remember me to her & your sister Miss Woole[r] [&] the Cockhills[8]

Nachrodt[9]—Feby 16 1843. Mary Taylor

MS Berg. W & S 153.
Address: not in MS.
PM: not in MS.
Text: the MS is torn. Missing words are supplied in square brackets.

1. Mary Taylor's letter provides a useful commentary on this period, when CB's own correspondence is lacking. Mary had travelled to Germany at the end of 1842. See her letter to EN of 30.10 and 1.11.1842 n.9.
2. Not identified.
3. An arpeggio or spread chord.
4. Emanuel Swedenborg (1688–1772), Swedish scientist, philosopher, and theologian.
5. 'Der Kohl', in the sense of twaddle or rubbish.
6. A courier or express messenger.
7. Miss Harriet Heald, sister of the Vicar of Birstall.

8. See MT to EN ?July 1842 and notes.
9. Nachrodt is a village 4 miles south-west of Iserlohn in North Rhine-Westphalia, Germany. See MT to EN, shortly before 24.9.1842. I am indebted to Sarah Fermi, who deciphered the name of the village.

To Ellen Nussey, 6 March [1843]

Bruxelles

Dear Nell

Whether you received my last billet or not I do not know, but as an opportunity [o]ffers of dispatching to you another I will [a]vail myself of it—I am settled by this time of course—I am not too much overloaded with occupation and besides teaching English I have time to improve myself in German[1] I ought to consider myself well off and to be thankful for my good fortune—I hope I am thankful—and if I could always keep up my spirits—and never feel lonely or long for companionship or friendship or whatever they call it, I should do very well—As I told you before Monsieur and Mde *Heger are the only two persons in the house for whom I really experience regard and esteem and of course I cannot always be with them nor even often—They told me when I first returned that I was to consider their sitting-room my sitting-room also and to go there whenever I was not engaged in the school-room—this however I cannot <room> 'do'—in the day-time it is a public-room—where music-masters and mistresses are constantly passing in and out[2] and in the evening I will not and ought not to intrude on Mr & Mde *Heger & their children[3]—thus I am a good deal by myself out of school-hours—but that does not signify—

I now regularly give 'English' lessons to Mr *Heger & his brother-in law Mr *Chappelle[4] (Mr H's first wife was the sister of Mr C's present wife) they get on with wonderful rapidity—especially the first—he already begins to speak English very decently—if you could see and hear the efforts I make to teach them to pronounce like Englishmen[5] and their unavailing attempts to imitate, you would laugh to all eternity.

The Carnival[6] is just over and we have entered upon the gloom and abstinence of Lent—the first day of Lent we had coffee without milk for breakfast—vinegar & vegetables with a very little salt-fish for dinner and bread for supper—The carnival was nothing but masking and mum[m]ery—Mr *Heger took me and one of the pupils into the town to see the masks—it was animating to see the immense crowds & the general gaiety—but the masks were nothing—

I have been several times to the *Dixons they are very kind to me—this letter will probably go by Mr Tom[7]—Miss *Dixon is certainly an elegant & accomplished person; my opinion of her is unchanged—for good &

otherwise—When she leaves Bruxelles I shall have no where to go to[8]—I shall be sorry to lose her society

I hear that Mary *Walker[9] is going to be married and that Mr *Joe Taylor* has been & is very poorly—what is the matter with him?

I have had two letters from Mary[10]—she does not tell me she has been ill & she does not complain—but her[11] letters are not the letters of a person in the enjoyment of great happiness—She has nobody to be so good to her as Mr *Heger is to me—to lend her books to converse with her sometimes &c.

Remember me to *Mercy & your Mother, tell me if any chances & changes have happened—remember me also to Mrs *George Allbutt[12] when you see her—

You do no[t] merit that I should prolong this letter—Good-bye to you dear Nell when I say so—it seems to me that you will hardly hear me—all the <heaving> wa[ves] of the Channel, heaving & roaring between must deaden the sound—

Go-o-d—b-y-e
C B[13]

MS BPM B.S. 50.4. W & S 154.
Address: not in MS.
PM: not in MS.

1. Two exercise books (BPM Bon 117 and 118) used by CB for German translations are dated 25 Apr. 1843 and May 1843. See her English version of Schiller's 'Der Taucher' and 'Der Graf von Hapsburg' in Neufeldt *CBP* 357–64, and her French translation of his 'Des Mädchens Klage', 'Der Alpenjäger', 'Ritter Toggenburg', and 'Nadowessische Totenklage', 365–9. cf. CB's use of Schiller's *Der Räuber* in *JE* ch. 28 and of 'Des Mädchens Klage' in *Villette* ch. 26.
2. In *Villette* 'Three pupils were . . . practising on three pianos in three proximate rooms—the dining room and the greater and lesser drawing-rooms.' (142.)
3. Marie Pauline, b. 20 Sep. 1837, d. 1886, Louise Florence, b. 14 July 1839, d. 1933, and Claire Zoë Marie, b. 23 July 1840, d. 1930. A son, Prospère Édouard Augustin (d. 1867), had been born on 28 Mar. 1842, soon after the Brontës' arrival at the pensionnat, and there would be two more children, Julie Marie Victorine, b. 15 Nov. 1843, d. 1928, and Paul François Xavier, 14 Dec. 1846–1925. For an attractive portrait of the Heger family by Ange François in 1847 see Fraser *CB* opp. 181, where the children are identified. For more information see Gérin *CB* 189–94. Marie, Louise, and Claire directed the Heger pensionnat after their mother's retirement. CB was fond of Louise Heger and portrayed her as Madame Beck's second child, Fifine, 'an honest, gleeful little soul', in *Villette* ch. 10.
4. M. Chapelle was a pianist and a professor at the Conservatoire Royal in Brussels; his wife was the sister of Marie-Josephine Noyer, M. Heger's first wife, who had died of cholera on 26 Sept. 1833. (Gérin *CB* 194.)
5. cf. M. Paul's attempts to speak English in e.g. *Villette* ch. 14.
6. The 8 days of festival and processions preceding the 'farewell to flesh' on Ash Wednesday (1 Mar. 1843).
7. Thomas Dixon (1821–65), fifth son of Abraham Dixon and brother of Mary. Abraham Dixon, in a letter from Ostend to Mary on 31.5.1842 and 3.6.1842, wrote: 'Tom is hard at work with his German & chance has given him a Royal Road to attain it, for the young Doctor of Languages, his Teacher [in Brussels], has got leave of absence, gone into Germany for a few weeks, & handed him over to his Father, the Librarian to the King, to whom at the King's Palace, he now goes to take his Lessons every other morning.' He was to be an engineer.

8. Since the Wheelwrights (see Heger to PB 5.11.1842 n. 7) did not leave Brussels until the end of Aug., it is surprising that CB does not mention them. The chaplain's wife, Mrs Jenkins, and her sons had found the Brontë sisters taciturn and difficult, and she had ceased her regular invitations to visit. See Gérin *CB* 200.
9. Mary Walker, daughter of the Revd John Walker, who was a cousin of Ellen's father, may be referred to here.
10. Mary Taylor.
11. These words form part of a corner of the second leaf, once cut off but now reattached. See n. 13 below.
12. The wife of Dr George Allbutt, b. 1812, LSA 1837, who had practised in his home-town of Hanley, Staffs., and then in Batley, Yorks., where he is listed as a surgeon in Pigot's *Directory* for 1842. He was the brother of the first Mrs William Moore Wooler, and of the Revd Thomas Allbutt, husband of Marianne (née Wooler). EN and her family were friendly with the Allbutts, and her *Diary* for 1844 records e.g. visits from 'Mrs G. Allbutt' on 16 May, 20, and 21 June, probably for meetings of the Batley Parish Dorcas Society. On this see *Whitehead* 157.
13. The last half-page of the letter contains a sketch by CB of herself, diminutive and plain, waving 'Good bye' across the sea to an attractively dressed Ellen Nussey, now 'Mrs O P Vincent', accompanied by a top-hatted bespectacled gentleman, 'The Chosen'. The names 'Ellen Nussey' and 'Vincent' have been deleted. Only the figures of CB and EN were left visible on the fragment which was later cut away. See illustration, pl. 3.

To Mary Dixon,[1] *[early 1843]*

[Brussels]

My dear Miss Dixon

I find I cannot come on Thursday; when I asked Mde Heger's leave, she said she had formed a prior engagement for me to go out with herself and Mr Heger. However I will come on Friday afternoon at two p.m if that hour will suit you—I must be back by four as M Heger will want his English lesson[2] after-dinner.

I surrender my unfortunate head to you with resignation—the features thereof may yield good practice as they never yet submitted to any line of regularity—but have manifested each a spirit of independance, <?won> edifying to behold—You are mistaken however in your benevolent idea that my portrait[3] will yield pleasure to Mary Taylor—do not give it to her, or if you do—do not expect thanks in return—she likes me well enough—but my face she can dispense with[4]—and would tell you so in her own sincere and truthful language if you asked her

Do not think I am quite disinterested in so readily consenting to serve you for a model—I shall have pleasure in coming and sitting with you for a little while, even though according to the custom of artists, you may not allow me to speak or turn my head.

I am dear Miss Dixon
Yours sincerely
C Brontë

Tuesday morning
I send a letter for Mary—to be enclosed in your packet.[5]

MS Berg, with envelope. Gérin *CB* 219.
Address (envelope): Miss Dixon.
PM: none.
Annotation on envelope by George Dixon: Lest you should think that this comes from some handsome mustachioued young gent^{n}. I beg to inform you that it is from Miss Brontè, & may be forwarded with propriety GD [Probably Mary's brother George was the bearer of her invitation to CB and of CB's reply and enclosure. For George Dixon, see MT to EN 30.10.1842 and 1.11.1842 n. 4.]
Date: between CB's arrival in Brussels on 30.1.1843 and Mary Dixon's departure from the city in June 1843. See *Stevens* 41. CB used mourning paper resembling that of her letter to EN of 10.11.1842, after Elizabeth Branwell's death.

1. For Mary Dixon see MT to EN 30.10.1842 and 1.11.1842 n. 4.
2. cf. the previous letter.
3. CB either drew or was given in exchange a portrait of Mary Dixon. See M. Dixon 16.10.1843.
4. Mary Taylor had been frankly uncomplimentary about CB's appearance. In a letter to Mrs Gaskell, Mary recalled that when they were both pupils at Roe Head, she had told CB 'she was very ugly. Some years afterwards, I told her I thought I had been very impertinent. She replied, "You did me a great deal of good, Polly, so don't repent of it".' (*Life* i. 109.)
5. See the next letter. Mary Dixon, a cousin of the Taylors, was probably able to send a 'packet' to Mary Taylor in Germany either by one of her own brothers or by Mary's.

To Ellen Nussey, [?April 1843]

[Brussels]

Dear Ellen

One ought to praise where praise is due and really that last letter of yours merits a good dose of panegyric–it was both long and interesting—send me quickly such another longer still if possible.

You will have heard of Mary *Taylor's resolute and intrepid proceedings[1]—Her public letters will have put you in possession of all details—nothing is left for me to say except perhaps to express my opinion of it—I have turned the matter over on all sides and really I cannot consider it otherwise than as very rational—Mind I did not jump to this opinion at once but was several days before I formed it conclusively.

You say you know what I shall say and think after having read the first part of your letter (which refers principally to *Joe *Taylor)—but that you do not mind—I may think what I please—Dear Nelly I should have thought nothing particular—if it had not been for this little defiance, and that made me think a good deal—Protect your heart Ellen—try to keep it whole and free—but this counsel is not needed—you are a sensible girl and will not surrender that citadel without capitulation

Is there ever any talk now of your coming to Brussels? During the bitter cold weather we had through February and the principal part of March—I did not regret that you had not accompanied me—If I had seen you shivering as I shivered myself—if I had seen your hands and feet as red and swelled as mine were—my discomfort would just have been doubled—I can do very well under this sort of thing—it does not fret me—it only makes me numb and silent—but if you were to pass a winter in Belgium you would be ill—However, more genial weather is coming now and I wish you were here—yet I never have 'pressed you' & never would press you too warmly to come—there are privations & humiliations to submit to—there is monotony and uniformity of life—and above all there is a constant sense of solitude in the midst of numbers—the Protestant the Foreigner is a solitary being <in th> 'whether' as teacher or pupil[2]—I do not say this by way of complaining of my own lot—for though I acknowledge that there are certain disadvantages in my present position, what position on earth is without them? and whenever I turn back to compare what I am with what I was—my place here with my place at Mrs *Sedgwicks[3] or *Mrs *White's[4]—I am thankful

There was one observation in your last letter which excited for a moment my wrath—at first I thought it would be folly to reply to it and I would let it die, afterwards—I determined to give one answer once for all—"Three or four people" it seems "have the idea that the future époux of Mademoiselle Brontë is on the Continent" These people are wiser than I am—They could not believe that I crossed the sea—merely to return as teacher to Mde *Heger's—I must have some[5] more powerful motive than respect for the character of my Master & Mistress, gratitude for their kindness to induce me to refuse a salary of 50£ in England and accept one of 16 in Belgium I must forsooth have some remote hope of entrapping a husband somehow—somewhere—if these charitable people knew the total seclusion of the life I lead—that I never exchange a word with any other man than Monsieur *Heger 'and seldom indeed with him'—they would perhaps cease to suppose tha[t][6] any such chimerical & groundless notion has influenced my proceedings—Have I said enough to clear myself of so silly an imputation? Not that it is a crime to marry—or a crime to wish to be married—but it is an imbecility which I reject with contempt—for women [who][7] have neither fortune nor beauty—to make marriage the principal object of their wishes & hopes & the aim of all their actions—not to be able to convince themselves that they are unattractive—and that they had better be quiet & think of other things than wedlock—[8]

I hope sincerely that all at Brookroyd are well—remember me to your Mother & *Mercy—any news of Anne yet?[9]

Good-bye—write to me soon and write nicely and pleasantly—don't cut me up with any secondhand nonsense

C B

MS HM 24432. W & S 155.
Address (integral): E. Nussey
PM: none.
Annotation in ink by ?EN: Brussels Ap —43
Date: ?EN's annotation, and para. 4 in the letter, indicate Apr. 1843. W & S 155, following *Shorter* 121, dates 1 Apr., but gives no evidence for this.

1. Mary's experiences in Germany must have been described in her 'public' letters, which have not been located: she refers to the letters and to her 'cheerful & active' life in her letter to EN of 16.2.1843, q.v. She taught English to German boys, took lessons in music from Friedrich Halle, and was learning algebra: 'I like it partly I believe because it is odd in a woman to learn it, & I like to establish my right to be doing odd things.' (MT to EN, winter 1843; *Stevens* letter 12.)
2. One of the main themes in *Villette*. See e.g. chs. 12 and 15.
3. CB uses this spelling in EN 21.3.1841. For Sarah Hannah Sidgwick see EJB 8.6.1839 n. 2.
4. See EN 3.3.1841 n. 1 and 21.3.1841 n. 1.
5. After these words CB began to use pencil instead of ink.
6. MS reads 'than'.
7. MS reads 'women to have'.
8. cf. CB's reflections on 'old maids' in *Shirley* ch. 10. *The Professor* and *Villette* are nevertheless concerned with 'wedlock', either achieved or baffled, between a pupil and a master. See also the poem 'At first I did attention give' (Neufeldt *CBP* 274 and *The Professor* appendix IV.)
9. EN's sister Ann.

To Branwell Brontë, 1 May 1843

Brussels

Dear B

I hear you have written a letter to me; this letter however as usual I have never received which I am exceedingly sorry for, as I have wished very much to hear from you—are you sure that you put the right address and that you paid the English postage 1s/6d without that, letters are never <sent> forwarded. I heard from papa a day or two since—all appears to be going on reasonably well at home—I grieve only that *Emily[1] is so solitary but however you & Anne[2] will soon be returning for the holidays which will cheer the house for a time—Are you in better health and spirits and does Anne continue to be pretty well—? I understand papa has been to see you[3]—did he seem cheerful and well? Mind when you write to me you answer these questions as I wish to know—Also give me a detailed account as to how you get on with your pupil and the rest of the family I have received a general assurance that you do well and are in good odour—but I want to know particulars—

As for me I am very well and wag on[4] as usual, I perceive however that I grow exceedingly misanthropic and sour—you will say this is no news, and that you never knew me possessed of the contrary qualities, philanthropy & sugariness—daß ist wahr (which being translated means that is true) but the fact is the people here are no go whatsoever—amongst 120 persons, which compose the 'daily' population of this house I can discern only 1 or 2 who deserve anything like regard—This is not 'owing to' foolish fastidiousness on my part—but to the absence of decent qualities on theirs—they have not intellect or politeness or good-nature or good-feeling—they are nothing—I don't hate them—hatred would be too warm a feeling—They have no sensations themselves and they excite none—but one wear[ie]s[5] from day to day of caring nothing, fearing nothing, liking nothing hating nothing—being nothing, doing nothing—yes, I teach & sometimes get red-in-the face with impatience at their stupidity—but don't think I ever scold or fly into a passion[6]—if I spoke warmly, as warmly as I sometimes used to do at Roe-Head[7] they would think me mad—nobody ever gets into a passion here[8]—such a thing is not known—the phlegm that thickens their blood is too gluey to boil—they are very false in their relations with each other—but they rarely quarrel & friendship is a folly they are unacquainted with—The black Swan Mr Heger is the sole veritable exception to this rule (for Madame, always cool & always reasoning is not quite an exception) but I rarely speak to Mr now for not being a pupil I have little or nothing to do with him—from time to time he shews his kind-heartedness by loading me with books[9]—so that I am still indebted to him for all the pleasure or amusement I have—

Except for the total want of companionship I have nothing to complain—of—I have not too much to do—sufficient liberty—& I am rarely interfered with—I lead an easiful, stagnant, silent life—for which when I think of Mrs Sedgwick[10] I ought to be very 'thankful'

Be sure you write to me soon—& beg of Anne to inclose a small billet in the same letter—it will be a real charity to do me this kindness—tell me every thing you can think of

It is a curious metaphysical fact that always in the evening when I am in the great Dormitory alone—having no other company than a number of beds with white curtains I always recur as fanatically as ever to the old ideas the old faces & the old scenes in the world below[11]

Give my love to Anne
and believe me
Yourn[12]

Dear Anne
Write to me

Your affectionate Schwester[13]
CB

Mr Heger has just been in & given me a little German Testament as a present[14]—I was surprised for since a good many days[15] he has hardly spoken to me—

MS BL Ashley 161. W & S 156.
Address: not in MS.
PM: not in MS.

1. 'Emily' deleted and 'papa' written above, probably by Mr Brontë himself at a later date.
2. EJB recorded in her Diary Paper of [31].7.45 that 'Branwell went to Thorpgreen as a tutor where Anne still continued—January 1843'. For their employers, the Revd Edmund Robinson and his wife Lydia, see EJB ?2.4.1841 n. 1. Anne taught the two younger daughters, Elizabeth Lydia (16.11.1826–16.1.1882) and Mary (b. 21.3.1828–1.2.1887), and may still have given lessons to the eldest daughter, Lydia Mary (b. 6.9.1825). Branwell was the tutor of the only son, Edmund (19.12.1831–February 1869).
3. Mr Brontë attended the York assizes on 11 and 20 Mar. 1843 as a witness at the trial of men accused of forging a deed of gift by John Beaver, a Haworth Church Land trustee. Sarah Fermi suggests that he visited Thorp Green at this time: Sarah Fermi and Dorinda Kinghorn, 'The Brontës and the Case of the Beaver Forgery' *BST* 21. 1 & 2. 15–24.
4. Jog along. cf. John Bunyan, *The Pilgrim's Progress*, ed. J. B. Wharey, rev. R. Sharrock, 'They made a pretty good shift to wagg along.' (Clarendon edn.; Oxford 1960) 296.
5. CB wrote 'wearys'; 'y' changed to 'i' by ?Branwell or PB.
6. Mrs Gaskell wrote: 'The Hégers have discovered, since the publication of "Villette", that, at this beginning of her career as English teacher in their school, the conduct of her pupils was often impertinent and mutinous in the highest degree. But of this they were unaware at the time, as she had declined their presence, and never made any complaint.' (*Life* i. 286–7.)
7. cf. CB's 'explosions' at Roe Head in her letter to EN of ?Oct. 1836, 'Weary with a day's hard work'.
8. cf. the descriptions of Belgian pupils in *The Professor* ch. 7 and 12.
9. Gifts of books from M. Heger included the works of Bernardin de St Pierre, given to CB on 15 Aug. 1843 (Sotheby's *Catalogue*, 16.12.1916) and *Les Fleurs de la poésie française depuis le commencement du XVIe siècle* (Tours, 1841), inscribed by CB 'Given to me by Monsieur Heger on the 1st January 1844, the morning I left Brussels'.
10. See EJB 8.6.1839 n. 2 and EN ?Apr. 43 n. 3. The words 'for which . . . thankful' were an afterthought, written from 'Sedgwick' onwards in CB's small print-style handwriting.
11. The fantasy world of Angria, shared with Branwell for many years. See CB's letters to Hartley Coleridge, Dec. 1840 and notes and Alexander *EW* and *EEW*.
12. Yours (northern dialect).
13. Sister (German).
14. *Das neue Testament* (London, printed for the British and Foreign Bible Society, 1835), inscribed by CB 'Herr Heger hat mir dieses Buch gegeben | Brußel | Mai 1843 | CB'. ('M. Heger gave me this book; Brussels, May 1843'). BPM, HAO BP, bb 98.
15. A Gallicism. cf. French 'depuis un bon nombre de jours', and see notes to CB's novels in the Clarendon and World's Classics edns. for her fairly frequent use of similar Gallicisms.

Emily J. Brontë to Ellen Nussey, [?22 May 1843]

[Haworth]

Dear Miss Ellen,

I should be wanting in common civility if I did not thank you for your kindness in letting me know of an opportunity to send "postage-free."

I have written as you directed though if "next Tuesday" means tomorrow, I fear it will be too late to go with Mr. Taylor.[1]

Charlotte has never mentioned a word about coming home if you would go over for half a year p[er]haps[2] you might be able to bring her back with you

Charlotte Brontë, 1850 by George Richmond

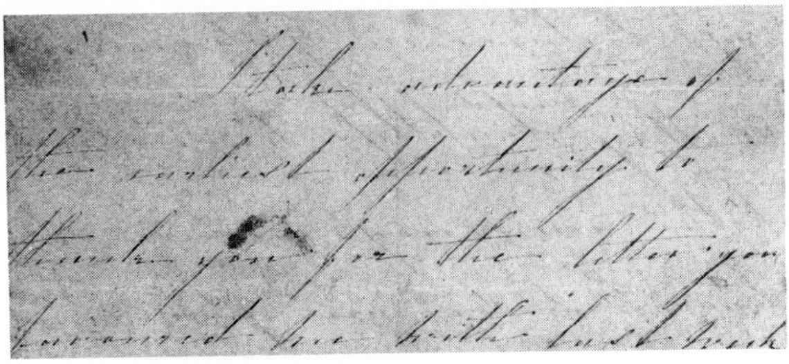

I take advantage of
the earliest opportunity to
thank you for the letter you
favoured me with last week

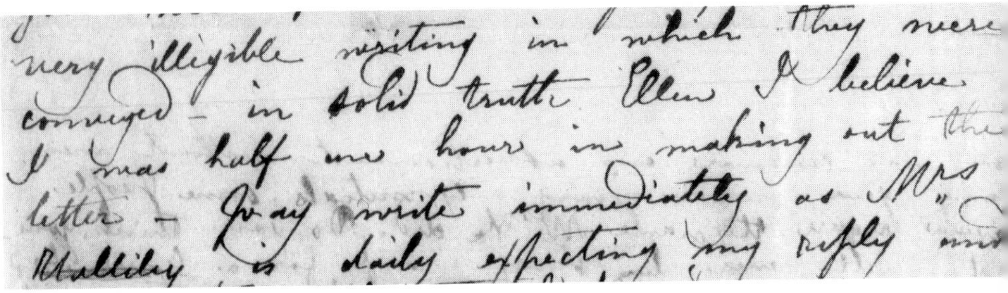

very illegible writing in which they were
conveyed — in solid truth Ellen I believe
I was half an hour in making out the
letter — Pray write immediately as Mrs
Ratliley is daily expecting my reply and

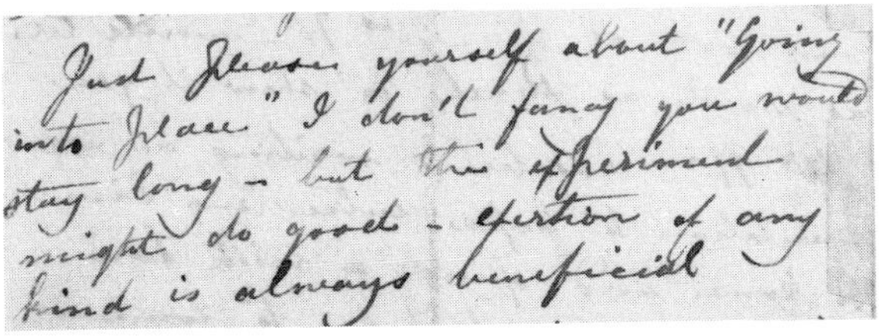

Just please yourself about "Going
into place" I don't fancy you would
stay long — but the experiment
might do good — exertion of any
kind is always beneficial

iiia

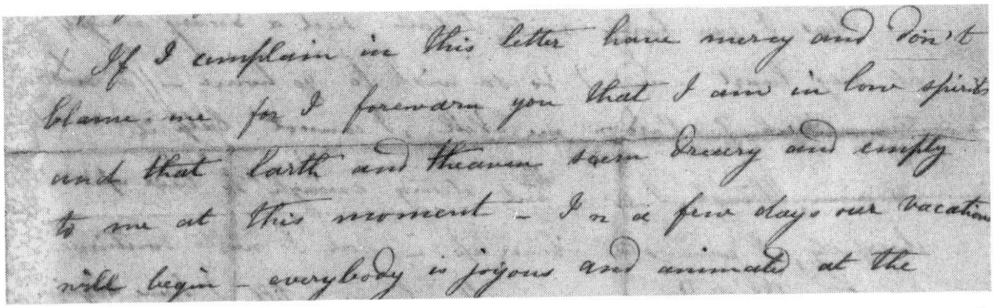

If I complain in this letter have mercy and don't
blame me for I forewarn you that I am in low spirits
and that Earth and Heaven seem dreary and empty
to me at this moment — In a few days our vacation
will begin — everybody is joyous and animated at the

iiib

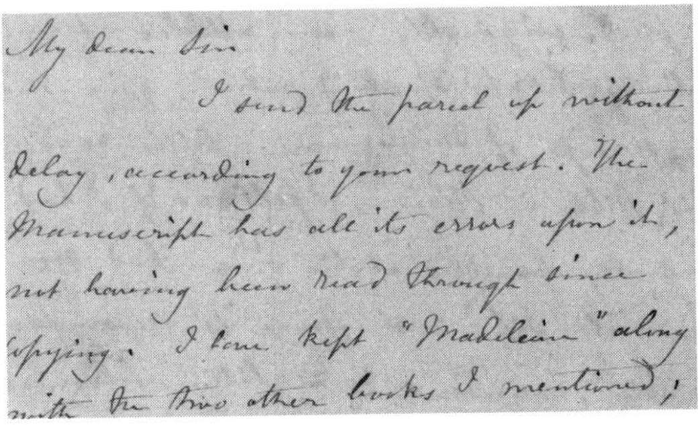

My dear Sir
I send the parcel up without
delay, according to your request. The
Manuscript has all its errors upon it,
not having been read through since
copying. I have kept "Madeleine" along
with the two other books I mentioned;

iv

Charlotte Brontë's handwriting in her letters:

i. To Ellen Nussey, 11 May 1831; MS B.S. 39
ii. To Ellen Nussey, 12 January 1840; MS B.S. 44
iii(a). To Ellen Nussey, May 1841; MS B.S. 48
iii(b). To Ellen Nussey, 6 August 1843; MS B.S. 50.6
iv. To W. S. Williams, 4 February 1849; MS B.S. 67

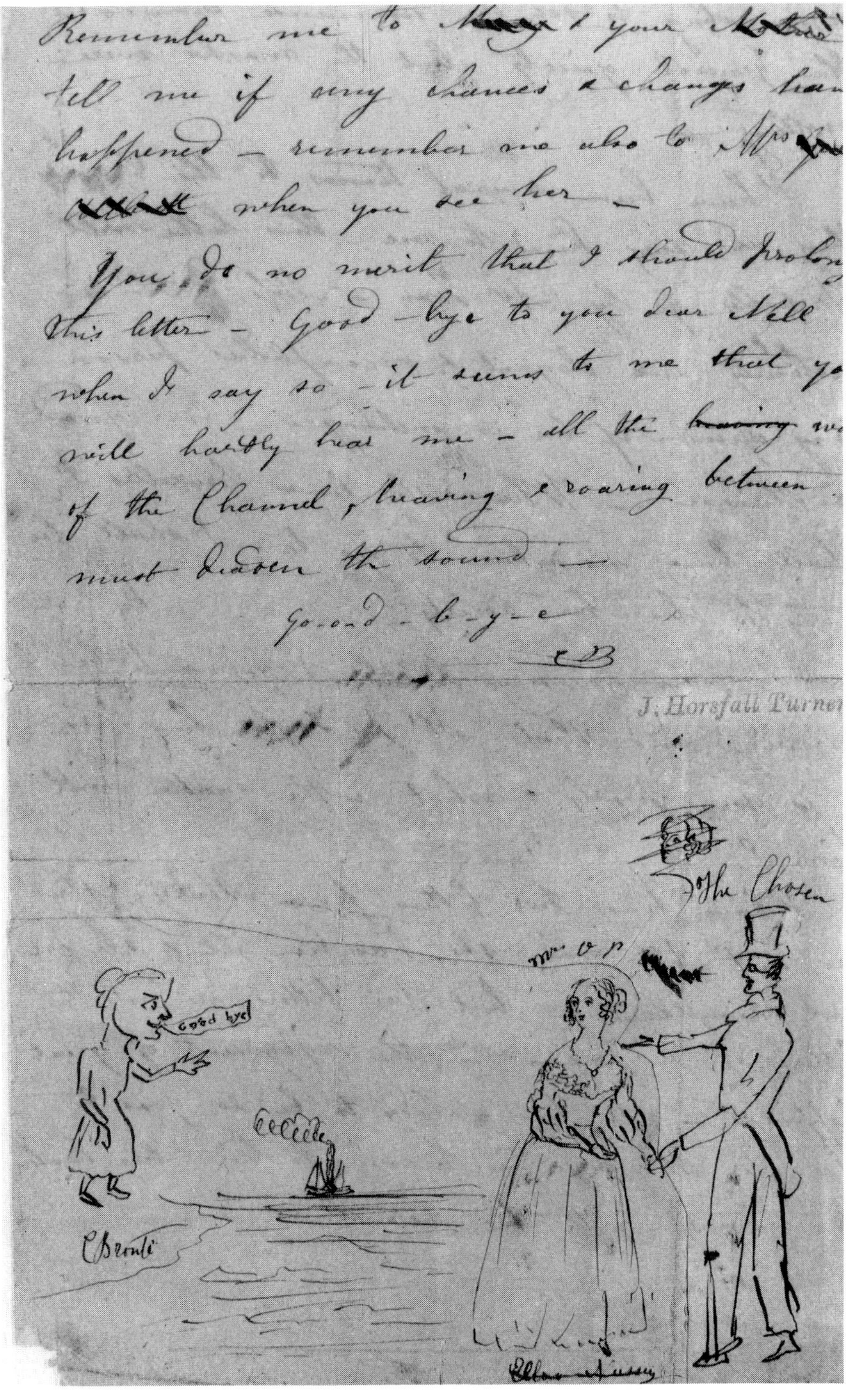
Remember me to [redacted] & your [redacted]
tell me if any chances & changes have
happened — remember me also to Mrs [redacted]
[redacted] when you see her —

You do no merit that I should prolong
this letter — Good-bye to you dear Nell
when I say so — it seems to me that you
will hardly hear me — all the ~~heaving~~ waves
of the Channel, heaving & roaring between
must deaden the sound —

Go-o-d-b-y-e

CB

J. Horsfall Turner

The last page of Charlotte's letter to Ellen Nussey of 6 March 1843, including a sketch of herself waving goodbye to Ellen across the sea from Belgium. MS BPM B. S. 50.4.

A portrait of Ellen Nussey as a young girl

otherwise she might vegetate 'there' till the age of Methusaleh[3] for mere lack of courage to face the voyage.

All here are in good health so was Anne according to the last accounts—the holydays will be here in a week or two and then if 'she' be willing I will get her to write you a proper letter—a feat that I have never performed.

With love and good wishes,
E J Brontë.

MS BL Ashley 177. W & S 157.
Address: not in MS.
PM: not in MS.
Annotation in ink by EN: Emily May 43
Date: based on EN's annotation, on EJB's reference to 'tomorrow' as a Tuesday, and on the approximate dates of AB's return from Thorp Green in other years—2 June in 1841 and mid-June in 1844 and 1845. See EN ?10.6.1841, 23.6.1844, and 18.6.1845. The mourning paper with its heavy black border no doubt dated from Elizabeth Branwell's death on 29.10.1842.

1. Probably Joe Taylor, who accompanied his sister Mary on a 'pleasant expedition' on the Continent until 26 June, when he left her in Hagen, Germany, to resume her teaching of English to 'nice dull' lads. See *Stevens* letter 11.
2. MS reads 'prehaps'.
3. i.e. until she was incredibly old. cf. Genesis 5: 27, 'And all the days of Methuselah were nine hundred sixty and nine years.'

To Emily J. Brontë, 29 May 1843

Brussels

Dear E. J.,—

The reason of the unconscionable demand for money is explained in my letter to papa. Would you believe it, Mdlle. Mühl[1] demands as much for one pupil as for two, namely, 10 francs per month. This, with the 5 francs per month to the Blanchisseuse,[2] makes havoc in £16 per annum. You will perceive I have begun again to take German lessons. Things wag on[3] much as usual here. Only Mdlle Blanche[4] and Mdlle Haussé[5] are at present on a system of war without quarter. They hate each other like two cats. Mdlle Blanche frightens Mdlle Haussé by her white passions (for they quarrel venomously). Mdlle Haussé complains that when Mdlle. Blanche is in fury, "elle n'a pas de lèvres."[6] I find also that Mdlle. Sophie[7] dislikes Mdlle Blanche extremely. She says she is heartless, insincere, and vindictive, which epithets, I assure you, are richly deserved. Also I find she is the regular spy[8] of Mme Heger, to whom she reports everything. Also she invents—which I should not have thought. I have now the entire charge of the English lessons. I have given two lessons to the first class. Hortense [Lannoy][9] was a picture on these occasions, her face was black as a "blue-piled thunder-loft,"[10] and her two ears were red as raw beef. To all questions asked her reply was, "je ne sais pas."[11] It is a pity but her friends could meet with a person qualified to cast out a devil. I am richly off for companionship in these parts. Of late days, M. and Mde Heger rarely speak to me, and I really don't pretend to care a fig for any body else in the establishment. You are not to suppose by that expression that I am under the influence of warm affection for Mde Heger. I am convinced she does not like me—why, I can't tell, nor do I think she herself has any definite reason for the aversion; but for one thing, she cannot comprehend why I do not make intimate friends of Mesdames Blanche, Sophie, and Haussé. M. Heger is wonderously influenced by Madame,[12] and I should not wonder if he disapproves very much of my unamiable want of sociability. He has already given me a brief lecture on universal bienveillance, and, perceiving that I don't improve in consequence, I fancy he has taken to considering me as a person to be let alone—left to the error of her ways; and consequently he has in a great measure withdrawn the light of his countenance,[13] and I get on from day to day in a Robinson-Crusoe-like condition—very lonely. That does not signify.[14] In other respects I have nothing substantial to complain of, nor is even this a cause for complaint. Except the loss of M. Heger's goodwill (if I have lost it) I care for none of 'em. I hope you are well and hearty. Walk out often on the moors. Sorry am I to hear that Hannah[15] is gone, and that she has left you burdened with the charge of the little girl, her sister. I hope Tabby[16] will continue to stay with you—give my love to her. Regards to the fighting gentry,[17] and to old asthma.[18]—Your

C. B.

I have written to Branwell, though I never got a letter from him.

MS untraced. W & S 158.
Address: not in source.
PM: not in source.
Text: *CBCircle* 114–15. Shorter had seen the MS. When he printed the complete letter as a footnote to the brief extract in *Life* 1900 (257–8) he wrote 'Here is the actual letter. The original, from *Charlotte Brontë and her Circle*, is in the possession of Mr. A. B. Nicholls.' *Shorter* 124 reproduces this text. W & S 158 follows Shorter's punctuation and is unlikely to be MS-based. Mrs Gaskell's 'extract' looks like a free version rather than an exact transcript. See Introduction p. 31

1. Not traced. In *Villette* ch. 26 Lucy and Paulina have German lessons from Fräulein Anna Braun, 'a worthy, hearty woman, of about forty-five' who is astonished by her pupils' progress but considers them 'a pair of glacial prodigies, cold, proud, and preternatural'. (435.) For the German lessons cf. EN 6.3.1843 n. 1.
2. The laundress.
3. Things jog on. See BB 1.5.1843 n. 4.
4. See EN May 1842 n. 5.
5. Probably the 'Mademoiselle Marie' referred to in the letter noted above.
6. Literally 'she has no lips'. In *Villette* ch. 14 Lucy says of the Parisienne, Zélie St Pierre, that she has 'lips like a thread' (176) and that she 'sneered again, in her cold, snaky manner' (194).
7. Mlle Sophie, the most likeable of the teachers, was fond of CB: see her letter of 17.12.1843.

8. Cf. *Villette* ch. 8: 'As Madame Beck ruled by espionage, she of course had her staff of spies.'
9. Shorter reads 'Jannoy', but the correction to 'Lannoy' in W & S 158 is confirmed by a reference to a lock of Hortense Lannoy's dark hair, a memento owned by her schoolfellows the Wheelwrights, in Joseph J. Green, *The Brontë–Wheelwright Friendship* (1916).
10. In *JE* ch. 24 Jane tells Rochester that his 'forehead resembles, what, in some very astonishing poetry, I once saw styled, "a blue-piled thunder-loft" ' (330). Mrs Elizabeth Buckley has found the source of the phrase in *Blackwood's Edinburgh Magazine* for Nov. 1830 (xxviii. 813) in Thomas Aird's poem, 'The demoniac', I.X.
11. 'I don't know'.
12. Mme Heger seems to have become increasingly distrustful of CB's attitude to her husband. cf. *Villette*, esp. ch. 38, where Mme Beck tries to separate Lucy and M. Paul.
13. cf. Psalms 4:6.
14. *Life* reads 'I get on here from day to day in a Robinson-Crusoe-like sort of way, very lonely, but that does not signify'. (i. 289.)
15. Not identified. The reference cannot be to Martha Brown's sister Hannah, who was born on 17 Apr. 1841. Mrs Gaskell adds: 'a servant-girl who had been assisting Tabby'. (*Life* i. 289.) According to reminiscences printed in the Halifax *Courier* of 8.12.1908 and reprinted in the *British Weekly* for 20.12.1908, 'two old servants and friends', Hannah Dawson and Martha Brown, were present at CB's deathbed in Mar. 1855.
16. Tabitha Aykroyd, who had returned to the parsonage after an absence. In her *Diary* for 30.7.1841 AB had written, 'Tabby has left us, Martha Brown has come in her place'. Tabby was 72 years old. See EN 21.12.1839 for her lameness, and EN 10.1.1842 for the Brontës' need for a 'good servant who will do all our work'.
17. Presumably the characters in the Gondal saga invented by Emily and Anne Brontë. No prose stories remain, but Emily's verse MSS show that many of her poems relate to Gondal. See EJB *Diaries* 30.7.1841 n. 11 and [31].7.1845: 'The Royalists . . . are hard driven at present by the victorious Republicans—The Gondals still flo[u]rish bright as ever I am at present writing a work on the First Wars.'
18. Emily's tendency to asthma is not mentioned elsewhere. When CB described Emily's state of health to Dr Epps on 9 Dec. 1848 she wrote: 'The patient has hitherto enjoyed pretty good health, though she has never looked strong . . . Her temperament is highly nervous.'

To Revd P. Brontë, [?2 June 1843]: Fragment

[Brussels]

I was very glad to hear from home.[1] I had begun to get low-spirited at not receiving any news, and to entertain indefinite fears that something was wrong. You do not say anything about your own health, but I hope you are well, and Emily also. I am afraid she will have a good deal[2] of hard work to do now that Hannah[3] is gone. I am exceedingly glad to hear that you still keep Tabby.[4] It is an act of great charity to her, and I do not think it will be unrewarded, for she is very faithful and will always serve you, when she has occasion, to the best of her abilities;[5] besides, she will be company for Emily,[6] who without her would be very lonely . . . [7]

MS untraced. W & S 159.
Address: not in source.

PM: not in source.
Date: as given in *Life*.
Text: Rylands MS *Life* fos. 260–1. The letter is not in *Shorter*. W & S 159 reproduces *Life* i. 289–90. The Hatfield typescript text, based on an addition to *Nussey* by EN, has minor variants, of dubious authenticity.

1. CB had received letters from Emily and her father, probably brought by Joe Taylor: see EJB to EN 22.5.1843. Her replies to each of them were probably enclosed in the same packet: if so, the later date of this letter, 4 days after that to Emily, may derive from a postmark.
2. Hatfield reads 'a great deal'.
3. ECG adds '(a servant-girl who had been assisting Tabby)'. See previous letter n. 15.
4. ECG adds '(considerably upwards of seventy)'. See previous letter n. 16.
5. Hatfield reads 'to the utmost of her ability'.
6. cf. BB 1.5.1843 n. 1.
7. The rest of this letter must have included an explanation of CB's 'unconscionable demand for money' for her German lessons. See the previous letter.

To a friend, 5 June 1843

Bruxelles 5 Juni

Meine lieber[1] Freundinn

Du hast ohne Zweifel gehört daſs ich bin nach Belgium wiederkehrt. Es machte mir Schmerz mein Vaterland zu verlaſsen, aber, wie du kennest[2] wohl, wenn[3] man nicht reich ist, man kann[4] nicht immer nach Haus bleiben, man muſst[5] in die Welt fortgehen und trachten mit Arbeitsamkeit und mit[6] Erwerbsamkeit zu verdienen, diese Unabhängigkeit die das Ungefahr ausgeschlagt[7] hat. Oftmals, wenn man von seinen Aeltern entfernt ist, man hat[8] viel Kummer zu[9] leiden, weil man nicht die selbe Gunst und das selbe Vergnügen unter Fremden finden kann, wie in der einigen Familie; allein ich habe das groſe Glück zu wohnen[10] bei einer Dame die mir sehr gut ist.[11]

Sonntag und Montag waren zwei Tage von Vacanz.[12] ' an' Sonntag ich bin[13] spazieren gewesen, mit Fraülein Hauße[14] un[d] drei der Schülerinn; wir haben auf dem Lande gespeist und des Abends sind wir nach Haus wieder[15] gekommen, durch die grüne Allee.[16] Da sahen wir viele Wagen und eine Menge von Herren und von[17] Damen sehr wohl geputz. Montag ich bin[18] nicht fortgegangen denn ich hatte den Schnupfen bekommen.

Heute ist es noch[19] Classe und weil wir alle unser[20] Beschäftigungen anfangen mussen, so habe ich nicht mehr[21] Zeit dir zu schreiben

Ich bin deine dienstwilliger[22] Freundinn
C Brontë

MS Berg. W & S 160.

To a Friend, 5 June 1843; Translation [German exercise]

Brussels, 5 June.

My dear[1] Friend,

No doubt you have heard that I have returned to Belgium. It gave me pain to leave my native land, but as you well know,[2] if[3] one is not rich one cannot[4] always stay at home: one must[5] go out into the world and endeavour, with diligence and with[6] industry, to earn that independence which Fate has denied.[7] Often, when we are separated from our parents, we suffer much distress,[8, 9] because we cannot find the same partiality and pleasure among strangers as in our [own] family. However, I have the great good fortune to live[10] with a lady who is very good to me.[11]

Both Sunday and Monday were holidays.[12] On Sunday I went for a walk[13] with Fräulein Hausse[14] and three of the pupils; we picnicked in the country, and returned[15] home in the evening through the Allée Verte.[16] There we saw many carriages, and crowds of very smartly dressed gentlemen and ladies.[17] On Monday I did[18] not go out because I had caught a cold.

Today it is school again,[19] and since we must all begin our[20] tasks, I have no more[21] time to write to you.

I am your friend [literally 'obliging'[22] friend]
C. Brontë

German text: MS Berg. W & S 160.
Address: not in MS.
PM: not in MS.
Text: This German exercise has been corrected in pencil by CB's teacher, presumably the Mlle Mühl referred to in EJB 29.5.1843. Legible substantive corrections are given in square brackets below. Where the teacher has indicated a changed word-order by adding '2 1' over the words concerned, the corrected version is given.

1. ['e' deleted].
2. [Deleted].
3. [?weil].
4. [kann man].
5. [muß].
6. [Deleted].
7. [ausgeschlagen].
8. [hat man].
9. [deleted].
10. [(zu wohnen)].
11. CB is probably being discreet about her real opinion of Mme Heger.
12. In 1843 Whit Sunday and Monday fell on 4 and 5 June. The last para. of the letter shows that this section at least was written on Tuesday 6 June: CB's date, '5 Juni' may be a slip, or the unchanged date of a rough draft. The letter could not have been written in 1842, when Whit Sunday was 15 May.
13. [bin ich].

14. See EN May 1842 n. 5 and EJB 29.5.1843 n. 5. In *Villette* ch. 33 Lucy Snowe describes a 'breakfast in the country' organized by M. Paul.
15. [Deleted].
16. The 'Allée Verte' or Green Walk was a popular promenade near the Canal de Willebroek, reached by way of the northern boulevards. In *The Professor* William Crimsworth seeks Frances 'on the Boulevards, in the Allée verte, in the Park'. (Ch. 19, 163.)
17. [Deleted].
18. [bin ich].
19. [Deleted].
20. [unsere].
21. [viel].
22. ['dienst' and 'r' deleted].

To Ellen Nussey, [?late June 1843]

[Brussels]

Dear Ellen

What a little sturdy body you are, and your sturdiness is a good thing if you are quite sure that you are in the right—but you should be very sure before you give yourself up to it.[1] I think it is a good thing that you have got your sister *Anne home—give my love to her—As well as I can see I think *Joe *Taylor is looking very well[2]—but that family always have colour—You are foolish to be so reluctant to go to *Hunsworth[3]—go—and don't be ashamed to say that you like *Joe *Taylor—he is worthy of being liked and admired also—which few men are—as to being desperately in love that is another thing—but I don't think you will tumble head over ears into that gulph—I get on here after a fashion—but now that *Mary *Dixon has left Bruxelles[4] I have nobody to speak to—for I count the Belgians as nothing—Sometimes I ask myself how long I shall stay here—but as yet I have only asked the question I have not answered it—However when I have acquired as much German as I think fit I think I shall pack up bag & baggage and depart—twinges of home-sickness cut me to the heart every now & then.

I do not give to the (I am forced to take a pencil—my pen is unmanageable) I say I do not give to the step Mary *Taylor has taken[5] the unqualified approbation you do—It is a step proving an energetic and active mind, proving the possession of courage, independence—talent, but it is not a prudent step—Often genius like Mary's triumphs over every obstacle without the aid of prudence—and she may be successful—hitherto she is so—but opinion & custom run so strongly against what she does—that I see there is danger of her having much uneasiness to suffer—if her pupils had been girls it would be all well—the fact of their being boys 'or rather young men'[6] is the stumbling-block—This opinion is for you only, mind—

The <likeness>portrait you send of *Henry is like—but not a likeness worth preserving—his notion of being a Missionary is amusing[7]—he would not live a year in the climates of those countries where Missionaries are wanted—

None of your family have much stamina in the constitution, on the contrary all are delicate and he one of the most so—

To-day the weather is gloomy and I am stupified with a bad cold and a headache

I have nothing to tell you my dear Ellen one day is like another in this place—I know you, living in the country can hardly believe that it is possible life can be monotonous in the centre of a brilliant capital like Brussels—but so it is—I feel it most on the holidays—when all the girls and teachers go out to visit—and it sometimes happens that I am left during several hours quite alone—with 4 great desolate schoolrooms at my disposition—I try to read, I try to write but in vain I then wander about from room to room—but the silence and loneliness of all the house weighs down one's spirits like lead[8]—you will hardly believe it when I tell you that Mde *Heger (good & kind as I have described her) never comes near me on these occasions—she is a reasonable and calm woman but Nelly as to warmheartedness She has as much of that article as Mrs *Allbutt[9]—I own I was astonished the first time I was left alone thus—when everybody else was enjoying the pleasures of a fête-day with their friends—and she knew I was quite by myself and never took the least notice of me—Yet I understand she praises me very much to everybody and says what excellent lessons I give &c.—She is not colder to me than she is to the other teachers—but they are less dependant on her than I am—they have relations & acquaintance in Bruxelles

You remember the letter she wrote me when I was in England how kind and affectionate it was[10]—is it not odd—? I fancy I begin to perceive the reason of this mighty distance & reserve[11] it sometimes makes me laugh & at other times nearly cry—When I am sure 'of it', I will tell it you

In the meantime the complaints I make at present are for your ear only, a sort of relief which I permit myself—In all other respects I am well satisfied with my position—and you may say so to people who inquire after me (if any one ever does)

Write to me dear Nell whenever you can—you do a good deed when you send me a letter—for you comfort a very desolate heart

Goodbye—love to your Mother & Sisters

[Unsigned]

MS Pierpont Morgan MA 2696. W & S 166 as 15 Nov. 1843.
Address: not in MS.
PM: not in MS.
Annotation in ink by EN: 82 Brussels —43
Date: probably late June. The letter is on similar paper to that of 6.8.1843 and must precede it, since CB has only just received the portrait of Henry Nussey, belatedly returned on 6 Aug.; but she has not yet heard of Sarah Walker Nussey's death on 16 June. It must follow Mary Dixon's departure in early or mid-June for a tour of the Continent. See n. 4 below. The misplacing/misdating of the

letter in the *Life*, *Shorter* 128 (Nov. 1843), and W & S 166 (15 Nov.) remained uncorrected partly because all three had failed to record the subsequent return of the portrait.

1. EN may have renewed her intention of 'going out' as a governess. cf. EN 24.1.1840.
2. Joe Taylor had begun a journey from Hagen in North Germany back to England on 26 June, as Mary Taylor's letter to EN of 25 June explains: 'I am sorry you will not get this letter by Joe; I had intended you should but I find myself so tired after a day's travelling . . . Joe leaves me tomorrow.' (MS Texas; *Stevens* letter 11.) He could well have returned via Brussels, collecting CB's letters on the way.
3. The village where John and Joe Taylor lived in the cottage next to their mill. See EN 3.1.1841 and n. 2.
4. Mary Dixon and her brother Abram were travelling for the sake of their health in Germany. Their father received letters from them on 6 July from Königswinter in the Rhineland and on 8 July from Laubach, about 50 miles further south, where Mary and Joe Taylor had earlier seen them 'both so much better for the cold water system that they recommended it to every one'. (MS Texas; *Stevens* letter 11 with the misreading 'Lambach'; and see Abram Dixon to Mary Dixon 24.7.1843, Dixon Collection, Leeds City Museum.)
5. Mary's unconventional insistence on earning her own living by teaching English to German boys had shocked some of her English friends. She wrote to EN on 25.6.1843 'When I am not engaged in teaching I am learning, Music & German; so that with sewing (only what I can't help) walking out, seeing my neighbours eating & sleeping I have not a moment to spare . . . I am not surprised to hear that Miss C. [Katherine] Wooler has cut me dead. Miss Wooler should have known better but she is timid & will probably come back again if ever I should make my appearance in your parts.' (MS Texas; *Stevens* letter 11.)
6. Mary described her German pupils as 'nice dull' lads. (*Stevens* letter 11.)
7. In his Journal for 25 June 1830 Henry Nussey had written: 'should it be the Lord's Will, I would for Christ's sake gladly be called to be a Missionary; if I could in any degree be an instrument in God's hands, of promoting the salvation of mankind.' (HN *Diary* fol. 2v.) Since then head injuries had caused some difficulties in public speaking, and Henry had experienced undue excitement at missionary meetings at Burton Agnes in 1838. His missionary aims must have revived during his curacy at Earnley; but in fact his next move was to Hathersage in Derbyshire in 1844.
8. cf. Lucy Snowe's description of the silent 'lifeless' pensionnat, and its 'house-roof . . . crushing as the slab of a tomb' in *Villette* ch. 15, 225.
9. Possibly Mrs George Allbutt, née Brook, the wife of a Batley GP. See EN 6.3.1843 n. 12. It is most unlikely that CB was referring to Miss Wooler's sister, Mrs Marianne Allbutt, who had died on 28 May 1843, and whom she recalled as a 'most tender and thoughtful' mother in a letter to Margaret Wooler of 30.8.1853. W & S 166 unaccountably reads 'Taylor' for 'Allbutt'.
10. This letter has apparently not survived, but cf. EN 30.1.1843, 'Mde Heger received me with great kindness'.
11. Mme Heger may have been aware of CB's increasing warmth of feeling for her husband. In CB's poem, 'At first I did attention give', the pupil's love for her schoolmaster is thwarted by a victorious rival. See *The Professor* appendix IV, and Neufeldt *CBP* 274–5.

To Ellen Nussey, 6 August, 1843

Brussels

Dear Ellen

You never answered my last letter but however forgiveness is a part of the Christian Creed and so having an opportunity to send a letter to England [I][1] forgive you and write to you again

If I complain in this letter have mercy and don't blame me for I forewarn you that I am in low spirits and that Earth and Heaven seem dreary and empty to me at this moment—In a few days our vacations[2] will begin—everybody is joyous and animated at the prospect because everybody is to go home—I know that I am to stay here during the 5 weeks that the holidays last and that I shall be much alone and consequently get downcast and find both days & nights of a weary length—It is the first time in my life that I have really dreaded the vacation

Last Sunday afternoon being at the Chapel Royal[3] in Brussels I was surprised to hear a voice proceed from the pulpit—which instantly brought all *Birstal and all *Battley[4] before my mind's eye—I could ?see nothing but I certainly thought that unclerical little Welsh pony *Jenkins[5] was there—I buoyed up my mind with the expectation of receiving a letter from you but however<J> as I have got none I suppose I must have been mistaken

Alas I can hardly write, I have such a dreary weight at my heart—and I do so wish to go home—is not this childish? Pardon me Nell, I cannot help it

However, though I am not strong enough to bear up cheerfully, I can still bear up—here I will continue to stay (DV) some months longer—till I have acquired German—and then I hope to see all your faces again Would that the vacation were well over—it will pass so slowly—

Do have the Christian charity to write to me a long, long letter—fill it with the minutest details nothing will be uninteresting—Do not think it is because people are unkind to me that I wish to leave Belgium—nothing of the sort, everybody is abundantly civil—but home-sickness keeps creeping over me—I cannot shake it off—

I beg ten thousand pardons for forgetting to return the likeness of *Henry—I enclose it in this letter be sure and keep it carefully—it is such a flattering likeness—may I ask who did it?[6]

You may scold me or say what you like to me about this being a scanty, shabby letter—if you had answered my last I might perhaps have had courage to write more—as it is I am incapable—

Remember me to your *Mother and *Mercy
and believe me
Very merrily, vivaciously, gaily
Yourn[7]
C B

Brussels Augst. 6th. —43
Since I wrote the preceding pages Mr *Jenkins has called—he brought no <news> 'letter' from you but said you were at Harrogate[8]—and that they could not find the letter you had intended to send—He informed me of two melancholy events[9]—Poor Sarah![10] when I last bid her good bye I little thought

I should never see her more—Certainly however she is happy where she is gone—far happier than she was here—when the first days of mourning are past you will see that you have reason rather to rejoice at her removal than to grieve for it—Your poor Mother I am sure will have felt her death much—and you also—I fear from the circumstance of your being at Harrogate that you are yourself ill—Write to me soon Ellen—

MS BPM B.S. 50.6. W & S 161 (part).
Address: not in MS.
PM: not in MS.
Annotation in ink by EN: Brussels Aug 6 —43

1. Text obscured by mounting.
2. cf. ch. 15 in *Villette*, 'The Long Vacation', where Lucy Snowe's 'heart almost died within' her in the desolate pensionnat. (218.)
3. For a description of this small rococo 'Chapelle de la Cour', begun in 1760 in what is now the Place du Musée, see Gérin *CB* 199–200. Anglican services alternated with 'Belgian Protestant and German Lutheran services', as CB recalled in *The Professor*, where William Crimsworth attends 'German, French and English services' in the hope of seeing Frances Henri. (Ch. 19, 163.)
4. The word is clumsily written, but a mis-spelling of 'Batley', the township between Birstall and Dewsbury, seems the most likely reading.
5. The Revd Evan Jenkins, MA, the English episcopal clergyman and 'Chaplain to H.M. King Leopold'. See CB to E. Branwell 29.9.1841, n. 7. His Welsh voice would recall that of his nephew, the Revd Joseph Walker Jenkins, curate of Batley. See MT to EN 4.4.1842 n. 9. Ellen Nussey would know the Revd Evan Jenkins, who visited his English relatives, as Abraham Dixon had noted on 3.6.1842: 'It is probable Mr Jenkins will be in Yorkshire next month, on a visit to his Brother at Pudsey, & nephew, the curate to Mr. Cassel at Batley.' (Letter to Mary Dixon, Leeds City Museum.) On 24 July 1843 Abraham Dixon wrote: 'Mr Jenkins has been very ill of a brain fever & confined several days to his bed, he was taken ill on the day after his return from London about ten days ago, Mrs Jenkins in consequence came up from Ostend. he is now better & they set off this morning from Ostend, from whence they go again to London, or rather to Greenwich for about a fortnight.' (Letter to Mary Dixon, Leeds City Museum.) These events help to explain CB's surprise. The Jenkins's absence must also have intensified her feeling of isolation.
6. 'I beg ten thousand . . . who did it?' *Shorter* 125 and W & S 161 omit this paragraph.
7. Yours. (Northern dialect.)
8. 'One of the principal watering places in the north of England.' Its springs were esteemed 'for curing scorbutic, cutaneous and chronic disorders' and the surrounding country was 'highly picturesque and beautiful, abounding with the residences of nobility and gentry', the situation of the town high, and the air 'cool and salubrious.' (*Dugdale* 934.)
9. CB refers in detail to only one event; but see the next note.
10. Sarah Walker Nussey (1809–43), Ellen's invalid sister, had died of a painful infection in the small intestine on 16 June. cf. EN 10.11.1834 where CB says that Sarah had been very ill, but that her death would be a gain for her. When Mary Taylor heard of her death she wrote to Ellen, 'Be comforted in this gloomy hour by the reflection of the care & kindness she received from you.' (*Stevens* letter 11, 25.6.1843; Texas MS.) Ellen's second cousin, also called Sarah Nussey (1819–43), the daughter of John Nussey of White Lee, Batley, had also died, on 21 July. In the letter quoted above, Mary Taylor wrote, 'I am very sorry to hear of Sarah Nussey's, to me, sudden illness. They will certainly lose the "flower of the flock" in losing her.'

To Emily J. Brontë, 2 September 1843

Bruxelles

Dear E. J.,

Another opportunity of writing to you coming to pass, I shall improve it by scribbling a few lines. More than half the holidays are now past, and rather better than I expected. The weather has been exceedingly fine during the last fortnight, and yet not so Asiatically hot as it was last year at this time. Consequently I have tramped about a great deal and tried to get a clearer acquaintance with the streets of Bruxelles. This week, as no teacher is here except Mdlle. Blanche, who is returned from Paris, I am always alone except at meal-times, for Mdlle. Blanche's character is so false and so contemptible[1] I can't force myself to associate with her. She perceives my utter dislike and never now speaks to me—a great relief.

However, I should inevitably fall into the gulf of low spirits if I stayed always by myself here without a human being to speak to, so I go out and traverse the Boulevards and streets of Bruxelles sometimes for hours together.[2] Yesterday I went on a pilgrimage to the cemetery,[3] and far beyond it on to a hill where there was nothing but fields as far as the horizon. When I came back it was evening; but I had such a repugnance to return to the house, which contained nothing that I cared for, I still kept threading the streets in the neighbourhood of the Rue d'Isabelle and avoiding it. I found myself opposite to Ste. Gudule,[4] and the bell, whose voice you know, began to toll for evening salut.[5] I went in, quite alone (which procedure you will say is not much like me), wandered about the aisles where a few old women were saying their prayers, till vespers begun. I stayed till they were over. Still I could not leave the church or force myself to go home—to school I mean. An odd whim came into my head.[6] In a solitary part of the Cathedral six or seven people still remained kneeling by the confessionals. In two confessionals I saw a priest. I felt as if I did not care what I did, provided it was not absolutely wrong, and that it served to vary my life and yield a moment's interest. I took a fancy to change myself into a Catholic and go and make a real confession to see what it was like. Knowing me as you do, you will think this odd, but when people are by themselves they have singular fancies. A penitent was occupied in confessing. They do not go into the sort of pew or cloister which the priest occupies, but kneel down on the steps and confess through a grating. Both the confessor and the penitent whisper very low, you can hardly hear their voices. After I had watched two or three penitents go and return I approached at last and knelt down in a niche which was just vacated. I had to kneel there ten minutes waiting, for on the other side was another penitent invisible to me. At last that went away[7] and a little wooden door inside the grating opened, and I saw the priest leaning his ear towards me. I was obliged to begin, and yet I did not know a word of the formula with which they always commence their confessions. It was a funny position. I felt precisely as I did when alone on the Thames at midnight.[8] I commenced with saying I was a foreigner and had been brought up a Protestant. The priest asked if I was a Protestant then. I somehow could not tell a lie and said 'yes.' He replied that in that case I could not '<u>jouir du bonheur de la confesse</u>';[9] but I was determined to confess, and at last he said he would allow me because it might be the first step towards returning to the true church. I actually did confess—a real confession.[10] When I had done he told me his address, and said that every morning I was to go to the rue du Parc[11]—to his house—and he would reason with me and try to convince me of the error and enormity of being a Protestant!!! I promised faithfully to go. Of course, however, the adventure stops there, and I hope I shall never see the priest again. I think you had better not tell papa of this. He will not understand that it was only a freak, and will perhaps think I am going to turn Catholic. Trusting that you and papa are well, and also Tabby and the [Hoyles][12], and hoping you will write to me immediately,—I am, yours,

C. B.

MS untraced. W & S 162.
Address: not in source.
PM: not in source.
Text: *CBCircle* 117–18, introduced as a 'newly-discovered Brontë treasure'. See p. 57. W & S 162 reproduces *Shorter* 126, except for 'Hoyles' in the last sentence, replacing Shorter's 'Holyes'. See n. 12 below.

1. For Mlle Blanche see EN May 1842 n. 5. To her paraphrase of parts of this letter, which omits the confession episode, Mrs Gaskell adds that Mlle Blanche 'was more profligate, more steeped in a kind of cold, systematic sensuality, than [Charlotte] had 'before' imagined it possible for a human being to be; and her whole nature revolted from <her> 'this woman's' Society.' (Rylands MS *Life* fol. 268.) It is not clear whether Mrs Gaskell based her comments on material in the holograph omitted by later editors, on reminiscences by CB, or on the descriptions of Zélie St Pierre in *Villette*.
2. In 1843 Brussels was still encircled by tree-shaded boulevards, dating from 1818, following the line of the city walls, and 'plantés de quatre rangées d'arbres . . . offrant sur les riants environs des points de vue ravissants'. (W. B. Craan, Map of Bruxelles, 1835; 'planted with four rows of trees [and] giving enchanting prospects of the smiling landscape beyond them'.)
3. The Protestant cemetery where Martha Taylor had been buried in Oct. 1842. See MT to EN 30.10.1842 and 1.11.1842 notes 1 and 2.
4. The rue d'Isabelle, the site of Mme Heger's pensionnat, had been created in 1625 'to provide a short cut for the general public to the Collegiate Church of S. Michel and Ste. Gudule' (founded in 1226). See Gérin *CB* 187–8. In *Life* Mrs Gaskell suppresses all references to the church, and uses in its place the description of Lucy Snowe exhausting herself by threading the streets of the city in *Villette* 221–2; see Rylands MS *Life* fol. 269.
5. The evening service.
6. CB uses this event in ch. 15 of *Villette* but adds to it by involving the priest in her heroine's later experiences.
7. The text may be corrupt.
8. cf. *Villette* ch. 6: 'Down the sable flood we glided . . . I asked myself if I was wretched or

terrified. I was neither . . . "How is this?" said I. "Methinks I am animated and alert, instead of being depressed and apprehensive?" I could not tell how it was.' (68.)

9. I could not enjoy the privilege of confession.
10. Biographers have speculated that CB confessed her love for M. Heger (e.g. Gérin *CB* 241–2) but the letter remains enigmatic. In the *Villette* confessional scene (225–8) Lucy Snowe's 'pressure of affliction' is said to be neither a sin nor a crime.
11. CB perhaps refers to the steep rue Montagne du Parc, not far from Ste Gudule, leading down from the park and the rue Royale towards the rue de la Chancellerie.
12. W & S 162 prints the name without a query, and adds a footnote: 'A family with whom the Rev. W. Weightman, curate of Haworth, is understood to have lived until his death on 6 Sept., 1842.' But the 1841 Census for Haworth shows that Mr Weightman was then lodging with the widowed Mrs Grace Ogden at Cook Gate. Shorter, who reads 'the Holyes' in *CBCircle* 118, *Life* 1900 266, and *Shorter* 126, believed that CB was making a 'playful reference to the curates'.

To Emily J. Brontë, [1 October 1843]

[Brussels]

This is Sunday morning. They are at their idolatrous "Messe";[1] and I am here, that is, in the Refectoire.[2] I should like uncommonly to be in the dining-room at home, or in the kitchen, or in the back kitchen. I should like even to be cutting up the hash, with the clerk and some register-people[3] at the other table, and you standing by, watching that I put enough flour, not too much pepper, and, above all, that I save the best pieces of the leg of mutton for Tiger and Keeper;[4] the first of which personages would be jumping about the dish and carving-knife, and the latter standing like a devouring flame on the kitchen-floor. To complete the picture, Tabby blowing the fire, in order to boil the potatoes to a sort of vegetable glue! How divine are these recollections to me at this moment! Yet I have no thoughts of coming home just now. I lack a real pretext for doing so; it is true, this place is dismal to me, but I cannot go home, without a fixed prospect when I get there; and this prospect must not be a situation; that would be jumping out of the frying pan into the fire. You call yourself idle! absurd, absurd! . . . Is Papa well? Are you well? And Tabby? You ask about Queen Victoria's visit to Brussels.[5] I saw her for an instant flashing through the Rue Royale in a carriage and six, surrounded by soldiers. She was laughing and talking, very gaily.[6] She looked a little, stout, vivacious Lady, very plainly dressed, not much dignity or pretension about her. The Belgians liked[7] her very well on the whole—They said she enlivened the sombre[8] court of King Leopold, which is usually as gloomy as a conventicle.[9] Write to me again soon. Tell me whether Papa really wants me very much to come home, and whether you do likewise. I have an idea that I should be of no use there; a sort of aged person upon the parish.[10] I pray, with heart and soul, that all may continue well at Haworth; above all, in our grey half-inhabited house. God bless the walls thereof. Safety, health, happiness, and prosperity to you, Papa, and Tabby. Amen.

C. B.

MS untraced. W & S 163.
Address: not in source.
PM: not in source.
Date: Mrs Gaskell dates 'Dec. 1st 1843' in *Life*, but the content, esp. the reference to Queen Victoria's visit (15–20 Sept. 1843), indicates Oct., when the 1st of the month was a Sunday. 'Oct' and 'Dec' are readily confused in CB's hand.
Text: Rylands MS *Life* i. fos. 273–4. W & S 163 begins 'Dear E. J.' but elsewhere reproduces printed editions of *Life*, with minor punctuation variants, and a redating from Dec. to Oct.

1. With this description of the Catholic Mass compare CB's hostile account of the 'solemn(?) rite' of the 'prière du midi' in *The Professor* ch. 14, and her references to 'chanting priests or mumming officials' in *Villette* ch. 36.
2. In *Villette* ch. 21 Lucy chooses to sit alone in the refectory, 'where the stove was lit and the air was warm; through the rest of the house it was cold'. (330.)
3. Probably Haworth villagers giving notice to the parish clerk of baptisms, deaths, and marriages.
4. The *Hatfield* text, an inaccurate copy of EN's transcript of this letter from the *Life*, reads 'the cat and keeper'. In her *Diary* for [31].7.1845 EJB notes 'got and lost Tiger . . . Tiger died early last year. Keeper and Flossey are well.' The 'tawny, strong limbed "Keeper" ' (the model for the dog Tartar in *Shirley*) was described by EN in her 'Reminiscences' as 'Emily's favorite, he was so completely under her control she could quite easily make him spring and roar like a lion'. (See Appendix.) John Stores Smith described Keeper as a 'conglomerate, combining every species of English caninity from the turnspit to the sheepdog, with a strain of Haworth originality superadded'. (*Free Lance* 14 Mar. 1868, quoted by Shorter in his note to *Life* (1900) ch. 24, 550; and see K. Tillotson, 'A Day with Charlotte Brontë in 1850', *BST* 16. 81. 22–30.)
5. Leopold I (1790–1865), elected King of the Belgians in 1831, was Victoria's uncle and trusted adviser. Prince Albert described the 6-day tour of Belgium, from 15 to 20 Sept. 1843, to Baron Stockmar: 'The old Cities of Flanders . . . had put on their fairest array, and were very tastefully decorated . . . Victoria was greatly interested and impressed; and the cordiality and friendliness which met us everywhere could not fail to attract her towards the Belgian people.' (Mrs Oliphant, Robert Wilson, and others, *The Life and Times of Queen Victoria* (4 Vols.; n.d. but *c.* 1900–3), i. 146.) See also Gérin *CB* 242–4.
6. The Queen wrote to King Leopold on 21 Sept.: 'It was such a joy for me to be under the roof of one who has ever been a father to me!' (Quoted in C. Woodham-Smith, *Queen Victoria: Her Life and Times* (1972), i. 244.
7. *Hatfield* reads 'like'.
8. *Hatfield* reads 'sedate'.
9. i.e. as gloomy as a Dissenters' meeting. Queen Marie-Louise of the Belgians had been deeply affected by the death of her favourite brother the Duke of Orleans in July 1842—an event which had prevented Queen Victoria from paying an intended visit to Belgium in that year. Compare also CB's description of the King as a 'nervous, melancholy man' in *Villette* ch. 20, 303.
10. Lit., like a pauper too old to work, who had to be supported by poor relief or workhouse accommodation, which it was the duty of the parish to provide.

The Revd Patrick Brontë to ?Mr Greenwood,[1] *4 October 1843*

Haworth,
October 4th, 1843.

Dear Sir,

When you see John Crabtree,[2] you will oblige me by desiring Him to pay the debt which he owes. Since you and Mrs. Greenwood call'd on me, on a particular occasion, I have been particularly, and more than ever guarded. Yet notwithstanding all I have done, even to the injury of my health, they keep propagating false reports—I mean to single out one or two of these slanderers, and to prosecute them, as the Law directs. I have lately been using a lotion for my eyes, which are very weak, and they have ascribed the smell of that, to a smell of a more exceptionable[3] character. These things are hard,[4] but perhaps under Providence, I may live to overcome them all. With all our kindest regards to you and your Family, I remain, Dear Sir,

Yours, very truly,
P. Brontë.

MS untraced. W & S 164.
Address: not in source.
PM: not in source.
Text: Maude Goldring, *Charlotte Bronte the Woman* (1915) 92–3. Goldring's punctuation probably reproduces that of the original MS more accurately than W & S 164 or *LD* 375.

1. The name of the recipient is not given by M. Goldring. W & S and *LD* both give 'Mr. Greenwood', the former with a query, *LD* without question, adding that he was 'the church trustee'. The trustee Joseph Greenwood of Spring Head was a widower, but there were many 'Mrs Greenwoods' in the area. M. Goldring prints the letter as one of two seen 'through the kindness of Mr. [Charles] Bairstow' of the Manor House, Stanbury, the grandson of George Taylor (1801–65), to whom the second of the two letters was sent by PB on 29.2.1844. A member of the Taylor family would seem to be a possible recipient for the present letter.
2. Not identified. The surname was a common one in Haworth and Keighley.
3. *LD* 375 reads 'objectionable'. For Ellen Nussey's belief that CB returned from Brussels because her father was drinking to excess with his curate, the Revd James William Smith, see EJB 19.12.1843 n. 4.
4. *LD* 375 reads 'hard to bear'.

To Ellen Nussey, 13 October [1843]

Brussels

Dear Ellen

I was glad to receive your last letter but when I read it—its contents gave me some <hu> 'pain'—it was melancholy indeed that so soon after the death of a sister[1] you should be called away from a distant county by the news of the severe illness of a <?a mother> brother [2]—and that after your return home your sister *Anne should fall ill too—A note I received yesterday from Mary Dixon[3] informs me that *Anne is now better but that *George is scarcely expected to recover—is this true—? I hope not—for his sake and for yours—His loss would indeed be a blow to his mother and sisters—a blow which I hope providence will long avert—do not my dear Ellen fail to write to me soon—to inform me how affairs get on at *Brookroyd—I cannot fail to be anxious on the subject—your family being amongst the number of the oldest & kindest friends I have. I trust the season of your afflictions will soon pass—it has been a long one—

Mary *Taylor is getting on well—as she deserves to [?do][4]—I often hear from her [5]—her letters and yours are one of my few pleasures—she urges me very much to leave Brussels and go to her—'but' at present however tempted to take such a step I should not feel justified in doing so—To leave a certainty for a complete uncertainty would be to the last degree imprudent

Notwithstanding Brussels is indeed desolate to me now—since Mary *Dixon left I have had no friend—I had indeed some very kind acquaintances in the family of Dr *Wheelwright[6]—but they too are gone now—they left in latter part of August—and I am completely alone—I cannot count the Belgians as anything—Madame *Heger is a politic—plausible and interested person[7]—I no longer trust her—It is a curious position to be so utterly solitary in the midst of numbers—sometimes this solitude oppresses me to an excess—one day lately I felt as if I could bear it no longer—and I went to Mde *Heger and gave her notice—If it had depended on her I should certainly have soon been at liberty but Monsieur *Heger—having heard of what was in agitation—sent for me the day after—and pronounced with vehemence his decision that I should not leave—I could not at that time have persevered in my intention without exciting him to passion—so I promised to stay a while longer—how long that while will be I do n[ot][8] know—I should not like to return to England [to][9] do nothing—I am too old for that now—but if I could hear of a favourable occasion for commencing a school—I think I should embrace it.

I have much to say Ellen—many little odd things queer and puzzling enough—which I do not like to trust to a letter, but which one day perhaps or rather one evening—if ever we should find ourselves again by the fireside at Haworth or at Brookroyd with our feet on the fender—curling our hair—I may communicate to you—

We have as yet no fires here and I suffer much from cold otherwise I am well in health—. Mr *George *Dixon[10] will take this letter to England—he is a pretty-looking & pretty behaved young man—apparently constructed without a back-bone—by which I don't allude to his corporeal spine—which is all right enough—but to his character

Farewell dear Ellen—I hope by the time you receive this Mr *George will be quickly gathering strength he has been severely tried—I hope also your Sister *Anne will be quite well—give my love to your Mother & Sisters and my good wishes to Mr *George anything you like to yourself dear Nell—

C B—

MS HM 24433. W & S 165.
Address (integral): E Nussey
PM: none.
Annotation in pencil by EN: Oct 13 | (1843) [on 2^{v}]: Brussels | Oct 43

1. Sarah Walker Nussey. See EN 6.8.1843 n. 10.
2. George Nussey, whose recurrent bouts of mental illness were becoming more frequent. He had been ill earlier in the year: writing on 25 June from Germany, Mary Taylor told EN that she had heard that George was going to try a water-cure at Ilkley. (*Stevens* letter 11.) See EN ?30.12.1844 n. 1.
3. See EN ?late June 1843, n. 4. Mary Dixon's father Abraham Dixon, writing to her from Brussels on 24.7.1843, had expected her to return to her brothers in Chad Road, Birmingham, but then to continue with the 'cold water system' she had begun on her travels. She had accordingly gone to Yorks. for further treatment, and had evidently visited or heard from the Nusseys—probably while she was in Leeds, on her way to Ilkley. See the next letter.
4. Paper torn.
5. Mary's letters to CB for this period do not survive, but her lively and amusing letters to EN of 25 June and winter 1843 (Texas and Berg MSS, *Stevens* letters 11 and 12) describe her life in Germany. She taught 42, and later 48 lessons a week, making more money than she needed to live on, and paying for tuition in music and German. Letter 12 mentions her reading of George Sand's novel, *Consuelo* (1842–3), and gives a spirited account of one of her music lessons from Friedrich Halle, father of Sir Charles Hallé.
6. See M. Heger's letter to PB, 5.11.1842, n. 7.
7. cf. CB's reference to Mme Heger as 'always cool and always reasoning' in BB 1.5.1843. On 14 Oct. CB wrote inside the back cover of her *Russell's General Atlas of Modern Geography* (London; n.d.): 'Brussels—Saturday Morning Octbr 14th 1843,—First Class—I am very cold—there is no Fire—I wish I were at home with Papa—Branwell—Emily—Anne & Tabby—I am tired of being amongst foreigners it is a dreary life—especially as there is only one person in this house worthy of being liked—also another who seems a rosy sugar-plum but I know her to be coloured chalk—'. (MS Pierpont Morgan.) Lucy Snowe says of Mme Beck in *Villette* ch. 8 that 'interest was the master-key' of her nature, and that she was 'secret, crafty, passionless'. (101, 102.) Mlle Reuter in *The Professor* is similarly described as a 'crafty little politician'. (91.)
8. Paper torn.
9. Paper torn.
10. For George Dixon see Mary Taylor's letter to EN, 30.10.1842 and 1.11.1842 n. 4. Far from spineless, he became in 1844 a partner in the Birmingham firm of Rabone and Company, export merchants, for which he had been working since 1838, and later became the head of the firm. He was to become an active educational reformer, mayor of Birmingham in 1866, Liberal MP for Birmingham from 1867 to 1876, and for the Edgbaston division of the city from 1885 until his death. See *DNB*. He was travelling to and from Belgium for his firm in 1842 and 1843.

To Mary Dixon, 16 October 1843

Brussels

Dear Miss Dixon

I certainly thought you would have forgotten me by this time for you have seen many new scenes and new faces since you left Brussels[1] but I, isolated as I am, am not likely soon to forget you—I think of you often, by way of refreshment and contrast when I am weary of the Belgians—

It grieves me to hear that the cold-water cure[2] has done you no good and that your health still continues so delicate—I really thought it would be beneficial to you—because it must be bracing in its nature—and strength I imagine is what you chiefly want—I trust the air and water of Ilkley[3] will be more successful—You have long been deprived of perfect health—but live in hope—where there is no actual disease—and where the age is not more mature than in your case[4]—I think health must return in time if care is taken—and severe remedies 'are' avoided.

I often hear from Mary Taylor[5]—as I daresay you do—she expresses herself as happy and contented in her present position—the number of her pupils continues to increase and she has consequently raised the price of her lessons—

She wishes me to go to her—because she knows I feel very lonely at Brussels and with a disinterested generosity, quite peculiar to herself—she has offered to share her lessons with me!

Of course however I shall not take advantage of this goodness.

The trials of the Nussey family are indeed very severe—poor Mr George[6] above all seems marked out for affliction—I do sincerely hope—both for his own sake and that of his family that the fears entertained on his account may prove unfounded—If they were to lose him—the tie that unites them would I fear be severed and the faggots would certainly fall asunder—I had a letter from Ellen some days since—in which she expresses good hopes of his recovery—

The other day being low-spirited—as I often am—and wishing very much for a little society—I went up-stairs and disinterred your portrait from the bottom of a trunk to which I had committed it—<It>I was comforted by discovering a certain likeness—notwithstanding what yourself and William Henry[7] affirmed to the contrary. If it were a little slenderer and paler—it would be very much like—

I suppose there is now no chance of Ellen Taylor[8] coming to Brussels How much longer I shall stay here—myself I do not know—probably till Spring—

In the meantime my dear Miss Dixon let me thank you again for your kindness to me whilst you were here—My note is short but it is unnecessary to make it longer—as I have nothing more to write which it would interest you to read—

Believe me yours with sincerity
C Brontë

MS Princeton, Taylor Collection. Unpublished.
Address: not in MS.
PM: not in MS.

1. See EN late June 1843 n. 4 and 13.10.1843 n. 3.
2. 'Hydropathy', originally developed by a farmer, Vincenz Priessnitz (1801–51) at Gräfenberg in Silesia, and widely used on the Continent, had been introduced into England in the early 1840s. Alfred Tennyson, who was subject to 'fits and trances', stayed at Prestbury, Cheshire, in 1844, at a hydropathic establishment founded by Priessnitz's nephew. His brother Horatio Tennyson described his own 'cure' there: 'You are packed in a wet sheet 2 or 3 times a day & each time on coming out you are plunged into a cold bath after which you have a wet bandage tightly bound around your waist, you are also occasionally thawed & dissolved into a dew by being swathed in 3 or 4 blankets on the removal of which . . . you are again plunged into stinging cold water'. Water-drinking was encouraged, smoking and alcohol forbidden. (See R. B. Martin, *Tennyson: The Unquiet Heart* (Oxford, 1980), 277.)
3. A small town on the river Wharfe, 16 miles north-west of Leeds. 'From a neighbouring hill issues a fine, clear, and cold stream, forming an excellent bath, which is much resorted to in the summer season.' (*Dugdale* 998.) Several hydropathic establishments were developed there, the first in 1843 under the care of Dr Rischack of Silesia.
4. Mary Dixon (1810–97) was 33.
5. See the previous letter n. 5.
6. George Nussey recovered physically, but from 1845 until his death in Oct. 1885 he was cared for in private asylums in York. See the previous letter n. 2.
7. William Henry Taylor (1828–99). His father, William Taylor (1777–1837) was the brother of Mary Taylor's father, Joshua Taylor (1766–1840), and of Mary Dixon's mother Laetitia (1780–1842). Since both his parents were dead he had lived in Brussels for a time in the household of his uncle Abraham Dixon 'in some kind of apprenticeship'. (*Stevens* 27.)
8. The sister of William Henry Taylor, 1826–51. Abraham Dixon wrote to Mary Dixon on 24.7.1843 that owing to the refusal of the Belgian government to 'use ?Kyan's process' he would have to withdraw financial support from the projected placing of Ellen Taylor at Mme Heger's school, at a cost of 'frs 1055 or £42' a year, with the additional cost of her clothes. (Dixon Collection, Leeds City Museum.) In Apr. 1850 Ellen joined Mary and Waring Taylor in New Zealand, becoming Mary's partner in her shop in Wellington, but she died of consumption in Mary's house on 27 Dec. 1851. See references to her in *Stevens*.

Mademoiselle Sophie to Charlotte Brontë,[1] *17 December 1843.*

Ma Chère Charlotte,

Veuillez me faire le plaisir d'accepter cette petite boîte en souvenir de moi. J'ai trop bonne opinion de votre cœur, pour oser supposer qu'il vous faille la vue d'un objet quelconque pour me rappeler à votre doux souvenir; non; je suis convaincue que l'amitié que vous m'avez toujours témoignée, a sa source dans les plus nobles Sentiments; néanmoins, vous me feriez de la peine, si vous refusiez de me donner encore cette marque de votre affection. Adieu, ma bonne Charlotte; j'aime à croire que je ne vous perdrai pas entièrement dans 15 jours[2] et que vous daignerez encore de temps en temps, lorsque vous aurez revu le sol natal, tourner votre pensée vers la triste Belgique où plus d'une personne pensera à vous.

Tout à vous
Votre amie Sophie.

Bruxelles, le 17 Decembre [*sic*] 1843.

MS BPM Bon 1. Gérin *CB* 589.

Mademoiselle Sophie to Charlotte Brontë [1]: Translation

17 December 1843.

My dear Charlotte,

Please do me the favour of accepting this little box as a memento of me. I have too good an opinion of your heart to dare to suppose that you need to see any object whatever to recall me to your indulgent memory; no; I am convinced that the friendship you have always shown me arises from the finest feelings; nevertheless, you would hurt me if you refused to give me one more token of your affection. Goodbye, my dear good Charlotte; I like to think that I shall not lose you completely in a fortnight's time[2] and that when you have seen your native land once more, you will deign from time to time to turn your thoughts again to poor Belgium where more than one person will be thinking of you.

All my love to you,
Your friend Sophie.

MS BPM Bon 1. Gérin *CB* 253 (an English translation; French text on 589.)
Address: Mademoiselle Charlotte Bruntë | Bruxelles
PM: none.

1. This letter was found in EJB's desk, now at the BPM. Mlle Sophie was a teacher at Mme Heger's pensionnat. See EN May 1842 and EJB 29.5.1843. Like CB, Sophie disliked the Parisian Mlle Blanche, and had evidently trusted CB sufficiently to confide in her. In *Villette* Lucy Snowe criticizes all the teachers at the pensionnat, allowing only that one of them was 'an honest woman, but a narrow thinker, a coarse feeler, and an egotist'. (175.)
2. CB intended to be at home on 2 Jan. 1844. See the next letter.

To Emily J. Brontë, 19 December 1843

Brussels

Dear E. J.,

I have taken my determination. I hope to be at home the day after New Year's Day.[1] I have told Mme [Heger]. But in order to come home I shall be obliged to draw on my cash for another £5. I have only £3 at present, and as there are several little things I should like to buy before I leave Brussels—which you know cannot be got as well in England—£3 would not suffice. Low spirits have afflicted me much lately,[2] but I hope all will be well when I get home—above all, if I find papa and you and B[ranwell] and A[nne] well. I am not ill in body.[3] It is only the mind which is a trifle shaken—for want of comfort.[4]

I shall try to cheer up now.—Good-bye.

C. B.

MS untraced. W & S 167.
Address: not in source.
PM: not in source.
Text CBCircle 119.
W & S 167 reproduces *CBCircle* 119 and *Shorter* 129, but corrects 'Héger' to 'Heger'.

1. On 30 Dec. 1843 Abraham Dixon wrote to his daughter Mary: 'I received your very little short letter dated Ilkley 28 Sep. this I send by Miss Bronté who leaves on Sunday for her home, and does not mean to return . . . Louisa [Bright] . . . dined at Mr Jenkins's on Xmas Day along with Miss Bronté & others with myself.' (Dixon Collection, Leeds City Museum.) CB eventually left Brussels on Monday 1 Jan. 1844.
2. Mary Taylor had urged CB's departure, as she explained in a letter received by Mrs Gaskell just before June 1857, in time for use in the 3rd ed. of the *Life*: 'When she had become acquainted with the people and ways at Brussels her life became monotonous, and she fell into the same hopeless state as at Miss W[ooler]'s, though in a less degree. I wrote to her, urging her to go home or elsewhere; she had got what she wanted (French), and there was at least novelty in a new place, if no improvement. That if she sank into deeper gloom she would soon not have energy to go, and she was too far from home for her friends to hear of her condition and order her home as they had done at Miss W—'s. She wrote that I had done her a great service, that she should certainly follow my advice, and was much obliged to me . . . More than once afterwards she mentioned the "service" I had done her.' (*Life* (3rd edn.), i. 282.) Mrs Gaskell misleadingly places the letter in her account of the year 1842, when CB was with Emily in Brussels.
3. Gérin points out that the decision to leave Brussels was taken only a few days after CB attended a concert in the Salle de la Grande Harmonie. See Gérin *CB* 248–52 and the adaptation of the concert experience in *Villette* ch. 20.
4. There is no evidence here of specific anxieties about Branwell or her father, in spite of Mrs Gaskell's allegations about the former in *Life* ch. 11 and 12, and Ellen Nussey's later assertion that Charlotte had hurried home because her father had begun to drink too much. EN's note to a letter from CB of 14.10.1846 reads: 'Charlotte suffered because conscience condemned her return to Brussels and absence from home on account of her Father. There were special reasons for her remaining at home discovered too late for immediate remedy. The truth, the real cause of C's sad suffering was in the fact that Mr. B. in conjunction with [the curate] Mr S[mith] (Peter Augustus Malone) had fallen into habits of intemperance.' (*Hatfield* 256–7; See EN's note in full, EN ?14.10.1846 n. 4.) Both Mrs Gaskell and EN were primarily concerned to

counter suspicions that CB had become emotionally involved with M. Heger; but it may be true that CB had been told that there were rumours about her father's drinking. See PB's defensive letter to ?Mr Greenwood of 4.10.1843.

To Ellen Nussey, [?January] 1844

Haworth—

Dear Ellen

I cannot tell what occupies your thoughts and time—are you ill? is some one of your family ill? are you married? are you dead? if it be so you may as well write a word to let me know—for my part I am again—in old England[1] [I shall tell you nothing further till you write to me

C Brontë]

Haworth—1844

Write to me directly that is a good girl I feel really anxious—and have felt so for a long time to hear from 'you'[2]—My apprehension has been that you have caught the infection of the typhus fever—kind remembrances to all your family.

MS Beinecke, Yale. W & S 168 (part).
Address: not in MS.
PM: not in MS.
Annotation in ink by EN: 83 1844
Text: The words in square brackets were added by EN to replace the missing text in this mutilated MS.

1. CB had left Brussels on 1 Jan., as her inscription in M. Heger's parting gift shows. It was *Les Fleurs de la poésie française depuis le commencement du XVIe siècle* (Tours, 1841) inscribed by CB 'Given to me by Monsieur Heger on the 1st January 1844, the morning I left Brussels'. CB sailed on the 'Earl of Liverpool' and Gérin notes that Mme Heger accompanied Charlotte 'to the boat at Ostend, which left on the morning's tide of Tuesday, 2 January'. See Gérin *CB* 255 and *The Times* 4.1.1844, 6, 'Custom House Jan 2. Vessels entered inwards: . . . Earl of Liverpool, from Ostend'.
2. EN was away from home, housekeeping for her brother Henry at Earnley Rectory in Sussex. See EN 23.1.1844.

To Ellen Nussey, 23 January 1844

[Haworth]

My dear Ellen

It was a great disappointment to me to hear that you were in the south of England[1]—I had counted upon seeing you soon as one of the great pleasures of my return home now I fear our meeting will be postponed for an indefinite time. Every one asks me what I am going to do now that I am returned home and every one seems to expect that I should immediately commence a school[2]—In truth Ellen it is what I should wish to do—I desire it of all things—I have sufficient money for the undertaking—and I hope now sufficient qualifications to give me a fair chance of success—yet I cannot yet permit myself to enter upon life—to touch the object which seems now within my reach and which I have been so long striving to attain—you will ask me why—It is on Papa's account—he is now as you know getting old—and it grieves me to tell you that he is losing his sight[3]—I have felt for some months that I ought not to be away from him—and I feel now that it would be too selfish to leave him (at least so long as Branwell and Anne are absent)[4] in order to pursue selfish interests of my own—with the help of God—I will try to deny myself in this matter and to wait.

I suffered much before I left Brussels—I think however long I live I shall not forget what the parting with Monsr *Heger cost me[5]—It grieved me so much to grieve him who has been so true and kind and disinterested a friend—at parting he gave me a sort of diploma[6] certifying my abilities as a teacher—sealed with the seal of the Athenée Royal[7] of which he is professor. He wanted me to take one of his little girls with me—this however I refused to do as I knew it would not have been agreeable to Madame[8]—I was surprised also at the degree of regret expressed by my Belgian pupils[9] when they knew I was going to leave I did not think it had been in their phlegmatic natures—

When do you think I shall see you Ellen—I have of course much to tell you—and I daresay you have much also to tell me things which we should neither of us wish to commit to paper I am much disquieted at not having heard from *Mary *Taylor[10] for a long time—*Joe[11] called at the Rue d'Isabelle with a letter from you—but I was already gone—he brought the letter back with him to England

I do not know whether you feel as I do Ellen—but there are times now when it appears to me as if all my ideas and feelings except a few friendships and affections are changed from what they used to be—something in me which used to be enthusiasm is tamed down and broken—I have fewer illusions—what I wish for now is active exertion—a stake in life—Haworth seems such a lonely, quiet spot, buried away from the world—I no longer regard myself as young, indeed I shall soon be 28—and it seems as if I ought to be working and braving the rough realities of the world as other people do—It is however my duty to restrain this feeling at present and I will endeavour to do so Write to me soon my dear Ellen

and believe me as far as it regards yourself
your unchanged friend
C Bronte

Jan[y] 23[d]—44

Remember me with kindness to your brother *Henry—Anne and Branwell have just left us to return to York—they are both wonderously valued in their situation[12]

MS Law-Dixon. W & S 169.
Address: [as given in *Nussey* 113–14]: Miss Ellen Nussey, Earnley Rectory, Chichester.
PM: not in source.

1. EN was with her brother Henry, who remained at Earnley, Sussex, until his appointment in Apr. 1844 as curate to the Revd John le Cornu (?1760–1844) at Hathersage in Derbyshire.
2. The original purpose of EJB's and CB's stay in Brussels was to acquire 'proficiency in foreign languages' so that they could attract pupils to their projected school. See E. Branwell 29.9.1841.
3. In his letter to ?Mr Greenwood of 4.10.1843 Mr Brontë had referred to his use of 'a lotion for my eyes, which are very weak'. He was to undergo a successful operation for cataract in Aug. 1846. See EN 9.8.1846 and notes.
4. Branwell Brontë was still the tutor to Edmund Robinson, and Anne Brontë the governess to his sisters at Thorp Green, near York. See BB 1.5.1843 n. 2.
5. The pain of parting from a beloved 'master' is a recurrent theme in CB's novels and poems: see e.g. *JE* ch. 23. EN, who like Mrs Gaskell was anxious to assert Charlotte's 'purity of mind', added a long note to one of the copies of *Nussey*:

   None but the basest minds could make evil out of the passage of regret just expressed. What are people worth who do not grieve at separation from tried and faithful friends?

   Oh! Ye clear beings! Who defamed C.B. You who must see farther than other people. What do you reach? Not the truth but a film of evil thought and injustice—sully the pure! and degrade the noble!

   Most offensive and unjust are the writers who can stigmatise C.B. With what minds can they have read the works of C.B.? It is incomprehensible! The high and rigorous moral tone of her writings ought to suffice in annihilating such ideal interpretations—Pure minded readers could never arrive at such a conclusion.

   It is quite true that affinity of talent was strongly attractive to C.B. who had never hitherto realised its power. She had never come in contact with a master mind that she could reverence and respect—acknowledge as her superior and do mental battle with on terms of equality and power. Here was the charm to C.B. and all the greater from being a new experience. (*Hatfield* 183–4.)

   EN unlike Mrs Gaskell, had not seen Charlotte's 4 surviving letters to M. Heger, written from Haworth in the 2 years following her return from Brussels, on 24 July and 24 Oct. 1844, 8 Jan. and 18 Nov. 1845.
6. Mrs Gaskell writes: 'There was some talk of one of Madame Héger's daughters being sent to [Charlotte] as a pupil if she fulfilled her intention of trying to begin a school. To facilitate her success in this plan . . . M. Héger gave her a kind of diploma, dated from, and sealed with the seal of the Athénée Royale de Bruxelles, certifying that she was perfectly capable of teaching the French language, having well studied the grammar and composition thereof, and, moreover, having prepared herself for teaching by studying and practising the best methods of instruction. This certificate is dated December 29th, 1843 . . .' (*Life* i. 304–5.) An empty envelope inscribed by CB 'Diploma given to me by Monsieur Heger Dec 29–1843' was found in EJB's desk. (BPM.)
7. A highly regarded academy for boys, under the patronage of the king. Since 1838 it had occupied buildings to the rear of Mme Heger's pensionnat, fronting on the rue des Douze Apôtres and the rue Terarcken. A M. Lebel was in charge of the boys' boarding-house attached to the Athénée, part of which overlooked the garden of the pensionnat. See Gérin *CB* 193, *Wroot* 198, and Henri Dorchy, *L'Athénée Royal de Bruxelles: son histoire* (Bruxelles, 1950). William Crimsworth and M. Paul Emanuel survey the pensionnat garden from the windows of schools resembling the Athénée in *The Professor* and *Villette* respectively.
8. 'this however . . . agreeable to Madame': W & S 169 reads simply 'but I refused', omitting CB's reason for doing so.

9. cf. CB's letter to Victoire Dubois of 18.5.1844, where she acknowledges a 'packet of affectionate letters . . . from the pupils of the First Class'.
10. See *Stevens* letter 12 and EN 13.10.1843 n. 5.
11. Joe Taylor. See EN Mar./Apr. 1842 n. 10.
12. MS may read 'situations'.

To Ellen Nussey, [?4 March 1844]

[Haworth]

My dear Ellen

I received your note this morning. I shall have great pleasure in accepting the kind invitation which it conveys from your Mother. I know nothing which can prevent me from coming on the day you fix viz. Thursday next—if therefore Mr. *George[1] will be kind enough to meet me at Bradford I shall (DV) be at the Talbot Inn[2] at ½-past four p.m. the time the Mail-Coach arrives from Keighley.

How glad shall I be to see you once more in good health—but I shall try to meet you gravely and quietly—no enthusiasm mind—all that shall be put by for our evenings when we curl our hair. Good-bye dear Nell—there's a warm corner remains in my heart for you at any rate   Remember me kindly to your Mother, Sisters and brothers—

C Brontë

Monday Morning

MS Princeton, Taylor Collection. W & S 171.
Address: not in MS.
PM: not in MS.
Date: EN was probably unsure of the date of this letter, which she annotated in ink '140   44', and placed, undated, after all the other letters of 1844 in *Nussey* 120, a position followed in *Shorter* 144. The date 4 Mar. (a Monday) is suggested in W & S 171. EN's Memorandum Book for 1844 (MS Texas) has no entries of daily events for Jan.–Mar. The paper used for this letter, an unwatermarked cream wove single sheet 117 mm. x 190 mm., resembles that used in the next two letters.

1. George Nussey.
2. One of the principal coaching-inns in Bradford, much used by wool-merchants since it was next to the Piece-Hall, at the West end of Kirkgate, not far from Market Street. It also served as the headquarters of the local Tories. See William Scruton, *Pen and Pencil Pictures of Old Bradford* (1889), 121, 170–1.

To Ellen Nussey, [?c7 March 1844]

[Haworth]

Dear Ellen

I will endeavour to be with you on Monday—should the weather be very bad of course I cannot come—I shall be in Bradford about 3 o'clock—p.m. from thence I shall either walk to Birstal if I can get any one to carry my box—or else take a conveyance if there is no coach—I hope nothing will happen to prevent me

Good-bye till Monday

C Brontë

MS BPM B.S. 50.7. No publication traced.
Address: not in MS.
PM: not in MS.
Annotation by EN in pencil: 45; p. 1845
Date: EN's date, 1845, is unlikely, since CB did not visit Brookroyd in that year. Her visit to EN in early 1844 had been completed by 25 March. The small neat handwriting and unwatermarked wove paper, with a leaf-size of approximately 95 mm× 116 mm, support the conjectural date suggested here. Possibly George Nussey's illness, referred to in EN 25.3.1844, caused Ellen to change the arrangements made in CB's previous letter.

To Ellen Nussey, [25 March 1844]

[Haworth]

Dear Nell

I got home safely[1] and was not too much tired on arriving at Haworth—I feel rather better to day than I have been—and in time I hope to regain more strength. I found Emily and Papa well and a letter from Branwell intimating that he and Anne are pretty well too.

Emily is much obliged to you for the flower-seeds you sent—she wishes to know if the Sicilian Pea[2] and Crimson Corn flower[3] are hardy flowers—or if they are delicate and should be sown in warm and sheltered situations

Write to me to-morrow and let me know how you all are—if your Mother continues to get better—if Mercy and Anne are well—and if *Mr George is better—Tell me also if you went to Mrs *John *Swain's[4] on Friday and if you enjoy[ed] yourself—talk to me in short as you would do if we were together

Good morning dear Nell—I shall say no more to you at present

C Brontë

Monday morning.
Our poor little cat[5] has been ill two days and is just dead—it is piteous to see even an animal lying lifel[ess] Emily is sorry—

MS BPM B.S. 50.8. W & S 172.
Address (integral): Miss Ellen Nussey | Brookroyd | Birstall | Leeds
PM: (i) HAWORTH (ii) BRADFORD YORKS | MR 26 | 1—4— | B (iii) LEEDS | MR 26 | 1844 | F
Text: conjectural readings of words obscured by mounting are given in square brackets.

1. If the previous letter is correctly dated, CB had planned a visit to Brookroyd starting on Monday 11 Mar.
2. The sweet pea.
3. Perhaps the 'Corn-rose or common Wild Poppy'. (*OED*.)
4. Sarah Dorothy, née Scott, the wife of John Swaine, son of the wealthy mill-owner Joseph Swaine of Brier Hall, Gomersal. Her son Joseph Henry Swaine was christened on 25 June 1845 at Birstall.
5. Tiger, the lively cat that CB recalled as one of the pleasures of home when she wrote to Emily from Brussels on 1.10.1843. Emily recorded in her Diary Paper for [31].7.1845 that 'Tiger died early last year'. Mrs Gaskell wrote: 'Charlotte was more than commonly tender in her treatment of all dumb creatures . . . The feeling, which in Charlotte partook of something of the nature of an affection, was, with Emily, more of a passion.' (*Life* i. 307–8.)

To Ellen Nussey, 7 April [1844]

[Haworth]

Dear Nell

I have received your note It communicated a piece of good news which I certainly did not expect to hear—I want however further enlightenment on the subject Can you tell me what has caused the change in Mary's plans and brought her so suddenly back to England?[1] Is it on account of *Mary *Dixon?[2] is it the wish of her brothers or is it her own determination—I hope whatever the reason be—it is nothing which can give her uneasiness or do her harm—Do you know how long she is likely to stay in England? Or when she arrives at Hunsworth?[3]

You ask how I am—I really have felt much better the last week—I think my visit to Brookroyd did me good.

What delightful weather we have had lately I wish we had had such while I was with you Emily and I walk out a good deal on the moors to the great damage of our shoes but I hope to the benefit of our health.

Good bye dear Ellen send me another of you[r] little notes soon

kind regards to all C B

MS Harvard H. E. W. 1.5.4. W & S 173.
Address: not in MS.
PM: not in MS.
Annotations in ink by EN: 90 Ap 7—44

1. The reason for Mary Taylor's sudden return from Germany is not known. EN must have heard news of her arrival from one of Mary's relatives: see the next letter.
2. Mary Taylor replied to EN's welcoming letter on 12 Apr., from Chad Road, Edgbaston, Birmingham, the home of her cousins the Dixon brothers. Mary Dixon, whose health had been causing concern, had probably returned to Birmingham from Yorks. cf. CB's letter to her of 16.10.1843.
3. See the next letter.

Mary Taylor to Ellen Nussey, [12]April 1844

Chad road.
[Edgbaston
Birmingham]

Dear Ellen

Many thanks for your welcome to England—How did you smell out so speedily that I was come? I shall see you & ask you this & a thousand other questions in about a fortnight & then I hope to see C. B. too. I am going to stretch the house at Hunsworth[1] & make it hold three or four people to sleep whereas I understand that now it only holds two (strangers). Wish M. Carr[2] much happiness for me, she will be married before I see her again. I have nothing to write & live in hopes of seeing you so I will not crack my brain to find anything.

Remember me to your Mama & sisters.
Yours M. Taylor.

MS Berg. W & S 174.
Address (integral): Miss E. Nussey | Brookroyd | Birstal | Leeds.
PM: (i) BIRMINGHAM | AP 12 | 1844 | B (ii) LEEDS | AP 13 | 1844 | A
Date: from the first postmark. A hole in the MS means that only 'April . . . 44' (in Mary Taylor's hand) can be read at the end of the letter.

1. John and Joe Taylor's bachelor cottage next to their mill at Hunsworth probably resembled Robert Moore's 'dingy cottage . . . converted into a neat, tasteful residence', with part of the 'steep rugged land' near it made into garden-ground. (*Shirley* 35.)
2. Mary Carr (1811–?54), daughter of the Gomersal solicitor Charles Carr senior (1777/8–1832). As EN noted in her diary, Mary Carr married the Revd William Margetson Heald (1803–75), the Vicar of Birstall, on 23 Apr. 1844. The Nusseys and Carrs were on friendly terms, and Mary's brother Charles was to marry EN's relative, Eleanor Walker, on 11 May 1848.

To Victoire Dubois,[1] 18 May 1844

[Haworth]

My dear little Victoire

You ask me how I do—and I answer I am much better I thank you—You tell me to return to Belgium—that is not possible I cannot return to you—but I can think of you all and love you

I cannot tell you my dear Victoire how much pleasure the packet of letters I received from the pupils of the first Class, gave me—I knew I loved my pupils—but I did not know that they had for me the affection those letters express[2]—I only fear now that they will exaggerate my good qualities and think me better than I really am.

It grieves me to hear that you are not quite satisfied with your present mistress—do not give way to this feeling—Be obedient, docile and studious and then I think she cannot fail to be kind to you—

I had intended to have written a long letter to you but I have not time so to do—I am afraid of missing the occasion to se[nd] these letters—[3]

If ever I return to Brussels, which is not likely, I shall certainly come to see you and Clémence—remember me kindly to her—I hope her health is better than it was—Write to me again my dear little Victoire the first opportunity and believe me

Your affectionate and sincere friend
C Brontë

MS BPM B.S. 51. *BST* 15. 77. 123–5.
Address (integral): M^{dlle} Victoire Dubois
PM: none.

1. A former pupil of CB at Mme Heger's pensionnat in Brussels.
2. CB had been surprised by the 'degree of regret expressed' by her Belgian pupils when she left the school. See EN 23.1.1844.
3. This letter was evidently enclosed with others in a packet: CB took advantage of Mary Taylor's return to Germany, planned for 22 May, to send letters to Brussels, through which Mary would no doubt pass. CB's letter to M. Heger of 24.7.1844 refers to previous correspondence with him.

Ellen Nussey to Mary Gorham,[1] *21 May [1844]*

Brookroyd.

My dear Polly

I should just like to know how many reproaches (of course unspoken ones) have passed your mind since my last letter—Be generous & forgive me, I feel I have sinned <u>though not willingly</u>—I would have written but could not—I have been in a perfect whirl of engagements[2] for the last ?3 weeks—In the first place we have been paying visits to Brides,[3] & meeting them in company—I have been also to Hathersage,[4] & lastly Mary Taylor has been staying with her Brothers 4 miles from here[5]—I said my adieu to her last night—She crosses the German Ocean[6] again tomorrow Miss Brontë has been a few days with Mary—I have been a good deal there too, & had the satisfaction of meeting Mary in nearly every visit ˋsheˊ made—It was a grievous disappointment Mary that you did not come, for I had resolved you should make up the quartette.—When I had certain information of Mary's arrival I set off with my youngest brother[7] at 9 o'clock at night to see her, & there I found Charlotte Brontë also, both, were walking & talking with all their might in the garden, it was so dark when I joined ˋthemˊ, that we could distinguish nothing but figures approaching & so afraid were we each of saluting a wrong individual that we cautiously peered into each other's faces—then, all at once a 'bless you' burst forth in all the power of friendship & affection.

One of Mary's brothers accompanies her to Germany & they attend the great musical festival at Cologne[8] next week.

My journey to Hathersage only occupied 3 days—I am going there again by & bye—I could ˋnot' help laughing at some ?paintings I saw in the Church—the Vicarage pew is elevated to a level with the reading desk, & is made the Vestry—fancy yourself upstairs in a pew curtained round & both Parson & Sexton occasionally walking in & robing &c & besides that, a sort of gentleman in a neighbouring pew every now & then popping a nose & a pair of eyes between the curtains during singing. The Church itself is very pretty, a good size, & most enchan[ting]ly situated—happily there is a good probability of the interior being entirely remodeled[9]—The Magistrate of the place has his plans drawn, & every thing in readiness for the good work of renovation—but the old Vicar will have nothing done, nor, will he hear of an additional curate being had, though there is nothing wanting but his consent. The country is very very beautiful I ˋwent' to the top of one hill & I quite longed for the time when Mary Gorham could join me in climbing the rocks & hills,[10] & tracing a course for ourselves among the ?heath, on the moors, or along the banks of the Derwent—I went to Derwent[11] where Henry's other church is, & there, I <u>had</u> a treat in seeing Derwent Hall, it is most beautifully furnished with old black oak—the state bed room exceeded anything I ever I saw of the kind, it was really a room fit for a lordly ghost to visit, if he had taste. Another room of tapestry pleased me very much, & also a library & some paintings—the place is to be sold but I hope not yet—the owners are friendly to Henry & I have set my heart on enjoying myself there when I visit Henry again—

I shall look forwards to next year, but don't you promise yourself too much pleasure lest I should fail in making Yorkshire realise ˋall' I paint to you

Now my dear Polly write very soon to me tell me how your Mama is, & anything you know about your neighbourhood.

I must use your last address for want of the right one But I hope this will find you some where. Tell me if you have enjoyed yourself & if your home-sickness increases if so it must have become a disease by this time.

My Sister joins in kindest love & I remain
My dear Mary ever yours affectionately
Ellen Nussey

Present my kind remembrances to your Aunt ?Rickman & Mrs Postlethwaite.[12] Do you hear anything of the Gibbses[13] I have not heard from any of them but Charlotte & Miss ?Isbister[14] Since my return I am reading Le Rhin[15] by Victor

Hugo. It is the most difficult french book I have met with to read but I like it. Good bye dear Polly

MS BPM Gorham Collection. *Whitehead* 109, 117 (short quotations).
Address: not in MS.
PM: not in MS.

1. Mary Gorham (1826–1917), the daughter of John Gorham, a gentleman farmer, was born in Kent. The family moved to Cakeham, near Chichester in Sussex in about 1831. Their home was about 1 mile from Earnley, Henry Nussey's curacy from Dec. 1838 to Apr. 1844, and EN probably first met Mary during her visit to her brother at Earnley from July to Nov. 1841. Mary married the Revd Thomas Swinton Hewitt (?1817–84) on 29 June 1852. The letter is included for its account of the reunion with Mary Taylor and CB, and for the references to Hathersage: CB's visit there in summer 1845 would be important for her writing of *JE*.
2. Ellen's Diary for 1844 includes the following entries: 'April 23 Tu. St George's Day. | Mr Heald & Mary Carr married | May 1 Wed. Mrs Burnley called | Went to see Mary Taylor | Charlotte at Hunsworth | May 4 Sa[t]. Arrived at Hathersage | 5 Su. at Hathersage & Derwent | May 6 Mon. Came for [=?from] Hathersage | Mr Healds Bride visit'. (EN *Diary* 1844)
Between 7 and 20 May EN met Mary Taylor 5 times either at home or on visits to mutual friends, and she records only 3 days 'at home' with no visitors or visits.
3. On Wednesday 15 May Ellen records in her Diary 'Met Mrs Heald & Mrs ?Micklenth[w]aite | at ?Marsh House'. Possibly both ladies were brides.
4. The announcement that the Revd Henry Nussey had been licensed to the curacies of Hathersage and Derwent was made in the *Leeds Intelligencer* on 13 Apr. 1844 (5); a further announcement in the same paper on 24 Aug. 1844 (5) gave the news of his preferment to the Vicarage of Hathersage by the Duke of Devonshire, the patron of the living. (I am indebted to Dr J. R. V. Barker for drawing my attention to the two announcements.) Henry's Hathersage curacy was to the Revd John Le Cornu (1760–1844) Vicar since 1796, who was in poor health. Henry Nussey performed most of his duties, reusing an Earnley sermon on 'Ministers desiring the Perfection of their people' on 16 June, the Sunday before Mr Le Cornu died on 19 June. (HN *Diary* fol. 90^r–97^v.)
5. At Hunsworth. See MT to EN 12.4.1844 and n. 1.
6. The name commonly used for the North Sea at this period. cf. the description of Lowestoft as a market-town 'situated on a lofty headland bordering on the German Ocean' in *Dugdale* 1156.
7. George.
8. The Niederrheinisches Musikfest (Lower Rhine Festival), first held in Düsseldorf at Whitsuntide in 1817, had been held in turn in Düsseldorf, Aachen, and Cologne since 1821. In 1844 Whit Sunday was 26 May.
9. The church of St Michael and All Angels, dating from the 14th cent., was restored in 1851–2. 'When Mr Le Cornu died the church was in a fairly ruinous condition, with the roof off and trees growing out of the walls. It is unlikely that Henry Nussey had done much to repair the neglect.' (M. F. H. Hulbert, *The Vicarage Family Hathersage 1627–1987* (Hathersage Parochial Church Council, 1988), 9.
10. Hathersage, a small town about 8 miles west of Sheffield, is in the hilly Peak District of Derby. Its church, hall, and vicarage are on the hillside above most of the other buildings. CB remembered the church with its Eyre brasses and its setting in a 'north-midland shire, dusk with moorland, ridged with mountain' in the Morton and Moor House chs. of *JE*. See e.g. chs. 28 and 31.
11. A picturesque village on the River Derwent, about 2 miles north of Hathersage: 'A high range of mountains bounds the vale on the west . . . It contains 31 houses, and 164 inhabitants.' 'The chapel, dedicated to St James, is a perpetual curacy . . . John Read, Esq., is the patron, and the Rev. Wilmot C.B. Cave, M.A., is incumbent.' (Samuel Bagshaw, *History, Gazetteer and Directory of Derbyshire* (1846), 505.) Derwent, like the hamlet of Ashopton, is now submerged beneath Ladybower Reservoir.

12. A long elegiac poem on the Duke of Wellington, headed 'In Memoriam November 18th 1852' and signed 'Ellen ?Rickman Postlethwaite' is in the Nussey collection at WYAS Sheepscar, Leeds.
13. The Gibbs family is referred to in Henry Nussey's Earnley Diary: 'Today going to call upon Mr. Fairles's Friend, I was invited by his Squire, Mr. Gibbs to dine at his house . . . Mr. Gibbs has nice property & a very fine family of eight children, 4 girls & 4 boys, educated at home, but I fear not for another & better world.' (HN *Diary* 21.1.1839, fol. 53^{v}–54^{r}.)
14. Not identified.
15. Victor Hugo's *Le Rhin* (2 vols.; 1842, rev. 1845) is based on letters written by Victor Hugo to his wife 'during his visits to the Rhineland in 1839 and 1840'. (*Oxford Companion to French Literature* (Oxford, 1984), 617.)

To Ellen Nussey, [23 June 1844]

[Haworth]

My dear Ellen

Anne and Branwell are now at home[1]—and they and Emily add their request to mine that you will join us in the beginning of next week[2]—write and let us know what day you will come and how—if by coach we will meet you at Keighley—Do not let your visit be later than the beginning of next week or you will see little of A & B—as their holidays are very short, they will soon have to join the family at Scarborough[3] Remember me kindly to your mother sisters and Mr *George—I hope they are all well

[admire my writing in haste C B][4]

MS BPM B.S. 52. W & S 176.
Address (integral): Miss Ellen Nussey | Brookroyd | Birstal | nr Leeds
PM: (i) HAWORTH (ii) BRADFORD YORKS | JU 23 | —44 | C (iii) LEEDS | JU 25 | 1844 | F

1. Anne and Branwell had returned from Thorp Green Hall, the home of their employers, the Robinsons.
2. i.e. on Monday 1 July, when EN did in fact come to Haworth: her Diary reads '[July] 1 M[on]. Came to Howarth All at home there.' (EN *Diary* 1844.)
3. For the Robinsons' visits to Scarborough, see EN ?10.6.1841 n. 2. They were usually accompanied by relatives, and in 1845, for example, took 2 apartments in Wood's Lodgings, nos. 2 (later 3) and 7A, the latter containing 'Drawing Room, Dining Room, Breakfast Parlour, and Twelve Beds'. (*Scarborough Record*, advertisement 7 June; visitors' lists 5, 12, 19, and 26 July, 2 and 9 Aug., 1845.)
4. Words in square brackets added by EN to replace words cut away.

To Mrs Taylor,[1] *Stanbury, [?17 July 1844]*

[Haworth]

Dear Mrs. Taylor,

I have asked Mr.[2] and Mrs. Rand[3] and Mrs. Bacon[4] to take tea with us on Friday afternoon—and should be glad if you and Miss Taylor[5] would come and meet them. Have the goodness to send word by Martha[6] if Friday will be a convenient day for you. Yours truly,

C. Brontë.

Wednesday morning.

MS untraced. W & S 175.
Address: not in source.
PM: not in source.
Text: from Maude Goldring, *Charlotte Brontë the Woman* (1915), 86–7, where it is described as a 'little note of Charlotte's . . . written to Mrs Taylor of Stanbury' on 'a thin scrap of paper, brown with age, in C's fine hand', doubtless owing its preservation to the 'recipe for chilblains on the back!'—'Chilblanes | Salve Spermaceti | And Sweete Oile | as a cure for Chilblanes'.
Date: Dr J. R. V. Barker suggests that the invitation was to a celebration tea after the public examination of the Haworth National School children, who had been taught by Mr Rand. This took place on Friday 19 July 1844; Wednesday would be 17 July. I am grateful to Dr Barker for this suggestion and for the references in n. 2.

1. Probably the widow of a former Haworth Church Trustee. See CB's letters to her of ?Dec. 1842, n. 1.
2. Ebenezer Rand, master of the recently opened National School. The *Bradford Observer* for 28.12.1843 carried the announcement:

   Haworth—Education—On the 2nd of January next we are to have a day school opened in the National School Room, to be conducted by Mr Rand, from the National Society's Central School, London. The posted advertisements inform us that the system will comprise a complete English education . . . The requisites for the school such as books, slates, pencils &c. are to be provided gratis; but the charge will be twopence a week for each child irrespective of age or proficiency. The Wesleyan Methodists are upon the alert to open a school in the Wesleyan school-room, West Lane. (5.)

   On 29.2.1844 the *Bradford Observer* reported that the school 'now contains upwards of 150 scholars'. (5.) Mr Rand's work was praised in the *Leeds Intelligencer* for 27.7.1844: 'The children were examined in the Scriptures, History, Geography, English Grammar, Arithmetic, &c., and the answering gave great satisfaction. The school has been open only for six months, yet within so short a time, owing to the excellency of the system, and the diligence of the master and mistress, the children have made considerable progress in learning, and in good manners. The school numbers 160 children.' (7.)
3. Sarah Ann Mary Elizabeth Rand.
4. ?Mrs Rand's mother.
5. Not identified. Perhaps Mrs Taylor's sister-in-law or her grandchild, Mary Ann Taylor (b. 1833, m. John Bairstow of Steeton 1860).
6. Martha Brown (1828–80), the younger of the 2 parsonage servants.

'Mathilde'[1] *to Charlotte Brontë, [?July 1844]*

[Brussels]

Ma chère Demoiselle.

Si je l'avais pu, il y avait longtemps que j'aurais profité de l'adresse[2] <?permission> 'que' vous m'avez donnée et dont l'envoi m'a fait tant de plaisir. En pension le mois d'Août approchant, nous avons plus d'ouvrage que de coutume,[3] mais ce ne serait rien, si je n'avais encore des maîtres à la maison, et de plus l'obligation, d'étudier mon piano[4] de toutes mes forces, car, par les maladies, un grand déficit se trouve dons nos pianistes, et il a bien fallu, faute de mieux, me prendre pour jouer à la fête de Madame.[5] Je ne sais comment je m'en tirerai; pour mon malheur, malgré toute ma bonne volonté, l'idée que quelqu'un m'écoute et me regarde, suffit pour me faire perdre la tête, et je crains bien que ce début ne soit pas heureux. Cependant, je désire de tout mon cœur réussir; une de mes cousines, qui a eu les plus grands malheurs, est maintenant ma maîtresse de piano elle a beaucoup d'élèves chez Mme Héger, mais dans le pays des aveugles les borgnes sont rois,[6] et par conséquent je suis la meilleure de toutes. Nous chérissons notre bonne maîtresse comme elle le mérite, bien réellement, et c'est beaucoup. Vous sentez combien je puis lui faire de peine et de tort en ne répondant pas à son attente. Allons, il faut prendre courage et espérer que Dieu me protégera dans une chose de si peu d'importance en elle-même, mais qui peut avoir des résultats bons ou mauvais pour ma cousine.

Il y a dans votre lettre, Melle Charlotte, un mot qui m'a fait bien plaisir. J'ai tort j'en suis sûre, car peut-être l'avez vous mis sans y ajouter une aussi grande signification que moi. Vous souvenez-vous m'avoir dit, I shall not cease to think of you with affection and even with estim.—Eh! bien, ce mot estime,[7] vous ne pourriez vous imaginer combien il m'a fait plaisir, je dirai même, il m'a rendue heureuse. Il m'avait semblé jusqu'ici que parfois je pourrais bien aspirer à l'amitié de <quelqu'un, mais n> certaines personnes qui ont mon estime, mais à la leur! l'estime, c'est selon moi, bien plus que l'amitié; quoique cependant je ne crois pas jusqu'à cette heure, avoir, malgré toutes mes fautes, rien fait qui puisse me rendre méprisable. Ce mot dit par vous, ma bonne maîtresse, m'a fait un bien! tenez, vous ne pouvez vous en faire d'idée.

Si vous saviez, il n'y a de cela que bien peu de temps, les pensées noires que j'avais! j'étais certaine par exemple, que personne ne pourrait jamais m'aimer, quoique une de mes anciennes compagnes, m'en ait bien désabusée; c'était de véritables accès de misanthropie, au point que Maman m'a cru malade. Heureusement, si cela n'a pas entièrement disparu, cela a du moins beaucoup diminué.

Ma chère demoiselle, permettez-moi de vous gronder, vous ne me donnez aucune nouvelle de votre santé! J'espère que vous m'en direz quelques mots la Iere fois que vous pourrez m'écrire, et pour vous en donner l'exemple, je vous dirai que moi je jouis d'une santé si bonne pour le moment que je souhaite que vous vous portiez de même. Adieu, Melle Charlotte, adieu, permettez-moi de vous embrasser de cœur,[8] puisque je ne puis même le faire en perspective.

Votre toute dévouée
Mathilde.

Melle Charlotte excusez-moi pour cette folie, mais il me semble que lorsque je vous écris la porte de mon cœur s'ouvre, et toujours le temps et le papier me forcent à la refermer.

MS BPM. Gérin *CB* 590–1.

'Mathilde'[1] to Charlotte Brontë, [?July 1844]: Translation

[Brussels]

My dear Mademoiselle,

If I could I would long ago have made use of the address[2] you have given me; your sending it gave me so much pleasure. At school, as August approaches, we have more work than usual,[3] but that would be no matter if I hadn't teachers at home as well, and if in addition I weren't obliged to practise my piano[4] as hard as I can—for illness has very much reduced the numbers of our pianists, and this has even led to my being chosen, for want of a better, to play for Madame's fête.[5] I don't know how I shall get through it; unluckily for me, in spite of all my good intentions, the idea that someone is listening to me and watching me is enough to make me lose my head, and I'm much afraid that this début may be a failure. Still, I long to succeed, with all my heart; one of my cousins, who has had very great misfortunes, is now my piano teacher. She has many pupils at Madame Heger's, but in the country of the blind the one-eyed man is king,[6] and so I am the best of the bunch. We love our good teacher as she deserves, and that is truly a great deal. You will realise how much I may distress and injure her if I do not come up to her expectations. Well, I shall have to be brave and hope that God will protect me in a matter of such small importance in itself, but which may have good or evil results for my cousin.

In your letter, Miss Charlotte, there is a word which has given me great pleasure. I am sure I am wrong, for perhaps you wrote it without attaching to it as much meaning as I do. Do you remember saying to me, 'I shall not cease to think of you with affection and even with esteem'—Well—this word 'esteem',[7] you could not imagine what pleasure it gave me; I will even say it has made me happy. It had seemed to me up to now that I might sometimes hope to have the friendship of certain people whom I esteem—but to receive their esteem! In my view, esteem is much more than friendship; though admittedly I don't believe that (in spite of all my faults) I have up to now done anything which might make me despicable. This word 'esteem' that you have used, my kind teacher, has done me good! You really can't conceive how much.

If you knew the black thoughts I had until quite a short time before you wrote! For example, I was certain that nobody could ever love me, though one of my old friends convinced me I was wrong; it was a real bout of misanthropy, even making my mother think I was ill. Fortunately, if this has not completely gone, it has at least greatly diminished.

My dear mademoiselle, allow me to scold you—you don't give me any news of your health! I hope that you will say a few words about it the first time you are able to write to me; and to set you an example, I will tell you that I myself enjoy such good health at the moment that I wish you may be just as well as I am. Goodbye, Miss Charlotte, goodbye; let me embrace you in my heart,[8] since there is no prospect of my doing so in person.

Your most devoted
Mathilde.

Miss Charlotte, forgive me for this folly, but it seems to me that when I write to you the door of my heart opens, but then time and paper compel me to close it again.

MS of original French version BPM. Gérin *CB* 590–1.
Address (integral): Mademoiselle Charlotte Brontë | Angleterre.
PM: not in MS.
Date: the reference to 'August approaching' and the impression of a strong affection for CB make July 1844 (rather than 1845) a likely date.

1. An embossed shield-shaped device bears indistinct initials in Gothic letters, but no identification of 'Mathilde' has yet been suggested. CB evidently valued the letter, since she kept it in her desk; she also used the name for one of Frances's pupils, 'heiress of a Belgian Count' in *The Professor* (251).
2. The incomplete address used here probably means that the letter was enclosed in a packet of correspondence. cf. CH 24.7.1844, where Charlotte refers to news she has received about M. Heger's overworking.
3. cf. *Villette* ch. 15: 'These two months, being the last of the "année scolaire", were indeed the only genuine working months in the year.' (213.)
4. For the high value placed on musical accomplishment at Mme Heger's pensionnat, see M. Heger's letter to PB of 5.11.1842 and n. 6.
5. Mme Heger's first name was Claire, that of the saint celebrated on 12 Aug.
6. Proverbial in both English and French. *ODEP*'s first quotation is from Skelton (1522).
7. In CB's poem, 'At first I did Attention give' the pupil's 'Observance' and 'deep esteem' for her schoolmaster develop into 'entire affection' and the 'mighty feeling' of love. (Neufeldt *CBP* 274–5; Berg MS.)
8. For the affectionate tone of the letter, cf. CB's letter to Victoire Dubois, 18.5.1844 and n. 2.

To Constantin Heger, 24 July [1844]

[Haworth]

Monsieur

Je sais bien que ce n'est pas à mon tour de vous écrire,[1] mais puisque Mde Wheelwright[2] va à Bruxelles et veut bien se charger d'une lettre—il me semble que je ne dois pas négliger une occasion si fav[o]rable pour vous écrire.

Je suis très contente que l'année scolaire soit presque finie et que l'époque des vacances approche—j'en suis contente pour vous Monsieur—car, on m'a dit[3] que vous travaillez trop et que votre santé en est un peu altérée—C'est pourquoi je ne me permets pas de proférer une seule pl[a]inte au sujet de votre long silence—j'aimerais mieux rester six mois sans recevoir de vos nouvelles que d'ajouter un atome au poids, déjà trop lourd, qui vous accable—Je me rappelle bien que c'est maintenant l'époque des compositions,[4] que ce sera bi[e]ntôt celle des examens et puis, des prix—et pendant tout ce temps, vous êtes condamné à respirer l'atmostphère desséchante des classes—à vous user.—<à parler> à expliquer, à interroger à parler toute la journée et puis le soir vous avez toutes ces malheureuses compositions à lire, à corriger,[5] presqu' à refaire—Ah Monsieur! je vous ai écrit une fois une lettre peu raisonnable, parceque le chagrin me serrait le cœur, mais je ne le ferai plus[6]—je tacherai de ne plus être égoïste et tout en regardant [vos][7] lettres comme un des plus grands bonheurs que je connaisse j'attendrai patiemment pour en recevoir jusqu'à ce qu'il v[o]us plaira et vous conviendra de m'en envoyer. En même temps je puis bien vous écrire de temps en temps une petite lettre—vous m'y avez <bien> autorisée—

Je crains beaucoup d'oublier le français, car je suis bien persuadée que je vous reverrai un jour—je ne sais pas comment ni quand—mais cela doit être puisque je le désire tant, et alors je ne voudrais pa[s] rester muette devant vous—ce serait trop triste de vous voir et de ne pas pouvoir vous parler[8][;] pour éviter ce malheur—*j'apprends, tous les jours, une demie page de français par cœur* dans un livre de style familier: *et j'ai un plaisir à apprendre cette leçon*—monsieur—*quand je prononce les mots français il me semble que je cause avec vous.*[9]

On vient de m'offrir une place comme première maîtresse dans un grand pensionnat à Manchester, avec un traitement de 100£[10] i.e. 2500 frs par an—je ne puis pas l'accepter—car en l'acceptant je dois quitter mon père et cela ne se peut pas—J'ai cependant mon projet—(lorsqu'on vit dans la retraite le cerveau travaille toujours—on désire s'occuper—on veut se lancer dans une carrière active) Notre Presbytère est une maison assez grande—avec quelques changements—il y aura de la place pour cinq ou six pensionnaires—[11] si je pouvais trouver ce nombre d'enfants de bonne famille je me dévouerais à leur éducation—Emilie n'aime beaucoup l'instruction mais elle s'occuperait toujours du ménage et, quoiqu'un peu recluse, elle a trop bon cœur pour ne pas faire son possible pour le bien-être des enfants—elle est aussi très généreuse et pour l'ordre, <l'exact> l'économie, l'exactitude—le travail assidu—toutes choses très essentielles dans un pensionnat—je m'en charge volontiers

Voilà mon projet Monsieur, que j'ai déjà expliqué à mon père et qu'il trouve bon—Il ne reste donc que de trouver des élèves—chose assez difficile—car nous demeurons loin des villes[12] et on ne se soucie guère de franchir les montagnes qui nous servent de barrière—mais [la] tâche qui est sans difficulté est presque sans mérite—il y a un grand intérêt à vaincre les obstacles—je ne dis pas que je réussirai mais je tâcherai de réussir—le seul effort me fera du bien *il n'y a rien*[13] *que je crains comme* la paresse—*le désœuvrement—l'inertie—la lethargie des facultés—quand le corps est paresseux, l'esprit souffre cruellement, Je ne connaîtrais pas cette lethargie si je pouvais écrire—autrefois je passais des journées, des semaines, des mois entiers à écrire et pas tout à fait sans fruit*<*s*> *puisque Southey,*[14] *et Coleridge*[15]*—deux de nos meilleurs auteurs, à qui j'ai envoyé certains manuscrits en ont bien voulu temoigner leur approbation—mais à present j'ai la vue trop faible*[16] pour écrire—*si j'écrivais beaucoup je deviendrais aveugle. Cette faibl[esse] de vue est pour moi une terrible privation—sans cela savez-vous ce que je ferais Monsieur?—j'écrirais un livre et je le dédierais à mon maître de litérature—au seul maître que j'ai jamais eu—à vous Monsieur. Je vous ai souvent dit en français combien je vous respecte—combien je suis redevable à votre bonté, à vos conseils, Je voudrais le dire une fois en Anglais—Cela ne se peut pas—il ne faut pas y penser—la carrière des lettres m'est fermée*—celle de l'instruction seule m'est ouverte—elle n'offre pas les mêmes attraits—c'est égal, j'y entrerai et si je n'y <irai> 'vais' pas loin, ce ne sera pas manque de diligence. Vous aussi Monsieur—vous avez voulu être avocat[17]—le sort ou la Providence vous a fait professeur—<vous ne> vous <en ' êtes pas tr> êtes heureux malgré cela

Veuillez presenter à Madame l'assurance de mon estime—je crains que Maria—Louise—Claire[18] *ne m'aient déjà oubliée*—Prospère et Victorine ne m'ont jamais bien connue—<c'est> moi je me souviens bien de tous les cinq—surtout de Louise—elle avait tant de caractère—tant de naïveté—tant de vérité dans sa petite figure[19]—

Adieu Monsieur—
votre élève reconnaissante
C Brontë

July 24th.
Je ne vous ai pas prié de m'écrire bientôt, parceque je crains de vous importuner—mais vous êtes trop bon pour oublier que je le désire tout le même—oui—je le désire beaucoup—c'est assez—après tout—faites comme vous voudrez monsieur—si, enfin je recevais une lettre et si je croyais que vous l'aviez écrite par pitié—cela me ferait beaucoup de mal—

Il parait que Mde Wheelwright va à Paris avant d'aller à Bruxelles—mais elle mettra ma lettre à la poste à Boulogne—encore une fois adieu monsieur cela fait mal de dire adieu même dans une lettre—Oh c'est certain que *je vous reverrai un jour*[20]—il le faut bien—puisque <la> *aussitôt que j'aurai gagné assez d'argent pour aller à Bruxelles j'y irai—et je vous reverrai si ce n'est que pour un instant.*[21]

MS BL Add. 38732A. W & S 179.

To Constantin Heger, 24 July [1844]: Translation

[Haworth]

Monsieur,

I am well aware that it is not my turn to write to you,[1] but since Mrs Wheelwright[2] is going to Brussels and is willing to take charge of a letter—it seems to me that I should not neglect such a favourable opportunity for writing to you.

I am very pleased that the school year is almost over and that the holiday period is approaching—I am pleased about it on your account, Monsieur—for I have been told[3] that you are working too hard and that as a result your health has deteriorated a little—That is why I refrain from uttering a single complaint about your long silence—I would rather remain six months without hearing from you than add an atom to the burden—already too heavy—which overwhelms you—I well remember that it is now the time for compositions,[4] that it will soon be the time for examinations and after that for prizes—and for the whole period you are condemned to breathe in the deadening aridity of the classes—to wear yourself out—in explaining, questioning, speaking all day long, and then in the evenings you have all those dreary compositions to read, correct,[5] almost re-write—Ah Monsieur! I once wrote you a letter which was hardly rational, because sadness was wringing my heart, but I shall do so no more[6]—I will try to stop being egotistical and though I look on your letters[7] as one of the greatest joys I know, I shall wait patiently to receive them until it pleases and suits you to send them. But all the same I can still write you a little letter from time to time—you have given me permission to do so.

I am very much afraid of forgetting French, for I am quite convinced that I shall see you again one day—I don't know how or when—but it must happen since I so long for it, and then I would not like to stay silent in your presence—it would be too sad to see you and not be able to speak to you;[8] to prevent this misfortune—every single day, I *learn by heart half a page of French from a book in a colloquial style: and I take pleasure in learning this lesson*, Monsieur—*when I pronounce the French words I seem to be chatting with you.*[9]

I have just been offered a position as principal teacher in a large boarding school in Manchester, with a salary of £100,[10] i.e. 2,500 francs a year—I cannot accept it—because acceptance would mean having to leave my father and that cannot be—Nevertheless I have made a plan: (when one lives in seclusion one's brain is always active—one longs to be busy—one longs to launch out into an active career) Our Parsonage is a fairly large house—with some alterations—there will be room for five or six boarders[11]—if I could find that number of children from respectable families—I would devote myself to their education—Emily is not very fond of teaching but she would nevertheless take care of the housekeeping, and though she is rather withdrawn she has too kind a heart not to do her utmost for the well-being of the children—she is also a very generous soul; and as for order, economy, strict organisation—hard work—all very essential matters in a boarding-school—I willingly make myself responsible for them.

There is my plan, Monsieur, which I have already explained to my father and which he considers a good one.—So all that remains is to find the pupils—a rather difficult matter—for we live a long way from towns[12] and people hardly wish to take the trouble of crossing the mountains which form a barrier round us—but the task which lacks difficulty almost lacks merit—it is very rewarding to surmount obstacles—I do not say that I shall succeed but I shall try to succeed—the effort alone will do me good *I fear nothing*[13] *so much as* idleness—*lack of employment—inertia—lethargy of the faculties—when the body is idle, the spirit suffers cruelly. I would not experience this lethargy if I could write—once upon a time I used to spend whole days, weeks, complete months in writing and not quite in vain since Southey*[14] *and Coleridge*[15]*—two of our best authors, to whom I sent some manuscripts were pleased to express their approval of them—but at present my sight is too weak*[16] *for writing—if I wrote a lot I would become blind. This weakness of sight is a terrible privation for me—without it, do you know what I would do, Monsieur?—I would write a book and I would dedicate it to my literature master—to the only master that I have ever had—to you Monsieur. I have often told you in French how much I respect you—how much I am indebted to your kindness, to your advice, I would like to tell you for once in English—That cannot be—it must not be thought of—a literary career is closed to me*—only that of teaching is open to me—it does not offer the same attractions—never mind, I shall enter upon it and if I do not go far in it, it will not be for want of diligence. You too, Monsieur—you wanted to be a barrister[17]—fate or Providence has made you a teacher—you are happy in spite of that.

Please assure Madame of my esteem—I am afraid that Maria,—Louise and Claire[18] *will have already forgotten me*—Prospère and Victorine have never known me well—I myself clearly remember all five—especially Louise—she had so much character—so much naïveté—so much truthfulness in her little face[19]—

Goodbye Monsieur—
Your grateful pupil,
C. Brontë

July 24th.
I have not asked you to write to me soon because I don't want to seem importunate—but you are too good to forget that I wish it all the same—yes—I wish for it very much—that is enough—after all, do as you please, Monsieur—if in fact I received a letter and thought that you had written out of pity for me—that would hurt me very much.

It seems that Mrs Wheelwright is going to Paris before going to Brussels—but she will put my letter in the post at Boulogne—once more goodbye, Monsieur—it hurts to say goodbye even in a letter—Oh it is certain that *I shall see you again one day*[20]—it really has to be—for *as soon as I have earned enough money to go to Brussels I shall go—and I shall see you again if it is only for a moment.*[21]

Original French version MS BL Add. 38732A. W & S 179.
Address: not in MS.
PM: not in MS.
Date: CB's date, 24 July, probably applies to the whole letter, though M. Heger applies it to his second quotation only and combines all his other quotations under the date 'Juin 24'. That the year is 1844 is confirmed by later references in this year to the plan for a school. CB was writing after EN left Haworth on 22 July 1844.
Text: The letter was torn up by M. Heger and thrown away, but found and stuck together with thin paper strips by Mme Heger, as her daughter explained to Marion H. Spielmann: see Introduction, p. 64. Square brackets indicate conjectural readings for text now concealed or torn away. Mrs Gaskell saw (or heard M. Heger read) this and other letters to him on her visit to Brussels in May 1856, and in spite of her dread that they might be published in full, wished to quote from them. M. Heger accordingly, in a very courteous letter to her of 22 May 1856 (Rylands MS EL B91) provided extracts from the first 2 letters. See CH 24 10.1844 and notes. From the present letter he quoted the words set in italic, slightly improving CB's French in the process.

1. There had been a previous exchange of letters: on 24.10.1844 CB refers to a letter written by her to M. Heger 'at the beginning of May'. M. Heger's daughter Louise thought there had been many more letters than those which have survived. See *BST* 11. 59. 258–61.
2. Elizabeth Wheelwright, née Ridge, the wife of Dr Thomas Wheelwright. The family had been friendly towards CB in Brussels in 1842–3. See CH to PB 5.11.1842 n. 7.
3. CB had received letters from other Belgian friends besides Victoire Dubois and 'Mathilde'. See the previous letter, and V. Dubois 18.5.1844.
4. cf. *Villette* ch. 15: 'To [these two months] was procrastinated . . . the main burden of preparation for the examinations preceding the distribution of prizes . . . the professor of literature, M. Paul . . . would not have help . . . [he] stood on the examiner's estrade alone.' (213–14.)
5. For M. Heger's method of teaching and correcting 'compositions' see *Life* ch. 11, which reproduces an essay by CB with M. Heger's marginal corrections, preceded by his explanation of his method of stylistic analysis. Part of this is a direct quotation from his letter to Mrs Gaskell of 22 May 1856, when he also sent her, at her request 'le travail des deux sœurs Emily et Charlotte', and a promise of 'quelques mots d'explication . . . sur la méthode suivie dans mes courses, en ce qui concerne les exercices de style'. (Rylands MS EL B91.)

6. CB was not able to keep her promise: see esp. her letters to M. Heger of 8.1.1845 and 18.11.1845. But she had probably not revealed her 'chagrin' to EN, whose diary records on 8 July 1844, during her stay with CB 'At Ponden Kirk plenty of fun & fatigue'. EN's entries for 13 and 22 July are cryptic, but may refer to a game: 'Went with Charlotte to Bradford—High Water' and 'High water in Charlotte's bedroom left Haworth'. (EN *Diary* 1844.)
7. MS reads 'regardant vous lettres'.
8. MS reads 'parler pour éviter'.
9. Mrs Gaskell used this quotation but omitted its conclusion, from 'quand . . . cause avec vous'. (*Life* i. 326.)
10. A generous sum. CB's salary as a governess at Upperwood House, Rawdon, was 'not really more than £16 per annum' (EN 3.3.1841), and Anne Brontë earned £40 p.a. at Thorp Green.
11. The parsonage had 5 rooms on the upper floor of the main part of the house, but there may also have been a servant's room above the back kitchen. See Jocelyn Kellett, *Haworth Parsonage: The Home of the Brontës* (Keighley, 1977), 34–6 and plan on 43.
12. Haworth was not easily accessible, especially in winter, though only 12 miles from Bradford. The term 'mountains' could be used for comparatively low hills at this period. See EN 20.6.1833 and n. 1.
13. 'Il n'y a rien . . . m'est fermée': Mrs Gaskell quoted this passage, not quite accurately, in *Life* ch. 13, using the extracts from CB's letters provided for her by M. Heger. (*Life* i. 321–2.)
14. See Southey to CB 12 Mar. 1837.
15. Hartley Coleridge, son of Samuel Taylor Coleridge. See HC draft Dec. 1840 and HC 10.12.1840.
16. CB was short-sighted, and had also spent much time in writing in a minuscule hand and in copying fine-lined engravings. She had to wear spectacles, but the extreme 'faiblesse' complained of here must have been of comparatively short duration.
17. M. Heger's father, once affluent, had lost his fortune through an unreturned loan. Before he became a teacher, Constantin Heger had to earn his living in Paris 'as secretary to a solicitor, an initiation into the legal world which greatly attracted him and into which, had he had money, he would have liked to qualify for admittance'. (Gérin *CB* 193.)
18. For the Heger children, see EN 6.3.1843 n. 3.
19. 'tant de vérité dans sa petite figure': omitted in W & S 179 and its source, *The Times* 19 July 1913. Louise Florence Heger 'loved CB . . . with a love that was returned'. (See M. H. Spielmann, 'Charlotte Brontë in Brussels', in Butler Wood (ed.), *Charlotte Brontë: A Centenary Memorial* (1917), 84 ff., and letters to and from Louise Heger in *BST* 11. 59. 258–61. Quiévreux describes her as 'une femme remarquable, peintre et musicienne'. (Louis Quiévreux, *Bruxelles, les Brontës et la famille Héger* (Bruxelles, 1953) ([3].) and Gustave Vanzype wrote 'Elle était douée d'une voix superbe, servie par une sensibilité délicate . . . Elle peignait avec maîtrise . . . Et elle écrivait avec précision, avec élégance, avec fermeté des lettres en lesquelles s'exprime une pensée très haute et très personelle'. Her conversation was 'alerte, malicieuse et nourrie d'un étonnant savoir'. ('Le Melilot Bleu', in *La Meuse* (Liège, 1933). Typescript in BPM Heger Papers B.S. X, H.) (She was 'a remarkable woman, an artist and musician.' 'She was endowed with a superb voice, enhanced by her delicate sensitivity. Her painting was masterly . . . and she wrote with precision, elegance and vigour letters that revealed a very lofty and individual mind. Her conversation was shrewd, mischievously witty, and enriched by an astonishing fund of knowledge.') Louise Heger and her brother Paul presented CB's letters to their father to the British Museum in 1913 because 'they put an end to wrongful suppositions . . . the *truth* should always be brought to light'. (*BST* 11. 59. 259.)
20. This confidence had been eroded by the time CB wrote to M. Heger on 18.11.1845. In fact she did not see the Heger family again.
21. Mrs Gaskell created a composite version of M. Heger's last 2 extracts, but she omitted the last 2 clauses, which he had improved to 'et je vous reverrai ne fût-ce que pour un instant'. (Rylands MS EL B91; *Life* i. 326–7.)

To Ellen Nussey, [?29 July 1844]

[Haworth]

Dear Nell

We were all very glad to get your letter this morning—We I say as both Papa and Emily were anxious to hear of the safe arrival[1] of yourself and the little varmint.[2]

As you conjecture Emily and I set to, to shirt-making the very day after you left and we have stuck to it pretty closely ever since—we miss your society at least as much as you miss ours depend upon it—would that you were within calling distance—that you could as you say burst in upon us in an afternoon—and being despoiled of your bonnet and shawl—be fixed in the rocking-chair for the evening once or twice every week—I certainly cherished a dream during your stay—that such might one day be the case but the dream is somewhat dissipating—I allude of course to Mr *Smith[3]—to whom you do not allude in your letter—and I think you foolish for the omission—I say the dream is dissipating—because Mr *Smith has not mentioned your name since you left—except once when papa said you were a nice girl—he said—"yes—she—is a nice girl—rather quiet——— I suppose she has no money"[4]—and that is all—I think the words speak volumes—they do not prejudice one in favour of Mr *Smith—I can well believe what papa has often affirmed—and continues to affirm—i-e that Mr *Smith is a very fickle man—that if he marries he will soon get tired of his wife—and consider her as a burden—also that money will be a principal consideration with him in marrying.[5]

Papa has two or three times expressed a fear that since Mr *Smith paid you so much attention he will perhaps have made <to great> an impression on your mind which will interfere with your comfort—I tell him I think not as I believe you to be mistress of yourself in those matters. Still he keeps saying that I am to write to you and dissuade you from thinking of him—I never saw papa make himself so uneasy about a thing of the kind before—he is usually very sarcastic on such subjects

Mr *Smith be hanged!—I never thought very well of him and I am much disposed to think very ill of him at this blessed minute—I have discussed the subject fully for where is the use of being mysterious and constrained—It is not worth while—

Be sure you write to me and immediately—and tell me whether you have given up eating and drinking altogether—I am not surprised at people thinking you looked pale and thin—I shall expect another letter on Thursday—don't disappoint me My best regards to your Mother and Sisters—

Yours somewhat irritated

C B

Monday morning

MS BPM Gr. E 6. W & S 177 as 16 July.
Address: not in MS.
PM: not in MS.
Annotation: (i) after 'varmint': pencilled note by EN, 'a King Charles Dog (gift of Mr B.)'; (ii) at the end of the letter: note in ink by EN: 'Mr Bronte used to amuse himself with his curates & play upon them—This one was Peter Augustus'.
Date: W & S 177 is wrongly dated 16 July 1844 (a Tuesday) when EN was still at Haworth. See n. 1 below. CB's 'Monday morning' may well be 29 July, a likely date for the receipt of EN's letter announcing her safe arrival at home on 22 July.

1. EN's *Diary* 1844 shows that she returned to Birstall on Monday 22 July. The entry reads, 'High water in Charlotte's bedroom left Haworth Henry with the Duke of Devonshire.'
2. The mischievous spaniel, Flossy junior, offspring of Anne Brontë's 'long, silky, black and white "Flossy" '; the latter is described by Anne in 1848 as 'fatter than ever, but still active enough to relish a sheep hunt'. (AB to EN 26.1.1848.) See annotation (i) above, and CB's charming watercolour of a lively looking dog said to be Flossy senior, BPM HAOBP P. Br. c30, reproduced in colour in *Sixty Treasures*, no. 17. 'Varmint', a dialectal variant of 'vermin', sounds like affectionate abuse, or a quotation. Perhaps it echoes a scolding of the dog by one of the Haworth servants.
3. The Revd James William Smith, MA (b. ?1815), a graduate of Trinity College Dublin. He may be the James Smith who was admitted as a pensioner on 'July 5 1832 aged 17; s[on] of John, Mercator [merchant]; b. Meath. B. A. Vern. [Spring] 1837; M. A. Vern. 1840.' (*Alumni Dublinenses*.) He was Mr Brontë's curate from Mar. 1843 until Oct. 1844, his first signatures in the Haworth Parish Registers being on 12 Mar. 1843 (burial of Mary Feather of Haworth) and his last as curate being on 13 Oct. 1844 (baptismal and burials registers). He then became a minister in Keighley, his position as perpetual curate of the newly formed parish of Eastwood, Keighley, being established on 17 Feb. 1846, when he was licensed to the 'District of Eastwood, County of York' having subscribed to the 39 Articles on 13 Feb. 1846. (Subscription Books, Diocese of Ripon, WYAS Sheepscar, Leeds.) On 26 Feb. 1848 CB told EN that Smith had 'absconded' from his ministry 'without the knowledge or sanction of his friends' and that 'His principles must have been bad indeed; he could have had no sense of honour—amongst other debts, it appears that he got £5 of Miss Sugden for some charitable purpose and that he appropriated the money for his own use.' He is said to have emigrated to Canada. See various, and conflicting, accounts in *Wroot* 124–6, *LD* 392. He was said to be the 'original' of Peter Augustus Malone, one of the curates in *Shirley*.
4. W & S 177 follows *Shorter* 133 in the erroneous reading 'I suppose she has money'.
5. cf. *Shirley* ch. 16: after Malone has discovered that Caroline will inherit little money, he transfers his attentions to the heiress Shirley.

To Ellen Nussey, [?10 August 1844]

[Haworth]

I did not "swear at the postman" when I saw another epistle from you Nell—and I hope you will not "swear" at me when I tell you that I cannot think of leaving home at present even to have the pleasure of joining you your Mother and Sisters at Harrogate,[1] but I am obliged to you for thinking of me—thank you Nell.

I have seriously entered into the enterprise of keeping a school[2]—or rather taking a limited number of pupils at home that is I have begun to seek in good earnest for pupils—I wrote to Mrs *White,[3] not asking her for her daughter[4]—I cannot do that—but informing her of my intentions I received an answer from Mr *White expressive of, I believe, sincere regret that I had not informed them a month sooner in which case, <they> 'he' said, they would gladly have sent me their own daughter and also Colonel *Stott's[5]—<That would> but that now both were promised to Miss *Cockhills'[6]—

I was partly disappointed by this answer—and partly gratified—indeed I derived quite an impulse of encouragement from the warm assurance that if I had but applied a little sooner they would certainly have sent me Sarah Louisa I own I had misgivings that nobody would be willing to send a child for education to Haworth—these misgivings are partly done away with—

I have written also to Mrs Busfield[7] of Keighley and enclosed the diploma[8] which Mr Heger gave me before I left Brussels—I have not yet received her answer but I wait for it with some anxiety—I do not expect that she will send me any of her children but if she would, I daresay she could recommend me other pupils—unfortunately she knows us only very slightly

As soon as I can get an assurance of only <u>one</u> pupil—I will have cards of terms printed—and will commence the repairs necessary in the house—I wish all that to be done before winter—

I think of fixing the board and English education at 25£ per annum[9] do you know what Miss Cockhill's terms are? If not I wish you could get to know and inform me.

I have nothing new to tell you about the Revd Mr Lothario-Lovelace *Smith[10]—I think I like him a little bit less every day—I am glad 'now' he did not ask you to marry him—you are far too good for him—Mr *Weightman[11] was worth 200 Mr *Smiths—tied in a bunch

Good-bye to you, remember me to "Mrs *Nussey & family."[12]

I fear by what you say Flossy Junr[13] behaves discreditably & gets his Mistress into scrapes—

C Brontë

MS HM 24434. W & S 178 as [20 July 1844].
Address: not in MS.
PM: not in MS.
Annotation: (i) in ink at the top of fol. 1^{r}: 44; (ii) on fol. 2^{v} in pencil by EN: of the school | ?keeping | Mr. Smith
Date: W & S is wrongly dated [20 July 1844], when EN was still at Haworth. On Sunday 11 Aug. EN noted in her diary, 'heard from Charlotte' and on 16 Aug., 'Preparing for Harrogate'. (EN *Diary* 1844.) A date of about 10 August is therefore probable.
Text: There is no sign that the MS is incomplete in spite of the lack of greeting or date.

1. See EN 6.8.1843 n. 8. EN's diary entries for Aug. 1844 include: '16 F[riday] Preparing for Harrogate | 17 Sa. Mother Anne Henry &c gone to Harrogate | 18 Su. At home alone | 19 M. Richard & George came from Harrogate | 24 Sa. Went to Harrogate'. On Monday 2 Sept. she records, 'Came from Harrogate with Richard & J.T. [?Joe Taylor]'. (EN *Diary* 1844.)
2. cf. CH 24.7.1844 and n. 11, and see the prospectus for 'The Misses Bronte's Establishment | for | The Board and Education | of a limited number of | young ladies'.

3. Mrs John White of Upperwood House, Rawdon, CB's former employer. See EN ?3.3.1841 n. 1 and EN ?21.3.1841 n. 1.
4. Sarah Louisa, b. 1832. See EN ?3.3.1841 n. 4.
5. Colonel George Stott, later Stott-Stanhope, who had inherited Eccleshill Hall and estate, about 2 miles from Upperwood House, from his uncle Walter Stott-Stanhope. One of his daughters was to marry Arthur Robson White, the baby of the household while CB was at Upperwood House.
6. The school at Oakwell Hall, near Birstall, kept from about 1838 or earlier by the 3 Misses Cockill, Hannah (1810/11–93, later Mrs John Battye), Sarah (1812–96), and Elizabeth (1813–54). Their mother Hannah (1784–1856), widow of Thomas Cockill, was a distant relative of EN, and a friend of the Taylors of Gomersal. Elizabeth Cockill had been a fellow-pupil with CB at Roe Head. See *BST* 17. 88. 210–13.
7. Probably Sarah Busfeild, née Bond (d. ?1883), the wife of the Revd William Busfeild (?1802–78) rector of Keighley from 2 July 1840 in succession to Theodore Dury.
8. See EN 23.1.1844 n. 6.
9. CB decided to ask £35 per annum for 'Board and Education'. See the prospectus.
10. James William Smith. See the previous letter. The original 'Gay Lothario' was a heartless libertine in Nicholas Rowe's *The Fair Penitent* (1703). He was the model for Richardson's rake, Robert Lovelace, in *Clarissa* (1747–9).
11. Mr Brontë's former curate, William Weightman (1814–42). See EN 17.3.1840 n. 4.
12. CB was probably imitating the typical local gazette entry for fashionable visitors to a watering-place.
13. See previous letter and n. 2. One of these 'scrapes' is recorded in EN's Diary for 29 Sept. 1844: 'Flossy eat Mrs B[rowne]'s bonnet'.

To Ellen Nussey, [?c. 22 August 1844]

[Haworth]

Dear Nell,

I am very glad to hear of Henry's good fortune[1]—It proves to me what an excellent thing perseverance is, for getting on in the world. Calm self-confidence (not impudence, for that is vulgar and repulsive) is an admirable quality, but how are those not naturally gifted with it to attain it? I am driving on with my small matter [2] as well as I can. I have written to all the friends on whom I have the slightest claim, and to some on whom I have no claim; Mrs Busfeild,[3] for example. On her, also, I have actually made bold to call. She was exceedingly polite; regretted that her children were already at school at Liverpool;[4] thought the undertaking a most praiseworthy one, but feared I should have some difficulty in making it succeed on account of the situation. Such is the answer I receive from almost every one. I tell them the retired situation is, in some points of view, an advantage; that, were it in the midst of a large town, I could not pretend to take pupils on terms so moderate; Mrs. B. remarked that she thought the terms very moderate, but that, as it is, not having house-rent to pay, we can offer the same privileges of education that are to be had in expensive seminaries, at little more than half their price; and, as our number must be limited, we can devote a large share of time and pains to each pupil Thank you for the very pretty little purse you have sent me. I make to you a

The Brontës' prospectus for a school at Haworth Parsonage, 1844

The Misses Bronte's Establishment
FOR
THE BOARD AND EDUCATION
OF A LIMITED NUMBER OF
YOUNG LADIES,
THE PARSONAGE, HAWORTH,
NEAR BRADFORD.

Terms.

	£. s. d.
BOARD AND EDUCATION, including Writing, Arithmetic, History, Grammar, Geography, and Needle Work, per Annum,	35 0 0
French, German, Latin } each per Quarter,	1 1 0
Music, Drawing, } each per Quarter,	1 1 0
Use of Piano Forte, per Quarter,	0 5 0
Washing, per Quarter,	0 15 0

Each Young Lady to be provided with One Pair of Sheets, Pillow Cases, Four Towels, a Dessert and Tea-spoon.

A Quarter's Notice, or a Quarter's Board, is required previous to the

Removal of a Pupil.

[Copy in BPM]

curious return, in the shape of half-a-dozen cards of terms. Make such use of them as your judgment shall dictate. You will see that I have fixed the sum at £35,[5] which I think is the just medium, considering advantages and disadvantages. What does your wisdom think about it? We all here get on much as usual. Papa wishes he could hear of a curate, that Mr S[mith][6] may be at liberty to go. Good bye, dear Ellen, I wish you and yours happiness, health, and prosperity.

Write again before you go to [?Harrogate].[7] My best love to Mary.[8]

C. Bronte.

MS untraced. W & S 181 as 29 July.
Address: not in source.
PM: not in source.
Text: *Nussey* 117–19, which may be closer than *Shorter* 139 to MS punctuation.
W & S 181 departs from *Shorter* only in reading 'Mercy' instead of 'Mary' in the last sentence.
Date: *Life* dates 24 July, *Hours at Home* xi. 205 'July', and *Nussey*, *Shorter*, and *W & S* 29 July; but EN did not hear 'of Henry's being made vicar' of Hathersage until 21 Aug. See EN *Diary* 1844 and n. 1 below. Perhaps EN misplaced an envelope postmarked 29 July, the likely date of CB's first letter to her after her return home from Haworth. (W & S 177; see p. 361.)

1. Henry Nussey had held curacies at Derwent and Hathersage in Derbyshire since Apr. 1844. After the death of the Revd John Le Cornu, the Vicar of Hathersage, on 19 June 1844, Henry's brother John, Apothecary to the Queen, may have used his influence to secure the living (in the gift of the Duke of Devonshire) for Henry. EN recorded in her Diary on 25 June 'A letter from John about the Living', on 22 July 'Henry with the Duke of Devonshire', and on 21 Aug. 'Heard of Henry's being made vicar'. (EN *Diary* 1844.) See EN to MG 21.5.1844 n. 4.
2. The plan to establish a school at the parsonage.
3. See the previous letter n. 7.
4. The Busfeilds had three sons and two daughters.
5. See the prospectus produced by the Brontë sisters.
6. The Revd J. W. Smith probably moved to Keighley in Nov. or Dec. 1844. See EN ?2.10.1844 and *c*.26.10.1844 notes.
7. *Nussey* reads 'Burlington'. There is no other reference to a visit by EN in 1844 to 'Burlington' (Bridlington on the East Yorks. coast), though she went there in early 1845: see EN 4.3.1845. The text is probably corrupt. A reference to Harrogate, where EN went on 24 Aug., is likely. See the previous letter.
8. Possibly, as the emendation in W & S 181 implies, a misreading for 'Mercy' rather than an exceptional use of Mercy's baptismal name. But textual corruption is likely: Mercy does not figure in EN's diary for this period, and may have been housekeeping for her brother Henry. Non-specific reference to Mary Dixon or Mary Gorham is unlikely, and Mary Taylor was away in Germany.

Mary Taylor to Ellen Nussey, [?late Summer/Autumn 1844]

[Germany][1]

Dear Ellen

I am just now in a terribly talking humour, & if you were here I should entertain you for hours with interesting trifles;—interesting <trifles> to me & if they were not so to you, why you would have to bear it! But as I can't enter into a long circumstantial explanation of the state of things here & there is nothing important going forward I have just nothing to say. I am alone & melancholy. We sometimes take it into our heads—at least I do, to wonder what we live for, to look all round & see nothing in this world worth getting up for in the morning. I am particularly apt to be of this opinion when something has occured to show me that those things which I value, those virtues I strive after, that moral beauty which makes <life> the charm [of ev]ery day life—all that is worth living for in fact is despised [& rejec]ted by other people. This sometimes gives me the idea that [I am mis] taken & always makes me feel alone in the world. [Another disco]very have I lately made. Persons whom I considered [. . .] their conduct that they had no more [. . .] sider virtue & morality than if they had me-[. . .] particulars cannot be written or are not [. . .] you them when I see you, & if I never tell [. . .] self the repetition of a vexatious history. [I think of] you when my outlandish friends de-[. . .] what Charlotte is doing. I think of her too. [. . .]—since I left England. What is the [. . .] nervous? I have heard of your being [. . .] you for a full account of her state of health & occupations. I can easily imagine that she is grown low spirited with solitude & want of interesting employment. Pray write—write sooner than I have done to you & tell me how she goes on. I half expect Joe[2] this Autumn but if M. Dixon and William[3] come as they talk of doing perhaps he will think that is enough. In any case write to me, particularly about Miss Bronte. I have neglected writing to Miss Cockhill.[4] Tell her I will do it shortly. The reason is we have had neither earthquake nor revolution here so I have nothing to say. My own affairs go on as usual. I teach & practise music.—You must have heard this till you are tired of it.

Yours truly, M. Taylor.

MS Berg. W & S 180.
Address: (integral): E Nussey
PM: none.
Date: if the clause 'I have heard of your being' should be completed 'at Haworth', this letter would be after 22 July, when EN returned from her visit there. This and the reference to autumn indicate a late Aug. or Sept. date.
Text: lacunae caused by the tearing away of a corner of the leaf. Some conjectural readings supplied in square brackets.

1. Mary Taylor had spent about 5 weeks in England in spring 1844 before returning to Germany where she evidently resumed her teaching, after a visit to 'the great musical festival at Cologne' at the end of May. See her letter to EN of [12].4.1844, and EN's letter to Mary Gorham of 21.5.1844.
2. cf. CH 24.10.1844 n. 1.
3. Mary Dixon and her brother William Taylor Dixon (1818–84). For Mary Dixon see E. Branwell 29.9.1841 n. 8. William was at St Catharine's College Cambridge from 1842 to 1846, and was to become curate of St Cuthbert's, Carlisle, from 1846 to 1848, headmaster and chaplain of the training school, Leeds 1848–50, and later a vicar at various churches in Yorks. and Som. On 11 July 1843 William had written a somewhat depressed note from Brussels to another member of his family: 'I think the nicest time will be when you are all at Hunsworth, there will be so many, you will kick up a row, but the few days that you will pass there will soon pass by like every thing else'. (Dixon Collection, Leeds City Museum.)
4. Hannah G. Cockill. See MT to EN ?July 1842 n. 6 and EN ?10.8.1844 n. 6.

To Ellen Nussey, [?2 October 1844]

[Haworth]

Dear Nell

I—Emily & Anne are truly obliged to you for the efforts you have made in our behalf[1]—and if you have not been successful you are only like ourselves—every one wishes us well—but there are no pupils to be had—We have no present intention however of breaking our hearts on the subject—still less of feeling mortified at defeat—The effort must be beneficial whatever the result may be—because it teaches us experience and an additional knowledge of the world—

I send you two additional circulars and will send you two more if you desire it when I write again

I have no news to give you—Mr *Smith leaves in the course of a fortnight[2]—he will spend a few weeks in Ireland[3] previously to settling at Keighley[4]—he continues just the same—often noxious & bad-tempered—sometimes <rather pleas> just supportable—

How did your party go off?[5] how are you?—How is *Joe *Taylor?[6] Write to me soon and at length for your letters are a great comfort to me—we are all pretty well—Remember me kindly to each member of the Houshold at Brookroyd—

Yours—C B—

MS Pierpont Morgan MA 2696. W & S 182 and 184.
Address: not in MS.
PM: not in MS.
Date: EN annotates in ink '89 Oct 44'; a later hand adds in pencil '?19 | Oct. 2', but the '2' may not be a date. A letter dated 16 Sept. may be missing: W & S 183, based on *Shorter* 141 ('Dear Ellen | I received your kind note', p. 372) is wrongly so dated, perhaps because an envelope with that postmark survived.
Text: W & S follow *Shorter* in splitting this letter into two: the first para. (*Shorter* 142, W & S 184, dated 2 Oct. 1844) and the remainder (*Shorter* 140, W & S 182, dated 15 Aug. 1844).

1. Since her return home from Harrogate on 2 Sept., EN had evidently tried to find pupils for the Brontës' projected school.
2. J. W. Smith officiated at a baptism and a burial at Haworth on 13 Oct.—his last entries in the registers for 1844, though he returned occasionally from Keighley in 1845.
3. Probably in Co. Meath, if he is the James Smith admitted to Trinity College Dublin on 5 July 1832. See EN 29.7.1844 n. 3.
4. Mr Smith's address is given as Keighley in the *Clergy List* for 1845, but he was not one of the Revd William Busfeild's curates there. See EN 29.7.1844 n. 3.
5. Several events might be so described: the Nusseys had entertained 'Mr. & Mrs. Browne' (perhaps Henry Nussey's former rector, the Revd Henry Browne and his wife from Sussex) from 28 to 30 September; on 2 October EN notes 'Dined at the Rydings', and on 3 October 'Dinner company at home J. T[aylor] Jun [or 'Jnr'] here.' (EN *Diary* 1844.)
6. 'J. T. ?Jun' visited the Nusseys on 4 and 10 Sept. and 3 Oct.: probably EN was distinguishing Joe Taylor, b. 1816, from his brothers Joshua (b. 1812) and John (b. 1813).

To Constantin Heger, 24 October 1844

[Haworth]

Monsieur

Je suis toute joyeuse ce matin—ce qui ne m'arrive pas souvent depuis deux ans— c'est parceque *un Monsieur*[1] *de mes connaissances va passer par Bruxelles* et qu'*il a offert de se charger d'une lettre pour vous*—laquelle lettre il vous remettra luimême, ou bien, sa sœur[2] de sorte que je serai <sure> certaine que vous l'avez reçue.

Ce n'est pas une longue lettre que je vais écrire—d'abord je n'ai pas le temps—il faut que cela parte tout de suite et ensuite je crains de vous ennuyer. Je voudrais seulement vous demander, si vous avez reçu de mes nouvelles au commencement du mois de Mai et puis au mois d'Aôut? Voilà six mois[3] que j'attends une lettre de Monsieur—six mois d'attente c'est bien long, cela! Pourtant je ne me plains ˋpas′ et je serai richement recompensée pour un peu de chagrin—si vous voulez maintenant écrire une lettre et la donner à ce monsieur—ou à sa sœur qui me la remettrait sans faute.

Quelque courte que soit la lettre *j'en serai satisfaite—n'oubliez pas* seulement *de me dire comment vous vous portez* Monsieur et *comment Madame et les enfants*[4] *se portent* et les maîtresses et les élèves.

Mon père et <mes>ma sœur[5] vous presentent leurs respects—l'infirmité de mon père augmente peu à peu[6]—cependant il n'est pas encore tout à fait aveugle—mes sœurs se portent bien mais mon pauvre frère est toujours malade.[7]

Adieu Monsieur, *je compte bientôt avoir de vos nouvelles—cette idée me sourit car le souvenir de vos bontés ne s'effacera jamais de ma memoire et tant que ce souvenir durera* <?l'affection> ˋ*le respect*′[8] *qu'*il m'a *inspiré*<e>*durera aussi*

Votre élève très dévouée
C Brontë

Je viens de faire relier tous les livres que vous m'avez donnés quand j'étais encore à Bruxelles j'ai un plaisir à les considérer—cela fait tout une petite bibliothèque—Il y a d'abord les ouvrages complets de Bernardin<e> St Pierre[9]—Les Pensées de Pascal[10]—un livre de poësie,[11] deux livres allemands[12]—et (ce qui vaut tout le reste) deux discours[13] de Monsieur le Professeur Heger—prononcés à la Distribution des Prix de l'Athénée royal—
Octbe. 24th 1844

MS BL Add. 38732B. W & S 185.

To Constantin Heger, 24 October 1844: Translation

[Haworth]

Monsieur,

I am full of joy this morning—something which has rarely happened to me these last two years—it is because *a gentleman*[1] *of my acquaintance will be passing through Brussels* and *has offered to take charge of a letter to you*—which either he or else his sister[2] will deliver to you, so that I shall be certain you have received it.

I am not going to write a long letter—first of all I haven't the time—it has to go immediately—and then I am afraid of bothering you. I would just like to ask you whether you heard from me at the beginning of May and then in the month of August? For all those six months [3] I have been expecting a letter from you, Monsieur—six months of waiting—<That> is a very long time indeed! Nevertheless I am not complaining and I shall be richly recompensed for a little sadness—if you are now willing to write a letter and give it to this gentleman—or to his sister—who would deliver it to me without fail.

However short the letter *may be I shall be satisfied with it*—only *do not forget to tell me how you are*, Monsieur, and *how Madame and the children*[4] *are* and the teachers and pupils.

My father and sister[5] send you their regards—my father's affliction is gradually increasing[6]—however he is still not completely blind—my sisters are keeping well but my poor brother is always ill.[7]

Goodbye Monsieur, *I am counting on soon having news of you—this thought delights me for the remembrance of your kindness will never fade from my memory and so long as this remembrance endures the respect*[8] it has *inspired in me will endure also.*

Your very devoted pupil,
C. Brontë

I have just had bound all the books that you gave me when I was still in Brussels. I take pleasure in looking at them—they make quite a little library—First there are the complete works of Bernardin de St. Pierre[9]—the Pensées of Pascal[10]—a book of verse,[11] two German books[12]—and (something worth all the rest) two speeches,[13] by Professor Heger—given at the Prize Distribution of the Athénée Royal.

Oct 24 1844.

Original French version MS BL Add. 38732B. W & S 185.
Address (integral): Monsieur Heger | N° 32 Rue d'Isabelle | Bruxelles
PM: not in MS.
Date: CB apparently first wrote '1843', then changed it to 1844. Her letter of 8.1.1845, lamenting Joe Taylor's return from Belgium without a reply from M. Heger, confirms the date of 1844 for the present letter, though CB's reference to two years of comparative unhappiness is unexpected.

Text: The letter was torn in pieces by M. Heger and sewn together again by his wife. Cf. the previous letter of 24 July 1844. The right lower corner of fol. 2 is missing, but there is no loss of text. Part of the postscript has been torn away and displaced, but remains adhering to the seal. M. Heger, rather surprisingly, copied out extracts (printed here in italic) for Mrs Gaskell's use in his letter of 22 May 1856. (Rylands MS EL B91.) Mrs Gaskell, however, discreetly limited her quotation to the last 2 sentences, from 'N'oubliez pas' and combined them with the letter of 24.7.1844. (*Life* i. 322.) In his 'Extraits des lettres que je possède' M. Heger altered 'la lettre' to 'votre réponse' in para. 3, and 'qu'il m'a inspiré' to 'vous m'avez inspiré' in para. 5.

1. Joe Taylor would travel through Brussels on his way to Switzerland. cf. EN 14.11.1844.
2. Perhaps CB expected Joe to hand the letter to Mary Taylor, who would then give it to M. Heger on her way back from Germany.
3. CB's letter to M. Heger of 24 July 1844 implies that he had not responded to her most recent letter—presumably one written in May along with the note to Victoire Dubois of 18 May.
4. See EN 6.3.1843 n. 3.
5. Emily, who remained at Haworth. Anne Brontë would be at Thorp Green.
6. Mr Brontë's eye-trouble had proved to be the gradual growth of cataract, at first on the right and then on both eyes. In his copy of Thomas John Graham's *Modern Domestic Medicine* (1826), after Graham's note on the use of *Sulphate of Zinc. or white vitriol*, 'This salt dissolved in rose-water forms an excellent collyrium', Mr Brontë added '—or ointment for the eyes . . . Dr Outhwaite recommended this to me in Oct. 1843–'. (BPM MS bb210 p. 63.)
7. This term is sometimes used by Branwell's sisters as a euphemism for 'the worse for drink', as in EN 31.7.1845: 'I found Branwell ill—he is so very often owing to his own fault'. At this period he was still at Thorp Green, where, as Anne later recorded, he 'had much tribulation and ill health'. (AB *Diary* 31.7.1845.)
8. This discreet alteration reverses the sequence of emotions in CB's draft poem, 'At first I did attention give': 'Respect to homage changed . . . I gave entire affection now'. (MS Berg; *The Professor* appendix IV, Neufeldt *CBP* 274–5.)
9. The works of Jacques-Henri Bernardin de Saint-Pierre (1737–1814) included *Voyage à l'Isle de France* (i.e. Mauritius) (1773), *Études de la nature* (1784), and *Paul et Virginie*, (1787), a highly popular sentimental romantic tale of parted lovers. In *Villette* M. Paul Emanuel takes his berth in the 'Paul et Virginie' for the voyage abroad which, like that of Virginie in the tale, will ultimately lead to death at sea. For Bernardin's influence on CB's writing, see Enid Duthie, *The Foreign Vision of Charlotte Brontë* (1975), esp. 190–2, 198. M. Heger gave his works to CB on 15 Aug. 1843, the Athénée speech-day. (Sotheby's *Catalogue*, among the 'effects of the late Mrs A. B. Nicholls', 16 Dec. 1916.)
10. *Les Pensées*, first published in 1670, were set down by the philosopher Blaise Pascal (1623–62) in preparation for an *Apologie de la religion chrétienne* which he never completed.
11. *Les Fleurs de la poésie française depuis le commencement du XVIe siècle* (Tours, 1841), inscribed by CB 'Given to me by Monsieur Heger on the 1st January 1844, the morning I left Brussels'. The copy was sold at Sotheby's on 15 Dec. 1916 among 'the effects of the late Mrs A. B. Nicholls'.
12. One of these was the 'little German testament' which CB was surprised to receive from M. Heger on 1 May 1843: see her letter to BB of that date, n. 14. The other German book was perhaps one by Schiller, or an anthology containing poems by him: cf. CB's references to Schiller in her novels (listed in *The Professor* 333) and her translations of several of his poems in 1843. (Neufeldt *CBP* nos. 217, 218, 220–3, and notes on pp. 489–90.)
13. M. Heger had the honour of being invited to give the prize-giving addresses at the Athénée Royal in 1834 and 1843: *Discours prononcé à la distribution des prix de l'Athénée Royal de Bruxelles, le 16 août 1834* and *Discours . . . Bruxelles, le 15 août 1843*. In her account of the speeches in *Foreign Vision* 164–7, Enid Duthie praises Heger's lucid expression of his 'passionate belief in the function of education'. Lucy Snowe praises the eloquence of M. Paul Emanuel's 'discours' and describes the 'long, loud, ringing cheer' which followed in *Villette* ch. 27 (444–6.) For the Athénée Royal, see EN 23.1.1844 n. 7.

To Ellen Nussey, [c.26 October 1844]

[Haworth]

Dear Ellen

I received your kind note last Saturday[1] and should have answered it immediately but in the meantime—I had a letter from Mary Taylor—and had to reply to her and to write sundry letters to Brussels to send by opportunity[2] my sight will not allow me to write several letters per day so I was obliged to do it gradually.

I send you two more circulars[3] because you ask for them—not because I hope their distribution will produce any result—I hope that if a time should come when Emily Anne or I shall be able to serve you—we shall not forget that you have done your best to serve us—

Mr Smith[4] 'curate' is gone hence—he is in Ireland at present and will stay there six weeks—he has left neither a bad nor a good character behind 'him'—nobody regrets him because nobody could attach themselves to one who could attach himself to nobody—I thought once he had a regard for you but I do not think so now—he has never asked after you since you left nor ever mentioned you in my hearing except to say once when I purposely alluded to you that you were "not very locomotive" the meaning of the observation I leave you to divine.

Yet the man is not without points that will be most useful to himself in getting through life—his good-qualities however are all of the selfish order—but they will make him respected where better and more generous natures would be despised—or at least neglected.

Mr Grant[5] fills his shoes at present decently enough—but one cares naught about these sort of individuals so drop them—

Mary Taylor is going to leave our hemisphere[6]—To me it is something as if a great planet fell out of the sky—Yet unless she marries in New Zealand she will not stay there long

[Signed][7]

Write to me again soon and I promise to write you a regular long letter next time

MS BPM B.S. 53. W & S 183 as 16 Sept.
Address: not in MS.
PM: not in MS.
Annotations include: 44 <or 5> [in EN's hand?]
Date: CB is writing some time after 13 Oct. 1844, the date of J. W. Smith's last entries as curate in the Haworth registers, and soon after sending 'sundry letters' to Brussels. These almost certainly included her hurried note to M. Heger of Thursday 24 Oct. Her reference to 'last Saturday' means that she is unlikely to be writing later than Friday 25 or Saturday 26 Oct.

1. Probably 19 Oct.
2. For a similar usage cf. Jane Austen, *Mansfield Park* (ed. R. W. Chapman; Oxford, 1923), 372: '[Mrs Norris] could not help thinking her poor dear sister Price would feel it very unkind of her not to come by such an opportunity.' Mary must have told CB that Joe Taylor would travel via Brussels.
3. cf. EN ?2.10.1844 where CB sends 'two additional circulars' about the projected parsonage school and promises 'two more if you desire it when I write again'.
4. See EN 29.7.1844 n. 3.
5. Joseph Brett Grant (d. ?1884). A pensioner at Emmanuel College Cambridge, he graduated BA in 1843 and MA in 1868. I am grateful to Dr Juliet Barker for pointing out that his appointment as Headmaster of the Free Grammar School near Oxenhope was announced in the *Leeds Intelligencer* on 27.7.1844 (7). His first entry as PB's curate in the Haworth Register of Burials was on 10 Nov. 1844, and the Subscription Books of the Diocese of Ripon show that he was ordained priest on 15 Feb. 1845. (WYAS Sheepscar, Leeds.) He became curate-in-charge of the new district of Oxenhope formed in that year, and by Mar. 1846 was the perpetual curate there, a position he retained until his death. He married at Woodford in Essex, on 13 Jan. 1846, 'Sarah-Ann, eldest daughter of C. R. Turner Esq.' of Woodford. (*Gentleman's Magazine* 1846, 308.) CB tacitly admitted that 'Mr Donne', one of the curates in *Shirley*, was based on J. B. Grant, and described his reaction to the novel in her letter to W. S. Williams of 3.4.1850 (MS Berg; W & S 541 and 537.) 'Mr Donne's' marriage to 'a most sensible, quiet, lady-like little woman' is said to have been 'the making of him'. (*Shirley* ch.37.) The Revd Walter Bell, who knew PB slightly and had preached in his church, told a clerical friend, George Hay Forbes, that the curates in *Shirley* were 'greatly caricatured' but 'it was still a likeness'. Mr Grant was 'the brother of Wm. Grant of Glasgow—J.B.G. is really a very zealous, hardworking parish priest'. (Letter from W. Bell, Little Weston, Beverley, 5.8.1857; MS St Andrews University Library.)
6. The possibility of Mary's emigration to 'Port Nicholson' in New Zealand had been mentioned in 1841. See EJB ?2.4.1841 notes 4 and 5.
7. The 'signature' looks like a large '3' below a curving line.

To Ellen Nussey, 14 November 1844

[Haworth]

Dear Ellen

Your letter came very apropos as indeed your letters always do—but this morning I had something of a head-ache and was consequently rather out of spirits[1]—and the epistle (scarcely legible[2] though it be—excuse a rub) cheered me; in order to evince my gratitude as well as to please my own inclination—I sit down to answer it immediately—

I am glad in the first place to hear that *Henry is really going to be married,[3] and still more so to learn that his wife elect has a handsome fortune—not that I advocate marrying for money in general—but I think in many cases (and this is one) money is a very desirable contingent of matrimony. In the 2nd place I have a word to say in your private ear—Do your best to restrain *Henry in the commencement of his career as Vicar of *Hathersage—advise him not to launch out too much in the way of expenses[4]—I always have a notion that the gentlemen of your family would be the better for a word of counsel from their sisters on this point—and you yourself often require a lesson in the art of saving—I have sometimes felt sorrowful when I saw how easily money slipt through your fingers—you like to give pleasure to others and I fear you sometimes do so at the expense of inconveniencing yourself—

These, however, are only surmises of mine and, perhaps, surmises that I have no right to express—Scold me if they offend you.

We have made no alterations[5] yet in our house—it would be folly to do so while there is so little likelihood of our ever getting pupils—I fear you are giving yourself far too much trouble on our account—Depend upon it Ellen if you were to persuade a Mamma to bring her child to Haworth—the aspect of the place would frighten her and she would probably take the dear thing back with her instanter We are all glad that we have made the attempt and we are not cast down because it has not succeeded.

I wonder when Mary *Taylor is expected in England—it surprises me to hear of Joe being in Switzerland[6]—probably she is with him there also—in that case it may yet be some weeks before they return—I trust you will be at home—part of the time at least while she is at Hunsworth[7]—and that you she and I may meet again somewhere under the canopy of heaven—I cannot, dear Nell, make any promises about myself and Anne going to *Brookroyd at Christmas—her vacations are so short she would grudge spending any part of them from home—

The Catastrophe, which you relate so calmly, about your book-muslin[8] dress lace bertha[9] &c. convulsed me with cold shudderings of horror—you have reason to curse the day when so fatal a present was offered you—as that infamous little *bitch[10]—the perfect serenity with which you endured the disaster—proves most fully to me that you would make the best wife, mother & mistress of a family in the world—you and Anne are a pair, for marvellous philosophical powers of endurance—no spoilt dinners—scorched linnen, dirtied carpets—torn sofa-covers 'squealing brats, cross husbands' would ever discompose either of you—You ought never to marry a good-tempered man—such a union would <have> 'be' mingling honey with sugar. Mr *Smith[11] now would have been a good contrast to you as far as temper goes—marrying you to him would have been like sticking one of his own white roses[12] upon a black thorn cudgel.

With this very picturesque metaphor I close my letter—Good-bye and write very soon

Yours C Brontë

I have received two French Newspapers[13] this week which I shall return to Hunsworth—I am very glad of them

MS HM 24435. W & S 186.

Address: not in MS.
PM: not in MS.

1. An additional cause for CB's low spirits would be her realization that some weeks must elapse before the Taylors could return with a letter from M. Heger.
2. EN's handwriting at this period is loosely formed and confusing, as her letters of 1844 and 1845 to Mary Gorham show. (BPM Gorham Collection.)
3. After previous refusals from at least 3 ladies, including CB, Henry Nussey's proposal to Emily Prescott (1811/12–1907) daughter of 'Richard Prescott, Gentleman, of Plumpton Terrace, Everton Lancs', had been accepted. Her father was dead by the time of her marriage on 22 May 1845, and she was married from the house of William Budd Prescott of 31 Plumpton Terrace, Everton Road, Liverpool, a merchant with premises at 20 Water Street, Liverpool. See CB's letter to HN of 5.3.1839, n. 1, M. F. H. Hulbert, *The Vicarage Family Hathersage 1627–1987* (Hathersage Parochial Church Council, 1988) 9, and Pigot and Slater, *Directory* for Liverpool and Environs, 1844.
4. Henry was to incur considerable expense in his alterations to Hathersage Vicarage in 1845: 'So the South wing was extended West, a wine cellar and food cellar, and two larger bedrooms squeezed under the same roofline.' (M. F. H. Hulbert, *Discovering Hathersage Old Vicarage* (n.d., ?*c*.1986), 11, and see *Whitehead* 116.)
5. See CH 24.7.1844 and n. 11.
6. Mary Taylor had expected a visit from her brother Joe while she was in Germany, as CB would know. See MT to EN, late Summer/Autumn 1844.
7. See MT to EN 30.10.1842 and 1.11.1842 n. 5.
8. A delicately woven cotton fabric, 'folded like a book when sold in the piece'. (*OED*.)
9. 'A deep falling collar, attached to the top of a low-necked dress.' (*OED*.) Flossy was later to 'nestle' in EN's 'portmanteau'—i.e. among the clothes hanging from a clothes-rack. (EN.5.4.1851, W & S 654.)
10. Flossy junior: see EN ?29.7.1844. Oddly, CB had referred to Flossy as a dog, not a bitch, in EN ?10.8.1844.
11. The curate J. W. Smith.
12. Probably a private joke at Mr Smith's expense. His fictional persona, Peter Augustus Malone, presents a 'huge bunch' of red cabbage-roses to Shirley in ch. 16 of the novel.
13. The Taylor brothers lent copies of French newspapers to their friends, including EN and CB, who welcomed them as a link with the language she had spoken with M. Heger. In *Shirley* Mr Yorke, based on the Taylors' father, is 'an adept in the French and Italian languages' and Robert Moore, a composite character who in some aspects recalls Joe Taylor, speaks 'English with a foreign, and French with a perfectly pure accent'. 58, 59.) CB never names the French papers. Possibilities would be the liberal *Le Moniteur universel* (1789–1868) to which Dumas *père* (1802–70) and Sainte-Beuve (1804–69) contributed, or the famous *Le Journal des débats* (1789–1939). *La Gazette de France* (founded 1631) was royalist in sympathy and unlikely to be taken by the Taylors, but they would approve of *Le National*, founded in January 1830 as an opposition newspaper, and established by 1840 as a republican paper advocating electoral reform; and probably also of the socialist and republican *La Réforme*, founded in 1843 and devoted to the amelioration of the lot of the working man.

To Ellen Nussey, [?30 December 1844]

[Haworth]

Dear Ellen

I have lately wondered very much why you did not write to me—I now know the cause—Mary Taylor is staying with us at present and she has told me the distressing circumstance[1] which absorbs both your time and thoughts at present

Poor Mr George—I am sorry for him—very sorry—he did not deserve this suffering—I know too what a calamity his severe illness will be for all the family—and most especially for you—

This morning—(Monday) Mary has had a letter from 'one of' her brothers which informs us that Mr George is rather better.

Do not write to me Ellen till you have time and composure to write without too much trouble What can be the cause of these severe attacks to which Mr George has been subjected. Does his medical attendant[2] treat him properly?

When you do write inform me how you all bear the fatigue of body & anxiety of mind you have had to go through—

Mary Taylor is looking very well and is in good spirits.

Good-by'e dear Ellen
C Brontë

MS BPM B.S. 53.5. W & S 187 as [6 Jan. 1845].
Address: not in MS.
PM: not in MS.
Annotation in pencil, partly erased and mostly illegible, by EN, ending 'January 45'.
Date: EN's date is accepted for W & S 187, which specifies '[January 6th, 1845]'.
But Mary Taylor had returned home by 4 Jan. 1845, when she asked EN how George was getting on, and reported 'Charlotte is very well she sends her love'. See *Stevens* 56 and n. 1 below. EN probably received the letter in early Jan.

1. CB refers to the onset of an acute phase of George Nussey's mental illness. His sisters cared devotedly for this most likeable of the brothers, and EN accompanied him to Harrogate and then Bridlington in search of rest and health in early 1845. (EN 13.1.1845 and 24.3.1845.) By 18 Aug. 1845 George was a patient at Dr Henry Stephen Belcombe's private asylum at Clifton Green on the outskirts of York: see EN 18.8.1845 n. 5. Ellen added a note to the present letter in one of the copies of *Nussey*, attributing George's illness to an accident, not recorded elsewhere: 'Private. A terrible accident laid low this dear, suffering brother,—one of the best and noblest of men,—a devoted son, and brother, handsome 'fascinating' man, always a perfect gentleman in every detail to the end of his sad life. Unfortunately to himself his injuries did not deprive him of acute sensibility to his misfortune, and loss of mental power. His memory was perfect up to the time of his accident, after that event his memory seemed to fail in connecting influences, and association for working, and reasoning purposes, though politely thoughtful to those around him in little acts of attention. | The bitterest part of his lot was in the consciousness of his affliction. | Strange it seems, that memory remained uninjured respecting all that happened before his accident. Medical skill 50 years ago was very defective.' (*Hatfield* 199–201.)
2. Probably the surgeon William Carr of Gomersal (1784–1861), husband of EN's cousin Sarah Nussey of White Lee, Batley (1791–1864).

Mary Taylor to Ellen Nussey, 4 January [1845]

[Hunsworth,
Yorkshire]

Dear Ellen

Here I am again & am very anxious to know how you are & how George is getting on.[1] When shall I come & see you?[2] Joe wishes to borrow George's gig & horse on Sunday night to go to Leeds on Monday morning. Could you not come in it or the day after? A. & T. Dixon[3] will be here on Sunday, to whom you will have nothing to say but the day following I shall be alone & very much want to see you   I think a night from home would do you good if you could be spared so long. Charlotte is very well   she sends her love.[4]

Remember me to your Mother & Sisters

M. Taylor.

MS Berg. *Stevens* letter 15.
Address: not in MS.
PM: not in MS.
Date: M. Taylor wrote ?'5', then changed it to '4', i.e. Saturday. She must have returned from Haworth to her brothers' house at Hunsworth on or just before this date. cf. EN ?30.12.1844. The year must be 1845, as the content indicates: Mary was in Germany in Jan. 1844 and in New Zealand in Jan. 1846.

1. See the previous letter, n. 1.
2. Hunsworth is about 3 miles from Ellen's home, Brookroyd, Birstall.
3. Probably Mary's cousins Abraham or Abram Dixon (1815–1907) and Tom Dixon (1821–65). Their father was also 'Abraham', but Mary would probably have referred to him as 'Mr' or 'my uncle Dixon'. Originally a Birstall family, they were now scattered in Belgium, America, Birmingham, and elsewhere. See E. Branwell 29.9.1841 n. 8 and MT to EN 30.10. and 1.11.1842 n. 4, and for Tom Dixon see EN 6.3.1843 n. 7.
4. Mary must have written after her return from a visit to CB, who was still at Haworth.

To Constantin Heger, 8 January 1845

Haworth—Bradford—Yorkshire

M. Taylor est revenu,[1] je lui ai demandé s'il n'avait pas une lettre pour moi—"Non, rien." "Patience"—dis-je—Sa sœur viendra bientôt["]—Mademoiselle Taylor[2] est revenue   "Je n'ai rien pour vous de la part de Monsieur Heger" dit-elle   "ni lettre ni message."

Ayant bien compris ces mots—je me suis dit, ce que je dirais à un autre en p[a]reille circonstance "Il faut vous résigner et, surtout, ne pas vous affliger d'un malheur que vous n'avez pas merité"   Je me suis efforcée à ne pas pleurer à ne pas me plaindre—

Mais quand on ne se plaint pas et qu'on veut se dominer en tyran[3]—les facultés se révoltent—et on paie le calme extérieur par une lutte intérieure presque insupportable

Jour et nuit je ne trouve ni repos ni paix—si je dors je fais des rêves tourmentants[4] où je vous vois toujours sévère, toujours sombre et irrité contre moi—

Pardonnez-moi donc Monsieur si je prends la partie de vous écrire encore—Comment puis-je supporter la vie si je ne fais pas un effort pour en alléger les souffrances?

Je sais que vous serez impatienté quand vous lirez cette lettre—Vous direz encore que je sui[s] exaltée[5]—que j'ai des pensées noires &c. Soit Monsieur—je ne cherche pas à me justifier, je me soumets a toutes sortes de réproches—tout ce que je sais—c'est que [j]e ne puis pas—que je ne veux pas me résigner à perdre entièrement l'amitié de mon maître—j'aime mieux subir les plus grandes douleurs physiques que d'avoir toujours le cœur, lacéré par des regrets cuisants. Si mon maître me retire entièrement son amitié je serai<s> tout à fait sans espoir—s'il m'en donne un peu—très peu—je serai contente—heureuse, j'aurais un motif pour vivre—pour travailler.

Monsieur, les pauvres n'[o]nt pas besoin de grand'chose pour vivre—ils ne demandent que les miettes de pain[6] qui tombent de la table des riches—mais si on leur refuse ces miettes de pain—ils meurent de faim—Moi non plus je n'ai pas besoin de beaucoup d'affection de la part de ceux que j'aime je ne saurais que faire d'une amitié entière et complète—je n'y suis pas habituée—mais vous me témoigniez, autrefois, un peu d'intérêt quand j'étais votre élève à Bruxelles—et je tiens à conserver ce peu d'intérêt—j'y tiens comme je tiendrais à la vie.

Vous me direz peutêtre—Je ne vous porte plus le moindre intérêt Mademoiselle Charlotte—vous n'êtes plus de Ma Maison—je vous ai oubliée"

Eh bien Monsieur dites-moi cela franchement—ce sera pour moi un choc—n'importe ce sera toujours moins hideux que l'incertitude.

Je ne veux pas relire cet[t]e lettre—je l'envoie comme je l'ai écrite—Pourtant j'ai comme la conscience obscure qu'il y a des personnes froides et sensées[7] qui diraient en la lisant—"elle déraisonne"—Pour toute vengeance—je souhaite à ces personnes—un seul jour des tourments [que] j'ai subis depuis huit mois—on verrait alors s'elles [ne] déraiso[n]neraient pas de même

On souffre en silence tant qu'on a la force et qua[nd] cette force manque on parle <?3 or 4 i.w.> sans trop mesurer ses paroles. <Je n'ai pas besoin de souhaiter à Monsieur le bonheur et la prosperité—il jouit de [?3 i.w.] ?autou[8]>

Je souhaite à Monsieur le bonheur et la prospérité

C B

MS BL Add. 38732D. W & S 188.

To Constantin Heger, 8 January 1845: Translation

Haworth—Bradford—Yorkshire

Mr Taylor returned,[1] I asked him if he had a letter for me—"No, nothing." "Patience"—I say—"His sister will be coming soon"—Miss Taylor[2] returned "I have nothing for you from M. Heger" she says "neither letter nor message."

When I had taken in the full meaning of these words—I said to myself, what I would say to someone else in such a case "You will have to resign yourself to the fact, and above all, not distress yourself about a misfortune that you have not deserved." I did my utmost not to cry not to complain—

But when one does not complain, and when one wants to master oneself with a tyrant's grip[3]—one's faculties rise in revolt—and one pays for outward calm by an almost unbearable inner struggle

Day and night I find neither rest nor peace—if I sleep I have tormenting dreams[4] in which I see you always severe, always saturnine and angry with me—

Forgive me then Monsieur if I take the step of writing to you again—How can I bear my life unless I make an effort to alleviate its sufferings?

I know that you will lose patience with me when you read this letter—You will say that I am over-excited[5]—that I have black thoughts etc. So be it Monsieur—I do not seek to justify myself, I submit to all kinds of reproaches—all I know—is that I cannot—that I will not resign myself to the total loss of my master's friendship—I would rather undergo the greatest bodily pains than have my heart constantly lacerated by searing regrets. If my master withdraws his friendship from me entirely I shall be absolutely without hope—if he gives me a little friendship—a very little—I shall be content—happy, I would have a motive for living—for working.

Monsieur, the poor do not need a great deal to live on—they ask only the crumbs of bread[6] which fall from the rich men's table—but if they are refused these crumbs—they die of hunger—No more do I need a great deal of affection from those I love—I would not know what to do with a whole and complete friendship—I am not accustomed to it—but you showed a little interest in me in days gone by when I was your pupil in Brussels—and I cling to the preservation of this little interest—I cling to it as I would cling on to life.

Perhaps you will say to me—"I no longer take the slightest interest in you Miss Charlotte—you no longer belong to my household—I have forgotten you."

Well Monsieur tell me so candidly—it will be a shock to me—that doesn't matter—it will still be less horrible than uncertainty.

I don't want to re-read this letter—I am sending it as I have written it—Nevertheless I am as it were dimly aware that there are some cold and rational people[7] who would say on reading it—"she is raving"—My sole revenge is to wish these people—a single day of the torments that I have suffered for eight months—then we should see whether they wouldn't be raving too

One suffers in silence so long as one has the strength and when that strength fails one speaks <?4 i.w>. without measuring one's words too much. <I do not need to wish Monsieur happiness and prosperity—he enjoys [2 or 3 i.w.] ?around[8] >I wish Monsieur happiness and prosperity

C B

MS BL Add. 38732D. W & S 188.
Address (integral): Monsieur Heger | N° 32 Rue d'Isabelle | Bruxelles | Belgique
PM: (i) HAWORTH (ii)B[RA]DFORD YORKS | JA 9 | 1845 | C (iii) PA— | 12 JAN | 5 (iv)— — | OSTENDE (v) BRUXELLES | 12 JANV | 1845
Text: has been slightly impaired by the tearing of the paper into 9 pieces, later sewn together with whitish cotton. A small piece of paper, about 30 mm. x 12 mm., has adhered to the back of the red sealing wax, leaving a hole in the second leaf. Missing letters have been conjecturally supplied in square brackets. M. Heger sent Mrs Gaskell no extracts from this letter. See CH 24.7.1844, note on text.

1. CB had hoped that her letter to M. Heger of 24.10.1844, taken to him by Joe Taylor, would elicit a reply, to be delivered to her by Joe or Mary.
2. Mary Taylor had decided to give up her teaching post in Germany and, after returning to Yorks., to emigrate to New Zealand. See EN *c*.26.10.1844 n. 6 and 20.2.1845 n. 5.
3. One may compare Lucy Snowe's attempt to control the 'strain of long expectancy' and her 'sick collapse of disappointment' when no letters arrive, in *Villette* 380–4.
4. Lucy Snowe is tormented by an 'avenging dream' in *Villette* 222–4, and speaks of the 'sinister band of bad dreams' which harass the solitary 'with horror of calamity, and sick dread of entire desertion' in 380–4.
5. Over-excited or neurotic. In her letter to Heger of 24.7.1844 CB perhaps implies that M. Heger had rebuked her for a previous 'lettre peu raisonnable'.
6. cf. Luke 16: 20–1, where the beggar Lazarus desired 'to be fed with the crumbs which fell from the rich man's table'. M. Heger seems to have written to CB at least once during 1845, in May; possibly he also replied earlier in the year to the present plea. See CH 18.11.1845 n. 1.
7. cf. CB's description of Mme Heger in BB 1.5.1843 as 'always cool & always reasoning', and her characterization of Mlle Reuter in *The Professor* and Mme Beck in *Villette*.
8. Conjectural readings for 2 heavily deleted lines of writing.

To Ellen Nussey, 13 January [1845]

[Haworth]

My dear Ellen

I have often said and thought that you have had many and heavy trials to bear in your still short life—you have always borne them with great firmness and calm so far—I hope fervently you will still be enabled to do so. Yet there is something in your letters that makes me fear the present is the greatest trial of all[1] and the most severely felt by you—I hope it will soon pass over—pass over completely and leave no shadow behind it—

A certain space of time—complete rest—such care as you will give to *George—must with God's blessing produce the best results—

I do earnestly desire to be with you—to talk to you—to give you what comfort I can—

I cannot go to you to Harrogate[2] but as—in a letter I had from Mary *Taylor this morning—she tells me *George will probably soon be going with *Henry to *Hathersage[3] and you will be returning to *Brookroyd I shall then in that case either go to you at Brookroyd—or have you to Haworth—as you at the time shall deem best—and in deciding whether you shall come to me or I go to you—let only one thing be consulted—namely your health & comfort.

The circumstance of *George's having so far recovered his strength as to be able to walk two miles—surprises me greatly—he must have great elasticity as well as strength of constitution—I should think it cannot be considered otherwise than as a favourable symptom—surely with such good muscular powers—his nervous vigour will soon be restored—

The worst thing is—that when he does recover instead of being in a position to live a life of calm & ease—he will be obliged again to plunge into the turmoil of business[4]—the members of the family who can assist him[5]—ought to look to this—if they have any brotherly regard for the best amongst them—A relapse would be dreadful—

Branwell and Anne leave us on Saturday—Branwell has been quieter and less irritable[6] on the whole this time than he was in Summer—Anne is as usual always good, mild & patient—I think she too is a little stronger than she was—

Shortly after B & A leave I shall go to Hunsworth[7] for a week—if all be well—

If you are likely to come home shortly I would put off my visit till that time—

Write to me as soon as you can and tell me how *George & yourself get on & what your plans are

Good bye dear Ellen
C Brontë

MS HM 24436. Envelope; BPM B.S. 104/5. W & S 189.
Address (envelope): Miss Ellen Nussey | Mrs Coupland's | High-Harrogate
PM: (i) HAWORTH (ii) BRADFORD | JA 13 | 1845 | C (iii) HARROGATE | JA 14 | 1845
Annotation (i) by EN on letter and envelope: 'Jan 13—45'; (ii) by another hand on the envelope: 'mentions Branwell and Anne Brontë'.

1. For George Nussey's illness see EN ?30.12.1844 n. 1.
2. See EN 6.8.1843 and notes. EN and her family had also stayed in Harrogate in late Aug. 1844.
3. Henry Nussey had been appointed Vicar of Hathersage in Aug. 1844. See EN ?22.8.1844 n. 1.
4. Joseph, Richard, and George Nussey had carried on the family's woollen manufacturing business after the death of their father. See EN 21.12.1839 n. 2.

5. Joseph Nussey seems to have been by this time a dissolute drunkard, and unlikely to assist George. See EN 31.7.1845 and n. 5. Apart from Richard, the eldest brother John (1794–1862), the Court Apothecary who lived in London, and the Revd Joshua Nussey (1798–1871) would probably be in a position to help.
6. cf. CH 24.10.1844 where CB says her brother is 'toujours malade'. Her guarded words may indicate that Branwell was drinking less, or revealing less anxiety about his predicament at Thorp Green, from which he was to be dismissed in disgrace in July this year. He and Anne would be returning to their posts at Thorp Green on Saturday 18 Jan.
7. CB would go to stay with Mary Taylor at her brothers' house.

To Ellen Nussey, [?20 February 1845]

[Haworth]

Dear Ellen,

You ought to have written to me before now—you promised I should hear from you soon—and the non-fulfilment of this promise makes me rather afraid that some disagreeable event or other is the occasion of the delay. I hope George continues to improve in health;[1] write soon and let me know whether such is the case or not. I spent a week at Hunsworth[2] not very pleasantly; headache, sickliness, and flatness of spirits made me a poor companion,[3] a sad drag on the vivacious and loquacious gaiety of all the other inmates of the house. I never was fortunate enough to be able to rally, for so much as a single hour, while I was there. I am sure all, with the exception perhaps of Mary, were very glad when I took my departure. I begin to perceive that I have too little life in me, nowadays, to be fit company for any except very quiet people. Is it age, or what else, that changes one so?[4] I had a note from Mary yesterday. She said she was to leave Hunsworth on Friday.[5] She asked for your address. I did not know the address of the lodgings, so I gave her that of Mr [?Hudson],[6] where I shall also send this note. If you have any French newspapers[7] send them soon. I had one sent, I think, direct from Hunsworth to-day; but there is one missed between, and I should like to read that one first. Write to me, if possible, immediately.

C. Brontë.

MS untraced. W & S 190.
Address: not in source.
PM: not in source.
Date: as in source; but 20 Feb. was a Thursday. CB's reference to Mary leaving 'on Friday' rather than 'to-morrow' or 'a week to-morrow' makes the date questionable.
Text: *Shorter* 148.
W & S 190 reproduces *Shorter* 148 except that *Shorter* omits the name 'Hudson'. *Nussey* 122 is incomplete, beginning 'I hope George continues'. *Life* i. 318 includes an extract beginning 'I spent a week' and ending 'changes me so?'—a variant which may provide the correct reading.

1. EN and her brother George were in Bridlington ('Burlington'). cf. EN 24.10.1839 notes 1 and 5.
2. cf. CB's comment on the 'malaria' of Hunsworth in EN 29.9.1846.
3. Ellen Nussey comments, using a slightly inaccurate quotation from Mary Taylor's letter to Mrs Gaskell in *Life* i. 319–20:

   It was about this time that a friend writes, 'When I last saw Charlotte she told me she had quite decided to stay at home. She owned she did not like it. Her health was weak. She said she should like any change at first, as she had liked Brussels at first, and she thought there must be some possibility for some people of having a life of more variety and more communion with human kind but she saw none for her. I told her very warmly she ought not to stay at home: that to spend the next 5 years at home, in solitude and weak health, would ruin her: and she would never recover it. Such a dark shadow came over her face when I said, Think of what you will be five years hence, that I stopped, and said, Don't cry Charlotte. She did not cry, but went on walking up and down the room, and said in a little while, "But I intend to stay [Polly]." '

   Dear Charlotte discovered that her Father's welfare depended very much on her presence at the parsonage. Her high principle and sense of duty determined her to self-sacrifice, whatever cost or loss it might bring upon her. Her admiration of the Great Duke was quite sympathetic she was herself a little Wellington in the cares and anxieties of life. Duty always first. (*Hatfield* 196–7.)
4. *Life* i. 318 reads 'changes me so?'.
5. Mary Taylor was to sail for New Zealand on the 'Louisa Campbell' from Gravesend on 12 Mar., calling at Plymouth on 17 Mar. and arriving in Wellington on 24 July. The information given in *Stevens* 57 does not tally with the dates recorded in *The Times* for 13, 14, and 19 Mar. 1845.
6. CB and EN had stayed with John and Sophia Hudson at Easton Farm near Bridlington in 1839. See EN 24.10.1839 and notes 5 and 6.
7. See EN 14.11.1844 n. 13.

To Ellen Nussey, [?4 March 1845]

[Haworth]

My dear Ellen,

I must just acknowledge your last note, though I have not, this morning, time to write a long letter.

From what you say of George's state of health,[1] it seems to me that decidedly the best plan would be (if possible) to isolate him for a time from all his relations—yourself included, and let him travel with a judicious and conscientious medical man; such a mode of cure would be expensive, but certainly it would be the surest and speediest.

It is an unvarying symptom in cases of diseased brain, for the patient to feel irritation[2] in the presence of his relations, and to be averse to receive their services, and I believe they often feel most antipathy to those whom, in health they were most attached to.

If you stay with George you will probably suffer much in mind, be worn down in body, and do no real good. Take the advice of the medical man you have consulted at Burlington, and let your other relations take it—otherwise they will probably repent hereafter. I believe it is of great importance not to lose time in such cases. All of course depends upon what resources there are for meeting expense, and of that you can judge.

Remember me very kindly to Mrs. Hudson,[3] to whom I shall again direct this letter—not knowing your address at the Quay. Tell her that our stay at E[aston] is one of the pleasant recollections of my life—one of the green spots that I look back on with real pleasure. I often think it was singularly good of her to receive me, a perfect stranger, so kindly as she did.

I know of no new books—unless it be "The Chimes," by Dickens,[4] which I have not read. I have had no news from Hunsworth since I last wrote to you, I should like to hear whether Mary is actually gone.[5] Write to me again soon, dear Ellen, as I am truly anxious to hear of you and of George, both for your sake and his own.

Yours,
C. Brontë.

MS untraced. W & S 191.
Address: not in source.
PM: not in source.
Date: from source.
Text: *Nussey* 122–3, with 'Easter' corrected to 'Easton', following EN's correction in the BPM Killick copy of *Nussey*. *Shorter* 149 and W & S 191 reproduce *Nussey*, with minor punctuation variants and the emendation to 'Easton'. Not in *Life*.

1. George Nussey was to become a patient in Dr H. S. Belcombe's Clifton House asylum near York later this year. CB's letter to EN of 18.8.1845 implies that he had been there some time.
2. EN wrote in the margin of the BPM *Nussey* Copy 2 'This was not the case'. She also deleted paras. 2 to 4 in BPM Copies 1 and 2, and the names 'Hudson' and 'George' in paras. 5 and 6.
3. See EN 24.10.1839. Easton is about 2 miles inland from the Quay, which is the area near Bridlington Harbour as distinct from the street of Georgian houses near Bridlington Priory.
4. *The Chimes: a Goblin Story | of | Some Bells, that rang an old year out and a new year in*; one of Dickens's Christmas stories, published in Dec. 1844 following the great success of *A Christmas Carol* in Dec. 1843.
5. See the previous letter n. 5.

To Ellen Nussey, 24 March [1845]

[Haworth]

Dear Ellen

I repeat to you what you say sometimes to me "Take care of yourself". You are not strong enough, not of sufficiently robust fibre to travel 70 miles[1] in an open gig in very cold weather Don't do it again.

You have done quite right to leave *George for a time 'your absence cannot harm him' —and a total estrangement from the persons and things that were about him in his illness—will in all probability do him good—Do not dear *Ellen be disheartened because *George's improvement in health is slow—When one thinks of the nature of his illness of the extreme delicacy of the organ affected (the brain) it is obvious that that organ after the irritation of fever & inflammation could not all at once regain its healthy state—it must have time—but with time I do believe a complete cure will yet be effected—I should not hope it, if *George were a man of irregular habits[2]—but as it is—I think there is the best ground for confident hope.

Have you heard any particulars of *Mary *Taylor's departure—what day she sailed[3]—what passengers were in the ship—in what sort of spirits and health she set off—&c. glean what intelligence you can and transmit it to me. Yesterday I was much surprised to receive a newspaper directed in *Mary *Taylor's hand—its date was of the 9th of March—the Post-Mark I could not make out—it was a Weekly Despatch.[4]

I can hardly tell you how time gets on here at Haworth—There is no event whatever to mark its progress—one day resembles another—and all have heavy lifeless physiognomies—Sunday—baking day & Saturday are the only ones that bear the slightest distinctive mark—meantime life wears away—I shall soon be 30—and I have done nothing yet—Sometimes I get melancholy—at the prospect before and behind me—yet it is wrong and foolish to repine—undoubtedly my Duty directs me to stay at home for the present—There was a time when *Haworth was a very pleasant place to me, it is not so now—I feel as if we were all buried here[5]—I long to travel—to work to live a life of action—Excuse me dear *Ellen for troubling you with my fruitless wishes—I will put by the rest and not bother you with them.

You must write to [me]—if you knew how welcome your letters are—you would write very often. Your letters and the French Newspapers[6]—are the only messengers that come to me from the outer world—beyond our Moors; and very welcome messengers they are.

Talking of the French Newspapers—it is a pity I never had any intimation that I was expected to send them to you—otherwise I should not have failed to do so—as it was I concluded of course that they would go to you from *Hunsworth—now however you will in all probability receive them first—be sure & send them regularly—

What did Mr & Mrs *Hudson[7] say about your looks when they saw you—? Did they not think it marvellous that after a lapse of near 7 years you should be looking nearly as young as ever?

Don't forget to tell me how George is when you write—Give my love to your Mother and Sister—is Mrs *Sykes[8] with you yet—Do you know anything about Miss *Wooler?[9] Write very soon—Good bye dear Ellen

C Bronte

When you see Joe *Taylor ask him for Ellen *Taylor's[10] address at Bradford March 24th—35[11]

I shall be sorry when you are gone to *Hathersage[12]—you will be so far off again how long will they want you to stay? I should say *Henry would do wisely to make sure of Miss *P[rescott][13] immediately 6 months is a long time to wait—adverse things might happen in the mean while.

MS Law-Dixon. W & S 192.
Address: not in source.
PM: not in source.
Annotation by EN in ink: Mar 24—45
Date: CB dated 'March 24th—35' in error. The content shows that EN's '45' is correct.

1. EN had returned to Birstall from Bridlington on the east coast of Yorks.
2. CB had referred to George as the best of the Nussey brothers in her letter of 13 Jan., whereas in contrast she was later to call Joseph Nussey's sufferings expiation for his errors: 'One shudders for him' (EN soon after 3 June 1846.)
3. See EN ?20.2.1845 n. 5.
4. The *Weekly Dispatch*, a leading popular Sunday paper founded in 1801 and owned from 1840 by Alderman James Harmer (1777–1853), who made it outspokenly radical. It was sympathetic to Chartism and critical of the financial provision made for Prince Albert, and would appeal to the radical and republican Mary Taylor. The number for 9 Mar. began with an indignant article on the misdirection of charity, the neglect of the poor at home, and in particular the misdoings of 'those odious pocket-gropers, called missionaries' who distributed Bibles but allegedly did nothing for the practical benefit of the negroes of West Africa; the leading article was a ferocious attack on the nepotism, jobbery, self-aggrandisement, and injustice attributed to 'the great Duke of Newcastle, the monstrous Tory who laid down the principle "that every man had a right to do what he pleased with his own" '. The reports in the same number of a shipwreck in a heavy squall at Dover, and the 'appalling shipwreck' of an East Indiaman and two transport ships in the Far East must have added to CB's anxiety about Mary's voyage.
5. cf. *Shirley* ch. 23 where Rose Yorke (modelled on Mary Taylor) tells Caroline of her intention to seek the other hemisphere: 'I am resolved that my life shall be a life: not . . . a long, slow death like yours in Briarfield Rectory . . . a place that, when I pass it, always reminds me of a windowed grave?' (451.)
6. See EN 14.11.1844 n. 13. CB had hoped for letters from M. Heger as 'messengers . . . from the outer world'.
7. See EN 24.10.1839 and notes 5 and 6.
8. Not identified. The surname was common in the locality.
9. CB renewed contact with Miss Wooler in April: see MW 23.4.1845.
10. Ellen Taylor (1826–51) was Mary Taylor's cousin, the orphan daughter of William Taylor (1777–1837) and his wife Margaret, née Mossman (1793–1834). Ellen's uncle Abraham Dixon took an interest in her welfare and in 1843 made abortive plans for her to attend Mme Heger's school in Brussels. See M. Dixon 16.10.1843 n. 8. Ellen was to join her cousin Mary in Wellington, New Zealand, in Aug. 1849 and to help her to plan and stock a shop there, but her health was poor and she died of TB on 27 Dec. 1851. For more information see *Stevens, passim*.
11. See the note on date, above.
12. Henry Nussey was planning to make improvements to his vicarage at Hathersage in preparation for his coming marriage, and would no doubt have welcomed Ellen's assistance in supervising them.
13. Illegible in source. See MW 23.4.1845. Henry did not delay long: he married Emily Prescott (1811/12–1907) at St George's Church, Everton, Lancs. on 22 May 1845. She was said to be

wealthy. See EN 14.11.1844 n. 3 and 1.6.1845. Everton, then a pleasant village 1 mile from Liverpool, was 'the favourite residence of the Liverpool merchants'. (*Dugdale* 754.)

To Ellen Nussey, [?27 March 1845]

[Haworth]

Dear Ellen,

I received the enclosed letters[1] from Mary this morning, with directions from Joe Taylor to send them on to you as soon as I had read them, and request you to despatch them instanter[2] back to Hunsworth.

He likewise says, I ought by all means to have sent you the French Newspapers, and no doubt thinks me exquisitely stupid because I did not.

Mary is in her element now—she has done right to go out to New Zealand.

[Unsigned][3]

MS untraced at the time of first publication; now Kent Bicknell. W & S 193.

Address: not in source.

PM: not in source.

Date: the content indicates a later date than the letter of 24 Mar. Evidence for the W & S date, 'March 27th, 1845' is lacking, but it is more likely than ?*Nussey* and *Shorter*'s 'March 21st, 1845'.

Text: *Nussey* 124, probably closer to the MS in accidentals than *Shorter* 150 and its derivative, W & S 193. See also n. 2. The letter is not in *Life*.

1. Letters to Mary Taylor's family and friends, perhaps posted on or about 17 Mar. when the 'Louisa Campbell' put into Plymouth.
2 *Shorter* 150 and W & S 193 read 'despatch instanter'.
3. *Shorter* 150 and W & S 193 add the signature 'C. BRONTË'.

To Ellen Nussey, 2 April [1845]

[Haworth]

Dear Ellen

I send you herewith a French Newspaper—which however will be of little interest to you as you have missed so many in consequence of your absence;[1] you should ask Joe *Taylor to give you those you have missed, I should think he still has them in his possession—At present however your occupations of dress-making &c.[2] will no doubt give you enough to do without reading old French Newspapers—

I am greatly obliged to your Mother for her kindness in asking me to come and see you now—but of course I would much rather put off my visit till after all stirs are over—till your bridesmaid duties are all discharged—and when you are quite alone—quite settled and quiet—somewhere about the latter end of Summer or the beginning of Autumn—I will if all be well—make shift to toddle over and see you.

How plainly it is proved to us, that there is scarcely a draught of unmingled happiness to be had in this world—*George's illness comes with *Henry's marriage—Mary *Taylor finds herself free—and on that path for adventure and exertion to which she has so long been seeking admission—Sickness—Hardship—Danger are her fellow-travellers—her inseparable companions. She may have been out of the reach of these S.W. & N.W. gales[3] before they began to blow—or they may have spent their fury on land and not ruffled the sea much—if it has been otherwise she has been sorely tossed while we have been sleeping in our beds or lying awake thinking about her.

Yet these real—material dangers 'when once past' leave in the mind the satisfaction of having struggled with a difficulty and overcome it—Strength—Courage—experience are their invariable results—whereas I doubt whether suffering purely mental [h]as any good result unless it be to make us by comparison less sensitive to physical suffering—I repeat then, that *Mary *Taylor has done well to go out to New-Zealand—but I wish we could soon have another letter from her—I hope she may write from Madeira[4]

Ten years ago I should have laughed heartily at your account of the blunder you made in mistaking the bachelor doctor of *Burlington for a Married Man I should have certainly thought you scrupulous over-much—and wondered how you could possibly regret being civil to a decent individual merely because he happened to be single instead of double. Now however I can perceive that your scruples are founded on common-sense. I know that if women wish to escape the stigma of husband-seeking they must act & look like marble or clay—cold—expressionless, bloodless—for every appearance of feeling of joy—sorrow—friendliness, antipathy, admiration—disgust are alike construed by the world into an attempt to hook in a husband—Never mind Nell—well-meaning women have their own Consciences to comfort them after all—Do not therefore be too much afraid of shewing yourself as you are—affectionate and good-hearted—do not too harshly repress sentiments & feelings excellent in themselves because you fear that some puppy may fancy that you are letting them come out to fascinate him—Do not <compel> condemn yourself to live only by halves because if you shewed too much animation some pragmatical thing in breeches (excuse the expression)[5] might take it into its pate to imagine that you designed to dedicate your precious life to its inanity—Still, a composed—decent equable <carriage> deportment is a capital treasure and that you possess

Write again soon—for I feel rather fierce and want stroking down—

Good-bye dear Nell.
[Unsigned]

MS HM 24437. W & S 194.
Address: not in MS.
PM: not in MS.
Annotation by ?EN: Ap 2nd. 45

1. At Bridlington. See EN 20.2.1845 n. 1.
2. In preparation for her brother Henry's wedding. See EN 24.3.1845. n. 13.
3. *The Times* for 28 and 31 Mar., 1 and 2 Apr., recorded 'severe squalls' and heavy gales, mainly westerly and west-north-westerly, off the English coast. On 1 Apr. it carried a 'Caution to Mariners' dated Bristol 28 Mar., warning that a buoy had broken adrift 'during the gale of the 26th inst.'. See also EN 24.3.1845 n. 4.
4. The harbour of Funchal in Madeira made it a natural port of call for ocean-going vessels before they continued the long passage to New Zealand by sailing down the west coast of Africa to the Cape of Good Hope. CB evidently followed Mary's probable route with interest: in *J E* she makes Jane's rich uncle the 'Funchal correspondent of his house'. (372.) In fact Mary wrote home soon after the ship had called at Santiago, one of the Cape Verde Islands, considerably further south than Madeira. See EN 1.6.1845.
5. Surprisingly, Mrs Gaskell omits this parenthesis in the *Life*, where she quotes the greater part of the letter soon after extracts from Charlotte's letters to M. Heger. P. 323 is headed 'Women's Conduct liable to Misconstruction'. (*Life* i. 322–4.)

To Margaret Wooler, 23 April 1845

[Haworth]

My dear Miss Wooler

Both Emily and I thank you for the kind promptitude with which you answered my last letter and for the clear information contained in your reply.

We have written to Mr Bignold[1]—he says the terms for female lives are very low he can only offer $4\frac{1}{2}$ per cent for annuities purchased at 25—and 5 per cent for those purchased at 30. As you say—an advantage so trifling would scarcely compensate for the loss of the principal.

Our rail-road investment[2] is not <yet> threatened with immediate danger—and as we have none of us yet quite attained the age of thirty—[3] we think it best to take a twelvemonth to consider the matter. Mr Bignold also says that an annuity purchased at 30—and deferred twelve years—would produce 10 per-cent. I should scarcely feel inclined to run so great a risk—it appears to me that, under favourable circumstances and with moderate economy <save the difference> one might in that space of time save the difference out of the interest. However a year will give time for reflection.

We have never hitherto consulted any one but you on our affairs—nor have we told any one else of the degree of success our small capital has met with, because, after all, there is nothing so uncertain as rail-roads; the price of shares varies continually[4]—and any day a small share-holder may find his funds shrunk to their original dimensions—Emily has made herself mistress of the necessary degree of knowledge for conducting the matter, by dint of carefully reading every paragraph & every advertisement in the news-papers that related to rail-roads and as we have abstained from all gambling, all 'mere' speculative buying-in & selling-out—we have got on very decently.

You do not, my dear Miss Wooler, say anything at all about your health in your last letter—When you write again tell me whether your prolonged residence at the sea-side[5] has alleviated the sufferings you endured from indigestion—I fear you must have felt severely the cold east winds that have been blowing lately—I think they must be very injurious to vegetation for as yet scarcely any signs of spring appear about Haworth—the grass is still bleached and withered and there is not a single tree in leaf—

I have heard no tidings of Mary Taylor since I last wrote to you—she must by this time be far beyond Madeira—therefore a <calc> letter is not to be calculated on for a year to come[6]—Ellen Nussey is staying with her brother Henry in Derbyshire[7]—his marriage is postponed till the 24th May[8] in consequence of a death in the lady's family. those sort of things never seem to me secure till the knot is actually tied.

The east wind has given me a head-ache which is the reason of my writing a singularly stupid letter. I have the greatest difficulty in drawing out one dull sentence after another and tacking each to its predecessor.

Goodbye my dear Miss Wooler till summer when I hope to see you face to face—

C Brontë

MS Fitzwilliam. W & S 196.
Address: not in MS.

PM: not in MS.

1. Not identified.
2. In the York and North Midland line; cf. MW 30.1.1846. George Hudson (1800–71) the York linen-draper who had become the 'Railway King', was the chief promoter of this line, which from its projection in 1835 he had seen as a future link in a fast route to London. The first section, from York to a connection with the Leeds and Selby railroad near Milford, was formally opened on 29 May 1839. (*Regional History*, iv. 31.) By late 1843 this had already paid dividends of 10%. The 'Railway Mania' was reaching its peak in early 1845 and by July 'it was not an uncommon thing for one hundred thousand railway shares to be sold in one day in the Leeds share market'. In the West Riding the crash came in Aug., as a result of railway company amalgamation and massive unsound speculation: 'thousands were ruined and scores of thousands suffered heavy loss'. (*Mayhall* i. 519.)
3. CB was 29 on 21.4.1845.
4. The York and North Midland shares remained generally high at this period, but there was a threat from the temporarily buoyant 'Great North of England Railway' stock, and some insecurity arising from the immense number of projected railway companies applying for incorporation, many of them unsuccessfully. See *The Times* for Mar. and Apr. 1845. However, the proposed York and North Midland-Bridlington branch line had been recommended by the Board of Trade on 27 Mar. for acceptance by Parliament. (See *The Times* 29 Mar. 1845, 5.)
5. Margaret Wooler 'lived for a time at Hornsea [on the East Yorks. coast] and then had a house in the North Bay at Scarborough'. (The Revd Max Blakeley, 'Memories of Margaret Wooler and her Sisters', *BST* 12. 62. 114.)
6. CB was unduly pessimistic. A letter was received from Mary in late May. See previous letter n. 4.
7. At Hathersage.
8. The marriage took place on Thursday 22 May 1845. See EN 24.3.1845 n. 13.

To Ellen Nussey, 24 April 1845

[Haworth]

Dear Ellen

You are a very good girl indeed to send me such a long and interesting letter In all that account of the young lady and gentlemen[1] in the rail-way carriage,[2] I recognise your faculty for observation which is a rarer gift than you imagine—you ought to be thankful for it—I never yet met with an individual devoid of observation whose conversation was interesting—nor with one possessed of that power in whose society I could not manage to pass a pleasant hour.

I was amused with your allusions to individuals at *Hunsworth—I have little doubt of the truth of the report you mention about Mr Joe paying assiduous attention to *Isabella *Nussey[3]—whether it will ever come to a match is another thing—Money would decide that point as it does most others of a similar nature—You are perfectly right in saying that Mr *Joe is more influenced by Opinion than he, himself suspects—I saw his lordship in a new light last time I was at *Hunsworth—sometimes I could scarcely believe my ears when I heard the stress he laid on wealth—Appearance Family—and all those advantages which are the acknowledged idols of the world—His conversation on Marriage (and he talked much about it) differed in no degree from that of any hackneyed Fortune-Hunter—except that with his own peculiar and native audacity he avowed views & principles which more timid individuals conceal. Of course I raised no argument against anything he said I listened and laughed inwardly to think how indignant I should have been 8 years since if any one had accused *Joe *Taylor of being a worshipper of Mam[m]on and of Interest. Indeed I still believe that the Joe *Taylor of 10 years ago—is not the Joe *Taylor of to-day—The world with its hardness and selfishness has utterly changed him—He thinks himself grown wiser than the wisest—in a worldly sense he is wise his feelings have gone through a process of petrifaction which will prevent them from ever warring against his interest—but Ichabod![4] all glory of principle and much elevation of character is gone!

I learnt another thing—fear the smooth side of *Joe *Taylor's tongue more than the rough side—he has the art of paying peppery little compliments—which he seems to bring out with a sort of difficulty as if he were not used to that kind of thing—and did it rather against his will than otherwise—these compliments you feel disposed to value on account of their seeming rarity—fudge—! They are 'at' any one's disposal—and are confessedly hollow blarney.

Now Ellen what I have said about *Joe T—and his marriage-views, is to <u>you</u> only be sure and not repeat it to <u>any third person</u>—especially your brothers—I know you will observe this caution and not forget it.

I have just received a note from Ellen *Taylor[5]—requesting me to write to you (as they do not know your address—) and beg you to send the French-papers when you have done with them to

Mr T *Dixon[6]
care of Mr?* Jee.[7] Civil Engineer.
Sheffield

Be sure & write to me again soon—No further news yet from Mary—I suppose we need not now expect to hear from her for a year to come[8]—

C Brontë

April 24th—45
Many happy returns of your birthday.[9] In my answer to Ellen Taylor I gave her your address in case she should want to make any other communication
Give my love to *Mercy[10]—and my kind regards to Mr *Henry—it is a pity the wedding is postponed.[11] Write again soon.

MS HM 24438. W & S 197.
Address: not in MS.
PM: not in MS.
Annotation by EN in ink: Ap 24—45

1. MS may read 'gentleman'.
2. EN would travel by train from Leeds via Rotherham to Sheffield and then complete her journey to Hathersage by road.
3. Isabel or Isabella Nussey (b. *c.*1821) second daughter of EN's cousin John Nussey of White Lee, Batley. Isabella's father was a prosperous woollen manufacturer. He had built a mill 'twice the size' of the Nussey family mill at Birstall Smithies, leased facilities in a mill at Mirfield, and was Treasurer to the Trustees of the Leeds White Cloth Hall. (Information by courtesy of the late Mr J. T. M. Nussey.) He could afford a tutor for his daughters, the Revd George Richardson (d. 1879) who later married Isabella. By contrast the financial state of EN's branch of the family was precarious.
4. 'The glory has departed'. See 1 Samuel 4: 19–22.
5. See EN 24.3.1845 n. 10.
6. Thomas Dixon (1821–65), fifth son of Abraham Dixon and cousin of the Taylors of Gomersal and of Ellen Taylor. See EN 6.3.1843. n. 7. A letter from him to his sister Mary of ?early 1842 bears out Mary Taylor's description of the Dixons as an affectionate family, refers to his lessons in German, and mentions a 'rotatatry' engine similar to one in the 'Mechanic's Magazines'. He was in training as an engineer. (Dixon Collection, Leeds City Museum.)
7. The name has been deleted and rewritten in brown ink as 'Joe', but the reference is probably to a relative of the Dixons' friends, the Jees of Smethwick, near Birmingham.
8. See MW 23.4.1845 n. 6.
9. 20 Apr.
10. Deleted and over-written 'Mary', but it was Mercy, EN's sister, who was with her at Hathersage.
11. See MW 23.4.1845 n. 8.

To Mrs Rand,[1] *26 May [1845]*

[Haworth]

Dear Mrs Rand

I was much pleased to get your little note; only the day before I received it papa and I were saying we wondered you did not write and I almost began to fear either you or Mr Rand[2] were ill.

It must indeed have been a great charge to you to have had 70 scholars put under your care while you were as yet hardly recovered from the effects of your confinement—I do not doubt however that when you become quite strong, you will discharge the duty without much 'difficulty' Mrs Bacon[3] too must have her hands full, having both baby and the house and cooking to attend to, while you are engaged in the school. I am glad to hear your little boy[4] is still healthy and thriving I should like much to see him.

Papa has got a new Curate lately a Mr Nicholls[5] from Ireland—he did duty for the first time on <Thurs> Sunday[6]—he appears a respectable young man, reads well, and I hope will give satisfaction I hear no complaints yet about the new school-master Mr Purnell;[7] but it does not appear that the number of children increases much—however I think it is very well that it does not diminish—considering the unceasing opposition of the Methodists[8] and Dissenters.[9]

I do hope you and Mr Rand will not have so much opposition[10] to contend with at Staley Bridge[11]—and indeed, even if you should, as it appears that the church-people are both more numerous and more active than they are here, you will no doubt be better supported.

With best regards to Mrs Bacon, Mr Rand and a kiss for your dear little baby

Believe me my dear Mrs Rand
Yours sincerely
C Brontë

May 26th.
Whenever you feel disposed to write, we shall always be happy to hear from you

MS Pierpont Morgan MA 2696. W & S 198.
Address: not in MS.
PM: not in MS.
Date: CB dates 'May 26th'. The year 1845 is indicated by the reference to Mr Nicholls's arrival in Haworth. See n. 5 below.

1. Sarah Ann Mary Elizabeth Rand, wife of the former schoolmaster at the Haworth National School, who had recently moved to the National School near Staley Bridge in Ches.
2. Ebenezer Rand. See CB's letter to Mrs Taylor, ?17.7.1844 n. 2. His appointment at Haworth had been the result of PB's initiative in 1843 in 'getting a daily teacher for the National Church Sunday School' (established largely through the efforts of PB in 1832), the salary to be paid by the 'London Institutes' along with that of a curate for Oxenhope. (Excerpts from a letter quoted in *LD* 327.) From the time of his appointment in Feb. 1844 the children at the National School had made 'considerable progress in learning' owing to 'the excellency of the system, and the diligence of the master and mistress' (probably Mrs Rand). (*Leeds Intelligencer*, 27 July 1844, 7.) PB's friendly letter of 5 June to Mr Rand shows that he was highly regarded and hard-working: 'You can, I know, do a good deal, and you would be disposed to do more than might be suited to your constitution'. (W & S 200.) His move to Staley Bridge from Haworth was followed by one to Ipswich some time before 29 Oct. 1859, when PB wrote to him, 'much pleas'd to learn that through Divine mercy, you are again able to see'. (W & S 1005.)
3. ?Mrs Rand's mother.
4. Ebenezer Bacon Rand (1845–1929). He was born in Haworth, where he was christened on 16 Apr. 1845. After attending a school in Ipswich he entered Gonville and Caius College Cambridge as a pensioner in 1864, gained his BA in 1868 and MA in 1871, and was ordained priest in the following year. His last ministry was at Southleigh, Oxon. from 1915 to 1929.
5. Arthur Bell Nicholls (1819–1906), who was to marry CB on 29 June 1854. He was licensed to the curacy of Haworth on 9 June 1845, but was officiating there before that date, his first entry in the Marriage Register being on 28 May 1845, and in the Burials Register on 29 May. He replaced the Revd Joseph Brett Grant, who officiated at a marriage in Haworth on 12 May before taking up his duties as minister-in-charge in the newly formed separate church district of Oxenhope. See EN *c*.26.10.1844 n. 5.
6. 25 May.
7. Joseph Purnell. Slater's Yorkshire *Directory* for 1848 shows that he was still the master at the National School in that year; the name of the mistress is given as Mary Wright.
8. Wesleyan Methodists were already holding cottage meetings in Haworth by 1742, when the Revd William Grimshaw (1708–63) became the Anglican incumbent there. He had been 'an entire stranger to the people called *Methodists*' but from that time 'he thought it his duty to countenance, and to labour with' them. (John Wesley's account of Grimshaw, quoted in Thomas Coke, LL D, and Henry Moore, *The Life of the Reverend John Wesley A. M.* (2nd edn.; 1792), 329.) He built a chapel for the Wesleyan Methodists in West Lane Haworth in 1758. In the 1840s the congregation was increasing, and a new chapel 'in the classical style' holding over

650 people would be opened in 1846. See D. Colin Dews, *A History of Methodism in Haworth from 1744* (Keighley, 1981), 15. The Methodists had bought extra land in 1838 and had built a large schoolroom, with a library, in which the Sunday School was held; it became a day school in 1847. See Eunice Skirrow, 'Upper Worth Valley Schools in the Nineteenth Century', *BST* 20. 3. 156–62.

9. The Baptists flourished in Haworth. The engraved stone on the front of West Lane Baptist Church reads 'Haworth Baptist Chapel Built MCCLII Enlarged MCCLXXV Rebuilt MCCCXLIV'. In addition a second Baptist chapel had been built for the Particular Baptists at Hall Green, opposite Haworth Old Hall, in 1824. In the 1830s the Baptist ministers had opposed PB on the levying of church rates and other matters, and by 1836 the Baptists had raised over £1,500 to establish a school for the religious instruction of their children. I am grateful to Dr Juliet R. V. Barker for her information on this matter.

10. National Schools had been established throughout England by the Church of England 'National Society for Promoting the Education of the Poor in the Principles of the Established Church', formed in 1811. Nonconformists generally supported the 'British and Foreign School Society', formed, as the 'Royal Lancasterian Society', in 1808, but their 'British Schools' were outnumbered by the National Schools. See S. J. Curtis, *History of Education in Great Britain* (1950), 208.

11. A cotton-manufacturing town in Ches., 9 miles from Manchester. Mr Rand was actually at 'St. Mark's School, Ducking Field' (Dukinfield), 2 miles from Staley Bridge, as a letter to him from PB on 26.2.1849 shows. (W & S 424.)

To Ellen Nussey, 1 June [1845]

[Haworth]

Dear Ellen

You probably know that another letter has been received from Mary *Taylor. It is however possible that your absence from home[1] will have prevented your seeing it so I will give you a sketch of its contents—It was written at about 4° N. of the Equator[2]—The first part of the letter contained an account of their landing at <?Stiago> Santiago[3]—Her health at that time was very good—and her spirits seemed excellent—they had had contrary winds at first setting out but their voyage was then prosperous—In the latter portion of the letter she complains of the excessive heat & says she lives chiefly on oranges but still she was well—& freer from head-ache & other ailments than any other person on board—The receipt of this letter will have relieved all her friends from a weight of anxiety.

I am uneasy about what you say respecting the French Newspapers—do you mean to intimate that you have received none since you went to *Hathersage—? I have despatched them regularly—Emily & I keep them usually 3 days sometimes only 2 & then send them forward to you—

I see by the cards you sent and also by the newspaper that *Henry is at last married[4] how did you like your office of bridesmaid? and how do you like your new sister and her family? You must write to me as soon as you can and give me an <u>observant</u> account of everything.

It seems strange that after all, *Henry should be married and well married—before *George—Who would have thought that such would have been the case ten years ago—? I saw in the papers some weeks since a notice of the death of a Mr *Ringrose Merchant of Hull[5]—is it the father of *Amelia *Ringrose?[6] If so in what way will the event affect *George's interests—[7] favourably? or otherwise?

I still believe that matters will terminate happily for him—I still fancy there is comfort in store for him somewhere—Should it turn out otherwise my ideas on the subject of Compensation and Providential care will be singularly baffled—Still I know that the course of events cannot be calculated by human sagacity nor the justice of destinies decided on by human opinion therefore it is absurd either to predict or prejudge, so I hold my tongue.

Write to me soon dear Ellen and don't forget to tell me about the Newspapers I sent one yesterday—And I shall send one with this letter to-morrow—How is your health & how is *Mercy—[8] remember me kindly to her—

C B—

June 1st. Sunday Even[in]g

MS BPM B.S. 54. W & S 199.
Address: not in MS.
PM: not in MS.
Annotation by EN in ink: 97 June 1st 45
Date: the reference to Henry Nussey's marriage confirms that the year is 1845.

1. EN had been at Hathersage, apart from the time needed for her 'bridesmaid's office' at Henry's wedding, since late Apr. See EN 24.4.1845.
2. i.e. approximately west of the Guinea coast of Africa. For Mary's voyage see EN 2.4.1845 notes 3 and 4.
3. One of the Cape Verde Islands, with a harbour at Praia on the south coast.
4. Henry Nussey, son of 'John Nussey, Gentleman' married Emily Prescott, daughter of 'Richard Prescott Gentleman' of Plumpton Terrace, Everton, on 22 May 1845 'at St George's Church Everton in the parish of Walton on the Hill in the County of Lancaster'. William Budd Prescott, Ellen Nussey, and Richard Nussey were among the 6 witnesses. (Copy of the Register entry reproduced in M. F. H. Hulbert, *The Vicarage Family Hathersage 1627–1987* (Hathersage Parochial Church Council, 1988), 9.) See EN 14.11.1844 n. 3.
5. This Mr Ringrose was not Amelia's father. *The Gentleman's Magazine* for June 1845, p. 677, records the death on 30 Apr. at Cottingham Grange of William Ringrose, Esq., aged 64, 'for many years one of the leading merchants of Hull'. He was Amelia's eldest Ringrose uncle, the son of John and Rebecca Ringrose, and had been christened at Cottingham Independent Chapel on 4 Feb. 1780. Pigot's Yorkshire *Directory* for 1841 lists William and Christopher Leake Ringrose (Amelia's father) as ship-owners, Hide, Bark, and Corn Merchants and Factors trading at 42 High Street, Hull. (138).
6. Amelia's parents were C. L. Ringrose (b. 1791) and Mary Ann, née Boyes, who were married at Holy Trinity Church, Hull, on 19 Mar. 1818. He and his son F. Philip Ringrose had added to the commodities listed above that of bone-importing, and they carried on a regular trade with Holland. The family had lived since 1841 at Tranby Lodge, Hessle, near Hull, but had previously lived in Rotterdam, where the two sons and two daughters living at home at the time of the 1851 Census had been born, and where Amelia's eldest brother Christopher Leake Ringrose married Euphemia Knowles on 12 Nov. 1845. Amelia, the eldest daughter, was born in 1818. The Dixons

and Taylors of Gomersal had family connexions with Cottingham, north of Hull, the Ringrose family's original home.

7. George Nussey was engaged to be married to Amelia Ringrose. Possibly his trading contacts in Hull, then the fourth most important port in England, had led to a personal acquaintance with the Ringroses.

8. The name has been deleted and incorrectly rewritten as 'Mary'.

To Ellen Nussey, 13 June 1845

[Haworth]

Dear Ellen

Your letter was, as usual, very interesting to me—You really must have a great deal to do[1]—but if the responsability does not harass your mind and the fatigue, your body—too much—it is on the whole rather a good thing for you—It is practice—in case you should soon marry yourself and have a house of your own to look after—and if you should not, it is still exercise of the faculties which is always beneficial. These brides—by the bye, are well off to have everything done to their hand so nicely—what I should like the least if I were in your place would be the choosing of servants and the ordering of furniture—the parish business I should object far less to.

I am very glad you like your new sister so well and I hope the longer you know her—the more meritorious she will appear—As to the Mrs ?Wm *Prescott[2] who—you say, is like me—I somehow feel no leaning to her at all—I never do to people who are said to be like me—because I have always a notion that they are only like me in the disagreeable outside—first-acquaintance part of my character—in those points which are obvious to the ordinary run of people and which I know are not pleasing   You say she is clever—"a clever person" how I dislike the term—it means a rather shrewd—very ugly—meddling, talking woman—

How long are you going to stay at *Hathersage   As to my going to see you there, it is quite out of the question—It is hardly worth while to take so long a journey for a week or a fortnight and longer I could not stay—I feel reluctant indeed to leave papa for a single day—his sight diminishes weekly[3] and can it be wondered at—that as he sees the most precious of his faculties leaving him, his spirits sometimes sink? It is so hard to feel that his few and scanty pleasures must all soon go—he now has the greatest difficulty in either reading or writing—and then he dreads the state of dependence to which blindness will inevitably reduce him—He fears that he will be nothing in his parish—I try to cheer him, sometimes I succeed temporarily—but no consolation can restore his sight or atone for the want of it. Still he is never peevish—never impatient only anxious and dejected.

I read Miss *Ringrose's[4] note attentively—there is great propriety and discretion in it—it seems to me somewhat calm—perhaps too calm for the circumstances—yet she may be an excellent and affectionate girl—notwithstanding that, to me, incomprehensible tranquillity—I should say she would precisely have suited *George as a wife—if she be lady-like, affectionate, and sensible—her decorum and touch of phlegm would have been decided recommendations not only to *George but to most men—as a wife—Those are the people that are made for marriage—such at least is my belief. I think if I were in your place—I would answer that 'one' letter—but by no means carry on a regular correspondence—it is evidently not a case in which a third person ought to interfere.

When you return to *Brookroyd I hope I shall be able to <?visit you> pay you a short visit—for I certainly long to see you—Write to me again as soon as you can—I was on the point of saying remember me to Mary *Gorham[5] as if she had been an acquaintance of mine—somehow from your description I always imagine her to resemble Mary *Taylor[6] and feel a respect for her accordingly.

You do not tell me how *Mercy is—is she still at *Hathersage? If she be give my love to her—

Good bye C Brontë

MS HM 24439. Envelope: BPM B. S. 104/6. W & S 201.
Address (envelope): Miss Ellen Nussey | Hathersage | Bakewell | Derbyshire
PM: (i) HAWORTH (ii) BRADFORD YORKS | JU ?13 | 1845 | C (iii) BAKEW[ELL] | JU 14 | 1845
Annotation in pencil on envelope by EN: June 45 | after H's marriage

1. Part of EN's task at Hathersage was to supervise the completion and furnishing of the new rooms Henry Nussey added to the vicarage. See EN 14.11.1844 n. 4 and EN to Mary Gorham 22.7.1845.
2. Perhaps the wife of William Budd Prescott, the Liverpool merchant from whose house Emily Prescott was married.
3. On 18.11.1845 CB wrote to M. Heger that her father's sight was 'presqu' éteinte, il ne sait plus ni lire ni écrire' ('almost gone; he can no longer read or write'). Mr Brontë's operation for cataract did not take place until Aug. 1846.
4. See previous letter, notes 6 and 7.
5. Mary Gorham (1826–1917) was the friend EN had made when she stayed with Henry Nussey in Sussex. See EN to Mary Gorham 21.5.1844 notes.
6. EN thought Mary Gorham would have made a congenial addition to the group of friends—CB, EN, and Mary Taylor. See EN to Mary Gorham 21.5.1844.

To Ellen Nussey, [?18 June 1845]

[Haworth]

Dear Nell

You thought I refused you coldly did you? It was a queer sort of coldness when I would have given my ears to be able to say yes, and felt obliged to say no.

Matters are now however a little changed, Branwell and Anne are both come home.[1] and Anne I am rejoiced to say has decided not to return to Mr *Robinson's[2]—her presence at home certainly makes me feel more at liberty—Then dear Ellen if all be well I will come and see you at *Hathersage—tell me only when I must come—mention the week and the day—have the kindness also to answer the following queries if you can—

How far is it from Leeds to Sheffield?[3]

What time 'in the morning' does the Sheffield train start from Leeds?

Can you give me a notion of the cost?—

I think with you that I had better go direct from Haworth and not spend a day at *Brookroyd—

Of course when I come you will let me enjoy your own company in peace and not drag me out a visiting.

I have no desire at all to see your medical clerical curate[4]—I think he must be like all the other curates[5] I have seen—and they seem to me a self-seeking, vain, empty race. At this blessed moment we have no less than three[6] of them in Haworth-Parish—and God knows there is not one to mend another.[7]

The other day they all three—accompanied by Mr* Smith[8] (of whom by the bye I have grievous things to tell you) dropped or rather rushed in unexpectedly to tea It was Monday and I was hot & tired—still if they had behaved quietly and decently—I would have served them out their tea in peace—but they began glorifying themselves and abusing Dissenters[9] in such a manner—that my temper lost its balance and I pronounced a few sentences sharply & rapidly which struck them all dumb. Papa was greatly horrified also—I don't regret it.

Give my respects (as *Joe *Taylor says) to Miss *Gorham[10]—By the bye I reserve the greatest part of my opinion of Master Joe's epistle till we meet

I can only say that <his> it is highly characteristic

C Brontë

Write soon Come to Sheffield to meet me if you can.

MS HM 24440. Envelope: BPM B.S. 104/7. W & S 202.
Address (envelope): Miss Ellen Nussey | Hathersage | Bakewell | Derbyshire
PM: (i) HAWORTH (ii) BRADFORD YORKS | JU 18 | 1845 | C (iii) BAKEWEL[L] | JU 19 | 1845
Annotation (i) on letter by EN: June—45 | Her opinion of curates; (ii), on envelope by EN: July 45 | before visiting Hathersage | 'Lullaby' 'Woman's Faith | God save the Queen | Peaceful slumbering on | oacean

Date: from postmarks.

1. For the Revd and Mrs Edmund Robinson, the employers of Branwell and Anne Brontë, see EN 2.4.1841 n. 1. Mr Robinson's Account Book for 1845 shows that he had paid 'Mr. Bronté's Sal[ar]y £20.0.0' on 21 Apr. and then, in advance on 11 June, 'Mr Brontè due July 21st £20.0.0'. (BPM Robinson Papers.) Branwell was due to have a holiday, as in 1844: see EN 23.6.1844. In EN *c*.27.6.45 CB explains that he was at home only a week, but would come back to Haworth when the Robinsons went to Scarborough. The Robinsons went to Scarborough on 4 July: see Helier Hibbs (ed.), *Victorian Ouseburn: George Whitehead's Journal* (York, 1990), 15g. The *Scarborough Herald* for 10, 17, 26, and 31 July records their presence at No. 7A, Cliff; Edmund had joined them by 16 July, when Mr Robinson records '12s. 6d. Given to Edmund'. Branwell's salary had been paid in full for the quarter, in contrast to the part payment to Anne, showing that he was expected to continue in the Robinsons' employment. See *Barker* for a full account of this period.
2. On 10 Feb. 1845 Mr Robinson had paid 'Miss Brontès Sal[ar]y' of £10, on 11 May 'Miss Brontè due 8th £10.0.0.', and on 11 June 'Miss Brontè £3.10.0.', evidently a final payment. (BPM Robinson Papers.)
3. The route via the North Midland line to Rotherham and then the Rotherham—Sheffield line would be about 42 miles.
4. The Revd James Yates Rooker, admitted in October 1844 to St Catharine's College Cambridge, but did not graduate. See EN's comments in her letter to Mary Gorham of 22.7.1845. Mr Rooker lived at Thorp Cottage, Outseats, near Hathersage, and was the curate at the neighbouring hamlet of Bamford, where a school, built in 1841, was also used as a church. When Henry Nussey wrote home on 12.6.1846 Mr Rooker had recently become a priest. Perhaps he had received medical training. The *British Medical Directory* for 1853, p. 427, includes J.Y. Rooker's father, Abel Rooker, in practice 'prior to 1815', of Darleston near Walsall, Staffs.
5. EN comments: 'The conduct of the three Curates was very aggravating at the time—and they were complained of to Bishop Longley. The air of Haworth and district was stimulating, and there was no Society to expend their spirits upon, so they threw themselves on each other with great gusto.' She adds, incorrectly, 'Theological training Colleges did not exist for them in those days'. (*Hatfield* 215.)
6. The Revd A. B. Nicholls was Mr Brontë's curate at Haworth, the Revd J. B. Grant was in charge of the neighbouring district of Oxenhope, and the Revd James Chesterton Bradley (1818–1913) was the perpetual curate at Oakworth, about 2 miles from Haworth, from 1844 to 1847. cf. the behaviour of the curates in *Shirley* ch. 7. For Mr Nicholls see CB to Mrs Rand 26.5.1845 n. 5, for Mr Grant EN *c*.26.10.1844 n. 5. Mr Bradley had graduated BA. from Queen's College Oxford in 1841, was ordained deacon and licensed to a curacy at Keighley in July 1842, ordained priest on 24. June 1843, and licensed to the Oakworth curacy on 9. Oct. 1844. He went on to become Curate of All Saints' Paddington from 1847 to 1855, Curate of Corfe Castle Dorset 1856–62, and Rector of Sutton-under-Brailes, Glo. from 1863 until his retirement in 1903. He is said to have worked assiduously at Oakworth 'to organise the parish and to build a church', but overwork led to illness, resignation, and a long rest. See *Wroot* 132–4. 'Little Mr. Sweeting', the flute-playing curate in *Shirley*, is said to be based on Mr Bradley.
7. A colloquialism: not one is better than the others.
8. The name has been scraped out, but is more likely to be 'Smith' than 'Smidt', the reading of W & S 202. For the Revd J. W. Smith and the culmination of his 'grievous' behaviour, see EN ?29.7.1844 n. 3 and Vol. ii, 26.2.1848. In *Shirley* CB refuses to be specific about the later history of Mr Smith's fictional persona, Malone, because the public would not digest the 'unvarnished truth' about him. (722–3.)
9. The curates were 'high Church', as were William Weightman and John Collins, who had 'banged the Dissenters most fearlessly and unflinchingly'. See EN ?7.4.1840 for CB's condemnation of such bigotry.
10. Mary Gorham was staying, or about to stay, with EN at Hathersage. See EN to Mary Gorham 21.5.1844 and 22.7.1845 and notes.

To Ellen Nussey, [?21 June 1845]

[Haworth]
Saturday morning

Dear Nell

When did you write your letter. I only got it to-day—therefore of course I cannot come till Tuesday—But on Tuesday if all be well I will endeavour to be with you

If anything should prevent me from coming on Tuesday I will come on Saturday[1]—D.V.

Mind—do not put yourself to any inconvenience to come to Sheffield to meet me—

I am sorry I shall not be in time to go with you to Chatsworth[2] & the Peak[3]—but observe Nell I will certainly make you go again

I feel shy at the thoughts of seeing Miss *Gorham[4]—though I am a middle-aged person and she is a young lady.

Good bye dear Nell
C Brontë

MS Princeton, Parrish Collection. W & S 203.
Address: not in MS; but CB was writing to EN at Hathersage.
PM: not in MS.
Text: there is a false start on the verso of the leaf—'Dear Nell'.
Date: CB's 'Saturday morning' could be 21 or 28 June; the former date best suits the eventual timing of CB's postponed 3-week stay at Hathersage, from about 3 to 26 July 1845. See EN *c*.27.6.1845 n. 1 and note on date.

1. i.e. CB planned to come on 24 or 28 June.
2. The grand baroque mansion of the Dukes of Devonshire, about 9 miles south of Hathersage. EN would have a special interest in taking visitors there, since the duke was the patron of Henry Nussey's living; but on 22.7.1845 EN wrote to Mary Gorham, 'We shall not see Chatsworth again whilst Charlotte is here.'
3. The Peak District of Derbyshire, with Kinder Scout (2,088 ft.) as its highest point, and the village of Castleton in the vale below to the east. CB would have read in Scott's *Peveril of the Peak* (1823) a description of the ruined 'Martindale Castle' with its massive towers and 'disjointed masses of building' up which 'slowly winded a narrow and steep path'. She was to see Castleton when she visited the caverns there with EN, and 'went a little way up' Cave Dale. (EN to Mary Gorham, 22.7.1845.)
4. Mary Gorham was 10 years younger than CB. She had left Hathersage by the time CB reached it.

To Ellen Nussey, [c.27 June 1845]

[Haworth]

Dear Ellen

It is very vexatious for you to have had to go to Sheffield[1] in vain—I am glad to hear that there is an Omnibus[2] on Thursday and I will try to come on that day—

The opening of the railroad[3] is now postponed till July the 7th.—I have told Emily and Anne that I should not like again to put you off—and for that and some other reasons they have decided to give up the idea of going to Scarbro' and instead, to make a little excursion next Monday & Tuesday to Ilkley[4] or elsewhere—so that the place only is changed the days remain the same If all be well they will be back on Wednesday—therefore if the day be fine on Thursday and all other things right I hope no other obstacle will arise to prevent my going to Hathersage—I do long to be with you and I feel nervously afraid of being prevented or put off in some way.

Branwell only stayed a week with us but he is to come home again when the family go to Scarbro'[5]

I will write to Brookroyd[6] directly—yesterday I had a little note from Henry inviting me to go to see you—This is one of your contrivances for which you deserve smothering—you have written to Henry to tell him to write to me—do you think I stood on ceremony about the matter?

Why won't you tell me whether *Mercy[7] is at Hathersage or not? I have asked you four times in four different letters—

The French papers have ceased to come here for which I am sorry

Good b'ye for the present C B.

MS BPM Bon 168. W & S 204 as [24 June, 1845].

Address: not in MS.

PM: not in MS.

Annotation includes, in EN's hand: [June 45]

Date: 24 June, the date given for *Shorter* 161 and W & S 204, is unlikely. Emily Brontë gives precise dates for her excursion with Anne: they left home 'on the 30th of June—monday sleeping at York—returning to Keighley Tuesday evening sleeping there and walking home on Wedensday morning' (i.e. 2 July). (EJB *Diary* [31].7.1845.) CB therefore planned to go to Hathersage on Thursday 3 July. Since she mentions an 'Omnibus on Thursday' she is unlikely to have been writing before Friday 27 June. Three letters must be missing, since in those extant CB asks only once (on 13 June) whether Mercy Nussey is at Hathersage, not 'four times in four different letters'.

1. CB must have warned EN too late that she could not after all travel to Hathersage (via Sheffield) on or before Tuesday 24 June. See previous letter.
2. A term first used in England for a horse-drawn public vehicle 'plying on a fixed route' in 1829. cf. French 'voiture omnibus = voiture pour tous' (1828). (*OED*).
3. The York and Scarborough Railway. The *Scarbro' Record and North Yorkshire Advertiser* for 21 June 1845 congratulates its readers 'on the completion of our Railway: for though not yet opened to the public, it is a road that *has been* traversed, and soon will come into general operation'. (3.) An advertisement on p. 2 in the number for 5 July announces that the railway

will be 'opened for passengers on and after July 8th, 1845'. The York and North Midland Railway had been open since 1839.

4. Emily and Anne could not have reached Ilkley (16 miles north-west of Leeds) by rail at this date; but in the event they went to York instead. See note on date above.
5. i.e. Branwell was due to return to Haworth on 2 or 5 July. See EN ?18.6.1845 n. 1. If he was to return to the Robinsons after his week at home in mid-June his early receipt, on 11 June, of salary not due until 21 July is puzzling.
6. Henry Nussey and his bride were at his mother's home in Birstall, Yorks. See CB to Mrs Nussey, 28.7.1845.
7. The probable reading of the original: the name has been deleted and over-written in another hand as 'Mary'.

Emily Brontë to Ellen Nussey, ?16 July [1845]

[Haworth]

Dear Miss Ellen,

If you have set your heart on Charlotte staying another week[1] she has our united consent: I for one will take everything easy on Sunday—I'm glad she is enjoying herself:[2] let her make the most of the next seven days ?& return[3] stout and hearty—

[Love to her and you from Anne & myself and tell her all are well at home[4]—Your affect—

E J Bronte][5]

MS BPM B.S. 108. Envelope: Mr G. A. Yablon. W & S 205 as 11 July. *BST* 12. 63. 193 (as 18th) + facs.
Address (envelope): Miss Ellen Nussey | Hathersage, | Bakewell, | Derbyshire
PM: (i) HAWORTH (ii) BRADFORD | JY 17 | 1845 | C (iii) BAKEWELL | JY 18 | 1845
Date: EJB's date is unclear—possibly '15' altered to '16' July. The postmarks show that the dates given in W & S 205 and *BST* 12. 63. 193 are incorrect.
Text: ?EN has written the last sentence and signature to supply the text lost when the lower part of the leaf was cut off.

1. CB would therefore stay for about 3 weeks (from ?3–26 July) instead of a fortnight. Her length of stay is confirmed by Anne Brontë's *Diary* for 31.7.1845: 'Charlotte has lately been to Hathersage in Derbyshire on a visit of three weeks to Ellen Nussey'; and her return on 26 July is confirmed by EN's letters to M. Gorham of 22 July: 'C.B. leaves me on Saturday' and 6 August: 'Charlotte Brontë stayed till the Saturday before the arrival [of Henry Nussey and his bride on Thursday 31 July].' W & S wrongly give the dates of CB's visit to Hathersage as 'from June 26th until July 19th, 1845'. (ii. 41.)
2. For CB's activities at Hathersage see EN to Mary Gorham 22.7.1845.
3. MS may read 'to return'.
4. Emily was evidently writing before Branwell received his dismissal from Mr Robinson. See EN 31.7.1845.
5. See text note above. MS may read 'Yours affect—'.

Ellen Nussey to Mary Gorham,[1] *22 July [1845]*

Vicarage Hathersage

My dear Mary,

I scarcely knew where to address you so I determined to give you time to get home[2] again, which I hope you all have done by this time. I have nothing very striking to tell 'you' except that Henry has been over from home & brought an architect to look at what the workpeople had done.[3] The Archdeacon[4] & rural dean[5] also came to view the church the day that Henry was here—& Mr. & Miss Rooker[6] were here—I accompanied the Archdeacon down to the village in order to make a call upon Mrs Shirley[7] in her carriage, & to ask her to take tea with 'us' which in truth I hoped she & hers would not do—for we had only the little room in use—Anne Allen the gardener's wife for servant & some very heavy bread of her making for tea. Fortunately after some hesitation they decided to proceed & we had only the rural dean in addition to our party & his servant Man in the kitchen. We have not taken tea at Thorp[8] since you left—at North Lees[9] we have paid 2 or 3 visits Miss Wright[10] has been very good in calling—Mrs Shuttleworth[11] did bring her cousins back with her & I have only seen her at Church—The little girl has spent an afternoon here with her nurse, she was very amusing & very good, I wished we had had her here when you were present. We have not daily visits from Mr R[ooker]. The workpeople don't require him now, so he has no pretence for coming so often We have made more discoveries in his character & our opinion is rather favourable—He is only too frank. The Archdeacon told him of his odious aspirations[12] but not in our presence—he asked us if we had noticed it whereupon I could not help laughing & I said we had noticed some<u>think</u> also—He then said he also had a provincialism he sounded the ou horribly broad—We had a long conversation on these & other points The church clock struck ten the moon shone brilliantly into the room & still his reverence stood with hat & whip in hand holding forth with great zeal Miss R[ooker] is we think rather shy about coming here Charlotte Brontè says I am to give her respects & say you are a subject of daily annoyance to her for I am so often talking of you She has great regrets she has not seen you. We have been to Castleton[13] & the Miss Halls[14] accompanied us through the caverns & were very lively & noisy—another party came in soon after—a gentleman & lady—they crossed the river Styx[15] together to our great amusement We could not discover whether 'they' were brother & sister or what, but the lady was very sweet looking, & the gentleman twice addressed a word or two to me once when we passed them in the caverns & to say good morning when they left—the <u>book</u> said they were from Newark—Charlotte was very much pleased with the caverns but the mirth of Miss Halls was rather displeasing to her—We had Mrs. Eyre's[16] pony & we went a little way up cave dale.[17] We shall not see Chatsworth again whilst Charlotte is here. Mrs. Cave the Vicar's lady from Hope[18] & a young lady have spent a 'day' with us they 'came' by the omnibus in the morning & we have called there—they say they shall call when Henry & his bride come so I hope all unpleasantness will be forgotten. The Plasterers have not yet finished their work—but the happy Pair are to come next Thursday week[19] whether we are ready or not for them—a new cook comes today—The little dog is become a most forward passionate little animal Flossy is looking very pretty we take her walks but do not allow her to visit us much in the room She has had another visit to 'the' ?Lion in company with the large dog from Thorp—she quite disgraced the immense animal with her courage.

I had another letter the other day from Miss Seymour[20] they have lost 10,000 from the villiany of one of Mr S.'s trustee's he & his family are off to America they are very thankful it is no worse. I think Mr. Ross[21] is quite a Jesuit from the many things I hear his duplicity is amazing Have you read the Monk of Cimiés[22] I should like 'you' to it is by Mrs Sherwood. My Mother & Sisters are quite charmed with Emily[23]—Now dear Mary I shall hope to have a very long letter soon—C.B. leaves me on Saturday[24]—Tell me how you left the Flints[25]—how your relations are in London & particularly how your own family are—When is Charlotte Gibbs[26] to marry? Ever believe me my dear Mary

Your very affet friend—
Ellen

My kindest love to your Mama Did she think you looking well?

MS BPM Gorham Collection. *Whitehead* 118–19 (part).
Address: not in MS.
PM: not in MS.

1. See EN to Mary Gorham 21.5.1844 n. 1. EN is writing during CB's visit to Hathersage.
2. Cakeham in Sussex, about 1 mile from Henry Nussey's former curacy in Earnley.
3. For Henry Nussey's alterations to the vicarage, see EN 14.11.1844 n. 4.
4. The Revd Walter Augustus Shirley, D D, (1797–1847), Archdeacon of Derby 1840–7, Bishop of Sodor and Man, 1847. A moderate evangelical.
5. Not identified.
6. See EN ?18.6.1845 n. 4.
7. Wife of the archdeacon.
8. Thorp Cottage, Outseats, where Mr Rooker lived.
9. The 16th-cent. North Lees Hall in Outseats near Hathersage, the home of the Eyre family. In 1845 the widow Mary Eyre was living there with her son George, a farmer, and her daughters Ann Mary and Harriet. CB would also see in Hathersage church the 15th-cent. memorial brasses of this family whose name she was to use in *JE*. North Lees Hall's first mistress, Agnes Ashurst, 'is reputed to have become demented and was confined to a room on the second floor where the walls were padded for her protection. Like the mad Mrs. Rochester of the novel, she too met her death in a fire.' (M. F. H. Hulbert, *Jane Eyre and Hathersage* (Hathersage, n.d.), 7. The battlemented hall is sketched on p. 9, and described by W. H. Hoult in 'Charlotte Brontë's Holiday in the Peak District', *BST* 14. 74. 24.)
10. Miss Hannah Wright of Brookfield Hall. She was also the owner of North Lees Hall.

11. A distant relation of Janet Shuttleworth, wife of Dr James Phillips Kay (1804–77) who had added his wife's name to his own in 1842 and who was an acquaintance and correspondent of CB from 1850 onwards. The Mrs Shuttleworth referred to here lived at Hathersage Hall, a 'handsome mansion' in the village, rebuilt in 1844, 'the property and seat of John Spencer Ashton Shuttleworth, Esq'. (Samuel Bagshaw, *Directory* for Derbyshire (1846), 504.)
12. Probably Mr Rooker's way of pronouncing or misapplying the letter 'h'.
13. This picturesque village about 5 miles west of Hathersage is most famous for the Peak Cavern at the base of the castle rock, with its great opening arch and limestone chambers extending deep into the mountain. Guides were available to the Peak, Speedwell, and 'Fluor, or Blue John' caverns.
14. Not identified. Slater's *Directory* for Derbyshire for 1850 includes Joseph Hall, an attorney, and Mr Richard Hall, both of Castleton.
15. Probably a reference to the dark Peakhole water of the Peak Cavern or 'Devil's hole', likened to the legendary river of hate in the Greek underworld.
16. The widow Mary Eyre. See n. 9 above.
17. Cave Dale or Covedale, at the foot of Castle Hill, entered through a narrow 'rocky portal, scarcely six feet wide'; 'the castle, seated on the extreme verge of a narrow ridge of rock, rises high above you, and here forms a landscape which, for picturesque wildness, has not its equal in any other part of this mountainous district.' (Samuel Bagshaw, *Directory* for Derbyshire, 457.)
18. A village between Hathersage and Castleton. Mrs Cave was the wife of the Revd Wilmot Cave Brown Cave, MA, Vicar of Hope and perpetual curate of Derwent. The 'unpleasantness' perhaps had something to do with Henry Nussey's curacy of Derwent, which he had held along with that of Hathersage, from Apr. 1844. See EN to Mary Gorham 21.5.1844 n. 4.
19. Thursday 31 July.
20. Not identified.
21. Possibly the Revd John Ross of Hathersage, a Catholic priest. (Samuel Bagshaw, *Directory* for Derbyshire, 510.)
22. A novel published in about 1837 by Mary Martha Butt, afterwards Sherwood (1775–51), writer of many ultra-Protestant tales and moral tracts.
23. Henry Nussey's wife.
24. 26 July.
25. Perhaps a family Mary Gorham had stayed with at Leek in Staffs. when she left Hathersage. See EN to MG 6.8.1845.
26. For the Gibbs family see EN to Mary Gorham 21.5.1844 n. 13.

To Mrs Nussey,[1] 28 July 1845

[Haworth]

(a) My dear Mrs Nussey

I lose no time after my return home[2] in writing to you and offering you my sincere thanks for the kindness with which you have repeatedly invited me to go and stay a few days at Brookroyd. It would have given me great pleasure to have gone, had it been only for a day, just to have seen you and Miss Mercy (Miss Nussey[3] I suppose is not at home) and to have been introduced to Mrs *Henry[4]—but I have stayed so long with Ellen at Hathersage that I could not possibly now go to Brookroyd I was expected at home and after all <u>home</u> should always have the first claim on our attention. When I reached home (at

10 o'clock on Saturday nig[ht]) I found papa, I am thankful to say pretty well—but he thought I had been a long time away.

I left Ellen well and she had gen[er]ally good health while I stayed with her but she is very anxious about matters of business and apprehensive lest things should not be comfortable against the arrival of Mr & Mrs *Henry[5]—she is so desirous that the day of their arrival at Hathersag[e] should be a happy one to both.

I hope my dear Mrs Nussey you are well and I should be very happy to receiv[e] a little note either from you or from Miss Mercy to assure me of this

Believe me
Yours affectionately & sincerely
C Brontë

July 28th

(b) Give my kind and respectful regards to Mr & Mrs H Nussey and my love to Miss Mercy.

MS (a) BPM B.S. 54.5. (b) Harvard. W & S 206 as 23 July, without postscript.
Address: not in source.
PM not in source.
Text: (a) MS B.S. 54.5, in the Bale Collection at BPM. (b) holograph MS of postscript in Houghton Library, Harvard, MS *69M–104. Both the letter and the fragment indicate that Mercy (but not Ann) Nussey was at Birstall with the newly married Henry Nusseys. The handwriting of the fragment matches that of the letter.

1. EN's mother, the widowed Mrs John Nussey, née Ellen Wade (?1771–1857).
2. CB was writing on Monday, 2 days after her return from Hathersage.
3. Ann Nussey, EN's eldest sister.
4. Henry Nussey and his bride would leave Brookroyd for Hathersage on Thursday 31 July.
5. See EN to Mary Gorham 6.8.1845 where the last-minute preparations for the arrival are described.

Emily J. Brontë, Diary Paper [31] July 1845

Haworth—Thursday—July 30th 1845.

My birthday—showery—breezy—coo[l]—I am twenty seven years old to day—this morning Anne and I opened the papers we wrote 4 years since on my twenty third birthday[1]—this paper we intend, if all be well, to open on my 30th three years hence in 1848—since the 1841 paper, the following events have taken place

Our school-scheme[2] has been abandoned and ?instead Charlotte and I went to Brussels on the 8th of Febrary 1842 Branwell left his place at Luddenden Foot[3] C and I returned from Brussels November 8th 1842 in consequence of

Aunt's death— Branwell went to Thorpgreen as a tutor where Anne still continued—January 1843 Charlotte returned to Brussels the same month and after staying a year came back again on new years day 1844 Anne left her situation at Thorp Green of her own accord—June 1845 Branwell <3 or 4 i.w.> '?left'—July 1845[4] Anne and I went our first long Journey by ourselves together—leaving Home on the 30TH of June—monday sleeping at York—returning to Keighley Tuesday evening sleeping there and walking home on Wedensday morning—though the weather was broken, we enjoyed ourselves very much except during a few hours at Bradford and during our excursion we were Ronald Macelgin,[5] Henry Angora, Juliet Augusteena, Rosobelle ?Esualdar, Ella and Julian Egramon[t] Catherine Navarre and Cordelia Fitzaphnold escaping from the palaces of Instruction to join the Royalists who are hard driven at present by the victorious Republicans—The Gondals still flo[u]rish bright as ever I am at present writing a work on the First Wars—Anne has been writing some articles on this and a book by Henry Sophona—We intend sticking firm by the rascals as long as they delight us which I am glad to say they do at present—I should have mentioned that last summer the school scheme was revived in full vigor—We had prospectuses printed.[6] despatched letters to all aquaintances imparting our plans and did our little all—but it was found no go—now I dont desire a school at all and none of us have any great longing for it. We have cash enough for our present wants with a prospect of accumolation[7]—we are all in decent health—only that papa has a complaint in his eyes and with the exception of B who I hope will be better and do better, hereafter. I am quite contented for myself—not as idle as formerly, altogether as hearty and having learnt to make the most of the present and hope for the future with less fidget[i]ness that I cannot do all I wish—seldom or ever[8] troubled with nothing to do ie <i.w.> and merely desiring that every body could be as comfortable as myself and as undesponding and then we should have a very tolerable world of it—

By mistake I find we have opened the paper on the 31st instead of the 30th Yesterday was much such a day as this but the morning was devine—

Tabby who was gone in our last paper is come back and has lived with us—two years and a half and is in good health—Martha who also departed is here too.[9] We have got Flossey,[10] got and lost Tiger[11]—lost the Hawk. Nero which with the geese was given away and is doubtless dead for when I came back from Brussels I enquired on all hands and could hear nothing of him[12]—Tiger died early last year—Keeper[13] and Flossey are well also the canary acquired 4 years since

We are now all at home and likely to be there some time—Branwell went to Liverpool on <Monday> 'Tuesday' to stay a week.[14] Tabby has just been teasing me to ?tu[r]n as formerly to—'pilloputate'.[15] Anne and I should have picked the black currants if it had been fine and sunshiny. I must hurry off now to my turning[16] and ironing I have plenty of work[17] on hands and writing and am altogether full of buis[ness] with best wishes for the whole House till 1848 July 30th and as much longer as may be I conclude

E J Brontë

MS William Self. W & S ii. 49–51.

Following the signature is a drawing of Emily seated, writing on her writing-desk which is on her knees. She faces the window, in front of which is a bed with a dog curled up on it. To the left is a chest of drawers, and on the floor to Emily's left is another dog, probably Keeper, lying with his head on his paws.

1. See EJB *Diary* 30.7.1841. Emily was actually writing on Thursday 31 July, the day after her birthday. See Anne Brontë's Diary Paper, which follows.
2. The idea of a school at Bridlington or Dewsbury Moor had been abandoned (EN 19.7.1841, 2.11.1841) but the stay in Brussels was originally designed to improve Emily and Charlotte's qualifications for teaching. In 1844 plans for a school in the parsonage had to be given up when no pupils could be obtained. (EN 14.11.1844.)
3. Branwell had been dismissed from his post at Luddenden Foot station. See EN 20.1.1842 n. 8.
4. Branwell had been dismissed from Thorp Green for 'proceedings . . . bad beyond expression'. See EN 31.7.1845 and notes 9–11.
5. The names of Emily and Anne's Gondal characters sound even more exotic than those of Charlotte and Branwell's Angrian saga, where names like Zorayda, Gabriella, and Isidore mingle with 'Rogue', 'Gravey', and 'Pigtail'. For Gondal, see EJB *Diary* 30.7.1841 n. 11, and many of the names used in Emily and Anne's poems.
6. See EN *c.* 22.8.1844 and the Brontës' Prospectus, p. 365.
7. The sisters had invested money left to them by Elizabeth Branwell in railway shares. See EN 10.11.1842 n. 2, MW 23.4.1845 notes 2 and 4.
8. For this locution cf. EN 15.5.1840 n. 6.
9. The servants Tabitha Aykroyd and Martha Brown.
10. A King Charles spaniel given to Anne Brontë by her pupils at Thorp Green. See *Sixty Treasures* 17.
11. The parsonage cat. See EJB 1.10.1843, EN 25.3.1844.
12. See EJB *Diary* 30.7.1841 notes 3 and 5.
13. See EJB 1.10.1843 n. 4.
14. Branwell 'thought of nothing but stunning or drowning his distress of mind' after his dismissal from Thorp Green, and was sent away for a week in the care of the Haworth sexton John Brown. See EN 31.7.1845 n. 13.
15. Emily and Anne had recorded in their Diary Paper of 24.11.1834 that 'Taby said just now come Anne pillopatate (ie pill [peel] a potato'. (BPM MS Bon 131; *Sixty Treasures*, 11.)
16. Collars, cuffs, etc. could be unpicked and reattached so as to conceal the worn side, garments could be turned inside out, and sheets turned 'sides to middle'.
17. Often used to mean 'needlework'.

Anne Brontë, Diary Paper 31 July 1845

Thursday July the 31st 1845

Yesterday was Emily's birthday and the time when we should have opened our 1845 [1841] paper but by mistake we opened it to day instead. How many things have happened since it was written—some pleasant some far otherwise—Yet I was then at Thorp Green[1] and now I am only j[us]t escaped from it. I was wishing to leave [?it] then and if I had known that I had four years longer to stay[2] how wretched I should have been—<?then ?too. I ?was writing the fourth volume of ?Sophala[3]> but during my stay I have had some very unpleasant and undreamt of experience of human <nature> nature[4]—Others have seen more changes Charlotte has left Mr White's and been twice to Brussels where she stayed each time nearly a year—Emily has been there too and stayed nearly a year—Branwell has left Luddendenfoot and been a Tutor at Thorp Green[5] and had much tribulation and ill health he was very ill on Tuesday but he went with John Brown to Liverpool where he now is I suppose and we hope he will be better and do better in future[6]—This is a dismal cloudy wet evening we have had so far a very cold wet summer—Charlotte has lately been to Hathersage in Derbyshire on a visit of three weeks to Ellen Nussy—she is now sitting sewing in the Dining-Room Emily is ironing upstairs I am sitting in the Dining Room in the Rocking chair before the fire with my feet on the fender Papa is in the parlour Tabby and Martha are I think in the Kitchen Keeper and Flossy are I do not know where[7] little Dick is hopping in his cage[8]—When the last paper was written we were thinking of setting up a school—the scheem <was dropped> 'has been' dropt and long after taken up again and dropt again because we could not get pupils—Charlotte is thinking about getting another situation—she wishes to go to Paris—[9] Will she go? she has let Flossy in by the bye and he is now lying on the sopha—Emily is engeaged in writing <the> the Emperor Julius's life[10] she has read some of it and I want very much to hear the rest—she is writing some poetry too I wonder what it is about[11]—I <am writin> 'have be-'gun the third volume of passages in the life of an Individual.[12] I wish I had <finnish> 'finish-' ed it—This afternoon I began to set about making my grey figured silk frock that was dyed at Keigthley—What sort of a hand shall I make of it? E. and I have a great deal of work[13] to do—when shall we sensibly diminish it? I want to get a hab<b> it of early rising shall I succeed? We have not yet finished our Gondal chronicles that we began three years and a half ago when will they be done?—The Gondals are at present in a sad state the Republicans are uppermost but the Royalists are not quite overcome—the young sovereigns with their brothers and sisters are still at the palace of Instruction—The Unique Society <we> 'above' half a year ago were wrecked on a dezart Island <?du> as they were returning from ?Gaaldin—they are still there but we have not played at them much yet—The Gondals in general are not yet in first rate playing condition[14]—will they improve? I wonder how we shall all be and where and how situated <when we open this pap> on the thirtyeth of July 1848 when if we are all alive[15] Emily will be just <thirty> '30' I shall be in my 29th year Charlotte in her 33 rd and Branwell in his 32nd and what changes shall we have seen and known and shall we be much chan[g]ed ourselves? I hope not—for the worse [a]t least—I for my part cannot well b[e] flatter or older in mind than I am n[o]w—Hoping for the best I conclude Anne Brontë

MS William Self. W & S ii. 52–3.

1. AB had been a governess in the family of the Revd Edmund Robinson of Thorp Green Hall near York from before 28 Aug. 1840, when she wrote the poem beginning 'O! I am very weary | Though tears no longer flow'. (Chitham *ABP* 75.) Chitham suggests that her employment there began about 8 May 1840. (*ABP* 10.) See AB *Diary* 30.7.1841 and notes.
2. Anne left Thorp Green in June 1845. See EN 18.6.1845 n. 1.
3. Perhaps this should read 'Solala'. cf. AB *Diary* 30.7.1841, 'I am now engaged in writing the fourth volume of Solala Vernon's Life'—i.e. part of the 'Gondal saga', for which see EJB *Diary* 30.7.1841 n. 11.
4. Anne had at some time pencilled into her Prayer Book the words 'Sick of mankind and their disgusting ways'. (Gérin *AB* 200.) Anne had been distressed by the uncongenial worldliness of the Robinsons' social milieu and still more by the behaviour of Branwell and (it seems) of Mrs Robinson. See *Barker*, and cf. Anne's presentation of the 'gentry' in *AG* and *Tenant*.
5. For these events see the *Chronology* and EJB *Diary* [31].7.1845 notes 2–4.
6. See EN 31.7.1845 notes 10 and 11.
7. See EJB *Diary* [31].7.1845 notes 9–13.
8. The canary 'acquired 4 years since' mentioned in EJB *Diary* [31].7.1845.
9. CB never, as far as is known, visited Paris. A note alleged to be by CB from Paris, dated 'Paris, le Juillet 3' and written on the flyleaf of a copy of *Les Psaumes de David mis en vers Français* (Neuchâtel, 1832) is almost certainly a forgery. See MGC *Census* p. 1, 197 and Jos Bemelmans, 'A Charlotte Brontë Manuscript', *Notes and Queries* 228 (August, 1983), 294–5. By 1842, the only likely year for such a visit, CB would not have committed the solecism in the date.
10. See EJB *Diary* [31].7.1845 and n. 5. The references in Emily's poems to Julius Brenzaida, once 'King of Almedore in Gaaldine' are listed by F. Ratchford in Hatfield *EBP* 18–19.
11. Some of Emily's finest poems were written in 1845, including 'Cold in the earth' (3 Mar.) and 'Silent is the House' (9 Oct.). See Hatfield *EBP* 220–42.
12. Possibly a version of *AG*, or part of the 'book by Henry Sophona' referred to in EJB *Diary* [31].7.1845. See the Clarendon *AG*, pp. [xi]–xii.
13. The usual term for 'needlework' at this period.
14. EJB took a more cheerful view of the Gondals: see her 1845 *Diary*.
15. Emily and Anne's other diary papers had been written on 24 Nov. 1834 and 26 June 1837, reproduced in *Sixty Treasures* 11 and Brian Wilks, *The Brontës* (1975) 55 respectively. *CB Circle* has good facsimiles of pages from Emily's 1841 and 1845 *Diaries* opp. 146 and 154. The brother and sisters were 'all alive' in July 1848, but all except Charlotte had, tragically, died by July 1849.

To Ellen Nussey, 31 July [1845]

[Haworth]

Dear Ellen

I was glad to get your little packet[1] it was quite a treasure of interest to me—I think the intelligence about *George is cheering[2] I have read the lines to Miss *Ringrose[3]—they are expressive of the affectionate feelings of his nature and are poetical in so much as they are true—faults in expression, rythm, metre were of course to be expected.

I cannot understand how your brother John[4] should withold assistance in the matter of ?Joseph[5]—I think he is ?deeply to blame—he ought from the first to have relieved your Mother entirely from the care of keeping him. It is true he has many calls upon ˋhim' but this call is certainly one of the most sacred he can have It is hard—it is wrong to leave such a burthen on his aged Mother's shoulders.

All you say about Mr *Rooker[6] amused me much—still I cannot put out of my mind one fear—viz. that you should think too much about him—faulty as he is and as you know him to be—he has still certain qualities which might create an interest in your mind before you <are> ˋwere' aware—he has the art of impressing ladies by something apparently involuntary in his look & manner—exciting in them the notion that he cares for them while his words and actions are all careless, inattentive and quite uncompromising for himself. It is only men who have seen much of life and of the world and are become in a measure indifferent to female attractions that possess this art—so be on your guard—these are not pleasant or flattering words—but they are the words of one who has known you long enough to be indifferent about being temporarily disagreeable provided she can be permanently useful—

I got home very well—There was a gentleman in the rail-road carriage whom I recognized by his features immediately as a foreigner and a Frenchman[7]—so sure was I of it that I ventured to say to him in French "Monsieur est français n'est-ce pas?" He gave a start of surprise and answered immediately in his own tongue. he appeared still more astonished & even puzzled when after a few minutes further conversation—I enquired if he had not passed the greater part of his life in Germany He said the surmise was correct—I had guessed it from his speaking French with the German accent.

It was ten o'clock at night when I got home—I found Branwell ill[8]—he is so very often owing to his own fault—I was not therefore shocked at first—but when Anne informed me[9] of the immediate cause of his present illness I was greatly shocked, he had last Thursday[10] received a note from Mr *Robinson sternly dismissing him <from> intimating that he had discovered his proceedings which he characterised as bad beyond expression[11] and charging him on pain of exposure to break off instantly and for ever all communication with every member of his family—We have had sad work with Branwell since—he thought of nothing but stunning[12] <his>, or drowning his distress of mind—no one in the house could have rest—and at last we have been obliged to send him from home[13] for a week with some one to look after him—he has written to me this morning and expresses some sense of contrition for his frantic folly—he promises amendment on his return—but so long as he remains at home I scarce dare hope for peace in the house—We must all I fear prepare for a season of distress and disquietude—When I left you I was strongly impressed with the feeling that I was going back to sorrow. I cannot now ask Miss *Wooler nor any one else.

Give my love to Miss *Rooker—ask her if she will forgive me for disfiguring her album[14] Write to me again as soon as you can after the Bride & Bride-groom are come home

Good-bye dear Nell
C Brontë

I would not send the lines to Miss Ringrose—they are too defective and ?unfinished as poetry to be seen.

MS BPM Gr. E 7. W & S 207 (part).
Address: not in MS.
PM: not in MS.
Annotation in ink by EN: 102 July 31–45
Text: Conjectural readings have been supplied for two heavily deleted passages, from 'I cannot understand . . . Mother's shoulders' and 'I would not send . . . be seen'.

1. EN had written from Hathersage.
2. It is not clear whether George Nussey was already being cared for by Dr Belcombe in York, but he may have been. In EN 24.3.1845 CB implies that the Nusseys had sought treatment for him away from his familiar surroundings. For Dr Belcombe see EN 18.8.1845 n. 5.
3. See EN 1.6.1845 notes 6 and 7.
4. As a general practitioner and 'Joint Apothecary in ordinary to her Majesty', with an address in Cleveland Row, St James's, London, John Nussey was presumably comfortably off. See EN 20.2.1834 n. 1. He was also the owner of several houses and other properties in Birstall.
5. Ellen's brother Joseph (1797–1846) was ill; in CB's view, as a consequence of his errors. (See EN soon after 3 June 1846.) In EN 7.10.1845 Charlotte ranges Joseph with other members of EN's family who would find it difficult to fend for themselves.
6. See EN ?18.6.1845 n. 4. CB's warnings seem to have been taken to heart: in an undated letter to Mary Gorham EN wrote 'I find Mr Rooker has vanity enough to imagine himself attractive so I shall carefully avoid anything like placing myself in his way'. (?Aug. 1845, BPM Gorham Collection)
7. EN passed on this news to Mary Gorham. See her letter of 6.8.1845.
8. CB's euphemism for Branwell's drinking and its consequences. In his letter to John Brown of 13.3.1840 (W & S 90) Branwell had boasted of drinking until 'the room spun round' though he had abstained for several months afterwards. On 22 May 1842 he had recalled his 'malignant yet cold debauchery' at Luddenden Foot in a letter to F. H. Grundy. (W & S 133.) CB had told M. Heger on 24 Oct. 1844 that her brother was 'toujours malade'.
9. Anne Brontë's Diary Paper for 1845, written on the same day as this letter, records that 'Branwell has left Luddenden foot and been a Tutor at Thorp Green and had much tribulation and ill health he was very ill on Tuesday'. (p. 410.)
10. Since CB was writing on Thursday 31 July, this should mean 24 July, with an interval of 4 days before Branwell was taken to Liverpool on Tuesday 29 July. But in his letter to F. H. Grundy of Oct. 1845 Branwell speaks of 'Eleven continuous nights of sleepless horror' before he was sent away. This would mean that he received his dismissal on Thursday 17 July, which was probably the day after his pupil Edmund Robinson joined his parents at Scarborough. (See EN 18.6.1845 n. 1.) CB's misleading reference, like the many slips of the pen in this MS, reflects her disturbed state of mind.
11. Branwell's explanation for the dismissal was that Mr Robinson had discovered an 'attachment' between Branwell and his wife, and had threatened to shoot him if he returned. (BB to FHG Oct. 1845.) Branwell convinced many of his friends and his family that Mrs Robinson had been strongly attracted to him—a belief that recently discovered evidence tends to support. CB and her father passed on their version of Branwell's account to Mrs Gaskell, who was compelled by a threat of legal action to retract statements made about the 'seduction' of Branwell in the 1st and 2nd edns. of the *Life*. William Shaen, acting as solicitor for Mr and Mrs Gaskell,

published in *The Times* of 30 May 1857 and the *Athenaeum* of 6 June 1857 a retractation of 'every statement . . . which imputes to a widowed lady, referred to, but not named [in the *Life*] any breach of her conjugal, of her maternal, or of her social duties'. See *Life* ch. 13. For the changes made in the 3rd edn. see the Penguin edn. of the *Life*, ed. by Alan Shelston (Harmondsworth, 1975), ch. 13 and appendix A. In a letter of 5 Mar. 1887 Mrs H. Rhodes, niece of the Brontës' former servants Nancy and Sarah Garrs, refers in a letter to J. Erskine Stuart to Branwell's being 'caught' in the boat-house with Mrs Robinson as the reason for his dismissal. [MS BPM B.S. xi, 48.] Various alternative speculations about his dismissal remain unproven—e.g. that Mrs Robinson bought her safety by traducing Branwell to her husband, that the young Edmund Robinson revealed that Branwell had made homosexual advances to him, that he had indulged in drunken excesses, or that he had forged Mr Robinson's signature in order to obtain money. See Rebecca Fraser's useful discussion in her *CB* ch. 12, and her article 'Mrs Robinson and Branwell Brontë: Some Mistaken Evidence', *BST* 19. 1 & 2. 29–31, where some of the assumptions made in Gérin *BB* ch. 16 are refuted. New evidence for Mrs Robinson's attraction to Branwell is given in *Barker*. See also EN 29.9.1840 n. 11. In the *Independent Magazine* for 20 Nov. 1993, p. 7, Diana Warren of Huddersfield claimed that her 'great-great grandmother, Sarah Wheelwright, née Verens, had an illegitimate child . . . Thomas Verens . . . by Branwell Brontë, whom she met and was seduced by in Bradford.' Thomas was born in 1845.

12. Mrs Gaskell alleged that Branwell took opium habitually for the last 3 years of his life: 'In procuring it he showed all the cunning of the opium-eater. He would steal out while the family were at church—to which he had professed himself too ill to go—and manage to cajole the village druggist out of a lump; or, it might be, the carrier had unsuspiciously brought him some in a packet from a distance.' (*Life* i. 332.) Mr Brontë did not request the removal or alteration of this account, which may therefore be factual.
13. E J Brontë recorded in her *Diary* for [31].7.1845 'Branwell went to Liverpool on <Monday> 'Tuesday' to stay a week' and Anne added in her *Diary* 'he was very ill on Tuesday but he went with John Brown to Liverpool where he now is I suppose and we hope he will be better and do better in future'. See also Branwell's letter to J. B. Leyland of 4.8.1845, and his poem 'Penmaenmawr', Winnifrith *BBP* 163–5, Neufeldt *BBP* 276–8.
14. An 'autograph album' in which friends wrote verses, drew sketches, or in some other way expressed their good will towards the album's owner. cf. EN to Mary Gorham 6.8.1845: 'Miss R[ooker] teased C.B. to write in her album so she wrote her a piece of German from Memory & a piece of French in mine.' For Ellen CB wrote verses from C-H Millevoye's 'Le Jeune Malade'—her title for his poem 'La Chute des feuilles', which she had previously copied in an exercise-book used in Brussels, and was to praise in the 1st edn. of *Shirley*. See *Shirley* 106, 755, and Appendix, p. 609.

Branwell Brontë to J. B. Leyland,[1] *4 August* 1845

Haworth,

Dear Sir,

John Brown[2] wishes to know whether, or not, you can make your intended visit to Haworth this week.

Of course he awaits, and will be ready for your own convenience, in naming your week or your day.

I need hardly add that I shall myself be most delighted to see you, as God knows I have a tolerably heavy load on my mind just now;[3] and would look to an hour spent with one like yourself as a means of at least, temporarily, lightening it.

I returned yesterday from a week's journey to Liverpool and North Wales,[4] but I found during my absence that wherever I went a certain woman robed in black, and calling herself "MISERY" walked by my side, and leant on my arm as affectionately as if she were my legal wife.[5]

Like some other husbands, I could have spared her presence.

yours most sincerely,
P. B. Brontë—

MS Brotherton. W & S 208.
Address: not in MS.
PM: not in MS.

1. Joseph Bentley Leyland (1811–51), a sculptor with a studio in Halifax, where BB had first met him, probably in 1839. He is remembered for his statue of Dr Beckwith in York Minster, and for a sculpted group of African bloodhounds. See *DNB*. His portrait medallion of BB can be seen at BPM. For his contacts with BB, see *Leyland*, by J. B. Leyland's brother Francis A. Leyland, and *Infernal World*, esp. 43–5. Gérin *BB* reproduces a photograph of the medallion as a frontispiece.
2. John Brown (1804–55) was the Haworth sexton and stonemason. BB was corresponding on his behalf with J. B. Leyland about the memorial tablet to the Revd William Weightman (now in Haworth church) which Leyland had been commissioned to design and execute.
3. See previous letter and n. 11.
4. See previous letter and notes 10 and 13.
5. 'Wife' is written in extra large letters. The letter as a whole, which is in BB's upright hand, is clearly legible but irregular in spacing, lineation and size of letters.

Ellen Nussey to Mary Gorham, 6 August [1845]

Vicarage Hathersage

My dear Mary

My time has been so fully occupied I really could not answer your welcome letter earlier Have you received the one which was on the way when yours arrived? I thought by your requesting to know further about the expenses to Buxton that one of my notes to you at Leek[1] miscarried—I told you of all I thought belonged to you—that was the 'sum' 16/ to Buxton & the 2/6 for the man—Besides that I paid for his dinner & his master has had the injustice to charge me 8/for my ride back again These t[w]o latter of course belong most strictly to me—& I only tell you because you wished to know all about the Journey. I have had a great deal to do to have all things comfortable for the happy Pair[2] who arrived here on Thursday last the bells rang for them nearly all the afternoon & all the people were out to watch them through the village—I was requested to meet them in Sheffield but the preparations here prevented me The carpenters were at work to the last Moment & the dining room was to carpet at 4 o'clock p.m. The door into the new room was only on the hinges just in time The Plasterers are yet working here & the only difference since you left is the presence of a little more furniture & 3 more people. We have sat for company two days on Monday we had several visitors & it was my duty to hand all the wine & cake—yesterday was wet & we had none. Today is fine & I am in the throes of anticipation. Charlotte Brontë stayed till the Saturday before the arrival[3]—Miss Rooker & I accompanied her to Sheffield The latter was very ill all the way home with sickness—You will be sorry to hear the large dog at Thorpe[4] & our dog at home have both died mad Miss Rooker's dog seized her arm but made no incision yet we have felt uneasy about her She has since been very poorly but is nearly recovered I am happy to say—She has had a violent cold & the death of the dog & its ?cause made her nervous—she has had a younger sister with her some time—Charlotte & I only took tea once with Miss R[ooker] when her brother was absent The daily visits too were given up during her stay—Henry employed an Architect to look after the workmen so Mr. R[ooker] had no pretext for visiting here so frequently Charlotte was amused with Mr R. She thought him in some respects like Joe Taylor & in others like Mr. Heald.[5]—Mr ?Dacy[6] of whom we heard so much called with his Vicar & Lady on Monday he did not prepossess me much in his favour he is little & consequential & I did not think him handsome. You will no doubt wish to know how I like my new relative on further acquaintance—I am glad to say the more I see & know of her the more I approve & like—She is very pious but very agreeably so & quite free from all affectation.—Charlotte Brontë did 'not' see so much of the neighbourhood as you by a very great deal She could not walk as you did—By the bye did your Mama think you looking well? I have had another letter from Miss Ringrose but in my answer I forgot to mention your brother for which I am very sorry as she says they have not heard of their dear boy—If your brother[7] speaks of his pupils will you 'tell' me what he says—Now dear Mary I shall be very anxious to hear from you I have been unreasonable enough to hope you would write again before I could write I will be a good correspondent on my return home which will be in the course of ?3 weeks or so I think—Is Charlotte Gibbs[8] married yet?—Give my affectionate regards to your Mama—Remember me to your Papa & James[9] What did Mrs Rogers say to the cake—& How are the Woodmans Remember me to the Dukes[10]—& Pray write me a very long letter with all news soon Tell me how Miss Flint[11] is for I fear I cannot write till I return home

Good bye dear Polly & believe me
Yours very affect. Ellen

I find Mary that Man & Wife are not actual company for me & I begin to sigh for you & Charlotte—time is less my own—& hearts are less responsive to me than yours were though of course it is all right that it should be so—I still think newly married folks are only fit company for themselves—however kind they may wish to be to others I took it into my head to leave them after dinner always to enjoy their love alone but they complain so I am obliged to sit by & look as grave as I can though I very often laugh & think to myself were it my position I would have rather less of the expression of love but they tell me I know nothing about it which is an argument I have no reply to. Henry desires his very kind regards to all. Miss R[ooker] teased C.B. to write in her album[12] so she wrote her a piece of German from Memory & a piece of French in mine When she returned home a French man[13] was in the railway carriage so 'she' refreshed herself with a long conversation in french which she says she enjoyed—I should have so much to talk of if you were here. I shall get you some Blue John[14] if I can—

Good bye
Nell

MS BPM Gorham Collection.
Address (envelope): Miss Gorham | Cakeham | Chichester | Sussex
PM: (i) *Hathersage* (ii) BAKEWEL[L] | AU 6 | 1845 (iii) CHICHESTER | AU 8 [?9] | 1845

1. A silk manufacturing and market-town in north Staffs. Mary Gorham would reach it via Buxton after her visit to Hathersage.
2. Henry and Emily Nussey reached Hathersage on 31 July.
3. 26 July.
4. Thorp Cottage, Outseats, where the curate Mr Rooker and his sister lived. The 'dog at home' was not Flossy junior. See EN to Mary Gorham 22.7.1845 and EN ?29.7.1844 n. 2.
5. The younger W. M. Heald, Vicar of Birstall.
6. Not identified.
7. John Gorham (1823–66) admitted pensioner at St John's Cambridge 1840; BA 1845, MA July 1848, ordained priest 21 Nov. 1848. He was curate to the Revd John Moss at Aldingbourne, near Chichester, Sussex, 1850–2, vice-principal of the Collegiate Institution, Cape Town, 1854–8, assistant master at St John's School, Hurstpierpoint and Fellow of St Nicholas College, Lancing, 1859–66. He paid some attention to EN during her visit to the Gorhams in June–Sept. 1848, went riding with her, and talked 'on looking to the future'. (21.8.1848, recorded in EN *Diary* 1849 BPM.) See also Vol. ii, EN 18.8.1848, W & S 387. In Aug. 1845 he seems to have been acting as tutor to one of the brothers of Amelia Ringrose. See Vol. ii, AR 26.2.1848.
8. See EN to Mary Gorham 21.5.1844 n. 14.
9. Mary Gorham's brother.
10. Acquaintances from the West Wittering area, near Henry Nussey's former curacy at Earnley in Sussex. Henry describes Mr Duke as a 'neighbouring kind & gentlemanly Farmer' and Mrs Woodman as a 'very kind, nice looking, and truly excellent [Christian], but imbued [with] Calvanistic sentiments' (HN *Diary* Jan. 1839, fol. 48^r and 23.2.1839, fol. 61^r.
11. One of the family with whom Mary had stayed at Leek.
12. See EN 31.7.1845 and n. 13.
13. cf. EN 31.7.1845 and CH 18.11.1845 n. 14.
14. Translucent violet fluorspar, mined in the Castleton area. It can be made into ornaments: CB describes 'vases of fine purple spar' in the dining-room at Thornfield in *JE* ch. 11.

To Ellen Nussey, 18 August [1845]

[Haworth]

Dear Ellen

You will think I have been long in writing to you and long in sending you the French Newspaper; I did not send you the paper because I did not get it myself. I have delayed writing because I have no good news to communicate.

My hopes ebb low indeed about Branwell—I sometimes fear he will never be fit for much—his bad habits[1] seem more deeply rooted than I thought—The late blow to his prospects and feelings has quite made him reckless.[2] It is only absolute want of means that acts as any check to him—One ought indeed to hope to the very last and I try to do so—but occasionally hope—in his case, seems a fallacy.

I am writing to you now—not because I have anything to tell you Nell—but because I want you to write to me—I am glad to see that you were pleased with your new Sister[3] and by this time you will be still better able to judge of her character—How does the house get on—? the wet weather we have had lately and still have, must be unfavourable for the plaster drying—

I was sorry to hear of poor Miss *Rooker's being ill[4] and also of the catastrophe of the two dogs—do you mean the large dog Norah—when you say Mr *Rooker's dog died mad?

As to Mr *Rooker himself you must be sure and give me all details about him—you will no doubt see more of him now as his Vicar is at home. Does he talk away in the old fashion? has any ar[row] of Cupid entered his heart yet?—I don't care if the pericardium be stuck as full as a quiver of them provided yours is free—

Have you yet received any answer from Dr *Belcombe[5] about poor *George or have you heard how he is getting on from any other source?

When I was at *Hathersage you were talking about writing a letter to Mary *Taylor,[6] I have lately written to her a brief, shabby epistle of which I am ashamed—but I found when I began to write I had really very little to say that I thought would interest her—I sent the letter to Hunsworth—and I suppose it will go some time.

You must write to me soon—a long letter Remember me respectfully to Mr & Mrs *Henry *Nussey & Give my love to Miss *Rooker when you see her

Yours C B

MS HM 24441. W & S 209.
Address (integral): Miss Ellen Nussey | Vicarage Hathersage | Bakewell | Derbyshire
PM: (i) HAWORTH (ii) BRADFORD YORKS | AU 18 | 1845 | C (iii) BAKEWELL | AU 19 | 1845 (iv) [illegible]
Annotation (i) by EN in ink: Aug 18 |—45; (ii) in pencil: Branwell never be fit for much

1. See EN 31.7.1845 n. 8.
2. Branwell wrote to J. B. Leyland on ?19.8.1845 'As to my own affairs I only wish I could see one gleam of light amid their gloom.' (MS Brotherton; W & S 210.) But his letter to Leyland of 10.9.1845 shows that he still wished to achieve something in his life: 'I have, since I saw you at Halifax, devoted my hours of time snatched from downright illness, to the composition of a three volume Novel . . . I felt that I must rouse myself to attempt some thing while <labouring under> roasting daily and nightly over a slow fire.' (MS Brotherton; W & S 213.)
3. Emily Nussey, whom EN at this stage approved and liked: see her letter to Mary Gorham of 6.8.1845.
4. See EN to Mary Gorham 6.8.1845.
5. Henry [Stephen] Belcombe, physician [1790–1856] of Minster-Yard, York; MD Edinburgh 1812; Senior Physician to the York County Hospital, to the Retreat, and to Clifton Asylum; former President of the Royal Medical Society of Edinburgh. The *Provincial Medical Directory* for 1847, which supplies these details, gives the name as 'Henry Septimus Belcombe', and adds that he contributed papers to various medical journals. I am grateful to Dr Juliet R. V. Barker for additional information from Barbara Hutton, *Clifton and its People in the Nineteenth Century* (Yorkshire Philosophical Society, 1969), 15–17: 'Clifton Asylum' was Clifton Green House, 'a private asylum for upper-class patients' founded in 1813 by H. S. Belcombe's father, Dr William Belcombe (1757–1828) and the surgeon Alexander Mather, who wrote of it in 1819 that 'all severity of discipline' was excluded from the plan of treatment. When Clifton Green House was sold in 1853 George Nussey was cared for at Lime Tree House, Acomb, York, by Dr Samuel Nelson and then by Dr W. J. Nelson until the end of his life. (Information by courtesy of Barbara Whitehead. See *Whitehead* 125, n. 16.)
6. Mary Taylor was aware of CB's depressed state earlier in 1845: see EN 20.2.1845 n. 3.

To Ellen Nussey, [?August 1845]

[Haworth]

Dear Ellen

I shall just scribble a line or two in answer to your last as you wished me to write soon.

Things here at home are much as usual—not very bright as it regards Branwell—though his health[1] and consequently his temper have been somewhat better this last day or two—because he is now forced to abstain.

Poor Miss *Ringrose's[2] note interested me greatly—your position with regard to her is a difficult one—and I feel it hazardous to advise you—I can only say that were you or I either of us in her place we should be most anxious to know the truth.[3] Still if you do tell her all Ellen—convey your intelligence in careful and guarded language—above all remove from her mind the idea that she is the cause of this disaster—otherwise the news would be too dreadful.

You are however far the best judge as to whether disclosures are advisable or not—and I would not, on this point bias your judgment one grain.

Dr *Belcombe's letter[4] did not please me much—it seems so cold, so formal—so little explanatory—yet we cannot judge[—]what to you is a matter where your very best affections are concerned—to him is only business; and if he discharges that business with integrity I suppose it is all we can expect from him

You must be sure and not leave *Hathersage till *Joe *Taylor has paid his visit—and tell me how he looks and what he says—if he comes out in the colours in which we have seen him[5] he will be a strong dose to Mrs *Henry—

I am not, just at present, disposed to augur so well of her as I was—It seems most astonishing to me that she should not be most desirous to ?retain[6] you

Write again very soon C B—

MS BPM Gr. E 8. W & S 211.
Address: not in MS.
PM: not in MS.
Annotation by EN: 103 Aug—45 | 48
Date: EN's date suits the content of the letter.

1. See EN 31.7.1845 and Branwell's letter to FHG of Oct. 1845.
2. CB had advised Ellen (on 13 June 1845) to answer a letter from Amelia Ringrose, but not to write regularly; in fact Ellen, and eventually CB, were to become her frequent correspondents.
3. Amelia had apparently been engaged to George Nussey, but did not yet know the truth about his mental illness.
4. A report on George Nussey's health. See previous letter, n. 5. Dr Belcombe's attendance at the humanely run Society of Friends' Retreat and at the York Asylum indicates at least that he was an experienced and trusted doctor.
5. For CB's opinion of Joe Taylor at this period see EN 24.4.1845.
6. W & S 211 reads 'receive'; the word is obscure, but in the context is likely to be 'retain'. See the next letter.

To Ellen Nussey, 8 September [1845]

[Haworth]

Dear Ellen

You will wonder why I have not sent the French Newspaper—I have had it sometime but did not finish reading it till yesterday—be so kind as to send it forward to Sheffield[1] as soon as you conveniently can—I have kept it just a week which is 3 days too long.

I am glad you are got home and yet I scarcely know why I should be—I neither intend to <come> 'go' and see you soon nor to ask you to come and see us—Branwell makes no effort[2] to seek a situation—and while he is at home I will invite no one to come and share our discomfort.

I was much struck with the account you gave me of the warm-hearted—sisterly kindness the justice and gratitude with which you were treated at Hathersage.[3] I see how it is—I could not live with one so cold and narrow though she were correct as a mathematical straight line and upright as perpendicularity itself—still I think she is just the person for *Henry—she will obtain influence over him and keep it—I had very much regretted the having after all neglected to pay for the broken window-pane—but when I read that you had nearly had to pay for your washing—my regrets ceased—It is most surprising to me that she should not have wished you to remain with her and been even fearful of losing your company—How a woman can be affectionately devoted to her husband and not feel some regard for that husband's sister is inexplicable—Depend upon it Nell—if we knew how much selfishness goes to the composition of such affection as this, we should be amazed.

I do not wonder at your feeling anxious about George's affairs—have you seen Joe Taylor and has he given you his opinion on the subject?[4]

Have you written to poor Miss Ringrose yet?[5] I think you should not delay answering her letter—and still your position is indeed a most difficult and unpleasant one in the matter—it is hard for you to be silent—it is harder still to speak.

Give my love to your Mother & Sisters—Emily & Anne regret as I do that we cannot ask you to come to Haworth [?We] think during this fine weather how we should enjoy your company—write to me soon dear Nell—

C Brontë

MS BPM B.S. 55. W & S 212 (part).
Address: not in MS.
PM: not in MS.
Annotation: W. [for T. J. Wise]; '45' added to CB's date, 'Sept^{br} $8^{\underline{th}}$.'

1. EN was expected to send the newspapers to the Taylors' cousin Tom Dixon 'c/o Mr ?Jee Civil Engineer Sheffield'. See EN 24.4.1845 n. 7.
2. Branwell eventually applied for the Secretaryship to a railway company on ?23 Oct. 1845. See his letter of that date. (p. 431.) F. H. Grundy's misdating of Branwell's letters to him makes it impossible to place the 'prayer for employment' on the railway referred to in *Grundy* 89. There it is followed by an excerpt from what may be an unrelated letter of ?June 1846. W & S print both fragments as part of their letter 252, dated June 1846.
3. *Nussey* 134–5, *Shorter* 166, and W & S 212 omit the greater part of paras. 3 and 4, on the sensitive subjects of Mrs Henry Nussey's character and George Nussey's illness.
4. Joe Taylor, who like George Nussey was in the wool trade, might be expected to understand his financial or business affairs. The Nussey scribbling and fulling mill at Birstall Smithies had employed 44 workers in 1840, and their Brookroyd Mill 42 workers.
5. See previous letter and notes 2 and 3.

To Ellen Nussey, [?10 September 1845]

[Haworth]

(a) Dear Ellen

I think Miss R[ingrose] certainly means next Saturday—her note was written on Friday she could not expect you to receive and answer it the day after. It is a pity she does not yet understand George's case—The circumstance of her being in the dark will make it a most difficult matter for you to correspond with her. You will I fear find it a most puzzling business if she writes to you often.

I do not relish Dr Belcombes[1] style of writing—yet no doubt much may be said in extenuation of his brevity & abruptness: he may sometimes have found relations 'injudiciously' interfering—He still holds out hope—but the hope seems as distant as ever.

It appears to me a most strange and inexplicable thing that there should be any difficulty about George's affairs—I trust Joe Taylor will be able to give useful information on the subject—but how far will his word avail? Books & papers will, I suppose, decide the matter—Surely—surely—Richard[2] will do justice to his sick brother, his aged Mother—his utterly unprotected sisters—but I remember I have often heard you say that George committed too little of his affairs to paper and depended far too much on his memory—this will complicate the (b) business—yet I should think an [ex]amination of <?letters> matters would be desirable if it were only to let you know clearly how you are likely to stand and what your resources are—For yourself personally Ellen I should say—act independently and take a situation[3]—I should say this, were I not aware that if you attempted to do such a thing you might find impediments[4] from your connections which you could scarcely surmount—knowing this Ellen I give you no dogmatical advice—you must 'act' for the best according to circumstances and it is well for You that you have the inestimable gift of Common Sense to gui[de] you—Write to me again as soon as you have anything to tell me Ellen—I feel most anxious to learn how matters progress. Give my best love to your Mother & Sisters.

C Brontë

Wednesday—

(a) MS Beinecke, Yale. No publication traced.

(b) MS BPM B.S. 55.5. No publication traced. Envelope BPM B.S. 104/8.

Address (envelope): Miss Ellen Nussey | Brookroyd | Birstal | Leeds

PM: (i) [HAW]ORTH (ii) BRAD[FOR]D YORKS | SP 10 | 1845 | C (iii) LEEDS | SP 10 | 1845 F

Annotation includes (i) by EN in ink, on the letter part(a): Sep 9–45; (ii) by EN in pencil, on the envelope: Sep 10–45. The envelope bears a blue lozenge-shaped wafer with the words 'To You' within a black line edging.

Date: the content shows that the letter is close in time to, and probably shortly after EN 8.9.1845; 'Wednesday', the day given by CB, corresponds to 10 Sept., the date of a surviving envelope.

Text: the content, paper, handwriting, and dimensions show that these two separated fragments form one letter.

1. See EN 18.8.1845 n. 5.
2. The remaining active partner in the Nussey brothers' business.
3. CB is advising Ellen to become a governess.
4. cf. CB's comments on similar 'impediments' to Mary Taylor's becoming a governess in EN

?10.6.1841: 'I offered the Irish Concern to Mary Taylor but she is so circumstanced that she cannot accept it—her brothers—like George—have a feeling of pride that revolts at the thought of their Sister "going out" I hardly knew that it was such a degradation till lately—'. EN did not in fact 'go out'.

Branwell Brontë to J. B. Leyland,[1] *10 September [?1845]*

Haworth

My dear Sir,

I was certainly sadly disappointed at not having seen you on the Friday you named for your visit; but the cause you allege for not arriving was justifiable with a vengeance—I should have been as cracked as my cast[2] had I entered a room and seen the labours of weeks or months destroyed (apparently—not, I trust, really) in a moment.

That vexation is I hope over and I build upon your renewed promise of a visit, for nothing cheers me so much as the company of one whom I believe to be a MAN, and who has known care <so far as> 'well enough' to be able to <pity> appreciate the discomfort of another, who knows it too well.

Never mind the lines I put into your hands; but come hither with them, and if they shall have been lost out of your pocket on the way, I won't grumble, provided you are present to apologise for the accident.

I have, since I saw you at Halifax, devoted my hours of time snatched from downright illness, to the composition of a three volume Novel[3]—one volume of which <has> is completed—and along with the two forthcoming ones, has been really the <work>'result' of half a dozen by past years of thought about, and experience in, this crooked path of life.

I felt that I must rouse myself to attempt some thing while <labouring under> roasting daily and nightly over a slow fire[4]—to wile away my torment and I knew that in the present state of the publishing and reading world a Novel is the most saleable article so that where ten pounds would be offered for <the> a work the production of which would require the utmost stretch of a man's intellect—two hundred pounds would be a refused offer for three volumes whose composition would require the smoking of a cigar and the humming of a tune.

My Novel is the result of years of thought and if it gives a vivid picture of human feelings for good and evil—veiled by the cloak of deceit which must enwrap man and woman—If it records as faithfully as the pages that unveil mans heart in Hamlet or Lear—<I shall ?be> the conflicting feelings and clashing pursuits in our uncertain path through life I shall be as much gratified (and as much astonished) as I should be if in betting that I could jump over the

Mersey I jumped over the Irish sea. It would not be more pleasant to light on Dublin instead of Birkenhead than to leap from the present bathos of fictitious literature on to the firmly fixed rock honoured by the foot of a Smollet or Feilding.[5]

That jump I expect to take when I can model a rival to your noble Theseus who haunted my dreams when I slept after seeing him—but meanwhile I can try my utmost to rouse from almost killing cares, and that alone will be its own reward.

Tell me when I may hope to see you and believe me, dear Sir,

Yours,

P. B. Brontë.

MS Brotherton. W & S 213.
Address: not in MS.
PM: not in MS.
Annotation: The printed transcript which accompanies this letter in the Brotherton Collection volume is followed by a note: 'William Thompson ("Bendigo"), born at Nottingham in the year 1811, was a champion pugilist of England. He beat Benjamin Caunt in 1845. Benjamin Caunt was born at Hucknall Torkard about the year 1815. A noted pugilist, standing 6 feet 2½ inches in height, and fighting at 14st. 7lbs., he became champion of England by defeating "Bendigo" after 75 rounds in April, 1838.' A further printed note reads: 'Below this pen-and-ink sketch, on the half-page now torn away, was another pen-and-ink sketch by Branwell representing a "bust of himself thrown down, and the lady of his admiration holding forth her hands towards it with an air of pity, while underneath it was the sentence: 'A cast, cast down, but not cast away.' " (F. A. LEYLAND).'
Text: The second leaf of the letter is incomplete. It includes a silhouette-sketch in ink of 2 figures, one all black, with chained wrists, the other with hands raised and splayed out as if directing attention to the first figure. The caption reads; 'Bendigo, "taking a sight".' 'Alas! poor Caunt!'

1. See BB to JBL 4.8.1845 n. 1.
2. Leyland's 'Theseus', mentioned in the penultimate paragraph. cf. BB to JBL 25.11.1845, where Branwell compares himself to the Theseus, which had 'lost its hands and feet'.
3. Probably the incomplete MS, 'And the Weary are at Rest', now in the collection of Harry B. Smith, New York; privately printed for J. A. Symington in 1924. See Alexander *EW* 190 and n. 45. Gérin dates the MS 1845 rather than 1842 because of BB's 'very exact description of "the little Circular Museum" at Scarborough' which he could have seen when he joined the Robinsons there in July 1844 (see EN 23.6.1844) and because of 'the reference to the conservatory at Chatsworth built only after Branwell had gone to Thorp Green in 1843'. (Gérin *BB* 253.) See Gérin's résumé of the story, where 'Mrs Thurston is represented as much attracted to Percy' as, according to Branwell, Mrs Robinson was attracted to him. (Gérin *BB*. 253–60.) The possibility that the 'three volume Novel' was *WH* is remote. Branwell's authorship was alleged by his friend the Halifax schoolmaster William Dearden in a letter of 15 June 1867 to the *Halifax Guardian*, where Branwell was said to have read to a group of friends, as his own work 'stray leaves' of a manuscript recognizable as *WH*. The unreliable F. H. Grundy added supporting 'evidence' in *Pictures of the Past*: 'Patrick Brontë declared to me, and what his sister [Emily] said bore out the assertion, that he wrote a great portion of *WH* himself.' (*Grundy* 80.) In her discussion in *Infernal World*, 135–9, Daphne du Maurier concludes that the 'full credit and the glory' of writing *WH* must go to Emily, 'though the germ of the idea could have sprung from her brother'; but she does not take into account CB's assertions that 'Ellis Bell produced *Wuthering Heights*' ('Biographical Notice of Ellis and Acton Bell' in *WH* 1850 ed.; Clarendon *WH* 437) and that Branwell 'was not aware that [his sisters] had ever published a line'. (Vol ii, WSW 2.10.1848; W & S 394.)
4. For Branwell's state of mind and the reasons for it see EN 31.7.1845, especially notes 10 and 11.
5. Unlike Branwell, CB disapproved of the novels of Henry Fielding (1707–54), Thackeray's 'false god' (Vol. iii, GS 11.3.1852). There are no references in her letters to the novels of Tobias George Smollett (1721–71).

To Ellen Nussey, [18 September 1845]

[Haworth]

Dear Ellen,

I have just read Mary's letters;[1] they are very interesting, and shew the vigorous and original cast of her mind,—there is but one thing I could wish otherwise in them, that is a certain tendency to flightiness[2]—it is not safe, it is not wise, and will often cause her to be misconstrued; perhaps flightiness is not the right word, but it is a devil-may-care tone;[3] which I do not like when it proceeds from under a hat, and still less from under a bonnet. I long to hear of Mary being arrived at her remote destination and occupied in serious business,[4] then she will be in her element; then her powerful faculties will be put to their right use. Write to me again soon, all continues the same here. Good bye.

C. B.[5]

MS untraced. Envelope: BPM B.S. 104/9. W & S 214.
Address (envelope): Miss Ellen Nussey | Brookroyd | Birstal | Leeds
PM: (i) HAWORTH (ii) BRADFORD YORKS | SP 18 | 184— | C (iii) [mutilated] 1— | 1845 | F
Annotation by EN in pencil on envelope: Sep 45 | of M Tayl[or] [+3 i.w.]. Oblong yellow wafer with the words 'Forget me not' within a line border.
Text: *Nussey* 134, probably closer to MS in punctuation than *Shorter* 167 and W & S 214, which may derive from *Nussey*. Not in *Life*. EN probably edited the letter: one would expect a reference to George Nussey's illness. The abridged *Hours at Home* text may retain some authentic readings. See notes 1 and 5.

1. Mary Taylor's letters for 1845–7 have not been located. She had left Gravesend on 12 Mar. 1845 and arrived in Wellington, New Zealand on 24 July. See EN 20.2.1845 n. 5. *Stevens* cites the *New Zealand Spectator* for 26 July 1845 for the arrival date. (57.) *Hours at Home* reads 'just received——'s letters'. (xi. 295.)
2. W & S 214 reads '*flightiness*'.
3. One of Mary Taylor's letters to CB from a later period, June–24 July 1848, may show what CB had in mind: 'If I could command £300 & £50 a year afterwards I would "hallock" about N.Z. for a twelvemonth then go home by way of India & write my travels which would prepare the way for my novel.' (MS Pierpont Morgan; *Stevens* 76.) 'Hallack' or 'hallock' is Northern dialect for 'to idle away time'.
4. Mary joined her brother William Waring Taylor (?1819–1903), who 'had arrived in Wellington in Apr. 1842, and by 1843 was conducting a general business and importing agency, living in and trading from his wooden cottage on Herbert Street, Te Aro, not far from the water-front'. (*Stevens* 63.)
5. The *Hours at Home* text ends: 'Write to me again soon, and I promise to write you a regular long letter next time.' (xi. 295.)

To Ellen Nussey, 7 October [1845]

[Haworth]

Dear Ellen

Your position seems to be one full of difficulties and embarrassments but how often does it happen that in situations precisely similar to yours—when a hedge of danger & trial seems to enclose us on every side—an opening is suddenly made and a way of escape afforded where we thought it least practicable—

I see you have courage and calmness this is the state of mind which will enable you best to take advantage of the means of safety should they offer—I have complete faith in your moral fortitude and I trust and believe God will grant you physical health and strength to bear up against whatever trial[1] may await you—You & your Sister Anne[2] could work your way well—you have each in a different way resources within yourselves—but your poor Mother, Mercy[3]—George—Joseph[4]—what can they do—what can be done for them? If these Swaines[5] are really acting a false & dishonest part—I would not be in their place for the wealth of a Rothschild—no one ever yet unjustly oppressed the defenceless without his sin being visited fearfully upon him—

Depend upon it dear Ellen it is better that you should have no visitors at present—not even one so insignificant as me—I have told you, without apology that I cannot ask you to Haworth at present—I told Miss Wooler the same.

It gave me a feeling of painful surprise to learn that you had not yet seen Joe Taylor—surely with a man so strong-minded & firm-principled as we have always been accustomed to believe Joe Taylor to be—even the circumstance of his being about to become closely connected with the Nusseys of White-Lee[6] ought not fairly to extinguish his regard for old friends—When is he likely to be married to Isabella Nussey do you think? Possibly it may be the pressure of business which prevents his coming to Brookroyd—I had a note from Ellen Taylor[7] to-day in which it was mentioned that John Taylor[8] was gone from home—

Let me hear from you again dear Ellen with as little delay as possible—such a long interval elapsed between your last letter & the one before that I began to grow quite uneasy—

I have scribbled this note by candle-light—my eyes are tired—which must plead my excuse for the almost illegible writing

Give my best love to your Mother & Sisters—Emily was wondering the other day how poor little Flossy[9] gets on—

Good night dear Nell

C B

MS BPM Gr. E 9. W & S 215.
Address: not in MS.
PM: not in MS.
Annotation (i) by EN: Oct 7–45; (ii) in another hand: W. [for T. J. Wise] 47.
Date: CB's date 'Oct^{br} 7th' must be 1845, as EN's note and the content show.

1. CB evidently feared that EN and her immediate family would be in financial straits now that George Nussey could no longer engage in trade. The expense of his care at Clifton House in York would also be a consideration. The apparent threat posed by the Swaines remains unclear.
2. Ellen's sister Ann seems to have been a capable woman, though CB's comments on her are equivocal; e.g. 'Ann has been originally a clever woman but her judgment has been corrupted.' (EN 30.4.1840.) Like Mercy Nussey, Ann is said to have done some schoolteaching, and she was normally in charge of the housekeeping at Brookroyd. (See EN's accounts for Sept.–Oct. 1849 when she was housekeeping in Ann's place; EN *Diary* 1849.)
3. Four pages of poems written out by 'MN' in a literate and fluent hand, followed by 'The Wandering Minstrel Translated from the German' by MN are to be found in the Nussey collection (WYAS Sheepscar, Leeds) and are possibly the work of Mercy Nussey. In 1847 CB twice refers to Mercy being unable to get to her school—presumably as an occasional or visiting teacher. (EN 7.10.1847, 2.12.1847.) Her recurrent bouts of illness may account for CB's opinion in the present letter. In later life Mercy's health deteriorated and she had to be cared for away from home.
4. See EN 31.7.1845 n. 5.
5. Probably Joseph Swaine (1781–1870) of Brier Hall, Gomersal, and his half-brother Edward Swaine (1790–1885) of Crow Trees, Gomersal; they were flannel and cloth merchants and manufacturers. EN and her family were personal friends of the Brier Hall Swaines, as both her 1844 and 1849 diaries show. Perhaps the suspicions of dishonesty were groundless, or concerned with another branch of the family. See references in H. A. Cadman, *Gomersal Past and Present* (Leeds, 1930), e.g., 18, 75, and 161.
6. See EN 24.4.1845 n. 3. Joe Taylor did not marry Isabella.
7. See CB to M. Dixon 16.10.1843 n. 8.
8. Joe Taylor's brother and business partner at Hunsworth Mill. See EN 7.8.1841 n. 4.
9. Ellen's King Charles spaniel, at first referred to as 'he', but evidently a bitch. See EN ?29.7.1844 n. 2 and 4.11.1845.

Branwell Brontë to Francis H. Grundy,[1] *[October 1845]*

[Haworth]

I fear you will burn my present letter on recognising the handwriting; but if you will read it through, you will perhaps rather pity than spurn the distress of mind which could prompt my communication, after a silence of nearly three (to me) eventful years.[2] While very ill and confined to my room, I wrote to you two months ago, hearing that you were resident engineer of the Skipton Railway,[3] to the inn at Skipton.[4] I never received any reply, and as my letter asked only for one day of your society, to ease a very weary mind in the company of a friend who always had what I always wanted, but most want now, cheerfulness, I am sure you never received my letter, or your heart would have prompted an answer.

Since I last shook hands with you in Halifax,[5] two summers ago, my life till lately has been one of apparent happiness and indulgence. You will ask, 'Why does he complain, then?' I can only reply by showing the under-current of distress which bore my bark to a whirlpool, despite the surface waves of life that seemed floating me to peace. In a letter begun in the spring of [?1844 or 1845], and never finished owing to incessant attacks of illness, I tried to tell you that I was tutor to the son of [Revd. Edmund Robinson], a wealthy gentleman whose wife[6] is sister to the wife of [William Evans], M.P. for the county of [Derbyshire], and the cousin of Lord [?Goderich].[7] This lady (though her husband detested me) showed me a degree of kindness which, when I was deeply grieved one day at her husband's conduct, ripened into declarations of more than ordinary feeling. My admiration of her mental and personal attractions, my knowledge of her unselfish sincerity, her sweet temper, and unwearied care for others, with but unrequited return where most should have been given, ... although she is seventeen years my senior,[8] all combined to an attachment on my part, and led to reciprocations[9] which I had little looked for. During nearly three years[10] I had daily 'troubled pleasure, soon chastised by fear.'[11] Three months since I received a furious letter from my employer, threatening to shoot me if I returned from my vacation, which I was passing at home; and letters from her lady's-maid[12] and physician[13] informed me of the outbreak, only checked by her firm courage and resolution that whatever harm came to her, none should come to me . . . . I have lain during nine long weeks utterly shattered in body and broken down in mind. The probability of her becoming free to give me herself and estate never rose to drive away the prospect of her decline under her present grief. I dreaded, too, the wreck of my mind and body, which, God knows, during a short life have been severely tried. Eleven continuous nights of sleepless horror reduced me to almost blindness, and being taken into Wales[14] to recover, the sweet scenery, the sea, the sound of music caused me fits of unspeakable distress. You will say, 'What a fool!' but if you knew the many causes I have for sorrow which I cannot even hint at here, you would perhaps pity as well as blame. At the kind request of Mr. Macaulay[15] and Mr. Baines,[16] I have striven to arouse my mind by writing something worthy of being read, but I really cannot do so. Of course you will despise the writer of all this. I can only answer that the writer does the same, and would not wish to live if he did not hope that work and change may yet restore him.

Apologizing sincerely for what seems like whining egotism, and hardly daring to hint about days when in your company I could sometimes sink the thoughts which 'remind me of departed days,'[17] I fear departed never to return,—I remain,

[P. B. Brontë]

MS untraced at the time of first publication; now Brotherton. W & S. 216.
Address: not in source.
PM: not in source.
Date: Grundy dates 'within a few months of January 1848' (*Grundy* 86), but Branwell had received his dismissal from Mr Robinson 'three months since' on 17 July 1845. See EN 31.7.1845 n. 10.
Text: *Grundy* 86–8. Grundy omits the names of the Robinsons' relatives.

1. Francis Henry Grundy (b. ?1822), a civil engineer and railway surveyor whom Branwell had met in Halifax in 1842. See BB to FHG 25.10.1842 n. 1.
2. Branwell had last written to Grundy on 29.10.1842, when he was at Haworth after his dismissal from Luddenden Foot station in Apr. 1842. See EN 20.1.1842 n. 8.
3. George Hudson's Leeds and Bradford Railway opened in 1846, 2 years after incorporation; extensions to Keighley and Skipton were in use by Mar. and Sept. 1847 respectively. A further extension from Skipton to Colne in Lancs. was opened in 1848. Grundy describes his position as one of 'far greater responsibility than before—that of resident engineer to some thirty-five miles of railway . . . It was then that I resumed my intimacy . . . with Patrick Branwell Brontë.' (*Grundy* 161.) Grundy's chronology is confused, but he recalled a gap of 'three years' in his contacts with Branwell. (81.)
4. Probably the Devonshire Hotel, where Grundy invited Branwell to visit him at the end of Oct. See the next letter.
5. Branwell's station at Luddenden Foot was about 4 miles from Halifax, where Grundy was lodging in 1841.
6. Mrs Robinson's sister Mary (née Gisborne) was the wife of William Evans of Allestree or Allestrey Hall near Derby, MP for North Derbyshire.
7. BB may refer to the Revd Edmund Robinson's relative, the politician and statesman Frederick John Robinson (1782–1859), created Viscount Goderich on the formation of Canning's ministry in Apr. 1827, briefly Prime Minster from late 1827 to 1828, and created Earl of Ripon in 1833.
8. Lydia Robinson was born in 1799, Branwell Brontë in 1817.
9. Branwell's allegations are discussed in M. C., 'Two Biographies of Branwell Brontë', *BST* 14.71.38–41, and Dame Myra Curtis and others, 'Further Thoughts on Branwell Brontë's Story', *BST* 14.72.3–16. In her biography Gérin accepts and embroiders Branwell's version; Daphne du Maurier takes the extreme opposite view, considering that his story was 'a fabrication from start to finish . . . used as a cover-up for some bad misdemeanour at Thorp Green'. (*BST* 14.72.16.) Important new evidence is presented and discussed in *Barker*.
10. Branwell exaggerates. He was at Thorp Green for $2\frac{1}{2}$ years, from Jan. 1843 until 17 July 1845, and his poem written at and entitled 'Thorp Green', dated 30 Mar. 1843, is a remarkably miserable one. See Neufeldt *BBP* 260–1, Winnifrith *BBP* 262–3.
11. Not traced. BB used a version of this line in his 'Letter from a father on earth to his Child in her grave'. (unlocated MS dated 3 Apr. 1846; Neufeldt *BBP* 280–1; Winnifrith *BBP* 168–70.) For the use of 'chastise' to mean 'chasten' (*OED* 5) cf. Pope, *Odyssey* xvi: 196, 'Then with surprise (surprise chastised by fears) . . . he cried'.
12. Ann Marshall (?1809–16.4.1847.)
13. John Crosby, MRCS 1818; listed as a 'surgeon' in Pigot's *Directory* for 1841. Gérin notes that he was a member of the society of Oddfellows' 'Loyal Providence Lodge, Great Ouseburn'. (*BB* 236.) If BB was a fellow-member, he might have received financial help through Dr Crosby, since Oddfellows assist members in sickness, distress, or other misfortune. George Whitehead records that 'Rev. E. Robinson was interred, June 5th [1846] There was about 60 Odd Fellows followed him, his Mrs and Misses Elizabeth and Mary and the young master followed him to the church'. (Helier Hibbs (ed.) *Victorian Ouseburn: George Whitehead's Journal* (York, 1990), 20 a.)
14. See EN 31.7.1845 notes 10 and 13; Branwell had seen the Welsh mountain Penmaenmawr on a boat-trip from Liverpool, and had prayed for strength like that of the 'moveless' mountain to withstand his grief. See his poem 'Penmaenmawr' in Neufeldt *BBP* 276–8, Winnifrith *BBP*. 163–5.
15. The historian Thomas Babington Macaulay (1800–59), whose poems, *Lays of Ancient Rome* had appeared in 1842. Branwell refers to a complimentary letter from him in his letter to J. B.

Leyland of 25.11.1845. Macaulay's father Zachary Macaulay and Lydia Robinson's father the Revd Thomas Gisborne had been fellow-members of the 'Clapham Sect' and friends of William Wilberforce; they were also distantly connected through marriage.

16. Edward (later Sir Edward) Baines (1800–90), editor of the *Leeds Mercury* from 1818. Like his father (Edward Baines, 1774–1848) he was a liberal in politics, an active supporter of Mechanics' Institutes, and the author of several historical and topographical works.

17. cf. Robert Burns, 'Ye banks and braes o' bonie Doon', ll 5–8:

Thou'll break my heart, thou warbling bird,
That wantons thro' the flowering thorn:
Thou minds me o' departed joys,
Departed, never to return.—

Branwell Brontë to F. H. Grundy, [?late October 1845]

Haworth.
Bradford.
Yorks.

My Dear Sir,

If I have strength enough for the journey and the weather be tolerable I shall feel happy in calling on you at the Devonshire Hotel[1] on Friday the 31st of the month

The sight of a face I have been accustomed to see \`and like' when I was happier and stronger, now proves my best medicine—

I am,
Dear Sir,
Yours sincerely,
P. B. Bronte.

MS BPM B.S. 140. W & S 255 as [July 1846].

Address: not in MS.

PM: not in MS.

Date: The letter is undated. In 1846 Friday 31st could only have been in July. In 1845 Friday 31st was the last day of Oct. This would follow BB's reference to 'the inn at Skipton' in his Oct. letter to Grundy, and the invitation would have been welcome since BB was again seeking railway employment. See CB's comments in EN 4.11.1845. Grundy, however, says that Branwell did not visit him at Skipton.

1. Grundy wrote, 'I invited him to come to me at the Devonshire Hotel, Skipton, a distance of some seventeen miles, and in reply received the last letter he ever wrote.' (*Grundy* 90.) Grundy's dates cannot be relied on.

Branwell Brontë to ?H. Robson, Solicitor to the Manchester, Hebden Bridge . . . & Carlisle Junction Railway Company, ?23 October 1845

Haworth.
Bradford.
Yorks.

Dear Sir,

I respectfully beg leave to offer myself as candidate for the situation of Secretary to the Manchester and Hebden Bridge and Keighley and Carlisle Junction Railway.[1]

I trust to be able to produce full testimonials as to my qualifications and Securities, if required, to any probable amount.[2]

I am,
Dear Sir,
Your most respectful and
obdt Servt,
P. B. Bronté—

MS BPM B.S. 139. Gérin *BB* 246–7.
Address: not in MS.
PM: not in MS.
Date: as given on acquisition by BPM in 1937. See *BST* 9.48.194, 199.

1. The full title included 'Leeds' before '& Carlisle'. 'The 1845 Leeds and Bradford Railway Act had authorised a branch to Haworth . . . in October of the same year the Manchester, Hebden Bridge . . . Junction Railway [Company] put forward a scheme following approximately the same route for its closing stages, proposing the atmospheric system as a possible form of traction . . . both these schemes were unsuccessful.' (*Regional History* viii; 71.) The line would have proceeded from 'a junction with the Leeds and Manchester Railway at Hebden Bridge' via the Hebden Bridge Valley 'and by a tunnel through Cock Hill into the Haworth Valley and thence by way of Haworth to Keighley' where it would join the 'Leeds and Bradford Railway Extension'. The advertisements stressed the 'commercial advantages and great facilities' of the proposed line, and its promoters included the local manufacturers Joseph, James, and W. C. Greenwood and Hartley Merrall of Spring Head, near Haworth, and other Haworth landowners and tradesmen, as well as the 'Rev. P. Brontë' and his curate J. B. Grant. (*Bradford Observer* 23.10.1845, 7.)
2. The *Bradford Observer* for 23 Oct. 1845 carried 5 separate announcements relating to the proposed line, including an advertisement for this secretarial post: 'MANCHESTER, HEBDEN BRIDGE & KEIGHLEY, AND LEEDS & CARLISLE JUNCTION | RAILWAY. | Provisionally Registered. | WANTED, an active, intelligent, respectable Gentleman as | SECRETARY to the above Company. Communications to be | addressed to Mr. H. ROBSON, Halifax, | Solicitor to the Company.' (7, col. 5.)

To Ellen Nussey, [4 November 1845]

[Haworth]

Dear Ellen

You do not reproach me in your last but I fear you must have thought me unkind in being so long without answering you—The fact is I had hoped to be able to ask you to come to Haworth—Branwell seemed to have a prospect of <being able to obtain> ˋgetting′ employment,[1] and I waited to know the result of his efforts in order to say, "dear Ellen come and see us—but the place (a Secretaryship to a Railroad Committee) is given to another person Branwell still remains at home and while he is here—you shall not come—I am more confirmed in that resolution the more I know of him—I wish I could say one word to you in his favour—but I cannot—therefore I will hold my tongue.

Poor Miss *Ringrose's letters interest me much—they are quiet and unpretending but seem affectionate and sincere—Will ˋshe′ and *George ever be married?[2] Such an event seems to human eyes very unlikely now—yet that is no proof that it will not one day take place—Oh I wish brighter days would come for all *your *family—and they may do so, sooner than we can calculate.

We ˋare′ all obliged to you dear Ellen for your kind suggestion about Leeds but I think our school-schemes are for the present at rest.[3]

Emily and Anne wish me to tell you that they think it very unlikely[4] for little Flossy to be expected to rear so numerous a family—they think you are quite right in protesting against all the pups being preserved—for if kept they will pull their poor little mother to pieces The French Newspaper[5] I send you to day is the first we have had for an age—two have missed—Be sure I shall always be punctual in dispatching them to you so that when there is a long gap—you will know to what quarter to ascribe the delay. I believe *Joe *Taylor is at present at Ilkley[6] or has been there lately—I saw his name in the newspaper in the list of visitors "at this fashionable watering place"

Do not think about my coming to Brookroyd for the present Ellen[7] Give my sincere love to your Mother Anne & *Mercy and believe me—

Yours faithfully

C B

MS Berg. Envelope: BPM B.S. 104/9.5. W & S 217.
Address (envelope): Miss Ellen Nussey | Brookroyd | Birstal | Leeds
PM: (i) HAWORTH (ii) BRADFORD YORKS | NO 4 | 1845 | C (iii) LEEDS | NO 4 | 1845 | F
Annotation (i) on letter by EN: Nov 4–45; (ii) on envelope: Nov 45. Wafer on envelope: yellow, with the words 'Hope is my Anchor'.

1. See the previous letter. F. H. Grundy, a railway engineer, commented on this or an earlier application for employment by Branwell: 'But Brontë got no situation with us. Indeed, it was altogether improbable, for the cause of his leaving his appointment [at Luddenden Foot] had been too notoriously glaring. His absence, carousing with congenial drinkers . . . had been of days' continuance. He had a porter . . . to whom he left all the work, and the result was that very serious defalcations were discovered.' (*Grundy* 86.) On the 'defalcations' see EN 20.1.1842 n. 8.
2. George Nussey never recovered sufficiently to leave Dr Belcombe's and later the Nelsons' care in York, and Amelia married Joe Taylor in ?Sept. 1850. See EN 18.8.1845 n. 5.
3. The plan to establish a school in the parsonage could not be fulfilled so long as Branwell was there; but see EJB's Diary Paper for 31.7.1845, which makes it clear that none of the sisters was enthusiastic about it in any case.
4. Unfitting, undesirable (Yorks. dialect). cf. *JE* ch. 9 where Jane is told it is not 'likely' for her to speak to the dying Helen Burns. (93.) For Flossy see EN 7.10.1845 n. 9.
5. Last referred to in EN 8.9.1845.
6. See CB to M. Dixon 16.10.1843 n. 3.
7. In this and her subsequent letters to EN in 1845 CB declines to visit Brookroyd, but does not admit to what was really preoccupying her. At some time in 'the autumn of 1845' she had 'accidentally lighted on' some of Emily's poems in manuscript; Anne had produced hers, and the sisters agreed to arrange 'a small selection' of their poems and if possible get them printed. They must have been preparing and fair-copying them from this time onwards. See CB to Aylott & Jones, 28.1.46 and notes.

To Constantin Heger, 18 November [1845]

Haworth Bradford Yorkshire

Monsieur

Les six mois de silence sont écoulés; nous sommes aujourd'hui au 18 Novbe., ma dernière lettre etait datée (je crois) le 18 Mai,[1] je puis donc vous écrire encore, sans manquer à ma promesse.

L'été et l'automne m'ont paru bien longs; à vrai dire il m'a fallu des efforts pénibles pour supporter jusqu'à present la privation que je me suis imposée: vous ne pouvez pas concevoir cela, vous, Monsieur, mais imaginez vous, pour un instant, qu<e> 'un de vos enfants est séparé de vous de 160 lieues de distance et que vous devez rester six mois sans lui écrire, sans recevoir de ses nouvelles, sans en entendre parler, sans savoir comment il se porte, alors vous comprendrez facilement tout ce qu'il y a de dure dans une pareille obligation. Je vous dirai franchement, qu'en attendant, j'ai tâché de vous oublier, car le souvenir d'une personne que l'on croit ne devoir plus revoir[2] et que, pourtant, on estime beaucoup, harasse trop l'esprit et quand on a subi cette espèce d'inquiétude pendant un ou deux ans, on est prêt à tout faire pour retrouver le repos. J'ai tout fait, j'ai cherché les occupations,[3] je me suis interdit absolument le plaisir de parler de vous—même à Emilie mais je n'ai pu vaincre ni mes regrets ni mon impatience—c'est humiliant cela—de ne pas savoir maîtriser ses propres pensées, être esclave à un regret, un souvenir, esclave à une idée dominante et fixe qui tyrannise son esprit. Que ne puis-je avoir pour vous juste autant d'amitié que vous avez pour moi—ni plus ni moins? je serais alors si tranquille, si libre—je pourrais garder le silence pendant dix ans sans effort<s>.

Mon père se porte bien mais sa vue est presqu'éteinte, il ne sait plus ni lire ni écrire; c'est, pourtant, l'avis des medecins d'attendre encore quelques mois avant de tenter une opération[4]—l'hiver ne sera pour lui qu'une longue nuit—il se plaint rarement, j'admire sa patience—Si la Providence me destine la même calamité[5]—puisse-t-elle au moins m'accorder autant de patience pour la supporter! Il me semble, monsieur, que ce qu'il y a de plus amère dans les grands malheurs physiques c'est d'être forcé à faire partager nos souffrances à tous ceux qui nous entourent; on peut cacher les maladies de l'âme mais celles qui attaquent le corps et détruisent les facultés, ne se cachent pas. Mon père me permet maintenant de lui lire et d'écrire pour lui, il me témoigne aussi plus de confiance qu'il ne m' 'en' a jamais témoignée, ce qui est une grande consolation.

Monsieur, j'ai une grâce à vous demander: quand vous répondrez à cette lettre, parlez-moi un peu de vous-même—pas de moi car, je sais, que si vous me parlez de moi ce sera pour me gronder et, cette fois, je voudrais voir votre aspect bienveillant; parlez-moi donc de vos enfants; jamais vous n'aviez le front sévère quand Louise et Claire et Prosper[6], étaient près de vous. Dîtes-moi aussi quelquechose du Pensionnat, des élèves, des Maîtresses—Mesdemoiselles Blanche, Sophie et Justine[7] restent-elles toujours à Bruxelles? Dîtes-moi où vous avez voyagé pendant les vacances—n'avez-vous pas été sur les bords du Rhin? N'avez-vous pas visité Cologne ou Coblentz? Dîtes-moi enfin ce que vous voulez mon maître mais dîtes-moi quelquechose. Écrire à une ci-devant sous-maîtresse[8] (non—je ne veux pas me souvenir de mon emploi de sous-maîtresse je le renie) mais enfin, écrire à une ancienne élève ne peut être une occupation fort intéressante pour vous—je le sais—mais pour moi c'est la vie. Votre dernière lettre m'a servi de soutien—de nourriture[9] pendant six mois—à present il m'en faut une autre et vous me le donnerez—pas parceque vous avez pour moi de l'amitié—vous ne pouvez en avoir beaucoup—mais parcequ[e] vous avez l'âme compatissante et que vous ne condamneriez personne à de longues souffrances pour vous épargner quelques moments d'ennui. Me défendre à vous écrire, refuser de me répondre ce sera m'arracher la seule joie que j'ai au monde, me priver de mon dernier privilège—privilège auquel je ne consentirai jamais à renoncer volontairement. Croyez-moi mon maître, en m'écrivant vous faites un bon œuvre[10]—tant que je vous crois assez content de moi, tant que j'ai l'espoir de recevoir de vos nouvelles je puis être tranquille et pas trop triste mais quand un silence morne et prolongé semble m'avertir de l'éloignement de mon maître à mon égard—quand de jour en jour j'attends une lettre et que de jour en jour le désappointement vient me rejeter dans un douloureux accablement et que cette douce joie de voir votre écriture, de lire vos conseils me fuit comme une vaine vision,[11] alors, j'ai la fièvre—je perds l'appétit et le sommeil—je dépéris

Puis-je vous écrire encore au mois de Mai prochain? j'aurais voulu attendre toute une année—mais c'est impossible—c'est trop long.

C Brontë

I must say one word to you in English—I wish I could write to you more cheerful letters, for when I read this over, I find it to be somewhat gloomy—but forgive me my dear master—do not be irritated at my sadness—according to the words of the Bible:[12] "Out of the fullness of the heart, the mouth speaketh and truly I find it difficult to be cheerful so long as I think I shall never see you more.[13] You will perceive by the defects in this letter that I am forgetting the French language—yet I read all the French books I can get, and learn daily a portion by heart—but I have never heard<it> French spoken but once since I left Brussels[14]—and then it sounded like music in my ears—every word was most precious to me because it reminded me of you—I love French for your sake with all my heart and soul.

Farewell my dear Master—may God protect you with special care and crown you with peculiar blessings

C B.

MS BL Add. 38732c. W & S 218.

To Constantin Heger, 18 November [1845]: Translation

Haworth
Bradford Yorkshire

Monsieur,

The six months of silence have elapsed; to-day is the 18th November, my last letter was dated (I believe) the 18th May;[1] therefore I can write to you again without breaking my promise.

The summer and autumn have seemed very long to me; to tell the truth I have had to make painful efforts to endure until now the privation I imposed on myself: you, Monsieur—you cannot conceive what that means—but imagine for a moment that one of your children is separated from you by a distance of 160 leagues, and that you have to let six months go by without writing to him, without receiving news of him, without hearing him spoken of, without knowing how he is, then you will easily understand what hardship there is in such an obligation. I will tell you candidly that during this time of waiting I have tried to forget you, for the memory of a person one believes one is never to see again,[2] and whom one nevertheless greatly respects, torments the mind exceedingly and when one has suffered this kind of anxiety for one or two years, one is ready to do anything to regain peace of mind. I have done everything, I have sought occupations,[3] I have absolutely forbidden myself the pleasure of speaking about you—even to Emily, but I have not been able to overcome either my regrets or my impatience—and that is truly humiliating—not to know how to get the mastery over one's own thoughts, to be the slave of a regret, a memory, the slave of a dominant and fixed idea which has become a tyrant over one's mind. Why cannot I have for you exactly as much friendship as you have for me—neither more nor less? Then I would be so tranquil, so free—I could keep silence for ten years without effort.

My father is well but his sight has almost gone, he can no longer read or write; nevertheless the doctors' advice is to wait a few months longer before attempting an operation[4]—for him the winter will be nothing but a long night—he rarely complains, I admire his patience—If Providence ordains that the same calamity[5] should be my own fate—may He at least grant me as much patience to endure it! It seems to me, Monsieur, that what is most bitterly painful in great bodily afflictions is that we are compelled to make all those who surround us sharers in our sufferings; we can hide the troubles of the soul, but those which attack the body and destroy its faculties cannot be hidden. My father now lets me read to him and write for him, he also shows more confidence in me than he has ever done before, and that is a great consolation.

Monsieur, I have a favour to ask you: when you reply to this letter, talk to me a little about yourself—not about me, for I know that if you talk to me about myself it will be to scold me, and this time I would like to see your kindly aspect; talk to me then about your children; your forehead never had a severe look when Louise and Claire and Prospère[6] were near you. Tell me also something about the School, the pupils, the teachers—are Mesdemoiselles Blanche, Sophie and Justine[7] still in Brussels? Tell me where you travelled during the holidays—haven't you been through the Rhineland? Haven't you visited Cologne or Coblenz? In a word, tell me what you will, my master, but tell me something. Writing to a former assistant teacher[8] (no,—I don't want to remember my position as an assistant teacher, I disown it) well then, writing to an old pupil cannot be a very interesting occupation for you—I know that—but for me it is life itself. Your last letter has sustained me—has nourished me[9] for six months—now I need another and you will give it me—not because you have any friendship for me—you cannot have much—but because you have a compassionate soul and because you would not condemn anyone to undergo long suffering in order to spare yourself a few moments of tedium. To forbid me to write to you, to refuse to reply to me—that will be to tear from me the only joy I have on earth—to deprive me of my last remaining privilege—a privilege which I will never consent to renounce voluntarily. Believe me, my master, in writing to me you do a good deed[10]—so long as I think you are fairly pleased with me, so long as I still have the hope of hearing from you, I can be tranquil and not too sad, but when a dreary and prolonged silence seems to warn me that my master is becoming estranged from me—when day after day I await a letter and day after day disappointment flings me down again into overwhelming misery, when the sweet delight of seeing your writing and reading your counsel flees from me like an empty vision[11]—then I am in a fever—I lose my appetite and my sleep—I pine away.

May I write to you again next May? I would have liked to wait a full year—but it is impossible—it is too long—

C. Brontë

[The remainder of the letter is in English as printed.]

Address: not in MS. Allegedly sent to M. Heger at the Athénée Royal. (*Chadwick* 274).
PM: not in MS.
Annotation in pencil in left margin by ?M. Heger: rue des 3 tete 2 | au second—?Talairier Cordonnier | rue de la ?Caserne 13 ?Trinon..e—| ?Corbitier M. ?Tuvalle[15]. M. Heger sent Mrs Gaskell no extracts from this letter. See CH 24.7.1844, note on text.
Date: 1845, indicated by the reference to PB's impending operation.
Text: M. Heger did not tear up this letter, and the text remains intact.

1. This letter does not survive, but was perhaps written in answer to one from M. Heger, since CB says she has been 'sustained' by his last letter for 6 months.
2. Possibly the phrase implies obligation as well as futurity. Contrast CB's letter to M. Heger of 24.7.1844: 'Oh c'est certain que je vous reverrai un jour—il le faut bien.'
3. One occupation was the transformation of CB's memories of M. Heger and Brussels into *The Professor* and poems on the theme of master and pupil. See the Clarendon *The Professor*, introduction, 215–21 and notes, and appendix IV (the poem 'At first I did attention give'). See also the previous letter, n. 7.
4. Mr Brontë was operated on for cataract on 25 Aug. 1846. See EN 26.8.1846.
5. In July 1844 CB had been concerned about her own weak eyesight, fearing that if she wrote too much she would become blind. See CH 24.7.1844.
6. See EN 6.3.1843 n. 3 and CH 24.7.1844 n. 18.
7. See EN May 1842 n. 5. CB has not referred to Mlle Justine in previous letters. Either she or 'Mdlle Marie' may be the 'Mdlle Haussé' referred to in EJB 29.5.1843.
8. After the first 6 months in Brussels CB taught English in return for lessons in French and German. See EN July 1842.
9. In *Villette* Lucy Snowe describes M. Paul's letters as 'real food that nourished, living water that refreshed'. (713.)
10. CB's intensely bitter lines, which almost certainly refer to M. Heger, 'He saw my heart's woe discovered my soul's anguish' were probably written some time after this letter in Dec. 1847. She goes on 'But once a year he heard a whisper low and dreary . . . He was mute as is the grave.' (Neufeldt *CBP* 340; Winnifrith *CBP* 244–5.) M. Heger may have rejected CB's plea to be allowed to write again in May 1846 for no more letters to him survive.
11. CB is recalling Ezekiel's words on false prophets. See Ezekiel 12: 24, 13: 7, and Job 20: 8.
12. Matthew 12: 34 and Luke 6: 45.
13. In *The Professor* Frances Henri's letter to her teacher, William Crimsworth, conveys a similar misery: 'how sorry I am that I shall probably never see you more . . . I am heart-broken to be quite separated from you.' (162.)
14. See EN 31.7.1845.

15. M. Heger's scribbled notes (if they are his) are almost illegible, and the readings given here are conjectural. They may refer to a M. Talairier or Talavrier, shoemaker ('cordonnier') in the 'Rue des Trois Têtes' off the Montagne de la Cour in Brussels, and to someone else, possibly another tradesman, in the 'Rue de la Caserne' (Barracks Street).

To Ellen Nussey, [20 November 1845]

[Haworth]

Dear Ellen,

I was very glad to get your little note, short as it was. I consider on the whole it contained good news; the last sentence concerning George,[1] is quite cheering. I persist in saying good times are still in store for Brookroyd, for I have ever remarked, that after much distress comes a proportionate degree of happiness; and so Joseph Taylor, Esq., of Hunsworth Mills, Cleckheaton, has re-discovered the way to Brookroyd. High time he did so. I am not surprised to hear that Mr. and Mrs. T[aylor][2] are about to leave the old lady,[3] her unhappy disposition is preparing for her a most desolate old age.

Good bye,—write directly. Once more I tell you not to ask me to go to Brookroyd. I have no thought of leaving home at present.

C. B.[4]

MS untraced. Envelope: BPM B.S. 104/10. W & S 219.
Address (envelope): Miss Ellen Nussey | Brookroyd | Birstal | Leeds
PM: (i) HAWORTH (ii) BRADFORD YORKS | NO 20 | 1845 | C (iii)— | NO 20 | 1845 | C
Annotation in pencil by EN on the envelope: Nov 45. Wafer: a blue lozenge, with the word 'Farewell' within a line border.
Date: from postmarks and content.
Text: *Nussey* 136. W & S 219 and *Shorter* 170 have minor punctuation variants and expand 'Mrs. T.' to 'Mrs. T[aylor]' Not in *Life*. The edited version in *Hours at Home* xi. 296 may retain two authentic readings: see notes 3 and 4.

1. See EN 4.11.1845 n. 2.
2. Joshua Taylor (1812–80), eldest brother of Mary Taylor, and his wife Jane Lister Charlesworth (1815–87), who were married at the Moravian church in Gomersal in 1838. Joshua Taylor carried on the Taylor family business, and was described by his son Edward as 'very well read and a theoretical chemist'. (*BST* 15.79.309.) He was said to be the model for Matthew Yorke in *Shirley*. (*Wroot* 141–2 is inaccurate in stating that Joshua Taylor lived at Hunsworth.)
3. *Hours at Home* xi. 296 reads 'the old woman—'. The reference is to the widowed Mrs Joshua Taylor, née Anne Tickell (?1781–1856), the 'Mrs Yorke' of *Shirley* and mother of Mary Taylor. Her 'unhappy disposition' had meant that all her other children had left home soon after their father's death in Dec. 1840. See EN 3.1.1841 n. 2 and *Wroot* 138–9.
4. The *Hours at Home* text ends '. . . old age. Write again soon. Good-by. Write directly'. (xi. 296.)

Branwell Brontë to J. B. Leyland, [?25 November 1845]

Haworth, Bradford, Yorks.

My dear Sir,

I send through yourself the enclosed scrap[1] for the Halifax Guardian—and I ought to tell you why I wish anything of so personal a nature to appear in print.

I have no other way, not pregnant with danger, of communicating with one whom I cannot help loving.[2] <?How> Printed lines with my usual signature 'Northangerland'[3] would excite no suspicion—as my late unhappy employer shrunk from the bare idea of my being able to write anything, and had a day's sickness after hearing that Macaulay[4] had sent me a complimentary letter so He won't know the <word> name.

I sent through a private channel one letter of comfort in her great and agonizing present afflictions, but I recalled it through dread of the consequences of a discovery.

These lines only have one merit—that of <*i.w*> really expressing my feelings while sailing under the Welsh mountain[5]—When the band on board the steamer struck up 'Ye banks and braes'[6]—and God knows that, for many different reasons, those feelings were far enough from pleasure.

I suffer very much from that mental exhaustion which arises from brooding on matters useless at present to think of—and active employment would be my greatest cure and blessing—for really after hours of thought which business would have hushed I have felt as if I could not live, and, if long continued, such a state will bring on permanent affection of the heart, which is already bothered with most uneasy palpitations.

I should like extremely to have an hours sitting with you, and if I had the chance, I would promise to try not to be gloomy. You said you would be at Haworth e're long but that 'e're' has doubtlessly changed to 'ne'er;' So I must wish to get to Halifax sometime to see you.

I saw Murray's monument[7] praised in the papers and I trust you are getting on well with Beckwith's,[8] as well as with your own personal statue of living flesh and blood. Mine, like your Theseus,[9] has lost its hands and feet, and, I fear, its head also, for it can neither move write or think as it once could.

I hope I shall hear of you on John Brown's[10] return from Halifax whither he has gone, and apologising honestly for putting 'you' to the trouble of placing the enclosed in the hands of the newspaper Editor—if you choose to do so.

I remain,
Dear Sir,
Yours most sincerely,
P. B. Bronté.

MS Brotherton. W & S 220.
Address: not in MS.
PM: not in MS.
Date: added in pencil in the MS by a later hand.

1. Branwell's poem 'Penmaenmawr', published in the *Halifax Guardian* on 20.12.1845. See Neufeldt *BBP* 276–8.
2. Mrs Robinson of Thorp Green. In the poem BB imagines her 'gentle breast and sorrowing face'.
3. Branwell took his pseudonym from his own Angrian creation, the anti-hero or rogue Alexander Percy, Earl of Northangerland. See Alexander *EW* 2, 131–3.
4. Thomas Babington Macaulay. See BB to F. H. Grundy Oct. 1845 and n. 15.
5. Penmaenmawr is near Conwy in North Wales. See EN 31.7.1845 and n. 13.
6. Burns's song, published in 1791, with the lines 'Thou minds me o' departed joys, | Departed, never to return' is echoed in Branwell's 'Penmaenmawr' ll. 15–16.
7. The tablet in memory of the Revd John Murray in Halifax Parish Church.
8. Leyland 'was to be paid £250 and find his own material'—fine white stone and marble—for the monument to Dr Stephen Beckwith in York Minster. See *Infernal World*, 177.
9. See BB to JBL 10.9.1845.
10. The Haworth sexton and stonemason. See BB to JBL 4.8.1845 n. 2.

To Ellen Nussey, ?14 December 1845

[Haworth]

Dear Ellen

I was glad to get your last note, though it was so short and crusty. Three weeks had elapsed without my having heard a word from you,[1] and I began to fear that some new misfortune had occurred—that George was worse, or something of that kind. I was relieved to find that such was not the case. Anne is obliged to you for the kind regret you express at not being able to ask her to Brookroyd; she wishes you could come to Haworth. I think you are a trifle 'out of your head.'[2] Do you scold me out of habit, Ellen, or are you really angry? In either case it is all nonsense. You know as well as I do that to go to Brookroyd is always a great pleasure to me, and that to one who has so little change and so few friends as I have, it must be a great pleasure—but I am not at all times in the mood or circumstances to take my pleasure. I wish so much to see you, that I shall certainly sometime after New Year's Day, if all be well, be going over for a day or two to Birstall. Now I could not go if I would. At the latter end of February or the beginning of March I may be able to do so. If you think I stand upon ceremony in this matter, you miscalculate sadly. I have known you, your mother and sisters, too long to be ceremonious with any of you.

Invite me no more now, Nell, till I invite myself, be too proud to trouble yourself, and if, when at last I mention coming (for I shall give you warning), it does not happen to suit you, tell me so with quiet hauteur.

I should like a long letter next time, with full particulars, and in the name of Common Sense, no more lover's quarrels.

Good-bye. C. B.

My best love to your mother and sisters.

MS untraced. W & S 221.
Address: not in source.
PM: not in source.
Text: *Shorter* 171. W & S 221 is identical with *Shorter*. Not in *Life*. *Hours at Home* xi. 296 and *Nussey* 136–7 are heavily edited and abridged, but see n. 2 below.

1. EN stayed in Leeds with her brother Richard's fiancée Elizabeth Charnock sometime in Nov. or Dec.—long enough to have 'many opportunities of hearing good Dr Hook', the Vicar of Leeds. (EN to Mary Gorham 29.12.1845, BPM Gorham Collection.) Her absence from home may help to account for the break in correspondence.
2. The otherwise corrupt *Nussey* text may record MS punctuation here: it reads 'a trifle out of your head! do you scold'.

To Ellen Nussey, [?30 December 1845]

[Haworth]

Dear Ellen,—

I don't know whether most to thank you for the very pretty slippers you have sent me or to scold you for occasioning yourself—in the slightest degree, trouble or expense on my account—I will have them made up and bring them with me—if all be well when I come to Brookroyd.

Reading your letter left me a somewhat 'sair[1] heart'—these Swaines[2] seem to be so selfish and mean a set—and it seems so hard that people like them should have it in their power to annoy you—I greatly fear they will not scruple to use such power—without reserve or delicacy—as far as they can—I only hope that their capability to injure your Mother may be limited.

Never doubt that I shall come to Brookroyd as soon as I <u>can</u> Nell—I dare say my wish to see you is equal to your wish to see me.

I had a note on Saturday[3] from Ellen Taylor[4] informing me that letters have been received from Mary and that she was well and in good spirits—I suppose you have not yet seen them as you do not mention them—but you will probably have them in your possession before you get this note. I am glad you are pretty well satisfied respecting George's position—I should think the calm, tranquil state of his mind is a favourable symptom—Miss Ringrose I suppose has ceased to write to you as you do not mention her now.[5]

You say well in speaking of Branwell that no sufferings are so awful as those brought on by dissipation—alas! I see the truth of this observation daily proved—Ann and Mercy must have a weary and burdensome life of it—in waiting upon their unhappy brother[6]—it seems grievous indeed that those who have not sinned should suffer so largely.

Write to me a little oftener Ellen—I am very glad to get your notes—Remember me kindly to your Mother and Sisters.—

Yours faithfully,
C. Brontë.

MS untraced. Envelope: BPM B.S. 104/11. W & S 222 as 31 Dec. 1845.
Address: (envelope): Miss Ellen Nussey | Brookroyd | Birstal | Leeds
PM: (i) HAWORTH (ii) BRADFORD YORKS | DE 30 | 1845 | C (iii) LEEDS | DE 30 | 1845 F
Annotation on envelope by EN in pencil: Dec 45. Wafer: yellow rectangle with the words 'Remember me' within a line border.
Date: from postmarks. CB or EN may have misdated the letter, since all printed sources date 31 Dec. 1845.
Text: Punctuation and capitalization of the copy-text, W & S 222, indicate a manuscript-based text. *Nussey* 137–8 and *Shorter* 172 are heavily edited. *Life* i. 330 has the paragraph beginning 'You say well', omitting proper names. *Hours at Home* prints a brief edited extract.

1. Sore or sad. cf. Burns, 'For the sake of somebody': 'My heart is sair, I dare na tell, | My heart is sair for Somebody.'
2. CB refers to the possible dishonesty of these Gomersal cloth merchants in EN 7.10.1845.
3. 28 Dec.
4. Mary Taylor's cousin. See CB to M. Dixon 16.10.1843 n. 8.
5. See EN 1.6.1845 notes 6 and 7.
6. Joseph Nussey. See EN 31.7.1845 n. 5.

To Mr Rand,[1] 22 January 1846

[Haworth]

Dear Sir

Papa's sight is still very bad[2] and consequently he wishes me to answer your last letter in his stead.

Papa sympathises with you sincerely in the recent affliction you have sustained in the loss of your father[3]—he trusts that God will continue to support you and yours under that and all other calamities—

The unsettled state of things at Staley-Bridge[4] must be very unpleasant for you—it is to be hoped you may soon be enabled to obtain a more comfortable situation—I should think the neighbourhood of London would be more likely to suit yourself and Mrs Rand than the North of England—I <recen> trust therefore your recent application in that quarter may prove successful—

The Haworth National School does extremely well—and the master Mr Purnell[5] is I believe much liked—Few changes of any moment have taken place at Haworth since you left—the arrival of a new peal of six bells[6] is, I believe, the principal—They ring them almost daily—and we, living so near the church—have the full benefit of their tones—

Mr Grant also is married[7]—but as it is only a few days since he brought his bride down from London we have not yet seen her.

<I am> Papa wishes me to say particularly that he is extremely glad to hear such a good account of the progress of your little boy[8]—he hopes he may continue to prove a great comfort to you and his mamma—

Give my very kindest regards to Mrs Bacon[9] and Mrs Rand—Papa also wishes to be remembered to you all—

Believe me yours truly
Charlotte Brontë

MS Knox College, Galesburg. No publication traced.
Address: (envelope): Mr Rand | Master of the National School | Staley-Bridge | Manchester
PM: (i) HAWORTH (ii) BRADFORD Y[ORKS] | JA 22 | 1846 | C (iii) [MANCHES]TER | JA 22 | 1846

1. See CB to Mrs Rand 26.5.1845 n. 2.
2. On 18.11.1845 CB had told M. Heger that her father was almost blind and could no longer read or write.
3. Not identified.
4. See CB to Mrs Rand 26.5.1845 n. 11.
5. See CB to Mrs Rand 26.5.1845 n. 7.
6. On 21 Apr. 1845 Mr Brontë had written to Joseph Rushworth of Mouldgreave 'In conformity with what appears to be the wish of the Inhabitants—respecting a Peal of six bells, in order to consider the propriety or impropriety of such a measure—it is requested that you will be so kind as to attend in the Vestry of the Church of Haworth on the 29th Instant, at six o'clock in the evening.' (MS BPM B.S. 192; *LD* 326.) By 5 June 1845 Mr Brontë could inform Mr Rand that 'Our school is getting on tolerably well—and we have raised £230—for a peal of new bells!!!' (*LD* 338–9.) The bells were cast in 1845 by C. and G. Mears of London and officially opened on 10 Mar. 1846. See the inscriptions in the belfry and on the tenor bell, quoted in *LD* 326.
7. The Revd Joseph Brett Grant of Oxenhope married Sarah-Ann Turner on 13 Jan. 1846. See EN *c.* 26.10.1844 n. 5.
8. Ebenezer Bacon Rand. See CB to Mrs Rand 26.5.1845 n. 4.
9. ?Mrs Rand's mother.

To Ellen Nussey, 23 January [1846]

[Haworth]

Dear Ellen

I must write to you to-day, whether I have anything to say or not—or else you will begin to think that I have forgotten you—whereas never a day passes, and seldom an hour, that I do not think of you and the scene of trial[1] in which you live—move and have your being.

I was amused with what you said in your last about Mrs H Nussey[2]—and her little piques and jealousies—She may be a well-principled and well-intentioned woman—but I should fear she is very narrow—otherwise she could not take offence at a Sister venturing to give good advice to her brother.

Mary Taylor's letter[3] was deeply interesting and strongly characteristic—it is one of those matters I hope to talk over with you, when I see you—I do not doubt that John & Joe's motives for not coming frequently to Brookroyd[4] are regulated chiefly by matters of business—I imagine that if they might follow their own inclinations they would appear there—much oftener—at least—I hope such is the case, they are surely not mere butterflies who hover about their acquaintance on sunny days and leave them in rainy seasons—

What news of George? you did not mention him in your last letter so I concluded there was no additional intelligence—All you say of Miss Ringrose leads one to regret more that obstacles should have arisen to prevent her marriage with George—I think she would have been so exactly the person to have made him happy.[5]

I hope poor Mrs George Allbutt[6] is better by this time—do their means increase with their family? Remember me to her when you happen to see her—

I have no news whatever to communicate—no changes take place here—Branwell[7] offers no prospect of hope—he professes to be too ill to think of seeking for employment—he makes comfort scant at home.

I hold to my intention of going to Brookroyd as soon as I can—that is provided you will have me for a day or two—

Give my best love to your Mother & Sisters—

Yours dear Nell
always faithful
C Brontë

MS HM 24442. Envelope: BPM B.S. 104/12. W & S 223.
Address (envelope): Miss Ellen Nussey | Brookroyd | Birstal | Leeds
PM: (i) HAWORTH (ii) BRADFORD YORKS | JA 26 | 1846 | C
Annotation by EN: (i) on letter in ink: Jan 3—46; in pencil: Branwell offers no prospect of hope &c; (ii) on envelope: Jan 46 | Emily | ?G & ?Tay[lors]. Wafer: blue lozenge with the words 'Be wise to-day' within a line border.
Date: *Nussey* 138 and *Shorter* 173 follow EN's incorrect date, 3 Jan., for their abridged versions of this letter. W & S 223 is accurate in dating 'Jany. 23rd [1846]'. EN's annotations on the envelope match the content. See n. 2.

1. The Nusseys were nursing EN's brother Joseph, whose illness CB regarded as a consequence of his sins. See EN 31.7.1845 n. 5 and 30.12.1845. Joseph died on 29 May 1846. CB ends her sentence with an adaptation of Acts 17: 28.
2. Emily Nussey, wife of EN's brother Henry. See EN 14.11.1844 n. 3. EN had advised Henry not to antagonize his curate, Mr Rooker: 'Mr Rooker is doing better again, I imagine . . . I wrote a long letter describing the line of conduct I thought would be for Henry's & Emily's happiness if they would pursue it I recommended a little attention (however disagreeable to them) to this vain & purse proud curate neglect him & he is a man to set a whole Parish at the heels of the Vicar—'. (EN to Mary Gorham 29.12.1845, BPM Gorham Collection.)
3. Mary's letters from New Zealand for 1845–7 have not been located.

4. John and Joe Taylor's cottage at Hunsworth was about 3 miles from Brookroyd.
5. CB praises Amelia Ringrose's 'propriety' and quiet 'unpretending . . . affectionate and sincere' letters in EN 13.6.1845 and 4.11.1845.
6. Wife of the Batley GP George Allbutt, a relative by marriage of the Woolers, and a friend of the Nusseys. See EN 6.3.1843 n. 12.
7. Later in the year Branwell told J. B. Leyland that he was thinking of a situation abroad, since 'The quietude of home, and the inability to make my family aware of the nature of most of my sufferings makes me write 'Home thoughts are not, with me | Bright as of yore'. (BB to JBL ?28.4.46.) See also Branwell's poems of late 1845, 'Lydia Gisborne', beginning 'Cannot my soul depart' (*Barker* 469, Neufeldt *BBP* 275–6), and 'Real rest', (8 Nov. 1845) beginning 'I see a corpse upon the waters lie', where he envies the corpse's 'cold oblivion'. (Neufeldt *BBP* 274–5; Winnifrith *BBP* 166–7.)

To Messrs Aylott and Jones,[1] *28 January* 1846

[Haworth]

Gentlemen

May I request to be informed whether you would undertake the publication of a Collection of short poems in 1 vol. oct—[2]

If you object to publishing the work at your own risk—would you undertake it on the Author's account?—

I am Gentlemen
Your obdt. hmble. Servt.
C Brontë

Address
Revd P Brontë
Haworth Bradford—Yorkshire

MS BPM Bon 169. W & S 227.
Address: not in MS.
PM: not in MS.
Annotation in unknown hand: N° 1

1. In ch. 14 of the *Life* Mrs Gaskell writes: 'The publishers to whom [CB] finally made a successful application for the production of "Currer, Ellis, and Acton Bell's poems," were Messrs. Aylott and Jones, Paternoster-row. Mr. Aylott has kindly placed the letters which she wrote to him on the subject at my disposal.' (i. 337.) Shorter added a note on the publishers, whom he describes as 'two young men . . . booksellers and stationers rather than publishers' in *Shorter* i. 320, where he quotes a letter from Mr Aylott's daughter, Mrs Martyn, describing her father's 'business life'. It is inaccurate in its references to CB, but useful as a personal account of the publisher:

   It is so many years since he died (1872) and many more years since his connection with Charlotte Brontë—for I was quite a young girl when he used to tell us about her, and how she would make a three days' journey from the Yorkshire Moors to come and see him about her books. I believe it was only her poems that my father published, for he refused her novels, as he was rather old-fashioned and had very narrow views regarding light literature, so that

> he suggested that she should take them to Messrs. Smith and Elder. My father much preferred publishing classical and theological books, and the enclosed list is the only one I have, showing some of his publications. He commenced business in 1828 in Chancery Lane, and from there he went to 8 Paternoster Row. Mr. Jones was his partner for a few years . . . that partnership was dissolved and the firm was Aylott and Co., as another partner was taken in, though not having his name known. After that my brother was made partner and the firm was then Aylott and Son until my father retired in 1866. (*Shorter* i. 320 n. 1.)

There is no evidence that CB ever met Aylott, and her first novel was not sent to Smith, Elder until it had been the round of 6 other publishers. Possibly Mrs Martyn was recalling the transfer of the *Poems* to Smith, Elder in 1848. Aylott and Jones published the first number of *The Germ: Thoughts towards Nature in Poetry, Literature, and Art* for D. G. Rossetti and his Pre-Raphaelite colleagues in Jan. 1850. By 1855 the firm had become 'Aylott & Co', booksellers and publishers. (See Hodson's *Booksellers, Publishers and Stationers Directory* 1855 (repr. in fascimile for the Oxford Bibliographical Society; Oxford, 1972), 67.) Mr Aylott allowed Mrs Gaskell to use CB's letters to the firm in the *Life* ch. 14, where she describes Charlotte's 'generous and full confidence, not misplaced, in the thorough probity of Messrs. Aylott and Jones'. (*Life* i. 339.) Their preference for publishing theological works is evident in the *Publishers' Circular*; e.g. in May 1846 they produced *Six Lectures on the Importance and Practicability of Christian Union, chiefly in relation to the Movements of the Evangelical Alliance* by J. Aldis, and in Jan. 1846 *Thirty-Six Nonconformist Sonnets* by a Young Englander; in Mar. *Notes on the Epistle to the Thessalonians* by A. Barnes.

2. In her 'Biographical Notice of Ellis and Acton Bell', prefixed to her edn. of her sisters' *WH* and *AG* in Sept. 1850, CB explained how the decision to publish came about:

> About five years ago, my two sisters and myself, after a somewhat prolonged period of separation, found ourselves reunited, and at home . . . formerly we used to show each other what we wrote, but of late years this habit of communication and consultation had been discontinued; hence it ensued, that we were mutually ignorant of the progress we might respectively have made.
>
> One day, in the autumn of 1845, I accidentally lighted on a MS. volume of verse in my sister Emily's handwriting. Of course, I was not surprised, knowing that she could and did write verse: I looked it over, and something more than surprise seized me,—a deep conviction that these were not common effusions, nor at all like the poetry women generally write. I thought them condensed and terse, vigorous and genuine. To my ear, they had also a peculiar music—wild, melancholy, and elevating.
>
> My sister Emily was not a person of demonstrative character, nor one, on the recesses of whose mind and feelings, even those nearest and dearest to her could, with impunity, intrude unlicensed; it took hours to reconcile her to the discovery I had made, and days to persuade her that such poems merited publication. I knew, however, that a mind like hers could not be without some latent spark of honourable ambition, and refused to be discouraged in my attempts to fan that spark to flame.
>
> Meantime, my younger sister quietly produced some of her own compositions, intimating that since Emily's had given me pleasure, I might like to look at hers. I could not but be a partial judge, yet I thought that these verses too had a sweet sincere pathos of their own.
>
> We had very early cherished the dream of one day becoming authors. This dream, never relinquished even when distance divided and absorbing tasks occupied us, now suddenly acquired strength and consistency: it took the character of a resolve. We agreed to arrange a small selection of our poems, and, if possible, get them printed . . .
>
> The bringing out of our little book was hard work. As was to be expected, neither we nor our poems were at all wanted; but for this we had been prepared at the outset; though inexperienced ourselves, we had read the experience of others. The great puzzle lay in the difficulty of getting answers of any kind from the publishers to whom we applied. Being greatly harassed by this obstacle, I ventured to apply to the Messrs Chambers, of Edinburgh, for a word of advice; *they* may have forgotten the circumstance, but *I* have not, for from them I received a brief and business-like but, civil and sensible reply, on which we acted, and at last made a way.

As Mrs Gaskell found, Mr Robert Chambers 'had entirely forgotten the application which had been made to him and his brother for advice; nor had they any copy or memorandum of the correspondence'. (*Life* i. 336.)

In her letter to W. S. Williams of Sept. 1848 CB recalled that Emily's poems had stirred her heart 'like the sound of a trumpet when [she] read them alone and in secret'. (MS BL Ashley 164; W & S 392.)

To Margaret Wooler, 30 January 1846

[Haworth]

My dear Miss Wooler

I have not yet paid my usual visit to Brookroyd—it is indeed more than a year since I was there, but I frequently hear from Ellen and she did not fail to tell me that you were gone into Worcestershire,[1] she was unable however to give me your exact address—had I known it I should have written to you long since.

I thought you would wonder how we were getting on when you heard of the Railway Panic[2] and you may be sure that I am very glad to be able to answer your kind enquiries by an assurance that our small capital is as yet undiminished. The York and N. Midland[3] is, as you say, a very good line—yet I confess to you I should wish, for my own part, to be wise in time—I cannot think that even the very best lines will continue for many years at their present premiums and I have been most anxious for us to sell our shares ere it be too late—and <inve> to secure the proceeds in some safer if, for the present, less profitable—, investment. I cannot however persuade my Sisters to regard the affair precisely from my point of view and I feel as if I would rather run the risk of loss than hurt Emily's feelings by acting in direct opposition to her opinion—she managed in a most handsome and able manner for me when I was at Brussels and prevented by distance from looking after my own interests—therefore I will let her manage still and take the consequences. Disinterested and energetic she certainly is and if she be not quite so tractable or open to conviction as I could wish I must remember perfection is not the lot of humanity and as long as we can regard those we love and to whom we are closely allied, with profound and never-shaken esteem, it is a small thing that they should vex us occasionally by, what appear to us, unreasonable and headstrong notions. You my dear Miss Wooler know full as well as I do the value of sisters' affection[4] to each other; there is nothing like it in this world, I believe, when they are nearly equal in age and similar in education, tastes and sentiments.

You ask about Branwell; he never thinks of seeking employment and I begin to fear that he has rendered himself incapable of filling any respectable station in life, besides, if money were at his disposal[5] he would use it only to his own injury—the faculty of self-government is, I fear almost destroyed in him You ask me if I do not think that men are strange beings—I do indeed, I have often thought so—and I think too that the mode of bringing them up i[s] strange, they are not half sufficiently guarded from temptation—Girls are protected as if they were something very frail and silly indeed while boys are turned loose on the world as if they—of all beings in existence, were the wisest and the least liable to be led astray.

I am glad you like Bromsgrove,[6] though I daresay there are few places you would not like with Mrs Moore for a companion. I always feel a peculiar satisfaction when I hear of your enjoying yourself because it proves to me that there is really such a thing as retributive justice even in this world—You worked hard, you denied yourself all pleasure, almost all relaxation in your youth and the prime of your life—now you are free—and that while you have still, I hope, many years of vigour and health in which you can enjoy freedom—Besides I have another and very egotistical motive for being pleased—it seems that even "a lone woman"[7] can be happy, as well as cherished wives and proud mothers—I am glad of that—I speculate much on the existence of unmarried and never-to-be married women nowadays and I have already got to the point of considering that there is no more respectable character on this earth than an u[n]married woman who makes her own way through life quietly pers[e]veringly—without support of husband or brother and who having attained the age of 45 or upwards—retains in her possession a well-regulated mind—a disposition to enjoy simple pleasures—fortitude to support inevitable pains, sym[p]athy with the sufferings of others & willingness to relieve want as far as her means extend—

I once had the pleasure of seeing Mrs Moore at Rouse-Mill[8]—will you offer her my respectful remembrances—I wish to send this letter off by today's post I must therefore conclude in haste—Believe me My dear Miss Wooler

Yours most affectionately
C Brontë

Write to me again when you have time—

MS Fitzwilliam. W & S 224.
Address: not in MS.
PM: not in MS.

1. Margaret Wooler was staying with Mrs Moore in Bromsgrove, Worcs. She may have been a relative or friend of Margaret Wooler's parents, who named their eldest son William Moore Wooler.
2. 'Towards the close of 1845, the whole of England was much disturbed by an unwholesome extension of railway enterprise, which ended in a panic and an alarming crash.' 788 schemes, many of them bubble companies, had been lodged with the Board of Trade by 30 Nov. 1845,

and many fraudulent speculators absconded, leaving shareholders impoverished or destitute. See [Robert Wilson] *The Life and Times of Queen Victoria* (4 vols.; n.d. [?1902]), i. 199–201. There had been a series of scandals: the subscription contract for the Dublin–Galway Railway had contained 'the names of entirely fictitious persons to the tune of half a million pounds.' A London and York line promoted by rivals of the York and North Midland line produced a subscription list which was shown to have 'nearly £30,000 worth of shares . . . signed for by persons who could not be found and another £45,000 by persons who did not have the means to pay for it'. (O. S. Nock, *The Great Northern Railway* (1958), 9–10.)

3. Opened in 1839, the line had by this time been extended to link with the North Midlands Railway, making possible rail travel from York to London. See MW 23.4.1845 n. 2.
4. For Margaret Wooler's sisters, see CB to Mrs Franks May 1831 n. 6.
5. Eventually very small sums of money had to be doled out to Branwell. See his note to John Brown of ?June 1848 where he asks Brown to get him 'Five pence worth of Gin' and promises to repay him 'Punctualy at Half-past Nine in the morning . . . out of a shilling given me then'.
6. A market-town about 11 miles south-west of Birmingham, described in *Dugdale* 291 as 'a large but dirty place, full of shops, and manufactories of needles, nails, sheeting, and other coarse linen. In the principal street are some good houses, while many of the more ancient buildings are wood, strangely decorated with black stripes, and other unusual ornaments, the effect of which is extremely grotesque.'
7. Caroline Helstone is more pessimistic about the lot of 'Old Maids' in *Shirley* ch. 10, written in 1848–9.
8. The Wooler family home and corn mill in Batley. See EN ?early 1837, n. 7.

To Messrs Aylott and Jones, 31 January 1846

[Haworth]

Gentlemen

Since you agree to undertake the publication of the work respecting which I applied to you—I should wish now to know as soon as possible the cost of paper and printing, I will then send the necessary remittance together with the manuscript.

I should like it to be printed in 1 octavo volume of the same quality of paper and size of type as Moxon's last edition of Wordsworth.[1] The poems will occupy—I should think from 200 to 250 pages. They are not the production of a Clergyman[2] nor are they exclusively of a religious character—but I presume these circumstances will be immaterial—

It will perhaps be necessary that you should see the manuscript in order to calculate accurately the expense of publication—in that case—I will send it immediately—I should like however previously to have some idea of the probable Cost—and if from what I have said—you can make a rough calculation on the subject—I should be greatly obliged to you

I remain Gentlemen
Yr obdt Servt
C Brontë

Address as before
Revd P Brontë
Haworth
Bradford
Yorkshire

MS BPM Bon 170. W & S 228.
Address: not in MS.
PM: not in MS.
Annotation: <N° 2>

1. Edward Moxon (1801–58) had worked for Longmans, but started his own publishing business in 1830. Himself a verse-writer, he published the work of many famous poets, including some of the work of Tennyson and Browning. Wordsworth's poems were published by Moxon from 1836: vols. i and ii of a heavily revised collected edn., *The Poetical Works of William Wordsworth*, appeared in 1836, vols. iii–vi in 1837; *Poems Chiefly of Early and Late Years* (vol. vii) was added in 1842, and the carefully revised collection of 1845 was in one vol., 'royal octavo', printed in double columns. G. D. Hargreaves writes: 'If [CB] had in mind Wordsworth's *Poems* (1845), a "royal octavo" (with a leaf size of about 10 in. x $6\frac{1}{4}$ in.) of over 600 pages, it would not be surprising that this proved unsuitable for the size and scale of the Bells' *Poems* which Charlotte considerably overestimated.' ('The Publishing of "Poems by Currer, Ellis and Acton Bell" ', *BST* 15. 79. 294–300.)
2. Aylott and Jones, with their preference for religious works, might have assumed this from the address. CB explains the decision to use pseudonyms in her preface to the 1850 edn. of *WH* and *AG*:

> Averse to personal publicity, we veiled our own names under those of Currer, Ellis, and Acton Bell; the ambiguous choice being dictated by a sort of conscientious scruple at assuming Christian names positively masculine, while we did not like to declare ourselves women, because—without at that time suspecting that our mode of writing and thinking was not what is called 'feminine'—we had a vague impression that authoresses are liable to be looked on with prejudice; we had noticed how critics sometimes use for their chastisement the weapon of personality, and for their reward, a flattery, which is not true praise. (See Clarendon *WH*, appendix I, 436.)

To Ellen Nussey, [?5 February 1846]

[Haworth]

Dear Ellen

I got a note from Hunsworth[1] yesterday—inquiring after Mary's letter which it appears has never yet reached Mrs Burnley[2]—would you have the goodness to brush up the Miss Cockills[3] about it—What can they be doing? they must have had it a month—Give my love to your Mother & [Sisters and write]

[Signature cut off]

MS Beinecke, Yale. Unpublished.
Address: not in MS.
PM: not in MS.

Annotation by ?EN in ink: Feb 5–46
Date: CB had read Mary Taylor's letter sometime between 30.12.1845 and 23.1.1846, as her letters of those dates show, giving a date in Feb. for the present letter to allow for the Cockills' keeping it for a month. The paper used is the same as that of Aylott 31.1.1846 and 6.2.1846, and EN's date of 5 Feb. is therefore not unlikely.
Text: Last line of text partly visible.

1. Mary Taylor's letters would have begun their circuit at her brothers' house.
2. Probably Mrs Thomas Burnley of Pollard Hall, next door to the Taylors' former home, the Red House, Gomersal. She was the wife of a worsted manufacturer, and a friend of the Taylors and Nusseys, as EN's references in her 1844 Diary show.
3. Hannah, Sarah, and Elizabeth Cockill, who had a school at Oakwell Hall, near Birstall. See MT to EN ?July 1842, n. 6.

To Messrs Aylott and Jones, 6 February 1846

[Haworth]

Gentlemen

I send you the M.S. as you desired.[1]

You will perceive that the Poems are the work of three persons[2]—relatives—their separate pieces are distinguished by their respective signatures—

I am Gentlemen
Yrs. truly
C Brontë

Feby. 6th. / 46
I am obliged to send it in two parcels on account of the weight[3]—

MS BPM Bon 171. W & S 229.
Address: not in MS.
PM: not in MS.
Annotation: N° 3

1. The MS sent to the publishers does not survive. See D. Roper, 'The Revision of Emily Brontë's Poems of 1846', *The Library* 6th ser., 6.2 (June 1984), 153–67. Roper points out that 'we do possess the holograph manuscripts from which Emily Brontë's poems were apparently transcribed to make her share of the copy', and that Emily probably revised and copied out her own poems for the printer.
2. The *Poems* consist of 21 poems by Emily, 21 by Anne (signed 'Ellis' and 'Acton' respectively), and 19 by Charlotte (signed 'Currer') including the long three-part poem 'Gilbert'. Most are arranged so that a poem by Currer is followed by one each by Ellis and Acton.
3. G. D. Hargreaves notes that 'The complete manuscript must have exceeded the 16 oz. postal maximum then in force'. ('The Publishing of "Poems by Currer, Ellis and Acton Bell" ', *BST* 15. 79. 295.) John Greenwood of Haworth (1807–63) told Mrs Gaskell that he began about 1843 to 'do a little in the stationery line . . . [The Brontë sisters] used to buy a great deal of writing paper, and I used to wonder whatever they did with so much . . . they seemed so distressed about it, if I had none. I have walked to Halifax (a distance of 10 miles) many a time, for half a ream of paper, for fear of being without it when they came.' (*Life* i. 336.)

To Ellen Nussey, [?13 February 1846]

[Haworth]

Dear Ellen,

Will it suit you if I come to Brookroyd next Wednesday, and stay till the Wednesday after;[1] if convenient tell me so at once and fix your own time. Is there a coach from Bradford to Birstall on Wednesday.[2] If so, do you know what time it leaves Bradford? I should be there at the Talbot about 4.30 p.m.[3]

[Unsigned]

MS untraced. Envelope BPM B.S. 104/13. W & S 225.
Address (envelope): Miss Ellen Nussey | Brookroyd | Birstal | Leeds
PM: (i) HAWORTH (ii) BRADFORD YORKS | FE 13 | 1846 | C (iii) LEEDS | FE—3 | 1846 | F
Annotation on envelope by EN in pencil: Feb 3 — 46. Wafer: blue lozenge with the words 'Si je puis' (If I can) within a line border.
Date: based on postmarks, appropriate wafer, and content, supported by the date 'Feb. 13th, 46' in *Nussey*.
Text: *Nussey* 138; *Shorter* 175 and W & S 225 substantially as *Nussey*.
Not in *Life* or *Hours at Home*.

1. The two Wednesdays after Friday 13 Feb. were 18 and 25 Feb., but CB was to stay 'a day or two longer', returning home on 2 Mar. See EN 3.3.1846 and EJB to EN 25.2.1846.
2. *Shorter* and W & S read 'Wednesday?'
3. 4.30 p.m. was 'the time the Mail-Coach arrives from Keighley', as CB explained in EN 4.3.1844. The 'Talbot' was a 'fine and well-conducted inn' in the Kirkgate, Bradford. See EN 4.3.1844 n. 2.

To Messrs Aylott and Jones, 15 February 1846

[Haworth]

Gentlemen

I sent the Manuscript in two parcels[1]—by Post—on Satdy. 7th. inst.—I should be obliged to you if you would send me a line to intimate whether it came safe to hand

I am Gentlemen
Yrs truly
C Brontë

MS BPM Bon 172. W & S 230.
Address: not in MS.
PM: not in MS.
Annotation: N° 4

1. See Aylott 6.2.1846.

To Messrs Aylott and Jones, 16 February 1846

[Haworth]

Gentlemen

I have received yours of the 13th. inst. The M.S. will certainly form a thinner vol. than I had anticipated—I cannot name another Model which I should like it precisely to resemble—yet I think a duodecimo[1] form and a somewhat reduced—though still clear type would be preferable—

It appears to me that if I were to refer the choice of type and size to your own judgment and experience—you would be better able to decide on what was suitable—I only stipulate for clear type—not too small—and good paper.

You have, I presume, received both the parcels—I was obliged to divide the M.S. on account of the weight

I am Gentlemen
Yrs truly
C Brontë

MS BPM Bon 173. W & S 231.
Address: not in MS.
PM: not in MS.
Annotation: N° 5

1. G. D. Hargreaves suggests that CB used the term 'loosely as indicating "rather small" . . . in the event the book was produced comfortably as a "foolscap octavo" (leaf size about $6\frac{3}{4}$ in. x $4\frac{1}{4}$ in.) with 165 pages of text, as opposed to the 200–250 estimated by Charlotte'. ('The Publishing of "Poems by Currer, Ellis and Acton Bell" ', *BST* 15. 79. 296.) Possibly CB had not yet acquired the practical handbook described by Mrs Gaskell: 'If the volume was to be published at their own risk, it was necessary that the sister conducting the negotiation should make herself acquainted with the different kinds of type, and the various sizes of books. Accordingly she bought a small volume, from which to learn all she could on the subject of preparation for the press.' (*Life* i. 339.)

To Messrs Aylott and Jones, 21 February 1846

[?Birstall][1]

Gentlemen

I select the long primer type[2] for the poems—I do not think it would be necessary to adopt a stouter paper nor would lines round the pages be required.

The remittance of £31—10s[3]—shall be made in a few days—

I am Gentlemen
Yrs truly
C Brontë

MS Princeton, Parrish Collection. Noted but not printed on W & S ii. 83.
Address: not in MS.
PM: not in MS.
Annotation: none. Not included in the numbered sequence of Aylott letters.

1. If CB went to Birstall on 18 Feb. as she planned, she must have written from there.
2. 'A size between Small Pica and Bourgeois, of 89 ems to a foot.' (*OED*.) Approximately the modern 10 pt. size. Aylott and Jones may have sent CB a type specimen, or she may have acquired the manual referred to by Mrs Gaskell. See previous letter, n. 1.
3. Aylott and Jones's estimate for the cost of paper and printing. CB paid another £5 on 25 May when the exact costs had been worked out. See Aylott 7 and 25 May 1846, notes.

Emily Brontë to Ellen Nussey, 25 February 1846

Haworth.

Dear Miss Ellen,

I fancy this note will be too late to decide one way or the other with respect to Charlotte's stay—yours only came this morning (Wedensday) and unless mine travels faster you will not receive it till Friday—Papa, of course misses C and will be glad to have her back. Anne and I ditto—but as she goes from home so seldom you may keep her a day or two longer if your eloquence is equal to the task of persuading her—that is if she be still with you when you get this permission[1]

love from Anne Yours truly E. J. Bronte

MS Harvard FMS Eng 870(98). W & S 226.
Address: not in MS.
PM: not in MS.

1. EN ?13.2.1846 shows that CB had planned to stay with EN from 18 to 25 Feb., the date of this letter. Perhaps she took her family's permission for granted, since she did not return until 2 Mar. See EN 3.3.1846.

To Messrs Aylott and Jones, 3 March 1846

[Haworth]

Gentlemen

I send a draft for £31—10s—being the amount of your Estimate—

I suppose there is nothing now to prevent your immediately commencing the printing of the work—When you acknowledge the receipt of the draft—will you state how soon it will be completed—

I am Gentlemen
Yrs truly
C Brontë

MS BPM Bon 174. W & S 232.
Address: not in MS.
PM: not in MS.
Annotation: N° 6

To Ellen Nussey, 3 March [1846]

[Haworth]

Dear Ellen

I reached home a little after 2 o'clock all safe and right[1]—yesterday—I found papa very well—his sight much the same—Emily & Anne were gone to Keighley to meet me—unfortunately I had returned by the old road[2] while they were gone by the new—and we missed each other—they did not get home till ½ past 4—and were caught in the heavy shower of rain which fell in the afternoon—I am sorry to say Anne has taken a little cold in consequence—but I hope she will soon be well—

Papa was much cheered by my report of Mr Carr's opinion[3] and of old Mrs Elam's[4] experience—but I could perceive he caught gladly at the idea of deferring the operation a few months longer.

I went into the room where Branwell[5] was to speak to him about an hour after I got home—it was very forced work to address him—I might have spared myself the trouble as he took no notice & made no reply—he was stupified—My fears were not vain Emily tells me that he got a sovereign from Papa while I have been away under pretence of paying a pressing debt—he went immediately & changed it at a public-house—and has employed it as was to be expected—she concluded her account with saying he was "a hopeless being"—it is too true—In his present state it is scarcely possible to stay in the room where he is—what the future has in store—I do not know—

I hope ** Mercy and Miss Bradbury[6] ** got home without any wet—Give my best love to your Mother & Sisters—let me hear from you on Thursday if possible

Believe me dear Nell
Yours faithfully
C B—

MS BPM Bon 175. W & S 233.
Address: not in MS.
PM: not in MS.

1. See EJB to EN 25.2.1846.
2. Beatrice E. Stanley suggests that the new road was 'the present direct road between Haworth and Keighley' and the old road 'possibly by way of Low Bridge and Park Lane, Keighley, and Hainworth Shay, to the cross roads on Cradle Edge, near the Guide Inn (Gaumless), and so by Barcroft to Cross Roads'. ('Changes at Haworth', *BST* 10. 54. 222–4.)

3. CB had sought medical opinion on the treatment of her father's cataracts. See her next letter. William Carr (1784–1861) and his sons are listed in Edward Baines's *History, Directory and Gazetteer, of the County of York* (1823), i. 509 as Surgeons, of Little Gomersal. The *Provincial Medical Directory* for 1847 gives no medical qualifications, noting that Carr was 'In Practice prior to the Act of 1815'. He is described by H. A. Cadman as 'to some extent eccentric in his ways, but clever in his profession'. (*Gomersal Past and Present* (Leeds, 1930), 121. His wife was Sarah Nussey of White Lee (1791–1864), EN's first cousin.
4. Probably 'the wife of Benoni Elam, who had kept the school which Ellen Nussey attended as a pupil.' (John T. M. Nussey, 'Notes on the Background of Three Incidents in the Lives of the Brontës', *BST* 15. 79. 335.)
5. 'In truth when I fall back on myself I suffer so mu[ch wre]tchedness that I cannot withstand any temptation to get out of myself.' (BB to J. B. Leyland, ?28.4.1846.)
6. The Bradburys were friends of the Nusseys and Taylors. See MT to EN 30.10 and 1.11.1842, and MT to EN 25.6.1843, *Stevens* letter 11.

To Eliza Jane Kingston,[1] *[?3 March 1846]*

[Haworth]

My dear Cousin

I should have answered your last kind note before but I have been a few weeks from home since I received it—now however on my return I will not delay a day replying to it.

You ask after papa's sight and wish to be informed whether he has yet undergone an operation—not yet—nor can he—for some months to come—During my absence from home I consulted an experienced surgeon[2] on papa's case—he did not doubt from what I said that an operation well performed would be successful—but advised delay as the cataract is not yet sufficiently hardened—meantime Papa's general health is very good—for which we ought to be, and I hope—are thankful.

Mr Branwell[3] wrote to inform us of his son's death[4]—it was indeed a distressing event for all more especially for my poor Aunt 'Charlotte'—when you write again tell me how She continues to support the affliction—I think Mr Branwell said that another of his sons[5] was at Sea and that they had received no tidings of him for some time—under such circumstances suspense must be doubly distressing to his parents—I remember no winter which can bear comparison in point of mildness with the one <we have> now leaving us—we have never had any snow[6] in Yorkshire except for a few days in November—and a slight sprinkling at the commencement of Feby which was gone in two or three hours—I hope the mild temperature has agreed with my Aunt Kingston[7] and yourself also.

Have you sold the shares you intended to dispose of—we are still frequently advised to get out of the Railroads before it is too late—but really the Y & N Midland[8]—as yet seems to present no signs of falling off to warrant selling out on the contrary it appears full as prosperous as ever—I shall be glad to hear from you again—

Believe me yr affecte Cousin C Brontë

MS BPM B.S. 56. *BST* 12. 64. 299.
Address: not in MS.
PM: not in MS.
Date: The date at the top of fol. 1^{r}, 'Feby 6th | 46' may be in CB's hand, but is in a darker ink than the rest of the letter; perhaps she had dated but not completed it before going to Brookroyd from ?18 Feb. to 2 Mar., the period when she 'consulted an experienced surgeon on papa's case'.

1. Elizabeth (Eliza) Jane Kingston (1808–78), one of CB's cousins, then living in Penzance. She was the fifth child of CB's Aunt Jane, née Branwell (1773–1855) and John Kingston (?1768–1824), a Methodist preacher who had 'fallen from grace' and who was expelled from the Methodist Connexion in 1807. The family emigrated, and Eliza was born in Baltimore, Maryland, where her father had become a bookseller and publisher. Jane Kingston left her husband in Apr. 1809 and brought Eliza, as a baby of 10 months, back to Penzance. For Eliza's gradual decline into extreme poverty, owing to the failure of various ventures and of her Cornish mining shares, see F. E. Ratchford, 'The Loneliness of a Brontë Cousin', *BST* 13. 67. 100–10.
2. William Carr of Gomersal. See previous letter.
3. Joseph Branwell (1789–1857), a cousin of the Brontës' mother, who had married his cousin Charlotte Branwell (1791–1848), CB's aunt. They were married on 29 Dec. 1812, the day of Patrick and Maria Brontë's marriage. He may be the Joseph Branwell, master of a day-school in Queen Street, Penzance, named in Pigot and Co., *National Commercial Directory* [for] Bedfordshire . . . Cornwall etc. (London, 1830).
4. Joseph Branwell, lost at sea early in 1846.
5. William Branwell, who later became a clerk in the General Post Office and died at Battersea, London in 1876. cf. CB to EJK 8.5.1846. There was also a son named Charles Henry Branwell, who is said to have been a midshipman. See C. W. Hatfield, 'The Relatives of Maria Branwell', *BST* 9. 49. 251.
6. *Shackleton* records a 'moderate' Nov. with no snow, and 7 days of snow or frost in an otherwise wet Dec. He sums up Jan. as 'wet, and very open and mild', Feb. as 'exceeding fine'. He confirms CB's observation that there was a little snow and frost from 8 to 10 Feb.—an additional proof that this letter must have been written after 6 Feb.
7. Eliza's mother, Jane Kingston.
8. George Hudson's York and North Midland line was prospering. In 1845 permission had been given for a new branch line from Church Fenton to Harrogate, and an additional application to construct 'a more direct line between York and Leeds', put forward in the same year, would be granted on 26 June 1846. For the railway panic, see MW 30.1.1846 n. 2.

To Messrs Aylott and Jones, 11 March 1846

[Haworth]

Gentlemen

I have received the Proof Sheet and return it corrected.

If there is any doubt at all about the printer's competency[1] to correct errors I would prefer submitting each sheet to the inspection of the Authors—because such a mistake for instance as tumbling stars instead of trembling[2] would suffice to throw an air of absurdity over a whole poem—but if you know from experience that he is to be relied on—I would trust to your assurance on the subject and leave the task of correction to him—as I know that a considerable saving both of time and trouble would be thus effected—

The Printing and Paper[3] appear to me satisfactory—of course I wish to have the work out as soon as possible—but I am still more anxious that it should be got up in a manner creditable to the Publishers and agreeable to the Authors.

I am Gentlemen
Yrs truly
C Brontë

MS BPM Bon 176. W & S 234.
Address: not in MS.
PM: not in MS.
Annotation: N° 7

1. The printer was John Hasler of Crane Court, Fleet Street. Four errors that eluded his and the authors' vigilance were listed in an *errata* slip inserted in the early copies. G. D. Hargreaves comments on these errors and other possible inaccuracies in 'The Publishing of "Poems by Currer, Ellis and Acton Bell" ', *BST* 15. 79. 296–7. See also D. Roper, 'The Revision of Emily Brontë's Poems of 1846', *The Library*, 6th ser., 6.2 (June 1984), 153–67.
2. See l. 22 of CB's 'Pilate's wife's dream', the first poem in the collection.
3. The printing and layout are clear, with generous margins, and the 'foolscap octavo' format accommodates 29 lines of text. G. D. Hargreaves points out that the ' "leading" or extra spacing between the lines of text' makes for easy reading. The paper is unwatermarked wove, 'inferior to that used in the first editions of *Jane Eyre* and *Shirley*, but it has lasted reasonably well'. ('Publishing of "Poems" ', *BST* 15. 79. 296.)

To Messrs Aylott and Jones, 13 March 1846

[Haworth]

Gentlemen

I return you the 2nd. Proof—The Authors have finally decided that they would prefer having all the proofs—sent to them in turn but you need not enclose the M.S. as they can correct the errors from memory[1]—

I am Gentlemen
Yrs truly
C Brontë

MS BPM Bon 177. W & S 235.
Address: not in MS.
PM: not in MS.
Annotation: N° 8

1. If Aylott and Jones did cease to send the MS, correcting from memory as well as deliberate revisions may account for some of the discrepancies between the surviving manuscripts and

the printed texts. For a discussion, see the articles cited in Aylott 11.3.46 n. 1; for variants in CB's poems see Neufeldt *CBP*, and for those in AB's poems, see Chitham *ABP* notes and appendix II. See also G.D. Hargreaves, 'The poems of Ellis Bell: the version printed in 1846 and the manuscript version', *BST* 21.3.49–62.

To Messrs Aylott and Jones, 28 March 1846

[Haworth]

Gentlemen

As the proofs have hitherto always come safe to hand—under the direction of C Brontë Esqre.—I have not thought it necessary to request you to change it, but a little mistake[1] having occurred yesterday—I think it will be better to send them to me in future under my real address which is

Miss Brontë

Revd P Brontë's &c,

I am Gentlemen

Yrs truly

C B—

MS BPM Bon 178. W & S 236.
Address: not in MS.
PM: not in MS.
Annotation: N° 9

1. See BB to JBL ?28.4.1846 and notes for the slight possibility that Branwell Brontë, who would be addressed as '— Brontë Esqre', had seen evidence of his sisters' literary transactions.

To Ellen Nussey, 31 March [1846]

[Haworth]

Dear Ellen

I begin to feel somewhat uneasy about your long silence[1]—Is all well at *Brookroyd? I have sometimes feared your Mother is worse, for the late sharp change in the weather[2] has been a most trying one for many weak & elderly persons about here—Our poor old servant Tabby[3] had a sort of fit a fortnight since but is <real> nearly recovered now—Martha[4] is ill with a swelling in her knee and obliged to go home—I fear it will be some time before she will be in working condition again—

I received the number of the Record[5] you sent—and despatched it forwards to Mr Young[6] &c. am I right? I read D'Aubignés[7] letter it is clever and in what he says about Catholicism[8] very good—the evangelical alliance[9] part is not very practicable yet certainly it is more in accordance with the spirit of the Gospel to preach unity amongst Christians than to inculcate mutual intolerance & hatred—

I have no news to tell you and I only scribble these few lines to entreat you to write to me immediately—

Any visits from Hunsworth lately? I begin to be anxious to hear again from Mary *Taylor the papers speak of letters received from N Zealand dated Novbr.—I sent you a French Newspaper yesterday

Good Morning

Love to all
March 31st.— C Brontë

I am very glad I went to Brookroyd when I did for the changed weather has somewhat changed my strength & health since—how do you get on? I long for mild south & west winds. I am thankful papa continues pretty well—though often made very miserable in mind by Branwell's wretched conduct—there—there is no change but for the worse—

MS HM 24443. W & S 237.
Address: not in MS.
PM: not in MS.

1. CB had last written (unless letters are missing) on 3 Mar. requesting a speedy reply.
2. This is confirmed by *Shackleton*, who records mainly rain or cloud up to 15 Mar., followed by frost, snow, sleet, and a little rain with a few fine days. He describes Mar. as 'seasonable'.
3. Tabitha Aykroyd was 75 years old. After a previous absence due to illness, she had returned to the parsonage sometime before 29 May 1843, and was in good health when EJB wrote her Diary Paper of [31].7.1845.
4. Martha Brown (1828–80), the young servant who now did most of the household work.
5. A Church of England newspaper published from 1828 to 1948. In *The Religion of the Heart* (Oxford, 1979) Elisabeth Jay describes *The Record* as militantly activist and ultra-Tory, firmly pro-Establishment and (in its early days) fanatically anti-Papist and with a tendency towards Calvinism. It 'was on the left wing' of the Evangelicals. (68.) Henry Nussey quotes at length from it in a journal kept in 1848. (WYAS Sheepscar, Leeds.)
6. Not identified.
7. Jean Henri Merle D'Aubigné (1794–1872), a Swiss pastor and historian. He was the pastor of the French Protestant Church at Hamburg from 1818 to 1823, a court preacher in Brussels from 1823 to 1830, and Professor of Church History in Geneva from 1830. He wrote *Histoire de la réformation au XVIe siècle* (5 vols.; Paris 1835–53.) He visited England on several occasions. He taught that the Church was 'not the clergy . . . [but] the Christian people'. See Marion J. Phillips, 'Charlotte Brontë and the Priesthood of All Believers', *BST* 20. 3. 145–55. CB had read D'Aubigné's long letter 'To the Right Rev. the Bishop of Chester', dated London, 28 July 1845, published in *The Record* for 12.3.1846, 3, cols. 3–5.
8. In his letter D'Aubigné gave examples of the continental movement of Catholics away from Rome and towards Evangelicalism, and he deplored what seemed to be a contrary movement in England. The Church of Rome was 'agitating' and its hierarchy showing new vigour: only a strong English Protestant church would avoid the fate of Protestantism in France and elsewhere in the 17th cent. He believed that the English church needed *apostolicity* (depend-

ence on the New Testament and not on the patristic writings), *catholicity*, embracing 'all those who confess the Lord', and *autonomy* or self-government. At present the established church in England was linked with a government which had to fulfil its 'new duties towards Roman Catholics and Dissenters'.

9. D'Aubigné envisaged an international movement of all Evangelical Christians, so that 'the various forms which the unchangeable truth of God' had taken should be united in the single new form. (See Phillips, 'Brontë and the Priesthood' 149.) In his letter D'Aubigné deplored a 'bigoted and sectarian spirit': 'The vocation of the Church is to assemble all the families of the earth in but one family . . . Let us leave sectarian Catholicity to the Greek Church and to the Roman Church.' Some Anglicans and Nonconformists had already joined the proposed Evangelical Alliance, for which a Provisional Committee had been formed by Feb. 1846, and *The Record* devoted a good deal of attention to the arguments for and against it. See e.g. the numbers for 26 Feb., 26 Mar., and 6 Apr.

To Messrs Aylott and Jones, 6 April 1846

[Haworth]

Gentlemen

C. E & A Bell[1] are now preparing for the Press a work of fiction—consisting of three distinct and unconnected tales[2] which may be published either together as a work of 3 vols. of the ordinary novel-size,[3] or separately as single vols—as shall be deemed most advisable.

It is not their intention to publish these tales on their own account.

They direct me to ask you whether you would be disposed to undertake the work[4]—after having of course by due inspection of the M.S. ascertained that its contents are such as to warrant an expectation of success.

An early answer will oblige as in case of your negativing the proposal—inquiry must be made of other Publishers—

I am Gentlemen
Yrs truly
C Brontë

MS BPM Bon 179. W & S 238.
Address: not in MS.
PM: not in MS.
Annotation: N° 10

1. Currer, Ellis, and Acton Bell. For the pseudonyms see Aylott 31.1.1846 n. 2.
2. Emily Brontë's *WH* and Anne Brontë's *AG* would be published together as 3 vols. in Dec. 1847, *AG* being vol. iii. CB's *The Professor* came out in 2 vols., but not until June 1857, after her death. The dates of composition of the 3 works must remain uncertain. The Clarendon editors conclude that the writing of *WH* 'is not likely to have started before October 1845', whereas Anne had begun the 3rd vol. of *Passages in the Life of an Individual* (which may be a version of *AG*) by 31 July 1845. See her Diary Paper of that date. The fair copy manuscript of *The Professor* was complete by 27 June 1846. All 3 novels must have been well on the way to completion by the date of this letter. CB's 'Biographical Notice' to her 1850 edn. of her sisters' works

misleadingly implies that the novels were begun only after the failure of the *Poems*. See Clarendon *WH* appendix I.

3. i.e. the 'three-decker' selling at *31s. 6d.* Henry Curwen notes in *A History of Booksellers* (c.1873–4) the apparently immutable law by which novels of this period 'were required to consist of three volumes of about three hundred pages each'. (293.) See J. A. Sutherland, *Victorian Novelists and Publishers* (1976), 11–18. CB's underestimate of *WH* as material for 1 vol. rather than 2 may mean that Emily had achieved, or planned, a shorter novel than the one we now have.
4. Aylott and Jones were unlikely to publish secular novels. See Aylott 28.1.1846 n. 1.

To Messrs Aylott and Jones, 11 April 1846

[Haworth]

Gentlemen

I beg to thank you in the name of C. E. & A Bell for your obliging offer of advice; I will avail myself of it to request information on two or three points.

It is evident that unknown authors have great difficulties to contend with before they can succeed in bringing their works before the public, can you give me any hint as to the way in which these difficulties are best met. For instance, in the present case, where a work of fiction is in question, in what form would a publisher be most likely to accept the M.S.—? whether offered as a work of 3 vols or as tales which might be published in numbers[1] or as contributions to a periodical?[2]

<is it usual to ?intr> What publishers[3] would be most likely to receive favourably a proposal of this nature?

Would it suffice to write to a publisher on the subject or would it be necessary to have recourse to a personal interview?

Your opinion and advice on these three points or on any other which your experience may suggest as important—would be esteemed by us a favour

I am Gentlemen
Yrs truly
C Brontë

MS BPM Bon 180. W & S 239.
Address: not in MS.
PM: not in MS.
Annotation: N° 11

1. The serial publication of fiction in cheap monthly or weekly parts had been given new prominence in the 1830s, principally by Dickens's use of the method in *Pickwick Papers* (in monthly parts dated Apr. 1836 to Nov. 1837).
2. Dickens's *Oliver Twist* came out in *Bentley's Miscellany* from 1837 to 1839, and CB's much-admired Thackeray had produced mainly pseudonymous fiction in e.g. *The New Monthly Magazine*, *Bentley's Miscellany*, *Ainsworth's Magazine*, *Punch*, and—most frequently—*Fraser's Magazine*, where *The Luck of Barry Lyndon* appeared in 1844.
3. Henry Colburn (d. 1855) and Richard Bentley (1794–1871) dominated the circulating library

fiction market; Bradbury and Evans, the printers of *Pickwick Papers*, had begun publishing in 1844, and the firm of Chapman and Hall was increasingly important from 1836 onwards. Smith, Elder and Co. and T. C. Newby, the Brontës' eventual publishers, must have been included in or added to the list of likely names at some point. See SE 15.7.1847 n. 2, WSW 10.11.1847 n. 8 and CB's letter to Henry Colburn, 4.7.1846.

To Ellen Nussey, 14 April [1846]

[Haworth]

Dear Ellen

I assure you I was very glad indeed to get your last note—for when three or four days elapsed after my second despatch to you and I got no answer, I scarcely doubted there was something wrong—It relieved me much to find my apprehensions unfounded—

I return you Miss R[ingrose]'s notes with thanks—I always like to read them—they appear to me so true an index of an amiable mind and one not too conscious of its own worth—beware of awakening in her this consciousness by undue praise—It is a privelege of simple-hearted—sensible but not brilliant people—that they can be and do good without comparing their own thoughts and actions 'too closely' with those of other people and thence drawing strong food for self-appreciation—Talented people almost always know full well the excellence that is in them—

I am very glad you have seen *George[1]—still the interview must have been a painful one to you in many respects—It disappointed me rather that you mentioned it so briefly—I should have liked more details—what did he say when he first saw you? how did he receive you? Did he give you the idea of being happy?

*Joe *Taylor has performed a good action in the best manner[2]—I cannot but approve of him—it proves that the *Joe *Taylor of 12 years ago still exists within the Joe Taylor of to-day. It was very unfortunate that you were not at *Brookroyd—you should have been there—

You ask if we are more comfortable—I wish I could say anything favourable—but how can we be more comfortable so long as Branwell stays at home and degenerates instead of improving?

It has been lately intimated to him that he would be received again on the same Rail-road where he was formerly stationed[3] if he would behave more steadily but he refuses to make an effort, he will not work[4]—and at home he is a drain on every resource—an impediment to all happiness—But there's no use in complaining—

Give my love to all—
Write again soon
C B—

MS HM 24444. Envelope: BPM B.S. 104/14. W & S 240.
Address (envelope): Miss Ellen Nussey | Brookroyd | Birstal | Leeds
PM: (i) HAWORTH (ii) BRADFORD YORKS | Ap 14 | 1846 | C (iii) L— | AP 14 1846 | F
Annotation (i) in ink by EN on the letter: Ap 14—46 | [in pencil] Branwell "refuses to make an effort, and will not work"; (ii) in pencil on the envelope: Ap 46 | On A's disposition &c. Wafer: yellow rectangle with the words 'Toujours le meme' within a line border.

1. EN must have visited York, where George was still being cared for in Clifton House asylum.
2. CB had hoped Joe Taylor would use his business knowledge to help the Nusseys when George's illness caused difficulties for them. See EN 8.9.1845, ?10.9.1845, and 7.10.1845. The nature of his present 'good action' is unknown.
3. The Manchester and Leeds Railway, which was to become the Lancashire and Yorkshire Railway in July 1847. Since Branwell's dismissal from Luddenden Foot station in Apr. 1842 several new stations had been opened, and the line had 'quickly achieved a high profit level, owing to the density of population along the route'. (*Regional History* viii. 103, 253–4.)
4. Branwell, however, was writing poems again, and by 28 Apr. was gathering information for an ambitious but never to be completed long poem, 'Morley Hall'. See BB to JBL 28.4.1846 and notes.

To Messrs Aylott and Jones, 15 April 1846

[Haworth]

Gentlemen

I have to thank you for your obliging answer to my last; the information[1] you give is of value to us and when the M.S. is completed your suggestions shall be acted on.

There will be no Preface to the Poems—the blank leaf may be filled up by a table of contents[2] which I suppose the Printer will prepare—It appears the volume will be a thinner one than was calculated on—

I am Gentlemen
Yrs truly
C Brontë

MS BPM Bon 181. W & S 241.
Address: not in MS.
PM: not in MS.
Annotation: N° 12

1. See Aylott 11.4.1846 and notes.
2. This was probably printed without proof-correction by the authors. It contains some errors, such as 'The Student's Life 140' instead of 'The Student's Serenade 143'.

To Messrs Aylott and Jones, 20 April 1846

[Haworth]

Gentlemen

When the work is completed will you have the goodness to send me 3 Copies by Post—

I shall then consult with you as to the measures necessary to be taken with regard to advertising—sending copies to Reviewers &c.

I am Gentlemen
Yrs truly
C Brontë

MS BPM Bon 182. W & S 242.
Address: not in MS.
PM: not in MS.
Annotation: N° 13

To Ellen Nussey, 20 April [1846]

[Haworth]

Dear Ellen

I send you the drawing and copy which is Anne's doing[1] Miss R[ingrose]'s letter is the most interesting I have yet seen—but I think when you write again you cannot give her too plain an explanation of the real state of matters—the longer she is suffered to indulge false hopes—the more bitter will be her final disappointment[2]—You said I was to think of you on Monday—why? The 20th. is not your birthday is it?[3] I thought it was the 22nd. I return your kind wishes on that point with interest—

It is to be hoped Mrs. Heald will now have better health[4]—What does Mrs. J. Swaine[5] know about J T[aylor] & I[sabella] N[ussey][6] what are her reasons for incredulity?

I had a very short note from Ellen Taylor[7] last week—she is at Hunsworth Joe Taylor was at Brussels—

No news yet from Mary[8]—

I suppose you have received my last—ere this—it crossed yours

Good bye dear Nell
C B—

MS BPM Bon 200. W & S 243.
Address: not in MS.
PM: not in MS.
Annotation in pencil by EN: includes 'Ap 20—48'.
Date: EN's attribution to 1848 is mistaken: 20 Apr. was a Monday in 1846, a Thursday in 1848. The paper is the same as that used for most of CB's letters to Aylott and Jones in 1846, i.e. an unwatermarked greyish wove sheet approximately 93 mm. x 139 mm with an embossed crown device.

1. For Anne Brontë's interest in drawing, and the skill in copying shown by her and CB, see Jane

Sellars, 'Art and the Artist as Heroine in the Novels of Charlotte, Emily and Anne Brontë', *BST* 20. 2. 72–4, and Christine Alexander and Jane Sellars, *The Art of the Brontës* (Cambridge, 1995).

2. EN and CB must have had grounds for their belief that George Nussey would never be well enough to marry Amelia Ringrose.
3. EN's birthday is usually given as 22 Apr., but the Nussey collection at WYAS Sheepscar, Leeds, includes doggerel verses by ?R. N. Chapman Jnr. entitled 'My birthday', probably copied by EN, and dated 'Ap 20th 1837'. CB's birthday was 21 Apr.
4. Mary Heald, née Carr (b. 1811) wife of the Revd W. M. Heald (1803–75) Vicar of Birstall, who had married on 23 Apr. 1844, as EN noted in *Diary* 1844.
5. See EN 25.3.1844 n.4.
6. cf. EN 24.4.1845, where Joe Taylor is said to be paying 'assiduous attention' to the (probably wealthy) Isabella, EN's cousin; but see also EN 26.8.1846.
7. An orphaned cousin of the Taylors of Gomersal and Hunsworth. See CB to M. Dixon 16.10.1843 n. 8.
8. Mary Taylor.

To Ellen Nussey, 25 April [1846]

[Haworth]

Dear Ellen

I was not at all surprised at the contents of your note—indeed what part of it was new to us—? J[oe] T[aylor] has his good and bad side like most others[1]—there is his own original nature and there are the alterations the world has made in him—Meantime why do<es> *Birstal and *Gomersal trouble themselves with matching him? Let him in God's name court half the country side and marry the other half—if such procedure seem good in his eyes, and let him do it all in quietness—he has his own botherations no doubt—it does not seem to be such very easy work getting married even for a man—since it is necessary to make up to so many ladies—More tranquil are those who have settled their bargain with celibacy.

I like Miss *Ringrose's letters more and more—her goodness is indeed better than mere talent—I fancy she will never be married[2] but the amiability of her character will give her comfort—to be sure one has only her letters to judge from and letters often deceive—but hers seem so artless and unaffected Still were I in your place I should feel uneasy in the midst of this correspondence—does a doubt of mutual satisfaction in case you should one day meet never torment you?

I am sure you have done right to be plain with her about *George—She seems at last to have caught a glimpse of the real truth.

Anne says it pleases her to think that you have kept her little drawing she would rather have done it for you than for a stranger—

I have got a trifle of a head-ache to day and can write only in the most stupid manner—

Good bye to you dear Nell Give my love to your Mother and sisters—
C Brontë

MS HM 24460. W & S 244.
Address: not in MS.
PM: not in MS.
Date: CB dates 'April 25th', EN (wrongly) 'Ap 25 48'. 1846 suits the content and the paper, a double sheet of that used for letters to Aylott and Jones in this year. See the previous letter, note on date.

1. CB's opinion of Joe Taylor varied. In EN 24.4.1845 she thought him changed by the hard selfish world, but she praised him in e.g. EN 14.4.1846.
2. CB was mistaken: Amelia Ringrose married Joe Taylor in ?Sept. 1850.

Branwell Brontë to J. B. Leyland,[1] *[?28 April 1846]*

Haworth,
Bradford,
Yorks.

My dear Sir,

As I am anxious—though my return for your kindness will be like giving a sixpence back for a sovereign lent—to do my best in my intended lines on 'Morley'[2] I want answers to the following qu[estion]s;

Ist. (As I can[not find] it in the map or Gazzeteer) In what dis[trict] of Lancashire is Morley situated?

IId. Has the Hall a particular name?

IIId. Do you know the family name of its owners when the occurrences happened which I ought to dwell on?

IVth. Can you tell in what century they happened?

Vth. What, told in the fewest words, was the nature of the leading occurrence?

If I learn these facts I'll do my best, but in all I try to write I desire to stick to probabilities and local characteristics.

Now, after troubling you so much, I doubt not that you will drive your fist through that damned medallion[3] in your Studio, as being the effigies of a regular bore.

I cannot, without a smile at myself, think of my stay for three days in Halifax on a business which need not have occupied three hours; but in truth when I fall back on myself I suffer so mu[ch wre]tchedness that I cannot withstand any temptation to get out of myself—and for that reason I am prosecuting enquiries about situations suitable to me whereby I could have a voyage abroad.[4] The quietude of home, and the inability to make my family aware of the nature of most of my sufferings[5] makes me write

'Home thoughts are not, with me
   Bright as of yore;
Joys are forgot by me,
   Taught to deplore!
My home has taken rest
   In an afflicted breast
Which I have often pressed,
   But—may no more!'[6]

Troubles never come alone—and I have some little troubles astride the shoulders of the big one.

Literary exertion would seem a resource, but the depression attendant on it, and the almost hopelessness of bursting through the barriers of literary <cliques> circles,[7] and getting a hearing among publishers, make me disheartened and indifferent; for I cannot write what would be thrown, unread, in to a library fire: Otherwise I have the materials for a respectably sized volume, and if I were in London personally I might perhaps try Henry Moxon[8] [sic]—a patronizer of the sons of rhyme; though I dare say the poor man often smarts for his liberality in publishing hideous trash.

As I know that, while here, I might send a manuscript to London, and say good bye to it I feel it <?useless to> folly to feed the flames of a printers fire.

So much for egotism!

I enclose a horrible ill-drawn daub[9] done to wile away the time this morning. I meant it to represent a very rough figure in stone.

When all our cheerful hours seem gone for ever,[10]
   All lost that caused the body or the mind
   To nourish love or friendship for our kind,
And Charon's boat, prepared—o'er Lethe's river—[11]
Our souls to waft, and all our thoughts to sever
   From what was once lifes light, still there may be
   Some well loved bosom to whose pillow we
Could heartily our utter self deliver:
And if—toward her grave—Death's dreary road
   Our darling's feet should tread, each step by her
Would 'draw' our own steps to the same abode,
   And make a festival of sepulture;
For, what gave joy, <to> and joy to us had owed,
   Should Death affright us from, when he would her restore?

Yours most sincerely,
P. B. Brontë

MS Brotherton. W & S 245.
Address: not in MS.
PM: not in MS.

1. See BB to JBL 4.8.1845 n. 1.
2. Probably suggested to BB as a topic for a poem by J. B. Leyland, whose 'ancestral connection' Anne Leyland of Morley Hall, Leigh, Lancs., had eloped to her lover's house. Daphne du Maurier considers that BB would have seen a resemblance to the elopement of the Robinsons' daughter Lydia with the actor Henry Roxby on 20 Oct. 1845. (*Infernal World* 183–4.) Only a 90-line introduction to Branwell's projected epic poem survives. The poet meditates on past times when the now ruined hall stood in a Lancashire of green fields unspoilt by the noise, grime, and brick buildings of the industrial age, and he reflects on mutability and mortality. (Neufeldt *BBP* 284–6, Winnifrith *BBP* 171–4.)
3. Leyland's bas relief portrait medallion of BB, now in BPM; reproduced as a frontispiece in Gérin *BB*.
4. No details of these enquiries are known; like his previous plans to go abroad in 1836, and in 1842, when he contemplated work on the French railways (BPM MS B.S. 138), they were unsuccessful.
5. Branwell's family felt that they also had cause for complaint. See e.g. EN 14.4.1846.
6. Branwell refers to Mrs Robinson of Thorp Green.
7. Four or more letters from Branwell to the Editor of *Blackwood's Edinburgh Magazine* had failed to elicit a response. See his letters of 7.12.1835 and 4.1.1837 in Neufeldt *BBP* pp. xxxv–xlii, and Mrs Oliphant's account in *William Blackwood and his Sons* (1907), ii. 176–85, where she says that Robert Blackwood probably thought BB's letter of 1836 showed he was crazy. But Branwell had several poems published in newspapers: see *Barker*, Neufeldt *BBP* pp. xxi–xxiii, and Selwyn H. Goodacre, 'The Published Poems of Branwell Brontë', *BST* 19.8.361–8.
8. Branwell means Edward Moxon (1801–58), referred to in Aylott 31.1.1846. The sisters must have discussed Moxon's edn. of Wordsworth's poems as an exemplar for their own publication. This and other matters may point to an awareness on Branwell's part of his sisters' project. By 11 Mar. CB was receiving proof-sheets, and on 27 Mar. a 'little mistake' occurred because the sheets had been addressed to 'C. Brontë Esqre'; on 11 Apr. CB refers (in terms echoed by BB) to the difficulties unknown authors have to contend with. On the other hand CB was to state categorically that her 'unhappy brother never knew what his sisters had done in literature—he was not aware that they had ever published a line'. (vol. ii, WSW 2.10.1848; W & S 394.)
9. F. A. Leyland comments, 'The sketch referred to in this letter is in Indian-ink, and is of a female figure, with clasped hands, streaming hair, and averted face. We need not entertain a doubt as to whom it is intended to represent [i.e. Mrs Robinson].' (*Leyland* ii. 135.) The sketch is on a page 181 mm. x 233 mm. and is entitled ' "Our Lady of greif" ' ' "Nuestra Sen'ora de la pena" '. The 2nd phrase is repeated on a tombstone-like slab beside the 'statue' figure, and what may be a castle is vaguely sketched in the background.
10. See Neufeldt *BBP* 283 and 514, Winnifrith *BBP* 170 and notes.
11. BB would recall, as well as classical references, Milton's description of the rivers of hell in *Paradise Lost* II 582–6, where 'Lethe the River of Oblivion roules | Her watrie Labyrinth'. The god Charon is usually said to conduct the 'souls of the dead in a boat over the rivers Styx and Acheron to the infernal regions' (John Lemprière's *Classical Dictionary* (1788)) whereas Lethe is 'farr off from these'. (*Paradise Lost* II 582.)

To Messrs Aylott and Jones, 7 May 1846[1]

[Haworth]

Gentlemen

The Poems may be neatly done up in Cloth[2]—

Have the goodness to send Copies and advertisements, as early as possible, to each of the undermentioned Periodicals

Colburn's New Monthly.
Bentley's Miscellany.
Hood's Magazine.
Jerrold's Shilling Magazine[3]

Blackwoods Magazine.
The Edinburgh Review.
Tait's Edinburgh Magazine.
The Dublin University Magazine.[4]

Also to the Daily News, and the Britannia Newspaper.[5]

If there are any other periodicals to which you have been in the habit of sending copies of works, let them be supplied also—with copies—I think those I have mentioned will suffice for advertising.

I have to mention that your three last communications and the parcel had all been opened—where or by whom, I cannot discover; the paper covering the parcel was torn in pieces and the books were brought in loose.

I enclose the estimate

I am Gentlemen
Yrs truly
C Brontë

MS BPM Bon 183. W & S 246.
Address: not in MS.
PM: not in MS.
Annotation: N° 14. After 'Jerrold's Shilling Magazine' someone in the publishing house has added 'Athenaeum', 'Lit^{y} Gazette', 'Critic', 'Times',[6] and at the foot of fol. 1^{r}:

4 Watts
4 Aldis ?Stationers Hall
4 Bell

---

1 of each ?GA

On fol 1^{v} there are calculations of costs:

	2. 1.	20. 10	
		1. 10. 9.	
$10\frac{3}{4}$ Sheets @ 41/-per Sheet—			22—0—9
Extra for small type, & corrections.			1—15—"
		11.5 17.6	
$10\frac{3}{4}$ Reams of Paper for Ditto—	@22/6		12—2—6

1. On 20 Apr. CB had asked for '3 Copies by Post' on completion of the work. A. M. F. Robinson describes what must be one of these early copies: 'There is a tiny copy of the "Poems" of Ellis, Currer, and Acton Bell, which was Emily's own, marked with her name and with the date of every poem carefully written under its title, in her own cramped and tidy writing.' (Robinson *EB* 128.) 'Emily Brontë's copy is dated May 7th, 1846.' (ibid. 141.) See *Barker* 930.
2. See D. F. Foxon, 'Binding Variants in the Brontës' *Poems*', *Book Collector* 2 (1953), 219–21, and 'The Publishing of "Poems by Currer, Ellis and Acton Bell" ', *BST* 15. 79. 297, where G. D. Hargreaves concludes that the earliest bindings are likely to be 'light *or* dark green cloth with a design of "geometrical" rules, lettered on the front but not the spine.' 'Harp' bindings are probably those of the 2nd issue by Smith, Elder in 1848, but the question is complicated by T. J. Wise's suspect claim that some of the 'harp' copies in light green cloth are rare first issue bindings.
3. 'Colburn's New Monthly' was founded by Henry Colburn (d. 1855) as *The New Monthly Magazine and Universal Register* in 1814. Its title in 1846 and until its demise in 1871 was *The New Monthly Magazine and Humorist*. *Bentley's Miscellany* (1837–68), founded by Richard Bentley (1794–1871) and edited by Dickens until Jan. 1839, had published *Oliver Twist* in serial form. The poet Thomas Hood (1799–1845) had begun *Hood's Magazine and Comic Miscellany* (1844–8), and Douglas William Jerrold (1803–57), friend of Dickens and writer for *Punch*, produced *Douglas Jerrold's Shilling Magazine* (1845–8).
4. *Blackwood's Edinburgh Magazine* (1817–1905), continued as *Blackwood's Magazine* until 1980, was begun by William Blackwood (1776–1834) as a Tory rival to the Whiggish *Edinburgh Review*. The Brontë children used it as a model for their juvenile 'books' in 1829 and 1830. See CB to Hartley Coleridge 10.12.1840 n. 2 and BB 17.5.1832 n. 7. The *Edinburgh Review* (quarterly, 1802–1929) was founded by Francis Jeffrey (1773–1850) Sydney Smith (1771–1845), and Henry Brougham (1778–1868). William Tait (1793–1864) published *Tait's Edinburgh Magazine* (1832–4; new ser. 1834–61) 'a literary and radical magazine, to which Mill, Cobden, and Bright contributed'. (See *DNB*.) *The Dublin University Magazine* (1833–77) was the only one of these journals to review the Bells' *Poems*. When on 6 Oct. 1846 CB thanked the editor for his 'indulgent notice' she signed herself 'Your Constant and grateful reader'. Conceivably Mr Brontë's curate, A. B. Nicholls, an alumnus of Trinity College Dublin, subscribed to his university's magazine, which was strongly Protestant and in favour of continuing union with England. It had a number of distinguished contributors, was edited by the novelist Charles Lever from 1842 to 1845, welcomed native Irish poetry, and published translations of works by German Romantic writers.
5. The *Daily News* (1846–1912), founded as a Liberal rival to the *Morning Chronicle*, was edited by Dickens for 17 numbers only. John Forster, Charles Wentworth Dilke (as manager), and Eyre Crowe eventually succeeded in establishing it as an influential and profitable newspaper. The *Britannia* (1839–56) was a weekly newspaper, incorporated in 1856 with the violently Tory *John Bull* (1820–92).
6. The influential *Athenaeum* (1828–1921) was to publish a 'not discouraging' review of the Bells' *Poems* on 4 July 1846, and *The Critic* (1844–63), subtitled the *Journal of British and Foreign Literature and the Arts*, welcomed the volume's 'genuine poetry' as a 'ray of sunshine' on the same day. See Aylott 10.7.1846 and notes. The poems were ignored by *The Times*, then edited by the 'Thunderer', John Thaddeus Delane (1817–79). They were not reviewed in Henry Colburn's *The Literary Gazette* (1817–62) until their reissue by Smith, Elder in 1848, when the reviewer concluded, 'We hope our Bells will leave off poetry . . . and stick to prose for the recreation of the public.' (*The Literary Gazette* 30.12.1848, 862.)

To Eliza Jane Kingston,[1] *8 May 1846*

[Haworth]

My dear Cousin

Papa wishes me to acknowledge for him the receipt of the Post-office order for the rent[2] and also to thank you for the very kind note accompanying it.

His eyes do not give him any pain and his health is still good—we all look forward to Summer as the period for the operation[3]—we shall be most thankful when it is well over for there is something formidable in the idea—and that feeling increases as the reality appears to approach.

I am sorry to hear that our Mining Shares[4] have only a nominal value Still as they yield a small dividend we cannot regard them as wholly worthless—The new 'railway' Shares are rising and on that account do you not think it would be better to sell an old share and retain them? I am not at all certain on this point therefore I only ask the question—I do not venture to suggest advice—

We are glad to hear my Cousin William[5] is returned safely from Sea and that my Aunt Charlotte is consequently in better health and spirits—It is well too I think that he is to abandon a sailor's career for had he again left England, after what has happened,[6] his Mother and Sisters would scarcely have known peace of mind during his absence.

The Spring has been very cold and wet[7] in Yorkshire also—but since May has set in we have had more genial weather—I trust it will continue so—for we too—all of us enjoy better health when the air is serene and mild—I fancy most of us possess the Constitution of Mamma's family—Myself and my sister Anne especially—

Give our united love to my Aunt Kingston[8] and accept the same yourself.

Believe my dear Cousin
Your affectionate Cousin
C Brontë

MS Berg. No publication traced.
Address (envelope): Miss Kingston | 17 St Clare Street | Penzance | Cornwall
PM: (i) HAWORTH (ii) BRADFORD YORKS | MY 8 | 18–6 | — (iii) [PENZ]ANCE |—Y 10 | 1846 | A

1. See EJK ?3.3.1846 n. 1.
2. Probably rent from property formerly owned by Elizabeth Branwell; or perhaps Mr Brontë had previously sent Eliza and her mother a loan towards their own rent. Eliza and the Brontë sisters had inherited equal shares of their Aunt Elizabeth Branwell's residual estate of less than £1,500, but Eliza's income from this, and her mother's annuity of £50, cannot have left much room for manœuvre. See F. E. Ratchford, 'The Loneliness of a Brontë Cousin', *BST* 13. 67. 100–10.
3. Mr Brontë's forthcoming operation for cataract. See EN 3.3.1846 n. 3.
4. Presumably these were shares in Cornish tin mines. Ratchford quotes from letters written by

Eliza in the 1860s describing the poor returns and precariousness of such ventures: 'So you see mining is a kind of lottery not fit for an inexperienced woman'; 'I have had no calls from the mines for the last six months. It will be two years in March next, since I received anything from them.' ('Loneliness of a Cousin', 108.)

5. See EJK ?3.3.1846 n. 5.
6. CB refers to the death at sea of Charlotte Branwell's son Joseph earlier in the year.
7. *Shackleton* recorded a cool and 'exceeding wet' Apr. with 26 days of rain and 2 of snow; but in early May light southerly and westerly winds brought more warmth, and Charlotte was writing on 'a fine day'.
8. Eliza's mother, Jane Kingston, née Branwell (1773–1855.) See EJK ?3.3.1846 n. 1.

To Messrs Aylott and Jones, 11 May 1846

[Haworth]

Gentlemen

The books may be done up in the style of Moxon's duodecimo edition of Wordsworth.[1]

The price may be fixed at 5s. or if you think that too much for the size of the volume—say 4s.[2]

I think the periodicals I mentioned in my last will be sufficient for advertising in at present and I should not wish you to lay out a larger sum than £2—especially as the estimate[3] is increased by nearly £5 in consequence it appears of a mistake—I should think the success of a work depends more on the notice it receives from periodicals than on the quantity of advertisements.

If you do not object—the additional amount of the estimate can be remitted when you send in your account at the end of the first six months.

I should be obliged to you if you could let me know how soon copies can be sent to the editors of the magazines and newspapers specified—

I am Gentlemen
Yrs trly
C. Brontë

MS BPM Bon 184. W & S 247.
Address: not in MS.
PM: not in MS.
Annotation: N° 15

1. 'Presumably that of 1836–7 in six volumes of the same size as the Bells' *Poems* . . . [which] appeared in *dark* green cloth.' (G. D. Hargreaves, 'The Publishing of "Poems by Currer, Ellis and Acton Bell" ', *BST* 15. 79. 297.) See also Aylott 31.1.1846 n. 1.
2. The price was fixed at 4 shillings. Copies of the 2nd issue (Smith, Elder 1848) were still being sold at '*4s. cloth*' in Apr. 1856, a year when the firm's ledgers show that they still had 556 copies, out of the original 1,000 printed, 'on hand'. By 1 July 1857 (i.e. after the publication of the *Life*) Smith, Elder had 450 of these copies bound in expectation of a surge in sales. (Smith, Elder ledgers, by courtesy of John Murray (Publishers) Ltd.)

3. CB had paid £31. 10*s*. on 3 Mar. Aylott's calculations on the back of her letter of 7.5.1846 show that the 'estimate' had been increased to £35. 18*s*. 3*d*.

To Messrs Aylott and Jones, 25 May 1846

[Haworth]

Gentlemen

I received yours of the 22nd. this Morning; I now transmit £5[1]—being the additional sum necessary to defray the entire expense of paper and printing—it will leave a small surplus of 11s. 9d which you can place to <our> 'my' account

I am glad you have sent copies to the newspapers[2] you mention—and in case of a notice <appearing> favourable or otherwise appearing in them or in any of the other periodicals to which copies have been sent—I should be obliged to you if you would send me down the number, otherwise as I have not the opportunity of seeing these publications regularly,[3] I might miss it and should the poems be remarked upon favourably it is my intention to appropriate a further sum to advertisements.[4] If, on the other hand they should pass unnoticed or be condemned, I consider it would be quite useless to advertise as there is nothing either in the title of the work or the names of the authors to attract attention from a single individual

I am Gentlemen
Yrs truly
C Brontë

MS BPM Bon 185. W & S 248.
Address: not in MS.
PM: not in MS.
Annotation: N° 16

1. See previous letter n. 3.
2. See Aylott 7.5.1846 and notes. Since review copies had been sent out by Friday 22 May the *Poems* were probably on sale to the public on or soon after that date. The title-page reads: 'POEMS | BY | CURRER, ELLIS, AND ACTON | BELL. | [rule] | LONDON: | AYLOTT AND JONES, 8, PATERNOSTER-ROW. | [rule] | 1846.' Curiously, the publication date is given as Sept. in the *Publishers' Circular* for 1846, p. 3: 'Bell (C. E. & A.) Poems, fcp. Sep. 0. 4. 0. Aylott' and p. 267, in the circular dated 15 Sept. 1846: 'POEMS. By Currer, Ellis, and Acton Bell. Fcp. pp. 170, cloth 4s.'
3. Two of the periodicals mentioned in or noted on Aylott 7.5.1846, *Blackwood's Edinburgh Magazine* and *The Literary Gazette*, were probably available at the Keighley Mechanics' Institute, as they had been in 1841. The Institute's copies of the *Edinburgh Review* ('6 parts') may have been back numbers. See Clifford Whone, 'Where the Brontës Borrowed Books', *BST* 11. 60. 344–58.
4. The £2 already spent was a pitifully small amount. 'A single insertion in a newspaper was of little use . . . About 1850 it could be said that £20 was the minimum and £150 the maximum

usually spent in advertising a new book, but that the outlay quite often reached £200 or £300.' (Marjorie Plant, *The English Book Trade* (2nd edn.; 1965), 408.)

To Ellen Nussey, [?Soon after 3 June 1846]

[Haworth]

Dear Ellen,

I hope all the mournful contingencies of death are by this time removed from Brookroyd, and that some little sense of relief is beginning to be experienced by its wearied inmates. Your brother [Joseph][1] suffered greatly I make no doubt, and I trust and even believe that his long sufferings on earth will be taken as sufficient expiation for his errors. One shudders for him, but it is his relations—his mother and sisters—whom I truly and permanently pity. I wish you all may get a little repose and enjoyment now. I should like to hear from you shortly, and whether any new plans are in contemplation about poor George. Give my love to all.

C. Brontë

MS untraced. W & S 249.
Address: not in source.
PM: not in source.
Date: 'June '46' in source.
Text: W & S 249, the fullest surviving version. The letter is not in *Life* or *Hours at Home*. *Reid* 72, *Nussey* 141–2, and *Shorter* 197 omit names and other details which would identify Joseph Nussey.

1. Joseph Nussey (1797–1846) and his brother Richard had for a time been partners in the woollen manufacturing industry. Joseph, the 2nd son of EN's father John Nussey, died unmarried on 29 May 1846 and was buried on 3 June. For his dissolute character see EN 31.7.1845, where he is already a 'burthen' on his aged mother, and EN 30.12.1845. He was probably an alcoholic. Whitehead notes that his cause of death was entered on his death certificate as 'phthisis'. (*Whitehead* 127.) This term was usually but not necessarily applied to the wasting caused by pulmonary TB.

Branwell Brontë to J. B. Leyland, [June 1846]

[Haworth]

My dear Sir,

I should have sent you "Morley Hall"[1] ere now, but I am unable to finish it at present from agony to which the grave would be far preferable.

Mr Robinson[2] of Thorp Green is <u>dead</u>, and he has left his widow in a dreadful state of health. She sent the Coachman[3] over to me yesterday, and the account which he gave of her sufferings was enough to burst my heart.

Through the will she is left quite powerless, and her eldest daughter[4] who married imprudently, is cut off without a shilling.

The Executing Trustees detest me, and one declares that if he sees me he will shoot me.[5]

These things I do not care about, but I do care for the life of the one who suffers even more than I do. Her Coachman said that it was a pity to see her, for she was only able to kneel in her bedroom in bitter tears and prayers. She has worn herself out in attendance on him, and his conduct during the few days before his death, was exceedingly mild and repentant, but that only distressed her doubly. Her consience has helped to agonize her, and that misery I am saved from.

You, though not much older than myself, have known life. I now know it with a vengeance—for four nights I have not slept—for three days I have not tasted food—and when I think of the state of her I love best on earth, I could wish that my head was as cold and stupid as the <bust> medallion[6] which lies in your studio.

I write very egotistically but it is because my mind is crowded with one set of thoughts, and I long for one sentence from a friend.

What I shall do I know not—I am too hard to die, and too wretched to live. My wretchedness is not about castles in the air, but about stern realities; my hardihood lies in bodily vigour; but, Dear Sir, my mind sees only a dreary future which I as little wish to enter on, as could a martyr to be bound to the stake.

I sincerely trust that you are well, and hope that this wretched scrawl will not make 'me' appear to you a worthless fool, or a thorough bore.

Believe me, Yours, most sincerely,
P B Brontë

MS Brotherton. W & S 250.
Address: not in MS.
PM: not in MS.
Annotation: The letter is accompanied by the full page pen and ink sketch entitled 'Myself' showing a bulky male figure with wrists bound, tied to a stake, in the midst of flames. See W & S ii. 97.
Date: soon after the death of the Revd Edmund Robinson of Thorp Green on 26 May 1846.

1. BB's poem, which remains fragmentary. See BB to JBL 28.4.1846.
2. Branwell's former employer had died on 26 May at the age of 46, having suffered from 'Dyspepsia many years Phthisis 3 months'. (*Infernal World*, 188.)
3. William Allison. George Whitehead of Little Ouseburn records in his journal that when Allison moved with Mrs. Robinson to Great Barr on 22.2.47 he had been at Thorp Green four years. (Helier Hibbs (ed.), *Victorian Ouseburn: George Whitehead's Journal* (York, 1990), 25b.) See also BB to FHG ?June 46 n. 1.
4. Lydia Mary Robinson, b. 6 Sept. (or Oct.) 1825, the eldest daughter. George Whitehead had recorded in his journal: 'Miss Lydia Robinson made her exit with Henry Roxby (a play actor) Monday morning, Oct 20th. They went to Gretna Green and got married that night. She was a fortnight turned 20 years that day. A bad job 1845.' (Hibbs (ed.), *Victorian Ouseburn*, 16k.) However, he makes a later entry: 'Mr & Mrs Roxby came to Thorp Green first time on

Tuesday Nov 18th, and left on Thursday, Nov 20th All right 1845.' (Ibid. 17e.) For the will see the next letter and notes.

5. It is impossible to know how much of this account Branwell himself believed to be true. In a poem written on 1 June 1846 he contrasts his state at Whitsuntide (11 May) 1845, when he had hoped love would keep his 'heart beside' Lydia Gisborne (i.e. Mrs Robinson) and his present loss of hope in 'woe's far deeper sea'. (Neufeldt *BBP* 282.) Daphne du Maurier gives persuasive reasons for her belief that Branwell fabricated a face-saving story. (*Infernal World* 188–93.) Mrs Gaskell believed, as did CB and her father, that Mrs Robinson had seduced Branwell and caused his moral and physical downfall, but she was compelled by Mrs Robinson's lawyers to retract her allegations. See EN 31.7.1845 notes 10 and 11, and new evidence in *Barker*.
6. See BB to JBL 28.4.1846 n. 3.

To Ellen Nussey, 17 June 1846

[Haworth]

Dear Ellen

I was glad to perceive by the tone of your last letter that you are beginning to be a little more settled and comfortable. I should think Dr Belcombe[1] is quite right in opposing George's removal home—if he has such an impression of suffering <con> connected with all recollections of Brookroyd—depend upon it, it would be misery to him to return there—and I fear misery to you to have him amongst you; you would all be too often, painfully and forcibly reminded of the difference between what he is and what he was;[2] and if there is a chance of his final recovery (which I would still hope) that chance is far more likely to become certainty if he remains in the hands of those who understand his complaint and can watch its symptoms.

We—I am sorry to say—have been somewhat more harrassed than usual lately—The death of Mr Robinson[3]—which took place about three weeks or a month ago—served Branwell for a pretext to throw all about him into hubbub and confusion with his emotions—&c. &c. Shortly after came news from all hands that Mr Robinson had altered his will[4] before he died and effectually prevented all chance of a marriage between his widow and Branwell by stipulating that she should not have a shilling if she ever ventured to reopen any communication with him—Of course he then became intolerable[5]—to papa he allows rest neither day nor night—and <his> 'he is' continually screwing money out of him sometimes threatening that he will kill himself if it is withheld from him—He says Mrs R—is now insane[6]—that her mind is a complete wreck—owing to remorse for her conduct towards Mr R— (whose end it appears was hastened by distress of mind)[7]—and grief for having lost him.

I do not know how much to believe of what he says but I fear she is very ill—Branwell declares now that he neither can nor will do anything for himself—good situations have been offered more than once[8]—for which by a fortnight's work he might have qualified himself—but he will do nothing—except drink, and make us all wretched—

Do not say a word about this to any one dear Ellen—I know no one but yourself to whom I would communicate it—

I had a note from Ellen Taylor[9] a week ago—in which she remarks that letters were received from New Zealand a month since or more and that <Mary> all was well—but that they were on business[10] and not sent anywhere—Mary's name was not mentioned—but I suppose she was included in the expression that all was well—I thought it singular that J Taylor had never intimated to any of Mary's friends that tidings of her had been heard—He was not aware I am sure of Ellen Taylor's writing to me—so don't mention this circumstance either—there may be reasons for the reserve with which we are unacquainted—at any rate do not speak of it unless you should hear others speak of it—

I should like to hear from you again soon
Believe me yrs
C B—

June 17th. —46
I am greatly obliged to your Sister Anne—for so kindly making me an exception to her rule of exclusion[11]—and I hope one day to see Brookroyd again—though I think it will not be just yet—these are not times of amusement. Love to all—

MS BPM Gr. E 11. W & S 251 (part). *BST* 17. 90. 356–7.
Address: not in MS.
PM: not in MS.
Text: the letter is not in *Nussey*, and is drastically cut in *Shorter* 198 and W & S 251.

1. See EN 18.8.1845 n. 5.
2. EN's much-loved youngest brother had been her companion in walking and riding, as her 1844 Diary shows, and he is never criticized by CB. See EN *Diary* (1844), and for EN's loyal account of him, EN 30.12.1844 n. 1.
3. See previous letter and notes.
4. Mr Robinson had altered his will on 2 Jan. 1846 to 'make certain that his daughter [Lydia Mary] and her actor husband [Henry Roxby] should not benefit from his own marriage settlement, which they would have done had the 1831 will stood unaltered . . . [In 1846] all Mr Robinson's money and other possessions were left to his wife, to his son and heir Edmund, and to his daughters Elizabeth and Mary'. There was no clause 'under which Mrs Robinson would forfeit her inheritance if she remarried.' (*Infernal World*, 188–9.) There were however trustees of the estate, Mr Robinson's brother-in-law, the Venerable Charles Thorpe, Archdeacon of Durham, and William Evans MP, the husband of Mrs Robinson's sister Mary. There was no stipulation about communication with Branwell Brontë. The 'news from all hands' must have been distorted rumours of the actual changes.
5. CB does not say that Branwell himself was the source of the false account of the will, but he may have been. For his state of mind, see his letters to FHG of ?June 1846 and JBL of *c.* June/July 1846.

6. The Robinson papers in the BPM show that Mrs Robinson, while mourning her husband's death, was coping fairly efficiently with business-matters after it, though there are errors and deletions in her account-book in the days immediately following his death. On 29 May she recorded £18 paid to 'Old Servants (for my Angel)'; in June she listed the expenses for 'Edm's sad funeral', wrote on the blotting-paper 'My Angel Edmund', and on 28 Aug. had paid for 'My locket for my Edmund's hair.' (Robinson Papers 93/2.) She also corresponded with her agent Daniel Seaton on business-matters, and arranged for the drawing up of her own will. See Robinson papers for 1846, esp. 93/2 and 94/1–7, and see Gérin *BB* 265–9, and *Infernal World* 188–94.
7. Branwell had built up an image of himself as Mrs Robinson's refuge from her husband's ill-treatment of her, which (Branwell alleged) he 'bitterly repented' on his death-bed. See BB to JBL *c.* June/July 1846.
8. Grundy comments on a letter from Branwell (see below) 'Here comes another prayer for employment, with, at the same time, a confession that his health alone renders the wish all but hopeless.' (*Grundy* 89.)
9. Ellen Taylor was staying with her cousins Joe and John Taylor at Hunsworth. See CB to M. Dixon 16.10.1843 n. 8.
10. Such letters would not be 'sent anywhere'—i.e. circulated amongst Mary's friends. Mary Taylor's brothers John, Joe, and Waring all helped her financially. See *Stevens* 76. In her letter to CB of June/July 1848 from New Zealand Mary writes, 'Moreover <I> in accordance with a late letter of John's I borrow money from him & Joe & buy cattle with it'. (MS Pierpont Morgan; *Stevens* 76.)
11. No doubt Ann Nussey made the 'rule' because of her family's exhaustion after their ordeal of nursing the dying Joseph Nussey.

Branwell Brontë to Francis H. Grundy, [?June 1846]: [Fragment]

Haworth, Bradford, York.

The gentleman with whom I have been is dead. His property is left in trust for the family, provided I do not see the widow; and if I do, it reverts to the executing trustees, with ruin to her. She is now distracted with sorrows and agonies; and the statement of her case, as given by her coachman,[1] who has come to see me at Haworth, fills me with inexpressible grief. Her mind is distracted to the verge of insanity,[2] and mine is so wearied that I wish I were in my grave.—

Yours very sincerely,
P. B. Brontë.

MS untraced. Part of W & S 252.
Address: not in source.
PM: not in source.
Date: Grundy places the letter from which he extracts this para. in 1848, confusing matters further by printing it as if it belonged to a letter beginning 'Dear Sir,—I must again trouble you with [a prayer for employment]'. The first part of the letter cannot be dated with certainty, but may

really be Jan. 1848; the second part—the present fragment—must from its content be soon after Mr Robinson's death in May 1846. See previous letter and notes, and p. 433. W & S 252 reproduces Grundy's composite text (89).

1. The Thorp Green coachman was William Allison, not the 'George Gooch' seen by Branwell at about the same period. For Gooch see BB to FHG ?July / Aug. 1846, n.1. Allison was evidently a trusted servant. An account book entry may corroborate Branwell's reference to his visit to Haworth. 6 days after her entry for 'Edm's sad funeral' on 5 June 1846, Mrs Robinson recorded that she paid £3 to 'Wm for journey' (11 June). Other entries such as 'Wm for a horse's expences' (3 July) make it likely that he was the 'W. Allison' who received wages of £25 on 7 Nov. 1846. (BPM Robinson Papers 93/2.) In 1847 George Whitehead recorded in his journal that 'William Allison (Mrs Robinson's coachman) left and went to live with Sir Edward Scott near Birmingham Feb 22nd He has been at Thorp Green 4 years.' (Helier Hibbs (ed.), *Victorian Ouseburn: George Whitehead's Journal* (York, 1990), 25b.) Sir Edward Scott was the relative of Mrs Robinson in whose house at Great Barr she lived for most of the time from Mar. 1847 until his wife's death in Aug. 1848, and whom she married on 8 Nov. 1848.
2. See previous letter n. 6.

Branwell Brontë to J. B. Leyland, c. June/July 1846

[Haworth]

Well, my dear Sir, I have got my finishing stroke at last—and I feel stunned into marble by the blow.

I have this morning recieved a long, kind and faithful letter from the medical gentleman[1] who attended Mr R—in his last illness and who has ˋsinceˊ had an interview with one whom I can never forget.

He knows me well, and he pities my case most sincerely—for he declares that though used to the rough ups and downs of this weary world, he shed tears from his heart when he saw the state of that lady and knew what I should feel.

When he mentioned my name she stared at him and fainted. When she recovered she in turns dwelt on her inextinguishable love for me[2]—her horror at having been the first to delude me into wretchedness, and her agony at having been the cause of the death of her husband,[3] who, in his last hours, bitterly repented of his treatment of her.

Her sensitive mind was totally wrecked.[4] She wandered into talking of entering a nunnery; and the Doctor fairly debars me from hope in the future.

It's hard work for me dear Sir; I would bear it—but my health is so bad that the body seems as if it could not bear the mental shock.

I never cared one bit about the property. I cared about herself—and always shall do.

May God bless her but I wish I had never known her!

My appetite is lost; my nights are dreadful, and having nothing to do makes me dwell on past scenes—on her own self, her voice, her person—her thoughts—till I could be glad if God would take me. In the next world I could not be worse than I am in this.

I am not a whiner dear Sir, but when a young man like myself has fixed his soul on a being worthy of all love—and who for years, has given him all love, pardon him for boring a friend with a misery that has only one black end.

I fully expected a change of the will, and difficulties placed in my way by powerful and wealthy men, but I hardly expected the hopeless ruin of the mind that I loved even more than its body.

Excuse my egotism, and believe me,

Dear Sir,
Yours,
P. B. Bronte

MS Brotherton. W & S 253.
Address: not in MS.
PM: not in MS.

1. The surgeon John Crosby. See BB to FHG Oct. 1845 n. 13.
2. See EN 17.6.1846 and notes.
3. Possibly Branwell believed this; but it was presumably John Crosby who had provided the more prosaic information on Mr Robinson's death certificate, 'Dyspepsia many years Phthisis three months'.
4. Either Branwell had been given a grossly distorted account of Mrs Robinson's grief for her husband or he was fantasizing. See EN 17.6.1846 n. 6 and BB to JBL 24.1.1847.

To Henry Colburn,[1] *4 July 1846*

[Haworth]

Sir

I request permission to send for your inspection the M.S of a work of fiction in 3 vols.[2] It consists of three tales, each occupying a volume and capable of being published together or separately, as thought most advisable. The authors of these tales have already appeared before the public.[3]

Should you consent to examine the work, would you, in your reply, state at what period after transmission of the M.S. to you, the authors may expect to receive your decision upon its merits—

I am Sir
Yours respectfully
C Bell

Address Mr Currer Bell
Parsonage.
Haworth
Bradford
Yorkshire.[4]

July 4th —46
Henry Colburn Esqr.

MS Princeton, Parrish Collection. W & S appendix II.
Address: not in MS.
PM: not in MS.
Annotation by Colburn on 2^{v}, lacking opening and closing words formerly written at the top and bottom of the mutilated sheet: [t]he Authors, & what they have written & state that this information is necessary before I can decide on allowing the M.S— to be sent to me Also to request them to state the nature of the stories | HC.
PS—I have answered the Lord Mayor & Lord Londonderry—I shall return to town on Thursday—?dinner on | D Hurst Esq [or ?'Hunt']

1. Henry Colburn (d. 1855). Of obscure origins, he was one of the most prominent publishers of fiction at this period, and was the chief rival of Richard Bentley (1794–1871) his former business partner from 1829. As the proprietor of various journals, such as Colburn's *New Monthly Magazine* (1814–36, continued as the *New Monthly Magazine and Humorist* until 1871) and as a publisher he was notorious for his shameless publicity methods, such as the promotion of his own publications at the expense of other works in magazine reviews. He had a shrewd eye for the market and became very wealthy. See Aylott 6.4.1846 and 11.4.1846 and notes.
2. CB's *The Professor*, EJB's *WH*, and AB's *AG*, none of which Colburn published. See Aylott 6.4.1846 n. 2. CB later described the long struggle to get their work accepted: 'These MSS. were perseveringly obtruded upon various publishers for the space of a year and a half; usually, their fate was an ignominious and abrupt dismissal.' ('Biographical Notice of Ellis and Acton Bell, September 1850'. See Clarendon *WH* 437.)
3. Colburn would not be impressed by the publication of *Poems* in May 1846.
4. MS reads 'Yorskshire'.

To Ellen Nussey, 10 July 1846

[Haworth]

Dear Ellen

I see you are in a dilemma and one of a peculiar and difficult nature—Two paths lie before you—you conscientiously wish to choose the right one—even though it be the most steep, strait and rugged[1]—but you do not know which is the right one—you cannot decide whether Duty and Religion command you to go out into the cold and friendless world and there to earn your bread by Governess drudgery[2]—or whether they enjoin your continued stay with your aged Mother—neglecting <u>for the present</u> every prospect of independency for yourself and putting up with daily inconvenience—sometimes even with privations.

Dear Ellen I can well imagine that it is next to impossible for you to decide for yourself in this matter—so I will decide it for you—at least I will tell you what is my earnest conviction on the subject—I will shew you candidly how the question strikes me.

The right path is that which necessitates the greatest sacrifice of self-interest—which implies the greatest good to others—and this path steadily followed will lead I believe in time to prosperity and to happiness though it may seem at the outset to tend quite in a contrary direction—

Your Mother is both old and infirm;[3] old and infirm people have few sources of happiness—fewer almost than the comparatively young and healthy can conceive—to deprive them of one of these is cruel—If your Mother is more composed when you are with her—Stay with her—If she would be unhappy in case you left her—stay with her—It will not apparently, as far [as] shortsighted humanity can see—be for your advantage to remain at Brookroyd—nor will you be praised and admired for remaining at home to comfort your Mother—Yet probably your own Conscience will approve you and if it does—stay with her.

I recommend you to do—what I am trying to do myself[4]—

Who gravely asked you "whether Miss Brontë was not going to be married to her papa's Curate"?

I scarcely need say that never was rumour more unfounded—it puzzles me to think how it could possibly have originated—A cold, far-away sort of civility are the only terms on which I have ever been with Mr *Nicholls[5]—I could by no means think of mentioning such a rumour to him even as a joke—it would make me the laughing-stock of himself and his fellow-curates for half a year to come—They regard me as an old maid, and I regard them, one and all, as highly uninteresting, narrow and unattractive specimens of the "coarser sex".

The coldness and neglect of your brothers for their struggling, suffering Mother and Sisters irritates me more than I can or at least ought to express—I had fully calculated on Joshua inviting you at least to pay him a lengthened visit.[6]

Write to me again soon whether you have anything particular to say or not—Give my sincere love to your Mother and Sisters

C Brontë

The enigmas are very smart and well-worded[7]—

MS BPM Gr. E 10. W & S 257 (part).
Address: not in MS.
PM: not in MS.

1. cf. Matthew 7: 13–14.
2. This idea was repeatedly canvassed but never acted upon. See e.g. EN 24.1.1840, and ?24.5.1841, when it was seriously considered for a time but quashed when George Nussey's pride revolted at the idea of such 'degradation' for his sister. (EN ?10.6.1841.)
3. Mrs Nussey was 75.
4. This is somewhat disingenuous on CB's part, in view of her literary ambitions, but her loyalty and devotion to her father are not in doubt.
5. The Revd Arthur Bell Nicholls (1819–1906), Mr Brontë's curate since May 1845. CB's early coolness had changed into a genuine affection by the time she married Mr Nicholls in June 1854, though she still had reservations: she could not conceal from herself that he was 'not

intellectual' and was a rigid Puseyite. (See M. J. Shaen (ed.), *Memorials of Two Sisters* (1908), Catherine Winkworth to Emma Shaen, 8 May 1854, 112–13.)

6. 'The coldness and neglect . . . lengthened visit': heavily deleted in MS. The reading is conjectural. Omitted from *Shorter* 199 and W & S 257. For CB's critical view of Ellen's brothers, cf. EN 31.7.1845 and 2.10.1838. The Revd Joshua Nussey (1798–1871), Vicar of Oundle since 1845, had at least visited his mother and sisters after his brother Joseph's death on 29 May 1846, and on his return via Hathersage, had urged Henry Nussey to do likewise. Henry wrote home, 'Josh. pressed us very much to come over & see you—but we must beg to be excused, on a/c of the expense to both yrselves & us. Otherwise we shd have been most happy to have paid this tribute of filial affection to my dear Mother, & of sympathy with ?yrselves. You will have a few friends calling upon you, & this will be some alleviation to y^{r} past anxieties & present distresses.' (HN to his mother and sisters, 12.6.1846; BL MS Egerton 3268A fol. 98^{r}.)
7. Polite riddles or enigmas could be found in some of the ladies' magazines and 'pocket companions' of the time, and in compilations such as *Riddles, Charades, and Conundrums* (1822) noted by R. W. Chapman in connection with Garrick's riddle, 'Kitty, a fair but frozen maid', recalled in ch. 9 of Jane Austen's *Emma*, ed. R. W. Chapman (Oxford, 1933; repr. 1986), 70 and 489–90.

To Messrs Aylott and Jones, 10 July 1846

[Haworth]

Gentlemen

I am directed by the Messrs. Bell to acknowledge the receipt of the <British> Critic[1] and the Athenaeum,[2] containing notices of the poems.

They now think that a further sum of £10 may be devoted to advertisements, leaving it to you to select such channels as you deem most advisable.

They would wish the following extract from the <British> Critic to be appended to each advertisement.

"They in whose hearts are chords strung by Nature to sympathize with the beautiful and the true will recognize in these compositions the presence of more genius than it was supposed this utilitarian age had devoted to the loftier exercises of the intellect["]

They likewise request you to send copies of the Poems to Frazer's Magazine[3]—Chamber's Edinburgh Journal[4]—The Globe[5] and the Examiner.[6]

I am Gentlemen
yrs truly C Brontë

MS BPM Bon 186. W & S 258.
Address: not in MS.
PM: not in MS.

Annotation: N° 17. The name of each periodical in the last sentence has been ticked in ink, no doubt indicating compliance with CB's request.

1. See Aylott 7.5.1846 n. 6. CB has selected part of the review in *The Critic* for 4 July 1846 pp. 6–8, quoting from a sentence which reads in full: 'To those whose love of poetry is more a matter of education than of heart, it is probable that these poems may not prove attractive; they too much violate the conventionalities of poetry for such as look only to form, and not to substance; but they in whose hearts are chords strung by nature to sympathize with the beautiful and the true in the world without, and their embodiments by the gifted among their fellow men, will recognize in the compositions of Currer, Ellis and Acton Bell, the presence of more genius than it was supposed this utilitarian age had devoted to the loftier exercises of the intellect.' The reviewer was generous in his praise: 'Indeed, it is long since we have enjoyed a volume of such genuine poetry as this . . . this small book of some 170 pages only has come like a ray of sunshine . . . Here we have good, wholesome, refreshing, vigorous poetry'. Miriam Allott prints the review in *Allott* 59–61, and notes that *The Critic* 'always remained kindly disposed to all the Brontës'. (18.)
2. See Aylott 7.5.1846 n. 6, and *Allott* 61–2. The reviewer, in *The Athenaeum* for 4 July 1846, 682, recognizes the 'instinct of song' in 'the three brothers', though in 'very unequal proportions; requiring in the case of Acton Bell, the indulgences of affection . . . and rising, in that of Ellis, into an inspiration . . . A fine quaint spirit has the latter, . . . and an evident power of wing that may reach heights not here attempted'. 'The Muse of Currer Bell walks half way betwixt the level of Acton's and the elevation attained by Ellis.' Lines 41–70, 79–82 of CB's 'The teacher's monologue' are quoted to give 'the tone and manner of his singing'.
3. *Fraser's Magazine* (1830–82), founded by William Maginn (1793–1842) and Hugh Fraser. It was taken by Elizabeth Branwell for the Brontë household from May 1832, but for how long is not known. Unlike Colburn's journals, its policy was to avoid literary 'puffery', and it was to begin its coverage of the Brontës' work with G. H. Lewes's lengthy, enthusiastic, and discriminating piece on *JE* in Dec. 1847. See WSW 11.12.1847 n. 1.
4. *Chambers's Edinburgh Journal* (1832–1938), dealing with literature, science, and the arts, was founded by Robert and William Chambers, of the Edinburgh publishing firm 'to take advantage of the universal appetite for instruction which at present exists'. See William Chambers, *Memoir of Robert Chambers* (rev. edn. 1872), 233.
   CB was grateful for the Chambers's advice on the publication of the *Poems*. See Aylott 28.1.1846 n. 2.
5. *The Globe and Traveller* (1803–1921) was founded (as *The Globe*) by a publishers' syndicate as an advertising medium, and in its early days was associated with Benthamite radicalism; T. L. Peacock had been a contributor. It was to carry an advertisement for *JE*, with laudatory quotations from reviews, on 3 Dec. 1847.
6. *The Examiner* (1808–81) was a radical weekly founded by Leigh Hunt (1784–1859) and his brother John (1775–1848), and noted for its perceptive and untiring advocacy of the new poets, and particularly of Shelley and Keats from 1816 onwards. See Ian Jack, *English Literature 1815–1832* (Oxford, 1963), 319–20. CB was 'gratified' by *The Examiner*'s intelligent appreciation of *JE*, the first of a number of reviews of the Brontës' work. See her letter to Smith, Elder of 1.12.1847, and the lengthy extracts printed in *Allott*.

To Messrs Aylott and Jones, 15 July 1846

Haworth
Bradford
Yorks

Gentlemen

I should be obliged to you to send me another copy of the Critic for the 4th. inst, containing the review of the poems.

I suppose, as you have not written, no other notices[1] have yet appeared—nor has the demand for the work increased.

Will you favour me with a line, stating whether any, or how many copies have yet been sold[2]

I am Gentlemen
Yours truly
C Brontë

MS BPM Bon 187. W & S 259.
Address: not in MS.
PM: not in MS.
Annotation: N° 18

1. The poems were to be briefly noticed after their reissue in 1848, and again after Charlotte republished *WH*, *AG* and a selection of her sisters' poems in 1850. See e.g. *The Literary Gazette* 30.12.1848, 862: 'We hope our Bells will leave off poetry', and Lewes's review in *The Leader* for 28.12.1850, 953. (*Allott* 291–3.) The only other review of the poems on their first appearance, apart from those in *The Critic* and *The Athenaeum*, was that in the *Dublin University Magazine* for Oct. 1846. See CB's letter to the magazine's editor of 6.10.1846 and notes. Mrs Gaskell rightly says that the poems 'stole into life'. (*Life* i. 348.)
2. When CB sent gift copies of *Poems* to De Quincey and others on 16.6.1847 she wrote, 'In the space of a year our publisher has disposed but of two copies'. Of 1,000 copies printed, 961 remained unsold when Smith, Elder purchased the stock from Aylott and Jones some time between 7 Sept. and early Nov. 1848. See John Carter, *Books and Book-Collectors* (NY, 1957), 177, where the figures are quoted from the Smith, Elder ledgers by courtesy of John Murray.

To Messrs Aylott and Jones, 18 July 1846

Haworth
Bradford

Gentlemen

The Critic and the note accompanying it are come to hand.

The Messrs. Bell desire me to thank you for your suggestion respecting the advertisements. They agree with you that since the season is unfavourable—advertising had better be deferred.

They are obliged to you for the information respecting the number of copies sold[1]

I am Gentlemen
Yours truly
C Brontë

MS BPM Bon 188. W & S 260.
Address: not in MS.
PM: not in MS.
Annotation: N° 19

1. Two copies. See previous letter.

To Messrs Aylott and Jones, 23 July 1846

[Haworth]

[Gentlemen]

The Messrs. Bell would be obliged to you to post the enclosed note in London. It is an answer to the letter you forwarded, which contained an application for their autographs from a person who professed to have read and admired their poems. I think I before intimated, that the Messrs. Bell are desirous for the present of remaining unknown, for which reason they prefer having the note posted in London to sending it direct, in order to avoid giving any clue to residence, or identity by post-mark, &c.

[I am Gentlemen Yours truly,
C. Brontë.]

MS untraced. Envelope: BPM B.S. 104/15 W & S 261.
Address (envelope): F. Enoch Esqre.[1] | Corn Market | Warwick
PM: (i) [illegible] (ii) WARWICK | JY 23 | 1846
Text: The envelope is mounted on card, along with the three signatures, 'Currer Bell | Ellis Bell | Acton Bell' (see p. 489). The location of the accompanying letter to Messrs Aylott and Jones (W & S 261) is not known. It was copied by Mrs Gaskell and the autographs were lent to the Brontë Museum by Alfred Gledhill of Brighton in 1896. See *BST* 1. 8., the catalogue for that year. Bracketed words in the present text are from W & S. 261.

1. Frederick Enoch was 'known as a song-writer' (Butler Wood, 'Some Biographical Notes on the Brontë Literature', *BST* 4.21.191) and as the 'author of the song, once famous, "My sweetheart when a boy" |'. (Herbert Wroot, 'The Brontë Society and its Work', in Butler Wood (ed.), *Charlotte Brontë: A Centenary Memorial* (1917), 133.) He was the son of John Enoch, listed in Pigot's *Directory* for Warwick, 1841, and Slater's *Directory* for Warwick, 1850, as a 'Boot & Shoemaker, Auctioneer & Appraiser'. The Census of 1851 describes John Enoch, aged 63, as in addition an Alderman of the Borough, and his son Frederick, aged 24, as unmarried, working as a Printer, Stationer, and shop-assistant. Frederick later wrote a number of songs that were set to music, including 'Sweet Vesper Hymn', set as a 4-part song by Henry Smart and

published by Novello. I am grateful to Kathleen Collins, Music and Drama Librarian at Warwick County Library, for her information about his published work.

To Ellen Nussey, 23 July [1846]

[Haworth]

Dear Ellen

A series of toothaches[1] prolonged and severe, bothering me both day and night have kept me very stupid of late and prevented me from writing to you—More than once I have sat down and opened my desk but have not been able to get up to par. to-day—after a night of fierce pain I am better—much better and I take advantage of the interval of ease to discharge my debt.

I wish I had £50 to spare at present and that you Emily, Anne and I were all at liberty to leave home without our absence being detrimental to anybody—How pleasant to set off en masse to the sea-side and to stay there for a few weeks taking in a stock of health and strength. We could all do with recreation.

I return Miss *Ringrose's "portrait",[2] it is skilfully painted—a little flattering to be exposed to the view of the original—but it gives a stranger a sweet and attractive idea of "notre Amélie" I will not attempt a companion picture of <u>my friend</u> for it is unnecessary. Miss *Ringroses' 'own' letters had delineated her clearly and faithfully enough without the aid of this finished miniature—and yours will I know do for you the same office—independently of elaborate assistance from me.

You have acted well—very well in telling Miss R. the simple truth[3] respecting the position of your family—Adversity agrees with you Ellen—your good qualities are never so obvious as when under the pressure of affliction.—Continued prosperity[4] might develop too much a certain germ of ambition latent in your character—I saw this little germ putting out green shoots when I was staying with you at *Hathersage—it was not then obtrusive and perhaps might never become so—Your good sense—firm principle and kind feeling might keep it down—but if riches were ever to accrue to you—I prophecy that your many virtues would have a severe struggle with this one defect—Still I wish Fortune would try you but not with too strong a temptation—

Holding down my head does not suit this toothache—Give my love to your Mother and Sisters—write again as soon as may be—I liked the extract from the Aunt's[5] letter much

Yours faithfully

C B.

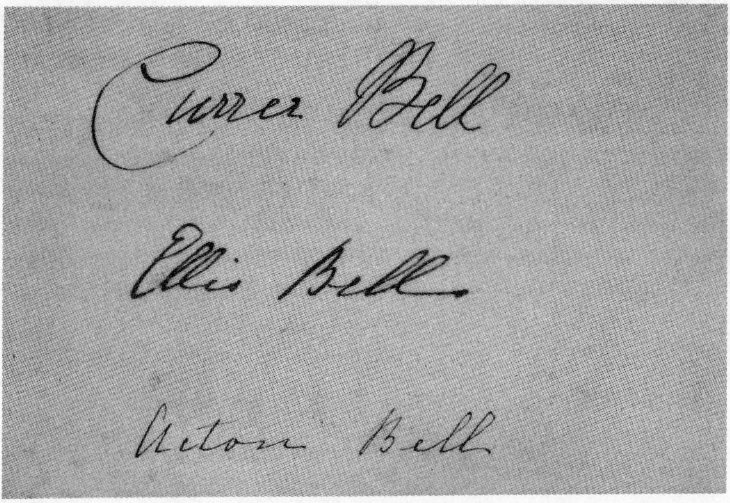

The signatures of the 'Bells'; BPM B.S. Picture 256.

MS Rosenbach. W & S 262 as 24 July.
Address: not in MS.
PM: not in MS.
Date: CB dates 'July 23rd', EN 'July 24–46. EN's date, probably derived from a postmark, is followed by *Shorter* 200 and W & S 262.

1. Mrs Gaskell later reported to Catherine Winkworth that Charlotte had a 'large mouth & many teeth gone'. (Letter of 25.8.1850, CP letter 75.)
2. Presumably a verbal 'miniature' of Amelia Ringrose. CB uses similar terms for verbal portrayal in *The Professor* ch. 14: 'I have left on your mind's eye no distinct picture of her; I have not painted her complexion . . . nor even drawn the outline of her shape.' (123.)
3. The truth about George Nussey's permanent mental illness, or about the Nussey family's financial difficulties, or both. cf. EN 25.4.1846.
4. CB had visited Hathersage while EN was supervising costly extensions to Hathersage Vicarage in preparation for the arrival of Henry Nussey and his wealthy bride. EN's letter to Mary Gorham of 22 July 1845 also shows a rather snobbish mockery of the curate's 'vulgar' speech-habits. See EN to M. Gorham 22.7.1845 and 6.8.1845.
5. Perhaps one of Christopher Ringrose's 4 sisters.

Branwell Brontë to Francis H. Grundy, [?July/August 1846]: [Extract]

[Haworth]

Since I saw Mr. George Gooch,[1] I have suffered much from the accounts of the declining health of her whom I must love most in this world,[2] and who, for my fault, suffers sorrows which surely were never her due. My father, too, is now quite blind,[3] and from such causes literary pursuits have become matters I have no heart to wield. If I could see you it would be a sincere pleasure, but . . . Perhaps your memory of me may be dimmed, for you have known little in me worth remembering; but I still think often with pleasure of yourself, though so different from me in head and mind.

P. B. Brontë.

MS untraced. W & S 254.
Address: not in source.
PM: not in source.
Date: not 1848, the date given by Grundy, but shortly before Mr Brontë's operation for removal of a cataract on 25 Aug. 1846.
Text: This extract is printed in *Grundy* 89 after that referring to 'the coachman's' account of Mrs Robinson's 'sorrows and agonies'. (BB to FHG ?June 1846.) He introduces it with the words 'Soon there is another letter, wearying for work, although illness of body and mind have brought on sleeplessness and disordered action of the heart'.

1. The juxtaposition of this letter with that referring to the Thorp Green coachman has led most commentators to identify the two men. Edward Chitham, to whom I am grateful for first pointing out that Mrs Robinson's coachman was William Allison, believes that Grundy may have misread 'the coachmn' or a similar phrase as 'Geo Gooch'. See his *A Life of Anne Brontë* (Oxford, 1991), 138 and 202 n. 15., and for William Allison, see BB to FHG ?June 1846 n. 1. But

Branwell's handwriting is usually clear and legible. Grundy was working with a railway engineer, George Gooch, in 1841 and 1847. See *Halifax Guardian* 6.3.1841 and 6.3.1847. I am indebted to Juliet Barker for these references.

2. Mrs Robinson. See EN 17.6.1846 n. 6.
3. See the next letter.

To Ellen Nussey, [9 August 1846]

[Haworth]

Dear Nell

Anne and I both thank you for your kind invitation—and our thanks are not mere words of course[1]—they are very sincere both as addressed to yourself and your Mother and Sisters—but we cannot accept it and I think even you will consider our motives for declining valid this time.

In a fortnight I hope to go with papa to Manchester to have his eyes couched[2]—Emily and I made a pilgrimage[3] there a week ago to search out an operator and we found one in the person of a Mr Wilson[4]—He could not tell from description whether the eyes were ready for an operation—Papa must therefore necessarily take a journey to Manchester to consult him—if he judges the cataract ripe—we shall remain—if on the contrary he thinks it not yet sufficiently hardened we shall have to return—and papa must remain in darkness a while longer.

Poor Bessie Hirst![5] I was thinking about her only a day or two before I got your letter. Do you know whether she suffered much pain or whether her death was easy?

I am sorry to hear so indifferent an account of Mrs *Henry[6]—I certainly never did expect she would make an agreeable addition to your family after reading Mrs *Prescott's[7] letter to you respecting her—yet though not agreeable she may still be well-principled and well intentioned—let us hope she is so—for in that case she will never go far wrong—There is a defect in your reasoning about the feelings a wife ought to experience **in paying money for her husband.**[8] Who holds the purse will wish to be Master, Ellen; depend on it whether Man or woman—Who provides the cash will now and then value himself (or herself) upon it—and even in the case of ordinary Minds, reproach the less wealthy partner—besides no husband ought to be an object of charity to his wife—as no wife to her husband *Sisterly affection makes you partial and misleads your usually correct judgment—No dear Nell—it is doubtless pleasant to marry well as they say—but with all pleasures are mixed bitters—I do not wish for you a very rich husband—I should not like you to be regarded by any man even as "a sweet object of charity"[9]

Give my sincere love to all
Yours
C Brontë

MS HM 24445. Envelope: BPM B.S. 104/16. W & S 263.
Address: (envelope): Miss Ellen Nussey | Brookroyd | Birstal | Leeds
PM: (i) HAWORTH (ii) BRADFORD YORKS | AU 10 | 1846 | C (iii) LEEDS | AU 10 | 1846 | F
Annotation (i) on the letter by EN in pencil: Aug 9 -46; (ii) on the envelope by EN in pencil: Aug 46 | Mr B's opera[tion] | on the—eyes | Money | between husband & wife | destroy.
Wafer: rectangular yellow with the words 'Time explains all' within a line border.

1. Customary or ordinary words—i.e. a mere empty formula. cf. the Clarendon *Tenant* (426): 'I merely honoured her with a careless salutation and a few words of course.'
2. To have the opaque crystalline lens depressed in order to restore vision, impaired by the opacity of the cataract.
3. The journey could have been by train to Manchester from Hebden Bridge, the nearest station to Haworth at this date on a line which had been fully open since Mar. 1841.
4. William James Wilson, MRCS (d. 1855) a skilful and respected oculist; an honorary surgeon at the Manchester Royal Infirmary from 1826 to 1855, with a private practice at 72 Mosley Street. He had helped to found the Manchester Institution for curing the Diseases of the Eye in 1814. Mr Wilson may have been recommended to PB by his former friends the Outhwaites, despite a coolness between them in Sept. 1844, evident in a letter from PB in private hands. Dr John Outhwaite (1792–1868), the brother of Anne Brontë's godmother Fanny Outhwaite, had 'spent some time with Mr. Wilson, an eminent surgeon, in Manchester', before graduating 'as Doctor of Medicine in the University of Edinburgh'. (Obit. of John Outhwaite, *Bradford Observer*, 20.2.1868, 4.)
5. Not identified.
6. Henry Nussey's wife, née Emily Prescott.
7. Possibly Mrs William Prescott, Emily's ?sister-in-law.
8. 'in paying money for her husband': a conjectural reading. EN has tried to scrape out the words. Emily's father had been a Liverpool merchant, and his daughter had a 'handsome fortune'. (EN 14.11.1844 notes.)
9. Not traced.

To Ellen Nussey, 21 August [1846]

Address—83 Mount Pleasant
Boundary Street
Oxford Road
Manchester

Dear Ellen

I just scribble a line to you to let you know where I am—in order that you may write to me here for it seems to me that a letter from you would relieve me from the feeling of strangeness I have in this big town.

Papa and I came here on Wednesday,[1] we saw Mr Wilson the Oculist[2] the same day; he pronounced papa's eyes quite ready for an operation and has fixed next Monday[3] for the performance of it—Think of us on that day dear Nell—

We got into our lodgings[4] yesterday—I think we shall be comfortable, at least our rooms are very good, but there is no Mistress of the house[5] (she is very ill and gone out into the country) and I am somewhat puzzled in managing about provisions—we board ourselves—I find myself excessively ignorant—I can't tell what the *deuce to order in the way of meat—&c.

I wish you or your Sister *Anne could give me some hints about how to manage—For ourselves< we> I could <man> contrive—papa's diet is so very simple—but there will be a nurse[6] coming in a day or two—and I am afraid of not having things good enough for her—Papa requires nothing you know but plain beef & mutton, tea and bread and butter but a nurse will probably expect to live much better—give me some hints if you can—

Mr. Wilson says we shall have to stay here for a month at least—it will be dreary—I wonder how poor Emily and Anne will get on at home with Branwell—they too will have their troubles—What would I not give to have you here One is forced step by step to get experience in the world Ellen—but the learning is so disagreeable—One cheerful feature in the business is that Mr Wilson thinks most favourably of the case[7]—

Write very soon—remember me kindly to all

Yours C Brontë

MS HM 24446. Envelope: BPM B.S. 104/17 W & S 264.
Address (envelope): Miss Ellen Nussey | Brookroyd | Birstal | Leeds
PM: (i) MANCHESTER | AU 21 | 1846 | 1 (ii) LEEDS | AU 22 | 1846 | A
Annotation: on the envelope by EN in pencil: Aug 4 <—> from Manchester | during Mr. B's stay. [Part cut away along with the stamp.]

1. Probably by the Leeds–Manchester railroad. See EN 9.8.1846 n. 3. CB was writing on Friday.
2. See EN 9.8.1846 n. 4.
3. The operation was postponed until Tuesday 25 Aug.
4. These were within half a mile of Mrs Gaskell's house in Rumford Street. She writes: '[Mr Wilson] recommended them to comfortable lodgings, kept by an old servant of his. These were in one of numerous similar streets of small monotonous-looking houses, in a suburb of the town.' (*Life* ii. 2–3.) See also Brian Kay and James Knowles, 'Where "Jane Eyre" and "Mary Barton" were born', *BST* 15. 77. 145–8, and the photograph of the house, renumbered 59 Boundary Street West, opp. 146. The authors comment that 'the outlook was not pleasant; it faced a large timber-yard, and the whole neighbourhood was completely built up'.
5. Mrs Ball, wife of Thomas Ball, who is listed as an 'agent' in Slater's *General and Classified Directory* for Manchester (Manchester, 1848).
6. Mr Brontë recorded in his copy of *Graham's Domestic Medicine* that he 'had to take three rooms at £1—5—0, per week, & to board myself, besides Mrs. ?Ryde the nurse, was paid 15^{s} per week, and her [*sic*] boarded besides, at Mr Balls'. (BPM Bon 38, p. 228; *LD* 389.) CB gives a formidable picture of a Mrs Horsfall, the professional nurse who attends Robert Moore in *Shirley* ch. 32.
7. Mr Brontë was fortunate in his doctor. Mr Wilson had 'the most agreeable courtesy of expression in conversation' as well as an immense capacity for work. 'Probably no person . . . was, during 40 years, more generally known and esteemed in Manchester'. (Gérin *CB*, 325, quoting from an obit. notice.) PB noted that Mr Wilson charged him only £10—'I believe he often ch-rg-s £20-or £30-'. (BPM Bon 38, p. 228; *LD* 389.)

To Ellen Nussey, 26 August [1846]

[Manchester]

Dear Ellen

The operation[1] is over—it took place yesterday—Mr Wilson performed it, two other surgeons[2] assisted—Mr Wilson says he considers it quite successful but papa cannot yet see anything—The affair lasted precisely a quarter of an hour—it was not the simple operation of couching Mr Carr[3] described but the more complicated one of extracting the cataract—Mr Wilson entirely disapproves of couching.[4]

Papa displayed extraordinary patience and firmness—the surgeons seemed surprised. I was in the room all the time, as it was his wish that I should be there—of course I neither spoke nor moved till the thing was done—and then I felt that the less I said either to papa or the surgeons, the better—papa is now confined to his bed in a dark room and is not to be stirred for four days—he is to speak and to be spoken to as little as possible—

I am greatly obliged to you for your letter and your kind advice which gave me extreme satisfaction because I found I had arranged most things in accordance with it—and as your theory coincides with my practice I feel assured the latter is right—I hope Mr Wilson will soon allow me to dispense with the nurse—She is well enough[5] no doubt but somewhat too obsequious &c. and not I should think to be much trusted—yet I am obliged to trust her in some things—

Your friend Charlotte has had a letter from Mary Taylor[6]—and she was only waiting to hear from one Ellen Nussey that she had received a similar document in order to communicate the fact—if the said Ellen had not got one too—Charlotte would have said nothing about it for fear of inflicting a touch of pain—I have not my letter here or I should send it to you it was written on the voyage—she refers me to "the long one" for later news—I have not yet seen it.

Greatly was I amused by your accounts of *Joe *Taylor's flirtations[7]—and yet something saddened also—I think Nature intended him for something better than to fritter away his time in making a set of poor, unoccupied spinsters unhappy—The girls unfortunately are forced to care for him and such as him because while their minds are mostly unemployed, their sensations are all unworn and consequently fresh and keen—and he on the contrary has had his fill of pleasure and can with impunity make a mere pastime of other people's torments. This is an unfair state of things, the match is not equal I only wish I had the power to infuse into the souls of the persecuted a little of the quiet strength of pride—of the supporting consciousness of superiority (for they are superior to him because purer) of the fortifying resolve of firmness to bear the present and wait the end. Could all the virgin population of *Birstal and *Gomersal receive and retain these sentiments—*Joe *Taylor would eventually have to vail his crest[8] before them.

Perhaps luckily their feelings are not so acute as one would think and the gentleman's shafts consequently don't wound so deeply as he might desire—I hope it is so.

Give my best love to your Mother and Sisters.

Write soon
C Brontë

MS HM 24447. Envelope: BPM B.S. 104/18. W & S 265.
Address (envelope): Miss Ellen Nussey | Brookroyd | Birstal | Leeds
PM: (i) MANCHESTER | AU 26 — 1 (ii) LEEDS | AU 27 | 1846 | A
Annotation (i) on the letter by EN in ink: Aug 26 — 46; [in pencil]: concerning the operation upon her father's eyes; (ii) on the envelope by EN in pencil: Aug 46 | On Mr B's—J T's flir—. [Part of the envelope has been cut away for the sake of the stamp.]

1. Mr Brontë described the operation for cataract in detail in the margins of his copy of Graham's *Domestic Medicine*. It was performed on the left eye, to which belladonna was applied to expand the pupil before the lens was extracted. See BPM Bon 38, pp. 226–9 (*LD* 389) for the full account. See also EN 13.9.1846 n. 6 for the return of *The Professor* 'curtly rejected by some publisher, on the very day when her father was to submit to his operation'.
2. PB names only 1 assistant surgeon, Mr ?Redicar, 'on whose proper management of the eye, during the operation, much depends'. (BPM Bon 38 p. 228.) Mr Brontë's handwriting is difficult to read. His reference may be to Charles Redfern, recorded in the *British Medical Directory* for 1853, p. 417 as an assistant surgeon at the Manchester Eye Hospital, MRCSE and LSA 1839, living at 23 Great Ducie Street, Manchester.
3. William Carr, the Gomersal practitioner. See EN 3.3.1846 n. 3.
4. PB noted: 'Mr Wilson said that in couching, catar[a]ct often return'd, and the operation had to be repeated.' (BPM Bon 38, p. 229.)
5. PB commented on the nurse's assiduity. (BPM Bon 38, p. 226.)
6. After a $4\frac{1}{2}$-month voyage from 12 Mar. to 24 July 1845, Mary had joined her brother Waring in his house and shop in Herbert Street, Wellington, New Zealand. 'Waring . . . dealt in land, wool, cattle, clothing and piece goods, and general commodities of every kind.' (*Stevens* 66.) Stevens notes that 'Waring was in Sydney early in 1846, so that [Mary] may have been left in charge during his absence.'
7. CB had grown impatient of the constant local gossip about Joe Taylor's philandering. See EN 25.4.1846.
8. cf. 1 *Henry VI*, v. iii. 24–6: 'Now the time is come, | That France must vail her lofty-plumed crest, | And let her head fall into England's lap.' (The lines are part of a speech by 'La Pucelle', the Virgin—Joan of Arc.)

To Ellen Nussey, 31 August [1846]

[Manchester]

Dear Ellen

Thank you for M[ary] T[aylor]'s letter—it contains later news than mine and very good news too—It is evident she is far from unhappy—May she prosper—

Papa is still lying in bed in a dark room with his eyes bandaged—No inflamation[1] ensued but still it appears the greatest care—perfect quiet and utter privation of light are necessary to ensure a good result from the operation—He is very patient but of course depressed and weary—He was allowed to try his sight for the first time yesterday—he could see dimly—Mr Wilson seemed perfectly satisfied and said all was right—

I am truly sorry for your toothache; I have had bad night[s] with the same wretched ailment since I came to Manchester but I am better now—

Give my sincere love to Miss *Wooler[2] when you see her—Give her my address too and tell her to write to me here indeed I shall enclose a scrap of paper which you must deliver to her—

In great haste—with love to all—and hopes and good wishes for poor *George[3]

Yrs
C B—

MS Beinecke, Yale. W & S 266 (part).
Address: not in MS.
PM: not in MS.
Annotation (i) by EN in ink: ?116 Aug 31—46; (ii) in pencil: P Mr B

1. Thus in MS. PB notes: 'I was bled with 8 leeches, at one time, & 6, on another, (these caused but little pain) in order to prevent inflamation—'. (BPM Bon 38, p. 226; *LD* 389.)
2. No letters to Miss Wooler from the Manchester period survive, but the undated fragment beginning 'it was fifteen years ago' (MW ?Nov. / Dec. 1846; W & S 275) refers to PB's 'eye which has been operated on' as if the operation was fairly recent.
3. The name has been deleted, but the outline remains just visible.

To Ellen Nussey, [13 September 1846]

[Manchester]

Dear Ellen

Papa thinks his own progress rather slow but the Doctor affirms he is getting on extremely well—he complains of extreme weakness and soreness in the eye but I suppose that is to be expected for some time to come—he is still kept in the dark—but he now sits up the greatest part of the day—and is allowed a little fire in the room from the light of which he is carefully screened—

Poor George![1] time passes—winter, spring and summer, and his ?natural self delays to return—How can his brothers decline to give assistance in his case? What is a little money compared with the mental and bodily health of one who should ?serve as the prop of his mother [line of writing cut off][2] sighted in their unnatural egotism[3]—

By this time you will have got Mary's letters—most interesting they are—and she is in her element—because she is where she has a toilsome task to perform, an important improvement to effect[4]—a weak vessel[5] (Waring) to strengthen—She will remain in New Zealand as long as she can there find serious work to do—but no longer—

You ask if I have any enjoyment here in truth I can't say I have[6]—and I long to get home—Though unhappily home is not now a place of complete rest—it is sad to think how it is disquieted by a constant phantom, or rather two[7]—Sin and Suffering—They seem to obscure the cheerfulness of day and to disturb the comfort of evening—

Give my love to all at Brookroyd and believe me

[Signature cut off]

P.S I am sorry for poor J. Taylor—does Ellen Taylor[8] live at Hunsworth now?

MS BPM Bon 189. W & S 267 (part).
Address: not in MS.
PM: not in MS.
Annotation in ink, by EN: Sep 13 —46
Date: EN's date, perhaps based on a postmarked envelope or on a now-missing date by CB, suits the content.
Text: The single sheet of paper lacks about 12 mm. at the foot (compared with the sheets of similar unwatermarked cream-wove paper used for EN 26.8.1846 and EN 31.8.1846) where CB's signature has been cut off. About 1 line of text is missing from 1[r] as a result. The postscript is written at the top of 1[r].

1. For George Nussey's mental illness see EN ?30.12.1844 n. 1. The whole para. has been heavily deleted.
2. See note on text above.
3. CB took a critical view of EN's older brothers, especially of Joshua. cf. EN 31.7.1845 and 10.7.1846. Henry Nussey's letter of 12.6.1846 to his mother and sisters also seems to show a willingness to shift responsibility for George to other shoulders: 'George, I hope, is in a fair way for Recovery—& let everything be done to get him to Bonn. Confer with the Taylors & Ringroses about the expense, & friends who might see him.' (MS BL Egerton 3268A fol. 98v.)
4. Perhaps Mary Taylor was trying to make her brother Waring's shop and trading activities more efficient during his absence in Sydney. See EN 26.8.1846 n. 6.
5. cf. 1 Peter 3: 7, where a wife is the 'weaker vessel'.
6. This may be true, but CB was at least fully occupied, for she had begun to write *JE*. Mrs Gaskell praises her determination: 'Charlotte told me that her tale [*The Professor*] came back upon her hands, curtly rejected by some publisher, on the very day when her father was to submit to his operation. But she had the heart of Robert Bruce within her . . . Not only did "The Professor" return again to try his chance among the London publishers, but she began, in this time of care

and depressing inquietude,—in those grey, weary, uniform streets . . . there and then, did the brave genius begin "Jane Eyre." ' (*Life* ii. 7.)

7. In *Paradise Lost* II. 743 the offspring of Satan and Sin is the 'Fantasm' Death. CB associates Branwell's suffering with sin, as she does that of Joseph Nussey in EN 30.12.1845 and June 1846.
8. The Taylors' cousin Ellen had been at Hunsworth when CB wrote to EN on 20.4.1846. It is not clear whether she is sorry for John or Joe Taylor, both of whom lived at Hunsworth.

To Ellen Nussey, [21 September 1846]

[Manchester]

Dear Ellen

I have nothing new to tell you except that papa continues to do well though the process of recovery appears to me very tedious—I daresay it will yet be many weeks before his sight is completely restored—yet every time Mr Wilson comes he expresses his satisfaction at the perfect success of the operation—and assures <us> me Papa will erelong be able both to read and write—he is still a prisoner in his darkened room[1]—into which however a little more light is admitted than formerly.

The nurse goes to day—her departure will certainly be a relief though she is I daresay not the worst of her class. I was much interested in your remarks on your new inmate Mrs N[oble][2] I do hope you will get on pretty well with her—though indeed it must at all times be a bore to have a stranger domesticated in one's family—but if she makes herself tolerably agreeable—the advantage in a pecuniary point of view is certainly not to be despised—

Give My best love to your Mother & Sisters—write to me again soon & believe me

Yours faithfully
C Brontë

In haste
Monday

MS HM 24448. Envelope: BPM B.S. 104/19. W & S 268 as 22 Sept.
Address (envelope): Miss Ellen Nussey | Brookroyd | Birstal | Leeds
PM (i) MANCHESTER | SP 21 | 1846 | I (ii) LEEDS | SP 22 | 1846 | A
Annotation: (i) on the letter by EN in ink: Sep 22—46; (ii) on the envelope by EN in pencil: Sep 22—Mrs Noble
Date: as the first postmark and CB's date, 'Monday', show, the date must be 21 not 22 Sept.

1. PB noted in his copy of *Graham's Domestic Medicine*: 'I was confined, on my back—a month in a dark room, with bandages over my eyes for the greater part of the time—and had a careful nurse, to attend me both night, & day—'. (BPM Bon 38, p. 226; *LD* 389.)
2. Mrs Noble had probably lived or visited relatives in Birstall. EN's 1844 Diary has an entry for 20 Sept., 'Flower show Mrs. Mills Mrs. Nussey Mrs Noble & children', and her 1849 Diary

refers to visits in Apr., July and Sept. from ?S. A. Noble, I. H. Noble, and M. Noble respectively. (EN *Diary* 1844, 1849.)

To Messrs. Aylott and Jones, [?late September 1846]

[?Manchester]

[Once more, in September, she writes]
As the work has received no farther notice from any periodical, I presume the demand for it has not greatly increased.

MS untraced. W & S ii. lll.
Address: not in source.
PM: not in source.
Text: Rylands MS *Life* fol. 318. The sentence is quoted by Mrs Gaskell at the end of *Life* ch. 14 following CB's letter to Aylott and Jones of 23 July 1846. W & S comment, 'At the same time [CB] appears to have asked for two more copies of the "Poems" to be sent to her'; they print in evidence the note beginning 'Gentlemen,—I have received the 2 copies of Bell's Poems', with the date 25 Sept. [1846]. See the next letter.

To Messrs. Aylott and Jones, [?25 September 1846]

Haworth—

Gentlemen
I have received the 2 copies of Bell's Poems—the binding is very neat.[1] I will thank you to send a number of the Dublin University Magazine in case it should contain a notice of the work to my usual address—Haworth—Bradford &c.

I am Gentlemen
Yrs. truly,
C Brontë

MS Mr G. A. Yablon. W & S 269.
Address: not in MS.
PM: not in MS.
Annotation: N° 21
Date: perhaps cut off, since the sheet is 92 mm. × 116 mm. instead of 92 mm. × 139 mm. like the other letters to Aylott and Jones (except that of 7.5.1846.) A May date is possible, but the sequence number 21 indicates a later date than Aylott 18.7.1846 (N° 19) and the missing accompanying letter (N° 20) to Aylott of 23.7.1846; the ref. to the *Dublin University Magazine* anticipates its review of the poems in Oct., and the implication that CB has been away from home suits the time of the Manchester visit. The letter is not in *Shorter*; W & S 269 gives the date 'Sept. 25th [1846]', provisionally accepted here.

1. Perhaps CB had requested 2 gift copies for friends; or this may be a special binding, possibly connected in some way with the listing of the *Poems* in the *Publishers' Circular* for 15 Sept. 1846 as if they had only just been published. See Aylott 25.5.1846 n. 2. The letter is laid in a copy of the poems with a 'geometrical' patterned binding, formerly belonging to the collector John A. Spoor, and later to Mr Arthur Houghton. For a discussion by D. F. Foxon of 'Binding Variants in the Brontës' *Poems*' see *Book Collector* 2 (1953), 219–21; and see also G. D. Hargreaves, 'The Publishing of "Poems by Currer, Ellis and Acton Bell" ', *BST* 15. 79. 297.

To Ellen Nussey, 29 September 1846

[Haworth]

Dear Ellen

When I wrote to you last our return to Haworth was uncertain indeed—but Mr Wilson was called away to Scotland—his absence set us at liberty—I hastened our departure, and now we are at home—Papa is daily gaining strength—he cannot yet exercise his sight much—but it improves and I have no doubt will continue to do so—I feel truly thankful for the good ensured and the evil exempted[1] during our absence—

What you say about J. *Taylor grieves me much and it surprises me too—I know well the malaria[2] of *Hunsworth it is an abominable smell of gas[3]—I was sick from it ten times a day while I stayed there—that they should hesitate to leave from scruples about furnishing new houses provokes and amazes me—is not the furniture they have very decent? The inconsistency of human beings passes belief—I wonder what their sister Mary would say to them if they told her that tale—? She sits on a wooden stool without a back in a log-house[4] without a carpet—and neither is degraded nor thinks herself degraded by such poor accommodation.

**I am glad[5] J. T. has been to see George for I believe he would look more ?sharply to his condition than one of his own brothers would do—do not despair Ellen I still think George may recover—though his restoration may be very gradual.

Mrs N[oble[6]] must be a regular bore with her unfortunate ?homophobia[7] (don't look for that word in the dictionary) She and it together are dear at the price—still the ?cash will be useful—**

I should say *Richard and Miss C[harnock][8] have done well to get spliced at last—long life to them and a harmonious union! Still look out for squalls occasionally—

[Unsigned]

MS BPM B.S. 57. Envelope: BPM B.S. 104/19.2. W & S 270 (part).
Address (envelope): Miss Ellen Nussey | Brookroyd | Birstal | Leeds
PM: (i) BRADFORD [YO]RKS | SP 29 | 18–6 | E (ii) LEEDS | SP 30 | 1846 | A

Annotation on the envelope by EN in pencil: Sep 46 | Of J T | ?Emily &c | amusing. Wafer: blue lozenge with the words 'All's well' within a line border.

Text: The letter is incomplete. EN's annotation shows that a passage referring to Emily Brontë or Emily [Prescott] Nussey, Henry's wife, may have been lost—unless the reference is to Mrs Noble. *Shorter* 207 is drastically abridged; W & S 270 contains only the first 2 paras. but the last para. is printed as part of the postscript of W & S 387 (EN 18.8.1848).

1. CB seems to mean 'removed' or 'averted', usages recorded as obsolete in *OED*.
2. An unhealthy atmosphere, especially associated with low-lying ill-drained areas.
3. Either in the general sense of 'noxious vapour', or literally coal-gas, which was used commercially from about 1815, and was installed in many of the mills in and near Leeds at this period. The Hunsworth cottage was close to the Taylors' mill.
4. Waring Taylor's house in Herbert Street, Wellington, New Zealand. It was a substantial house of sawn timber 'finished on the outside with overlapping weatherboards' and was built well enough to survive an earthquake in 1848. (*Stevens* 63.)
5. 'I am glad J. T. has . . . be useful': a conjectural reading for a heavily deleted passage.
6. See EN 21.9.1846 n. 2.
7. CB may mean 'fear or dislike of men' (from the Latin 'homo' = 'man' rather than the Greek = 'same') on the analogy of 'hydrophobia'. The word is unclear and may be 'monophobia', which should mean a fear of being alone; but compare CB's curious use of 'phobia' instead of 'mania' in *The Professor* 235, where Hunsden describes Frances Henri's enthusiastic love of or mania for England as 'Anglophobia'.
8. EN's elder brother Richard Nussey (1803–72) and Elizabeth, daughter of John Charnock of Leeds, christened at St Peter's Church, Leeds, 4 Apr. 1803. After his marriage Richard Nussey moved to Mr Charnock's home at 103 Woodhouse Lane, Leeds. Local directories for 1847 and 1848 list Richard Nussey as a 'commission agent' connected with the wool trade, with premises at 4 Bond Street, Leeds.

To the Editor of the Dublin University Magazine,[1] *6 October* 1846

[Haworth]

Sir

I thank you in my own name and that of my brothers, Ellis and Acton, for the indulgent notice[2] that appeared in your last number of our first, humble efforts in literature;[3] but I thank you far more for the essay on Modern poetry which preceded that Notice—an essay in which seems to me to be condensed the very spirit of truth and beauty: if all or half your other readers shall have derived from its perusal the delight it afforded to myself and my brothers—your labours have produced a rich result.

After such criticism an author may indeed be smitten at first by a sense of his own insignificance—as we were—but on a second and a third perusal he finds a power and beauty therein which stirs him to a desire to do more and better things—it fulfils the right end of criticism—without absolutely crushing—it corrects and rouses—I again thank you heartily and beg to subscribe myself

Your Constant and grateful reader[4]
Currer Bell.

MS BPM Bon 190. W & S 271.
Address: not in MS.
PM: not in MS.

1. For the *Dublin University Magazine* see Aylott 7.5.1846 n. 4. The editor was John Francis Waller (1810–94), an Irish barrister and poet, who had taken over the editorship in July 1845. The magazine had been founded in 1833 by a group of graduates and undergraduates of Trinity College Dublin. Strongly Protestant and anti-revolutionary, it had been an immediate success in Ireland, and would appeal to the Brontës.
2. This review, in an article entitled 'Evenings with our younger poets—the first evening' (vol. 28, Oct. 1846, 383–98) was by William Archer Butler (*c*.1814–48) a founder of the magazine who had been Professor of Moral Philosophy at Trinity College Dublin since 1837. He reviewed poems by Mrs Crosland (Camilla Dufour Toulmin, 1812–95) and Richard Hengist Horne (1803–84) in the same article. Butler's allusion to one of the Brontës' favourite poets, William Cowper, would have pleased them: he found the poems 'uniform in a sort of Cowperian amiability and sweetness, no-wise unfragrant to our critical nostrils', was discriminating in his choice of quotations—3 of them taken from poems by EJB—found Currer Bell's 'Gilbert' 'impressively told', and concluded that the Bells' verses were 'full of unobtrusive feeling; and their tone of thought . . . unaffected and sincere.' See *Allott* 63–4, *Dublin University Magazine* 28 (Oct. 1846) 392–3.
3. The *Poems* were the Bells' first published work apart from 2 untraced poems by CB, but they were not by any means their 'first . . . efforts'.
4. CB sounds sincere: the magazine was not taken at the parsonage, for she had to ask Aylott and Jones to send her a copy 'in case it should contain a notice of the work' (Aylott ?25.9.1846), but someone in Haworth—possibly A. B. Nicholls—may have been a subscriber. The magazine does not appear in the list of periodicals taken by the Keighley Mechanics' Institute in 1841, though it could have been added later. See Clifford Whone, 'Where the Brontës Borrowed Books', *BST* 11. 60. 344–58.

To Ellen Nussey, 14 October 1846

[Haworth]

Dear Ellen

I read your letter with attention—not on my own account—for any project which infers the necessity of my leaving home is impracticable to me[1]—but on yours.

If your brother Richard has really interest to get you—I will not say several—but two or three pupils—he would be performing a really kind and brotherly act to secure you that number—Be assured Ellen that you could instruct them[2] without mine or any other assistance—if they were not more advanced than it is at all usual for children to be, at the ages of 10—11—12—There would not be work for two teachers—and what is more to the purpose—there would assuredly not be profit for two—after deducting an equitable sum for your Mother—At the present rate of competition it would be vain to expect a great number of pupils at first[3]—nor would a great number be necessary if there were only yourself to be maintained out of your earnings—<whereas> £20 clear gain—would be a very comfortable thing in that case, but if at the end of the year—you had to halve it with another, it would be a very different <thing> 'affair'—A Master or two might be necessary to help you with the accomplishments—but the expense of paying them would be nothing to the subtraction of an equal share for a regular co-adjutor.

Take courage—try the matter by yourself—Your Sisters can keep the house—you can devote yourself to the schoolroom.

I talk in this wise way, and yet to say the truth—had I no will or interest to consult but my own were I an isolated being without ties or duties connected with others I should probably with pleasure and promptitude have cast in my lot with yours—and struggled to double the £20 which I should scruple to share—But if I could leave home Ellen—I should not be at Haworth now—I know life is passing away and I am doing nothing—earning nothing a very bitter knowledge it is at moments—but I see no way out of the mist—More than one very favourable opportunity has now offered which I have been obliged to put aside—probably when I am free to leave home I shall neither be able to find place nor employment—perhaps too I shall be quite past the prime of life—my faculties will be rusted—and my few acquirements in a great measure forgotten—These ideas sting me keenly sometimes—but whenever I consult my Conscience it affirms that I am doing right in staying at home—and bitter are its upbraidings when I yield to an eager desire for release—I returned to Brussels after Aunt's death against my conscience—prompted by what then seemed an irresistible impulse—I was punished for my selfish folly by a total withdrawal for more than two year[s] of happiness and peace of mind[4]—I could hardly expect success if I were to err again in the same way—

I should like to hear from you again soon—Bring Richard to the point and make him give you a clear not a vague account of what pupils he really could procure you—people often think they can do great things in that way till they have tried—but getting pupils is unlike getting any other sort of goods.

C Brontë

MS HM 24449. W & S 273.
Address: not in MS.
PM: not in MS.

1. CB continued to make her duty to her father her primary concern to the end of her life. She agreed to marry Mr Nicholls in 1854 on condition that she should not leave her father, and for her father's sake 'proposed a plan of residence—which should maintain his seclusion and convenience uninvaded'. (Vol. iii, EN 11.4.1854.)
2. EN's school project did not materialize, though her brother Richard's marriage into a wealthy family may have given him an increase of influence and 'interest'. See EN 29.9.1846 n. 8.
3. CB speaks from experience; in 1844 she had found that there were 'no pupils to be had'. (EN 2.10.1844.)
4. EN commented, probably in the 1890s:

   Charlotte suffered because conscience condemned her return to Brussels and absence from home on account of her Father. There were special reasons for her remaining at home discovered too late for immediate remedy. The truth, the real cause of C's sad suffering was in the fact that Mr. B. in conjunction with Mr S. (Peter Augustus Malone) had fallen into habits of intemperance. This was known to very few persons, and is only now named for Charlotte's dear sake. She was indeed a brave little woman. She remedied the evil so quietly and firmly that her dearest friend and guest never had a suspicion of what was being done—till told long after by C. B. herself. The evil began in her absence. Such consequences ensuing on her absence, conscience accused her of dereliction of duty. (*Hatfield* 256–7.)

Mr Nicholls apparently endorsed these allegations of PB's drinking. (*CBCircle* 109.)

It is true that Mr Brontë had to deny rumours that he was drinking too much, e.g. in a letter, possibly to a Mr Greenwood, of 4.10.1843, where he attributes the slanders to his use of an eye-lotion. (W & S 164.) There is no evidence that the curate J. W. Smith ('Malone') was a heavy drinker. EN did not know of CB's letters to M. Heger, which revealed a primary cause of her 'more than two years' loss of peace of mind, but like Mrs Gaskell EN was anxious not to hint at a cause that implied less than perfect 'purity of mind'. *Villette* was to lead to speculation about an emotional entanglement on CB's part with her Brussels schoolteacher.

To Ellen Nussey, 17 November 1846

[Haworth]

Dear Ellen

I will just write a brief despatch to say that I received yours and that I was very glad to get it—I do not know when you have been so long without writing to me before—but I had begun to imagine that you were perhaps gone to your brother Joshua's[1]—I wish you may have a pleasant visit while you are there something that will do you good—I am afraid "a new kind of botheration" would not answer that purpose—Do you think of staying long? Tell me when you write how they receive you especially Mrs Joshua—[2]

Your visit to George must have been a mournful one—[h]is delusion is of the most painful kind for his relations—how strange that in his eye affection should be <convert> 'transformed' into hatred—it is as if the mental vision were inverted—and such is no doubt the case—the change in his brain distorts all impressions—Depend on it it would not be well for him to come home under such circumstances. Papa continues to do very well—he read prayers in the Church twice last Sunday—Next Sunday he will have to take the whole duty of the three services himself[3] as Mr Nicholls is in Ireland—

Remember me to your Mother and Sisters—write as soon as you possibly can after you get to Oundle—Good luck go with you.

C Brontë

MS BPM Gr. E 12. W & S 274 (part). *BST* 17. 90. 358.
Address: Not in MS.
PM: not in MS.

1. See EN 24.8.1838 n. 4. The Revd Joshua Nussey became the Vicar of Oundle, Northants. in 1845. CB had earlier deplored his failure to invite EN for a 'lengthened visit'. (EN 10.7.1846.)

2. Mrs Anne Elizabeth Nussey, née Alexander (1788–1875), a sister of Henry Alexander, a director of the East India Company.
3. Mr Brontë's ministerial duties had probably ceased on or just after 20 July 1846, when his signature in the Haworth Baptismal Register is almost illegible. They had been resumed by 19 Oct. The Revd A. B. Nicholls, his curate, was the chief officiating minister between these two dates, as he had been since Oct. 1845, and he was still taking most of the Sunday services until this visit to Ireland. For his family connections in Ireland see vol. ii, Biographical Notes.

To Margaret Wooler, [?November/December 1846]: [Fragment]

[Haworth]

it was fifteen years ago[1]—and his spirits are improved since his restoration to sight This last circumstance alone furnishes a continual subject for gratitude; those were indeed mournful days[2]—when Papa's vision was wholly obscured—when he could do nothing for himself and sat all day-long in darkness and inertion—Now—to see him walk about independently—read, write &c. is indeed a joyful change.

There is still one point on which I do not feel quite easy—it is that he continues to see spots[3] before the very eye which has been operated on and from which the lens is removed—he mentioned the circumstance to Mr. Wilson[4]—who put it off as a matter of no consequence, but without offering any explanation of the cause or nature of the appearance. I should much like to know Mr. Wm. Wooler's[5] opinion on the point—will you ask him some day when you have an opportunity.

I pity Mr. Thomas[6] from my heart. For ten years—he has now, I think, been a sufferer from nervous complaints—For ten years he has felt the tyranny of Hypochondria[7]—A most dreadful doom, far worse than that of a man with healthy nerves buried for the same length of time in a subterranean dungeon—I endured it but a year—and assuredly I can never forget the concentrated anguish of certain insufferable moments and the heavy gloom of many long hours—besides the preternatural horror which seemed to clothe existence and Nature—and which made Life a continual waking Night-mare—Under such circumstances the morbid Nerves can know neither peace nor enjoyment—whatever touches—pierces them—sensation for them is all suffering—A weary burden nervous patients consequently become to those about them—they know this and it infuses a new gall[8]—corrosive in its extreme acritude, into their bitter cup—When I was at Dewsbury-Moor[9]—I could have been no better company for you than a stalking ghost—and I remember I felt my incapacity to impart pleasure fully as much as my powerlessness to receive it—Mr Thomas, no doubt, feels the same—How grievous that with his principles, talents and acquirements the want

MS Fitzwilliam, W & S 275.
Address: not in MS.
PM: not in MS.
Date: The content and paper indicate late Nov. 1846 or early Dec. 1846. The handwriting, while not ruling out this period, would allow for a date in 1847–8. Content: CB writes of the cataract operation of 25 Aug. and the resulting 'joyful change' as if they were recent events. Paper: the size of the sheet is the same, within 2 mm., as that used in EN 28.12.1846 and 19.1.1847. All 3 letters are cream wove, and the fragment, like EN 28.12.1846, is watermarked JOYNSON, with a date of which the last digit is not clear; it may be 1845 or 1846.
Text: an undated fragment. The annotations in pencil suggesting dates of late 1846 or 1852 have no authority.

1. CB may refer to her father's serious illness in 1831, the year in which she first attended Miss Wooler's school. PB had written to Mrs Franks on 28.4.1831, 'I have for nearly a year past, been in but a very delicate state of health . . . For the six months, last past, I have been weak in body, and my spirits have often been low.'
2. Mr Brontë recorded in his copy of *Graham's Domestic Medicine*: 'After a year of <nearly total blindness> blindness—I was so far restored to sight, as to be able to read, and write, and find my way, without a guide—'. (227.) 'Before the operation, for about a year, I could neither see to read, or write, or walk without a guide—Jany. 1847. P.B.' (BPM Bon 38, p. 228; *LD* 389.)
3. Perhaps these were 'floaters', the commonly occurring perception of small specks floating in front of the eye, 'due to cells and fragments of débris in the vitreous cavity of the eye'. (*Encyclopaedia Britannica* (1982), 7. p. 123.)
4. William James Wilson, the surgeon who had performed the operation. See EN 9.8.1846 n. 4.
5. Margaret Wooler's brother William Moore Wooler, a retired general practitioner living in Dewsbury. See EN 21.7.1832 n. 7.
6. Thomas Wooler (13.7.1803–1895), a younger brother of Margaret Wooler, to whom CB wrote on 12.3.1852: 'I am truly glad to learn that satisfactory tidings have been received regarding Mr Thomas . . . foreign scenes and faces may prove a salutary stimulus; ere now I have observed that persons of diffident, self-doubting character are more at ease amongst total strangers than with those to whom they are partially known.'
7. CB uses this word to mean intense depression, not necessarily accompanied by preoccupation with imaginary ailments. In ch. 23 of *The Professor* William Crimsworth's Hypochondria is imagined as a being of preternatural horror 'with arms of bone' who discourses of 'her own Country—The Grave'. (228.)
8. The recurrent biblical imagery of the 'cup', as in Isaiah 51: 17, Revelation 16: 19, is combined here with the 'vinegar . . . mingled with gall' offered to Christ on the cross (Matthew 27: 34). The metaphors recur in CB's novels, most memorably in *Villette* 223–4.
9. Miss Wooler's school at Heald's House, where CB was a teacher until 22 Dec. 1838. Her statement that she 'endured [Hypochondria] but a year' may support other indications that the school moved from Roe Head early in 1838, not in 1837. See EN 4.1.1838 and 20.1.1839, notes.

To Ellen Nussey, [13 December 1846]

[Haworth]

Dear Ellen

I hope you are not frozen up in Northamptonshire[1]—the cold here is dreadful I do not remember such a series of North-Pole-days—England might really have taken a slide up into the Arctic Zone[2]—the sky looks like ice—the earth is frozen, the wind is as keen as a two-edged blade—I cannot keep myself warm—We have all had severe colds and coughs in consequence of the severe weather—Poor Anne has suffered greatly from asthma—but is now I am glad to say rather better—she had two nights last week when her cough and difficulty of breathing were painful indeed to hear and witness and must have been most distressing to suffer—she bore it as she does all affliction—without one complaint—only sighing now and then when nearly worn out—she has[3] an extraordinary heroism of endurance. I admire but I certainly could not imitate her.

Meantime, I fear you dear Nell, must have had your own share of miseries; the habitation of economical gentility[4] would not be the most desirable in the world at this season—and I imagine you must often have longed to be back in your Mother's warm room or at Brookroyd drawing-room[5] comfortable fire-side—Write soon again and let me know how you are—

You say I am "to tell you plenty"—What would you have me to say—nothing happens at Haworth—nothing at least of a pleasant kind—one little incident indeed occurred about a week ago to sting us to life—but if it gives no more pleasure for you to hear than it did for us to witness—you will scarcely thank <you> 'me' for adverting to it—

It was merely the arrival of a Sheriff's Officer[6] on a visit to Branwell—inviting him either to pay his debts or to take a trip to York—Of course his debts had to be paid—it is not agreeable to lose money time after time in this way but it is ten times worse—to witness the shabbiness of his behaviour on such occasions[7]—But where is the use of dwelling on this subject it will make him no better.

I am glad to hear that Mary *?Hurst[8] is likely to marry well—is her intended a clergyman? I have not heard of any further tidings from *Mary *Taylor—I send you the last French Newspaper[9] several have missed coming—I don't know why—Do you intend paying a visit to Sussex[10] before you return home?—Write again soon—your last epistle was very interesting—

[I am dear Nell
Yours in spirit & flesh
C B—

Dec 13th/46][11]

MS HM 24450. W & S 276.
Address: not in MS.
PM: not in MS.
Annotation (i) by EN in ink: Dec ?15 —46; (ii) by EN in pencil: Anne's illness and her "indurance." Story of Sheriff's officer's visit to Branwell "Either pay his debts or take a trip to York".
Date: At the end of the letter EN copied words which had been cut out, including what was

probably CB's original date, 'Dec 13th./46'. Her note at the head, 'Dec 15 —46' may be taken from a postmark.

1. EN was staying at her brother Joshua's vicarage in Oundle. See EN 17.11.1846 n. 1.
2. CB was fascinated by Bewick's description of the Arctic zone, with its 'multiplied rigors of extreme cold' in his *History of British Birds* ii. p. xii, and quoted it tellingly in *JE* ch. 1. In Yorks. frosts and snow in late Nov. had heralded a severe, very frosty Dec. with cold winds on 13 days. *Shackleton* noted that 13 Dec. was 'clear nearly', with a 'v. hard frost'.
3. CB changed 'had' to 'has'.
4. EN and CB considered that Mrs Joshua Nussey's chilly house matched her temperament. See EN ?19.1.1847.
5. MS may read 'drawing-rooms'.
6. After the passing of the County Court Act of 28 Aug. 1846 County Courts empowered to recover small debts replaced the old courts of request. BB apparently risked accumulating debts in the expectation of receiving money 'through the hands of one whom I may never see again'. (BB to JBL *c.*Jan. 1847; W & S 278.) When Mr Nicholson of the Old Cock Inn at Halifax threatened a court summons on ?17.6.1848 Branwell asked Leyland to tell him that his 'receipt of money on asking, through Dr Crosby' was morally certain. (W & S 376.) For Dr Crosby see BB to FHG Oct. 1845 n. 13. Branwell implies that the doctor would act as an intermediary for Mrs Robinson.
7. Branwell had sunk into a state of self-pitying lethargy in Oct. 1846, when he wrote to J. B. Leyland: 'All is yet with me clouds and darkness . . . Constant and unavoidable depression of mind and body sadly shackle me in even trying to go on with any mental effort.' (W & S 272.)
8. Perhaps Mary Hirst, daughter of a clothier, Abraham Hirst of Birstall, b. 22 Mar. 1817 and baptized by the elder W. M. Heald on 4 May that year; but Hirst was a common name in the Birstall area. In EN's 1849 Diary there is a 'reminder' entry for 20 Apr.: 'Mary Hirst married 1847'. (EN *Diary* 1849.)
9. The newspaper, which is never named, was circulated among friends by the Taylors of Hunsworth; it was last referred to in EN 31.3.1846.
10. i.e. to Mary Gorham's home at Cakeham.
11. The bracketed words were written by EN to replace the original text, which has been cut away.

To Ellen Nussey, 28 December 1846

[Haworth]

Dear Ellen

I feel as if it was almost a farce to sit down and write to you now with nothing to say worth listening to—and indeed if it were not for two reasons I should put off the business a[t] least a fortnight hence—

The first reason is, I want another letter from you for your letters are interesting, they have something in them, some information—some results of experience & observation—one receives them with pleasure and reads them with relish—and these letters I cannot expect to get unless I reply to them—I wish the correspondence could be so managed as to be all on your side—The second reason is derived from a remark in your last that you felt lonely, something as I was at *Stonegappe[1] and Brussels,[2] and that consequently you had a peculiar desire to hear from old acquaintance—I can understand and sympathise with this—I remember the shortest note was a treat to me when I was at the above-named places—therefore I now write—

I have also a third reason—it is a haunting terror lest you should imagine I forget you—that my regard cools with absence—&c. nothing irritates and stings me like this—It is not in my nature to forget your nature—though I daresay I should spit fire and explode sometimes if we lived together continually, and you too would be angry now & then and then we should get reconciled and jog on as before—Do you ever get dissatisfied with your own temper Nell when you are long fixed to one place, in one scene subjected to one monotonous species of annoyance? I do; I am now in that unenviable frame of mind—my humour I think is too soon overthrown—too sore—too demonstrative and vehement—I almost long for some of the uniform serenity you describe in Mrs *Joshua's disposition[3]—or at least I would fain have her power of self-control and Concealment—but I would not take her artificial habits and ideas along with her composure—no—after all I would prefer being as I am.

I can fancy that you have not much in common with those you see at *Oundle—You do right not to be annoyed at any nuisances of conventionality you meet with amongst them—regard all their ways in the light of fresh experience for you—if you see any honey amongst them, gather it, and never mind their snobbishness[4] (see Punch.[5]) But you don't want this advice—you practise, while I preach. Yet I don't after all consider that we ought to despise everything we see in the world merely because it is not what we are accustomed [to]—I suspect on the contrary—that there are not unfrequently substantial reasons ?underhand[6] for customs that appear to us absurd—and if I were ever again to find myself amongst strangers—I should be solicitous to examine before I condemned. Indiscriminating irony and fault-finding is just sumphishness[7] and that is all—

Anne is now much better—but Papa has been for near a fortnight far from well with the Influenza—he has at times a most distressing cough and his spirits are much depressed—I am sorry to hear of your Sister *Anne's ill health—but this cold weather would try any body[8]—

I wish you a happy Christmas[9]—write again soon—

C B—

MS HM 24451. Envelope: BPM B.S. 104/20. W & S 277.
Address (envelope): Miss Ellen Nussey | The Vicarage | Oundle | Northamptonshire
PM: (i) HAWORTH (ii) BRADFORD YORKS | DE 28 | 1846 (iii) WAKEFIELD | DE 29 | 1846 | A
Annotation on the envelope by EN in pencil: Oundle | 46 | On pleases [*sic*] of Society | good.
Wafer: a pink rectangle with the words 'Absent not forgot' within a line border.

1. The Sidgwicks' house at Lothersdale, Yorks., where CB had been a governess from late May to July 1839. See her letters for that period.

2. CB had felt especially isolated during her second year at the Pensionnat Heger in Brussels. On 29 May 1843 she had written to EJB: 'I get on from day to day in a Robinson-Crusoe-like condition—very lonely.'
3. cf. CB's comments on EN's sister-in-law in EN 13.12.1846 and 19.1.1847.
4. W. M. Thackeray's satirical papers, 'The Snobs of England by One of Themselves' appeared in *Punch* from 7 Mar. 1846 to 27 Feb. 1847. He 'reinterpreted the word "snob", turning the mere swaggering vulgarian (the sense hitherto) into the careful imitator of his superiors, the sham gentleman.' (Alan Horsman, *The Victorian Novel* (Oxford, 1990), 81.) In 'Snobs and Marriage' on 26 Dec. Thackeray had found snobbery ubiquitous: 'Art not thou, too, a Snob and a brother?' Earlier, in 'Clerical Snobs and Snobbishness' on 23 May, he had asked 'What is worldliness but snobbishness?', had deplored 'snobbishness . . . carried to quite an awful pitch' in the 'odious, mean, and disgusting' *Court Circular*, and satirized clerics who toadied to the nobility. CB would perhaps know that Joshua Nussey had been the domestic chaplain to Lord Blayney.
5. *Punch, or the London Charivari*, founded on 17 July 1841, was at this date still fairly radical.
6. W & S 277 reads 'underlaid', but no i-dot is visible in the MS. 'Underhand' can mean 'unobtrusive, secret'.
7. *OED* and Chambers's *Dictionary* derive the word from 'sumph', a provincial word for 'a blockhead, a soft, sheepish fellow'. *Wright* defines 'sumph' as a simpleton or a surly or sullen person.
8. See EN 13.12.1846 n. 2. 'Much snow', north winds, and very hard frosts had returned on 22 Dec. after a brief respite, and lasted until 28 Dec., when there were signs of a thaw. (*Shackleton*.)
9. Christmas is celebrated from 25 Dec. until the Feast of the Epiphany, 6 Jan.; CB's Christmas wishes, though belated according to modern usage, must have been regarded as timely. They do not imply that the letter should be redated.

To Ellen Nussey, ?19 January 1847

[Haworth]

Dear Ellen

I thank you again for your last letter which I found as full or fuller of interest than either of the preceding ones—it is just written as I wish you to write to me—not a detail too much—a correspondence of that sort is the next best thing to actual conversation—though it must be allowed that between the two there is a wide gulph still—

I imagine your face—voice—presence very plainly when I read your letters—still—imagination is not reality and when I return them to their envelope and put them by in my desk—I feel the difference sensibly enough—

My curiosity is a little piqued about that Countess you mention[1]—what is her name? you have not yet given it—I cannot decide from what you say whether she is really clever or only eccentric—the two sometimes go together but are often seen apart—I generally feel inclined to fight very shy of eccentricity and have no small horror of being thought eccentric myself—by which observation I don't mean to insinuate that I class myself under the head clever—God knows a more consummate ass in sundry important points has seldom browzed the green herb of his bounties[2] than I—Oh Lord Nell—I'm in danger sometimes of falling into self-weariness—

I used to say and to think in former times times that you would certainly be married—I am not so sanguine on that point now—It will never suit you to accept a husband you cannot love or at least respect—and it appears there are many chances against your meeting with such a one under favourable circumstances—besides from all I can hear and see Money seems to be regarded as almost the Alpha and Omega of requisites in a wife—Well Nell if you are destined to be an old maid I don't think you will be a repining one—I think you will find resources in your own mind and disposition which will help you to get on[3]—

As to society <it seems> ʽI don'tʼ understand much about it—but from the few glimpses I have had of its machinery it seems to me to be a very strange, complicated affair indeed—wherein Nature is turned upside down—Your well-bred people appear to me figuratively speaking to walk on their heads—to see everything the wrong way up—a lie is with them truth—truth a lie—eternal and tedious botheration is their notion of happiness—sensible pursuits their ennui—

—But this may be only the view ignorance takes of what it cannot understand—I refrain from judging them therefore—but if I was called upon to swop (you know the word I suppose?) to swop tastes and ideas and feelings with **Mrs Joshua Nussey**[4] for instance—I should prefer walking into a good Yorkshire kitchen fire—and concluding the bargain at once by an act of voluntary combustion—Is she a frog or a fish—? She is certainly a specimen of some kind of cold-blooded animal—**To live with a ?decent[5] girl like you day after day and never to ?thaw is intolerable**—All here is as usual—

Write again soon
Yours faithfully
C Brontë

MS BPM B. S. 57.5. W & S 279 (part).
Address: not in MS.
PM: not in MS.
Annotation (i) by EN in ink: 124 Jan 19—47; (ii) in pencil: ?Society
Date: CB's date, at the end of the letter, is probably 'Jany. 19 47'.

1. Not identified.
2. cf. Job 6: 5, 'Doth the wild ass bray when he hath grass?' and Genesis 1: 30, 'And to every beast of the earth . . . I have given every green herb for meat'.
3. CB recurred to the topic of old maids in *Shirley* ch. 10.
4. The name is heavily deleted, as is the sentence 'To live with . . . intolerable'. For Mrs Joshua Nussey see preceding letters to EN and notes.
5. MS may read 'dear'.

Branwell Brontë to J. B. Leyland, [24 January 1847]

[Haworth]

My dear Sir,

I am going to write a scrawl, for the querulous egotism of which I must intreat your mercy; but, when I look upon my past, present, and future, and then into my own self I find much, however unpleasant, that yearns for utterance.

This last week an honest and kindly friend has warned me that concealed hopes about one lady <may> should be given up let the effort to do so cost what it may. He is the Family Medical attendant,[1] and was commanded by Mr Evans M.P. for North Derbyshire[2] to return me, unopened, a letter which I addressed to Thorp Green and which the Lady was not permitted to see. She too, surrounded by powerful persons who hate me like Hell, has sunk into religious melancholy, believes that her weight of sorrow[3] is Gods punishment, and hopelessly resigns herself to her doom. God only knows what it does cost, and will, hereafter, cost me, to tear from my heart and remembrance the thousand recollections that rush upon me at the thought of four years gone by. Like ideas of sunlight to a man who has lost his sight they must be <visions>bright phantoms not to be realized again.

I had reason to hope[4] that ere ꜛveryꜛ long I should be the husband of a Lady whom I loved best in the world and with whom, in more than competence, I might live at leisure to try to make myself a name in the world of posterity, without being pestered by the small <by> but countless botherments, which like mosquitoes sting us in the world of work-day toil. That hope, and herself are gone—She to wither into patiently pining decline—It, to make room for drudgery falling on one now ill fitted to bear it.

That ill-fittedness rises from causes which I should find myself able <to> partially ꜛtoꜛ overcome had I bodily strength, but with the want of that, and with the presence of daily lacerated nerves the task is not easy. I have been in truth too much petted through life, and in my last situation I was so much master, and gave myself so much up to enjoyment that now when the cloud of ill health and adversity has come upon me it will be a disheartening job to work myself up again through a new lifes battle, from the position of five years ago to which I have been compelled to retreat with heavy loss and no gain. My army stands now where it did then, but mourning the slaughter of Youth, Health, Hope and both mental and physical elasticity.

The last two losses are indeed important to one who once built his hopes of rising in the world <to> on the possession of them. Noble writings, works of art, music or poetry now instead of rousing my imagination, cause a whirlwind of blighting sorrow that sweeps over my mind with unspeakable dreariness, and if I sit down and try to write all ideas that used to come clothed in sunlight now press round me in funeral black; for really every pleasureable excitement that I used to know has changed to insipidity or pain.

I shall never be able to realize the too sanguine hopes of my friends, for at 28 I am a thouroughly old man—mentally and bodily—Far more so indeed than I am willing to express. God knows I do not scribble like a poetaster when I quote Byron's terribly truthful words[5]—

> "No more, no more, oh! never more on me
> The freshness of the heart shall fall like dew,
> Which, out of all the lovely things we see
> Extracts emotions beautiful and new!"

I used to think that if I could have for a week the free range of the British Museum—the Library included—I could feel as though I were placed for seven days in paradise, but now really, dear Sir, my eyes would roam over the Elgin marbles, the Egyptian saloon and the most treasured volumes like the eyes of a dead cod fish.

My rude rough aquaintances here ascribe my unhappiness solely to causes produced by my sometimes irregular life, because they have known no other pains than those resulting from excess or want of ready cash—They do not know that I would rather want a shirt than want a springy mind, and that my total want of happiness, were I to step into York Minster now, would be far, far worse than their want of a hundred pounds when they might happen to need it; and that if a dozen glasses or a bottle of wine drives off their cares, such cures only make me outwardly passable in company but never drive off mine.

I know, only that it is time for me to be something when I am nothing. That my father cannot have long to live, and that when he dies my evening, which is already twilight, will become night—That I shall then have a constitution still so strong that it will keep me years in torture and despair when I should every hour pray that I might die.

I know that I am avoiding, while I write, one greatest cause of my utter despair—but by God Sir it is nearly too bitter for me to allude to it!

For four years (including one year of absence) a lady intensely loved me[6] as I did her, and each sacrificed to that love all we had to sacrifice, and held out to each other HOPE for our guide to the future. She was all I could wish for in a woman, and vastly above me in rank, and she loved me even better than I did her—Now what is the result of these four years? UTTER WRECK—The "Great Britain"[7] is not so thoroughly stranded as I am. I have recieved today, since I began my scrawl—a note from her maid Miss Ann Marshall and I know from it that she has been terrified by vows which she was forced to swear to, on her husband's deathbed, (with every <ghastly> addition of terror which the ghastly dying eye could inflict upon a keenly sensitive and almost worried woman's mind) a complete severance from him in whom lay her whole hearts feelings. When that husband was scarce cold in his grave her relations, who controlled the whole property overwhelmed her with their tongues, and I am quite consciou[s] that she has succumbed in terror, to what they have said.

To no one living have I said what I now say to you, and I should not bother yourself with my incoherent account did I not believe that you would be able to understand somewhat of what I meant—though not all Sir—for he who is without hope, and knows that his <?sky> clock is at twelve at night, cannot communicate his feelings to one who finds his at twelve at noon.

I long to be able to see you, and I shall try to do so on Friday next—the 29th inst. ˋor on Saturdayˊ if I am at all able to take the journey.

Till then I am,
Dear Sir,
Yours sincerely,
P. B. Brontë.

MS Brotherton. W & S 280.
Address: not in MS.
PM: not in MS.
Date: There are 4 possible months in 1846–8 in which 'Friday 29th', the date when Branwell hoped to meet Leyland, might occur: May 1846, which is too near the date of Mr Robinson's death; Sept. 1848, when Branwell himself died; and Jan. or Oct. 1847. Since Brunel's ship the *Great Britain* was no longer stranded by Oct. 1847, the Jan. 1847 date given by W & S is confirmed.

1. John Crosby. See BB to FHG Oct. 1845 n. 13.
2. William Evans. See BB to FHG Oct. 1845. n. 6 and to JBL June 1846 notes.
3. No evidence for Mrs Robinson's alleged religious melancholy has come to light, nor did she 'wither into patiently pining decline'. In Nov. and Dec. 1846 she had been consulting her solicitor Henry Newton about her powers under her marriage settlement, and adding codicils to her will as a result of her daughter Lydia's Gretna Green marriage with the actor Henry Roxby. In Jan. 1847 she settled her lawyer's bill and continued to write energetic letters on business matters connected with the estate. On 8 Nov. 1848 she was to marry Sir Edward Dolman Scott, whose first wife had died on 4 Aug. that year. See BPM Robinson Papers and EN 17.6.1846 notes 4 and 6.
4. By 1846 Branwell was linking his love with despair, not hope. In the sonnet 'When all our cheerful hours seem gone for ever' Branwell imagines himself joining his 'well loved' one on 'Death's dreary road': 'each step by her | Would draw our own steps to the same abode, | And make a festival of sepulture'. (Neufeldt *BBP* 283, Winnifrith *BBP* 170.)
5. Slightly misquoted from *Don Juan* c. 1. ccxiv.
6. Branwell's immediate family, and Mrs Gaskell, believed that Mrs Robinson had been a 'cold-hearted seductress'. Mrs Gaskell withdrew her allegations only after Mrs Robinson's lawyers threatened legal action. See EN 31.7.1845 n. 11.
7. Isambard Kingdom Brunel's great iron ship had left Liverpool for New York on 22 Sept. 1846, but within a few hours ran aground in Dundrum Bay, Co. Down, Ireland. Though holed, it did not break up, and no lives were lost, but it proved impossible to refloat until 27 Aug. 1847, when it was towed into Liverpool docks and eventually repaired.

To Ellen Nussey, ?28 January 1847

[Haworth]

Dear Nell,

I got your letter, but it had been opened—the paper was burnt in melting the wax, and an unsuccessful attempt had been made to reseal it with a blank seal—fortunately the contents were not abstracted. The pretty little cuffs were safe, and I am obliged for them—they are just the sort of thing I wanted to keep my wrists warm.

I am truly glad you are safe at home.[1] Was not your mother delighted to see you? I wish somebody would have the sense to leave you a fortune of £10,000 or so—it would be fun to witness the servile adulation of such people as Mr and Mrs—.[2] There—I am afraid, however, there is no chance of such a prize falling to your share out of the wheel of fortune. I must say that from what you say of the coldness, dreariness, and barrenness of these respected individuals' minds and hearts, I pity them full as much as I dislike them.

To-day you will be at [Woodhouse].[3] It is too late to tell you to adopt the white and scarlet by all means—you know I always consider that white suits you. Be sure and tell me all about the party—I hope Joe and John Taylor will not fail to be there, and to lay themselves out properly to your observation.

I had a note—a very short one—from Ellen Taylor[4] yesterday—I had not heard from her before for months. They had just received letters from Waring,[5] but none from Mary—both were well. Don't think of my coming to Brookroyd yet, Ellen—perhaps before the summer is over we may meet again, but let the matter rest at present. I am sorry to hear of your sister Ann's bad health—I fear she makes herself too anxious, and constant anxiety will wear any nerves and fibres. Give my very best love to them all, and say I thank them sincerely for their kind remembrance of me.

What is it that makes Mrs. . . . [6] such a very disagreeable person, and that renders her own friends so anxious to be rid of her? Is her upper story sound? Write again to me as soon as ever you can.—

Yours faithfully,
C. Brontë.

MS untraced. Envelope: BPM B.S. 104/21. W & S 281.
Address (envelope): Miss Ellen Nussey | Brookroyd | Birstal | Leeds
PM: (i) BRADFORD YORKS | JA 28 | 1847 | F (ii) LEEDS | JA 29 | 1847 | A
Annotation on envelope by EN in pencil: Jan 47. Wafer: blue lozenge with the words 'Post Paid' within a line border.
Text: *Shorter* 214. W & S 281 follows *Shorter* 214 except that *Shorter*'s 'W—' is correctly given as 'Woodhouse'. Not in *Life* or *Nussey*, but *Nussey* and *CBCircle* mistakenly print an extract from EN 14.2.1847 as 'January 28th, 1847'.

1. EN had returned to Birstall from her visit to the Joshua Nusseys at Oundle.

2. Perhaps the Joshua Nusseys. cf. CB's indignant references to them in EN 28.12.1846 and 19.1.1847.
3. In 1847 Woodhouse was still a village about 1 mile west of Leeds. The recently married Richard Nussey lived at 103 Woodhouse Lane, his father-in-law's house.
4. CB referred to a note from Ellen Taylor in EN 17.6.1846.
5. John and Joe Taylor's brother Waring would keep in touch with them on business connected with his shop in Wellington as well as on family matters.
6. Not identifiable, in the absence of a MS.

To Ellen Nussey, [14 February 1847]

[Haworth]

Dear Ellen

I shall scribble you a short note about nothing just to have a pretext for screwing a letter out of you in return.

I was sorry you did not go to Woodhouse[1] firstly because you lost the pleasure of observation and enjoyment and secondly because I lost the second-hand indulgence of hearing your account of what you had seen—it was stupid of Mr. & Mrs. Richard not to think of asking you when they asked the Taylors—

I laughed at the candour with which you give your reason for wishing to be there—Thou hast an honest soul Nell—as ever animated human carcase—and a clean one for it is not ashamed of shewing its inmost recesses—only be careful with whom you are frank—some would not rightly appreciate the value of your frankness, and never cast pearls before swine[2]—

You are quite right in wishing to look well in the eyes of those whom you desire to please—it is natural to desire to appear to advantage (honest not false advantage of course) before people we respect—long may the power and the inclination to do so be spared you—long may you look young & handsome enough to dress in white dear Nell—and long may you have a right to feel the consciousness that you look agreeable—I know you have too much judgment to let an over-dose of vanity spoil the blessing and turn it into a misfortune—After all though, Age will come on and it is well you have something better than a nice face for friends to turn to when that is changed—

I hope this excessively cold weather[3] has not harmed you or yours much—It has nipped me severely—taken away my appetite for a while and given me toothache in short put me in the ailing condition in which I have more than once had the honour of making myself such a nuisance both at *Brookroyd and *Hunsworth—the consequence is that at this present speaking I look almost old enough to be your mother—grey sunk and withered—To-day however it is milder and I hope soon to feel better—indeed I am not ill now and my toothache is quite subsided—but I experience a loss of strength and a deficiency of spirit which would make me a sorry companion to you or any one else I would not be on a visit now for a large sum of money—Write soon Give my best love to your Mother & Sisters—I return the French letter[4] it is pretty well but not much in it Poor Miss *Ringrose, I am sorry to hear of her sisters illness for her sake[5]—**Poor George too—still an alien from his home and himself—I do wish he might recover and be restored to you all—I hoped it once—indeed I hope it still and so must you.**[6]

Good bye dear Nell
C Brontë

I think you ought by all means to go to Burley Hall[7] if invited again

MS HM 24452. Envelope: BPM B.S. 104/22. W & S 282.
Address (envelope): Miss Ellen Nussey | Brookroyd | Birstal | Leeds
PM: (i) HAWORTH (ii) BRA[D]FORD YORKS | FE ?15 | 1847 (iii) LEEDS FE—— | 1847 | ?A
Annotation (i) on the envelope by EN in pencil: Feb '47 | on personal appearance | amusing; (ii) On the letter by EN in ink: Feb 14—. Wafer: yellow rectangle with the word 'L'esperance' within a line border.

1. See the previous letter, n. 3.
2. Cf. Matthew 7: 6.
3. *The Times* for mid-Feb. reported widespread severe frosts and heavy snowfalls, with drifts up to 5 ft. deep blocking railway lines. See e.g. the number for 13.2.1847.
4. Possibly a letter from Amelia Ringrose.
5. One of Amelia's younger sisters, Margaret Rosetta (Rosy) aged 17, Clara (13), or Laura (11).
6. The passage is heavily deleted. Cf. EN 17.11.1846, where CB refers to George Nussey's painful delusion that his relatives' affection had become hatred.
7. Burley Hall in Burley-in-Wharfedale, about 12 miles from Leeds, had been destroyed by fire 'with all its costly furniture' on 7 Dec. 1822, but had been rebuilt in 1832. In 1847 it was occupied by John Peele Clapham, who had leased it in 1834 from the lord of the manor, Thomas Horsfall. Perhaps there was a family connection: for the Nusseys' Wharfedale ancestry see *Whitehead* 22. Ann Nussey was to marry a land-agent, Robert Clapham, on 26 Sept. 1849. For Burley Hall see *Mayhall* i. 298 and Harry Speight, *Upper Wharfedale* (1900), 148–9.

To Ellen Nussey, 1 March 1847

Haworth

Dear Ellen

Even at the risk of appearing very exacting I can't help saying that I should like a letter as long as your last every time you write—Short notes give one the feeling of a very small piece of a very good thing to eat—they set the appetite on edge and don't satisfy it—a letter leaves you more contented—and yet, after all, I am very glad to get notes so don't think, when you are pinched for time and materials that it is useless to write a few lines—be assured a few lines are very acceptable as far as they go—and though I like long letters I would by no means have you to make a task of writing to me.

Dear Nell—as you wish to avoid making me uneasy—say nothing more about my going to Brookroyd at present—Let your visit to Sussex[1] be got over—let the summer arrive—and then we shall see how matters stand by that time. To confess the truth I really should like you to come to Haworth before I again go to Brookroyd—and it is natural and right that I should have this wish—to keep friendship in proper order the balance of good offices must be preserved—otherwise a disquieting and anxious feeling creeps in and destroys mutual comfort—In summer—and in fine weather your visit here might be much better managed than in winter—we could go out more be more independent of the house and of one room—Branwell has been conducting himself very badly lately—I expect from the extravagance of his behaviour and from mysterious hints he drops[2] <that>—(for he never will speak out plainly) that we shall be hearing news of fresh debts contracted by him soon—

The Misses *Robinson[3]—who had entirely ceased their correspondence with Anne for half a year after their father's death have lately recommenced it—for a fortnight they sent her a letter almost every day—crammed with warm protestation[4] of endless esteem and gratitude—they speak with great affection too of their Mother—and never make any allusion intimating acquaintance with her errors—It is to be hoped they are and always will remain in ignorance on that point—especially since—I think—she has bitterly repented them. We take special care that Branwell does not know of their writing to Anne.

Have you yet found any document which will give you a claim to a larger proportion of the sum you expect from the Railway people?[5] What a grievous pity it seems that you could not get the whole—It could never have come in better—

Poor George's condition[6] from what you say seems stationary—if he does not improve ?much neither does he retrograde—perhaps he may ?when it is least expected—take a sudden turn for the better—the brain may resume its proper healthy action ?and all may yet be well—

Give my love to your Mother and Sisters—Write again soon

I am yours faithfully
C Brontë

My health is better—I lay the blame of its feebleness on the cold weather more than on an uneasy mind. For after all I have many things to be thankful for

MS Law-Dixon. Envelope: BPM B.S. 104/23. W & S 283.
Address (envelope): Miss Ellen Nussey | Brookroyd | Birstal | Leeds
PM: (i) HAWORTH (ii) BRADFORD [YOR]KS | MR 2 | 1847 | D (iii) LEEDS | MR 3 | 1847 | A
Annotation (i) on the letter by EN in ink: 124 Mar 1 —47; (ii) in pencil: "Mrs Robinson Branwell's mistress"?; (iii) at the end of the letter: on letters Branwell &c Mrs G. Wafer: pink rectangle with the words 'Forget not' within a line border.
Date: The envelope is appropriate for CB's date, 'March 1st | 47. EN's annotation on the envelope, 'Mar 47 amusing | Letters ?a Countess | Society Mrs G' does not apply to this letter but to that of ?19 Jan., q.v.

1. No visit to Mary Gorham at Cakeham is recorded in 1847.
2. In Jan. 1847 Branwell had written to J. B. Leyland, 'I wish Mr Thos Nicholson of the "Old Cock" [Halifax] would send me my bill of what I owe to him, and, the moment that I recieve my outlaid cash, or any sum which may fall into my hands through the hands of one whom I may never see again, I shall settle it.' (MS Brotherton; W & S 278.) For Branwell's state of mind, see his letter to JBL 24.1.1847.
3. The eldest daughter of Mrs Robinson, Lydia Mary, was now married to the actor Henry Roxby and was unlikely to be in touch with Anne, but the two younger girls, Elizabeth Lydia and Mary, were to visit the parsonage in Dec. 1848, when 'they seemed overjoyed to see Anne . . . clinging round her like two children'. (Vol. ii, EN 10.12.1848; W & S 409.) By 18 Aug. 1848 they were no longer speaking affectionately of their mother. In a letter to EN of that date, incompletely published in W & S 387, CB writes: 'The Misses R— say that their mother does not care in the least what becomes of them; she is only anxious to get them husbands of any kind that they may be off her hands, and that she may be free to marry Sir E. Scott—whose infatuated slave, it would appear, she is. They assert that she does not appear to have the least affection for them now—formerly she professed a great deal, and was even servilely submissive to them—but now she treats them quite harshly—and they are often afraid to speak to her.' (BPM MS Gr. E 13.)
4. MS may read 'protestations'.
5. Brookroyd and probably other Nussey properties abutted on or formed part of land needed for new railroads. The Leeds, Dewsbury, and Manchester line, to be opened on 18.9.1848, was to have a station at Batley, and its Act of Incorporation (1845) provided for a branch from there to Birstall, eventually opened on 30.9.1852. See *Regional History* viii. 86, 248, and 254.
6. This para. is heavily deleted. The conjectural reading is that of MGC, who saw the MS.

To Ellen Nussey, [24 March 1847]

[Haworth]

Dear Nell

As I am going to send the French Newspaper to-day I will send a line or two with it—just to ask you how you are and to request you to let me have another letter or note, as soon as may be—I am sorry for poor Miss *Ringrose—Do you think there is any chance of her father[1] permitting her to visit you at *Brookroyd—? I wish he would, both for your sake and hers—she would have a comforter and you a companion—and then you would let me alone awhile—I should like you to be occupied pleasantly—till I can ask you to come to Haworth with some prospect of making you decently comfortable—It is at Haworth, if all be well, that we must next see each other again—

There was a word in your last note which I could not make out—after remarking that two of Miss *Ringroses younger sisters[2] are far from well, you said Amy[3] was very—something—I don't know what—and then asked could Miss *Ringrose have learnt this superstition in Holland—?

What superstition is it?

Did Miss *Wooler come to *Brookroyd on the occasion of your Mother's birthday? If so—was she well and in good spirits?—I owe you a grudge for giving her some very exaggerated account about my not being well—and setting her on to urge my leaving home as quite a duty—I'll take care not to tell you next time when I think I am looking 'specially' old and ugly—as if people could not have that privilege without being supposed to be at the last gasp!

I shall be 31 next birthday—My Youth is gone like a dream—and very little use have I ever made of it[4]—What have I done these last thirty years—? Precious little—

No arguments in the next epistle

Yours faithfully C. B

MS BPM Bon 191. W & S 284.
Address: not in MS.
PM: not in MS.
Annotation by EN in ink: 128 Mar 24 —47
Date: as given by EN.

1. Christopher Leake Ringrose, a wealthy merchant living at Tranby Lodge, Hessle, Hull. (See EN 1.6.1845 n. 6.) The family had formerly lived in Rotterdam, and Amelia may have been born there. See EN 1.6.1845 n. 6.
2. See EN 14.2.1847 n. 5.
3. Presumably Amelia Ringrose.
4. CB was, ironically enough, on the brink of her great fame as 'Currer Bell' because of what she had achieved 'these last thirty years'. She must have written in draft form the greater part of *JE* and she had begun to copy out the earlier chs. The first leaf of the fair copy MS, now in the BL (Add. MSS 43474–6) bears the date 16 Mar. 1847. For an account of its composition, begun while CB was with her father in Manchester in Sept. 1846, see *Life* ii. ch. 1, the introduction to the Clarendon edn. of *JE*, and EN 13.9.1846 n. 6. *The Professor*, however, was still going the rounds of publishing-houses in vain.

To Ellen Nussey, [?4 April 1847]

[Haworth]

Dear Nell

Your last letter both amused and edified me exceedingly—I could not but laugh at your account of the <u>fall</u> in *Birstal—yet I should by no means have liked to have made a third party in that exhibition—I have endured one fall in your company and undergone one of your ill-timed laughs and don't wish to repeat my experience.

What difference will the decease of old Mr *Charnock[1] make in the prospects of Mr. & Mrs. R[ichard] *Nussey? I hope he has left his daughter a handsome fortune—your letter of condolence I thought was well managed—and I am sure it could not have been an easy one to concoct—

Allow me to compliment you on the skill with which you can seem to give an explanation without enlightening one—one whit on the question asked—I know no more about Miss *Ringrose's supersti[ti]on now than I did before—what is the supersti[ti]on—when a dead body is limp what is the inference drawn?[2]

I hope the old lady at White Lea[3] is better—how is the young lady?[4] Do you ever see or hear anything of her—? What you say about John <Nussey> `*Taylor[5]' is deplorable and it seems strange that Joe—should attemp[t] to gloss it over—such efforts are vain and they never answer—We should not unnecessarily expose relations under such circumstances but neither should we degrade ourselves and them by inventing false excuses.

Do you remember my telling you or did I ever tell you about that wretched and most criminal Mr *Collins[6]—after running an infamous career of vice both in England and France—abandoning his wife to disease and total destitution in Manchester—with two children and without a farthing in a strange lodging house—?

Yesterday evening Martha[7] came up stairs to say—that a woman—"rather lady like" as she said wished to speak to me in the kitchen—I went down—there stood Mrs *Collins[8] pale and worn but still interesting looking and cleanly and neatly dressed as was her little girl who was with her—I kissed her heartily—I could almost have cryed to see her for I had pitied her with my whole soul—when I heard of her undeserved sufferings, agonies and physical degradation—she took tea with us stayed about two hours and entered frankly into the narrative of her appalling distresses—her constitution has triumphed over the hideous disease[9]—and her excellent sense—her activity and perseverance have enabled her to regain a decent position in society and to procure a respectable maintenance for herself and her children—She keeps a lodging-house in a very eligible part of the suburbs of Manchester[10] (which I know) and is doing very well—she does not know where Mr *Collins is and of course can never more endure to see him—She is now staying a few days at *Eastwood-House[11] with the *Sugdens[12] who I believe have been all along very kind to her—and the circumstance is greatly to their credit

I wish to know whether about Whitsuntide[13] would suit you for coming to Haworth—we often have fine weather just then—at least I remember last year `it' was very beautiful at that season—Winter seems to have returned with severity on us at present[14]—consequently we are all in the full enjoyment of a cold—much blowing of noses is heard and much making of gruel goes on in the house—how are you all? [Remainder of leaf cut off.][15]

MS Princeton, Taylor Collection. W & S 285 (part).
Address: not in MS.
PM: not in MS.
Annotation by EN in ink: 129 Ap 4—47
Date: as given by EN.

1. Richard Nussey's father-in-law, John Charnock of Woodhouse Lane, Leeds, is described as a 'gentleman' in local directories, e.g. in Parson and White's *Directory* for the Clothing District of Yorkshire (1830), 31, and (for the last time) in White's *Directory* for 1847, 57.
2. The inference is that there will soon be another death in the same house.
3. Probably Sarah Clapham Nussey (1765/6–1851), widow of EN's eldest uncle Joshua Nussey (1757–1814) who had gained substantial property by his marriage with the heiress of White Lee, Batley. Their son John (1786/7–1879), EN's cousin, was a wealthy mill-owner.
4. Isabel or Isabella Nussey, born *c.*1821/2, second daughter and only surviving child of John of White Lee. For Joe Taylor's assiduous attention to her in 1845, see EN 24.4.1845 and 7.10.1845.
5. John Taylor (1813–1901), brother of Joe Taylor. The nature of his 'deplorable behaviour' is unknown. He is said to be CB's model for Mark Yorke in *Shirley*, 'bonnie-looking', but phlegmatic, joyless, with a 'heavy brow' that 'speaks temper'. (169.) Mary Taylor was to acknowledge the likeness of the Yorkes to her own family in a letter to CB of 13.8.1850: 'There is a strange feeling in reading [*Shirley*] of hearing us all talking.' (*Stevens* 97.) John Taylor was apparently not a success in life, and his sister Mary bequeathed him an annuity on her death in 1893; he died unmarried.
6. The Revd John Collins MA, of Trinity College Dublin (b. ?1801), the talented but dissolute Irishman who had been curate to the Revd T. Dury and then to the Revd W. Busfeild, rectors of Keighley, from 5 Jan. 1840 until 1846. The Clergy Lists for 1847 and 1848 include his name in the alphabetical lists of clergymen, but give no curacy or place of residence. For his wife's complaints of his profligacy see EN 12.11.1840.
7. Martha Brown, the younger of the parsonage servants.
8. Mrs Collins was known to and probably on friendly terms with the Greenwoods of Keighley, who were related to the Sugdens (n. 12). See EJB 8.6.1839 n. 9.
9. *Shorter* 218, an abridged and bowdlerized version of the letter, does not refer to this disease, which was no doubt venereal. The fuller text in W & S 285 prints simply 'her constitution has triumphed over her illness'.
10. CB knew the area round Boundary Street, where she had stayed with her father during his operation for cataract. See EN 21.8.1846 n. 4.
11. The house now known as Victoria Hall, in the Aire valley about half a mile from the centre of Keighley. Pigot's *Directory* for 1841 describes it as 'a beautiful mansion' on 'a small plain' which at one period formed a race-ground. 'In 1848 . . . Eastwood House stood serene in its own park, with the wind blowing across a rural landscape.' (H. Bancroft, A. Briggs, and E. Treacy, *One Hundred Years: The Parish of Keighley 1848–1948* (Keighley, 1948) 11.)
12. Wealthy manufacturers. The William Sugden of Eastwood who died in 1834 had left an enormous estate. His son William (1811–52) also lived at Eastwood House. The 1851 Census names the residents there as 'William Sugden unmarried age 39; Sarah Sugden unmarried sister 37, Maria L. Sugden unmarried sister 35 and Elkanah Armitage brother-in-law 34.' For more information see Sarah Fermi, 'A "Religious" Family Disgraced: New Information on a Passage Deleted from Mrs Gaskell's *Life of Charlotte Bronte*', *BST* 20. 5. 289–95.
13. In 1847 Whit Sunday was 23 May.
14. March had ended with snow, hail, and northerly winds, and *Shackleton* recorded 'much snow' on 1 Apr., followed by hard frosts and snow until 4 Apr.
15. After 'how are you all?' W & S print in conclusion 'Give my best love to your mother, and believe me, yours, | C. BRONTË.' These words are not in the MS.

To Ellen Nussey, ?21 April 1847

[Haworth]

Dear Nell,

I am very much obliged to you for your gift, which you must not undervalue, for I like the articles, they look extremely pretty and light. They are for wrist frills,[1] are they not? Will you condescend to accept a scrubby[2] yard of lace—made up into nothing? I thought I would not offer to spoil it by stitching it into any shape. Your creative fingers will turn it to better account than my destructive ones. I hope such as it is they will not pick it out of the envelope at the Bradford Post Office,[3] where they generally take the liberty of opening letters when they feel soft as if they contained anything. I had forgotten all about your birthday and mine,[4] till your letter arrived to remind me of it. I wish you many happy returns of yours. Are both Ann and Mercy from home? Of course, your visit to Haworth must be regulated by Miss Ringrose's movements. I was rather amused at your fearing I should be jealous. I never thought of it, Nell. She and I could not be rivals in your affections. You allot her, I know, a different set of feelings to what you allot me. She is peculiarly amiable and estimable, I am not amiable, but still we shall stick to the last I don't doubt. In short, I should as soon think of being jealous of Emily and Anne in these days as of you.[5] If Miss Ringrose does not come to Brookroyd about Whitsuntide,[6] I should like you to come about the middle of the week before Whitsunday, if it suits you. I shall feel a good deal disappointed if the visit is put off—I would rather Miss Ringrose fixed her time in summer, and then I would come to see you (D.V.) in the autumn. I don't think it will be at all a good plan to go back with you. We see each other so seldom,[7] that I would far rather divide the visits. I wish Mrs N—'s[8] daughter may be a nice child, and that you may get her for a pupil. Remember me to all. Any news about poor George lately?—Yours faithfully,

C. Brontë.

MS untraced. W & S 286.
Address: not in source.
PM: not in source.
Text: *Shorter* 219. W & S 286 is identical with *Shorter*. *Nussey* 157–8 and *CBCircle* 225 are much edited and abridged. Not in *Life*. The edited version in *Hours at Home* xi. 301 may retain 2 authentic readings: see notes 5 and 7.

1. EN's birthday gift. cf. *The Professor*, where Mlle Reuter's 'delicate little collar and manchettes of lace . . . showed her neck [and] wrists to complete advantage'. (83.)
2. Paltry or shabby. For CB's jocular or slang use of the word, cf. EN 29.9.1840, where she recalls 'some fable . . . by a scrubby old knave, yclept Aesop', and EN 7.10.1847, 'scrubby notes'.
3. A previous letter containing a pair of cuffs had been opened. See EN 28.1.1847.
4. 20 and 21 Apr. EN's birthday is sometimes given as 22 Apr., but she copied out some verses entitled 'My Birthday' on 20.4.1837. See EN 20.4.1846 n. 3.
5. *Hours at Home* reads 'as of you, dear E.'

6. 23 May.
7. *Hours at Home* reads 'seldom now that'.
8. Not identified, though Mrs Noble, a former paying guest in the Nussey household, is a possibility. See EN 21.9.1846 n. 2.

To Ellen Nussey, [4 May 1847]

[Haworth]

At last there is another letter from Mary Taylor, I send it to yo[u] you are to return it to Hunsworth[1]

MS Harvard Hilles Library *69M-104. MGC *Census* pt. 4, [133].
Address (envelope): Miss Ellen Nussey | Brookroyd | Birstal | Leeds
PM: (i) HAWORTH (ii) [BRADFOR]D YORKS | MY 4 | 1847 (iii) LEEDS | MY 5 | 1847 | A (iv) BIR[STAL]
Annotation: the text of the letter was written on the verso of the envelope by CB. Wafer: a blue lozenge with the words 'Chacun a son gout' within a line border.

1. Probably the envelope contained only Mary Taylor's letter: CB asked EN in her letter of 12 May if she had received it. No letters from Mary Taylor dating from late 1846 or early 1847 have been located.

To Ellen Nussey, 12 May [1847]

[Haworth]

Dear Ellen

We shall all be glad to see you on the Thursday or Friday[1] of next week, whichever day will suit you best—About what time will you be likely to get here,—and how will you come—by coach to Keighley—or by a gig all the way to Haworth?

There must be no impediments now—I could not do with them; I want very much to see you, I hope you will be decently comfortable while you stay. Branwell is quieter now—and for a good reason—he has got to the end of a considerable sum of money[2] of which he became possessed in the Spring—and consequently is obliged to restrict himself in some degree—You must expect to find him weaker in mind and the complet[e] rake in appearance[3]—I have no apprehension of his being at all uncivil to you, on the contrary, he will be as smooth as oil

I pray for fine weather that we may be able to get out while you stay

Good bye for the present—prepare for much dulness and monotony—Give my love to all at Brookroyd

Did you get M[ary] T[aylor]'s letter—?

C Brontë

MS Berg. W & S 287.
Address: not in MS.
PM: not in MS.
Annotation by EN in ink: 131 May 12 —47
Date: CB dates 'May 12th'; EN gives the year.

1. 20 or 21 May, as CB had suggested on 21 Apr.
2. See EN 1.3.1847 n. 2. The money was either Branwell's 'outlaid cash'—perhaps part of his earnings at Thorp Green which had been saved and banked in some way—or a sum obtained 'through the hands of one whom' he might 'never see again'. Branwell seems to hint at a gift from Mrs Robinson; or he might have received money through the hands of Dr Crosby from the Oddfellows Lodge to which he is said to have belonged while at Thorp Green. See Gérin *BB* 236. Mrs Gaskell believed that the money came from Mrs Robinson: 'She had offered to elope with him; she had written to him perpetually; she had sent him money—twenty pounds at a time.' (*Life* i. 331, 1st and 2nd edns.; omitted from 3rd edn.)
3. For F. H. Grundy's melodramatic picture of Branwell with 'wildly floating' hair, cheeks 'yellow and hollow' and 'thin white lips not trembling but shaking' see *Grundy* 91.

To Ellen Nussey, [?14 May 1847]

[Haworth]

Dear Ellen

Your letter and its contents were most welcome. It will however suit us better if you can come on Wednesday in next week—we fix this day because it is the only one on which there is a carrier who can take charge of your luggage from Keighley Station—You must direct it to Mr. Brontë's Haworth—and we will tell the carrier to inquire for it—The railroad[1] has been opened some time but it only comes as far as Keighley—the remaining distance you will have to walk—there are trains from Leeds—I believe at all hours—if you can arrive at Keighley by about 4 o'clock in the afternoon Emily, Anne & I will all three meet you at the station—we can take tea jovially together at the Devonshire Arms[2] and walk home in the cool of the evening—this, with fine weather will I think be a much better arrangement than fagging through four miles in the heat of noon Write by return of post if you can & say whether this plan suits you and mention the precise hour when you will be at Keighley

Yours
C Brontë

MS Columbia. W & S 288.
Address: not in MS.
PM: not in MS.
Annotation by EN in ink: May —47
Date as in *Shorter* 221 and W & S 288. There may have been a postmarked envelope. The letter is marked 'W.', showing that it had belonged to T. J. Wise.

1. The Aire valley line from Leeds to Shipley had been open since July 1846, and its extension from Shipley to Keighley since 16 Mar. 1847. In 1845 there had been 2 proposals for a branch line

to Haworth, one of them, supported by Mr Brontë, using the 'atmospheric system of traction'; but the Keighley–Oxenhope line through the Worth valley via Haworth would not be built until 1867. See BB to H. Robson, ?23.10.1845 notes 1 and 2.

2. The coaching-inn in Church Street, Keighley. The building survives under another name—currently, 'The Grinning Rat'.

To Ellen Nussey, [?17 May 1847]

[Haworth]

Dear Nell,

Friday[1] will suit us very well. I do trust nothing will now arise to prevent your coming. I shall be anxious about the weather on that day; if it rains, I shall cry. Don't expect me to meet you; where would be the good of it? I neither like to meet, nor to be met.[2] Unless, indeed, you had a box or a basket for me to carry; then there would be some sense in it. Come in black, blue, pink, white, or scarlet, as you like. Come shabby or smart; neither the colour nor the condition signifies; provided only the dress contain E[llen] N[ussey] all will be right: à bientôt.

C. Brontë.

MS untraced. Envelope: BPM B.S. 104/24. W & S 289.
Address (envelope): Miss Ellen Nussey | Brookroyd | Birstal | Leeds
PM (i) HAWORTH (ii) BRADFORD YORKS | MY 17 | 1847 (iii) LEEDS | MY 18 | 1847 | A (iv) BIRSTAL
Annotation on the envelope by EN in pencil: May 47 | lively letter ?Mr Ringrose | Mrs G. Wafer: blue lozenge with the words 'Delay not' within a line border.
Date: the date 'May 17th, 47' given in *Nussey* suits the annotation and wafer on the surviving envelope reasonably well. EN may have deleted a reference to Mr Ringrose. 'Mrs G' indicates that the letter was used in the *Life*.
Text: *Nussey* 159. *Shorter* 222 and W & S 289 have minor punctuation variants. *Life* omits greeting, 'Nussey', 'à bientôt' and signature. Not in *Hours at Home*.

1. 21 May.
2. CB was evidently annoyed that her plans for a meeting and a 'jovial' tea at the Devonshire Arms had been upset by EN's change of date. An edited-out allusion to Mr Ringrose might have helped to explain EN's behaviour; but see the next letter.

To Ellen Nussey, 20 May [1847]

[Haworth]

Dear Ellen

Your letter of yesterday did indeed give me a cruel chill of disappointment. I can not blame you—for I know it was not your fault—but I must say I do not altogether exempt your sister Anne from reproach—I do not think she considers it of the least consequence whether little people like us of Haworth are disappointed or not, provided great nobs like the *Briar Hall gentry[1] are accommodated—this is bitter, but I feel bitter—

As to going to *Brookroyd—it is absurd—I will not go near the place till you have been to Haworth—

My respects to all and sundry accompanied with a large amount of wormwood and gall—from the effusion of which you and your Mother alone are excepted—

C B—

May 20th.

You are quite at liberty to tell your sister *Anne what I think if you <think> 'judge' proper—Though it is true I may be somewhat unjust for I am deeply annoyed—I thought I had arranged your visit tolerably comfortably for you this time—I may find it more difficult on another occasion

MS BPM Bon 192. W & S 290.
Address: not in MS.
PM: not in MS.
Annotation by EN in ink: 132 May 20 —47

1. The family of the wealthy woollen merchant Joseph Swaine of Brier Hall, Gomersal. EN's 1844 and 1849 diaries quite often refer to Mrs Swaine and her younger daughters Mary and Catherine, who were on friendly visiting terms with the Nusseys. For CB's reservations about the family, see EN 7.10.1845 and 30.12.1845.

To Ellen Nussey, [?25 May 1847]

[Haworth]

Dear Ellen,

I acknowledge I was in fault in my last letter, and that it was as you say quite unreasonable, especially as it regards Ann. After all, I cannot deny that she was in the right to take the chance that offered of going from home.[1] I forgive her, and I hope she will forgive me for my cross words . . . [2] I have a small present for Mercy. You must fetch it, for I repeat you shall come to Haworth before I go to Brookroyd.

I do not say this from pique or anger, I am not angry now, but because my leaving home at present would from solid[3] reasons be difficult to manage. If all be well I will visit you in the autumn, at present I cannot come. Be assured that if I could come I should, after your last letter, put scruples and pride away and 'go over into Macedonia'[4] at once. I never could manage to help you yet[5]. You have always found me something like a new servant, who requires to be told where everything is, and shown how everything is to be done.

My sincere love to your mother and Mercy.—

Yours,
C. B.

MS untraced. W & S 291.
Address: not in source.
PM: not in source.
Date as in source. See also n. 2.
Text: *Shorter* 224. W & S 291 reproduces *Shorter* 224, which is fuller than *Nussey* 160. Not in *Hours at Home*.

1. Ann Nussey had been invited to visit the Swaines of Brier Hall and to join Mary Swaine on an 'excursion', possibly to York. See the next letter and EN 7.10.1845 and notes.
2. The nature of the omission is indicated in a Dodd, Mead (New York) catalogue for Mar. 1895, when the autograph MS, '4pp. small 12mo' was offered for sale for $25: 'Brontè (Charlotte). Autograph letter signed with initials, dated "1847, May 25," to Miss Ellen Nussey, asking forgiveness for cross words, inviting her to come and visit, thanking her for a present of some garters, etc.' (Handwritten copy of catalogue entry in WYAS Bradford, Deed Box 28 Case 1.)
3. A dubious reading, perhaps for 'sound'. One good reason, not to be revealed to EN, must have been that CB was working hard to finish *JE*. She had begun her fair copy on 16 Mar., as the MS shows, and had 'nearly completed' the novel when she mentioned it to Smith, Elder on 7 Aug.
4. See Acts 16: 9.
5. EN had probably asked for help in running the Nussey household during Ann's absence.

To Ellen Nussey, 5 June 1847

[Haworth]

Dear Ellen

I return you Mary *Taylor's letter[1]—it made me somewhat sad to read it—for I fear she is no longer quite content with her existence in New Zealand—she finds it too barren—I believe she is more homesick than she will confess—Her gloomy ideas respecting you and me[2] prove a state of mind far from gay. I have also received a letter—its tone was similar to your own—and its contents too—an allusion or two to points on which she enjoins secrecy but which concern herself alone—prevent my sending it—you lose nothing, however,—for the two letters with that slight exception are nearly alike—

Is Miss *Ringrose coming to Brookroyd? I sincerely hope she is—her presence—would cheer your Mother and soothe you—You would find her also a better household companion than me—more handy--more even-humoured, more amiable in short—

What brilliant weather we have had—Ah, Nell! I do indeed regret you could not come to Haworth at the time I fixed—These warm sunny days would have suited us exactly—But it is not to be helped—

I hope Ann will derive benefit from her excursion[3]—I am convinced she greatly required a change—could she learn anything that would do poor George good—it would indeed be a blessing that she went with Mary Swaine[4]—

Give my best love to your Mother and Mercy—

Yours faithfully
C Brontë

MS HM 24453. Envelope: Professor Mark Seaward. W & S 292.
Address: Miss Ellen Nussey | Brookroyd | Birstal | Leeds
PM: (i) HAWORTH (ii) BRADFORD [YOR]KS | JU 5 | 1847 | ?D (iii) LEEDS | JU 6 | 1847 | A
Annotation: on the letter by EN in ink: June 5 —47. Wafer on the envelope: blue lozenge with the words 'Dinna forget' within a line border.
Date in CB's hand at the end of the letter: <May> 'June' 5th./ 47

1. This does not survive, but Mary's letter to CB of June/July 1848 conveys her dissatisfaction with her life: 'Has the world gone so well with you that you have no protest to make against its absurdities?' 'Did you never notice that the women of the middle classes are generally too ignorant to talk to?' 'It's a pity you don't live in this world that I might entertain you about the price of meat . . . This is the only legitimate subject of conversation we have the rest is gossip'. Mary admits, however, that her life is 'not disagreeable'. (*Stevens* 73–9.)
2. Mary emphasized the sadder aspects of CB's life in the letter Mrs Gaskell used in the 3rd edn. of the *Life*: 'She said she did not know how people could bear the constant pressure of misery.' [In Brussels] 'she fell into the same hopeless state as at Miss W[ooler's] though in a less degree,' and so on. But Mary's attempts to spur CB to action were, she says, gratefully acknowledged as the valuable service Mary had done for her. (*Life* i. 281–2 (3rd edn.)
3. Ann Nussey's excursion must have included a visit to Clifton House asylum in York, where her brother George was a patient.
4. See EN 20.5.1847 n. 1.

To Thomas De Quincey,[1] *16 June* 1847

[Haworth]

Sir

My Relatives, Ellis and Acton Bell and myself, heedless of the repeated warnings of various respectable publishers,[2] have committed the rash act of printing a volume of poems.

The consequences predicted have, of course, overtaken us; our book is found to be a drug; no man needs it or heeds it; in the space of a year our publisher has disposed but of two copies,[3] and by what painful efforts he succeeded in getting rid of those two, himself only knows.

Before transferring the edition to the trunk-makers,[4] we have decided on distributing as presents a few copies of what we cannot sell—we beg to offer you one in acknowledgment of the pleasure and profit we have often and long derived from your works—

I am Sir
Yours very respectfully
Currer Bell.

MS Berg. W & S 293.
Address (integral): T. De Quincey Esqr.
PM: not in MS.

1. De Quincey (1785–1859) was one of several authors to whom CB and her sisters sent copies of their poems. Her letters to Tennyson and J. G. Lockhart were substantially the same as that to De Quincey, and are not reprinted here; those to Wordsworth and Ebenezer Elliott have not been located. Notes on each of these recipients are given below. The letter to Hartley Coleridge, which has slight variants in wording, follows.

Thomas De Quincey's *Confessions of an English Opium Eater*, published in *The London Magazine* in 1821, had been followed by many contributions to other magazines, notably to *Blackwood's Edinburgh Magazine* in 1829–30, when the Brontës were both reading and imitating it in their own writings. Branwell Brontë had sent a copy of his poem, 'Sir Henry Tunstall', with translations of five of Horace's *Odes*, to De Quincey on 15 Apr. 1840, and the Brontës are said to have written to him many times. See Alexander H. Japp, *De Quincey Memorials* (1891), ii. 207–31, where the letter of 16 June 1847 is printed on pp. 207–8.

In 1847 Tennyson (1809–92) was preparing *The Princess* for publication in Dec., and was already being considered as a future laureate. Some of his finest work, such as 'Ulysses' and 'Morte d'Arthur', had appeared in his *Poems* of 1842. The 'Bells' ' gift may have been suggested by EJB, for whom her sisters were to bring back a copy of Tennyson's poems after their visit to London in July 1848. (BPM B.S. 22, CB's notebook of expenses.) Mrs Gaskell later reported to Charlotte Froude that CB 'can not bear Tennyson'. (Letter of *c*.25.8.1850, CP letter 78.) CB's letter to 'Alfred Tennyson Esqre' is dated 'June 16th. / 47'; the MS is in the Beinecke Library at Yale, and it was printed in [Hallam Tennyson] *Alfred Lord Tennyson: A memoir* (1897), i. 262, with the comment, 'For the sisters Brontë my father had the highest admiration.'

John Gibson Lockhart (1794–1854), son-in-law and biographer of Sir Walter Scott, was admired by the Brontës for his contributions to *Blackwood's Edinburgh Magazine* (from 1817), his *Life* of Burns (1828), and his *Life* of Scott (1838). In 1829 EJB had chosen Lockhart and his son John, along with Scott, to live on her imaginary island, and on 4 July 1834 CB advised EN to read his *Life* of Burns. In 1847 he was the editor of the *Quarterly Review*, a position he held from 1825 to 1853. He described CB's letter to him as a 'queer little note by Currer, who said the book had been published a year, and just two copies sold, so they were to burn the rest [*sic*], but distributed a few copies, mine being one . . . I think the poems of Currer much better than those of Acton and Ellis.' (Lockhart to Miss Rigby [Lady Eastlake] 13.11.1848, in Charles Eastlake Smith (ed.), *Journals and Correspondence of Lady Eastlake* (1895), i. 221.) The MS of the letter to Lockhart, now in BPM, is substantially the same as that to De Quincey. It accompanies a copy of the *Poems*, 1st edn. 1846, a letter from Fanny A. Beckett to Lockhart of 3.4.1848 praising the poems, and one from Harrison Ainsworth of 15.11.1848 reporting rumours about the authors' identity, and concluding that 'Currer Bell, I agree with you is not a *belle*; and there must be more than one hand at work to ring all these changes'.

According to *Shorter* i. 329, a copy was also sent to William Wordsworth (1770–1850). His poems were loved by CB, who wrote of his 'deep, serene and sober mind' and often quoted his work. (See the Clarendon *Professor* 253 and 335.) She was to make notable use of his sonnet, 'Great men have been among us' in her letter to W. S. Williams of 25 Feb. 1848. (Vol. ii; and see also BB to Wordsworth 10.1.1837.) Wordsworth had been the Poet Laureate since Southey's death in 1843, and he had carefully revised his work for the Moxon edn. of 1845 on which CB had probably hoped to model the Bells' *Poems* (Aylott 31.1.1846 n. 1.) But from May to 9 July 1847 Wordsworth suffered the agony of watching his beloved daughter Dora dying of TB—a death that followed a 'terrible list' of other bereavements. (See Stephen Gill, *William Wordsworth: A Life* (Oxford, 1989), 419–21.) It is said that he did not even open his copy of the Bells' *Poems*, but evidence is lacking.

Ebenezer Elliott (1781–1849), a Sheffield ironmaster and former Chartist, was famous for his *Corn-Law Rhymes* of 1831, trenchant verses supporting the abolition of the Protectionist corn laws which caused distress and deprivation among the poor. A copy of the Bells' *Poems* in the 'first issue' binding (BPM Bon 294) inscribed by CB 'Presented to Ebenezer Elliott by the Misses Brontë', was presumably accompanied by the usual letter.

2. See Aylott 28.1.1846 notes.
3. See Aylott 15.7.1846 n. 2.
4. For use as an inner lining for leather travelling trunks. CB later feared that the rejected *Professor* might 'prematurely find his way to the "buttermen" and trunkmakers'. (Vol. ii GS 5.2.1851.)

To Hartley Coleridge,[1] *16 June* 1847

[Haworth]

Sir

My relatives Ellis and Acton Bell and myself, heedless of the repeated warnings of various respectable publishers, have committed the rash act of printing a volume of poems.

The consequences predicted have, of course, overtaken us; our book is found to be a drug; no man needs it or heeds it; in the space of a year our publisher has disposed but of two copies and by what painful efforts, he succeeded in getting rid of those two himself only knows.

Before transferring the edition to the Trunk-makers, we have decided on distributing as presents, a few copies of what we cannot sell. We beg to offer you one in acknowledgment of the pleasure and profit we have often derived from your writings.

I am, Sir
Yours respectfully
Currer Bell.

MS Texas. cf. W & S 293 to De Quincey.
Address (integral): Hartley Coleridge Esqr.
PM: not in MS.

1. This is one of several letters accompanying gifts of the Bells' *Poems* to a number of different authors. See the previous letter and notes. For Hartley Coleridge (1796–1849) son of S. T.

Coleridge, see CB's draft letter to him of Dec. 1840, n. 1. In 1847 Hartley Coleridge was living with William and Eleanor Richardson at Grasmere in the Lake District.

To Ellen Nussey, 29 June 1847

[Haworth]

Dear Ellen

I return you Miss *Ringrose's letter which, like all her former ones, bears with singular clearness the stamp of goodness and candour. I hope by this time it is settled when she is to visit you[1]—she speaks rather vaguely on the subject in this letter—her father's word seems hardly to be depended on—and will not her mother stand in the way of an early and favourable decision—?[2]

I was amused by what she says respecting her wish that when she marries, her husband will at least have a will of his own, even should he be a tyrant[3]—Tell her when she forms that aspiration again she must make it conditional—if her husband has a strong will, he must also have strong sense—a kind heart—a thoroughly correct notion of Justice—because a man with a weak brain <and a> chill affections and strong will—is merely an intractable fiend—you can have no hold of him—you can never lead him right. A tyrant under any circumstances is a curse.

When can you come to Haworth? another period of fine weather is passing without you—I fear now your visit will be dull indeed—for it is doubtful whether there will even be a Curate to enliven you—Mr. *Nicholls is likely to get a district erelong[4] and then papa will be left without assistance for how long I do not know—This rather troubles me—the whole duty is too much for him at his age—he is pretty well but often complains of weakness—

When your Sister Anne returns write again and tell me how soon you are likely to come—

Yours faithfully
C Brontë

MS HM 24454. Envelope: BPM B.S. 104/25. W & S 294.
Address (envelope): Miss Ellen Nussey | Brookroyd | Birstal | Leeds
PM: (i) HAWORTH (ii) BRADFORD YORKS | JU 29 | 1847 | ?L (iii) LEEDS | JU 30 | 1847 | A
Annotation on the envelope by EN in pencil: June 47 | A's letter about her first visit | Mrs G. Wafer: blue lozenge with the words 'Seek and find' within a line border.

1. Amelia Ringrose eventually reached Brookroyd sometime between 12 and ?23 Aug. See CB's letters to EN on those dates.
2. See EN 1.6.1845 n. 6 and 24.3.1847.
3. cf. *The Professor* ch. 25: when William Crimsworth asks Frances her opinion of marriage to 'a profligate, a prodigal, a drunkard or a tyrant', she responds that against such 'slavery all right thinkers revolt'. (255.)

4. At the age of 29, Mr Nicholls might have been expected to move to a living elsewhere after 2 years as a curate at Haworth; but he remained there until May 1853, when Mr Brontë's opposition to his wish to marry CB drove him to find a curacy at Kirk Smeaton, near Pontefract. He resumed the Haworth curacy after his marriage to CB in June 1854.

To Ellen Nussey, ?14 July 1847: envelope only

MS BPM BS 104/25.2
Address: Miss Ellen Nussey | Woodhouse | Leeds[1]
PM (i) HAWORTH (ii) BRADFORD YORKS | JY 14 | 1847 | D (iii) LEEDS | JY 15 | 1847 | A
Annotation by EN in pencil: July 15 —47 first visit to ?Keighley by rail. Wafer: blue lozenge with the words 'You're Welcome' within a line border.

1. EN was staying at 103 Woodhouse Lane, Leeds, the home of Mr and Mrs Richard Nussey. The missing letter evidently arranged for her visit to Haworth. On 29 June CB had asked when EN could come, and the visit had been completed by 12 Aug. Ellen would be able to travel by train directly from Leeds to Keighley. See EN ?14.5.1847 n. 1, and 18.7.1847 (envelope).

To Messrs Smith, Elder and Co.,[1] 15 July 1847

Haworth

Gentlemen

I beg to submit to your consideration the accompanying Manuscript[2]—I should be glad to learn whether it be such as you approve and would undertake to publish—at as early a period as possible—

[Signature cut out]

Address—Mr Currer Bell[3]
Under cover to Miss Brontë
Haworth
Bradford
Yorkshire

MS BPM SG 1. W & S 297.
Address on fol. 2^r: Messrs. Smith & Elder | Cornhill
PM: not in MS.
Annotation on fol. 1^v: Currer Bell | Haworth | Bradford | July 15. 1847

1. The firm was founded in Oct. 1816 as a bookseller's and stationer's by two young Scotsmen, George Smith the elder (1789–1846), a 'model of industry and method, but not brilliant' and Alexander Elder (1790–1876), 'a man of some taste and discrimination' in books and art, but 'not a very capable man of business'. (*Huxley* 2, 7, 32.) Smith and Elder became publishers in Mar. 1819, and moved to 65 Cornhill in Nov. 1824. Under the energetic leadership of the younger George Smith (1824–1901) head of the firm from 1846, publishing and other activities had rapidly expanded. In 1868 the banking, Indian trading, and export departments that he had developed were sold off, and the firm published from 15 Waterloo Place until business was

transferred to John Murray in Jan. 1917. See *Huxley* and *DNB*—a publication which was conceived, planned, and largely financed by George Smith, with Leslie Stephen as its first editor in 1882. A 40-page memoir of G. Smith by Sir Sidney Lee introduces the first supplement to *DNB* (vol. xxii).

2. This was the MS of *The Professor*, which with *WH* and *AG* had, according to CB, been 'perseveringly obtruded upon various publishers for the space of a year and a half; usually, their fate was an ignominious and abrupt dismissal . . . something like the chill of despair began to invade [Currer Bell's] heart. As a forlorn hope, he tried one publishing house more—Messrs. Smith and Elder'. ('Biographical Notice of Ellis and Acton Bell' 1850; see Clarendon *WH* 437). CB forgot that *The Professor* at least was not completed until 27 June 1846; see CB to H. Colburn 4.7.1846 and Aylott 6.4.1846 n. 2. There had been 6 refusals by 15 July 1847.
3. The younger George Smith recalled the arrival of the parcel containing the MS of *The Professor*, 'addressed to the firm, but bearing also, scored out, the addresses of two or three other publishing houses; showing that the parcel had been previously submitted to other publishers. This did not tend to prepossess us in favour of the MS . . . But it was a rule that every MS. sent to the firm should be faithfully considered.' (*Huxley* 57.) The MS, now in the Pierpont Morgan Library, New York, is described in the Clarendon edn. of the novel, pp. xxix–xxxviii.

To Ellen Nussey, ?18 July 1847: envelope only

MS BPM BS 104/26
Address: Miss Ellen Nussey | Woodhouse | Leeds[1]
PM: (i) KEIGHLEY | JY 18 | 1847 (ii) LEEDS | JY 18 | 1847 | F
Annotation by EN in pencil: July 2 18 —47

1. For the address, see EN ?14.7.1847 n. 1. The missing letter was probably the final arrangement for EN's visit to Haworth, which had begun by 21 July. Memoranda in EN's 1849 Diary read: '[July] 21 Saw 2 suns on Haworth Moor 1847 [July] 22 lost an amythist brooch at Haworth 1847.' Mrs Gaskell writes: '[Ellen] was with them at the beginning of the glowing August of that year. They were out on the moors for the greater part of the day, basking in the golden sunshine.' She ends a paragraph of lyrical description, possibly based on notes provided by EN, by referring to 'the relish with which they welcomed their friend to their own true home on the wild and open hills. There, too, they could escape from the Shadow in the house below'. (*Life* ii. 25–6.) When EN recalled the parhelion seen on 21 July for Mme Duclaux (A. M. F. Robinson) the episode was considerably embroidered: the two suns became three, and the sisters were carefully posed, 'Emily a little higher, standing on a heathery knoll. "That is you!" said Ellen at last. "You are the three suns." . . . [Emily] was still standing on her knoll, quiet, satisfied; and round her lips there hovered a very soft and happy smile.' (Robinson, *EB* 143.)

To Messrs, Smith, Elder and Co., 2 August 1847

[Haworth]

Gentlemen

About three weeks since I sent for your consideration, a M.S. entitled "The Professor, a Tale, by Currer Bell."[1] I should be glad to know whether it reached your hands safely—and likewise to learn at your earliest convenience whether it be such as you can undertake to publish

I am—Gentlemen
Yours respectfully
C Bell—

I enclose a directed Cover for your reply[2]

MS BPM SG 2. W & S 298.
Address (integral): Messrs. Smith, Elder & Co.
PM: not in MS.
Annotation in ink on 2ᵛ: Currer Bell | Haworth | Augt 2. 1847

1. See SE 15.7.1847 and notes.
2. George Smith thought he recalled that CB's letter contained 'a postage stamp for our reply, it having been hinted to the writer by "some experienced friend" that publishers often refrain from answering communications unless a postage stamp was furnished for the purpose!' (*Huxley* 57.) Smith was probably remembering Mrs Gaskell's account of an earlier period when the inexperienced CB, failing to receive a reply from a publisher, 'consulted her brother as to what could be the reason for the prolonged silence. He at once set it down to her not having enclosed a postage stamp in her letter.' (*Life* ii. 24.) Perhaps CB had prudently affixed a stamp to the 'directed Cover'.

To Messrs Smith, Elder and Co., 7 August 1847

[Haworth]

Gentlemen

I have received your communication[1] of the 5th. inst. for which I thank you.[2]

Your objection to the want of varied interest in the tale is, I am aware, not without grounds—yet it appears to me that it might be published without serious risk if its appearance were speedily followed up by another work from the same pen of a more striking and exciting character. The first work might serve as an introduction and accustom the public to the author's name, the success of the second might thereby be rendered more probable.

I have a second narrative[3] in 3 vols. now in progress and nearly completed, to which I have endeavoured to impart a more vivid interest than belongs to the Professor; in about a month I hope to finish it—so that if a publisher were found for "the Professor", the second narrative might follow as soon as was deemed advisable—and thus the interest of the public (if any interest were roused) might not be suffered to cool.

Will you be kind enough to favour me with your judgment on this plan—

I am Gentlemen
Yours very respectfully
C Bell—

MS BPM SG 3. *BST* 18.92.101–2. *Life* ii. 25 (part).
Address (integral): Messrs. Smith Elder & Co.
PM: not in MS.
Annotation in ink on 2^{v}: Currer Bell Esq | Haworth | Augt 7. 1847

1. George Smith writes: 'Mr. Williams, the "reader" to the firm, read the MS. [of *The Professor*] and said that it evinced great literary power, but he had grave doubts as to its being successful as a publication. We together decided that he should write to Currer Bell a letter of appreciative criticism of the MS., declining the work but expressing an opinion that the writer *could* produce a book which would command success.' (*Huxley* 57.)
2. In 1850 CB described 'Currer Bell's' 'dreary expectation of finding two hard hopeless lines . . . instead, he took out of the envelope a letter of two pages. He read it trembling. It declined, indeed, to publish that tale, for business reasons, but it discussed its merits and demerits so courteously . . . that this very refusal cheered the author better than a vulgarly-expressed acceptance would have done. It was added, that a work in three volumes would meet with careful attention.' ('Biographical Notice', Clarendon *WH* 437.)
3. *JE*, begun in Aug. 1846. See EN 13.9.1846 n. 6.

To Ellen Nussey, [12 August 1847]

[Haworth]

Dear Ellen

Your letter made us all serious enough for though truly thankful that you escaped so well—one cannot but reflect with a degree of horror upon what might have happened—had a limb been broken or had something worse <i.*w.*> taken place, what a dreadful conclusion to your visit here![1] What tidings to send to your Mother! what news to send back to Haworth—! Indeed—I am grateful it is no worse—May you be protected from every peril as effectually!

It is evidently urgent that Amelia *Ringrose[2] should have change of scene—the sadness and oppression of mind is part of her complaint, which it appears to me certain is all on the nerves—and by that [I] do not mean that she is fanciful—but that her mind is cramped in some points and overwrought in others and wants freedom and repose, both of which advantages she will enjoy at *Brookroyd—and therefore to *Brookroyd it is to be hoped her parents will immediately let her migrate, without the children.[3]

I received yesterday a letter from Miss *Wooler—it is written under the impression that you were still with me—and she desires me to tell you with her love that [s]he has at length procured a copy of the Sunday Scholar's Christian year[4] and hopes soon to take it to Brookroyd—Miss Catherine[5] it appears is gone on a visit to Scotland—and Miss Sarah[6] has been spending some time at the house of a former pupil in London—where she had a livery servant daily at her disposal to accompany her to see all the Lions of the Capital—of which privilege, Miss W— says—, she availed herself freely—Give my best love to your Mother and Sisters. Emily & Anne unite in love to you

Yours thankfully C B

Thursday

MS BPM Bon 193. Envelope: BPM B.S. 104/27. W & S 299.
Address (envelope): Miss Ellen Nussey | Brookroyd | Birstal | Leeds
PM: (i) HAWORTH (ii) BRADFORD— | AU 12 | 1847 | D (iii) LEEDS | AU 13 | 1847 | A (iv) BIRSTAL
Annotation on the letter by EN in ink: Aug 12 —47. Wafer: a blue lozenge with the word 'Truth' within a line border.

1. EN had been staying with CB since about 20 July. See EN 18.7.1847 notes. She later added a note to a copy of *Nussey*: 'A carriage accident occurred on E.N's return from Haworth.' (*Hatfield* 281.) She had probably travelled by rail from Keighley to Leeds, and then by road from Leeds to Birstall.
2. Amelia's illness had taken the form of 'religious hypochondria' according to CB's letter to EN of ?15.10.1847.
3. Amelia's younger sister Clara was 13, and Laura 11.
4. By the Revd. Thomas Allbutt.
5. Margaret Wooler's sister and fellow-teacher Katherine Harriet (1796–1884). Both CB and Mary Taylor refer disparagingly to her. See EN May 1842 and MT to EN 25.6.1843 (*Stevens* letter 11) where Mary describes her disapproval of such unconventional 'proceedings' as teaching German boys and leading an independent life in Germany': 'Miss C. Wooler has cut me dead. Miss [Margaret] Wooler should have known better but she is timid.'
6. A younger sister of Margaret Wooler, born 6 Apr. 1798. She may have been a governess in a private house.

To Messrs Smith Elder & Co., 24 August 1847

Haworth

Gentlemen

I now send you per. Rail—a M.S. entitled "Jane Eyre, a novel, in 3 vols. by Currer Bell.[1]

I find I cannot pre-pay the carriage of the parcel as money for that purpose is not received at the small Station-house[2] where it is left.

If, when you acknowledge the receipt of the M.S. you will have the goodness to mention the amount charged on delivery—I will immediately transmit it in postage stamps

It is better in future to address Mr. Currer Bell—under cover to Miss Brontë—Haworth—Bradford Yorks—as there is a risk of letters otherwise directed, not reaching me at present—

To save trouble I enclose an envelope—

I am Gentlemen
Yours respectfully
C Bell

MS privately owned. W & S 300.
Address (integral): Messrs. Smith Elder & Co.
PM: not in MS.

1. Smith, Elder had rejected CB's idea of publishing *The Professor* before *JE*. See SE 7.8.1847 and 12.9.1847. The fair copy MS of *JE*, BL Add. MSS 43474–6, marked at intervals with the names of the compositors in the Stewart and Murray printing house, formed part of the George Smith Memorial Bequest of works by the Brontës and by Robert and Elizabeth Browning. George Smith's widow, Mrs Elizabeth Smith (d. 1914), bequeathed the MSS to the British Museum subject to a life-interest of her children. In 1933 her 3 surviving children relinquished their further life-interest, and transferred them to the Museum. The first fol. of *JE* is dated 16 Mar. 1847, and the last 19 Aug. 1847. Mrs Gaskell aptly described the 'clear, legible, delicate traced writing, almost as easy to read as print'. (*Life* ii. 10.) See the Clarendon edn. introduction, pp. ix–xx, with a facsimile of fol. 179 opp. p. xiv.
2. A temporary structure at Keighley, perhaps like that at Bingley on the same line, where, in Nov. 1849, the clerks' room was a wretched wooden hut 'about three yards square', and where 'during wet weather the clerks transact business with an umbrella over their heads'. (*Regional History* viii. 62.)

To Ellen Nussey, [?23 August 1847]

[Haworth]

Dear Ellen

I am very glad to hear Miss *Ringrose has come at last[1]—glad both for your sake and hers—I know it would have been a severe disappointment to you had she failed to come and I believe it would have been an injury to her had her visit been prohibited. You do not say how she is now—but I trust her health is improved since her arrival at Brookroyd—cheerful change and congenial society is, I have no doubt, the best thing for her complaints.

As to my visit, Nell—I certainly do think in my own mind it would be more judicious to place an interval between Miss *Ringrose's departure and my arrival—than to have us immediately one treading on the other's heels[2]—I should—it is true have liked to have seen Miss *Wooler—but I have written to her and told her that I do not think it probable we shall meet this time—nor will it—if she was to go to Scarbro'[3] in a fortnight from the time you saw her last—

Consider the matter, and when you have considered it ripely—I will be guided by your deliberate judgment, only be sure and give me a few day's notice whatever time you fix—and be sure also to take into consideration the convenience and inclinations of your Mother and Sisters as well as your own.

We have glorious weather here, for which we cannot be too thankful—I sincerely hope a day of general thanksgiving will be appointed after the harvest is got in.[4] Write to me again soon—

[Signature cut off]

MS BPM Bon 194. W & S 301 as 29 Aug.
Address: not in MS.

PM: not in MS.
Annotation by EN in ink: 136 Aug 29 —47
Date: EN probably confused 2 letters (1 now missing) and their envelopes. She annotated an envelope postmarked 28 and 29 Aug. 'Aug 23 —47'—a likely date for the present letter, written on a 'glorious' day soon after Amelia Ringrose's arrival. See notes 1 and 4.
Text: the signature has been cut off, along with the corresponding part of fol. 2.

1. Amelia Ringrose's visit had been hoped for since Mar.: see EN 24.3.1847. She arrived at Brookroyd on 14 Aug. and left on 2 Sept., according to memoranda notes in EN *Diary* 1849. A letter from Amelia's sister Rosie to EN of 21.9.1847 reports that Amelia is in 'much better spirits, I think her visit to you has been the cause of this very great improvement'. (MS BPM.)
2. cf. *Hamlet* IV. vii. 164–5. CB's visit began on 9 Sept.
3. Margaret Wooler had a house in the North Bay at Scarborough. See the article by her great-nephew, the Revd Max Blakeley, 'Memories of Margaret Wooler and her Sisters', *BST* 12. 62.113–14.
4. *Shackleton* recorded a 'fine & warm' Aug., with a 'v fine D[ay]' on the 23rd, and fine but sometimes overcast days thereafter. The 28th (the other possible date for this letter) was a fine day with cumulus clouds and a west wind.

To Ellen Nussey, [?28 August 1847]: envelope only

MS BPM B.S. 104/28
Address: Miss Ellen Nussey | Brookroyd | Birstal | Leeds
PM: (i) HAWORTH (ii) BRADFORD YORKS | A[U] 28 | 1847 | O (iii) LEEDS | AU 29 | 1847 | A (iv) BIRSTAL
Annotation by EN in pencil: Aug 23 —47 | Mrs G.[1] Wafer: blue lozenge with the words 'Look Within' (partly deleted and apparently altered to 'Swithin',) surrounded by a line border.

1. EN probably confused 2 letters and their envelopes. See the previous letter, note on date. One would expect CB to make definite arrangements for her visit to Brookroyd on 9 Sept., and a letter of 28 Aug. (now missing) would be appropriate. A holograph MS now in BPM (MS B.S.58.5) may have been written on 28 August 1847. It reads:

Dear Ellen | I will (D.V.) come to Brookroyd on Thursday—I shall endeavour to come by the first conveyance—I trust I shall find you all well—Love to all—|
Yrs. C Brontë | You left a brooch here—the broken one which I will bring

To Messrs Smith, Elder and Co., 12 September 1847

[Brookroyd, Birstall][1]

Gentlemen

I have received your letter and thank you for the judicious remarks and sound advice[2] it contains. I am not however in a position to follow the advice; my engagements will not permit me to revise "Jane Eyre" a third time,[3] and perhaps there is little to regret in the circumstance; you probably know from personal experience that an author never writes well till he has got into the full spirit of his work, and were I to retrench, to alter and to add now when I am uninterested and cold, I know I should only further injure what may be already defective. Perhaps too the first part of "Jane Eyre" may suit the public taste[4] better than you anticipate—for it is true and Truth has a severe charm of its own. Had I told <u>all</u> the truth,[5] I might indeed have made it far more exquisitely painful[6]—but I deemed it advisable to soften and retrench many particulars lest the narrative should rather displease than attract.

I adopt your suggestion respecting the title; it would be much better to add the words "an autobiography."[7]

In accepting your terms,[8] I trust much to your equity and sense of justice. You stipulate for the refusal of my two next works at the price of one hundred pounds each. One hundred pounds is a small sum for a year's intellectual labour, nor would circumstances justify me in devoting my time and attention to literary pursuits with so narrow a prospect of advantage did I not feel convinced that in case the ultimate result of my efforts should prove more successful than you now anticipate, you would make some proportionate addition to the remuneration you at present offer. On this ground of confidence in your generosity and honour, I accept your conditions.

I shall be glad to know when the work will appear. I shall be happy also to receive any advice you can give me as to choice of subject or style of treatment in my next effort—and if you can point out any works peculiarly remarkable for the qualities in which I am deficient, I would study them carefully and endeavour to remedy my errors.

Allow me in conclusion to express my sense of the punctuality, straightforwardness and intelligence which have hitherto marked your dealings with me

And believe me Gentlemen
Yours respectfully
C Bell.

Since you have no use for "the Professor",[9] I shall be obliged if you will return the MS.S. Address as usual to Miss Brontë &c.

MS BPM SG 3/1B. *BST* 18. 92. 102–3.
Address (integral): Messrs. Smith Elder & Co.
PM: not in MS.
Annotation: the accompanying cover is endorsed: 'Currer Bell's | Acceptance of S. E & C's Terms | for copyright of Jane Eyre | Septr. 12th 1847'. (MS BPM SG 3/2B.)

1. Smith Elder's letter had been forwarded from Haworth. A memorandum in EN *Diary* 1849 reads: '9 [September] CB came 1847.'
2. George Smith gives no hint that any advice was needed. W. S. Williams, he says, recommended the novel to him, and he 'could not put the book down . . . before I went to bed that night I had finished the MS. My literary judgment was perfectly satisfied.' (*Huxley* 58–9.) Mrs Gaskell, however, writes that Smith was 'much amused' by Williams's strong admiration of the tale, but 'when a second reader, in the person of a clear-headed Scotchman, not given to enthusiasm . . . became so deeply interested in it, as to sit up half the night to finish it, Mr. Smith's curiosity was sufficiently excited to prompt him to read it for himself'. Either George Smith 'forgot' the reading by (probably) James Taylor, with whom he later parted on less than cordial terms, or Mrs Gaskell misunderstood a verbal account. (*Life* ii. 29.)
3. Nothing is known about previous revisions of *JE*, apart from the very few alterations or insertions of single words or short phrases in the remarkably clean copy MS sent to the printers. See the Clarendon edn. introduction, and for a comparison with the much-revised MSS of *Shirley* and *Villette*, see Margaret Smith, 'The Manuscripts of Charlotte Brontë's

Novels', *BST* 18. 93. 189–205. Perhaps in the present letter CB implies that she had revised in the process of fair-copying from her first rough pencil drafts. See *Life* ii. 10.

4. CB told George Henry Lewes on 6.11.1847 that *JE* 'was rather objected to at first' because 'it would never suit the circulating libraries'.
5. Lowood school in *JE* is based upon the Clergy Daughters' School, founded in 1824 by the Revd William Carus Wilson and others at Cowan Bridge in Lancs. It was a charitable institution, to which Maria, Elizabeth, Charlotte, and Emily Brontë were sent soon after it opened. CB recalled and elaborated on her experience there as a child of 8, and on what she had heard and seen of her sister Maria's character and of the sufferings she had undergone. In the *Life* Mrs Gaskell sought to modify this impression of Cowan Bridge, because she had 'heard dear Miss Brontë herself regret that her account had . . . so bitten into people's thoughts & recollections'. (Letter to George Smith, [?July 1855], CP letter 256.) But Mrs Gaskell's account of the people and events in the 1st and 2nd edns. of her biography caused an immense fracas, which necessitated the revision of the 4th ch. See the Penguin edn. of *Life*, i. 4 and appendix A, the Clarendon *JE* appendix II, and W & S appendix I.
6. One reason for such pain would be that in reality 2 of CB's sisters, Maria and Elizabeth, died as a result of illnesses which began or became worse at Cowan Bridge; in *JE* only 1 intimate friend, Helen Burns (based on Maria Brontë), dies.
7. The first page of the MS is headed 'Jane Eyre | <by Currer Bell | Vol. 1st>. Perhaps CB had provided a covering page with the title 'Jane Eyre, a novel, in three vols. by Currer Bell', as she had described it to Smith Elder in her letter of 24 Aug. The 1st edn. title-page begins 'JANE EYRE. | An Autobiography. | EDITED BY | CURRER BELL.' From the 2nd edn. onward this was altered to 'BY | CURRER BELL.' See the 'Descriptive List of Editions', Clarendon *JE* pp. xxi–xxvi.
8. In the typescript of George Smith's *Recollections*, the account of Smith's first reading of *JE* is followed by a statement of his terms: 'The next day we offered Currer Bell £100 for the copyright which was promptly accepted, and we subsequently paid—in excess of our agreement—additional sums amounting in all to £500: an amount which was not then so inadequate as it would appear at the present day.' (i.e. in the 1880s and 1890s.) (p. 100; National Library of Scotland MS 23191.)
9. Having retrieved the MS of *The Professor*, CB made 2 attempts to revise it, the first about Dec. 1847 after *JE* was published, and the second sometime after *Shirley* came out in Oct. 1849. When the Revd A. B. Nicholls edited the novel for publication in 1857, after consultation with Mr Brontë, he deleted some expletives and obliterated, or confirmed CB's deletion of, some 'improper' passages. See WSW 14.12.1847, Vol. iii, GS 5.2.1851 and notes, and the Clarendon *The Professor* pp. xxix–xxxviii.

To Messrs Smith, Elder and Co., 18 September 1847

[Brookroyd, Birstall]

Gentlemen

I return the proof sheets, I like their appearance; the errors are not numerous.[1]

I regret that the circumstance of my being from home[2] has occasioned a day's delay—after next week[3] this hindrance will not, I trust again recur.

I perfectly understand that I am not to publish "The Professor" or any other work till after the appearance of the two books of which you are to have the refusal

I am Gentlemen
Yrs. respectful[l]y
C Bell.

MS BPM SG 3/3B. *BST* 18. 92. 103.
Address (integral): Messrs. Smith Elder & Co.
PM: not in MS.
Annotation in ink on 2v: Currer Bell | Sept 18. 1847

1. The 1st edn. of *JE*, based on the clear fair copy MS, is on the whole accurately printed, and CB made very few revisions in proof. See the Clarendon *JE* pp. xii–xx for these and for the occasional errors and omissions.
2. See previous letter, n. 1. Mrs Gaskell wrote: 'While [*Jane Eyre*] was in the press, Miss Brontë went to pay a short visit to her friend at B[irstall]. The proofs were forwarded to her there, and she occasionally sat at the same table with her friend, correcting them; but they did not exchange a word on the subject.' (*Life* ii. 28.)
3. CB was writing on Saturday. She returned home on 23 Sept. See the next 2 letters, and EN 7.10.1847 n. 11.

To Messrs Smith, Elder and Co., 24 September [1847][1]

[Haworth]

Gentlemen

I have to thank you for punctuating[2] the sheets before sending them to me as I found the task very puzzling—and besides I consider your mode of punctuation a great deal mo[re] correct and rational than my own.

I am glad you think pretty well of the first part of "Jane Eyre" and I trust, both for your sakes and my own the public may think pretty well of it too.

Henceforth I hope I shall be able to return the sheets promptly and regularly.

I am Gentlemen
Yours respectfully
C Bell

MS BPM SG 4. W & S 302.
Address (integral): Messrs. Smith, Elder & Co.
PM: not in MS.
Annotation: in ink on verso: Currer Bell | Haworth | Sept 24.1847

1. CB was writing on the day after her return from her visit to EN at Birstall.
2. The printers replaced much of CB's light pointing with a more formal deployment of colons, semi-colons, and full-stops, and corrected her inaccurate and sometimes misleading punctuation of quoted speech.

To Ellen Nussey, [?24 September 1847]

[Haworth]

Dear Nell

I got to Leeds all right at 10[1] but the train was just gone and I had to cool my heels at the station for 2 hours as the next train did not start till 12.

I had a very wet, windy walk home from Keighley—but my fatigue quite disappeared when I reached home and found all well—Thank God for it.

My boxes came safe this morning—I have distributed the presents Papa says I am to remember him most kindly to you—the screen[2] will be very useful and he thanks you for it—

Tabby was charmed with her cap she said <you> she never thought of naught o' t' sort as Miss Nussey sending her aught—and she is sure she can never thank her enough for it—

I was infuriated on finding a jar[3] in my trunk—at first I hoped it was empty but when I found it heavy and replete I could have hurled it all the way back to Birstal—however the inscription A— B— softened me much—it was at once kind and villanous in you to send it—you ought first to be tenderly kissed and then afterwards as tenderly whipped—

<him most> Emily is just now sitting on the floor of the bed-room where I am writing, looking at her apples—she smiled when I gave <that> them and the collar to her as your presents with an expression at once well-pleased and slightly surprised—Anne thanks you much—All send their love—

It appears Emily did send off a letter for me yesterday under the delusion that it would reach me by the evening-post—tell me what you had to pay for it and I will send the amount in postage stamps.

Give my best love to your Mother & *Anne and *Mercy and believe me

[Yours in a mixture of anger & love
CB
Sep 25—47]

MS Pierpont Morgan MA 2696. W & S 303 as 25 Sept.
Address (integral): Miss Ellen Nussey | Brookroyd | Birstal | Leeds
PM: (i) [?KEIGH]LEY (ii) BIRSTAL
Annotation by EN in ink: 137 Sep—47. Wafer: blue lozenge, with the word '?L'AMOUR' carefully obliterated.
Date: EN may have dated from a postmark. CB had apparently travelled the day before she wrote this letter, on a wet day, and therefore not on 24 Sept. which was cloudy but fine. If the date '25th' was originally CB's, she must have made a slip in her reference to Emily's letter of 'yesterday'.
Text: words in square brackets supplied by EN in pencil to replace those cut away for the sake of the signature.

1. CB would travel from Birstall by road, in a gig or a coach. She had stayed with EN from 9 Sept. until Thursday 23rd, an overcast day with some rain, according to *Shackleton*.
2. Probably a small face-screen, 'a frame covered with paper or cloth, or a disk of thin wood, etc., with a handle by which a person may hold it between his face and the fire'. (*OED*.)
3. A jar containing crab-apple cheese, as Anne Brontë's letter to EN of 4 Oct. makes clear.

To Messrs Smith, Elder and Co., 29 September 1847

[Haworth]

Gentlemen

I trust you will be able to get "Jane Eyre" out next month[1]—Have the goodness to continue to send the sheets of the 3rd. Vol. along with those of the 2nd.

I again thank you for your attention in punctuating the sheets.

I am Gentlemen
Yours respectfully
C Bell

MS BPM SG 5. W & S 304.
Address (integral): Messrs. Smith, Elder & Co.
PM: not in MS.
Annotation in ink on verso: Currer Bell | Septr. 29 —1847

1. Mrs Gaskell writes: ' "Jane Eyre" was accepted, and printed and published by October 16th.' (*Life* ii. 27.) *The Athenaeum* for Saturday 16.10.1847 announced it as a new book to be published '*On Tuesday*' (i.e. 19 Oct.) (p. 1066 col. 3); while the *Supplement to The Times*, 19.10.1847, p. 10 col. 3, announced 'This day is published, and may be had at all the libraries, Jane Eyre: an Autobiography'.

Anne Brontë to Ellen Nussey, 4 October 1847

Haworth

My dear Miss Ellen,

Many thanks to you for your unexpected and welcome epistle. Charlotte is well, and meditates writing to you. Happily for all parties the east wind no longer prevails—during its continuance she complained of its influence as usual. I too suffered from it, in some degree, as I always do, more or less; but this time, it brought me no reinforcement of colds and coughs which is what I dread the most. Emily considers it a dry uninteresting wind, but it does not affect her nervous system. Charlotte agrees with me in thinking the note about Mr Jenkin's[1] a very provoking affair. You are quite mistaken about her parasol; she affirms she brought it back, and I can bear witness to the fact, having seen it yesterday in her possession. The one you have dis-covered may possibly have been left by Miss Ringrose. As for my book, you are welcome to keep it as long as you, or your friends can derive any benefit from its perusal, I have no wish to see it again, till I see you along with it, and then it will be welcome enough for the sake of the bearer. We are all here much as you left us; I have no news to tell you, except that Mr Nicholl's[2] begged a holiday and went to

Ireland three or four weeks ago, and is not expected back till Saturday—but that I dare say is no news at all.—We were all severally pleased and grateful for your kind and judiciously selected presents—from papa down to Tabby;—or down to myself, perhaps I ought rather to say. The crab-cheese is excellent, and likely to be very useful, but I don't intend to need it.[3] It is not choice, but necessity that has induced me to choose such a tiny sheet of paper[4] for my letter, having none more suitable at hand; but perhaps it will contain as much as you need wish to read or I to write, for I find I have nothing more to say except that your little Tabby must be a charming creature,—and when the wedding fever[5] reaches <u>you</u> I hope it will be to some good purpose and give you no cause to regret its advent, and—that is all, for as Charlotte is writing or about to write to you herself I need not send any message from her. Therefore, accept my best love and believe me to be your affectionate friend

Anne Brontë

I must not omit the Major's[6] compliments

MS BPM B.S. 3. W & S 306 (part).
Address: not in MS.
PM: not in MS.

1. Probably the Revd David Jenkins, or one of his relatives. His son the Revd Joseph Walker Jenkins, curate of Batley in 1844, was no longer there; the Revd Evan Jenkins, brother of David, still lived in Brussels as chaplain to Leopold of the Belgians, but returned to England for visits. See CB to E. Branwell 29.9.1841 n. 7 and EN 6.8.1843 n. 5.
2. The Revd A. B. Nicholls's relatives lived at Banagher and Killead in Northern Ireland.
3. Crab cheese is a preserve made with 'crab-apple pulp, sugar and a little butter, sometimes flavoured with oak-geranium leaves', according to information kindly provided by Mrs Victoria Fattorini. Perhaps it could be used in the treatment of the 'colds and coughs' dreaded by Anne Brontë, though I have found no evidence for such a use.
4. Anne crossed each of her 2 pages to make the most of the paper's small dimensions (76 mm. × 113 mm.).
5. Unexplained. Perhaps Ellen's relative Eleanor Walker, who was to marry the solicitor Charles Carr of Gomersal in May 1848, had announced her engagement.
6. EN added a note to this letter in *Nussey*: 'Emily [Brontë] was dubbed Major—because of some personal prowess she exhibited on a special occasion, which was highly amusing, because it was teasing to Mr W[eightman] and unique behaviour on her part.' (*Hatfield* 286.) Ellen told A. M. F. Robinson of Emily's 'dauntless protection of the other girls from too pressing suitors. Never was duenna so gallant, so gay, and so inevitable. In compliment to the excellence of her swashing and martial outside on such occasions, the little household dubbed her "The Major" '. (Robinson, *EB*, 69.)

To W. S. Williams,[1] *4 October 1847*

[Haworth]

Dear Sir

I thank you sincerely for your last letter; it is valuable to me because it furnishes me with a sound opinion on points respecting which I desired to be advised: be assured I shall do what I can to profit by your wise and good counsel.

Permit me however, Sir, to caution you against forming too favourable an idea of my powers or too sanguine an expectation of what they can achieve. I am, myself, sensible both of deficiencies of capacity and disadvantages of circumstance which will, I fear, render it somewhat difficult for me to attain popularity as an author. The eminent writers you mention[2]—Mr. Thackeray,[3] Mr. Dickens,[4] Mrs. Marsh[5] &c., doubtless enjoyed facilities for observation such as I have not; certainly they possess a knowledge of the world, whether intuitive or acquired, such as I can lay no claim to—and this gives their writings an importance and a variety greatly beyond what I can offer the public.

Still—if health be spared and time vouchsafed me, I mean to do my best, and should a moderate success crown my efforts, its value will be greatly enhanced by the proof it will seem to give that your kind counsel and encouragement have not been bestowed on one quite un[worthy.

Yours respectfully,

C. Bell.]

Oct$^{\underline{b}}$ 4$^{\underline{th}}$/ 47
W. S. Williarns Esq$^{\underline{r}}$

MS BPM B. S. 59. W & S 307.
Address (integral): W. S. Williams Esq$^{\underline{r}}$
PM: not in MS.
Text: About one quarter of fol. 2 has been cut away, leaving only the words 'Oct$^{\underline{b}}$ 4$^{\underline{th}}$/47 | W. S. Williams Esq$^{\underline{r}}$' on the recto. The text given here has been completed from W & S 307, which appears to be MS-based.

1. William Smith Williams had written the previous letters to CB on behalf of the firm of Smith, Elder; she now for the first time addresses him personally. See the Biographical Notes.
2. CB had asked her publishers to 'point out any works peculiarly remarkable for the qualities in which' she was deficient, so that she could 'endeavour to remedy' her errors. (SE 12.9.1847.)
3. William Makepiece Thackeray's published *œuvre* had begun in 1836. CB probably knew and admired some of his pseudonymous work in *Fraser's Magazine* and *Punch*; see EN 28.12.1846 n. 4. *Vanity Fair: Pen and Pencil Sketches of English Society* by W. M. Thackeray appeared in monthly parts from Jan. 1847 to July 1848, and was therefore still incomplete when CB dedicated the 2nd edn. of *JE* to Thackeray in Dec. 1847, praising him in her preface as a man of profound intellect, and the 'first social regenerator of the day'. See WSW 28.10.1847 notes 1 and 2.
4. By Dec. 1840, when CB referred flippantly to him as sometimes writing like a 'boarding-school miss', Charles Dickens had published *Sketches by Boz, Pickwick Papers, Oliver Twist*, and *Nicholas*

Nickleby: see her letter to Hartley Coleridge of 10.12.1840. Since then he had produced *The Old Curiosity Shop*, *Barnaby Rudge*, *Martin Chuzzlewit*, *A Christmas Carol*, and *The Chimes*. By Oct. 1847 he had completed about two-thirds of *Dombey and Son*, having published 13 parts since Sept. 1846.

5. Mrs Anne Marsh, née Caldwell (1791–1874), author of a recent best-selling novel, *Emilia Wyndham* (1845), and of the *Two Old Men's Tales* (1834) which had established her reputation. On 28 Oct. CB told Mr Williams that she had not read 'a line of Mrs Marsh's' in her life.

To Ellen Nussey, 7 October 1847

[Haworth]

Dear Ellen

I have been expecting you to write to me—but as you don't do it and as moreover you may possibly think it is my turn, and not yours—though on that point I am far from clear—I shall just send you one of my "scrubby[1] notes" for the express purpose of eliciting a reply.

Anne was very much pleased with her letter—I presume she has answered it before now—I would fain hope that her health is a little stronger than it was—and her spirits[2] a little better—but she leads much too sedentary a life, and is continually sitting stooping either over a book or over her desk[3]—it is with difficulty one can prevail on her to take a walk or induce her to converse—I look forward to next Summer with the confident intention that she shall—if possible—make at least a brief sojourn at the sea-side.

I am sorry that I inocculated you with fears about the east wind, I did not feel the last blast so severely as I have often done—My sympathies were much awakened by the touching anecdote respecting you, Dr. *?Senior[4] and Mr. *?Jenkins[5]—Did you salute your boy-messenger with a box on the ear the next time he came across you—? I think I should have been strongly tempted to have done as much—.

Mr. *Nicholls[6] is not yet returned but is expected next week. I am sorry to say that many of the parishioners express a desire that he should not trouble himself to re-cross the channel but should remain quietly where he is—This is not the feeling that ought to exist between shepherd and flock—it is not such as is prevalent at Birstal[7]—it is not such as poor Mr. *Wightman[8] excited.

Mr. & Mrs. *Grant[9] called a day or two since—and Mrs. *Grant was full of unintelligible apologies about not having paid you more attention. One cannot owe a grudge where no suffering is inflicted.

When you write, dear Nell, be sure and tell me how Miss *Ringrose is getting on—I certainly know few persons whom I have not seen that excite in me more interest than she does. Has Miss *?R—[10] yet written to say how

George bore your visit[11] and whether it had any subsequent bad effect *on *him?—

I am afraid your Mother will be suffering from Rheumatism to-day—it is so wet and damp—and *Mercy too—will never have been able to get to her school[12] through this rain. Give my best love to all of them and believe me

Yours faithfully
C Brontë

MS HM 24455. Envelope: WYAS Kirklees. W & S 308.
Address (envelope): Miss Ellen Nussey | Brookroyd | Birstal | Leeds
PM: (i) HAWORTH (ii) [BRA]DFORD | OC 7 | 1847 | D (iii) LEEDS | OC 8 | 1847 | A (iv) BIRSTAL
Annotation (i) on the letter by ?EN in ink: Mr Nicholls | Oct 7 —47; (ii) on the envelope by EN in ink: Oct 8th 47; (iii) in pencil: destroy | of AB | Mr N &c. Wafer: puce-coloured rectangle with the words 'Never repine' within a line border.
Text: proper names heavily deleted or scraped out.

1. Paltry, shabby. cf. EN 29.9.1840 and 21.4.1847.
2. Anne's depression is evident in her poem, 'The three guides', dated 'August 11th 1847', where she prays for Faith to guide her through the 'pain and woe' of life, for 'who like thee can rise | Above this restless, clouded scene,— | Beyond the holy skies?' (Chitham *ABP* 144–52.)
   In a long, brooding poem written between Nov. 1847 and 17 Apr. 1848, Anne contemplates in 'Self-Communion' 'the wasting power of time'. (Chitham *ABP* 152–61.)
3. Anne's sedentary labour would include the proof-correcting of *AG*, accepted for publication, along with *WH*, by Thomas Cautley Newby. See WSW 10.11.1847, where CB complains that though 'the first proof-sheets were already in the press at the commencement of last August' publication had been held up by Newby's 'exhausting delay and procrastination'.
4. The name has been scraped out and 'Lewis' pencilled in, as in W & S 308, but no Dr Lewis is traceable. The reference may be to the Revd Dr Joseph Senior, LL D, master of the Free Grammar School in Batley by 1841; by 1845 he was also Campden Lecturer of Wakefield, Yorks., according to the Clergy Lists for 1845 and 1846.
5. See AB to EN 4.10.1847 n. 1.
6. See AB to EN 4.10.1847 n. 2.
7. The Vicar of Birstall was the Revd W. M. Heald (1803–75), a prototype of the amiable Cyril Hall in *Shirley*.
8. The spelling indicates the usual pronunciation of the former curate William Weightman's name; it is so spelt in Pigot's *Directory* for 1841. For the affection he inspired at Haworth, see EN 29.9.1840 and BB to FHG 25.10.1842 and notes.
9. For the Revd Joseph Brett Grant, Mr Brontë's former curate, and perpetual curate at Oxenhope since Mar. 1846, see EN ?26.10.1844 n. 5. He had married Sarah Ann Turner of Woodford, Essex, on 13.1.1846.
10. The name has been scraped out and over-written in pencil as 'Ringrose', but Amelia Ringrose had 'not yet been' to York to see George Nussey when CB wrote to EN on 26.2.1848. The reference is more likely to be to the manager of the Clifton House asylum.
11. A memorandum in EN *Diary* 1849 may read '20 [September] Went to see dear G ?1847', but CB was still at Birstall on that date. EN may have made an incorrect entry.
12. Mercy is said to have started a school for poor children at Carlinghow, not far from Brookroyd. See *Whitehead* 135.

To Messrs Smith, Elder and Co., 8 October 1847

[Haworth]

Gentlemen

There will be no preface to "Jane Eyre".[1] If you send me six copies of the work, they will be amply sufficient and I shall be obliged to you for them

I am Gentlemen
Yrs respectfully
C Bell

MS BPM SG 6. W & S 305 as 2 Oct. 1847.
Address (integral): Messrs. Smith, Elder & Co.
PM: not in MS.
Annotation in ink on verso: Currer Bell | Haworth | Octr 9. 1847

1. There was no preface to the 1st edn. of *JE*, but on 21 Dec. CB wrote a revised preface to the 2nd edn., dedicating her novel to Thackeray and defending it from the charge of immorality. See WSW 18 and 23.12.1847 and the Clarendon *JE* pp. [xxviii]–xxx. Her 'Note to the Third Edition', dated 'April 13th, 1848' explained that her 'claim to the title of novelist' rested on *JE* alone (and not, as Newby and others had implied, on the novels of 'Ellis' and 'Acton Bell' in addition).

To W. S. Williams, 9 October 1847

[Haworth]

Dear Sir

I do not know whether the Dublin University Magazine[1] is included in the list of periodicals to which Messrs. Smith & Elder are accustomed to send copies of new publications, but, as a former work[2]—the joint production of myself and my two relatives, Ellis and Acton Bell—received a somewhat favourable notice in that magazine, it appears to me that if the Editor's attention were drawn to "Jane Eyre", he might possibly bestow on it also a few words of remark—.

The Critic[3] and the Athenæum[4] also gave comments on the work I allude to; the review in the first mentioned paper was unexpectedly and generously eulogistic, that in the Athenæum, more qualified—but still not discouraging.

I mention these circumstances and leave it to you to judge whether any advantage is derivable from them.

You dispensed me from the duty of acknowledging your last letter—but my sense of the justness of the views it expresses will not permit me to neglect this opportunity both of acknowledging it and thanking you for it.

[Signature cut off]

MS Brotherton. W & S 309.
Address: not in MS.
PM: not in MS.
Annotation on 2^{v}: Currer Bell | Haworth | Oct 13 1847

1. See Aylott 7.5.1846 n. 4. The belated review of *JE* which appeared in the *Dublin University Magazine* for May 1848 praised its 'remarkable power and beauty' in spite of the lack of 'flashes of wit, [or] piquancy of dialogue', the imperfectly delineated character of Rochester, and some improbability towards the end; Jane herself was 'perfect', recalling the Consuelo of George Sand, but very much superior to her. See CB's comment in Vol. ii, WSW 1.5.1848. (W & S 366.), and *Dublin University Magazine* vol. 31, 608–14.
2. *Poems by Currer, Ellis, and Acton Bell* (1846).
3. See Aylott 7.5.1846 n. 6 and WSW 6.11.1847 n. 6.
4. See Aylott 10.7.1846 notes 1 and 2, and SE 26.10.1847 n. 2.

To Ellen Nussey, [?15 October 1847]

[Haworth]

[(i) a] Dear Ellen

Miss Ringrose's letters are distressing indeed. It appears to me most desirable that either you should go to her or she should come to you. It would seem as if there was no one to look after her—no one to take care of her at home. If her Mother is so absorbed in her wretched cravings and indulgences[1] as to be incapable of perceiving her daughter's state—has the father no eyes and no understanding? The poor girl is more to be pitied than many a beggar's child[2]—and it is hard indeed that one who deserves all affection and care should be so solitary—so neglected as she apparently is—

Probably by this time you will know more of her condition—and [(ii)a] if you are not already with her—and indeed whether you are or not—I hope you will soon acquaint me how she gets on—whether she is become downright ill or is a little better.

It is not religion which turns her head—it is a derangement of 'the' bodily and mental functions which, owing to her habits of thought, has taken the form of <u>religious</u> hypochondria[3]—had she never heard of religion she would still have been ill—but would have shewn her malady in some other way. She ought most certainly to go from home—change of scene is, I believe in such cases, almost indispensable for relief. If you went to see her at *Tranby[4]—she would be better while you stayed but would infallibly fall back into her old state as soon as you left her.

If Mr. *Ringrose had a spark of intelligence or good feeling—he would send his daughter to some cheerful watering-place—with you for a companion [(i)b] Such a plan would, I am morally certain be most efficient for her welfare—and it is a pity there is not some one to suggest it to him.

We are getting on here the same as usual—only that Branwell has been more than ordinarily troublesome and annoying of late—he leads papa a wretched life.[5] Mr. Nicholls is returned[6] just the same—I cannot for my life see those interesting germs of goodness in him you discovered, his narrowness of mind always strikes me chiefly—I fear he is indebted to your imagination for his hidden treasures.

I am sorry to hear that Mercy occasionally spits blood but I should think it is more likely to proceed from the lungs than from the stomach. She ought however to be [(ii)b] careful—Give My best love to your Mother, Anne and Mercy

Yours faithfully
C Brontë

MSS (i) a and b: WYAS Kirklees. W & S 310. (ii) a and b: Beinecke, Yale. Unpublished. Envelope: WYAS Kirklees.
Address (envelope): Miss Ellen Nussey | Brookroyd | Birstal | Leeds
PM: (i) HAW[ORTH] (ii) BRADFORD YORK[S] | OC 1— | 18—7 | ?D (iii) LEED[S] | OC 1— | 1847 | A (iv) BIRSTAL
Annotation (i) on the letter by EN in ink (Kirklees fragment): Oct—47; (ii) on the envelope by EN in ink: Oct 15th 47; (iii) in pencil: destroy | of A's ailment | & Mr Nicholl
Text: The full text is published for the first time, the separation of the MS into 2 fragments having hitherto obscured their connection. This is confirmed by the content, by EN's annotation on the letter and envelope, and by the paper—two leaves of identical unwatermarked greyish paper, each 115 mm × *c*.123 mm., with crossed writing on both sides.

1. Mrs Ringrose either was or later became ill. When she died in Mar. 1850, CB, with Branwell's death in mind, wrote very sympathetically to Amelia: 'most truly do you describe the oblivion of faults which succeeds to Death . . . we forget what anxiety, what anguish, what shame the frailties and vices of that poor unconscious mould of clay once caused us'. (Vol. ii, AR 31.3.1850.)
2. Amelia's father was in fact a wealthy man. See EN 1.6.1845 n. 6.
3. For CB's use of 'hypochondria' to mean 'nervous depression', see MW ?Nov/Dec 1846 notes 7 and 9.
4. Tranby Lodge, Heads Lane, Hessle, a substantial house standing in its own wooded grounds in the country about 6 miles west of Hull. It was built in the early 19th cent. by a Hull merchant, Samuel Cooper, and sold by him to Amelia's father Christopher L. Ringrose in 1841. (I am indebted for this information to Peter J. Ainscough, Humberside County Librarian, who kindly provided details of the sale and maps of the area.)
5. In EN 11.1.1848 CB described Branwell's 'absurd and intolerable conduct' when he had money to spend: 'Papa is harrassed day and night—we have little peace—he is always sick, has two or three times fallen down in fits—what will be the ultimate end God knows—'. (MS Law-Dixon; see Vol. ii.) John Greenwood, the Haworth stationer, heard that on one occasion Branwell accidentally set his bed on fire, and had to be rescued by Emily. See A. H. Preston, 'John Greenwood and the Brontës', *BST* 12.61.35–8.
6. Mr Nicholls had been staying with relatives in Ireland. See EN 7.10.1847.

To Messrs Smith, Elder & Co., 19 October 1847

[Haworth]

Gentlemen

The six copies of "Jane Eyre" reached me this morning.[1] You have given the work every advantage which good paper, clear type and a seemly outside can supply—if it fails—the fault will lie with the author—you are exempt.

I now await the judgment of the press and the public.

I am Gentlemen
Yrs. respectfully
C Bell.

MS Princeton, Parrish Collection. W & S 311.
Address: not in MS.
PM: not in MS.
Annotation on verso: Currer Bell | Oct 19. 1847

1. CB was writing on the day of publication, if the advertisement in *The Athenaeum* for Saturday 16 Oct. is to be believed: 'New books published by Smith, Elder & Co. . . . Jane Eyre. An autobiography. Edited by Currer Bell. 3 vols. post 8vo. *On Tuesday.*' (i.e. 19 Oct.) The price, like that of most three-decker novels, was £1. 11*s*. 6*d*. (*c*£1. 58p.) For more details see the Clarendon edn. pp. xxi–xxvi.

To Messrs Smith, Elder and Co., 26 October 1847

[Haworth]

Gentlemen

I have received the newspapers. They speak quite as favourably of "Jane Eyre" as I expected them to do. The notice in the Literary Gazette[1] seems certainly to have been indited in rather a flat mood, and the Athenæum[2] has a style of its own which I respect, but cannot exactly relish; Still when one considers that journals of that standing have a dignity to maintain which would be deranged by a too cordial recognition of the claims of an obscure author—I suppose there is every reason to be satisfied

Meantime a brisk sale would be an effectual support under the hauteur of lofty critics—

I am Gentlemen
respe[c]tfully yours
C Bell

MS BPM SG 7. W & S 312.
Address (integral): Messrs. Smith, Elder & Co.

PM: not in MS.
Annotation on 2^v: Currer Bell | Haworth | Oct 27. 1847

1. *The Literary Gazette*, founded by Henry Colburn, and edited from its inception in 1817 until 1850 by William Jerdan (1782–1869), tended to puff works published by Colburn. See Aylott 7.5.1846 n. 6. The *Gazette*'s praise of *JE*'s 'novelty and talent' in the number for 23.10.1847, 748–9, was qualified by reference to 'ingredients of a less attractive nature' and to its mixture of styles. Mrs Gaskell shrewdly commented that the reviewer was 'uncertain as to whether it was safe to praise an unknown author' (*Life* ii. 30), but he did conclude that the novel displayed 'an observant insight into the workings of the human heart'. (749.)
2. The review in *The Athenaeum* for 23.10.1847, 1100–1, was by Henry Fothergill Chorley (1808–72), musical and literary critic for *The Athenaeum* from 1830 to 1868. (*Allott* 71–2.) Chorley considered that the power of the novel atoned for 'certain eccentricities in the invention, which trench in one or two places on what is improbable, if not unpleasant'. He found 'reality' in the novel until the secret of the maniac was revealed: 'From that point forward, however, we think the heroine too outrageously tried, and too romantically assisted in her difficulties:—until arrives the last moment, at which obstacles fall down like the battlements of *Castle Melodrame*.'

To W. S. Williams, 28 October 1847

[Haworth]

Dear Sir

Your last letter was very pleasant to me to read, and is very cheering to reflect on. I feel honoured in being approved by Mr. Thackeray[1] because I approve Mr. Thackeray. This may sound presumptuous perhaps, but I mean that I have long recognized[2] in his writings genuine talent such as I admired, such as I wondered at and delighted in. No author seems to distinguish so exquisitely as he does dross from ore, the real from the counterfeit. I believed too he had deep and true feelings under his seeming sternness—now I am sure he has. One good word from such a man is worth pages of praise from ordinary judges.

You are right in having faith in the reality of Helen Burns's character:[3] she was real enough: I have exaggerated nothing there: I abstained from recording much that I remember respecting her, lest the narrative should sound incredible. Knowing this, I could not but smile at the quiet, self-complacent dogmatism with which one of the journals lays it down that "such creations as Helen Burns are very beautiful but very untrue."[4]

The plot of "Jane Eyre may be a hackneyed one; Mr. Thackeray remarks that it is familiar to him;[5] but having read comparatively few novels, I never chanced to meet with it, and I thought it original—. The critic of the Athenaeum's work,[6] I had not had the good fortune to hear of.

The Weekly Chronicle[7] seems inclined to identify me with Mrs. Marsh. I never had the pleasure of perusing a line of Mrs. Marsh's in my life—but I wish very much to read her works and shall profit by the first opportunity of doing so. I hope I shall not find I have been an unconscious imitator.

I would still endeavour to keep my expectations low respecting the ultimate success of "Jane Eyre"; but my desire that it should succeed augments—for you have taken much trouble about the work, and it would grieve me seriously if your active efforts should be baffled and your sanguine hopes disappointed: excuse me if I again remark that I fear they are rather too sanguine; it would be better to moderate them. What will the critics of the Monthly Reviews and Magazines be likely to see in "Jane Eyre" (if indeed they deign to read it) which will win from them even a stinted modicum of approbation? It has no learning, no research, it discusses no subject of public interest. A mere domestic novel will I fear seem trivial to men of large views and solid attainments.

Still—efforts so energetic and indefatigable as yours ought to realize a result in some degree favourable, and I trust they will.

I remain, dear Sir
Yours respectfully
C Bell.

Octbr. 28th. / 47

I have just recd. "the Tablet"[8] and the "Morning Advertiser"[9]—neither paper seems inimical to the book—but I see it produces a very different effect—on different natures. I was amused at the analysis in the Tablet—it is oddly expressed in some parts—I think the critic did not always seize my meaning—he speaks for instance of "Jane's inconceivable alarm at Mr. Rochester's repelling manner—I do not remember that

MS Pierpont Morgan MA 2696. W & S 313.
Address: not in MS.
PM: not in MS.

1. CB's publishers had presented copies of *JE* 'to a few private literary friends'. (*Life* ii. 29.) Thackeray wrote to W. S. Williams on 23 Oct. that he had 'lost (or won if you like) a whole day in reading it . . . with the printers I know waiting for copy . . . It is a fine book though—the man & woman capital . . . The plot of the story is one with wh. I am familiar. Some of the love passages made me cry—to the astonishment of John who came in with the coals . . . It is a woman's writing, but whose? . . . Give my respects and thanks to the author.' (G. N. Ray (ed.), *The Letters and Private Papers of W. M. Thackeray* (4 vols., 1945), Letter 417.) After CB's death Thackeray recalled in his introduction to her novel-fragment 'Emma' 'the delight, and wonder, and pleasure with which I read *Jane Eyre*'. (*Cornhill Magazine*, 1 (Apr. 1860), 487.)
2. See EN 28.12.1846 n. 4 and WSW 4.10.1847 n. 3. Even before 1843, when the *Irish Sketch Book* appeared pseudonymously but with a preface in his own name, Thackeray's hand had been generally recognized in the writing of 'Michael Angelo Titmarsh', 'George Savage Fitzboodle', etc. CB had not read the early chs. of *Vanity Fair* (Jan. 1847–July 1848) before writing *JE*, according to her letter to WSW of 2.3.1849. (See Vol. ii, W & S 426.)
3. Mrs Gaskell had CB's authority for saying that her eldest sister Maria was 'the original of Helen Burns in "Jane Eyre" '. (Letter to John Forster of Sept. 1853, *CP* letter 166.) In the *Life* she wrote that CB's heart, 'to the latest day on which we met, still beat with

unavailing indignation at the worrying and the cruelty to which her gentle, patient, dying sister had been subjected' at Cowan Bridge school. (*Life* i. 73.)

4. 'Helen Burns is just one of those idealities in which young writers are fain to revel . . . dream-children . . . Creations such as these are very beautiful, but very untrue.' (*Atlas* 23.10.1847, 719; *Allott* 68.) But the review is full of high praise for the novel as a whole: 'It is one of the most powerful domestic romances which have been published for many years . . . It is a book to make the pulses gallop and the heart beat, and to fill the eyes with tears.' (*Allott* 67–8.)
5. See n. 1 above. The editor of Thackeray's letters, Gordon Ray, comments: 'Thackeray's phrasing is ambiguous, but it seems likely that he refers, not to a literary parallel, but to the similarity between his own history and certain parts of *Jane Eyre*.' (Ray, *Letters and Papers* ii. 319 n. 102.) Thackeray had been devoted to his wife Isabella, née Shawe, whom he had married in 1836, and had been deeply distressed when she became insane in 1840. In 1847 she was being cared for in a private home, and she remained in this or similar homes until her death. A personal familiarity with the plot of *JE* rather than an obvious parallel with (e.g.) Richardson's *Pamela or Virtue Rewarded* (1740) does seem to be implied. *Pamela* was in fact one of the 'comparatively few' novels CB had read. See HC Draft ?Dec. 1840 n. 6 and *JE* 5.
6. See SE 26.10.1847 n. 2. H. F. Chorley writes of *JE*, 'Some such tale as this was told in a now forgotten novel—*Sketches of a Seaport Town*.' (*The Athenæum* 23.10.1847, 1101.) Chorley's novel, published in 1834, drew on his experiences as a clerk in Liverpool before he moved to London in 1833.
7. The *Weekly Chronicle* was published from 1836 to 1851, then continued with various changes of name until 1867. After praising *JE* as 'extraordinary' and 'full of power' in the number for 23.10.1847, 3, the reviewer continued: 'We were tempted more than once to believe that Mrs. Marsh was veiling herself under an assumed editorship, for this autobiography partakes greatly of her simple, penetrating style, and, at times, of her love of nature; but a man's more vigorous hand is, we think, perceptible . . . From the first page to the last, it is stamped with the same vitality, and there is a minuteness and detail in every point, which makes this picture of a life so true and interesting beyond any other work that has appeared for very many years.' For Mrs Anne Marsh, see WSW 4.10.1847 n. 5.
8. *The Tablet*, the official organ of the Roman Catholic church in England, was founded by Frederick Lucas (1812–55) in 1840. A 'bold challenge to the writers of the day' by 'a new Knight in the lists of Literary Fiction', *JE* was 'not at all a conventional novel'; the reviewer found that the story invited the reader 'into the recesses of the human heart' and concluded 'The reading of such a book as this is a healthful exercise, and we sincerely hope may prove as attractive as it must be profitable.' Jane's original 'inconceivable alarm' at Rochester's repelling manner is followed by 'various phases of amusement at enduring and defying his haughty abruptness, delight in the exercise of power over him, and absorbing admiration of all that the outward shell concealed'. It would be 'marvellous' if Rochester were a 'portrait from a man's hands, notwithstanding the masculine firmness of the touch and the breadth of the handling'. (*The Tablet* 23.10.1847, 675.)
9. *The Morning Advertiser* was founded in 1794 by the Society of Licensed Victuallers of London to raise money for their charities, and was devoted primarily to trade interests. It was a paper with Liberal sympathies and an enormous circulation though 'not to be found in clubs, nor in the best stationers' shops, nor in the houses of the respectable . . . the journal *par excellence* of the public-house'. (Alexander Herzen [Aleksandr Ivanovich Gertsen], *My Past and Thoughts*, trans. Constance Garnett (1924), pt. 6, ch. 7, quoted in G. M. Young (ed.), *Early Victorian England* (1934), ii. 33.) The reviewer found *JE* 'deeply interesting and exciting', fresh and original, though occasionally 'melo-dramatic'. 'The author writes in a natural and unaffected style, and yet there are displayed throughout an earnestness and depth of feeling which the reader finds it impossible to resist.' Fact and fiction are mingled with 'ingenuity and success . . . There are occasional faults of exaggeration, and some specimens of oddity and eccentricity. They, however, are but minor evils amid great and conspicuous excellences.' (*The Morning Advertiser*, 26.10.1847, [3].)

To Ellen Nussey, [?29 October or early November 1847]

[Haworth]

Dear Ellen

The old pang of fearing you should fancy I forget you drives me to write to you—though heaven knows I have precious little to say and if it were not that I wish to hear from you and hate to appear disregardful where I am not so—I might let another week or perhaps two slip away without writing.

Rosetta *Ringrose's[1] letter as you say, does her credit—like her sister's there is a pleasing simplicity and absence of affectation in the style—I should think she is amiable—though probably not so unusually and remarkably so as Amelia—I should think she hardly possessed Amelia's devotedness of character and generous warmth of heart.

There is much in Rosy's letter which I thought very melancholy: Poor Girls—theirs, I fear, must be a very unhappy home—Yours and mine, Ellen, with all disadvantages, all absences of luxury and wealth and style <is> 'are' I doubt not happier.

I wish to goodness you were rich and independent that you might give Miss *Ringrose a temporary asylum and a relief from uneasiness, suffering and gloom.

As to that father—I cannot but despise him—he is a weak man I am certain. What good does it do to go and upbraid the mother he ought rather to comfort and sustain his daughters. They have it is plain, no support in either parent.

What you say about the effects of ether[2] on Catherine *Swaine[3] rather startled me—I had always consoled myself with the idea of having my front teeth extracted and rearranged some day under its soothing influence—but now I should think twice before I consented to inhale; one would not like to make a fool of oneself—

When you write again—and let it be soon—don't forget to give me a bulletin always about Miss *Ringrose's health—say also whether you have again had any tidings respecting *George. I am glad to hear *Henry's health is improving—and I trust a residence at Nice may benefit him still more.[4]

With best love <from> 'to' your Mother, Anne and *Mercy I am

Yours faithfully
C Brontë

MS HM 24456. W & S 321 as 29 Nov.
Address: not in MS.
PM: not in MS.
Annotation by EN in ink: <Oct> 'Nov'. | 29 —47.
Date: EN was uncertain of the date. *Shorter* 249 and W & S accept 29 Nov., but this is too close to

CB's letter of 2 Dec., written when EN had clearly been at Tranby for some time. Late Oct. or early Nov. would suit the content of the present letter: the extract in *CBCircle* 226 is dated *'November 10th, 1847'*, which may be right.

1. Margaret Rosita or Rosetta, b. 1830, a younger sister of Amelia. Her letter of 21.9.1847 to EN (MS BPM) speaks affectionately of Amelia, and expresses the wish to meet EN 'although from description I almost know you'.
2. By 1847 ether was in general use as an anaesthetic in England; in the 1850s it was for a time replaced by chloroform, introduced as an alternative method by Sir James Simpson in Nov. 1847, and praised for its superiority over ether in its rapid action and 'more agreeable' flavour in e.g. *John Bull* 20.11.1847, 742.
3. The youngest daughter of Joseph and Mary Swaine of Brier Hall, Gomersal. See EN 7.10.1845 n. 5.
4. EN would have heard of Henry's intention to go to Nice, and by early Nov. she could have heard of his arrival there. The first page of Henry's commonplace book in WYAS Sheepscar, Leeds, is headed 'Observations of a travel made on the Continent of Europe in the year 1847'; he begins: 'This was accomplished by my wife myself & a friend as far as to Geneva, where our friend left us for England again, & thence by ourselves to Nice, where I write this from memory, commencing it on the 12$^{\underline{th}}$ day of November, 1847, having been here about a fortnight . . . We left London for Ostend on the 13$^{\underline{th}}$ of July in the present year.' But Henry completed only the first page of his observations, and filled most of the rest with a miscellany of random facts and quotations, dated 1848–50. In March–May 1850 he and his wife were well enough to holiday in Italy. Henry found Rome a 'wonderful & wicked place', but felt so much better as to hope that 'in two years hence' he might 'resume duty in some shape or other w^{h} wd be a great comfort to all of us.' (BL MS Egerton 3268A, Henry Nussey to his sisters Ann (Mrs Clapham) and Mercy, 13.3.1850, fol. 100^{v}.) For whatever reason, he never resumed his 'duty' as a clergyman. Emily Nussey died at Nice in 1907; the place of Henry's death in ?1867 is not known.

To W. S. Williams, 6 November 1847

[Haworth]

Dear Sir

I shall be obliged to you if you will direct the enclosed to be posted in London,[1] as <at present> I wish to avoid giving any clue to my place of residence, publicity not being my ambition.

It is an answer to the letter I received yesterday, favoured by you; this letter bore the signature G. H. Lewes,[2] and the writer informs me that it is his intention to write a critique on "Jane Eyre" for the Decbr. number of Frazer's Magazine[3]—and possibly also, he intimates, a brief no—[. . . ? the Westminster] Review[4] Upon the whole he seems favourably inclined to the work though he hints disapprobation of the melo-dramatic portions.

Can you give me any information respecting Mr. Lewes—? what station he occupies in the literary world and what works he has written?[5] He styles himself "a fellow-novelist". There is something in the candid tone of his letter which inclines me to think well of him.

I duly received your letter containing the notices from "the Critic"[6] and the two Magazines[7]—and also the Morning Post.[8] I hope all these notices will work together for good:[9] they must at any rate give the book a certain publicity.

[Signature cut off]

MS Brotherton. W & S 314.
Address: not in MS.
PM: not in MS.
Text: the missing words before 'Review' were cut away along with the signature. *Shorter* 240 and W & S 314 read 'a brief notice to the "Westminster Review" '.

1. CB had made a similar request when Frederick Enoch asked for the 'Bells' ' signatures. (Aylott 23.7.1846.)
2. George Henry Lewes (1817–78), happily married to Agnes, née Jervis, whose later infidelity led to Lewes's partnership with 'George Eliot' from 1854. He was already a well-known critic and author, and had published a 1-vol. novel, *Ranthorpe*, in May 1847, with an affectionate dedication to his wife.
3. See the next letter, notes 1 and 2.
4. The *Westminster Review* (1824–1914), the journal of the 'philosophical radicals', was founded by James Mill and Jeremy Bentham. Lewes had written articles for it since 1840. Earlier in 1847 he and Thornton Hunt had planned to buy the journal, but could not raise enough money. His notice of *JE*, in the number for Jan. 1848, praised the natural tone, originality, freshness, and life-like characters of 'the best novel of the season'. It was certainly 'from the pen of a lady, and a clever one too'. (*Westminster Review*, 48 (1848), 581–4; *Allott* 87–8.)
5. Lewes had done good work in introducing European writing and philosophy to British readers through his journalism. His *Biographical History of Philosophy* (1845–6) was popular and sold well, though it was sneered at by some conventionally educated scholars for its superficiality. See Rosemary Ashton, *G. H. Lewes: A Life* (Oxford, 1991), 49. Lewes was a versatile and intelligent journalist, but his ill-plotted, over-ambitious, and uneven novel *Ranthorpe* did not add to his reputation. W. S. Williams responded to CB's enquiry with a favourable account of him. See WSW 10.11.1847.
6. See Aylott 7.5.1846 n. 6 and WSW 9.10.1847. *The Critic* praised Currer Bell for 'fertile invention, great power of description, and a happy faculty for conceiving and sketching character', found *JE* 'very far indeed above the average', and concluded that it was 'sure to be in demand'. (*The Critic* 30.10.1847, 277–8; *Allott* 73.)
7. If one of these was *Douglas Jerrold's Shilling Magazine* for Nov., CB would have found high praise modified by criticism of the 'extravagant contortions of melodrama' in the 'latter portion' of the novel (vi. 474). *The New Monthly Magazine* found *JE* 'one of the most powerfully written novels that have lately issued from the press', and concluded, 'The action is oftentimes improbable, but the passion is always true to life'. (80 (Nov. 1847), 374.)
8. The *Morning Post* (1772–1937) was a popular conservative daily paper. The review, one of those included in 'Opinions of the Press' at the end of the 3rd edn. of *JE*, was enthusiastic: 'The characters introduced are strongly marked, the incidents are various, and of a kind which enlist the sympathies, the style is fresh and vigorous, and scarcely anything is overdone. There is no regular plot; but, what is better, a thrilling interest is excited in each division or department of the story'. (*Morning Post* 3.11.1847, 2. Like many of these early 'reviews', the article is mainly a summary of the plot, with long quotations from the Thornfield chs.)
9. cf. Romans 8: 28.

To G. H. Lewes, 6 November 1847[1]

[Haworth]

Dear Sir

Your letter reached me yesterday; I beg to assure you that I appreciate fully the intention with which it was written, and I thank you sincerely both for its cheering commendation and valuable advice.

You warn me to beware of Melodrame[2] and you exhort me to adhere to the real. When I first began to write, so impressed was I with the truth of the principles you advocate that I determined to take Nature and Truth as my sole guides and to follow in their very footprints; I restrained imagination, eschewed romance,[3] repressed excitement: over-bright colouring too I avoided, and sought to produce something which should be soft, grave and true.

My work (a tale in 1 vol.) being completed, I offered it to a publisher. He said it was original, faithful to Nature, but he did not feel warranted in accepting it, such a work would not sell. I tried six publishers[4] in succession; they all told me it was deficient in "startling incident" and "thrilling excitement",[5] that it would never suit the circulating libraries,[6] and as it was on those libraries the success of works of fiction mainly depended they could not undertake to publish what would be overlooked there—"Jane Eyre" was rather objected to at first [on] the same grounds[7]—but finally found acceptance.

I mention this to you, not with a view of pleading exemption from censure, but in order to direct your attention to the root of certain literary evils—if in your forthcoming article in "Frazer" you would bestow a few words of enlightenment on the public who support the circulating libraries,[8] you might, with your powers, do some good.

You advise me too, not to stray far from the ground of experience[9] as I become weak when I enter the region of fiction; and you say "real experience is perennially interesting and to all men . ."

I feel that this also is true, but, dear Sir, is not the real experience of each individual very limited? and if a writer dwells upon that solely or principally is he not in danger of repeating himself, and also of becoming an egotist?

Then too, Imagination is a strong, restless faculty[10] which claims to be heard and exercised, are we to be quite deaf to her cry and insensate to her struggles? When she shews us bright pictures are we never to look at them and try to reproduce them?—And when she is eloquent and speaks rapidly and urgently in our ear are we not to write to her dictation[?]

I shall anxiously search the next number of "Frazer" for your opinions on these points.

Believe me, dear Sir,
Yours gratefully
C Bell

MS BL Add. 39763. W & S 315.
Address: (integral): G. H. Lewes Esqr
PM: not in MS.

1. This letter was enclosed in that of the same date to W. S. Williams, q.v. Mrs Gaskell introduced it as follows in *Life* ch. 16:

   Mr Lewes 'has' politely <sends> 'sent' me the following explanation of that letter of his, to which the succeeding one of Miss Brontë is a reply. "When 'Jane Eyre' <was> first <published> appeared, the publishers courteously sent me a copy. The enthusiasm with which I read it, made me go down to Mr. Parker, and propose to write a review of it for "Frazer's Magazine." He would not consent to an unknown novel—for the papers had not yet declared themselves—receiving such importance; but thought it might make one on Recent Novels: English and French—which appeared in "Frazer," December, 1847.—Meanwhile, I had written to Miss Brontë to tell her the delight with which her book filled me; and seem to have 'sermonized' her, to judge from her reply." (Rylands MS *Life* fol. 350.)

   Lewes's copy of the 1st edn. of *Jane Eyre* is in the Sterling Library of the University of London.
2. Thus in MS. G. H. Lewes found that the 'deep, significant reality' of *JE* brought its defects into stronger relief: 'There is, indeed, too much melodrama and improbability, which smack of the circulating-library,—we allude particularly to the mad wife and all that relates to her, and to the wanderings of Jane when she quits Thornfield; yet even those parts are powerfully executed.' (*Fraser's Magazine*, 36 (Dec. 1847), 691–2; *Allott* 84–5.) Lewes's theory was sounder than his practice. His own novels, *Ranthorpe* (1847) and *Rose, Blanche, and Violet* (1848) are too often marred by melodramatic scenes and inflated style.
3. CB's early writings, as C. Alexander's edn. shows, are full of unrestrained 'imagination . . . romance . . . excitement'; but in 1839 she wrote her 'Farewell to Angria': 'still I long to quit for a while that burning clime where we have sojourned too long its skies flame—the glow of sunset is always upon it the mind would cease from excitement & turn now to a cooler region—where the dawn breaks grey and sober & the coming day for a time at least is subdued in clouds'. (MS BPM Bon 125(1.) In *The Professor*, the 'tale in 1 vol' referred to in the present letter, she determined to write in this new mood of restraint; as she explained in the preface, 'I had come to prefer what was plain and homely . . . my hero should work his way through life as I had seen real living men work theirs.' She had anticipated Lewes's advice in ch. 19 of *The Professor*: 'Novelists should never allow themselves to weary of the study of real Life.' (Clarendon edn., 159; the novel was completed in 1845–6.)
4. See e.g. CB's letter to Henry Colburn, 4.7.1846, and SE 15.7.1847 notes 2 and 3.
5. Publishers show 'a passionate preference for the wild wonderful and thrilling'. (Preface to *The Professor*, 4.)
6. The circulating libraries, esp. that founded by Charles Edward Mudie (1818–90) in 1842, strongly influenced 19th-cent. publication of fiction by an effective moral censorship in the books selected, and purchased in quantity, for their thousands of subscribers. See J. A. Sutherland, *Victorian Novelists and Publishers* (1976), esp. 24–30, and R. D. Altick, *The English Common Reader* (1957, 1963), 295–8.
7. See SE 12.9.1847. MS reads 'one the same'.
8. In his review Lewes implies that many circulating library novelists cater for an undiscriminating taste for 'empty phantasmagoria' rather than 'breathing flesh and blood', and finds that 'St. John Rivers, the missionary, has a touch of the circulating-library, but not enough to spoil the truth of the delineation'. (*Fraser's Magazine*, 36 (Dec. 1847), 692; *Allott* 85.)

9. 'Unless a novel be built out of real experience, it can have no real success.' (Lewes in *Fraser's Magazine*, 36 (Dec. 1847), 691; *Allott* 84.)
10. cf. William Crimsworth's reference to 'my Darling, my Cherished-in-secret, Imagination, the tender and the mighty' in *The Professor* 30.

To W. S. Williams, 10 November 1847

[Haworth]

Dear Sir,

I have received the ["Britannia"][1] and the "Sun,"[2] but not the "Spectator,"[3] which I rather regret, as censure, though not pleasant, is often wholesome.

Thank you for your information regarding Mr Lewes.[4] I am glad to hear that he is a clever and sincere man; such being the case, I can await his critical sentence with fortitude: even if it goes against me, I shall not murmur; ability and honesty have a right to condemn where they think condemnation is deserved. From what you say, however, I trust rather to obtain at least a modified approval.

Your account of the various surmises respecting the identity of the brothers Bell,[5] amused me much: were the enigma solved, it would probably be found not worth the trouble of solution; but I will let it alone; it suits ourselves to remain quiet and certainly injures no one else.

The Reviewer, who noticed the little book of poems, in the "Dublin Magazine,"[6] conjectured that the soi-disant three personages were in reality but one, who, endowed with an unduly prominent organ of self-esteem, and consequently impressed with a somewhat weighty notion of his own merits, thought them too vast to be concentrated in a single individual, and accordingly divided himself into three, out of consideration, I suppose, for the nerves of the much-to-be-astounded public! This was an ingenious thought in the Reviewer; very original and striking, but not accurate. We are three.

A prose work[7] by Ellis and Acton will soon appear: it should have been out, indeed, long since, for the first proof-sheets were already in the press at the commencement of last August, before Currer Bell had placed the M.S. of "Jane Eyre" in your hands. Mr N<ewby>,[8] however, does not do business like Messrs. Smith and Elder; a different spirit seems to preside at 72. Mortimer Street[9] to that which guides the helm at 65. Cornhill.[10] Mr. N<ewby> shuffles, gives his word and breaks it; Messrs. Smith and Elder's performance is always better than their promise. My relatives have suffered from exhausting delay and procrastination, while I have to acknowledge the benefits of a management, at once business-like and gentlemanlike, energetic and considerate.

I should like to know if Mr. N<ewby> often acts as he has done to my relatives, or whether this is an exceptional instance of his method. Do you know, and can you tell me anything about him? You must excuse me for going to the point at once, when I want to learn anything; if my questions are importunate,[11] you are, of course, at liberty to decline answering them.—I am yours respectfully,

C. Bell.

MS untraced. W & S 316.
Address: not in source.
PM: not in source.
Text: Rylands MS *Life*, fos. 354–6. Unlike the Rylands MS, the printed *Life* omitted Newby's name and address, and the sentence beginning 'Mr Newby shuffles'. *Shorter* 242, based on the printed *Life*, adds the name and part of the address, but not the missing sentence. W & S 316, which has some minor variants, is probably based on Symington's transcript (now at Rutgers), made while the holograph manuscript of the letter was in the Law Collection 'album-de-luxe' at Honresfeld. See e.g. notes 9 and 11 below.

1. Rylands MS *Life* reads ' "Brittania" '. See Aylott 7.5.1846 n. 5. The *Britannia*'s full title at this date was *The Britannia, and Conservative Journal*. The reviewer began grudgingly with a criticism of the novel's autobiographical form and consequent 'total want of the construction which we are accustomed to expect' in a novel: most of Jane's adventures seem 'totally purposeless'. Nevertheless the book has considerable ability: 'it exhibits deep insight into character, and much skill in its portrayal; and it displays a deeper vein of thought, more matured power of reflection, and a higher tone of feeling than we usually meet with in modern novels' in spite of 'some passages which are simply revolting in themselves' relating to the maniac wife. Having praised the opening chs. and the 'pathos and heart' of the conclusion, the reviewer concludes: 'Both the mind and the pen of the writer seem to us to require practice; but there is assuredly sufficient merit in the book to entitle the author to every encouragement to continue a literary career commenced with so much promise.' (*The Britannia* 6.11.1847, 710.)
2. A daily newspaper, 1793–1871. The reviewer praised *JE*'s interest, originality, natural and simple manner of narration, 'the vigorous way in which feelings and passions are portrayed', and the 'very admirable delineation and nice discrimination of character', especially that of St John Rivers. Though some portions of the tale were 'not of a very pleasing character, and many, very many, of the incidents are most unnatural' and the story lacked a definite object, it entertained the reader and contained 'many sublime and beautiful thoughts, and inculcate[d] some most ennobling sentiments'. (*The Sun* 6.11.47, [3].)
3. The weekly periodical begun in 1828 by the Scottish journalist Robert Stephen Rintoul (1787–1858), with funds provided by Joseph Hume and others, as an organ of 'educated radicalism'. (*OCEL* 926.) The reviewer thought *JE* was unnatural, with too much artifice and contrived dialogue; Mr Rochester was 'hard, peculiar' and hardly proper in his conduct towards Jane. The story's truth was 'not probable in the principal incidents', there was 'a low tone of behaviour (rather than of morality) in the book; and . . . neither the heroine nor hero' attracted sympathy. The reviewer conceded however that there was 'considerable skill in the plan, and great power'. (*The Spectator* 6.11.47, 1074–5.) W. S. Williams might well have consoled CB for this review by recalling his own experience as a reviewer for Rintoul, a man of a 'chilly temperament' who 'used to say, in the most impressive manner, " 'The Spectator' is *not* enthusiastic, and must not be"!' (George Smith, typescript *Recollections*, National Library of Scotland MS 23191.)
4. CB's publishers would be well-informed. Lewes and George Smith were fellow-members of Douglas Jerrold's Museum Club, founded in 1847, and according to Sir Sidney Lee, W. S. Williams was 'always on very friendly terms' with Lewes, who was his neighbour in Campden Hill Terrace, Kensington, from June 1843 to June 1846. They had a number of acquaintances in common, such as Leigh and Thornton Hunt and Richard Hengist Horne. (See *Huxley* 55–6.)
5. J. G. Lockhart reported 2 surmises to Miss Rigby (later Lady Eastlake) on 13.11.1848: 'the common rumour is that they are brothers of the weaving order in some Lancashire town. At first it was generally said Currer was a lady, and Mayfair circumstantialised by making her the *chère amie* of Mr. Thackeray.' (Charles Eastlake Smith (ed.), *Journals and Correspondence of Lady Eastlake*, (1895), i. 222.) For the second rumour, see WSW 23.12.1847 n. 2; it was probably

not in circulation until the 2nd edn. of *JE*, with its dedication to Thackeray, appeared in Jan. 1848.

6. 'Whether [the triad of versemen] be in truth but one master spirit . . . that has been pleased to project itself into three imaginary poets,—we are wholly unable to conjecture . . . The tone of all these little poems is certainly uniform.' (See *Dublin University Magazine* 28 (1846), 385–7; *Allott* 63.) See Aylott 7.5.1846 n. 4.
7. *WH* and *AG* were published together in Dec. 1847, *AG* forming the third of the 3 vols. See WSW 14.12.1847 n. 5.
8. Thomas Cautley Newby (?1798–1882) began publishing in the late 1820s at 72 Mortimer Street, Cavendish Square, London, moved to 30 Welbeck Street in 1850, and retired in 1874. His tardy publication of 'Acton and Ellis Bell's' novels, delayed until *JE* proved to be a best seller, his hard bargaining, and his advertisements in 1848 implying that AB's second novel was the work of the highly successful Currer Bell, have earned him a bad press. But G. D. Hargeaves points out that Newby 'did give many unknown authors . . . some sort of a chance, while some novelists (like Mrs Grey, Ellen Pickering, and Mr and Mrs Mackenzie Daniel) published regularly with him in the eighteen-forties.' (*The Tenant of Wildfell Hall* (Penguin edn., 1985), 496.) Anthony Trollope commented drily but without rancour that Newby did not wrong him in paying nothing for his first novel, *The Macdermots of Ballycloran* in 1847: 'It is probable that he did not sell fifty copies of the work.' (*Autobiography* (World's Classics edn.; 1987), 75.) See also Geoffrey Larken, 'The Shuffling Scamp', *BST* 15. 80. 400–7.)
9. W & S 316 mistakenly prints '172 Mortimer Street'; Symington's typescript omits the number.
10. The premises to which Smith, Elder moved from 158 Fenchurch Street on or soon after 21 Nov. 1824, and where they remained until towards the end of 1868. (*Huxley* 7.)
11. The printed *Life*, *Shorter* 242, *Symington*'s typescript, and W & S 316 all read 'impertinent', which may well be correct.

To Messrs Smith, Elder and Co., 13 November 1847

[Haworth]

Gentlemen

I have to acknowledge the receipt of yours of the 11th. inst. and to thank you for the information it communicates. The notice from the "People's Journal"[1] also duly reached me, and this morning I received "the Spectator"

The critique in the Spectator[2] gives that view of the book which will naturally be taken by a certain class of minds; I shall expect it to be followed by other notices of a similar nature. The way to detraction has been pointed out and will probably be pursued—Most future notices will in all likelihood have a reflection of "the Spectator" in them.

I fear this turn of opinion will not improve the demand for the book—but time will shew: if "Jane Eyre" has any solid worth in it—it ought to weather a gust of unfavourable wind—

I am Gentlemen,
Yours respectfully
C Bell.

MS BPM SG 8. W & S 317.
Address (integral): Messrs. Smith Elder & Co.

PM: not in MS.
Annotation on 2^{v}: Currer Bell | Haworth | Nov 13. 1847

1. Founded in 1846 by the dramatist and poet John Saunders (1810–95), an associate of William Howitt and Charles Knight. The journal was incorporated with *Howitt's Journal* in 1849. The reviewer praised almost every aspect of *JE* and found its moral sentiments 'pure and healthy'; its 'great, if undisciplined, powers' went far beyond the promise shown in the *Poems* of 1846, and Jane's homely name indicated 'a departure from the sickly models of the Minerva Press'. (*The People's Journal* 13.11.1847, 268–72; *Allott* 80–1.)
2. See WSW 10.11.1847 n. 3.

To W. S. Williams, 17 November 1847

[Haworth]

Dear Sir

The perusal of the "Era"[1] gave me much pleasure, as did that of the "People's Journal".[2] An Author feels peculiarly gratified by the recognition of a right tendency in his works; for if what he writes does no good to the reader, he feels he has missed his chief aim, wasted, in a great measure, his time and his labour. The "Spectator"[3] seemed to have found more harm than good in "Jane Eyre", and I acknowledge that distressed me a little.

I am glad to be told that you are not habitually over-sanguine: I shall now permit myself to encourage a little more freely the hopeful sentiment which your letters usually impart, and which hitherto I have always tried to distrust. Still I am persuaded every nameless writer should "rejoice with trembling"[4] over the first doubtful dawn of popular good-will; and that he should hold himself prepared for change and disappointment: Critics are capricious, and the Public is fickle; besides one work gives so slight a claim to favour.

Ellis and Acton beg to thank you for the kind offer of your services with Mr. Newby[5]—but as the last of the proof-sheets has at length been sent down for correction, they deem it useless to trouble you on the subject— <sure>trusting that the publication of the work cannot now be delayed much longer.

Believe me, dear Sir
Yours very respectfully
C Bell.

MS Princeton, Parrish Collection. W & S 318.
Address: not in MS.
PM: not in MS.

1. A journal specializing in theatre news and reviews, 1838–1939. The reviewer considered that *JE* had 'nothing but nature and truth about it' and that in 'power of thought and expression' it surpassed 'Bulwer, [G. P. R.] James, D'Israeli, and all the serious novel writers of the day'. Currer Bell's pictures were 'like the Cartoons of Raphael . . . true, bold, well-defined, and full of life', and *JE*'s 'obvious moral thought' was that 'laws, both human and divine, approved in our calmer moments, are not to be disobeyed when our time of trial comes' and that 'the

practice of simple propriety, founded on strict morality and religious principles, is the sure road to ultimate bliss'. (*Era* 14.11.1847, 9; *Allott* 78–80.)

2. See SE 13.11.1847 n. 1.
3. See WSW 10.11.1847 n. 3.
4. Psalm 2: 11.
5. See WSW 10.11.1847 n. 8.

To W. S. Williams, 22 November [1847]

[Haworth]

Dear Sir

Will you have the goodness to post the enclosed letter for Mr. Lewes.[1]

I have received "Howitt's Journal"[2] "The Literary Circular"[3] "The Manchester Examiner"[4] and to-day the "Nottingham Mercury".[5]

I am dear Sir
Yrs. respectfully
C Bell

MS Bodleian Eng. lett. e. 30, fol. 185. *Bodleian Library Record* v. 4. 222–3.
Address (integral): To W. S. Williams Esqr.
PM: not in MS.
Annotation on 2^{v}: Currer Bell | Haworth | Nov 22 1847

1. G. H. Lewes. See the next letter.
2. *Howitt's Journal of Literature and Popular Progress*, ed. by William and Mary Howitt; founded in 1847 by William Howitt (1792–1879), prolific author of popular historical works, poems, short stories, and miscellaneous journalism. The journal was incorporated with the *People's Journal* in 1849. The reviewer considered *JE* 'One of the freshest and most genuine books which we have read for a long time. It is a domestic story, full of the most intense interest, and yet composed of the simplest materials, the worth of which consists in their truth.' (*Howitt's Journal* 20.11.1847, 333.)
3. A journal of 'Advertisements connected with literature and art' begun in Aug. 1836. I have not located the relevant number.
4. An influential liberal newspaper (1846–1922), issued twice weekly in 1847, and known as the *Manchester Examiner and Times* between 1848 and 1855. The reviewer was one of the few at this early date to link the novel, 'far beyond the average of its class', with the *Poems*: 'Currer Bell is one of those three brothers Bell, who lately published in concert, a volume of rhymes;—with success enough, it would seem, to make the name, on the title-page of an anonymous book, a respectable passport for it into the literature of the day. . . . It is a novel—a very clever and striking one, moreover, though written in the quiet, sober style of the old school, and, in its interest, entirely independent of contemporary commotions and discussions.' The reviewer praised the vivid portrayal of Jane's wretchedness as 'a shy and tormented child' in her aunt's household, and considered Lowood 'a picture, drawn to the life, of an English proprietary girls' school'. (*Manchester Examiner* 16.11.1847, 3, col. 1.)
5. A weekly paper, *The Nottingham Mercury and General Advertiser for the Midland Counties*, 1841–52. The reviewer provided one of the most extravagantly flattering of the 'Opinions of the Press' appended to the 3rd edn. of *JE*. He considered that the novel was a masterly performance whose writer promised 'beyond all doubt to be one of the most distinguished [competitors] of the present day' in the field of fiction. 'Of the many excellent and noble productions of the class

alluded to, we have read few of a more thrilling, edifying, and purifying character . . . Without the slightest approach to cant it is eminently religious—without any strained attempt at sentimentality it is truly pathetic . . . The doctrines of self-reliance, self-denial, and genuine humility, are powerfully exemplified in the career and demeanour of the heroine, and shown as thoroughly consistent with pious confidence in the over-ruling hand of Providence.' (*Nottingham Mercury* 19.11.1847, 6.)

To G. H. Lewes, 22 November 1847[1]

[Haworth]

Dear Sir

I have now read "Ranthorpe",[2] I could not get it till a day or two ago, but I have got it and read it at last; And in reading "Ranthorpe", I have read a new book; not a reprint, not a reflection of any other book, but a new book. I did not know such books were written now. It is very different to any of the popular works of fiction. It fills the mind with fresh knowledge.[3] Your experience and your convictions are made the [reader's], and to an author at least they have a value and 'an' interest quite unusual.[4]

I await your criticism on "Jane Eyre" now with other sentiments than I entertained before the perusal of "Ranthorpe." You were a stranger to me—I did not particularly respect you—I did not feel that your praise or blame would have any special weight—I knew little of your right to condemn or approve—now I am informed on these points.

You will be severe—your last letter taught me so much—. Well—I shall try to extract good out of your severity; and besides, though I am now sure you are a just, discriminating man, yet, being mortal, you must be fallible, and if any part of your censure galls me too keenly to the quick, gives me deadly pain, I shall for the present disbelieve it and put it quite aside till such time as I feel able to receive it without torture

I am, dear Sir
Yours very respectfully
C Bell

MS BL Add. 39763. W & S 319.
Address (integral): To G. H. Lewes Esq$^{\underline{r}}$
PM: not in MS.

1. Enclosed with the previous letter. For Lewes see WSW 6.11.1847 notes 2–5, and GHL 6.11.1847 notes 1 and 2.
2. Lewes's first novel, a single vol., was published anonymously by Chapman and Hall in May 1847, and by Tauchnitz later the same year. For an account of its composition and its lukewarm critical reception see Rosemary Ashton, *G. H. Lewes: A Life* (Oxford, 1991), 69–73. Ashton notes that 'Lewes was soon admitting the awfulness of *Ranthorpe* himself'. (72.)
3. In this inchoate novel, autobiographical and satirical elements mingle disconcertingly with didactic philosophizing, supported by a great display of multilingual quotations.

4. CB wrote 'readers'. Her interest would perhaps be aroused by the wording of Lewes's dedication of *Ranthorpe* to his wife (Agnes, née Jervis) as well as by the narrative. Lewes dedicated the novel, 'To her who has lightened the burden of an anxious life, this work is inscribed by her husband'.

To W. S. Williams, 27 November 1847

[Haworth]

Dear Sir

Will you have the goodness in future to direct all communications to me Haworth near Keighley instead of Bradford. With this address they will, owing to alterations in local post-office arrangements, reach me a day earlier than if sent by Bradford.

I have received this week the "Glasgow Examiner",[1] the "Bath Herald"[2] and "Douglas Jerrold's Newspaper".[3] The Examiner,[4] it appears, has not yet given a notice.

I am dear Sir
Yrs. respectfully
C Bell

MS BPM SG 9. W & S 320.
Address (integral): To W. S. Williams Esqr.
PM: not in MS.
Annotation on 1^v: Currer Bell | Haworth | Nov 27. 1847

1. Published 1844–64. The reviewer found this work of a new novelist 'one of surpassing power and interest'. Few recent novels exhibited 'characters so strongly marked—incidents so various and extraordinary, and yet so truthful—and a plot so skilfully, and, at the same time, so naturally conceived, and so effectively worked out; or display such a fresh and vigorous style . . . The story is remarkably well sustained throughout . . . We predict that this skilfully-planned and powerfully-told novel will be a favourite at all the libraries, and that it is but the precursor of better works to come from the same accomplished pen.' (*Glasgow Examiner* 20.11.1847, 4, col. 1.)
2. *The Bath Herald and General Advertiser*, 1792–1862. The 'engrossing charm' of *JE* was 'unconnected with factitious "remarkable adventure". It possesses as little of the marvellous as may be: and has neither a beauty for a heroine nor a demi-god for a hero.' The reader is 'chained' to the book because it exhibits 'the workings of a pure and gifted intelligence'. It is 'a study of character,—a picture-book of human emotions,—the mirror of a mind'. (*Bath Herald* 20.11.1847, 4.)
3. A weekly paper, radical in outlook, started by Douglas William Jerrold (1803–57) in 1846. It survived, with two changes of name, until 1851. The reviewer found *JE* 'original, vigorous, edifying, and absorbingly interesting . . . edifying from its moral truth and beauty . . . we think . . . that a woman's experience or invention furnished the materials of the book; but, there has been a man's hand, we imagine, in the arrangement and conduct of the work . . . [Lowood school] allowing for some exaggeration, is not unlike a real establishment of the kind known to many of our readers'. Though Rochester sometimes uses 'quite unjustifiable means of testing' Jane, 'it is in vain; the grand motive power of Jane's character—high principle or a sense of duty, prevails over her passionate love'. 'We must, however, enter our protest against Miss Eyre's Pamela-fashion of calling Mr. Rochester her master . . . before she loves him.' (*Douglas Jerrold's Weekly Newspaper* 20.11.1847, 1458–9.)
4. See Aylott 10.7.1846 n. 6.

To Messrs Smith, Elder and Co., 30 November 1847

[Haworth]

Gentlemen

I have received "the Economist"[1] but not "the Examiner";[2] from some cause that paper has missed as "the Spectator" did on a former occasion: I am glad however to learn through your letter that its notice of "Jane Eyre" was favourable and also that the prospects of the work appear to improve.

I am obliged to you for the information respecting "Wuthering Heights".[3]

[Signature cut off]

MS BPM SG 10. W & S 322.
Address (integral): To Messrs. Smith, Elder & Co.
PM: not in MS.
Annotation on 1^{v}: Currer Bell | Haworth | Dec. 1. 1847
Text: a strip of paper about 38 mm. deep has been cut from the bottom of the first leaf, evidently for the sake of the signature.

1. The weekly review established in 1843 by the politician and political economist James Wilson (1805–60); its full title from Sept. 1843 to 28 Dec. 1844 was *The Economist: or, the Political, Commercial, Agricultural, and Free-Trade Journal.* The reviewer was enthusiastic: 'Of all the novels we have read for years this is the most striking . . . Its style as well as its characters are unhackneyed, perfectly true and lifelike . . . It is thoroughly English—even somewhat provincial—which latter leads, in some of the scenes, to a certain raciness decidedly agreeable. It must be said that the drawing in some cases approaches to coarseness, and that in others the art employed in the construction of the story is too evident; but these are venial faults'. (*The Economist, Weekly Commercial Times, and Bankers' Gazette*, 27.11.1847, 1376.)
2. *The Examiner*'s review had appeared on 27 Nov. See next letter and notes.
3. Publication of *WH* and *AG* was imminent. The authors had received their 6 copies by 14 Dec., as CB informed W. S. Williams in her letter of that date.

To Messrs Smith, Elder and Co., 1 December 1847

[Haworth]

Gentlemen

"The Examiner" reached me to-day; it had been missent on account of the direction which was to Currer Bell, Care of Miss Brontë. Allow me to intimate that it would be better in future not to put the name of Currer Bell on the outside of communications; if directed simply to Miss Brontë they will be more likely to reach their destination safely. Currer Bell is <un> 'not' known in this district and I have no wish that he should become known.

The notice in the Examiner gratified me very much;[1] it appears to be from the pen of an able man who has understood what he undertakes to criticise; of course approbation from such a quarter is encouraging to an Author and I trust it will prove beneficial to the work.

I am Gentlemen
Yours respectfully
C Bell

I received likewise seven other notices from provincial papers enclosed in an envelope.[2] I thank you very sincerely for so punctually sending me all the various criticisms on "Jane Eyre"

MS BPM SG 11. W & S 323.
Address (integral): To Messrs. Smith, Elder & Co.
PM: not in MS.
Annotation on 2ᵛ: Currer Bell | Haworth | Dec 2. 1847

1. See Aylott 10.7.1846 n. 6. John Forster (1812–76) had recently taken over the editing of *The Examiner* from the radical journalist Albany William Fonblanque (1793–1872), who nevertheless still contributed, and probably wrote this review. cf. CB's reference to him in WSW 11.12.1847. The thoughts in *JE* were said to be 'true, sound, and original', the style 'resolute', and the object and moral excellent. 'Though relating to a woman, we do not believe [it] to have been written by a woman'. 'Whatever faults may be urged against the book, no one can assert that it is weak or vapid. It is anything but a fashionable novel. It has not a Lord Fanny for its hero, nor a Duchess for its pattern of nobility . . . The sentences are of simple English . . . Taken as a novel or history of events, the book is obviously defective; but as an analysis of a single mind . . . it may claim comparison with any work of the same species.' It differs altogether from 'the fictions of Sir Walter Scott or Sir Edward Lytton or Mr Dickens' and should rather be compared with 'the autobiographies of Godwin and his successors'. Jane Eyre has 'less rhetoric' than they have, but 'more graphic power, more earnest human purpose, and a more varied and vivid portraiture of men and things'. (*The Examiner* 27.11.1847, 756–7; *Allott* 76–8.)
2. Several of the 'Opinions of the Press' were drawn from provincial papers, whose praise must have increased the sales of the novel throughout the country. The *Liverpool Standard*, for example, found it 'most striking' and original: 'The gradual unfolding of the character of the heroine is not surpassed in any autobiography with which we are acquainted.' (*JE* 3rd edn., 'Opinions of the Press', 8.)

To Ellen Nussey, 2 December [1847]

[Haworth]

Dear Ellen

I send you the portraits[1] which I received this morning. I am of your opinion—the one you prefer is decidedly the most like and a very good likeness too: the other looks too tall a personage for you. A little note from Mercy accompanied the pictures—She says Mrs. Richard Nussey[2] is ill—Is she dangerously ill? Poor Mercy regrets the necessity of staying away from her school[3] in consequence of Ann's absence.

How much longer <will> do you remain at Hull—?[4] How does Miss Ringrose get on—and how does the change benefit yourself?

Yours faithfully
C Brontë

MS Montague. Envelope: BPM B.S. 104/29. No publication traced.
Address (envelope): Miss Ellen Nussey | C. Ringrose's Esqr. | Tranby | Hessle | Hull
PM: (i) HAWORTH (ii) KEIGHLEY | DE 2 | 1847 (iii) LEEDS | DE 2 | 1847 | F (iv) [HE]SSLE. Wafer on envelope: pink rectangle with the words 'Faithful and true' within a line border.

1. Two of the portraits sent on to Haworth by Mercy Nussey were evidently of EN; perhaps another was of Amelia Ringrose, since CB wrote on 24.12.1847 that 'the portrait' helped her to get a notion of Amelia's 'person'. The 140 mm. × 93 mm. envelope, larger than is needed for the tiny letter, indicates the probable size of the portraits.
2. For Mrs Richard Nussey see EN 29.9.1846, n. 8. She recovered from this illness but was seriously ill again in 1854; on 22.3.1854 CB was pleased to hear of her convalescence following a 'paralytic stroke'.
3. See EN 7.10.1847 n. 12. Mercy would have to take charge of the household since her sister Ann was normally the housekeeper.
4. EN's visit to Amelia Ringrose had probably begun in mid-Nov. For Tranby Lodge see EN 15.10.1847 n. 4.

To Messrs Smith, Elder & Co., 10 December 1847

[Haworth]

Gentlemen

I beg to acknowledge the receipt of your letter enclosing a Bank Post Bill for £100,[1] for which I thank you.

Having already expressed my sense of your kind and upright conduct, I can now only say that I trust you will always have reason to be as well content with me as I am with you. If the result of any future exertions I may be able to make should prove agreeable and advantageous to you, I shall be well satisfied, and it would be a serious source of regret to me if I thought you ever had reason to repent being my publishers.

You need not apologize, Gentlemen, for having written to me so seldom: of course I am always glad to hear from you, but I am truly glad to hear from Mr. Williams likewise; he was my first favourable critic;[2] he first gave me encouragement to persevere as an author, consequently I naturally respect him and feel grateful to him.

Excuse the informality of my letter and believe me, Gentlemen,

Yours very respectfully
Currer Bell.

MS BPM B.S. 60. W & S 324.
Address (integral): To Messrs Smith, Elder & Co.
PM: not in MS.
Annotation on 2^v: Currer Bell | Haworth | Decr 10. 1847

1. The sum agreed for the copyright of *JE*. CB eventually received £500 altogether. See SE 12.9.1847 n. 8.
2. See SE 7.8.1847 n. 2 and 12.9.1847 n. 2.

To W. S. Williams, 11 December 1847

[Haworth]

Dear Sir

I have delayed writing to you in the hope that the parcel you sent would reach me, but after making due inquiries at the Keighley, Bradford and Leeds Stations and obtaining no news of it, I must conclude that it has been lost.

However I have contrived to get a sight of Frazer's Magazine[1] from another quarter—so that I have only to regret Mr. Horne's kind present:[2] will you thank that gentleman for me when you see him, and tell him that the railroad is to blame for my not having acknowledged his courtesy before

Mr. Lewes is very lenient: I anticipated a degree of severity which he has spared me. His notice differs from all the other notices—he must be a man of no ordinary mind: there is a strange sagacity evinced in some of his remarks—yet he is not always right. I am afraid if he knew how much I write from intuition, how little from actual knowledge, he would think me presumptuous ever to have written at all. I am sure such would be his opinion—if he knew the narrow bounds of my attainments—the limited scope of my reading.

There are moments when I can hardly credit that anything I have done should <'have'> be found worthy to give even transitory pleasure to such men as Mr. Thackeray[3], Sir John Herschel[4], Mr. Fonblanque,[5] Leigh Hunt[6] and Mr. Lewes—that my humble efforts should have had such a result is a noble reward.

I was glad and proud to get the Bank Bill Mr. Smith sent me yesterday—but I hardly ever felt delight equal to that which cheered me when I received your letter containing an extract from <one> 'a note' by Mr. Thackeray[7] in which he expressed himself gratified with the perusal of "Jane Eyre". Mr. Thackeray is a keen, ruthless satirist—I had never perused his writings but with blended feelings of admiration and indignation—Critics, it appears to me, do not know what an intellectual boa-constrictor he is—they call him "humorous", "brilliant"—his is a most scalping humour, a most deadly brilliancy—he does not play with his prey—he coils round it and crushes it in his rings. He seems terribly in earnest in his war against the falsehood and follies of "the World"—I often wonder what that "World" thinks of him. I should think the faults of such a man would be, distrust of anything good in human Nature—galling suspicion of bad motives lurking behind good actions—are these his failings?

They are at any rate the failings of his written sentiments, for he cannot find in his heart to represent either Man or woman as at once good and wise. Does he not too much confound benevolence with weakness and wisdom with mere craft?

But I must not intrude on your time by too long a letter.

Believe me Yours respectfully
C Bell

I have received the Sheffield Iris,[8] the Bradford Observer,[9] the Guardian[10] the Newcastle [Gua]rdi[an][11] and the Sunday Times[12] since you wrote. The contrast between the notices in the two last named papers made me smile.[13] The Sunday Times almost denounces "Jane Eyre" as something very reprehensible and obnoxious, whereas the Newcastle Guardian seems to think it a mild potion which may be "safely administered to the most delicate invalid."[14]

I suppose the public must decide when critics disagree.

MS Lowell, Harvard. W & S 325 (without the postscript.)
Address (integral): To W. S. Williams Esq.
PM: not in MS.

1. See GHL 6.11.1847 and notes. *JE* is one of 5 'Recent Novels: French and English' reviewed by G. H. Lewes in *Fraser's Magazine* 36 (Dec. 1847), 686–95, and has the lion's share both of space and praise. Lewes regards Fielding and Jane Austen as greater than Scott in their 'truth in the delineation of life and character'—his prerequisite for good fiction—and proceeds to damn the first novel on his list, Marmion Savage's *The Bachelor of the Albany*, as a witty but forgettable display of fireworks with a farcical mixture of 'true' characters and stagey action. In contrast *JE* has 'almost all that we require in a novel . . . perception of character, and power of delineating it; picturesqueness; passion; and knowledge of life'. He believes that the writer, 'evidently a woman', is setting forth her own experience; if she 'has led a quiet, secluded life' her future novels will need to be planned and executed with 'circumspection; for, unless a novel be built out of real experience, it can have no real success'. Though he finds 'too much melodrama and improbability' in *JE*, he is generous with his praise and selects 'singularly fine' passages for quotation. The 'quiet truth' of this novel is compared with the exaggeration of Soulié's *Olivier Duhamel* ('a poor affair'), and the improbability of George Sand's *Piccinino* is condemned, as is that of the second part of Balzac's *Le Cousin Pons*—though the earlier part is a triumphant example of Balzac's 'astonishing faculty of observation'.
2. Richard Henry (later Hengist) Horne (1802–84) had sent a copy of his highly praised allegorical epic poem *Orion*, which he had published in 1843 at a farthing per copy 'to mark the public contempt into which epic poetry had fallen'. Horne's *New Spirit of the Age* (1844), George Smith's 'first venture' when he took charge of the firm, had led to his personal acquaintance with the 'quaint and picturesque' author. (*Huxley* 32–4.) See CB's letter to Horne of 15.12.1847.
3. See EN 28.12.1846 and WSW 4.10.1847 and notes. Thackeray was not yet one of George Smith's authors, though Smith admired his work. W. S. Williams had a 'slight acquaintance' with him. (*Huxley* 67.)
4. Sir John Frederick William Herschel (1792–1871), the astronomer. His *Results of Astronomical Observations made during the Years 1834–8 at the Cape of Good Hope* was one of several famous

illustrated scientific works published by Smith, Elder in the 1840s. It had appeared earlier in 1847, and was expensive to produce, even with the help of more than £1,000 from the Duke of Northumberland; George Smith wrote that he 'took a good deal of pains with the book'. (*Huxley*, 24.) It was advertised along with *JE* in e.g. Smith, Elder's 'List of New Books by Popular Authors' in May 1848.

5. See SE 1.12.1847 n. 1.
6. James Henry Leigh Hunt (1784–1859), essayist, editor, and poet. His recent work had been published by George Smith, who writes with amusement of his impracticality and with appreciation of his poems. Hunt's volume of essays, *Men, Women and Books*, had been praised on its publication in May 1847. See *Huxley* 35–7.
7. See WSW 28.10.1847 notes 1 and 2. In her preface to the 2nd edn. of *JE*, dated 'Dec. 21st, 1847', CB praised Thackeray as a satirist of prophet-like power, hurling the 'Greek fire of his sarcasm' and flashing 'the levin-brand of his denunciation' against the 'great ones of society'.
8. A weekly paper (1826–56) which carried an impressively long quotation from Milton's *Areopagitica* on the 'liberty to know . . . above all liberties' below its title. The reviewer considered that the novel was no common work: *JE* shows that 'conventional accomplishments [are] valueless contrasted with depth and originality of mind united to high moral purpose . . . Its style is polished and eloquent, its dialogues vivacious . . . each [character] makes known his individual qualities through the medium of speech, and in his own way . . . The incidents . . . are most powerfully worked up . . . a treat of no ordinary kind is in reserve for each and all who carefully read its rich, glowing, and eloquent pages.' (*Sheffield Iris* 2.12.1847, 6.)
9. A Liberal weekly newspaper published from 1834 to 1901. The reviewer found *JE* both instructive and realistic, in spite of some '*rather* exaggerated' incidents: 'the writer has an easy, graceful, and vigorous style, a keen eye for natural beauty, and the power of delineating and sustaining individual character.' 'The interest of the narrative is sustained to the last. The reflections of the chief character are forcible, just, and reassuring. Feeling and passion are subordinated to duty: the struggle is well depicted, but the victory is complete, and the weapons with which it is achieved are finely tempered and irresistible.' (*Bradford Observer* 2.12.1847, 7, col. 3.)
10. A religious paper published between 1846 and 1951, speaking for 'moderate and liberal-minded High Anglicanism'. Gladstone was one of its chief promoters. (G. M. Young (ed.), *Early Victorian England* (1934), ii. 83.) The reviewer had 'rarely met with a more deeply interesting story'; he praised the 'rare reality' of the descriptions, the admirably drawn characters, and the 'natural, easy and unflagging' dialogue; and he thought 'the mystery such as would baffle the keenest-scented reader'. But *JE* had 'one very prominent fault': Helen Burns's speech on the rising of the human spirit 'through gradations of glory' lacked reality, and as a creed could do 'much mischief'. The placing of 'In the days when we went gipsying' in the same year as *Marmion* (1808), and the improbable conversion of Eliza Reed to Rome, were also faults, though harmless ones. (*The Guardian* 1.12.1847, ii. 716–17.)
11. *The Newcastle Guardian and Tyne Mercury*, 1846–72, a moderately liberal weekly. *JE* was 'much superior to the ordinary run' and the style, though occasionally objectionable, was 'on the whole, agreeably natural', the tone 'quite healthy and moral'. The novel was 'a simple and well-told narrative of events common in every-day life' which could be recommended for a 'prominent place in the circulating libraries and other quarters where light literature is appreciated'. (*Newcastle Guardian* 4.12.1847, 6.)
12. The *Sunday Times* was begun on 20 Oct. 1822 by Henry White as a rival to *The Observer*; both papers were mildly liberal. Though the reviewer grudgingly admitted that *JE* was clever and original, he found in it 'as many faults as any novel we remember to have seen'. It was '*outré*, both in description, character, and plot', unnatural, with a 'morose and reserved' heroine and a 'morose and savage' hero 'with the repulsive manners of a boor' whose interview with his mad wife 'confined in an upper story of Rochester Castle' was too disgusting to be quoted. The authoress boasts of having dared to overstep conventional rules, and 'There are some scenes so exaggerated that they pass all credible bounds. As a whole, "Jane Eyre" is a mass of improbable incidents and exaggerated characters.' (*Sunday Times* 5.12.1847, 2.)
13. Mrs Gaskell contrasted London readers of *JE*, who found it exaggerated, with Northerners

who 'were sure, from the very truth and accuracy of the writing, that the writer was no Southeron'. (*Life* ii. 39.)

14. CB mockingly uses the current style of patent-medicine advertisements, such as that for the 'elegant tonic' 'Dr. Collier's Orange Quinine Wine, for cases of Impaired Constitution, Debility attended with Nervousness, &c . . . This medicine may be taken by persons of the most delicate constitution'. (*Douglas Jerrold's Weekly Newspaper* 23.10.1847, 1350.)

To W. S. Williams, 14 December 1847

[Haworth]

Dear Sir

I have just received your kind and welcome letter of the 11th. I shall proceed at once to discuss the principal subject of it.

Of course a second work has occupied my thoughts much. I think it would be premature in me to undertake a serial[1] now; I am not yet qualified for the task: I have neither gained a sufficiently firm footing with the public, nor do I possess sufficient confidence in myself, nor can I boast those unflagging animal spirits, that even command of the faculty of composition, which, as you say and I am persuaded, most justly, is an indispensable requisite to success in serial <fiction> literature. I decidedly feel that ere I change my ground, I had better make another venture in the 3 vol. novel form.

Respecting the plan of such a work, I have pondered it, but as yet with very unsatisfactory results. Three commencements have I essayed,[2] but all three displease me. A few days since I looked over "The Professor." I found the beginning very feeble, the whole narrative deficient in incident and in general attractiveness; yet the middle and latter portion of the work, all that relates to Brussels, the Belgian school &c. is as good as I can write; it contains more pith, more substance, more reality, in my judgment, than much of "Jane Eyre". It gives, I think, a new view of a grade, an occupation, and a class of characters—all very common-place, very insignificant in themselves, but not more so than the materials composing that portion of "Jane Eyre" which seems to please most generally—.

My wish is to recast "the Professor", add as well as I can, what is deficient, retrench some parts, develop others—and make of it a 3-vol. work[3]; no easy task, I know, yet I trust not an impracticable one.

I have not forgotten that "the Professor" was set aside[4] in my agreement with Messrs. Smith & Elder—therefore before I take any step to execute the plan I have sketched, I should wish to have your judgment on its wisdom. You read or looked over the M.S.—what impression have you now respecting its worth? And what confidence have you that I can make it better than it is?

Feeling certain that from business reasons as well as from natural integrity you will be quite candid with me, I esteem it a privilege to be able thus to consult you.

Believe me, dear Sir,
Yours respectfully
C. Bell—

"Wuthering Heights" is, I suppose, at <last> 'length' published[5]—at least Mr. Newby has sent the authors their six copies—I wonder how it will be received. I should say it merits the epithets of "vigorous" and "original" much more decidedly than "Jane Eyre" did. "Agnes Grey" should please such critics as Mr. Lewes—for it is "true" and "unexaggerated" enough.

The books are not well got up—they abound in errors of the press.[6] On a former occasion I expressed myself with perhaps too little reserve regarding Mr. Newby[7]—yet I cannot but feel, and feel painfully that Ellis and Acton have not had the justice at his hands that I have had at those of Messrs. Smith & Elder

MS Princeton, Taylor Collection. W & S 327.
Address: not in MS.
PM: not in MS.

1. Mr Williams presumably had in mind publication in separate monthly parts rather than serialization in a magazine, since George Smith's *Cornhill Magazine* was not founded until 1860. The firm no doubt hoped to rival such profitable best-selling serializations as Chapman and Hall's ventures with Dickens's *Pickwick Papers*, published in 20 monthly parts dated Apr. 1836 to Nov. 1837, and *Nicholas Nickleby* (Apr. 1838–Oct. 1839). George Smith had tried but failed to secure the publication of works by Thackeray, whose *Vanity Fair* was currently being published in monthly parts by Bradbury and Evans. See J. A. Sutherland, *Victorian Novelists and Publishers* (1976), 52, 101, and *Huxley* 67.
2. These 'commencements' have not been located, unless CB is referring to her attempts to recast *The Professor*, 2 of which survive. One is a single-page pencil draft entitled 'Preface' (BPM MS Bon 109) beginning 'I had the pleasure of knowing Mr Crimsworth very well'. The narrator explains that he has cut out 'the whole of the first ?seven chapters with one stroke', but the fragment breaks off before the 'first interview' of the Crimsworth brothers. See the Clarendon *Professor* appendix III. A longer pencil draft of $2\frac{1}{2}$ chs. (18 leaves), known as 'John Henry', is in Princeton University Library. In it CB renames the Crimsworth brothers John Henry and William Moore, and begins to develop the character of John Henry's wife Julia. See the Clarendon *Shirley* appendix D.
3. *The Professor* is a short novel, which had to be very spaciously printed to fill 2 vols. when it was eventually published in 1857. The standard 3-vol. format would have suited the circulating libraries. On the verso of a later preface to *The Professor*, written after the publication of *Shirley* in 1849, CB calculates that she must write either 134 or 182 manuscript pages to produce the 'equivalent to 300 pages printed book'—i.e. one standard vol. (Pencil draft MS, Pierpont Morgan Library.) See the Clarendon *Professor* appendix II.
4. See SE 18.9.1847.
5. *WH* was published in 2 vols., along with *AG* as the 3rd vol. The title-page of vol. i begins, misleadingly, 'WUTHERING HEIGHTS | A NOVEL, | BY | ELLIS BELL, | IN THREE VOLUMES'; the vol. iii title-page begins 'AGNES GREY. | A NOVEL, | BY | ACTON BELL, | VOL. III'. For bibliographical details of the early edns., see the 'Descriptive Lists' in the Clarendon edns. of the novels. They were published in the week ending 15 Dec. The *Publishers' Circular* for that

date reads: 'WUTHERING HEIGHTS by Ellis Bell and Agnes Grey. By Acton Bell. 3 vols. post 8vo. pp. 1128, boards, 31s. 6d.'

6. The Clarendon eds. note in *WH* the ubiquitous presence of superfluous commas, inadequate hyphenation, and a number of mis-spellings; in *AG* they find similar punctuation and literal errors. See e.g. *AG* pp. xv–xviii. Michael Sadleir lists comparable printing errors in Newby's edition of Trollope's *The Macdermots of Ballycloran*, and he notes the 'amateur printing' of the vols. (*Trollope: A Bibliography* (1928), 8–9.)
7. See WSW 10.11.1847.

To W. S. Williams, 15 December 1847

[Haworth]

Dear Sir

I write a line in haste to apprise you that I have got the parcel.[1] It was sent, through the carelessness of the railroad people, to Bingley,[2] where it lay a fortnight—till a Haworth carrier happening to pass that way, brought it on to me.

I was much pleased to find that you had been kind enough to forward "the Mirror"[3] along with "Frazer". The article on "the last new novel" is in substance similar to the notice in the Sunday Times.[4] One passage only excited much interest in me: it was that where allusion is made to some former work which the author of "Jane Eyre" is supposed to have published:[5] there, I own my curiosity was a little stimulated. The Reviewer cannot mean the little book of rhymes to which Currer Bell contributed a third—but as that and "Jane Eyre" and a brief translation of some French verses sent anonymously to a Magazine[6] are the sole productions of mine that have ever appeared in print, I am puzzled to know to what else he can refer.

The Reviewer is mistaken, as he is in perverting my meaning, in attributing to me designs I know not—principles I disown[7]

I have been greatly pleased with Mr. R. H. Horne's poem of "Orion"[8]. Will you have the kindness to forward to him the enclosed note[9] and to correct the address if it is not accurate.

Believe me dear Sir
Yours respectfully
C Bell.

MS BPM Bon 195. W & S 328.
Address (integral): To W. S. Williams Esqr.
PM: not in MS.

1. See WSW 11.12.1847.
2. Bingley is a market-town about 6 miles from Haworth and 4 from Keighley. Its railway station, on the Shipley–Keighley extension of the Leeds–Bradford line, had been opened in Mar. 1847.

3. *The Mirror of Literature, Amusement and Instruction*, 1823–47, continued as *The Mirror Monthly Magazine* from 1847 to 1849. See 4th ser., ii. 376–80 (Dec. 1847.) This sharp and hostile review was by George Searle Phillips ('January Searle', 1815–89), a prolific journalist who had returned from America to England in 1845, when he became the editor of the liberal *Leeds Times*. Since 1846 he had been the Secretary of the People's College at Huddersfield. He found CB immoral in seeking to show 'how impossible it is to reconcile love of religion with love of mankind' through the despicable Brocklehurst who 'pockets the funds' intended for the school, and through the unfeeling St John Rivers. The scenes with the madwoman were 'ludicrously extravagant' or disgusting beyond belief. 'There is not a single natural character throughout the work . . . Religion is stabbed in the dark—our social distinctions attempted to be levelled, and all absurdly moral notions done away with. The authoress is unacquainted with the commonest rules of society . . . The language she puts into the mouth of Blanche Ingram would disgrace a kitchen maid . . . The foundation of the story is bad, the characters are ill-drawn, and the feelings false and unnatural.' (380.) Phillips later claimed that he was a friend of Branwell Brontë. See *Infernal World* 220–3 for an account of his unreliable article on BB in *The Mirror* for 28.12.1872. Phillips became insane in 1873.
4. See WSW 11.12.1847 n. 12.
5. 'We have undoubtedly once before met with this authoress. Though appearing under a new guise, there are resemblances . . . to another production quite as bold, quite as daring, quite as much distinguished for its insidious tendency, as the present volume . . . It is the boast of its writer that she knows how to overstep conventional usages . . . to trample upon customs respected by our forefathers.' (*Mirror of Literature* ii. 376.)
6. No such publication has been traced. At various times CB copied, referred to, or translated a number of French poems, including works by Voltaire, André Chénier, Charles-Hubert Millevoye, Auguste Barbier, and La Fontaine. See the Clarendon *Shirley* 106, 558–9, and notes, and Neufeldt *CBP* appendix A. Neufeldt *CBP* no. 216, 'Napoleon', has 56 lines, but might perhaps be called a brief translation of Auguste Barbier's 'L'Idole'. Trial lines in a draft MS, BPM Bon 116, show that CB took special care with her English version and made a revised copy in Mar. 1843. (Pierpont Morgan MS, 'O Corsican! thou of the stern contour!') CB's appreciation of French poetry was stimulated by M. Heger's parting gift to her on 1 Jan. 1844, *Les Fleurs de la poésie française depuis le commencement du XVIe siècle* (Tours, 1841).)
7. In his review Phillips had written of *JE*: 'on every occasion a blow is sought to be struck at true religion'. (*Mirror of Literature* ii. 377.)
8. For R. H. Horne see WSW 11.12.1847 n. 2. Phenomenally successful owing to Horne's astute publicity techniques, *Orion* had been sold in 1843 at the price of one farthing, but only to those who had 'a good face and proper accent. A man with a horse-nose and boar's mouth who asked for "Hōrĭōn" would certainly not obtain it.' (Horne to Leigh Hunt, 3.6.1843, BL Add. MS 38110 fos. 39, 40.) The central image of this partly autobiographical epic was that of 'Blind Orion hungering for the Dawn', and its theme the notion that 'conflict and eventual reconciliation led to progress'. (Ann Blainey, *The Farthing Poet* (1968), 131.)
9. See the next letter.

To R. H. Horne, 15 December 1847

[Haworth]

Dear Sir

You will have thought me strangely tardy in acknowledging your courteous present, but the fact is it never reached me till yesterday:[1] the parcel containing it was missent; consequently it lingered a fortnight on its route.

I have to thank you, not merely for the gift of a little book of 137 pages, but for that of a <u>poem</u>. Very real, very sweet is the poetry of "Orion":[2] there are passages I shall recur to again and yet again, passages instinct both with power and beauty. All through it is genuine—pure from one flaw of affectation, rich in noble imagery. How far the applause of critics has rewarded the author of "Orion" I do not know;[3] but I think the pleasure he enjoyed in its composition must have been a bounteous meed in itself. You could not, I imagine have written that epic without at times deriving deep happiness from your work.

With sincere thanks for the pleasure its perusal has afforded me.

I remain, dear Sir
Yours faithfully
C Bell.

MS with envelope: Princeton, Taylor Collection. W & S 329.
Address (envelope): R. H. Horne Esqr. | Fallow Lodge | Finchley
PM: (i) [i.w.] | DE 17 | 1847 | B [overstamped:] Chief Office (ii) [i.w.] | DE 17 | 1847 | C
Annotation (i) in unknown hand on letter: Currer Bell, the name first adopted by the Authoress of "Jane Eyre"; (ii) on the envelope: *Charlotte Brontë*

1. See the previous letter.
2. Elizabeth Barrett Browning, who was a friend and correspondent of Horne, wrote to Mary Russell Mitford praising the poem's 'noble beauty' and 'unity of design'; but she criticized the 'want of action; & the personality fades off in a mist of allegorism, until at last we are scarcely surprised at seeing Time standing & talking on the brown-ribbed sea sand.' (P. Kelley and R. Hudson (eds.), *The Brownings' Correspondence* (Winfield, Kan.; 1989), vii. 173, 7 June 1843.) To Horne himself she wrote that it was a 'true poem', with 'passages scarcely to be exceeded in sculpturesque beauty'. (*ibid.* vii. 175, 9 June 1843.)
3. Many critics were rapturous in their praise of *Orion*. The favourable though not unqualified critique by E. B. Browning in *The Athenaeum* for 24 June 1843 (no. 817, 583–4) was quite outshone by a long and fulsome review in the *Monthly Magazine* for June 1843 (490–501); and Douglas Jerrold praised the poem as a 'social epic' in *The Illuminated Magazine* for June 1843, 119–21. See Ann Blainey, *The Farthing Poet* (1968), 134–7 and 270.

Draft letter to W. S. Williams, [?18 December 1847][1]

[Haworth]

Dear Sir

Your advice merits and shall have my most serious attention—I feel the <full> force of your reasoning—it is my wish to do my best in the career on which I have entered So I shall study and strive—and by dint of time, thought and effort—I hope yet to deserve in part the encouragement <I have> 'you and others have' so generously <received>accorded me. But Time will be necessary—that I feel more than ever—

In case of "Jane Eyre" reaching a second edition I should wish some few 'slight[2]' corrections to be made and will prepare an errata—Would the accompanying preface suit—I thought it better <not to be too lengthy> 'to be brief'—If you <wish alterations or additions to be made—name them> 'deem any' part objectionable let me know—[3]

MS Berg. cf. W & S 326 as 13 Dec. 1847.
Address: not in MS.
PM: not in MS.

1. This fragmentary pencil draft is on the verso of CB's draft of her poem, 'He saw my heart's woe' (Neufeldt *CBP*, 340; Winnifrith *CBP*. 244–5); it follows a deleted draft of part of her preface to the 2nd edn. of *JE*, for which see WSW 21.12.1847 n. 1.
2. MS may read 'style'.
3. For other notes, see the final version, which follows.

To W. S. Williams, 18 December 1847

[Haworth]

Dear Sir

Your advice[1] merits and shall have my most serious attention. I feel the force of your reasoning. It is my wish to do my best in the career on which I have entered; So I shall study and strive, and by dint of time, thought and effort, I hope yet to deserve in part the encouragement you and others have so generously accorded me. But Time will be necessary: that I feel more than ever.

In case of "Jane Eyre" reaching a second edition,[2] I should wish some few corrections[3] to be made and will prepare an errata. How would the accompanying preface do?[4] I thought it better to be brief.

The Observer has just reached me.[5] I always compel myself to read the Analysis[6] in every newspaper-notice. It is a just punishment—a due though severe humiliation for faults of plan and construction. I wonder if the analyses of other fictions read as absurdly as that of "Jane Eyre" always does

I am dear Sir
Yours respectfully
C Bell.

MS Princeton, Taylor Collection. W & S 326 as 13 Dec. 1847.
Address: not in MS.
PM: not in MS.

1. On 14 Dec. CB had asked Mr Williams for his candid opinion of her plan to convert *The Professor* into a 3-vol. novel. He must have dissuaded her from this project.
2. The 2nd edn. was published on or by 22 Jan. 1848.
3. For examples of these, see the Clarendon *JE* p. xv and textual footnotes; World's Classics *JE* (Oxford, 1980) note on the text. CB also made minor revisions: e.g. in ch. 25 Bertha Mason's 'visage' is 'dark' in the MS, 'wild' in the 1st edn., and 'lurid' in the 2nd and 3rd edns.
4. See the next letter, n. 1.
5. *The Observer and Sunday Advertiser* was begun on 4 Dec. 1791 by W. S. Bourne, and by 1847 was influential and widely read. The reviewer praised the variety and rapidity of the novel's action

and its vivid style, and found the 'impress of the events' so deep that the reader was 'carried away irresistibly'. Lowood was a ' "Do-the-Girls Hall" . . . How many similar establishments are there at this moment in "merry England" . . . The matter and moral of this book is good, and the style is also forcible and impressive. It is here and there deformed by some improbabilities, and occasionally a touch of fatuity in the personages makes the reader feel that the pen which traced those lineaments is not a practised one; but withal it may well be termed an extraordinary book of its kind; and as truly of a most noble purpose, considerable originality, and high promise. It will be read by most people with pleasure, and laid down by all with regret.' (*The Observer* 31.10.1847, 2.)

6. 'Analysis' here means the plot-summary, which is appreciative but robust in tone and occasionally so condensed as to sound satirical: Rochester 'ultimately professes his love, and asks Jane to wed him; which she reciprocates on the instant, and agrees to do in due season.' The wedding rite was 'promptly forbidden', but Jane and Rochester eventually married, and 'Happiness and a bouncing boy was the fruit of their union'. (*The Observer* 31.10.1847, 2.)

To W. S. Williams, 21 December 1847

[Haworth]

Dear Sir

I am, for my own part, dissatisfied with the preface I sent[1]—I fear it savours of flippancy. If you see no objection, I should prefer substituting the enclosed. It is rather more lengthy, but it expresses something I have long wished to express.

Mr. Smith is kind indeed to think of sending me "the Jar of honey";[2] when I receive the book I will write to him.

I cannot thank you sufficiently for your letters, and I can give you but a faint idea of the pleasure they afford me; they seem to introduce such light and life to the torpid retirement where we lie like dormice.[3] But—understand this distinctly; you must never write to me except when you have both leisure and inclination. I know your time is too fully occupied and too valuable to be often at the service of any one individual.

You are not far wrong in your judgment respecting "Wuthering Heights" & "Agnes Grey". Ellis has a strong, original mind, full of strange though sombre power: when he writes poetry that power speaks in language at once condensed, elaborated and refined—but in prose it breaks forth in scenes which shock more than they attract[4]—Ellis will improve, however, because he knows his defects. "Agnes Grey" is the mirror of the mind of the writer. The orthography & punctuation of the books are mortifying to a degree[5]—almost all the errors that were corrected in the proof-sheets appear intact in what should have been the fair copies. If Mr. Newby always does business in this way, few authors would like to have him for their publisher a second time.

Believe me, dear Sir,
Yours respectfully
C Bell.

MS Pforzheimer. W & S 331.
Address: not in MS.
PM: not in MS.

1. Perhaps this version resembled the deleted and incomplete draft preface in the Berg Collection, which is close to the final version at the beginning but ends in 'flippancy': 'I would point out to <them> 'their observation' these simple facts—Conventionality is not Morality—<Hypocrisy> 'Profession [i.w.] of Righteousness' is not Religion—to attack the first is not to stab the last—to take/remove the mask from the face of the Pharisee''s mask' is not to lift a profane hand to the crown of thorns—Let <my Censors> 'them' reflect and they will see where the difference lies—they will if <candid> '?conf' discover their mistake. Let them keep a good heart—and be assured that no harm is meant and no harm done Moreover to narrate the simple truth is not to devise an insidious fiction—Courage then ?dispirited friends—keep a good heart—lay aside the green-tinted spectacles of prejudice. ?Look a [i.w.] regard both books and men through a true medium—and you will 'in most instances' find their hue less morbid than you now imagine'. (Pencil MS, Berg; the last sentence is very faint and the reading given is conjectural. 'Take' and 'remove' are alternatives: CB had not decided which word to use.) The final version ends in a solemn tribute to Thackeray. (Clarendon *JE* pp. xxviii–xxx.)
2. Leigh Hunt's *A Jar of Honey from Mount Hybla*, a Christmas gift-book 'in a novel and elegant binding', illustrated by Richard Doyle, was issued by Smith, Elder by 15 Dec. ready for the Christmas market but was dated on the title-page '1848'. Golden opinions from a variety of journals praising the 'delicate and noble fancies' of Hunt's mélange of pastoral poetry and legends were used to advertise the work in Smith, Elder's list of new books for May 1848. The essays in the vol. had originally appeared in *Ainsworth's Magazine* in 1844. See SE 25.12.1847 and notes 1, 2, 3.
3. cf. *Villette* ch. 24, where Lucy knows that she should, like the dormouse, 'creep into a hole of Life's wall', there to wait for either 'kindly resurrection' or death. (382.)
4. cf. CB's 'Biographical Notice of Ellis and Acton Bell' and her 'Editor's Preface to the New Edition of Wuthering Heights' of 1850. (Printed in the Clarendon *WH* 435–45.)
5. See WSW 14.12.1847 and n. 6.

To W. S. Williams, 23 December 1847

[Haworth]

Dear Sir

I am glad that you and Messrs. Smith & Elder approve the second preface.

I send an errata of the 1st. Vol. and part of the 2nd: I will send the rest of the corrections as soon as possible.[1]

Will the enclosed dedication suffice?[2] I have made it brief because I wished to avoid any appearance of pomposity or pretention.

The notice in "the Church of England Journal"[3] gratified me much, and chiefly because it was the Church of England Journal—Whatever such critics as He of the Mirror[4] may say, I love the Church of England. Her Ministers, indeed I do not regard as infallible personages, I have seen too much of them for that—but to the Establishment, with all her faults—the profane Athanasian Creed[5] excluded—I am sincerely attached.

Is the forthcoming critique on Mr. Thackeray's writings in the "Edinburgh

Review"[6] written by Mr Lewes? I hope it is. Mr Lewes with his penetrating sagacity and fine acumen ought to be able to do the Author of "Vanity Fair" justice. Only he must not bring him down to the level of Fielding[7]—he is far, far above Fielding. It appears to me that Fielding's style is arid, and his views of life and human nature coarse, compared with Thackeray's.

With many thanks for your kind wishes and a cordial reciprocation of them,

I remain, dear Sir,
Yours respectfully
C Bell

On glancing over this scrawl—I find it so illegibly written that I fear you will hardly be able to decipher it—but the Cold is partly to blame for this—my fingers are numb.[8]

MS Berg. W & S 332.
Address: not in MS.
PM: not in MS.

1. These were for the 2nd edn. of *JE* (Jan. 1848). See WSW 18.12.1847 n. 3. Unfortunately new printing errors appeared in the new edn.
2. 'TO | W. M. THACKERAY, ESQ. | This Work | IS RESPECTFULLY INSCRIBED, | BY | THE AUTHOR.' Though Thackeray described this dedication as 'the greatest compliment I have ever received in my life' (G. N. Ray (ed.), *The Letters and Private Papers of W. M. Thackeray* ii. 341, 1945), it led to embarrassing speculation that *JE* was written by a former governess in his family. His wife's insanity, though quite unlike Bertha Rochester's, seemed to support this hurtful idea. CB knew nothing whatever of Thackeray's 'domestic concerns', as she explained to Mr Williams on 28 Jan. 1848, but the rumours were still circulating, with embellishments, in 1850. Thackeray wrote to Mrs Brookfield on 8.10.1850: 'Do you remember my telling you how my friend Gale at a dinner of Winchester big wigs had heard that I was a wretch with whom nobody should associate, that I had seduced a Governess by the name of Jane Eyre by whom I had had ever so many &c? The bishop . . . and a number of the clergy are coming here tomorrow and I thought I would like to make my appearance among them and give the lie to that story.' (Ray, *Letters and Papers* ii. 697–8.)
3. Originally *The Manx Guardian and Church of England Journal*; a 'Family newspaper, review and literary gazette' (1846–8), published in Douglas, Isle of Man, and intended by its editor, the Revd John Marshall, to serve the cause of 'true religion'. Its motto was 'Pro Ecclesia Dei'. The reviewer found *JE* 'one of the best works of its class that has appeared for years . . . the style is fresh and vigorous, and the whole tone of the work is marked by earnestness'. He praised CB's 'knowledge of human nature', individualization, and the 'dramatic constructiveness' of her plot; the incidents, though extraordinary, had an 'air of truth and reality'. The novel's insight into the female mind showed that the writer was probably a lady, and one who had lived in Scotland, since she used some 'Caledonian Doric' words. It was not surprising that *JE* had 'excited a great sensation in literary circles', and the reviewer hoped 'soon to see another work of fiction from the same talented author'. (*Church of England Journal* 16.12.1847, ii. 629–31.)
4. See WSW 15.12.1847 and n. 3.
5. This begins with a dogmatic affirmation that 'Whosoever will be saved [must] . . . hold the Catholick Faith. Which Faith except every one do keep whole and undefiled: without doubt he shall perish everlastingly'. It goes on to make a complex and difficult analysis or series of definitions of the nature of the Trinity. Though the creed was not formulated by St Athanasius, CB may have associated it with Roman and Anglo-Catholicism: both before and after his conversion to Rome in 1845 John Henry Newman regarded St Athanasius (*c.* AD 296–373) as a

heroic champion against the Arian heresy, a heresy with which he came to believe the Church of England was tainted.

6. This formidable Whig journal, most famously edited by Francis Jeffrey (1773–1850) from 1803 to 1829, was now under the editorship of William Empson (1791–1852). The article on Thackeray in vol. 87, no. 175 for Jan. 1848 was not by Lewes but by Abraham Hayward (1801–84). Lewes reviewed *Vanity Fair* in the *Morning Chronicle* in Mar. 1848. See Rosemary Ashton, *G. H. Lewes: A Life* (Oxford, 1991), 66.
7. Henry Fielding (1707–54), author of *Joseph Andrews*, *Tom Jones*, etc. CB was later to be disturbed by Thackeray's 'worship of his Baal-Bel-Beëlzebub . . . his false god of a Fielding'. (Vol. iii, GS 11.3.1852.) After Thackeray's lecture on Fielding she felt he was 'dangerously wrong' in his 'way of treating Fielding's character and vices'. (Letter to George Smith, vol. iii, 26.3.1853, printed in W & S 848 as to W. S. Williams, May 1853.) CB is recalling Lewes's dictum, in his review of *JE* in *Fraser's Magazine* 36 (Dec. 1847), that the *sine qua non* of novel-writing was 'a correct representation of life' and for this reason he considered 'Fielding and Miss Austen are the greatest novelists in our language'. (687.)
8. *Shackleton* recorded frost on 21 Dec. and a 'little small snow' on 22 and 23.

To Ellen Nussey, [24 December 1847]

[Haworth]

Dear Ellen

It was high time you wrote, I should soon have begun to think something was wrong, if you had delayed much longer.

I am glad Miss Ringrose has returned with you,[1] both for her sake and yours—Still with two visitors in the house you must have plenty to do—it is really most desirable to be able to provide attendance on such occasions without having constantly to deprive oneself of the pleasure of one's guests company.

People who can afford servants—who can comfortably trust the preparation of meals to the superintendence of a Cook, enjoy a very great privilege under such circumstances.

I have no patience with either your brother John[2] or the Duke of Devonshire.[3] In the first place what an illogical ass the Duke must be to make one brother responsible for the acts of another—to cut John because Henry had made what seems to me a not unreasonable demand—that of compensation for improvements on a living in the Duke's gift![4]

In the second place what earthly business had John to write his mother and sisters an unpleasant letter on the subject?

What right has he to annoy them?

I intensely dislike some of his conduct to the female members of his family—it is unjust—it is coldly tyrannous. His brothers wrong him and annoy him? It is possible—but why mix up his sisters—his mother with conduct in which they had no share—why lavish his revenge on them?

I should think Rosy Ringrose[5] from what you say, must be a very attractive personage to the "worthier sex" as some say or the "coarser sex" as others phrase it—much more so probably than her sister—though for sterling worth Amelia no doubt bears away the palm. A pretty Martha Taylor[6] (for Martha though piquant was not pretty) must be a very charming creature indeed.

I had a letter from Mary Taylor[7] last week—short and without one word of news in it except that she was in better health and spirits than she had usually enjoyed in Europe—she asks after you.

I wish all Brookroyd a happy Christmas and to yourself double good wishes

[Signature cut off]

MS Fales Library, New York University. W & S 330 as 'December—, 1847'.
Address (envelope): Miss Ellen Nussey | Brookroyd | Birstal | Leeds
PM: (i) HAWORTH (ii) KEIGHLEY | DE 24 | 1847 (iii) LEEDS | DE 24 | 1847 | F (iv) BIRSTAL
Annotation on the envelope by EN in pencil: Dec 24 47 | of Servants The [i.w.] of [i.w.] | John—R Ring[rose]

1. EN had returned from a visit to Amelia Ringrose's home at Tranby Lodge near Hull. See EN 15.10.1847 n. 4 and 2.12.1847.
2. On 31.7.1845 CB had written disparagingly of EN's brother John, the royal apothecary. John had probably used his influence with the Duke to secure the Hathersage living for his brother Henry, and he would be angered by the behaviour of both men. See EN ?22.8.1844 n. 1.
3. William George Spencer Cavendish, 6th Duke of Devonshire (1790–1858). He was the patron of the living at Hathersage, which Henry Nussey had now relinquished. There had been signs of discord in the parish as early as 29 Dec. 1845, when EN had recommended Henry and his wife to pay 'a little attention' to the 'vain & purse proud curate' Mr Rooker, who could otherwise 'set a whole Parish at the heels of the Vicar'. Henry had already 'resigned the School' by that date; 'the Master behaved extremely ill & as Henry had but one voice among the Trustees . . . he could not succeed in making it a Church of England School.' (EN to Mary Gorham 29.12.1845, BPM Gorham Collection.)
4. Henry Nussey, who was now in France, had substantially extended the vicarage in 1845 during his first year as vicar of Hathersage: see EN 14.11.1844 n. 4 and EN to Mary Gorham 6.8.1845. It was Henry's successor, the Revd Henry Cottingham, vicar from 1847 to 1859, who had 'plans drawn up for the rebuilding of the parish church at Hathersage and the building of the school'. (M. F. H. Hulbert, *The Vicarage Family Hathersage 1627–1987* (Hathersage Parochial Church Council, 1988), 9.)
5. See EN 14.2.1847 and ?29.10.1847 notes.
6. Mary Taylor's sister Martha had died in Brussels in 1842. See EN 13.1.1832 and 10.11.1842 notes.
7. Mary Taylor, who was still living above and probably helping in the shop kept by her brother Waring in Herbert Street, Wellington, had also offered 'Instructions on the Piano Forte' via advertisements in the *New Zealand Spectator* for Mar. 1847. She was building or about to build a 5-roomed house in Cuba Street, to be let to tenants. See *Stevens* 66.

To Amelia Ringrose, 24 December [1847][1]

[Haworth]

Dear Miss Ringrose

It was an excellent thought of Ellen to set you to write to me, especially as I perceive by the easy flow of your note that it is no task for you to have to address an entire stranger—I correct myself—we are not strangers: at least I seem to know you well, for you have been the theme of many a conversation and many a letter between Ellen and myself. I have long had a definite and vivid idea of your mind, disposition &c. and the portrait[2] helped me to get a notion of your person. It did not in the least surprise me to hear you were at Brookroyd; for I was sure that whenever Ellen left Tranby,[3] she would wish to take you with her, and I am well aware that if she once resolves on a thing, it is not easy to baffle her endeavours to get it accomplished.

Besides, I doubt not you were willing to come: it is much pleasanter to meet Ellen any day than to part with her. When she quits a place, she generally leaves an uneasy vacuum behind her, for though not a rattling or dazzling, she is a very acceptable companion. I understand well the feeling you affectionately express, that when you are a little depressed[4] it does you good to look at Ellen and know that she loves you. I am not acquainted with any one whose influence is at once so tranquil and so genial as hers. Faults she has, because she is human, but I daresay in your pilgrimage through life,[5] you will meet with few whose slight defects are counterbalanced by so many sterling excellencies.

You must excuse the brevity of this note, I do not possess your fluent pen in correspondence. With sincere wishes for your welfare, and earnest hopes that both your health and spirits may rapidly and permanently improve, that your prospects may brighten and that your disinterested goodness both to Ellen and many others may meet a prompt and abundant reward both here and hereafter,

I am, my dear Miss Ringrose
Yours very sincerely
C Brontë

MS Brotherton. W & S 333.
Address (integral): Miss Ringrose | Brookroyd
PM: not in MS.

1. Enclosed with the previous letter.
2. Probably the portrait returned with two portraits of EN on 2.12.1847.
3. See the previous letter n. 1.
4. cf. EN 12.8.1847, 15.10.1847 and notes.
5. CB frequently used this image, and other ideas associated with Bunyan's *The Pilgrim's Progress*, in her writings. See the Clarendon *Professor* appendix VII, 331.

To Messrs Smith, Elder and Co., 25 December 1847

[Haworth]

Gentlemen

Permit me to thank you for your present[1] which reached me yesterday. I was not prepared for anything so truly tasteful, and when I had opened the parcel, removed the various envelopes, and at last got a glimpse of the chastely attractive binding, I was most agreeably surprised. What is better; on examination, I find the contents fully to answer the expectation excited by the charming exterior;[2] the Honey is quite as choice as the Jar is elegant. The illustrations[3] too are very beautiful—some of them peculiarly so. I trust the Public will shew itself grateful for the pains you have taken to provide a book so appropriate to the Season.

I return the Preface to "Jane Eyre";[4] the remainder of the corrections I will send, if all be well, on Tuesday.[5] It gave me real pleasure to have the opportunity of publicly expressing my sense of your kindness and justice, and the circumstance of Mr. Williams' having suggested to me the propriety of such a step adds another item to the debt I owe him—

Believe me, Gentlemen
Yours respectfully
C Bell.

MS BPM SG 12. W & S 334.
Address (integral): To Messrs. Smith & Elder
PM: not in MS.
Annotation on fol. 2^{v}: Currer Bell | Haworth | Dec 27. 1847

1. Smith, Elder's Christmas gift-book, *A Jar of Honey from Mount Hybla* by Leigh Hunt. See WSW 21.12.1847 n. 2.
2. Other readers agreed. The reviewer in *The Examiner* (the paper founded by Hunt) wrote, 'A luxury of taste pervades the illustration, the printing, even the binding.' Smith, Elder had evidently 'spared no expense': the engravers included G. and E. Dalziel and W. J. Linton, and the printers were Vizetelly, Brothers, and Co. The binding, designed by Owen Jones, showed a cobalt blue jar wreathed with green tendrils against a honey-yellow background, within an ivy-clad framework.
3. These were by Richard Doyle (1824–83), the talented *Punch* caricaturist who was to work closely with Thackeray on his 1849 Christmas Book, *Rebecca and Rowena*, and on *The Newcomes* in 1852–3. In his later work Doyle developed his taste for fanciful and delicate 'faery' scenes. The frontispiece of the *Jar* is in this style, with a cloud of winged fairy and satyr figures rising from a honey-jar, and the other illustrations are equally fanciful.
4. Presumably a proof of the preface to the 2nd edn., where CB thanks her publishers 'for the aid their tact, their energy, their practical sense, and frank liberality have afforded an unknown and unrecommended Author . . . to my Publishers and the select Reviewers, I say cordially, Gentlemen, I thank you from my heart'.
5. 28 Dec.

To ?W. S. Williams, 31 December 1847

[Haworth]

Dear Sir

I think, for the reasons you mention, it is better to substitute Author for Editor.[1] I should not be ashamed to be considered the author of "Wuthering Heights" and "Agnes Grey", but, possessing no real claim to that honour, I would rather not have it attributed to me, thereby depriving the true authors of their just meed.

You do very rightly and very kindly to tell me the objections made against "Jane Eyre"; they are more essential than the praises. I feel a sort of heart-ache when I hear the book called "godless" and "pernicious" by good and earnest-minded men[2]—but I know that heart-ache will be salutary—at least I trust so.

What is meant by the charges of "trickery" and "artifice" I have yet to comprehend.[3] It was no art in me to write a tale—it was no trick in Messrs. Smith & Elder to publish it. Where do the trickery and artifice lie?

I have received the Scotsman,[4] and was greatly amused to see Jane Eyre likened to Rebecca Sharp[5]—the resemblance would hardly have occurred to me.

I wish to send this note by to-day's post and must therefore conclude in haste

I am, dear Sir
Yours respectfully
C Bell

MS Princeton, Parrish Collection. W & S 335.
Address: not in MS.
PM: not in MS.

1. The title-page of the 2nd edn. begins 'JANE EYRE: | **An Autobiography** | BY | CURRER BELL.' Rumours that the Bell brothers were in fact one author had circulated since the publication of their poems in 1846, as CB recalled in assuring W. S. Williams that such conjectures were unfounded: 'We are three.' (WSW 10.11.1847.) Newby fostered the rumours in order to boost the sales of the *WH* vols., advertised as 'By the successful New Novelist' in *Douglas Jerrold's Magazine* for 5.2.1848, and as 'Mr Bell's new novel' in *The Examiner* (19.2.1848.) In America Harper and Brothers announced *WH* 'By the Author of "Jane Eyre" ' and the *Tenant* 'By ACTON BELL, Author of Wuthering Heights'. (See e.g. the review in *North American Review*, 67 (Oct. 1848), 354–69.) When the rumours had been dismissed once and for all by CB's preface to her 1850 edn. of her sisters' works, the *Eclectic Review* recalled that the authorship of the Bells' works had 'sometimes been pronounced on with a dogmatism which would have been amusing, had it not indicated a sad lack of modesty and intelligence'. (*Eclectic Review*, NS 1 (Feb. 1851), 223.) Edwin Whipple, for example, had believed that all three Bells wrote *JE*, Acton being 'the author of Wuthering Heights, The Tenant of Wildfell Hall, and . . . of certain offensive but powerful portions of Jane Eyre'. (*North American Review*, 67 (Oct. 1848), 358.)
2. 'January Searle' wrote of *JE*: 'Religion is stabbed in the dark'. See WSW 15.12.1847 n. 3 In Apr. 1848 the *Christian Remembrancer* was to find *JE* coarse and morally questionable (vol. 15, 396–409); in Sept. that year the *Rambler*, the self-styled organ of 'English Catholicism', called it 'one of the coarsest books which we ever perused'. (vol. 3, pt. 9, 65.), and in Dec. 1848 Elizabeth

Rigby, writing in the influential *Quarterly Review*, condemned it as 'pre-eminently an anti-Christian composition'. (vol. 84, 153–85.)

3. See the *Spectator* 6.11.1847, 1074. *JE* is said to have 'too much artifice'; its author 'resorts to trick', and 'everything is *made* to change just in the nick of time'.
4. Founded in 1817 by Charles Maclaren (1782–1866) as a bi-weekly, *The Scotsman* was now a widely circulated and highly regarded daily paper. The reviewer found *JE* a 'striking and powerful novel . . . the production of a mind of considerable originality and strength'. 'Externally, Jane Eyre is a kind of superior Lilly Dawson [in the novel by Catherine Crowe], mentally, she is a sort of better Becky Sharpe . . . in her self-possession and dexterous management. Occasionally she *manages* too much, she sometimes wants geniality; one would like her better if she were not quite so cautious and careful.' There are 'some very doubtful points' about Mr Rochester, yet he is 'well *individualised*'. (*The Scotsman* 22.12.1847, [3].)
5. In the Nov. 1847 no. of *Vanity Fair* Becky Sharp, as Mrs Rawdon Crawley, had been received by the Pitt Crawleys and had decided she 'could be a good woman' if she had 'five thousand a year'—which, coincidentally perhaps, was the sum that Jane Eyre retained for herself from her legacy. See *Vanity Fair* ch. 42. Elizabeth Rigby was also to compare the 2 heroines, to Jane's disadvantage: 'There is none of that harmonious unity about [Jane's character] which made little Becky so grateful a subject of analysis.' In slyness, 'Jane outgovernesses them all—little Becky would have blushed for her.' (*Quarterly Review* 84, pp. 166, 169.)

Appendix: Reminiscences of Charlotte Brontë by 'a schoolfellow' [Ellen Nussey]

I

[Text from *Scribner's Monthly* May 1871, 18–24, dealing with the years 1831–2. Ellen intended to show that Charlotte Brontë was 'a Christian heroine': see the 'History of the Letters', pp. 36–8.]

SCHOOL DAYS AT ROE HEAD

Arriving at school about a week after the general assembling of the pupils, I was not expected to accompany them when the time came for their daily exercise, but while they were out, I was led into the school-room, and quietly left to make my observations. I had come to the conclusion it was very nice and comfortable for a school-room, though I had little knowledge of school-rooms in general, when, turning to the window to observe the look-out I became aware for the first time that I was not alone; there was a silent, weeping, dark little figure in the large bay-window; she must, I thought, have risen from the floor. As soon as I had recovered from my surprise, I went from the far end of the room, where the book-shelves were, the contents of which I must have contemplated with a little awe in anticipation of coming studies. A crimson cloth covered the long table down the center of the room, which helped, no doubt, to hide the shrinking little figure from my view. I was touched and troubled at once to see her so sad and so tearful.

I said *shrinking*, because her attitude, when I saw her, was that of one who wished to hide both herself and her grief. She did not shrink, however, when spoken to, but in very few words confessed she was 'home-sick'. After a little of such comfort as could be offered, it was suggested to her that there was a possibility of her too having to comfort the speaker by and by for the same cause. A faint quivering smile then lighted her face; the tear-drops fell; we silently took each other's hands, and at once we felt that genuine sympathy which always consoles, even though it be unexpressed. We did not talk or stir till we heard the approaching footsteps of other pupils coming in from their play; it had been a game called 'French and English,' which was always very vigorously played, but in which Charlotte Brontë never could be induced to join. Perhaps the merry voices contesting for victory, which reached our ears in the school-room, jarred upon her then sensitive misery, and caused her ever after to dislike the game; but she was physically unequal to that exercise of muscle, which was keen enjoyment to strong, healthy girls, both older and younger than herself. Miss Wooler's system of education required that a good deal of her pupils' work should be done in classes, and to effect this, new pupils had generally a season of solitary study; but Charlotte's fervent application made this period a very short one to her,—she was quickly up to the needful standard, and ready for the daily routine and arrangement of studies, and as quickly did she outstrip her companions, rising from the bottom of the classes to the top, a position which, when she had once gained, she never had to regain. She was first in everything but play, yet never was a word heard of envy or jealousy from her companions; every one felt she had won her laurels by an amount of diligence and hard labor of which they were incapable. She never exulted in her successes or seemed conscious of them; her mind was so wholly set on attaining knowledge that she apparently forgot all else.

Charlotte's appearance did not strike me at first as it did others. I saw her grief, not herself particularly, till afterwards. She never seemed to me the unattractive little person others designated her, but certainly she was at this time anything but *pretty*; even her good points were lost. Her naturally beautiful hair of soft silky brown being then dry and frizzy-looking, screwed up in tight little curls, showing features that were all the plainer from her exceeding thinness and want of complexion, she looked 'dried in.' A dark, rusty green stuff dress of old-fashioned make detracted still more from her appearance; but let her wear what she might, or do what she would, she had ever the demeanor of a born gentlewoman; vulgarity was an element that never won the slightest affinity with her nature. Some of the elder girls, who had been years at school, thought her ignorant. This was true in one sense; ignorant she was indeed in the elementary education which is given in schools, but she far surpassed her most advanced school-fellows in knowledge of what was passing in the world at large, and in the literature of her country. She knew a thousand things in these matters unknown to them.

She had taught herself a little French before she came to school; this little knowledge of the language was very useful to her when afterwards she was engaged in translation or dictation. She soon began to make a good figure in French lessons. Music she wished to acquire, for which she had both ear and taste, but her nearsightedness caused her to stoop so dreadfully in order to see her notes, she was dissuaded from persevering in the acquirement, especially as she had at this time an invincible objection to wearing glasses. Her very taper fingers, tipped with the most circular nails, did not seem very suited for instrumental execution; but when wielding the pen or the pencil, they appeared in the very office they were created for.

Her appetite was of the smallest; for years she had not tasted animal food; she had the greatest dislike to it; she always had something specially provided for her at our midday repast. Towards the close of the first half-year she was induced to take, by little and little, meat gravy with vegetable, and in the second half-year she commenced taking a very small portion of animal food daily. She then grew a little bit plumper, looked younger and more animated, though she was never what is called lively at this period. She always seemed to feel that a deep responsibility rested upon her; that she was an object of expense to those at home, and that she must use every moment to attain the purpose for which she was sent to school, *i.e.*, to fit herself for governess life. She had almost too much opportunity for her conscientious diligence; we were so little restricted in our doings, the industrious might accomplish the appointed tasks of the day and enjoy a little leisure, but she chose in many things to do *double* lessons when not prevented by class arrangement or a companion. In two of her studies she was associated with her friend, and great was her distress if her companion failed to be ready, when she was, with the lesson of the day. She liked the stated task to be over, that she might be free to pursue her self-appointed ones. Such, however, was her conscientiousness that she never did what some girls think it generous to do; generous and unselfish though she was, she never whispered help to a companion in class (as she might have done), to rid herself of the trouble of having to appear again. All her school-fellows regarded her, I believe, as a model of high rectitude, close application, and great abilities. She did not play or amuse herself when others did. When her companions were merry round the fire, or otherwise enjoying themselves during the twilight, which was always a precious time of relaxation, she would be kneeling close to the window busy with her studies, and this would last so long that she was accused of seeing in the dark; yet though she did not play, as girls style play, she was ever ready to help with suggestions in those plays which required taste or arrangement.

When her companions formed the idea of having a coronation performance on a half-holiday, it was Charlotte Brontë who drew up the programme, arranged the titles to be adopted by her companions for the occasion, wrote the invitations to those who were to grace the ceremony, and selected for each a title, either for sound that pleased the ear or for historical association. The preparations for these extra half-holidays (which were very rare occurrences) sometimes occupied spare moments for weeks before the event. On this occasion Charlotte prepared a very elegant little speech for the one who was selected to present the crown. Miss W.'s younger sister consented after much entreaty to be crowned as our queen (a very noble, stately queen she made), and did her pupils all the honor she could by adapting herself to the rôle of the moment. The following exquisite little speech shows Charlotte's aptitude, even then, at giving fitting expression to her thoughts:—

'Powerful Queen! accept this Crown, the symbol of dominion, from the hands of your faithful and affectionate subjects! And if their earnest and united wishes have any efficacy, you will long be permitted to reign over this peaceful, though circumscribed, empire.

[Signed, &c., &c.]
'Your loyal subjects.'

The little fête finished off with what was called a ball; but for lack of numbers we had to content ourselves with one quadrille and two Scotch reels. Last of all there was a supper, which was considered very *recherché*, most of it having been coaxed out of yielding mammas and elder sisters, in addition to some wise expenditure of pocket-money. The grand feature, however, of the supper was the attendance of a mulatto servant. We descended for a moment from our assumed dignities to improvise this distinguishing appanage. The liveliest of our party, 'Jessie York,' volunteered this office, and surpassed our expectations. Charlotte evidently enjoyed the fun, in her own quiet way, as much as any one, and ever after with great zest helped, when with old school-fellows, to recall the performances of the exceptional half-holidays.

About a month after the assembling of the school, one of the pupils had an illness. There was great competition among the girls for permission to sit with the invalid, but Charlotte was never of the number, though she was as assiduous in kindness and attention as the rest in spare moments; but to sit with the patient was indulgence and leisure, and these she would not permit herself.

It was shortly after this illness that Charlotte caused such a panic of terror by her thrilling relations of the wanderings of a somnambulist. She brought together all the horrors her imagination could create, from surging seas, raging breakers, towering castle walls, high precipices, invisible chasms and dangers. Having wrought these materials to the highest pitch of effect, she brought out, in almost cloud-height, her somnambulist, walking on shaking turrets,—all told in a voice that conveyed more than words alone can express. A shivering terror seized the recovered invalid; a pause ensued; then a subdued cry of pain came from Charlotte herself, with a terrified command to others to call for help. She was in bitter distress. Something like remorse seemed to linger in her mind after this incident; for weeks there was no prevailing upon her to resume her tales, and she never again created terrors for her listeners. Tales, however, were made again in time, till Miss W. discovered there was 'late talking.' That was forbidden; but understanding it was 'late talk' only which was prohibited, we talked and listened to tales again, not expecting to hear Miss C[atherine] H[arriet] W[ooler] say, one morning, 'All the ladies who talked last night must pay fines. I am sure Miss Brontë and Miss—were not of the number.' Miss Brontë and Miss—were, however, transgressors like the rest, and rather enjoyed the fact of having to pay like them, till they saw Miss [?Margaret] W[ooler]'s grieved and disappointed look. It was then a distress that they had failed where they were reckoned upon, though unintentionally. This was the only school-fine Charlotte ever incurred.

At the close of the first half-year, Charlotte bore off three prizes. For one she had to draw lots with her friend—a moment of painful suspense to both; for neither wished to deprive the other of her reward. Happily, Charlotte won it, and so had the gratifying pleasure of carrying home three tangible proofs of her goodness and industry. Miss W. had two badges of conduct for her pupils which were wonderfully effective, except with the most careless. A black ribbon, worn in the style of the Order of the Garter, which the pupils passed from one to another for any breach of rules, unlady-like manners, or incorrect grammar. Charlotte might, in her very earliest school-days, have worn 'the mark,' as we styled it, but I never remember her having it. The silver medal, which was the badge for the fulfillment of duties, she won the right to in her first half-year. This she never afterwards forfeited, and it was presented to her on leaving school. She was only three half-years at school. In this time she went through all the elementary teaching contained in our school-books. She was in the habit of committing long pieces of poetry to memory, and seemed to do so with real enjoyment and hardly any effort.

In these early days, whenever she was certain of being quite alone with her friend, she would talk much of her two dead sisters, Maria and Elizabeth. Her love for them was most intense; a kind of adoration dwelt in her feelings which, as she conversed, almost imparted itself to her listener.

She described Maria as a little mother among the rest, superhuman in goodness and cleverness. But the most touching of all were the revelations of her sufferings,—how she suffered with the sensibility of a grown-up person, and endured with a patience and fortitude that were Christ-like. Charlotte would still weep and suffer when thinking of her. She talked of Elizabeth also, but never with the anguish of expression which accompanied her recollections of Maria. When surprise was expressed that she should know so much about her sisters when they were so young, and she herself still younger, she said she began to analyze character when she was five years old, and instanced two guests who were at her home for a day or two, and of whom she had taken stock, and of whom after-knowledge confirmed first impressions.

The following lines, though not regarded of sufficient merit for publication in the volume of poems, yet have an interest as they depict her then desolated heart:—

MEMORY

When the dead in their cold graves are lying
Asleep, to wake never again!
When past are their smiles and their sighing,
Oh, why should their memories remain?
Though sunshine and spring may have lightened
The wild flowers that blow on their graves,
Though summer their tombstones have brightened,
And autumn have palled them with leaves,
And winter have wildly bewailed them
With his dirge-wind as sad as a knell,
And the shroud of his snow-wreath have veiled them,
Still—how deep in our bosoms they dwell!

The shadow and sun-sparkle vanish,
The cloud and the light fleet away,
But man from his heart may not banish
Even thoughts that are torment to stay.
When quenched is the glow of the ember,
When the life-fire ceases to burn,
Oh! why should the spirit remember?
Oh! why should the parted return?

During one of our brief holidays Charlotte was guest in a family who had known her father when he was curate in their parish. They were naturally inclined to show kindness to his daughter, but the kindness here took a form which was little agreeable. They had had no opportunity of knowing her abilities or disposition, and they took her shyness and smallness as indications of extreme youth. She was slow, very slow, to express anything that bordered on ingratitude, but here she was mortified and hurt. 'They took me for a child, and treated me just like one,' she said. I can now recall the expression of that ever honest face as she added, 'one tall lady *would* nurse me.'

The tradition of a lady ghost who moved about in rustling silk in the upper stories of Roe Head had a great charm for Charlotte. She was a ready listener to any girl who could relate stories of others having seen her; but on Miss W. hearing us talk of our ghost, she adopted an effective measure for putting our belief in such an existence to the test, by selecting one or other from among us to ascend the stairs after the dimness of evening hours had set in, to bring something down which could easily be found. No ghost made herself visible even to the frightened imaginations of the foolish and the timid; the whitened face of apprehension soon disappeared, nerves were braced, and a general laugh soon set us all right again.

It was while Charlotte was at school that she imbibed the germ of many of those characters which she afterwards produced in *Shirley*; but no one could have imagined that, in the unceasing industry of her daily applications, she was receiving any kind of impress external to her school-life.

She was particularly impressed with the goodness and saintliness of one of Miss W.'s guests,—the Miss Ainley of *Shirley*, long since gone to her rest. The character is not of course a literal portrait, for the very reasons Charlotte herself gave. She said, 'You are not to suppose any of the characters in *Shirley* intended as literal portraits. It would not suit the rules of art nor of my own feelings to write in that style. We only suffer reality to *suggest*, never to *dictate*. Qualities I have seen, loved, and admired, are here and there put in as decorative gems, to be preserved in that setting.' I may remark here that nothing angered Charlotte more, than for any one to suppose they could not be in her society without incurring the risk of 'being put in her books.' She always stoutly maintained she never thought of persons in this light when she was with them.

In the seldom recurring holidays Charlotte made sometimes short visits with those of her companions whose homes were within reach of school. Here she made acquaintance with the scenes and prominent characters of the Luddite period; her father materially helped to fix her impressions, for he had held more than one curacy in the very neighborhood which she describes in *Shirley*. He was present in some of the scenes, an active participator as far as his position permitted. Sometimes on the defensive, sometimes aiding the sufferers, uniting his strength and influence with the Mr. Helstone of *Shirley*. Between these two men there seems to have been in some respects a striking affinity of character which Charlotte was not slow to perceive, and she blended the two into one, though she never personally beheld the original of Mr. Helstone, except once when she was ten years old. He was a man of remarkable vigor and energy, both of mind and will. An absolute disciplinarian, he was sometimes called 'Duke Ecclesiastic,' a very Wellington in the Church.

Mr Brontë used to delight in recalling the days he spent in the vicinity of this man. Many a breakfast hour he enlivened by his animated relations of his friend's unflinching courage and dauntless self-reliance,—and how the ignorant and prejudiced population around misunderstood and misrepresented his worthiest deeds. In depicting the Luddite period Charlotte had the power of giving an almost literal description of the scenes then enacted, for, in addition to her father's personal acquaintance with what occurred, she had likewise the aid of authentic records of the eventful time, courteously lent to her by the editors of the *Leeds Mercury*.

I must not forget to state that no girl in the school was equal to Charlotte in Sunday lessons. Her acquaintance with Holy Writ surpassed others in this as in everything else. She was very familiar with all the sublimest passages, especially those in Isaiah, in which she took great delight. Her confirmation took place while she was at school, and in her preparation for that, as in all other studies, she distinguished herself by application and proficiency.

At school she acquired that habit which she and her sisters kept up to the very last, that of pacing to and fro in the room. In days when out-of-door exercise was impracticable, Miss Wooler would join us in our evening hour of relaxation and converse (for which she had rare talent); her pupils used to hang about her as she walked up and down the room, delighted to listen to her, or have a chance of being nearest in the walk. The last day Charlotte was at school she seemed to realize what a sedate, hard-working season it had been to her. She said, "I should for once like to feel *out and out* a school-girl; I wish something would happen! Let us run round the fruit garden [running was what she never did]; perhaps we shall meet some one, or we may have a fine for trespass." She evidently was longing for some never-to-be-forgotten incident. Nothing, however, arose from her little enterprise. She had to leave school as calmly and quietly as she had there lived.

II

[Text from Ellen Nussey's holograph MS, now in the Walpole Collection, the King's School, Canterbury. Fols. 48–67 contain a longer version of the account in *Scribner's Monthly* May 1871, 24–31, entitled 'CHARLOTTE'S EARLY LIFE AT HAWORTH'. Ellen describes CB's visit to Ellen's home, The Rydings, Birstall, in Sept. 1832, and her own visit to Haworth in July–Aug. 1833.]

Charlotte's first visit <made> from Haworth was made about three months after she left school. She travelled in a two wheeled gig, the only conveyance to be had in Haworth except the covered cart which brought her to school.

Mr Brontë sent Branwell as an escort; he was then a very dear brother, as dear to Charlotte as her own soul; they were in perfect accord of taste and feeling, it was mutual delight to be together. Branwell probably, had never been far from home before, he was in wild ecstasy with everything; he walked about in unrestrained boyish enjoyment: taking views in every direction of the old turret roofed house, the fine chesnut trees on the lawn (one of which was iron 'garthed' having been split by storms but still flourishing in great majesty) a large rookery gave a good background to the house, all these he noted and commented upon with perfect enthusiasm. He told his Sister 'he was leaving her in Paradise and if she were not intensely happy she never would be'. Happy indeed she was then in himself, for she, with her own enthusiasms looked forward to what <his> ˋher brother'sˊ great promise and talent might effect. He would at this time be between fifteen and sixteen years of age. The visit passed without much to mark it at this distance of time except that, we crept away together from household life as much as we could. Charlotte liked to pace the plantations or seek seclusion in the fruit garden, she was safe from visitors in these retreats. She was so painfully shy she could not bear any special notice, one day on being ˋledˊ in to dinner by a stranger she trembled and nearly burst into tears, but notwithstanding her excessive shyness, which was often painful to others as well as herself, she won the respect and affection of all who had opportunity enough to become acquainted ˋwith her.ˊ Charlotte's shyness did not arise I am sure, <in> either ˋfromˊ vanity, or self-consciousness, as some suppose shyness to arise, <but> its source was, (as Mr. Arthur Helps very truly says in one of his recent Essays) in 'not being understood'. She felt herself apart from others, they did not understand her, and she keenly felt the distance.

My first visit to Haworth was full of novelty and freshness. The scenery for some miles before we reachèd Haworth was wild and uncultivated with hardly any population, at last, we came to what seemed a terrific hill, such a steep declivity no one thought of riding down it, the horse had to be carefully led, we no sooner reached the foot of this hill than we had to begin to mount again, over a narrow, rough, stone-paved road, the horse's feet seemed to catch at the boulders as if climbing; when we reached the top of the village, there was apparently no outlet, but we were directed to drive into an entry that just admitted the Gig, we wound round in this entry and then saw the church close at hand, and entered on the short lane which led to the Parsonage gate way, here Charlotte was waiting having caught the sound of 'the' approaching gig. When greetings and introductions were over, Miss Branwell (the Aunt of the Brontës) took possession of their guest and treated her with the care and solicitude due to a weary traveller. Mr. Brontë also was stirred out of his usual retirement by his own kind consideration, for, not only the guest, but the manservant, and the horse were to be made comfortable—he <came to ?maked> 'made' enquiries about the man 'his length of service &c' with the kind purpose of <holding> 'making' a few moments of conversation agreeable to him.

Even <th>at this time, Mr. Brontë struck me as looking very venerable with his snow white hair and powdered coat collar. His manner and mode of speech always had the tone of high-bred courtesy. He was considered somewhat of an invalid, and always lived in the most abstemious and simple manner. His white cravat was not then so remarkable as it grew to be afterwards, he was in the habit of covering this cravat himself, we never saw the operation, but we always had to wind for him the white sewing [silk] which he used, Charlotte said it was her Father's one extravagance—he cut up yards and yards of white lutestring (silk) in covering his cravat, and like Dr. Joseph Woolffe (the renowned traveller) who when on a visit, and in a long fit of absence "went into a clean shirt every day for a week without taking one off" so Mr. Brontë's Cravat went into new silk and new size without taking any off, till at <last> 'length' nearly half of his head was enveloped in cravat; his liability to bronchial attacks no doubt attached him to this increasing growth of cravat.

Miss Branwell was a very small antiquated little lady, she wore caps large enough for half a dozen of the present fashion, 'and' a front of light auburn curls over her forehead. 'She probably had been pretty.' She always dressed in silk. She talked a great deal of her younger days, the gaities [*sic*] of her native town, Penzance in Cornwall, the soft warm climate &c She very probably had been a belle 'among her acquaintance,' the social life of her younger days she appeared to recall with regret. She took snuff out of a very pretty little gold snuff box, which she sometimes presented with a little laugh as if she enjoyed the slight shock and astonishment visible in your <face> 'countenance.' In Summer she spent part of her afternoons in reading aloud to Mr. Brontë, and in winter the evenings, she must have enjoyed this, for she and Mr. Brontë had sometimes to finish their discussions on what she had read when we all met for tea, she would be very lively and intelligent 'in her talk', and tilted argument without fear against Mr. Brontë.

'Tabby' the faithful trustworthy old Servant was very quaint in appearance—very active, and in these days was the general servant and factotum.

'We were all 'Childer' and 'Bairns' in her estimation.' She still kept to her duty of walking out with the 'Childer' if they went any distance from home, unless Branwell were sent by his Father as protector. 'In later days after she had been attacked with paralysis, she would anxiously look out for such duties as she was still capable of—The Post-man was her special point of attention, she did 'not' approve of the inspection which the younger eyes of her fellow servant bestowed on his deliveries, she jealously seized them '(when she could)' & carried them 'off' with hobbling step and shaking head and hand to the safe custody of Charlotte.'

Emily Brontë had by this time acquired a lithesome graceful figure, She was the tallest person in the house except her Father, her hair which was naturally as beautiful as Charlotte's was in the same unbecoming tight curl and frizz, and there was the same want of complexion. She had very beautiful eyes, kind<ly>, kindling, liquid eyes, 'sometimes they looked grey, sometimes dark blue' but she did not often look at you, she was too reserved. She talked very little, she and Anne were 'like twins,' inseparable companions, 'and' in the very closest sympathy which never had any interruption.

Anne, dear gentle Anne, was quite different in appearance to the others. She was her Aunt's favorite. Her hair was a very pretty light brown and <in falling curls> fell on her neck in graceful curls. She had lovely violet blue eyes, fine pencilled eye-brows, a clear, almost transparent complexion. She still pursued her studies, and especially her sewing, under the surveilliance [*sic*] of her Aunt. Emily had now begun to have the disposal of her own time. Branwell studied regularly with his Father, and used to paint in oils, which was regarded as study for what might eventually be his Profession—All the household entertained the idea of his becoming an Artist, and hoped he would be a distinguished one.

<We used to have> 'In fine & suitable weather' delightful rambles over the moors and down into the glens and ravines that here and there broke the monotony of the Moorland. The rugged bank and rippling brook were treasures of delight. Emily, Anne, and Branwell used to ford the streams and sometimes placed stepping stones for the other two—there was always a lingering delight in these spots, every moss, every flower, every tint and form, were noted and enjoyed, Emily especially had a gleesome delight in these nooks of beauty, her reserve 'for the time' vanished. One long ramble made in these early days was, far away over the moors to a spot familiar to Emily and Anne which they called the "Meeting of the Waters". It was a small oasis of emerald green turf broken here and there by small <rippling> 'clear' springs, a few large stones served us as resting places, seated here, we were hidden from all the world, nothing appearing in view but miles and miles of heather: a glorious blue sky and brightening sun: a fresh breeze wafted on us its exhilarating influence, we laughed and made mirth of each other, and settled we would

call ourselves the quartette, Emily half reclining on a slab of stone played like a young child with the tad-poles in the water, making them swim about, and 'then' fell to moralising on the big and the little, the brave and the cowardly as she chased them 'about' with her hand. No serious care or sorrow had so far cast its gloom on natures youth and buoyancy, and nature's simplest offerings were fountains of <pleasure> '&' enjoyment.

You will desire to know something of the now far-famed Parsonage. The interior lacked drapery of all kinds. Mr. Brontë's horror of fire forbad curtains to the windows, they never had these accessories to comfort and appearance till long after Charlotte was the only inmate of the family sitting room. She then ventured on the innovation when her friend was with her, it did not please her Father, but it was not forbidden. There was not much carpet any where except in the sitting room, and on the centre of the study floor. The hall floor and stairs were done with sand stone, always beautifully clean as everything about the house was, the walls were not papered but coloured in a pretty dove-coloured tint, hair-seated chairs and mahogany tables, bookshelves in the Study but not many of these elsewhere. Scant and bare indeed many will say, yet it was not a scantness that made itself felt—mind and thought, yes, I had almost said elegance, but certainly refinement diffused themselves over all, and made nothing really wanting. Mr. Brontë's health caused him to retire early, he assembled his household for family worship at eight o'clock, at nine he locked and barred the front door, always giving as he passed the sitting room door, a kindly admonition to the 'children' not to be late, half way up the stairs he stayed his steps to wind up the clock, the clock that in after days seemed to click like a dirge in the refrain of Longfellows poem "The old clock on the stairs" "Forever – never! Never – forever!"

A little later on there was the addition of a Piano. Emily played with precision and brilliancy when she did play 'which was not often if other<s were present> than the family circle were within hearing' Anne played also but she preferred soft harmonies—she sang a little her voice was 'weak but' very sweet <but> in tone.

Every morning was heard the firing of a pistol from Mr. Brontë['s] room window, it was the discharging of the loading which he made every night. 'From' Mr. Brontë's 'conversation it was evident he' delighted in the perusal of Battle scenes and in the artifice of war, had he entered on Military instead of Ecclesiastical service he would probably have had a very distinguished career. The self-denials and privations of camp life would <certainly> have <accorded> 'agreed entirely' with his nature, for he was remarkably independent of the luxuries and comforts of life—the only dread he had was fire and this dread was so intense, it caused him to prohibit all but silk or woollen dresses for his daughters, indeed for any one to wear any other kind of fabric was almost to forfeit his respect.

Mr. Brontë at times would relate strange stories which had been told to him by some of the oldest inhabitants in the Parish, of the extraordinary lives and doings of people who resided in far off out of the way places but in contiguity with Haworth—stories which made one shiver and shrink from hearing, but they 'were' full of grim humour & interest to Mr. Brontë and his children, they revealed the characteristics of a class of human beings, and 'as' such Emily has stereotyped 'them' in her "Wuthering Heights"

During Miss Branwell's reign at the Parsonage the love of animals had to be kept in due subjection, there was then but one dog, which was admitted into the parlour at stated times—Emily and Anne always gave him a portion of their breakfast which was the old north country diet of oat-meal porridge; later on, there were three <animal> 'household' pets, the tawny strong limbed 'Keeper' Emily's favorite, he was so completely under her control she could quite easily make him spring and roar like a lion, she 'had' taught him this kind of play without any coercion. 'Flossy' long silky haired black and white Flossy was Anne's favorite, and black 'Tom' the tabby was every-body's pet, it received such gentle treatment it seemed to have lost cat's nature and subsided into luxurious amiability and contentment. The<ir> 'Brontës'' love of dumb creatures made them very sensitive of the treatment bestowed upon them, for any one to offend in this respect was with them an infallible bad sign, and blot in 'their' disposition.

The services in church in these days were such as can only be seen <in localities> (if ever seen again) in localities like Haworth. The people assembled, but it was apparently to listen, any part beyond that was quite out of their reckoning. All through the Prayers a stolid look of apathy was fixed in the generality of their faces, then they sat or leaned in their pews; (some few perhaps were resting after a long walk over the moors). The children from the school pattered in after Service had commenced, and pattered out again before the sermon. <began.> The sexton with a long staff continually walked round in the aisles "knobbing" sleepers when he dare, shaking his head at and threatening unruly children, but when the sermon began there was a change, attitudes took the listening form, eyes were turned on the speaker. It was curious now to note the expression, a rustic untaught intelligence gleamed in their faces, in some a daring doubting questioning look as if the lips would like to say something defiant. Mr Brontë always addressed his hearers in extempore style, very often he selected a parable 'from one of the Gospels' which he explained in the simplest manner, sometimes going over his own words and explaining them also, so as to be perfectly intelligible to the lowest comprehension. The Parishioners respected <their Pastor> Mr Brontë <but> 'because, as' one of them said <it was because>, "He's a grand man he lets other folks business alone" no doubt Mr Brontë's knowledge of human nature made him aware that this was the best course to pursue till their independance had acquired a more civilised standard.

There were exceptions however among the villagers, two or three individuals deserve particular note—they were men remarkable 'for' self-culture and intelligence—one it was said vied with Mr. Brontë himself in his knowledge of the dead languages, he and another, had in addition to their mental stamina, such stalwart frames & stature, they looked capable of doing duty as guards to the whole village—the third individual was an ailing suffering man, but he wrote such a critique on Charlotte's writings when they became known, that it was valued more than any other—coming from such a source.

The villagers would have liked to <gossip> 'make Tabby talk to them' about the family in the Parsonage, but Tabby was invincible [and] impenetrable When they asked her "If the family was 'not' fearfully larn'd?" she left them in a "huff", but she did not deny her "childer" the laugh she knew they would have if she told them the village Query.

The Haworth of the present day has made a step onwards like many other places, in that it has its railway station, and its institution for the easy acquirement of learning Politics & literature—The Parsonage is quite another <Parson> habitation from the Parsonage of former days. The garden which was nearly all grass—<&> ' and possessing only ' a few stunted thorns and shrubs, and a few currant bushes which Emily and Anne treasured as their bit of fruit garden, is now a perfect arcadia of floral culture & beauty. At first the alteration in spite of its improvement strikes one with heart-ache & regret, for it is quite impossible even in imagination to people those beautified rooms with <its> their former inhabitants—but afterthought, shews one the folly of such regrets, for the Brontës did not live 'in' their house except for its uses of eating, drinking, and resting. They lived in 'the' free expanse 'of hill' moorland, its purple heather, its dells and glens and brooks, The broad sky view, the whistling winds, the snowy expanse, The starry heavens, and in the charm of that solitude '& seclusion' which sees things from a distance without the disturbing atmosphere <created by> 'which' lesser minds are apt to create. It was not the seclusion of a solitary person which becomes in time awfully oppressive—it was seclusion shared & enjoyed by intelligent companionship and intense family affection.

III

[Text from the King's School Canterbury MS by Ellen Nussey, fols. 1–47. Ellen describes the visit to Bolton Priory referred to in EN 11.9.1833, and her holiday with Charlotte at Easton and Bridlington in Aug.–Sept. 1839. Mr. Brontë first showed CB her mother's letters (p. 608) in Feb. 1850: see Vol. ii, EN 16.2.1850. The Haworth Sunday School was opened in 1832.]

Charlotte and Anne Brontë were steady and faithful to their posts as Sunday-School teachers both now, and whenever they were at home 'at this time';

some of the 'village' girls as they grew up to womanhood evinced an affectionate appreciation of their labours—the female teachers also, in their way, displayed a sense of the favours they enjoyed; they were all invited once a year to tea at the Parsonage. Their first visit was made when Charlotte's friend was staying with her. About four o'clock in the afternoon, half a dozen young women were ushered into the parlour; they were as fresh '& buoyant' as a moorland breeze, cheerful, healthy, bright-complexioned young creatures, with an astonishing amount of brusquerie in their manner; they were nearly all, earners of their daily bread at the factories, but manifested none of that deferential respect towards their employers which was the general tone of the well-employed in most other localities. They talked very freely of their masters but always by their christian names, as 'Jack' or 'Joe'; when it was suggested that they should be taught better manners, the Brontës were greatly amused, Emily especially so, who said in her way, (which was always peculiarly quiet), 'Vain attempt!' They shewed however a rough respect to their entertainers, and great good nature also, for on discovering that the<y all> 'Miss Brontës' were willing to play games with them but did not know how, they undertook to initiate them. The Brontë faces were worth anything as a study (if only an artist could have sketched them) during this attempt at learning to play; they had such a puzzled, amused, submissive expression, intently anxious though, to give pleasure and gratify others.

It was I believe at the close of this '(E's)' visit that, there was a clubbing together of pocket-money to secure an excursion to Bolton Abbey. Branwell Brontë undertook to procure a conveyance at a cheap rate which would carry all the party, and which, including the driver, would be six in number. The daily anticipation of the coming treat, mixed with apprehensions about the weather, was perfect excitement to all.

Branwell seemed to know every inch of the way, could tell the names of the hills that would be driven over, or walked over, their exact height above the sea, the views to be seen, and the places to be passed through; it was an event to <all> 'each' that, they were about to cross part of the range of hills which are designated the Back-bone of England.

The party started from the Parsonage between five and six in the morning, in a small double-gig or phaeton—it was partly a loan as well as a hire to Branwell. They were to meet friends and relatives who were to take Charlotte's friend home. The Haworth party chanced to drive up to the Hotel just before them, but in plenty of time to note, and go through what to 'their' young and enthusiastic hearts was 'quite' a new experience, (ie) that, their crowded and <rather> shabby-looking conveyance 'which had been of no import whatever till now' was regarded with disdain by the Hotel attendants, till they saw that they were cordially recognised by the handsome carriage-and-pair arrivals; all 'the party' breakfasted, and 'then' started on their stroll through the grounds. As this is written for those who do not know the charming parts of Yorkshire scenery, and for many who never can know it personally, they will probably welcome some description of Bolton. [EN has adapted parts of Thomas Dunham Whitaker's *The History and Antiquities of the Deanery of Craven* (1805, revised edn. 1812) to produce an 8½-page description of Bolton Priory and its setting. Each page has been crossed through, but is still clearly legible. EN continues:]

Emily and Anne hardly spoke during the whole excursion except to each other, but it was easy to see how they were drinking 'in' pleasure and treasuring up the scenery in their minds. Charlotte who was acquainted with all the party, was less shy. Branwell who probably never knew the feeling of shyness, amused every one; he was in a phrensy of pleasure, his eyes flashed with excitement, and he talked fast and brilliantly; a friend who was present and herself a great admirer of scenery, 'was so much amused by his ecstacies' said, she had never passed such a day of enjoyment in her life.—She thought Branwell very eccentric, but recognised his rare talent and genius, she presaged though, the danger of those flashing impulses, a danger which came so sorely and surely in after time. He had any amount of poetry ready for quotation, and this day he was well off in an appreciative audience whenever he chose to recite; it was one of the things he did well.

(Branwell's appearance up to this time was grotesque rather than otherwise; he was neither full-grown man nor yet a boy, and he had not acquired the art of attending to his appearance, none of the Brontës understood dress with its right and simple advantages, till Charlotte and Emily had been in Brussels; they then began to perceive the elegance of a well-fitting garment made with simplicity and neatness, <and> 'when' they adopted the better style for themselves it was a manifest improvement.) The Haworth party were first started on their return journey—they left their friends (whose route lay in another direction) full of grateful pleasure and happiness for the day's enjoyment which had proved to all, a[n] even greater treat than had been anticipated.

About this time Charlotte passed a great part of almost every day in drawing or painting; she would do one or the other, for nine hours with scarcely an interval, if she were greatly interested in her subject—her style was not bold or broad, it was minute and finished. At one period she set her heart on miniature painting but she did not succeed to her own approval, and sometimes, when a head or figure was nearly completed she would allow no remonstrance to prevent her committing 'it' to the flames, if she failed in her own estimate her work was doomed, she did not however act in sullen wrath or disappointment, she cheerfully set to work again intent on achieving her ideal if possible. But few of her drawings or paintings survived her; she permitted acquaintances to carry them off as a loan, <and> 'who' forgot to return them, she regretted the loss of some, but she would not ask to have them returned. Emily and

Anne were fond of the pencil, but chiefly as a recreation, or for the sake of acquiring the art so as to be 'able to' teach others when the need should arise.

Mr. Brontë was frequently making efforts, and trying to stir up his Parishioners to efforts, for the sanitary improvement of the village, but for years all he could do appeared to be unavailing; the needful outlay was not to be thought of, Haworth like many other places refused to acknowledge the real remedy for prevalent sickness and epidemic—the inhabitants persisted in ignoring evils which necessitated a free use of their money, they would not listen to the wisdom of a reform which Mr. Brontë's higher intelligence would fain have obtained by friendly persuasion—The Passing-bell was often a dreary accompaniment to the day's engagements, and must have been trying to the sensitive nervous temperaments of those who were always within sound of it as the Parsonage inmates were, but everything around, and in immediate vicinity was a reminder of man's last bourne, as you issued from the Parsonage gate, you looked upon the Stone-cutter's chipping shed which was piled with slabs ready for use, and to the ear there was the incessant sound of the chip, chip, of the recording chisel as it graved in the In Memoriams of the departed.

From the Parsonage-windows the first view, was the plot of grass edged by a wall, a thorn tree or two, and a few shrubs and currant-bushes that did not grow; next to these was the large and half-surrounding church yard, so full of grave-stones that hardly a strip of grass could be seen in it; twice or thrice in the week there was a diversion from this saddening prospect, though in itself a very undesirable one, and one that proved as much as anything could do, how familiar to the Villagers were the scenes of death and its accompaniments. The village house-wives made the old Church-yard their general drying-ground on washing- days, but in process of time they were compelled to better arrangements. Great was Mr. Brontë's amusement when the expulsion of the house-wives was effected, and he commemorated the incident in the following dogrel.

"CHURCH REFORM"

In Haworth, a parish of ancient renown,
Some preach in their surplice and others in their gown;
Othersome with due hatred of tower and steeple,
Without surplice or gown hold forth to the people;
And "High Church" and "Low Church" and no church at all
T'would puzzle the brain of St Peter and St Paul—
The Parson an old man, but hotter than old,
Of late in reforming had grown very bold,
And in his fierce zeal as report loudly tells
Through legal resort had reformed the bells—
His curate who follows—with all due regard
Though foiled by the church has reformed the church yard

Then let all schismatics, look on in mute wonder;
Nor e'er dream the church, shall in terror, knock under;
T'will go on reforming what e'er be their clatter
Till cleansed is the outside, both cup and platter—
The dead all deserted, their ghosts heavy moan
Oft shakes to the centre each slumbering stone—
The females all routed have fled with their clothes
To stack yards and back yards; where no one knows—
And loudly have sworn by the suds which they swim in
They'll wring off his head for his warring with women,
Whilst their husbands combine and roar out in their fury,
They'll Lynch him at once, without trial by jury,
But saddest of all the fair maidens declare,
Of marriage or love he must ever despair."

So ceased this long trespass on "God's Acre"
[There follows a gap in the folio numbering of the MS; leaves 23–5 are missing.]

Charlotte's first visit to the sea coast deserves a little more notice than her letters give of the <event—> 'circumstances—' it was an event eagerly coveted, but hard to attain. Mr. Brontë and Miss Branwell had all manner of doubts and fears and cautions to express, and Charlotte was sinking into despair—there seemed only one chance of securing her the pleasure: her friend must fetch her;—this she did through the aid of a dear relative, who sent her to Haworth under safe convoy, and in a carriage that would bring both Charlotte and her luggage—this step proved to be the very best thing possible, the surprise was so good in its effects, there was nothing to combat,—every body rose into high good humour, Branwell was grandiloquent, he declared "it was a brave defeat, that the doubters were fairly taken aback" and he added <the ?bad philosophy> 'what is sometimes right but not always' that, "You have only to will a thing to get it" &c Charlotte's luggage was speedily prepared, and almost before the horse was rested there was a quiet but triumphant starting; the brother and sisters at home were not less happy than Charlotte herself in her now secured pleasure. It was the first act of real freedom 'to be' enjoyed either by herself or her friend, a first experience in railway travelling, which however only conveyed them through half of the route, the stage coach making the rest of the journey. Passengers being too numerous for this accommodation, Charlotte and her friend were sent on in an open "Fly"; the weather was most delightful, the drive was enjoyed immensely, but they were unconsciously hastening on to a severe disappointment. Friends in the vicinity of the coast whither they were bound, had been informed of their coming, and were ready to seize upon them: they waited for 'met' the coach, but it did not bring their expected young friends, and they had to depart, but not without leaving orders at the Hotel where the coach stopped, for the capture of the occupants of the "Fly"; a post-chaise was in readiness, in which they were to be driven off not to the bourn they were longing for (the seaside), but two or three miles away from it, here they were (though most unwilling) hospitably entertained and detained for a month.—The day but one after their capture they walked to the sea, & as soon as they were near enough for Charlotte to see it in its expanse, she was quite overpowered, she could not speak till she had shed some tears—she signed to her friend to leave her and walk on; this she did for a few steps, knowing full well what Charlotte was passing through, and the stern efforts she was making to subdue her emotions—her friend turned to her as soon as she thought she might without inflicting pain; her eyes were red and swollen, she was still trembling, but submitted to be led onwards where the view was less impressive; for the remainder of the day she was very quiet, subdued, and exhausted. Distant glimpses of the German ocean had been visible as the two friends neared the coast on the day of their arrival, but Charlotte being without her glasses, could not see them, and when they were described to her, she said, 'Don't tell me any more.' 'Let me wait.' Whenever the sound of the sea reached her ears in the grounds around the house wherein she was a captive guest, her spirit longed to rush away and be close to it. At last their kind and generous entertainers yielded to their wishes and permitted them to take wing and go into Lodgings for one week, but still protecting them by every day visits, and bounteous provision from their dairy. What Charlotte and her friend had desired for themselves was, to be their own providers, believing in their inexperience that, they could do great things with the small sum of money they each had at their disposal, but at the end of the week when bills were asked for, they were thoroughly enlightened as to the propriety of the kind care which had guarded them—they discovered that moderate appetites and modest demands for attendan[ce] were of no avail as regarded the demands made upon their small finances. A week's experience sufficed to shew them the wisdom of not prolonging their stay, though the realisation of enjoyment had been as intense as anticipation had depicted.

The conventionality of <the generality> 'most' of the sea-side visitors amused Charlotte immensely. The evening Parade on the Pier struck her as the greatest absurdity. It was an old pier in those days, and of ?short dimensions, but thither all the visitors seemed to assemble in such numbers, it was like a packed ball-room; people had to march round and round in regular file to secure any movement whatever. Charlotte and her friend thought they would go away from this after making one essay to do as others did; they took themselves off to the cliffs to enjoy the moonlight but they had not done this long, ere some instinct as to safety warned them to return; on entering their lodgings another novelty impressed itself upon them, they encountered sounds which came from a Ranter's Meeting-house across the street, there was <wild> \violent/ excitement within its walls, and Charlotte was wild to go in amongst the<m> \congregation/ and see as she said, "What they were up to", but was restrained by the reflection that, these people who were making such awful noises were acting as they believed on religious impulse, and ought neither to be criticised nor ridiculed in their midst. Charlotte's impressions of the Sea never wore off; she would often recall her views of it, and wonder what its aspect would be just at the time she was speaking of it.

There was a little incident in Charlotte's early life which she sometimes recurred to with great amusement; it was when she was about five years old. She had familiarised herself with the description of the "Golden City" in the Book of Revelation and she had also read "The Pilgrim's Progress". She heard the servants (for there were ?two at the Parsonage in those days) talking much of Bradford, a town ten miles off, as a place that afforded them every conceivable delight—her imagination seized upon the idea that Bradford must be the "Golden City" she had read about, and she must walk to it as the Pilgrims did; off she went and had gone about a mile, and was rising the hill opposite the Parsonage, when she was all at once thrown into deep shadow by the approach of a team of horses drawing a huge waggon-load; the tramping of the horses and the engulphing darkness, as she thought, terrified her so, \that/ she sank down on the road-side, and there she was found by the maid who had followed in search of her, ready for that time to give up her pilgrimage. The sight of commercial, ?industrious, but murky Bradford would have been a cruel dissipation of ideas had she reached it. She afterwards became familiar enough with its aspect, for she had to pass through it in her journeyings to and from school and in her visits to her friends at B[irstall] and G[omersal]

[A "recent anecdote" intended to show the "Yorkshire love of 'Fair play' " follows.]

[Ellen goes on]:

Stories have been related of Mr. Brontë and his method of working off powerful passions, which are considered incredible, but a good deal of the ugliness of these facts would vanish if people more fully knew the <man> character of the man.

He could not be said to be a man of many sympathies; he never entered into details, they annoyed him, feeling in most aspects was to him a weakness, if he analysed, it was on general principles, he ruled his opinions by maxims which made no allowance for idiosyncrasies unless it were \that he had/ <u>one</u> exception—may we not be permitted to think that he <u>did understand</u> his <u>own</u> idiosyncracy, and so well too, that he thought it prudent to live the ascetic life which he adopted. He was quite capable of enforcing such rule upon himself when the time came for him to ?cease [or "use"] the unusual course of firing off pistols &c That he did <u>do</u> the things told of him, it is certain, for about the premises in early days were to be seen the bullet-holes in such objects as he had made targets of. Charlotte herself used to relate the story of the mutilated dress, as a strong proof of her Father's iron will and determination to carry <his point> through his purpose—his wife was never again to wear the obnoxious dress which had been a present 'to her,' and he made it impossible that she should wear it—he would quietly persuade himself that he was putting his gentle wife out of the reach of <temptation> a very 'feminine' temptation, and take no cognisance of his own hard and inflexible will, which ran itself into tyranny and cruelty. There is not the slightest doubt that he would have gained his object quite as surely by kinder and wiser methods of action, but it was not his nature to woo obedience, nor did he ever coerce it except as a general might, by stratagem. His 'outward' demeanour was always <externally> perfectly under control and quiescent. It is well to relate here, though it occurred after Charlotte became the solitary survivor of brother and sisters, that one day Mr. Brontë placed a packet of letters yellowed with age, in the hands of Charlotte as she was standing by the sitting room 'fire' along with her friend, saying, "These are your Mother's letters, perhaps you and Miss—will be interested in reading them." Interested indeed they were; the readers experienced a heart-ache of sympathy with the writer. Her gentleness and lovingness, her purity and refinement, her goodness and modesty, all shone forth so forcibly, they could not help thinking and feeling how hard her lot had been, torn from her children ere she could reap for herself any of that sweetness and goodness which they had derived from her, and long ere she could have the gratifications and joys <the> 'her' Mother's heart would feel in the unusual talents and gifts of her children. Her intelligence and cultivation were such, there can be no doubt that the Brontë family were, as is usually the case, eminently indebted to their Mother for their manifold excellencies if not for their talents likewise.

Miss Branwell's letters shewed that her engagement, though not a prolonged one, was not as happy as it ought to have been—there was a pathos of apprehension, (though gently expressed) in part of the correspondence, lest Mr. Brontë should cool in his affections towards her, and the readers perceived with some indignation, that there had been some just cause given for this apprehension. Mr. Brontë, with all his iron strength and power of will, had his weaknesses, and one <failing>, which, wherever it exists, spoils and debases the character—he had personal vanity. Miss Branwell's finer nature <was> 'rose' above such weakness, but she suffered all the more from evidences of it in one to whom she had given her affections, and 'whom she' was longing to look up to in all things. Charlotte was sometimes stirred into avenging her Mother, for when her Father boasted, as he did occasionally, of the conquests made in his earlier days, she put his <boast> 'self- complacency' down with <a> strong <hand> 'emphasis of disaproval' [*sic*]. Mrs. Brontë had the inestimable blessing of a well-balanced mind, yet she <possessed> 'was imbued with' a degree of superstition, and Charlotte inherited its influence, presentiments made deep impressions upon her, she gave <full bent> 'the reins' to herself in this respect when she wrote "Jane Eyre": its escape seemed to have done her good, <'just'>as if she had braced herself up for ever after. This fragile delicate little woman found time in the midst of her young family & busy household to write poetry & small articles for a Cottage Magazine 'in' which her husband was 'interested & ' also a contributor

It has been said that Charlotte would 'sometimes' dramatise when her spirits rose to the necessary pitch of excitement. She both charmed and fascinated her school friends and their immediate connections when she did this—but unfortunately it was repeated to her when a meeting of young friends was in anticipation, that, "Martin York" [Joe Taylor] had said, "He was going to stir Miss Brontë up to the exhibiting point, and he should have a rare evening of enjoyment." But Martin utterly failed then and thenceforward: Charlotte merely replied to her laughing informant, "Is he!" But her resolve was taken, and it was immutable; her self-respect had received a blow, and no tactics on "Martin's" part ever again prevailed to win the entertainment he coveted.

Charlotte probably had begun even now to contemplate the possibility of assuming a nom de plume at some distant time, for she liked when in E's home, to be playfully addressed as "Charles" and in cheerful moods would sign herself "Charles Thunder".

<It> 'We' may <be> indicate<d> here, for it belongs to this period, some of the Poems <she> 'Charlotte' had a preference for, and which, she used to repeat to herself when busy with her needle in soft audible cadence.

Heber's "Missionary Hymn" [? 'From Greenland's icy mountains'], which was a very great favourite with her, and some of Moore's Poems such as—

"O Thou who driest the mourners tears" "The bird let loose in Eastern skies" and "While here in shade and grief we roam". She did not as yet know the gem of sacred poetry, Keble's "Christian Year" but afterwards, when she did know it, she felt the power and gentle influence of many of the Poems, and could not endure to hear any one recite or read them who did not feel their beauty & meaning.

In <forty-five> the year of forty-five she wrote in her friend's note book the following French <Poem> 'Verses,' adding these remarks—"Millevoye died young—a short time after having written these verses—in my opinion the French language does not possess anything more truly poetical than this effusion."

LE JEUNE MALADE

De la dépouille de nos bois
L'automne avait jonché la terre:
Le bocage était sans mystère,

Le rossignol était sans voix.
Triste et mourant à son aurore
Un jeune malade, à pas lents,
Parcourait une fois encore
Le bois cher à ses premiers ans.
"Bois que j'aime! Adieu! je succombe,
"Votre deuil me prédit mon sort,
"Et dans chaque feuille qui tombe
"Je vois un présage de mort.
"Fatal oracle d'Epidaure!
"Tu m'as dit, les feuilles de bois
"A tes yeux jauniront encore,
"Mais c'est pour la dernière fois!
"Ta jeunesse sera flétrie
"Avant le pampre du coteau."
Et je meurs—de leur froide haleine
M'ont touch[é] les sombres autans,
Et j'ai vu, comme une ombre vaine,
S'évanouir mon beau printemps.
Tombe, tombe, feuille éphémère!

Index